CONTEMPORARY SOCIAL PROBLEMS

CONTEMPORARY SOCIAL PROBLEMS

Fourth Edition

Harold A. Phelps, PH. D.

PROFESSOR OF SOCIOLOGY
UNIVERSITY OF PITTSBURGH

David Henderson, PH. D.

ASSISTANT PROFESSOR OF SOCIOLOGY
UNIVERSITY OF PITTSBURGH

PRENTICE-HALL, INC. NEW YORK 1952

L. C. Cat. Card No. 52-8614

PREFACE TO THE FOURTH EDITION

As in previous editions, this revision follows the point of view that any social problem must be defined clearly before solutions can be found. Between these two steps of definition and solution in social study, it is necessary to collect and analyze the facts and to note what other problems are associated with the particular problem that is being redefined. Each chapter from 2 to 19 inclusive follows this plan.

Problems omitted from this revision or combined with other topics are poverty, unemployment, standards of living, and transients. The first three appear in Chapter 13, "Occupations," and transiency is reviewed in Chapter 10 under Migrations. The five chapters of the former Part Four in the third edition are omitted, and all summaries of theory and method are limited to Chapter 1 or 20.

New chapters include Chapters 6, "Children's Problems," 7, "Problems of College Youth," 11, "Minorities," 13, "Occupations," 15, "Family Problems—Personal," and Chapters 1 and 20. New sections of other chapters are Migrations in Chapter 10 and Inflations in Chapter 12.

Many students are disturbed about the obsolescence of data in books of this character. The impression of the authors, however, during this and prior revisions, is that the essential facts change very slowly. Readers may be interested in knowing that in the opinion of the authors the problems that have changed least either in factual content or in recommended treatment are mental deficiency, depressions, divorce, and crime. The most apparent change in social problems as a whole is the practical disappearance of what may be called the poverty or depression approach. At present the most prevalent emphasis is the urgent need for objective study. As a rule when problems are actually identified, there is opportunity for effective treatment, or the groundwork necessary to prevention becomes clear.

Harold A. Phelps
David Henderson

PREFACE TO THE FIRST EDITION

THE MAIN PURPOSE OF THIS BOOK IS TO SHOW THAT SOCIAL PROBLEMS must be redefined before they can be stated as problems to be solved. Hence, more attention is given to an analysis of different problems into their several component factors than to current methods that are recommended for their treatment.

Because of this selective approach, *Contemporary Social Problems* does not assume that its subtitle is *The Causes and Cures of Social Problems.* Causes and solutions are discussed, but only when they contribute to our understanding of a problem; that is, to its analysis and redefinition. Many major problems or their imputed causes are omitted, although they may be significant obstacles to human welfare, because they have not been, or cannot be, stated as scientific problems or subjected to the methods now available to social investigation.

Contemporary Social Problems is organized into two divisions, one being devoted to the theoretical analysis of social problems and their solubility (Chapters 1 and 19 to 23), the other to specific social problems (Chapters 2 to 18 inclusive). These specific problems are classified as economic, physical, mental, or cultural problems, because economic, physical, mental, or cultural criteria of social well-being are used in their definition. They are also arranged in an order that indicates their relative definiteness, as problems to be analyzed or solved.

All of these specific social problems cover a wide variety of social facts. For this reason, they should be regarded less as typical social problems than as our nearest current approximation to their definition and analysis. Each problem in reality is a cluster of problems. Thus, from this point of view, the problem of poverty is classified as economic, but is redefined as a mixture of physical, mental, and cultural, as well as of economic, disabilities. This procedure is followed as closely as possible in each chapter. It is particularly advantageous when the question of reform is raised, since a problem that is classified under one category may require for its adequate solution some remedial agencies from all of the other factors contributing to human welfare. Any social problem, adequately analyzed in its cause-and-effect relationships, presents a fair cross-section of almost every other problem, and because of these interrelationships it can be most clearly conceived as a central zone of social ill-being, rather than as a specific problem to be solved.

For the presentation of these materials in the classroom, an Appendix has been added. It contains two suggestions. The first refers to the advantage of organizing classroom discussion about a few problems, and employing others (suggested in this book or in the bibliography) for illustrative purposes; the other refers to the connection between the practical and theoretical implications of social problems.

Since social problems are always combinations of specific individual or group disabilities and of society's attitude concerning its own responsibility for them, both social theory or social policy, as well as the immediate problem, must be given some attention in a complete description of social problems. This emphasis upon the theoretical or practical, however, must be tempered by the purpose of the course or by the maturity of the students, and can be regulated most effectively by the degree to which it encourages the student to read critically and to search for supplementary data in recent social investigations.

HAROLD A. PHELPS

TABLE OF CONTENTS

PART 3 · PROBLEMS IN ECONOMIC ADJUSTMENT

PART 4 · PROBLEMS ACCENTED BY SOCIAL POLICY

INTRODUCTION

Did you know that:

1. Americans spend twice as much for alcohol as for medical care?
2. Cancer is the most curable of all major degenerative diseases causing death?
3. Nearly two million children in the United States are partially or totally deaf?
4. About 3,500 reputable practicing psychologists and psychiatrists are competing with 25,000 others, many of whom are charlatans and who advertise that they can cure nearly every mental illness?
5. California has saved an estimated 100 million dollars through its selective sterilization program during the last four decades?
6. More than four million children of school age do not attend school?
7. One out of every eight children is not living with both parents?
8. Between 50 and 65 per cent of high-school graduates who enter college do not complete their work in the regular four-year course?
9. There are seven ages: chronological, anatomical, physiological, psychological, pathological, hereditary, and statistical?
10. Two-thirds of the present population of the world is chronically undernourished?
11. Facts are helpless against prejudice; reason is even more helpless; and most helpless of all is justice?
12. In the last 50 years real wages per hour in the United States have increased more than three-fold?
13. The buying power of a 1951 dollar was equal to 39¢ of the 1914 dollar?
14. For every accidental death, three persons are permanently crippled, and 90 are injured seriously enough to require medical care?

15. The personal traits of sociability and conventionality are considered to be the two most important determinants of marital success?
16. More than two-thirds of the nation's children live in low-income families?
17. One in every eight married persons has been married more than once?
18. The F. B. I. reported 1,790,000 serious crimes in 1950?
19. For every 100 major offenses there are on the average about 27 arrests, 19 prosecutions, and 14 convictions?
20. "There is no short-cut to truth; no way to gain a knowledge of the universe except through the gateway of scientific method?"—Karl Pearson.

These statements are either direct quotations or close paraphrases of observations by reputable authorities. They are used to introduce an analytic statement of the nature of social problems in order to show their variety, extent, costs, and inconsistencies more than to indicate truisms.

CHAPTER 1

KEYS TO SOCIAL PROBLEMS

A SOCIETY'S PROBLEMS ARE GENERALLY OF THREE VARIETIES. THEY MAY be personal failures or defects. They may be the needs or liabilities of social groups. In addition, they may also be the programs that are supposed to correct or avoid these conditions. Problems become social when the community or some representative group of people accepts responsibility for them.

Each of these classes of disorders is illustrated constantly in newspapers. Let us suppose the following are parts of headlines in today's paper:

RISING COSTS	MENTAL	UNITED NATIONS . . . .
INFLUENZA	SOCIAL SECURITY	TRAFFIC . . . .

Examples of a society's problems are questions about costs, mental conditions, political relations, health, social legislation, mobility, carelessness, selfishness, and indifference. Many other synonyms suggested by these terms are social or personal problems in present-day society.

There are numerous historical cues to the nature of problems. The Chinese Wall, an Aztec temple, medieval crusades, a Maginot line, a research foundation, or the Atlantic Charter are evidences of their extent in time and space. They are monuments to human problems of social invention.

Obviously each age invents and defines its own problems. An objective of sociological study is to redefine each problem. This step is imperative if the problem is to be analyzed adequately or eventually to be solved.

One of many approaches [1]

Any list of social problems indicates how they must be observed and studied. Each problem must be clearly stated. Each problem must be analyzed in terms of its basic composition. Associated conditions and problems must be detected as a necessary step in analysis and as a further limitation of the primary problem. Finally, a remedy, treatment, prevention, or solution may be suggested.

These keys in the sociology of social problems can be made more specific by the following interpretations:

Statement: All social problems:

1. may be regarded as either normal or abnormal conditions.
2. are relative, that is, they are constantly changing.
3. involve questions of human values.
4. may be interpreted as conflicts within and between the social institutions and specifically in competing moral codes.
5. appear at first under conditions that seem to be wholly benign. The first symptoms are innocent enough, but unless the actual problem is detected and treated promptly its course may duplicate the history of a chronic disease until it becomes uncontrollable.

Analysis:

1. Problems may be individual and personal as well as social disorders.
2. Most problems have a long social history.
3. Problems have numerous and startlingly different effects.
4. Problems as a rule appear so rapidly that people are not able to deal with them effectively.
5. Problems arise generally in a maze of many causes (multiple causation).
6. Problems may spread widely through a population.

[1] Studies of social problems have followed one or more of five different approaches. According to A. P. Herman, *An Approach to Social Problems,* Ginn, Boston, 1949, Chap. 1, they are (1) the social-problems approach (a general survey); (2) the social-disorganization approach; (3) the cultural-lag approach; (4) the value-structure approach (a conflict analysis); (5) the community approach. If a student observes the elementary rules of scientific method and avoids the impression that a problem develops in a vacuum and has no connection with its "web of social relations," almost any of these approaches can be followed profitably.

7. Problems are persistent and for this reason appear to be inevitable characteristics of human society.

Associated conditions:

1. A general observation is that every problem is generated from a background of numerous problems and tends to appear regularly with other social problems as causes, correlates, or consequences.
2. Almost without exception, any problem is disastrous in its consequences if it is allowed to follow an uninterrupted course.

Solutions:

1. Although few social problems can be solved and even fewer can be prevented, human society has a long history of proposed remedies and treatments.
2. Skill in the understanding of human problems, their causes, and their modifications is one of the most accurate tests of social ingenuity, adaptation, and inventiveness.

A classification

In an introductory survey, essential social problems may be clarified to some extent by noting their primary sources. This is the point of view adopted in the opening paragraph. Problems may be considered as personal and subjective, as impersonal and objective, or as accidents.

In the sociology of social problems, this elementary approach was accorded early recognition. One of the first systematic outlines of sociology regrouped the human problems of society as:

1. Problems of organization and administration: problems of business, government, and social welfare.
2. Problems of policy and polity: problems of politics and legislation, of social reform, and of institutional change.
3. Problems of human nature: problems of culture, which are the conditions that determine a society's basic social problems.[2]

A comparison

It is possible to note the primary similarity of all social problems by comparative inventories. During the last century the following

[2] R. E. Park and E. W. Burgess, *Introduction to the Science of Sociology,* University of Chicago Press, Chicago, 1924, pp. 46-47.

lists of problems have been stated and numerous efforts to cope with them have been launched.

The first statement is essentially a historical review. Problems recognized a century ago for the two decades, 1840-1860, were:

1. Abolition of slavery
2. Bigotry
3. Blindness
4. Child labor
5. Class hatred
6. Corrupt social institutions
7. Drunkenness
8. Equality of women
9. Exploitation of the masses
10. Factory conditions
11. Gambling
12. Housing
13. Indian disputes
14. Labor unrest
15. Migrations
16. Monetary policies and inflation
17. Orphans
18. Political disorder
19. Poverty
20. Prostitution
21. Riots
22. Slavery [3]

At the turn of the century—during the decades 1890-1910—social problems were:

1. Administration of public institutions for the dependent
2. Aims of philanthropy
3. Blindness
4. Causes of degeneration
5. Child labor
6. Children, dependent, delinquent, defective
7. Crime
8. Deafness
9. Divorce
10. Drunkenness
11. Epilepsy
12. Feeblemindedness
13. Heredity and eugenics
14. Homeless dependents
15. Illegitimacy
16. Immigration
17. Insanity
18. Labor problems
19. Poor relief, public and private
20. Poverty
21. Prisoners and prisons
22. Prostitution
23. Sickness
24. Suicide
25. Unemployment
26. Urban problems [4]

Present-day problems, as noted in the indexes to periodical literature, include:

1. Accidents
2. Aged
3. Alcoholism
4. Bankruptcy
5. Blindness
6. Business cycles

[3] Adapted from: Vernon L. Parrington, *Main Currents in American Thought,* Harcourt, Brace, New York, 1927 and 1930, Vol. 2, Chap. 3, pp. 350 ff; Vol. 3, Bk. 1, pp. 3 ff.; Dixon Wecter, *The Saga of American Society,* Scribner's, New York, 1937, pp. 89-134; p. 463; p. 472.

[4] Adapted from: Charles R. Henderson, *Introduction to the Study of the Dependent, Defective and Delinquent Classes,* Heath, Boston, 1901. Samuel G. Smith, *Social Pathology,* Macmillan, New York, 1911. Amos Warner, *American Charities,* Crowell, New York, 1894.

7. Children—abnormal
8. Conflict in laws
9. Costs of living
10. Crime
11. Cripples
12. Deafness
13. Disasters
14. Disease
15. Displaced people
16. Divorce
17. Drug addiction
18. Employment
19. Epidemics
20. Eugenics
21. Euthanasia
22. Family problems
23. Farm prices
24. Fatigue
25. Feeblemindedness
26. Fraud
27. Gambling
28. Graft
29. Health
30. Homicide
31. Housing
32. Illiteracy
33. Income
34. Inflation
35. Insurance
36. Juvenile delinquency
37. Labor laws
38. Leadership
39. Leisure
40. Longevity
41. Lynching
42. Marriage
43. Mental disease
44. Mental health
45. Migrants
46. Narcotics
47. Neuroses
48. Occupations
49. Parole
50. Pensions
51. Physical defects
52. Planning
53. Police
54. Politics—corruption in
55. Population
56. Poverty
57. Prejudice
58. Prices and price supports
59. Prisons
60. Prisoners
61. Probation
62. Prohibition
63. Propaganda
64. Prostitution
65. Psychoses
66. Public Health
67. Public Welfare
68. Public Works
69. Punishment
70. Race relations
71. Racketeering
72. Reconstruction
73. Recreation
74. Refugees
75. Regional planning
76. Safety movement
77. Sex
78. Slums
79. Social hygiene
80. Social legislation
81. Social planning
82. Social security
83. Speech defects
84. Suicide
85. Taxation
86. Traffic problems
87. Unemployment
88. Venereal disease
89. Vocational problems
90. War

These illustrations of social defects in contemporary society are examples of several classes of social maladjustments for which a definition must be provided. They suggest the primary defects in social institutions, policy, or administration that are probably responsible for the chronic repetition of these problems. At the same time they suggest the redefinition of institutions, policy and administration from time to time. For example, poverty appears in all three of the lists but, certainly, concepts of causes and policies of amelioration have changed in the hundred-year period.

Zones of occurrence

When these problems are examined in terms of their sources and types, ten areas of social adjustment can be observed. These zones of occurrence include the different problems of:

1. Age groups—children, youth, adults, aged.
2. Social classes—migrants, uneducated, the poor.
3. Places—urban, rural, suburban, village, open country or neighborhood areas.
4. Religious, sex, or ethnic groups—conditions peculiar to men, women, Negroes, Orientals, native whites, Protestants, Catholics, Jews.
5. Periods of time—the social problems of Ancient Greece, of France at the beginning of its decline in population, of Fascist Italy, of the United States as the West became settled.
6. Occupations or industries—problems of textile workers, American farmers, of professional people.
7. Systems of legislation, as noted by the coverage of social legislation or social security programs, or within the functioning of other social institutions, such as the church, school, or family.
8. Economic philosophies—labor-management relations, social control of business or of the professions, economics of population and migration.
9. Political policies—fair employment practices, price fixing, isolationism.
10. Cultures or periods of social development—problems occurring with war, depression, inflation, industrial conflict.

These divisions are not mutually exclusive. Almost any problem belongs as much to all of them as to one particular area. These zones supply a convenient perspective or point of initial approach.

Summary

The social problems of every society have been general conditions of human misery and unrest. Only in rare instances would they be simple or single questions or the most obvious ills of a person or group. In general, they are established solidly in the composition of a people, in its social history, and in the success of its economic adjustment. Such conditions always demand careful study and all available technical skills.

In order to survive, a society must seek to preserve a balance in its strengths as well as to minimize its weaknesses. People must be healthy. They must be socially adjusted. Material resources must be abundant and wisely administered. Social institutions, individually and collectively, must be efficient and well coordinated. Every defect or deficiency in these desirable achievements may be either an actual problem or a menace to social and personal security.

A social problem, therefore, may be identified when an obvious and widely recognized evil threatens the well-being of a large number of people, and promises to be costly in time, money, and effort either to tolerate or to avoid.

A social problem is always a challenge to the techniques of social study as well as to the resources of public policy. As such the first questions to be asked are:

1. How is this problem to be defined and limited in order to merit scientific consideration?
2. What relevant facts are needed?
3. What other problems are so connected with it either as causes or as results that they too must be included?
4. What can society do about them?

Man probably can solve some of the problems for which he is responsible. Possibly he can also solve some of those that are created by his natural environment. But nature, as MacIver has stated, "solves no problem which man creates." [5]

Bibliography

Cuber, J. F., and R. A. Harper, *Problems of American Society,* Holt, New York, 1950.

Elliott, Mabel A., and Francis E. Merrill, *Social Disorganization,* Harper, New York, 1950.

Faris, R. E. L., *Social Disorganization,* Ronald, New York, 1948.

Herman, Abbott P., *An Approach to Social Problems,* Ginn, Boston, 1949.

Lemert, E. M., *Social Pathology,* McGraw-Hill, New York, 1951. Chap. 1 reviews different interpretations of social problems.

Merrill, Francis E., and others, *Social Problems,* Knopf, New York, 1950.

. . . . .

Astbury, B. E., "Great Britain's Postwar Social Problems," *Proc. Nat'l. Conf. Soc. Work,* (1946): 18-30.

Brooks, Lee M., "Fifty Years' Quest for Social Control," *Social Forces,* Vol. 29 (1950): 1-8.

Eaton, Walter H., "Alternative Meanings of Adjustment," *Am. Soc. Rev.,* Vol. 12 (1947): 75-81.

Fuller, Richard C., "The Problem of Teaching Social Problems," *Am. Jour. Soc.,* Vol. 44 (1939): 415-435.

[5] R. M. MacIver, *Community,* Macmillan, New York, 1917, p. 242.

Homans, George C., "A Conceptual Scheme for the Study of Social Organization," *Am. Soc. Rev.*, Vol. 12 (1947): 13-26.

Kramer, Ralph, "The Conceptual Status of Social Disorganization," *Am. Jour. Soc.*, Vol. 48 (1943): 466-474.

Merrill, Francis E., "The Study of Social Problems," *Am. Soc. Rev.*, Vol. 13 (1948): 251-262.

Mowrer, E. R., "Social Crises and Social Disorganization," *Am. Soc. Rev.*, Vol. 15 (1950): 60-66.

Queen, Stuart A., "Social Participation in Relation to Social Disorganization," *Am. Soc. Rev.*, Vol. 14 (1949): 251-257.

Riemer, Svend, "Social Planning and Social Organization," *Am. Jour. Soc.* Vol. 52 (1947): 508-516.

Selznick, Philip, "Foundations of the Theory of Organization," *Am. Soc. Rev.*, Vol. 13 (1948): 25-35.

Warren, R. L., "Social Disorganization and the Interrelationship of Cultural Roles," *Am. Soc. Rev.*, Vol. 14 (1949): 83-87.

Questions

1. How many different social problems can you name from the suggested phrase: "Rising Cost of . . ."? What problems are associated with the other partial headlines mentioned on p. 3?
2. In your judgment, are the five customary approaches different? Explain how an exponent of these approaches would begin the study of particular problems.
3. Can a social problem be studied methodically? Objectively? Scientifically?
4. What conditions in the 1840-1860 list would you not consider to be current problems?
5. Are there any topics in the most recent list that you would also delete?
6. What are the most publicized problems in your community?
7. Is it possible to define the problem of racial discrimination according to the three topics suggested by Park and Burgess? The problem of crime? Of divorce?
8. Can one problem be a cause of another problem? The result?
9. Why are problems described as relative? To what are they relative?
10. Can you mention problems that continue to be regarded as critical even though they are comparatively rare? Or the reverse, conditions that are not particularly critical yet appear in the lives of increasing numbers of people?

PART 1

PROBLEMS IN PHYSICAL AND MENTAL HEALTH

Introduction

ILLNESSES AND DEFECTS OF THE BODY ARE AMONG SOCIETY'S MOST costly burdens. They are also among the oldest of man's enemies. No region or period has been exempt. In brief, they are typical social problems.

They are typical because they illustrate each aspect of a basic social disorder in (1) their widespread occurrence, (2) the universal recognition of their harmfulness, and (3) the personal and social misery that appears with them.

The challenge of these conditions is both individual and social.

How to live, according to two observers, is largely a personal problem. Each individual is responsible for (1) his own contacts with the world (skin, clothing, housing, cleanliness), (2) his diet, (3) the poisons that he tolerates (alcohol, tobacco, tea, coffee), and (4) his habits of work, play, rest, and sleep.[1]

But living also has its larger community responsibilities, which are represented in today's public health movement.

This movement is interested in two broad activities. One is the study of health and disease as medical problems. The other is their study as bio-social questions.[2]

[1] I. Fisher and H. Emerson, *How to Live,* Funk and Wagnalls, New York, 1946, preface.

[2] Iago Galdston, *Social Medicine: Its Derivations and Objectives,* The Commonwealth Fund, New York, 1949.

A most important result of this movement is preventive medicine. This program has demonstrated already that most diseases can be prevented. But neither it nor any known system of treatment is able to cope with a large number of obscure and uncontrollable ills.

Accordingly, there are two important prospects in public health. One is the study of the health problems of a society in their connection with other social problems. The other suggests a more fundamental consideration, namely, the need of every society for some planned policy of population and social organization. This policy will tend, on the one hand, to lessen current health hazards and, on the other, to produce in coming generations a people that will be biologically and socially more immune, at least to the deteriorating and degenerating forms of physical and mental sickness.

CHAPTER 2

PHYSICAL HEALTH

IF A LOW DEATH RATE AND AN IMPROVED LIFE EXPECTANCY ARE SUFFICIENT evidence, the United States is one of the healthiest nations. Yet nowhere is there more apparent dread of illness or popular concern for ways to better health. Cigarette advertising cultivates both emotions. National and reputable health societies use the public's half-knowledge in their campaigns—to encourage mass examinations, as in the case of tuberculosis; to stimulate drives for funds, as in the March of Dimes; or to arouse suspicion ("Did you know that there are two million unknown cases of diabetes?").

These attitudes and reactions are always present in the social problems of illness. They are created and intensified by the number of illnesses, their distribution among different classes of people, direct and indirect burdens required by treatment or attempted elimination, and their enormous annual dollar expense.

According to records of the United States Public Health Service, nearly three million persons from fourteen to sixty-four years of age are incapacitated by illness to such an extent that they must be considered out of the labor force permanently or at least for ten years or longer. Four of every $100 that the consumer spends is for health needs—an annual health bill of $7.4 billion, when the maintenance of the world's largest physical plant of hospitals, clinics, and laboratories is also included.[1]

Illness and its results are often classified among the "inner enemies" of a nation. There is nothing surprising about the claim of

[1] T. D. Woolsey, "Estimates of Disabling Disease Prevalence," *Pub. Health Rpts.*, Vol. 65 (1950), No. 6, p. 181.

many a historian that an endemic disease can so reduce the vitality of a people as to bring about depopulation or ultimate disappearance.

Illness and social problems

Physical illnesses and their results are both social problems and causes of social problems. This statement is practically self-evident when the broad classes of disease are considered apart from their numerous social disorders—viz., acute, chronic or degenerative; infectious or communicable; deficiency or nutritional; glandular; social and occupational; diseases that are well understood and preventable, or the incurable.

Problems that are directly associated with illness are of equal importance to nation, family, or the individual. First of all, they bring about the need for a large percentage of national income in the support of hospitals and clinics for treatment and rehabilitation. At the same time they add to the tax burden when those who are ill and their dependents must be maintained by private or public insurance or poor-relief programs. They reduce the national labor force both in size and productivity, and they weaken the military strength of the country both in available manpower and in its operating effectiveness.

Illness ranks among major problems of the family. This is obvious when the wage earner is the victim and the family's income is reduced or cut off entirely. It is equally apparent if the mother is ill and is unable to provide adequate child care. In other, less-obvious cases, the disease may be communicable or degenerative and may lead to sterility and finally to the extinction of the family.

In the case of every individual, the social involvements of illness become major problems when normal growth, education, marriage, or vocational adjustment is retarded or restricted, or when his life expectancy is reduced.

From all these points of view, illnesses become social problems in terms of their own history. Some illnesses are increasing in spite of every known precaution. Others remain major hazards because they do not decrease more promptly. Minor illnesses, too, can take on primary significance. They are so recognized when they are frequent enough to cause a great loss of time, or when they are disabling illnesses, or when in some obscure way they weaken resistance or expose the body to the serious, chronic, and fatal diseases. Illness can also be socially significant when it is rare and, primarily for this reason, one of the little-known and puzzling medical questions.

Extent and causes of illness

Problems of ill health can be judged from each of these points of view: by the numbers who are ill, by the extent of the serious and disabling illnesses, or by their social and personal results.

If the first index is used, there are two sources of information: namely, mortality reports and the frequency of sickness. Mortality rates or death records, the most reliable sources of information concerning the leading causes of death and illness, are now available in comparable form for several decades, owing to the establishment of the death registration area by the Federal Bureau of the Census in 1880. The death registration area is organized on the basis of uniform reporting of deaths, following the International Classification of the Causes of Death. It now includes every state. Accordingly, the registration area reports are accurate indications of the trend of illness and death in this country.

Current reports of deaths and sickness surveys supply three outstanding facts that assist materially in reducing the problem of illness to one of reasonable proportions. (1) A few diseases are the leading causes of death and account for the greatest amount of permanent incapacity. (2) Sickness surveys show that temporary illness and inefficiency are due to minor ailments about which the public has little information. (3) The most significant fact is that the major causes of death are traced more often to such minor illnesses, which are not adequately cared for and which expose the body to the inroads of communicable and degenerative disease, than to any other specific causal factor.

The general causes of disease have been classified in ten groups, as follows: (1) heredity; (2) infection; (3) poisons; (4) food deficiencies or excesses; (5) air deficiencies; (6) hormone deficiency or excess; (7) physical trauma or strain; (8) physical apathy or disuse; (9) psychic trauma or strain; (10) psychic apathy or disuse.[2]

Causation is reduced further to six agencies: (1) injury, (2) malformation, (3) defect of diet, (4) poisoning, (5) infection, and (6) neoplasm (a growth, such as a tumor). Only the first four are primary causes. During the last seventy years of medical research

[2] E. L. Fisk, "Possible Extension of the Human Life Cycle," *Annals, Am. Acad. Pol. and Soc. Sci.*, Vol. 145 (1929): 177.

the two outstanding causes that have been found are vitamin deficiency and microbic infection. These two causes help to explain many specific diseases as well as broad groups of diseases.

Extent as indicated by mortality.[3] During the last fifty years, six diseases have received considerable attention because of their frequency and because they rank among the most seriously disabling illnesses. These are heart diseases, cancer, influenza and pneumonia, intracranial lesions, nephritis, and tuberculosis.

In this fifty-year summary and comparison, ten causes of death have been the leading health problems. Trends in each are important because they clarify both the achievements and failures in the public health movement.

During these five decades, the frequency of today's No. 1 killer, the diseases of the heart, has increased rapidly. The frequency of cancer has increased steadily, more than doubling since 1900. Influenza and pneumonia, the leading causes of death in 1900, continued to increase in frequency until 1920; thereafter they decreased gradually until 1940, and since then more rapidly to less than one-fourth their 1900 figure. Tuberculosis has decreased steadily in frequency over the entire period, and its rate is now less than one-sixth of its rate in 1900, when it was the second leading cause of death. Intracranial lesions (cerebral hemorrhage) have maintained a high and constant rate. Nephritis has had a slightly fluctuating rate, with a small decrease in the last decade. This is the order of the six leading causes of death, according to their frequency in recent years. Each illness (intracranial lesions to be omitted because it is a defect or a result of illness) will be discussed briefly.

One of the most significant experiences of medicine and sanitation during the first half of the twentieth century is their success with infectious diseases. This achievement is demonstrated in the case of the respiratory diseases as a whole and in the practical elimination of diarrhea and enteritis, diphtheria, and typhoid, each of which was an important cause of death in 1900. Other problems remain unsolved, however; for instance, public health has not been able to exercise greater control over congenital malformations and diseases of infancy.

Extent as indicated by illnesses. Illnesses that do not appear prom-

[3] For annual summaries and comparisons by decades, consult: *Statistical Abstract of the United States,* United States Department of Commerce, Washington, D.C. (published annually).

inently in death reports are recognized as important problems for two reasons. They are causes of disability that keeps the individual from his usual occupation, or they reduce the individual's efficiency. Although there is no report on the extent of illness which can compare in accuracy with mortality records, various sickness surveys supply a useful index of total incidence.

In the table on page 18 an abbreviated summary is given of one of the most complete of these sickness surveys. It is a classification of the illnesses reported in the Eastern Health District of Baltimore during the period 1938-1943. Its accuracy and completeness are insured in part by the fact that it represents numerous resurveys of the same population, and in part by comparison with other surveys conducted elsewhere in this country.

Evidence of the total amount of illness in the American population is supplied by this study. For the entire group, there were 1,379 illnesses each year per 1,000 population. Of this total, 650 were disabling illnesses, that is disabling the person for one day or longer; and 729 illnesses were nondisabling. The extent and severity of the disabling illnesses are stressed by the fact that there were nearly 25 days (24.4) of disability for each disabling case.

As shown by the table, the twelve most frequent illnesses or disorders are colds, bronchitis, sore throat, influenza, digestive disturbances, diarrhea and enteritis, headache, menstrual disorders, infected teeth, skin conditions, tonsillitis, and arthritis.

The most disabling conditions, as shown in the original chart from which the table was adapted, are tuberculosis, epilepsy, mental deficiency, psychoses, heart disease, rheumatic fever, arthritis, rheumatic heart, and hypertension. Although some of these conditions are comparatively rare, they rank high in annual days of disability since some of them incapacitate the individual permanently. Likewise, top ranking in social significance must be given to some of the minor disorders, since their frequency gives them a nearly equivalent rank for days of disability.

Aside from colds, which are the greatest cause of illness in every age group, each period of life has its own distribution of illnesses. In childhood—that is, under 14 years of age—communicable diseases are most frequent. Diseases of the skin, ears, eyes, and teeth, and nervous and digestive disorders are also common in this period. Illnesses are at their lowest level during adolescence and young adulthood. Certain specific diseases, however, have their highest

THE FREQUENCY OF SPECIFIC ILLNESSES

	Rates per 1,000 Population of Total Cases
Minor respiratory:	
Coryza and colds	240.2
Bronchitis	215.1
Sore throat	101.7
Influenza	72.1
Tonsillitis	19.4
Other respiratory:	
Tonsillectomy	12.2
Sinusitis	8.7
Pneumonia	8.6
Allergy and related disorders:	
Asthma	9.4
Hay fever	9.3
Dermatitis	7.1
Infectious, parasitic:	
German measles	16.1
Measles	16.0
Chickenpox	9.1
Whooping cough	8.6
Tuberculosis	3.1
Syphilis	2.6
Non-Infectious, general:	
Malignant neoplasm	3.3
Thyroid diseases	3.1
Diabetes	2.7
Nervous system:	
Nervousness	10.7
Neuritis	7.6
Psychoneurosis	5.9
Eye, inflammation, etc.	14.3
Ear:	
Otitis media	14.8
Earache	10.9
Heart and circulatory:	
Other heart diseases	17.1
Hypertension, arteriosclerosis	7.6
Other circulatory	7.3
Rheumatic fever	7.1
Minor digestive:	
Digestive disturbances	51.8
Diarrhea, enteritis	26.3
Other digestive:	
Infected teeth	20.3
Appendicitis	10.5
Nephritis	4.6
Menstrual disorders	20.4
Skin conditions (other)	19.6
Arthritis	19.3
Headache	27.9

Source: S. D. Collins, "Specific Causes of Illness Found in Monthly Canvasses of Famil es," *Pub. Health Rpts.*, Vol. 65 (1950): No. 39, 1256. This table is abbreviated from Figure 4.

incidence at this time—for example, puerperal conditions, venereal disease, typhoid fever, and pulmonary tuberculosis. Yet, on the whole, this period of life is the healthiest. In old age, particularly after age 45, degenerative and organic diseases are the chief causes of disability and death. Among the more prominent of these are diseases of the circulatory system, nervous diseases, nephritis, and diseases of the bones and locomotive organs.

The social, economic, and physical significance of this distribution of minor and major illnesses in different age groups, and its cause, are well summarized by Dr. Morris Fishbein:

> The chief factors in death after forty-five years of age are heart disease, pneumonia, high blood pressure, cancer, brain hemorrhage and kidney disease. Among the causes of these conditions, so far as known, are infections sustained early in life, particularly of the nose, throat, tonsils and sinuses, infections of the teeth, and spots of infection elsewhere in the body from which germs are carried to the heart, the kidneys and blood vessel walls. These early infections are themselves associated with poor personal hygiene, with overcrowded living conditions, with residence in damp places and with undue exposure to the elements. Any of these factors, as can easily be realized, is controllable only by social and economic movements which are only secondarily within the province of medicine.[4]

Chronic diseases

In a report to one of the first meetings of the World Health Organization, which was established by the United Nations to deal with all aspects of health, one of the directors said: "The major world health problem is not death but the chronic infection and infestation which converts man from a productive unit to a liability in society." [5]

This statement is also true for the United States. Chronic diseases exceed all others as a national burden and as sources of economic and social insecurity. They cause nearly one million deaths annually and one billion days of disability annually. Their victims require 750,000 hospital beds and the services of one third of the nation's doctors. More than twenty-five million persons suffer from one or more of the disabling or nondisabling chronic ailments. And it is estimated that by 1980 this total will be forty million people.

[4] *The Human Body and Its Care,* American Library Association, Chicago, 1919, pp. 15-16. Quoted by permission.

[5] *Pub. Health Rpts.,* Vol. 65 (1950), No. 49, p. 1613. V. A. Getting, "A Coordinated State Program for Chronic Illness," *Am. Jour. Pub. Health,* Vol. 40 (1950): 1251.

The chief chronic diseases are heart disease, arteriosclerosis, high blood pressure, nervous and mental diseases, arthritis, kidney disease (nephritis), tuberculosis, cancer, diabetes, and asthma. They are also called constitutional diseases to distinguish them from the diseases that are caused by conditions outside of the body. These diseases are chiefly the result of injuries and wear and tear sustained by the body as a normal result of aging. They are also known as that class of diseases on which scientific research has made little or no headway.

Although the chronic diseases increase with age and have their highest incidence in old age, they are found in all age groups. Sixteen per cent of the chronically ill are under 25 years of age; 50 per cent are under 45 years of age; 75 per cent are in the productive years, 15 to 64.

Prevention of chronic diseases is necessarily general and is nearly as extensive as the whole public health program. It includes nutrition, housing, school health programs that aim to correct defects as soon as they are discovered, educational programs to encourage people to seek early diagnosis and treatment, mental health, industrial clinics, and clinical provisions for each variety of chronic ailment.

Heart diseases

Diseases of the heart and blood vessels kill about 600,000 people each year. This is three times as many deaths as from cancer, six times as many deaths as from accidents, seven times as many deaths as from kidney diseases, nine times as many deaths as from pneumonia, and ten times as many deaths as from tuberculosis.

There are at least five different heart diseases. The three leading types or causes are rheumatic fever; hypertension, which is related to high blood pressure and arteriosclerosis; and coronary thrombosis. The other two are congenital malformations of the heart and syphilitic heart conditions. These two are either limited or are decreasing. Hence, the primary problems are to be located in the three leaders. Hypertension and arteriosclerosis are the most difficult, because they are degenerative. They are concentrated in middle and later life, and after age sixty they account for ninety per cent of all heart cases. The most hopeful from the standpoint of control are those associated with rheumatic fever, which is the chief type of heart disease before age forty.

These facts can be most graphically shown by contrasts. Among children under fifteen years of age, heart ailments are not only numerous but they present serious complications in other health conditions of youth. Here, then, heart disease ranks with the so-called diseases of childhood, such as scarlet fever, whooping cough, and diphtheria. Its fatality rate is more than three times that of tuberculosis. Among adults, heart disease has increased markedly in the colored population and among white females. After the age of thirty-five, heart disease far exceeds tuberculosis as a cause of death among both men and women, and after the age of forty it exceeds all other causes of death.

In addition to its direct contribution to the death rate, heart disease is an important secondary cause of death (in the case of influenza-pneumonia) and is a primary cause of disability. For every death from heart disease, there are ten living persons who are incapacitated and who are unable to continue normal productivity. In consequence, heart disease ranks high among the illnesses contributing to poverty and family disorganization.

The high incidence, economic losses, and remedial costs of heart disease have stimulated considerable research and preventive work, organized by the American Heart Association. The program of the Association has been directed toward three objectives: (1) complete physical examination in order to discover the ailment as soon as possible and to allow for early treatment; (2) the treatment of infections which occur with heart ailments; (3) occupational readjustment of persons with structural heart defects. The first line of attack has been followed with successful results by insurance companies. Aside from congenital defects, which are largely uncontrollable, the other causes of heart disease—diseases of childhood, acute and chronic infectious diseases of adults, focal infections and toxins—are thus minor and largely preventable conditions. Consequently, the control of heart disease can be achieved most directly by a general health program seeking to eliminate illnesses popularly considered of no great importance.[6]

[6] Since none of the specific causes of heart disease is known, both controls and therapy are experimental. The approaches are microbial, nutritional, and therapeutic, including such problems as (1) the relation of streptococci to rheumatic fever, (2) the relation that obesity and/or a high blood content of cholesterol (a fatlike substance) has to the coronary diseases, (3) the value of a saltless diet, (4) correcting the heart disorders of children by surgery, (5) treatment of coronary thrombosis with dicumarol (an anticoagulant therapy). Consult the series

Rheumatic fever. This disease has assumed considerable importance, not only because of its role in the heart disease of adults but also because of its role as a children's disease. According to the American Heart Association, this disease accounts for forty per cent of all heart diseases and kills more children than most of the other children's diseases combined. In addition, the Association reports that one million individuals are victims either of this disease or of rheumatic heart disease; that one fifth of its victims die within ten years and another fifth are crippled permanently; and that 40,000 G.I.'s during World War II acquired rheumatic fever, although it occurs primarily in the age group from six to fourteen.

To date the chief source of rheumatic fever is supposed to be repeated streptococcal infections of the nose and throat. There is also some evidence that it is favored or induced by generally poor home conditions and that broken homes or homes demoralized by alcoholism, promiscuity, and neglect supply a disproportionately large number of cases. Since there is no known cure, the recommended treatment is rest, sunlight, a wholesome diet, the correction of poor home conditions, and penicillin or sulfa drugs.

Cancer

Cancer resembles the preceding diseases in that little is known about it or its causes. One of the most widely accepted facts is that it appears in all age groups and that it increases rapidly after age thirty in all age groups. Insurance statisticians for some time have stated that most of this increase is actual and not due to better diagnosis or classification.

Another fact that may be of use in research is its distribution. Cancer occurs in animals as well as in humans, and this distribution affords researchers one of their most hopeful resources in animal research. Among humans, cancer is somewhat more frequent among women than men. Another difference is the greater frequency of skin cancer among whites than Negroes. Cancer is also found more often in southern than in northern states, the explanation being the higher incidence of cancer of the skin and mouth in the South.

"Statistical Studies of Heart Disease," by S. D. Collins, T. D. Woolsey, M. Gover, and M. Y. Pennell, in *Pub. Health Rpts.,* Vol. 64 (1949), No. 46, pp. 1439-1492; Vol. 65 (1950), No. 17, pp. 555-568; Vol. 65 (1950), No. 26, pp. 819-832. See also "Survivorship in Heart Disease," *Statis. Bull.,* Metropolitan Life Insurance Company, Vol. 31 (Sept. 1950): 8-11.

Other geographical comparisons have also been made showing the possible influences of occupations, climate (sunlight, especially), social and economic status, diet, clothing, housing (overheating), and any other source of physiological irritation arising from the habits of civilization.[7]

Cancer, often called neoplasm in mortality reports, is described as "an ungovernable, erratic growth and destructive migration of cells which are normally present in the body." From recent studies, the following facts are accepted generally by research workers: it arises *de novo,* not by transmission from person to person; it cannot be prevented by limiting exposure; it is the result of many factors operating over a long period of time. Except in its early stages, when it may be treated by surgery, X-ray, and radium, there is scant hope of recovery from cancer. Three suggested methods of prevention are: (1) proper mating of individuals devoid of a hereditary predisposition to cancer; (2) the elimination of prolonged irritation; (3) early diagnosis and treatment.

One of the most promising cures is suggested in the use of atomic energy in the treatment of cancer. Several projects are now being supported by the American Cancer Society in the hope that some form of this energy or some radioactive substance can be discovered that will explode the cancer cells without injuring normal cells.[8]

Influenza and pneumonia

Among the most acute and deadly of communicable diseases are the respiratory infections, influenza and pneumonia. They are not caused by a specific germ, but represent a group of diseases and a group of causes, some of which have been identified. These diseases occur in all latitudes, and are endemic and often epidemic. Control is difficult because they are spread by human contacts and frequently by healthy carriers. Both point to the common cold as the real problem in immediate prevention, and to its sequence of acute infections of the respiratory tract, which include sore throat, bron-

[7] H. C. Lombard, "Major Cancer Control Problems," *Am. Jour. Pub. Health,* Vol. 39 (1949): 1098. "The Geography of Cancer," *Time,* Aug. 14, 1950. Othe suggested inquiries include individual constitutional differences, either as causes of cancer or as factors causing differences in responses to treatment, milk as a factor, early marriage (associated with cancer of the cervix), individual habits, and heredity.

[8] *Health Bull. for Teachers,* Metropolitan Life Insurance Company, Vol. 20 (May 1949): 20.

chitis, and whooping cough. In combination, influenza-pneumonia is the most prevalent and damaging of all respiratory diseases in causing both sickness and death.

Influenza has been known to medical science for several centuries. It was brought to public attention in 1918, under the name "Spanish influenza" (Spain having been the country of its origin) in one of its most virulent forms. Although influenza is rarely a fatal disease but is usually only a precursor of some other (fatal) complication, during the world epidemic in 1918 twenty-eight per cent of the population were affected and several million people died from it. Influenza is definitely cyclical. Since 1627 there have been nineteen epidemics in the United States; and fourteen worldwide epidemics have been recorded since 1510. Influenza cannot be prevented, because its germinal causes have not been isolated. They are supposed to be a filtrable virus. Recently, thirty-three types of pneumonia have been identified, eight of which cause eighty per cent of all lobar pneumonia and four of which are usually fatal.

The decreasing death rate is a result of many years of research. Within the last decade the use of a serum treatment reduced the death rate by one half. Although vaccines have been used experimentally, they have not been very successful. The discovery of the sulfa drugs, introduced in 1936, marked the beginning of effective treatment through chemicals. Penicillin (1942) and aureomycin and terramycin (1949) have been used with great success. The result of these drugs is both prompt and dramatic and is responsible for the continued reduction of this disease.

Tuberculosis

Although tuberculosis is no longer one of the four leading causes of death, and has been declining steadily during the last sixty years, this decline has not been so spectacular as to eliminate it from the group of chief health hazards. For years the "Great White Plague" was the leading cause of death, far in excess of others. It is still an important health and social problem because of its connection with economic dependency and because there is no adequate preventive. Tuberculosis has been widely prevalent in every historical group and is well described in early medical works. After the isolation of the tubercle bacillus in 1882 by Koch, and the advance in curative and preventive measures and in living conditions, the decline in its incidence has been general, without regard to race, sex, or age groups. However, it remains a tremendous burden among the industrial population, where it is doubly injurious, affecting young adults at the period when their earnings are highest and most needed by their families.

This peculiar incidence of tuberculosis among industrial workers has made it one of the major occupational diseases. From ages twenty to fifty-five the death rate among male industrial workers is greatly in excess of that among the general population, and is greater among males than among females. At present this correlation between relative poverty and tuberculosis and its greater prevalence in cities indicate the chief social problems of this disease. They are the primary reasons for current demands for mass examinations and mass vaccination (such as the BCG vaccine which has been given to thirty-one million Japanese since V-J Day).

Insurance statisticians predict that further environmental controls will eventually place tuberculosis among the minor causes of death. The declining death rate was not interrupted by either of the two World Wars, except temporarily in some of the European countries —belligerent as well as nonbelligerent—where unusual increases did occur, most noticeably among children.

Nephritis

Nephritis (or Bright's disease), the fourth ranking cause of death, is even more well known as various diseases of the kidneys. The forms of this disease are both acute and chronic, and are generally classified as inflammatory, degenerative, and less frequently as renal insufficiency. All are obscure in origin and onset, difficult to diagnose, resistant to treatment, and consequently fatal in most cases. Nephritis is associated with anemia, variations in blood pressure, and several different disorders of the heart and lungs. Deaths occur most often because of hypertension, uremia, cardiac decompensation, and bronchopneumonia. Nephritis becomes most fatal after age thirty, and this fact, as well as its associations with other physical disabilities, classifies it as a typical degenerative disease.

Other significant bio-social illnesses

There are a number of specific illnesses or groups of illnesses that are not especially noteworthy in death reports or sickness surveys. These conditions of ill health continue to receive a lot of attention, either because they represent challenges to medical research or because they are looked upon as major sources of social demoralization. Examples are poliomyelitis, the venereal diseases, occupational diseases, and the deficiency diseases.

Poliomyelitis, or infantile paralysis, is a typical family of diseases. Health campaigns have made it one of the best known and most dreaded among all the hazards of childhood. However, it is actually relatively uncommon, judged by the frequency of other diseases or of accidents among children.

As to its incidence, little is known, but there are some definite trends in the reported cases. It tends to be cyclical. During the last 50 years, there were three periods of high incidence, namely, in 1916-1917, in 1931, and in 1949-1950. There were lesser epidemics in 1911, 1920, 1927, 1930, 1933, 1943, and 1946. A further encouraging character of the disease is to be noted in the fact that when it is epidemic it is generally limited to certain areas.

Infantile paralysis is misnamed if recent incidence proves to be typical. One reason is its peak of concentration at the age fifteen, with other years of considerable infection being the school, and not the preschool, or infantile, years. Furthermore, there has been a recent shift toward upper age groups, particularly young adults.

In this family of diseases, three viruses have already been identified. There are presumably other, undiscovered virus sources. These viruses attack nerve cells. However, the course of the infection is not well understood, and the reason why nerve cells are injured remains unknown. This question is the most important problem in medical research. For every case of nerve injury, there are five to ten cases in which carriers suffer no ill effect.

It is also known that this disease is transmitted by intimate personal contacts, such as those that take place in the home. But the mode of transmission is not known. Some individuals are apparently immune, and some who manifest the early symptoms recover completely. Another fact is that there are probably many more cases per year than those that are reported; that is, individuals can be carriers of the disease without showing its symptoms.

According to discoveries announced by the National Foundation for Infantile Paralysis, the prospect of control is most favorable. This opinion is based upon the fact that polio viruses produce antibodies that protect nerve cells. Current research is directed toward the exploitation of this process in the quest for an effective vaccine.[9]

Venereal diseases. In contrast to the situation at the turn of the century, the two important venereal diseases, syphilis and gonorrhea, have been given increasing publicity in recent decades. Nevertheless, they are not particularly well-known diseases. Ignorance, fear, and quackery, along with unsolved medical problems, continue to rank as major obstructions to control. As yet, little attention is given to the minor venereal diseases.[10]

Because of this history, the incidence of the venereal diseases continues to be stated in estimated round numbers. In the case of syphilis, annual attack rates vary from 150,000 to 500,000 per year. Attack rates of gonorrhea are never based on actual count or report, and are put at two million per year. The total number of victims amounts to an estimated twelve to eighteen million, of whom 3 million have syphilis and 15 million have gonorrhea. Estimates vary because of the recognition of unreported and unrecognized cases. It is agreed, however, that on the basis of death rates and new cases both diseases are declining. This decrease would be viewed more optimistically if the rate of new cases among children did not continue to shock the public.

Years ago Dr. William Osler placed syphilis among the leading causes of death. He wrote:

> Know syphilis, in all its manifestations and relations, and all other things clinical shall be added unto you.

Concerning gonorrhea, he said:

> From the standpoint of race conservation, gonorrhea is a disease of the first rank. . . . While not a killer, as a misery producer Neisser's coccus is king among germs.

When the problems of these diseases are compared with the characteristics of any social problem, they fulfill each requirement completely—in the number of persons involved, the serious physical and

[9] "What Do We Know about Poliomyelitis?," *Survey,* Vol. 85 (1949): 489. A. G. Gilliam and others, "Average Poliomyelitis Incidence," *Pub. Health Rpts.,* Vol. 64 (1949), No. 49, pp. 1575-1584. "Poliomyelitis Epidemic Recurrence," *Pub. Health Rpts.,* Vol. 64 (1949), No. 49, pp. 1584-1595.

[10] H. Packer, "The Minor Venereal Diseases," *Hygeia,* Vol. 27 (1949): 406 ff. W. H. Aufranc, "Are Venereal Diseases Disappearing?" *Jour. Soc. Hyg.,* Vol. 36 (1950): 344. H. A. Kahn and A. P. Iskrant, "Syphilitic Mortality Analysis," *Jour. Ven. Dis. Infor.,* Vol. 29 (1948): 193-200. J. J. Wright and C. G. Sheps, "Role of Case Finding in Syphilis Control Today," *Am. Jour. Pub. Health,* Vol. 40 (1950): 844-849.

social complications, the costly economic and physiological consequences, and the need for corrective measures. Moreover, since the causes, agencies of transmission, and medical treatment of these diseases are well known, there is no obstruction to prevention as in the case of some other physical diseases. Preventive measures are rarely employed, because the problems of social hygiene are entangled with many unsolved moral, legal, and social problems. Consequently, no other diseases, infectious or degenerative, present more immediate difficulties. Syphilis and gonorrhea continue to be major causes of personal and social maladjustment, while their eradication awaits a social policy which will be mutually agreeable to several competing social institutions. Educational campaigns have been successful in disseminating information concerning venereal disease. The Public Health Service, through its Division of Venereal Disease, and The American Social Hygiene Association are two of the principal organizations which channel information on venereal disease to the public. However, because of their prevalence and our cultural resistance to their prevention, the venereal diseases are sometimes called the Third Great Plague.

Associated problems. The social hygiene movement represents the approach to a group of connected problems. These problems involve: (1) the law and its violation, (2) morals, (3) prostitution, (4) subnormal classes, (5) ignorance, (6) economic status, (7) marriage and family relations, (8) abortion, miscarriage, and stillbirths, (9) acquired and congenital illness and defectiveness, (10) destitution and dependency, (11) health resources. Until recently little or no attention was given to these problems as related social conditions. There have been many independent controls, each being introduced in a piece-meal fashion and with consequent ineffectiveness. As a rule, control now includes three related steps. One is an educational program to persuade individuals to seek examinations voluntarily. This plan is most effective among males. A second is contact investigation and study in the clinic when individuals do not go to the clinic voluntarily. This plan is most effective among females. The third plan is the mass examination of large groups of people, but it is the least effective of the three.

While this coordinated program apparently has reduced the total number of cases in a population, it has not been able to reduce appreciably the number of new cases.

Medical aspects. From a biological and medical point of view there are several, at least five, diseases that are classified as venereal, and some chronic pathological conditions that are caused by venereal infections. Only three of these—syphilis,* gonorrhea, and chancroid—are mentioned in prevalence studies, and most attention is devoted to the first two. In their history, evidences of both can be traced indirectly and generally by their consequences to their occurrence many years before the Christian era.

Prior to 1905 the clinical nature of syphilis had been thoroughly described, but little had been learned of its causes. For this reason, syphilis and other venereal diseases were still improperly described as hereditary. Isolation or quarantine was employed to limit their spread. In 1905 the cause was traced to an animalcule (called *spirochaeta pallida* or the *pale spiral*) and in 1910 a specific was discovered (salvarsan, a combination of arsenic and benzol). Recent reports by Schaudinn have suggested that infection in syphilis is caused by an invisible virus, of which the spirochete is only the visible manifestation.

Gonorrhea is ranked with syphilis as being its equal in seriousness to the infected person and in social consequences. In most prevalence studies, gonorrhea is three to five times as frequent as syphilis. This disease was well known to the classical writers on medicine, and there are many references in the classical literature to its appearance and treatment. Its bacterial cause was isolated in 1879. Until recently gonorrhea was considered a minor local infection; but the contrary is now known to be true. Investigations show that it can be transmitted by the blood to almost every organ of the body. Gonorrheal "rheumatism" is its most frequent result. Owing to its frequency, virulence of the germ after apparent cure, and its biological and social sequelae, some medical authorities are of the opinion that gonorrhea is more resistant to treatment than syphilis.

Both of these diseases are leading secondary causes of death, and both cripple and disable patients by their many complications. Because there has been no specific cure for either disease except after early, persistent, and costly treatment, there is considerable hope in recently reported cures (either by newly discovered drugs or by artificially induced fever) that this plague will eventually be controlled.

Both sulfa drugs and penicillin have been experimented with extensively. Though effective results have been demonstrated, none of the authorities in this field is willing to admit that the cures are absolutely reliable. One of the most effective attacks is now being operated under the National Venereal Control Act (passed in 1938), which has established clinics throughout the nation.

Social consequences. In their physical, biological, mental, and social complications, the effects of both syphilis and gonorrhea are very extensive. Although syphilis results in higher mortality and is a primary cause of death, in other respects the consequences of syphilis and gonorrhea are practically identical.

Syphilis and its poisons involve the entire human organism. They attack the deeper organs, causing a great proportion of diseases of the heart, arteries, kidneys, and liver. Fifty per cent of the cardiac diseases and those of the circulatory system, ninety per cent of aneurysm, and forty per cent of cerebral hemorrhage and apoplexy are traced to these causes. They attack the central nervous system, resulting in locomotor ataxia, general paralysis, other spinal cord diseases, and mental disease. To syphilis is attributed ten per cent of the cases admitted to hospitals for mental diseases. It causes extensive damage to the eye. Fifteen per cent of blindness and many impairments of vision are traced to congenital or acquired syphilis. Among the latter impairments are optic atrophy, acute inflammation, iritis, adhesions, cloudiness of the lens capsule, and inflammation of the ciliary muscle or of the retinal lining. Syphilis attacks the reproductive system and becomes an important cause of sterility, premature births, and infant mortality.[11]

The principal conclusions of the Solomons as to the consequences of syphilis are in fundamental agreement with recent clinical observations:

1. The family of the late syphilitic abounds with evidence of syphilitic damage.
2. At least one fifth of the families of syphilitics have one or more syphilitic members in addition to the original patient.
3. Between one third and one fourth of the families of syphilitics have never given birth to a living child. This is much larger than the percentage obtained from the study of a large group of New England families taken at random. Here it is shown that only one tenth were childless.
4. More than one third of the families of syphilitics have accidents to pregnancies: namely, abortions, miscarriages, or stillbirths.
5. The birth rate in syphilitic families is 2.05 per family, whereas the

[11] H. C. and M. H. Solomon, *Syphilis of the Innocent,* United States Interdepartmental Hygiene Board, Washington, 1922, p. 128.

birth rate in the New England families mentioned above is 3.8 per family, or almost twice as high.

6. Over one half of the families show defects as to children (sterility, accidents to pregnancies, and syphilitic children).
10. Between 1 in 12 and 1 in 6 of the children examined show syphilitic involvement.
11. One fifth of all children born alive in syphilitic families were dead at the time the families were examined. This does not differ materially from the general average in the community.
15. A syphilitic is a syphilitic, whether his disease is general paresis, cerebrospinal syphilis, or visceral syphilis without involvement of the central nervous system, and the problems affecting his family are the same in any case.

Similarly, gonorrhea is held responsible for many chronic diseases and irreparable physical defects. Of these, blindness is most often associated with this infection. Six of every ten infections of the eyes among the newborn are due to gonorrhea, and so is slightly more than three per cent of adult blindness. A considerable but unknown proportion of chronic diseases in both men and women and a large percentage of the pelvic infections of women are of gonorrheal origin. Seventeen to twenty-five per cent of childlessness among married persons is due to sterility of men with a history of this infection, as are many cases of one-child sterility and about fifty per cent of sterility in women. Gonorrhea is also a factor in stillbirths, premature births, arthritis, rheumatism, endocarditis; and gonorrheal vulvovaginitis is a frequent and serious defect among young female children.

There are other damaging results to personal and family welfare that are joint products of both diseases. Venereal disease cuts in half the life expectancy of the individual; it shortens life by an average of eighteen years. It is an important factor in broken homes and divorce. In addition, it causes long periods of disability, chronic invalidism, and industrial inefficiency, and is mentioned as a probable cause of industrial accidents and increasing compensation payments in industry.

Social and personal characteristics. In the social histories of venereal disease patients, many are found to be of an inferior personality type. This observation is most usual in the case of the repeater who is described as "a weakly organized personality," that is, the type ordinarily called the psychopathic personality. Venereal infection, consequently, is an indicator of both social maladjustment and personal deterioration.

In a series of comparative studies in England, San Francisco, Chicago, and St. Louis, the venereal patient was found to be educationally as well as intellectually retarded—conditions that are sufficient to account for the indifference of the patient to treatment in the clinic. Moreover, these individuals also had inferior socio-economic status, an irregular work history, a record of alcoholism, abnormal childhood conditions, such as broken homes, and a record of sexual promiscuity. These studies also showed higher rates of venereal infection among the divorced, separated, widowed, and single (after age twenty-five) than among the married, and higher rates among delinquent and retarded children.[12]

In a special analysis of male victims, all these characteristics were noted in their histories. In addition, such particular personal traits were reported as "carefree, ready to take chances, more easily influenced, and unrestrained." As civilians they had a record of frequent arrests. In the Army they were poorly adjusted and frequently the subject of punishments or courts martial. They began their sex life early, engaged often in extramarital intercourse, and frequented prostitutes often and with little discrimination.[13]

Occupational diseases. Both the health and well-being of the American wage earner have improved steadily since 1910. General and specific death rates have decreased. Life expectancy has increased by at least twelve years. Moreover, some of the illnesses that were major risks to the industrial population forty years ago are now either under control or are capable of much more efficient management. This conclusion applies especially to the entire class of respiratory diseases that formerly were the ranking fatal illnesses among industrial workers.

This record would be interpreted as actual achievement, if at the same time it were not admitted that the mortality of industrial workers remains higher and their life expectancy less than for other

[12] H. N. Bundesen and others, "Psychosomatic Approach to Venereal Disease Control," *Am. Jour. Pub. Health,* Vol. 39 (1949): 1535-1540. N. R. Ingraham and others, "Juvenile Delinquency and Venereal Disease in Philadelphia," *Jour. Ven. Dis. Infor.,* Vol. 29 (1948): 362-371.

[13] C. D. Bowdoin and others, "Socio-Economic Factors in Syphilis," *Jour. Ven. Dis. Infor.,* Vol. 30 (1949): 131-139. M. W. Brody, "Men Who Contract Venereal Disease," *Jour. Ven. Dis. Infor.,* Vol. 29 (1948): 334-336. P. W. Tappan, "The Sexual Psychopath," *Jour. Soc. Hyg.,* Vol. 35 (1949): 354-367.

workers. The inescapable conclusion, therefore, is that occupational diseases continue to be significant social, economic, and health problems.

The term *occupational diseases* refers to the health hazards in particular industries or occupations rather than to new diseases. Both diseases and deaths vary considerably in different occupations. As a social problem, occupational diseases have two manifestations. First is the excessive incidence of common (or primary) diseases in a given vocation. Examples of these are pneumonia and heart diseases among steel workers; tuberculosis in the dusty trades, in the clothing industry, and among barbers; "rheumatism" among molders; lead poisoning among painters; asthma in the pottery industry; and dermatitis among boot and shoe workers, rubber handlers, and millers. The second is the occurrence of rare and degenerative diseases with unusual frequency under the abnormal working conditions of certain vocations—for example, among workers exposed to lead, benzine, turpentine, brass, acids, analin oil, arsenic, phosphorus, mercury, and carbon monoxide gas. Trachoma among mill workers, hookworm disease among miners, anthrax among wool sorters, eye defects among welders, ulcers among electroplaters, and caisson disease among divers and tunnel workers are illustrations of diseases caused by such exposure. Industrial hygienists justify this classification of diseases by occupations because of the unusual risks and exposure that some require.

Dublin and Leiboff, in an enumeration of 700 hazardous occupations, classified the following nine major hazards with their most frequent disabilities:

1. ABNORMALITIES OF TEMPERATURE:
   Hazards: (a) extreme dry heat; (b) sudden variations in temperature.
   Associated diseases or symptoms: anemia, general debility, catarrh, Bright's disease, pneumonia, neuralgia and rheumatic affections.
2. COMPRESSED AIR:
   Associated conditions: vertigo, paralysis of arms and legs, hemorrhage.
3. DAMPNESS:
   Associated conditions: diseases of the respiratory passages, neuralgia and rheumatic affections.
4. DUST:
   Hazards: (a) Inorganic dust.
   Associated conditions: inflammatory conditions of eyes, ears, nose, and throat, chronic catarrh, colds, pleurisy, tuberculosis.
   (b) Organic dust.

Associated conditions: dryness of nose, throat, and mouth, cough, asthma, bronchitis, tuberculosis.

5. EXTREME LIGHT:
   Associated conditions: cataracts, dermatitis, ulceration of the skin, cancer.
6. INFECTIONS:
   Hazards: (a) Anthrax (external and internal).
   Associated conditions: malignant pustule, malignant edema, hay fever.
   (b) Hookworm.
   (c) Septic infections.
7. POOR ILLUMINATION:
   Associated conditions: nystagmus, eyestrain, headache.
8. REPEATED MOTION, PRESSURE, SHOCK, ETC.:
   Associated conditions: muscular strains, partial paralysis.
9. POISONS:
   Hazards: Fifty-four poisons are enumerated, of which the more common are: ammonia, alcohol, aniline, arsenic, brass (zinc), lead, phosphorus, tar, turpentine.
   Associated conditions: headache, paralysis, nervous symptoms, skin diseases, irritation of the mucous membranes, digestive disturbances, sclerosis of the bones, bronchitis.[14]

There are no complete figures on the incidence or costs of these diseases, although it is generally accepted that skin diseases amount to more than two thirds of the total. Abroad, a few other diseases run a close second to skin diseases either in frequency or severity. Germany and Switzerland have experienced poisoning as a chief industrial hazard. In England, miner's nystagmus (a disease of the eye) and chrome ulceration have occasionally exceeded lead poisoning. Silicosis (respiratory diseases due to dusts) is the most frequent disease in South Africa and Australia. In tropical countries, parasitic ailments, such as hookworm, are most prevalent. In the United States, dermatitis is the principal disease from the standpoint of frequency, while lead poisoning is the most serious of occupational diseases. Others appearing more frequently in the reports are "industrial back," hernia, occupational cancer, conditions due to extreme heat, electrical injuries (burns, brain injury), and caisson disease. The following is a typical distribution of the reportable occupational diseases, enumerated in the order of their frequency:

1. Industrial dermatitis—hazards are oils, chemicals, dyes, paints, solvents, metals, fabrics, rubber, heavy dusts, cement, lead.

[14] L. I. Dublin and P. Leiboff, "Occupational Hazards and Diagnostic Signs," *United States Dept. of Labor Statistics,* Bulletin No. 306 (1922): 12-31.

2. Lead poisoning—hazards are reported in 150 occupations by the United States Department of Labor, such as printing, smelting, refining, making of pottery, varnish, tile.
3. Acid, oil, and fume poisoning—hazards are airplane dope, aniline dyes, artificial leather, bronzing, rubber cement mixing, degreasing, drycleaning, electroplating, enameling, engraving, varnishing, vulcanizing.
4. Chrome poisoning—hazards are coal-tar dyes, wallpaper, electric batteries, explosives, lithography, photography, electroplating, and certain paints.
5. Benzol poisoning—hazards are like those in 3 above.
6. Industrial eczema—hazards are found in all occupations in which there is exposure to a dye, fungus, plant, or solution.
7. Tuberculosis—hazards are dusts (coal, cement, asbestos, tobacco) and such inert dusts as carbon, iron, limestone rock, marble, chalk.
8. Anthrax—hazards are associated with occupations dealing with livestock.
9. Cyanide poisoning—hazards are fumigation, hardening of metals, cleaning or coating silver, tanning, dyeing, electroplating.
10. Dust in lungs—hazards are mineral, metal or vegetable dusts which are found in mining, quarrying, pottery-, glass- and brick-making, industrial sprays, stone-finishing, work with sand, sandstone, and talc, and construction work.[15]

Brief descriptions of a few of these diseases will be sufficient to show why occupation must be taken into consideration in explaining the greater morbidity and mortality rates of the industrial population.

Lead poisoning (plumbism) is one of the oldest and most destructive of industrial hazards. Its forms and modes of transmission are multiple. Lead may be inhaled as a fume or dust, or swallowed as a result of uncleanly work habits. This poison is widely distributed, both by the number of occupations exposed and by the variety of compounds in which lead is used. Susceptibility varies. In some instances, a week or so of exposure is sufficient. In others, the toxin operates slowly, involving many organs of the body. Its lesions are known to affect the arteries, kidneys, blood, and nervous system, and plumbism is associated with arteriosclerosis, nephritis, neuritis, anemia, tuberculosis, and pleurisy. A high incidence of nervous and mental diseases is also found among workers coming in contact with lead and more recently with the fumes of carbon disulphide, which is used in the manufacture of rayon.

The occupations most exposed are smelting, printing, electrotyping, and painting. However, the poison is also spread indirectly,

[15] *Cf.* R. T. Johnstone, *Occupational Diseases*, Saunders, Philadelphia, 1942, Chaps. 4-36.

and cases of lead poisoning are frequently reported among children. The greater incidence of cases of lead poisoning among males than among females is due to occupational differences. There is a growing body of evidence to prove that women are actually more susceptible than men to some poisons, and among them is lead. Studies in England showed that the rate of lead poisoning among women in paint factories and potteries was twice that of men. Women also had the more severe cases and were susceptible to the most serious form of poisoning, which attacks the brain, producing delirium, convulsions, and blindness. A high frequency of stillbirths, abortions, and infant mortality is also traced to the same condition in women. Lead is sometimes connected with sterility in both sexes. This conclusion was reached after a series of animal experiments and from cases in which the transmission of lead poisoning from either the father or the mother was demonstrated.[16]

Of the diseases that are usually not assigned to any particular industry, tuberculosis and pneumonia are most frequently classified as occupational hazards. For years the rate of tuberculosis in the industrial population has been more than twice that among the nonindustrial population. Although working conditions, home conditions, and economic status are often confused in explaining the occupational significance of this disease, the fact that the male death rate is greater than the female death rate after the age of twenty four throws the weight of the evidence toward certain occupations. Workers exposed to dusts, especially silica dust—lead and zinc miners, granite and sandstone cutters, pottery workers, and iron and steel foundry workers—have abnormally high death rates.

In a summary of the historical connection between respiratory diseases and dusty trades, Greenburg says:

> It is an interesting and significant fact that in every instance in which a heavy incidence of tuberculosis has been shown to result from exposure to industrial dust, the dust in question has been in part at least made up of crystalline rock. It is silicosis which lies at the basis of miners' phthisis, and silicosis is probably the chief predisposing factor in tuberculosis among ax grinders. . . .[17]

Dusts also are responsible for the extreme frequency of colds, bron-

[16] L. I. Dublin and R. J. Vance, "Occupational Mortality Experience of Insured Wage Earners," *Mo. Lab. Rev.,* Vol. 64 (1947): 1003-1018.

[17] L. Greenburg, "*Studies on the Industrial Health Problem,*" United States Public Health Service, Reprint No. 990 (1925): 10.

chitis, influenza, and grippe among the industrial population. In a survey of the effects of the common cold in industry, the Metropolitan Life Insurance Company reports that it exceeds all other diseases as a cause of lost time. Various surveys indicate that forty to fifty per cent of all lost days can be assigned to colds and their complications. They are responsible for at least one lost day per employee per year—an obviously serious loss in wages, productivity, and family expenditures for medical treatment.[18]

Occupational diseases are a matter of concern to the public health worker because of their widespread incidence, and to employers because of their contribution to absences, inefficiency, and labor turnover. For several reasons, they constitute a more serious menace than accidents. First, there are many difficulties involved in diagnosis. Workers are unable to diagnose their own conditions, and often physicians cannot find the causes of their disabilities until their occupations are known, as is illustrated by the following case:

> A man, suffering from continuous headaches, visits his physician. The latter can find no cause for the patient's illness. The patient shows no signs of disease other than the subjective symptoms which he describes. Perhaps the physician will recommend an examination of the subject's eyes, ears, and sinuses, which will prove negative. A puzzling diagnosis such as this becomes very simple when the occupation is ascertained. . . . Garage work . . . represents the hazard poisons—carbon monoxide and gasoline. Both produce headaches. . . . The effective remedy lies in the removal of the two poisons.[19]

A second major difficulty is compensation. Compensation legislation now recognizes both industrial accidents and diseases as compensable. But the latter are not so fully covered, because it is less easy to distinguish industrial from non-industrial health hazards. Moreover, the two are not comparable for other reasons, since diseases may secure such a foothold that all remedial measures are ineffectual. The obscurity, deceptive symptoms, and delays in diagnosis of these diseases are the main reasons why so little advance is being made in their eradication.

[18] "Cost of the Common Cold," *Statis. Bull.,* Metropolitan Life Insurance Company, Vol. 28 (Nov. 1947): 6. In this article the total cost of the common cold to the people as a whole is estimated to be "well over a billion dollars a year."

[19] L. I. Dublin and P. Leiboff, *op. cit.,* p. 2.

Social correlates of illness

Heretofore, numerous social problems have already been noted as being significantly related to illness. They may be related as causes or as effects. In both connections there is need for further exploration. The value of these correlations is that they may be concealing important explanations of disease. They may also suggest new approaches to old and puzzling conditions.

In the numerous reports of the National Health Survey, a variety of pertinent correlations are mentioned.[20] One, for example, is the general and specific relationship between disease and poverty. Migrants are found to have more illnesses than nonmigratory individuals or families. When the population is divided into economic classes, following the general categories well-to-do to the very poor, without exception the lowest economic class has the greater incidence of illness, and relief families have a greater incidence than nonrelief families. Above this lowest class, however, there is no correlation between the distribution of illnesses and income. Moreover, families that suffer a reduced income will commonly have a significantly higher proportion of illnesses than those families that are able to maintain their economic position. In noting this correlation, it is admitted that a major factor in the reduction of economic status may be chronic illness.

It has already been noted that chronic illness increases with age. In conjunction with this relationship is the further discovery that husbands and wives in the age group forty-five and above tend to have the same chronic illnesses more often than would occur by chance. This conclusion holds especially for arthritis and hypertensive vascular diseases, and to a lesser extent for heart diseases. This relationship suggests possible predisposing factors in the home.

Negroes have more disabling illnesses than whites, which may point to any of the above economic and social conditions as causes.

[20] Jean Downes, "Social and Environmental Factors in Illness," *Milbank Mem. Fund Quart.*, Vol. 26 (1948): 366-385. D. C. Wiehl, "Mortality and Socio-Environmental Factors," *Milbank Mem. Fund Quart.*, Vol. 26 (1948): 335-365. P. S. Lawrence, "Chronic Illness and Socio-Economic Status," *Pub. Health Rpts.*, Vol. 63 (1948), No. 47, pp. 1507-1521. M. Terris, "Relation of Economic Status to Tuberculosis Mortality by Age and Sex," *Am. Jour. Pub. Health,* Vol. 39 (1948): 1061-1070. S. Bloom, "Some Economic and Emotional Problems of the Tuberculosis Patient and His Family," *Pub. Health Rpts.,* Vol. 63 (1948), No. 14, pp. 448-455. S. J. Axebrod, "Health Problems of Industrialized Agriculture," *Am. Jour. Pub. Health,* Vol. 39 (1949): 1172-1175.

Rheumatic fever has a marked association with income, being most frequent in the lowest income groups. Among the particular personal problems of children, rheumatic fever is given some responsibility for excessive anxiety, frustration, dependence on the mother, and for some asocial behavior when the child is confronted with too-difficult tasks.

Both pneumonia and tuberculosis continue to be associated with crowding in the home and with occupation. Tuberculosis is also higher among adult males than females. These associations suggest such other possible causes as specific strains, tensions, dusts, or poisons in occupational exposures, and the postponement of medical examination.

Chronic disease of the parents is recognized as one of the most dangerous social environments for children. Many more illnesses among the children of such families are discovered than among the children of the nonsickly families.

When urban-rural contrasts are reviewed, rural children and young adults do not fare as well as comparable urban groups. Mortality in the rural areas has not been reduced as rapidly as in urban communities, and there is more preventable mortality in rural areas and small cities. For these differences, the greater availability of medical and health services in cities is generally given as a reason. Another rural-urban difference is the greater health needs of workers in agriculture. They have one of the highest occupational death rates, numerous illnesses of occupational origin, high rates of venereal infections, and an unusually large number of digestive disturbances. They are not protected in most states against work-connected disabilities, although twenty-four states do have voluntary plans for such coverage.

In comparing sexes, males have the poorer record both in death and sickness rates. This finding is considered important because it has been increasing in recent years. In addition, males suffer more breakdowns that interfere with occupational usefulness—a complex of problems that is connected with the financial status of the home, marital problems, and the need to change occupations in mid-career.

Specific personal and social correlates of tuberculosis. Many sources assert that, as tuberculosis develops, the patient becomes unusually optimistic, has an increasing sex urge, and experiences an intellectual stimulation. Comparisons of case records do not confirm these opinions, but they do reveal that such personality traits as anxiety, neurasthenia, mild neuroticism, emotionality, conflict, selfishness, and a limited range of interests are somewhat more frequent among the tuberculous than in control groups.[21]

Case studies support the contention that there are a number of social problems related to tuberculosis. Among its causes are such social conditions as overwork, family problems, financial problems, overambition, and unsuitable housing, living, and recreational conditions. Enormous variations in the incidence of tuberculosis in different economic, educational, social and nativity groups point to them as being of some causal significance or as sources of causes. Since its onset is higher in younger age groups, it creates vocational problems and imposes financial burdens on those least able to manage them. It obliges separation from families and friends. The combined ill effects of all these circumstances are regarded as sufficient reasons for some of the observed personality difficulties noted above.

Summary

In many respects physical disease and its associated problems present a dismal outlook for humanity. Practically no disease, however, is the equivalent of a death sentence if it is diagnosed early, and this conclusion has led to the axiom that early recognition is nine tenths of the cure. Another conclusion emphasizes the same point of view by giving an important position in the causes of the major communicable and degenerative diseases to the acute infections. By themselves, acute infections are secondary, but their damage to the entire system is chiefly responsible for the rapid advances of disease and mortality in middle life. The new diseases of civilization are primarily the consequences of minor infections, and preventive programs are being directed against them rather than against their incurable results.

Curative and preventive agencies are now concerned with two major and two minor classes of diseases. The first two are the communicable and degenerative diseases. The others are deficiency diseases and diseases caused by the malfunctioning of the ductless glands.

[21] R. G. Barker and others, *Adjustment to Physical Handicaps and Illness,* Social Science Research Council, New York, 1946. Bull. No. 55, Table 3, p. 129 and p. 130.

Communicable diseases are further subdivided according to whether the infecting agent is known or unknown. When the source of infection or the infecting organism is known, there are four methods of treatment. The first is the elimination of the source of infection. Such infectious diseases as malaria, yellow fever, dysentery, and sleeping sickness, all of which are due to animal parasites, are prevented by the elimination of the host—the parasite—or by quarantine. The second method is preventive inoculation, as in the case of typhoid fever, or treatment by chemicals; as in pneumonia and the venereal diseases. The third is the use of antitoxic sera, as in diphtheria and tetanus. Tuberculosis illustrates the fourth method, namely, the prevention of infecting contacts. Although tuberculosis is a bacterial disease, the infecting agency cannot be attacked directly. Tuberculosis is primarily a disease contracted during childhood under unwholesome living conditions, and prevention is directed toward sanitation. Much of the preventive work in this disease depends upon the development of immunity.

A second type of communicable disease is called the undetermined group, because the infecting organism is unknown or is doubtful. Many common diseases are classed in this group: influenza, measles, chickenpox, the common cold, epidemic encephalitis, mumps, poliomyelitis, smallpox, typhus fever, trench and similar fevers, and some diseases of animals, such as rabies. The theory accounting for these diseases is that the germs are ultra-microscopic in some part of their history and are filtrable. Two of these diseases, smallpox and rabies, are preventable by vaccines; the other diseases are treated by isolation or quarantine.

Degenerative diseases are now receiving more attention, because mortality due to them is increasing while the general death rate is decreasing. These diseases differ from the infectious group in causes and in treatment. A complete list of probable causes would include many environmental and hereditary factors. Those usually considered are heredity, infection, food, drugs, occupational poisons or toxins, injuries, and social habits, and are classified as immediate, or as indirect or predisposing. Little is known about the specific contribution of any of these causes, owing primarily to the fact that degenerative diseases appear late in life when original constitutional characteristics have been modified by a variety of social and economic conditions.

The prevention of degenerative diseases requires a program that will cover every cause; it should consist of eugenics, control over minor infections and the serious chronic infections, improved dietetics, food and drug laws, industrial sanitation, and mental hygiene.

Deficiency and glandular diseases are another group of puzzling health problems. They are mainly dietary problems and they are sometimes called "metabolic" diseases. Many of these conditions have a long biological and social history.[22]

Scurvy originally called the attention of the medical profession to the importance of a well-balanced diet. Rickets, beriberi, pellagra, and diabetes are the more commonly recognized deficiency diseases; in addition there are such glandular diseases as goiter, Addison's disease, brain tumor, Cushing's disease, and genital dystrophy. Gout, gallstones, and obesity are also occasionally included under this classification.

Although this group of diseases is vague both in content and treatment, deficiency diseases have important connections with other physical illnesses and with some of the mental diseases.

A general program of public health is charged with the study and prevention of all deficiency diseases. It is now handicapped in reaching the goal, which is medically possible, because of the inability of many sick persons to pay the costs of medical care and because of the infrequency with which well persons assume responsibility for their own health. Consequently, the current and unsolved problems in public health for which the National Health Program has been proposed (1945) include:

1. The uneven costs of medical care.
2. The uneven distribution of medical services.
3. Inadequate care of many illnesses.
4. Extensive use of inferior services.
5. Insufficient attention to prevention.
6. Unfairness to practitioners under the current health organization.
7. Organized plans for the payment of medical costs and for compensation for loss of earnings during sickness.

The present-day public health program recognizes the desirability of ten supplementary activities in medical and social research:

[22] E. H. Ackerknecht, "The History of Metabolic Diseases," *Ciba Symposia,* Vol. 6 (1944), Nos. 3 and 4, pp. 1834-1844. H. D. Kruse, "A Concept of the Etiological Complex of Deficiency States," *Milbank Mem. Fund Quart.,* Vol. 27 (1949): 5-94. C. L. Walker, "A Million Unknown Diabetics," *Harper's,* Vol. 198 (1949): 54-60.

1. Early diagnosis and immediate treatment.
2. Adequate medical service and adequate nutrition.
3. Control over population to restrict the spread of disease.
4. Positive and negative eugenic programs.
5. Accurate reporting of the incidence of illness and death.
6. Personal, sex, and mental hygiene.
7. Public health education.
8. Coördinated state and local public health services.
9. Sickness insurance.
10. Promotion of professional education and research in medicine.

As of 1951, nearly half of the American population was covered by some form of voluntary health insurance, but less than four million people were protected for all medical expenses. Private insurance therefore paid for about one fourth of the private hospitals' bill, which amounted to two billion dollars annually; one tenth of the physicians' bill, which amounted to two and one-fourth billion dollars; and nothing for dental services, nurses, drugs and appliances, which cost another two billion more. Continuing defects in the operation of these insurance plans are high administrative costs and the absence of stress on preventive medicine.

Research. Nearly all the diseases are being studied by coordinated research programs. In diseases of the heart and blood vessels, there are four: the Life Insurance Medical Research Fund, which was organized in 1945 by companies in Canada and the United States; the National Heart Institute, which is part of the United States Public Health Service created by an act of Congress in 1948; the American Heart Association; and the National Research Council of Canada. In cancer research there is a program jointly supported by the National Research Council and the American Cancer Society. The United States Public Health Service operates an even larger program in the National Cancer Institute. There is a similar public and private program in Canada. In the diseases of the kidney and arteriosclerosis, research is being carried on at the Goldwater Memorial Hospital in New York City and by the United States Public Health Service in Boston and adjacent communities. Examples of other research agencies are the National Foundation for Infantile Paralysis, the New York Foundation, the National Tuberculosis Association, the National Society for Crippled Children and Adults, The Commission on Chronic Illness (Chicago), the American Social Hygiene Association, Industrial Hygiene Foundation (Pittsburgh), and the Chronic Disease Program of the State of California. In addition there are numerous community agencies, such as the Cleveland Health Council, the Public Health Committee of the Chamber of Commerce (Honolulu), Arthritis and Rheumatism Foundation (Tucson), Detroit Fund for Crippling Diseases, Playtex Park Research Institute (New York), which is devoted to health problems of children, and Committee for Research on Medical Treatment of Alcoholic Patients (New York City).[23]

Bibliography

American Public Health Association, *The Control of Communicable Diseases,* The Association, New York, 1945.

Bachman, G. W., and L. Meriam, *The Issue of Compulsory Health Insurance,* The Brookings Institution, Washington, 1948.

Corwin, E. H. L., *Ecology of Health,* The Commonwealth Fund, New York, 1949. Chap. 4.

Dublin, L. I. (Ed.), *Health Progress,* 1936-1945, Metropolitan Life Insurance Company, New York, 1948.

Ewing, O. R., *The Nation's Health: A Ten Year Program,* Federal Security Agency, Washington, 1948.

Ewing, O. R., and G. F. Lull, *How Shall We Pay for Health Care?* Public Affairs Committee, Inc., New York, 1949. Bull. No. 152. An analysis of various health plans.

Hollingworth, Helen, and others, *Medical Care and Costs in Relation to Family Income,* Social Security Administration, Washington, 1947.

Hubbard, J. P., and others, *Health Services for the Rural Child,* American Medical Association, Chicago, 1948.

National Health Assembly, *America's Health,* Harper, New York, 1949.

Proudfit, F. T., and C. H. Robinson, *Nutrition and Diet Therapy,* Macmillan, New York, 1950.

Sigerist, H. E., *Civilization and Disease,* Cornell University Press, Ithaca, 1943.

Simmons, J. S., and I. M. Kinsey, *Public Health in the World Today,* Harvard University Press, Cambridge, 1949.

Sokolov, B. F., *Civilized Diseases,* Thorsons, London, 1949.

Stieglitz, E. J., *A Future for Preventive Medicine,* The Commonwealth Fund, New York, 1945.

Thomas, E. W., *Syphilis: Its Course and Management,* Macmillan, New York, 1949.

Tobey, J. A., *Public Health Law,* The Commonwealth Fund, New York, 1947. Chap. 15 deals with occupational diseases and compensation.

[23] H. M. Cavins, *National Health Agencies,* Public Affairs Press, Washington, 1945. S. M. Gunn and P. S. Platt, *Voluntary Health Agencies,* Ronald, New York, 1945. National Health Assembly, *America's Health,* Harper, New York, 1949.

United States Department of Agriculture, *Better Health for Rural America,* Washington, 1945.

Winslow, C. E. A., *The Conquest of Epidemic Disease,* Princeton University Press, Princeton, 1943.

World Health Organization, *Manual of the International Classification of Diseases, Injuries, and Causes of Death,* Columbia University Press, New York, 1948.

. . . . .

Darley, Ward, "Denver Rheumatic Fever Diagnostic Service," *Pub. Health Rpts.,* Vol. 64 (1949), No. 51, pp. 1631-1642.

De Delube, S. M., "Family Size in Some Hereditary Disorders," *Annals of Eugenics,* Vol. 15 (1950): 184-85.

Deevey, E. S., "The Probability of Death," *Sci. Am.,* Vol. 182 (1950): 58-60.

Hartz, J., "Human Relationships in Tuberculosis," *Pub. Health Rpts.,* Vol. 65 (1950), No. 40, pp. 1292-1305.

Hoffer, C. R., and Schuler, E. A., "Measurement of Health Needs and Health Care," *Am. Sociol. Rev.,* Vol. 13 (1948): 719-724.

Pack, G. T., and F. R. Grant, "The Influence of Disease on History," *Bull., New York Acad. Med.,* Vol. 24 (1948): 523-540.

Richardson, W. H., "How One State Fights Cancer," *Today's Health,* Vol. 28 (1950): 22 ff.

Scheele, L. A., "Arthritis as a Public Health Program," *Pub. Health Rpts.,* Vol. 65 (1950), No. 42, pp. 1351-58.

Thompson, C. H. (Ed.), "Health Status and Health Education of Negroes," *Jour. Negro Education,* Vol. 18 (Summer 1949): 197-443.

Williams, J. F., "Health and Heredity," *Eugenical News,* Vol. 34 (1949): 14-20.

Legislative and Other Health Plans

Bride, T. H., "Rhode Island Cash Sickness Compensation Program," *Am. Jour. Pub. Health,* Vol. 39 (1949): 1011-1015.

Davis, B. M., "The British National Health Service," *Pub. Health Rpts.,* Vol. 64 (1949), No. 6, pp. 161-191.

Deardorff, N., "Health Insurance Plan of Greater New York," *Am. Jour. Pub. Health,* Vol. 40 (1950): 1536-45.

Draper, W. F., "Voluntary Health Insurance on the National Scene: the United Mine Workers Health Program," *Am. Jour. Pub. Health,* Vol. 40 (1950): 595-601.

Goldman, Franz, and others (Eds.), "Medical Care for Americans," *Annals, Am. Acad. Pol. and Soc. Sci.,* Vol. 273 (Jan. 1951). Public medical care, medical care insurance, planning for the future.

Kaiser, R. F., "Proposed Elements of a State Cancer Control Program," *Pub. Health Rpts.,* Vol. 64 (1949) No. 37, pp. 1169-1181.

Miller, M. D., "Voluntary Health Insurance on the National Scene: A Program of the Insurance Companies," *Am. Jour. Pub. Health,* Vol. 40 (1950): 1125-28.

Roemer, M. I., "Pattern of Organized Medical Care Programs in a Rural County," *Am. Jour. Pub. Health,* Vol. 40 (1950): 812-26.
Thorp, W. L., "New International Programs in Public Health," *Am. Jour. Pub. Health,* Vol. 40 (1950): 1479-85.
Weinerman, E. R., "Appraisal of Medical Care Programs," *Am. Jour. Pub. Health,* Vol. 40 (1950): 1129-34.

Questions

1. Analyze the current status of public and private health insurance plans. As a guide, consult "The Price of Health: Two Ways to Pay It," *Time,* Feb. 20, 1950, pp. 9 ff.
2. What is the Rhode Island Cash Sickness Compensation Program?
3. How do plans for health insurance in the United States compare with the British National Health Service?
4. How does your state rank with the others in death rate, sanitation, medical facilities, and health insurance? As a guide in formulating your answer, consult the pamphlet, "Our National Health Problem," Research Council for Economic Security, Chicago, 1946.
5. Do you consider the Blue Cross plan a sufficient health insurance program?
6. What diseases have been considered at various times endemic? Could an endemic disease be a possible explanation of national suicide? What is the difference between an endemic and an epidemic disease?
7. In what ways has the International Classification of the Causes of Death contributed to an understanding of public health needs?
8. How would you account for the great difference in available research funds for the study of different illnesses?
9. Is any disease actually new?
10. Outline some state medical plan (some of which are suggested in the chapter bibliography or in footnotes, such as the North Carolina Syphilitic Campaign). Does the plan seem to be adequate and successful?
11. Collect all the information that you can find about some obscure disease, such as progressive muscular dystrophy. Classify the facts and outline a plan of research.
12. What do average families in different income groups spend for medical care?

CHAPTER 3

PHYSICAL DEFECTIVENESS

A TUBERCULOUS PATIENT WAS ONCE DESCRIBED BY DR. WILLIAM OSLER AS a person with many social problems and tuberculosis. The same can be said of nearly all persons with physical and mental illnesses and defects. Only in a comparatively few cases is any one illness or defect the individual's most conspicuous difficulty.

At present there is no accurate count of the total burden of the physical handicaps. In the population of the United States, according to one estimate, there are twenty-six million physically or mentally handicapped individuals, and their ranks are increased each year by 350,000. The experts agree from this evidence that "an atypical physique constitutes a social problem of vast magnitude." [1]

In the novel *Of Human Bondage,* the main character, a lame man, is a person with many social problems, and this disability is made the most of in explaining him as a personality. He is persistent, aggressive, and patient to a degree considerably beyond the average. In many other instances, similar associations are made between handicaps and personality. Frequently, the effects of handicaps are as significant as the handicap itself to the health of the individual.[2]

[1] H. A. Rusk, "But the Spirit Giveth Life," *The Survey,* Vol. 85 (1949): 213. For a description of this total group of handicapped people of which the physically disabled are a part, consult: "Disability: Who Makes up the Great Army of Disabled?" *Research Council for Economic Security,* Chicago, 1947. For specific incidence and annual trends, consult: "Rehabilitation and Placement of Handicapped Workers," *Mo. Lab. Rev.,* Vol. 67 (1948): 282-285; L. I. Dublin, "Salvaging Damaged Lives," *Am. Mercury,* Vol. 65 (1947): 355-362; "Physically Handicapped Persons in the United States," *Int'l. Labor Rev.,* Vol. 55 (1947): 124-127.

[2] W. S. Maugham, Grosset and Dunlap, New York, 1935. E. R. Carlson, *Born That Way,* John Day, New York, 1941. Frances Perkins, *The Roosevelt I Knew,*

There are numerous classes and types of physical defects. Those having such defects include (1) persons with orthopedic defects, which are defined as permanent handicaps that deprive the individual of the use of some part of his skeletal system, (2) the blind and partially sighted, (3) the deaf and hard of hearing, (4) speech defectives, and (5) persons whose vitality is impaired by the less obvious defects, such as the cardiac cripple, the arrested tuberculous, the aged infirm, the malnourished, and occasionally even persons with minor conditions of facial disfigurement.

These conditions are mainly problems of health from the standpoint of preventive medicine, but they are also economic and educational problems involving need for special training and vocational adaptation. And in many cases they present serious problems in social isolation, requiring long and resourceful treatment to offset the development of abnormal traits of personality.

Either as medical or as social problems, consequently, the occurrence of physical handicaps is an indication of a major liability to any society. They represent primary evidence of the inability to control infectious and degenerative diseases or to prevent industrial and other accidents. Accordingly, their absence or tendency to decrease is proof of a healthy and vital population.

Defectiveness as a social problem

In many ways physical defects are typical of all chronic social problems. In their antiquity, constant recurrence, and various complications and ill effects, they rival the claim of syphilis as the great imitator. Initially, they can be described as problems from at least seven points of view.

First of all they distinguish special social groups. These different classes of people require different services. In addition, they call attention to health needs of the population as a whole, if prevention is ever to be achieved. There are, for example, the defects of children, adolescents, young adults, the aged, housewives, the industrial or agricultural population, military personnel, or veterans. Or there are groups within each of these categories, such as speech defectives, amputees, spastics, the feebleminded, or the neurotic.

From another approach, the presence of defects represents a constant menace to national health and security. Attention to the

---

Viking, New York, 1946. See also "The Case of the Ugly Thief," *Time,* April 11, 1949, p. 69. In this article an unpleasant facial appearance is associated as a cause of personal maladjustment, delinquency, and crime.

hazard of having a large number of handicapped persons in the population is revived during and after every national emergency. This hazard is advanced as one of the chief reasons for the development of a national health program.

The economic significance of physical defects is rarely forgotten. This approach is stressed by wage and other losses, expenditures for rehabilitation, and other direct or indirect costs, the total of which could not be reckoned without a considerable margin of error. An illustrative example appears in the article in *Time,* mentioned in footnote 2, wherein the cost of the plastic surgery to improve the appearance of the "Ugly Thief" was given as $3,000.

Defects are also significant factors in family adjustments. For one reason or another, they tend to appear more often in some families as a sort of genetic or constitutional liability. Moreover when they do occur by chance or accident, the required reorganization of personal-social relations between members of the family is of so radical a nature that many families are completely demoralized.

Emotional upsets are another threat. They are numerous, subtle, and obscure. They are rarely recognized or admitted by their victims. As a matter of fact, emotional defects can be reserved as a separate class of social disorders or as their causes or results. In children, for example, they are noted by unusual degrees of overdependence, infantilism, insecurity, feelings of inferiority, and overprotection. These characteristics develop without any necessary relation to the defect. They are due to an obvious combination of unwholesome social conditions. Such unwholesome social conditions are the concern of professional groups, like medical social workers, operating in public and private clinics.

And, finally, the tasks that they present to the family, education, industry, and government, in questions of social adjustment, rehabilitation, re-education, vocational adjustment, and prevention, are sufficient to make them major enterprises in the operations of each of these institutions.

Main types of physical defectiveness

The current problem of the handicapped is totally unlike its historical antecedents. Although the blind, the deaf, and the crippled are still recognized within its limits and are important because they are always responsible for a certain amount of economic and social incompetency, they constitute by no means a majority of those whose handicaps are now thought worthy of social study and control.

Recent investigations have revealed a new group of physical defects; namely, those minor conditions that are temporarily less serious but more frequent than the three classical handicaps. In one sense, moreover, they are actually more serious, because they are associated causally with gross defects and fatal illness. In fact, medical workers have decided that the ultimate control over blindness, deafness, and serious crippled conditions depends largely upon the early detection and elimination of the minor defects. From this approach to the problems of the handicapped, a conclusion is reached similar to that reached in the study of physical illness. In the long run, prevention in either case depends upon control over minor defects and illnesses.

Many gross and minor handicaps are of comparatively little social significance. Some infirmities are the natural consequence of advancing age; others are too widely distributed to be sufficiently unusual to be included within the range of social problems. The natural failure of eyesight as people grow old, partial blindness or deafness, and some relatively gross crippling conditions are not always causes of poverty or social incompetency. Often their most serious consequence is a reduced earning capacity. They do not interfere with the individual's participation in the world's work, because of social compensations which the individual is able to make, or because society itself is adjusted to fairly wide variations in individual capacity.

The cases of partial and, from the economic point of view, adjusted handicaps interfere more directly with a census of the types and frequency of the physical defects that do disable their victims. Extreme handicaps—such as total blindness, absolute deaf-mutism, or other total physical incapacities—are found easily, usually within public institutions or in the enumeration of the United States Census. The discovery of other handicaps, in which the line between physical normality and defectiveness fluctuates, is beset with many difficulties. For example, it is hard to discriminate between poverty, mental defectiveness, and physical defectiveness as factors in social unadjustment when those conditions are found in the same person.

Frequency of major and minor defects

Records of the National Health Survey are considered the most accurate estimates both of the types of physical defects and their distribution. Statisticians accept these results because they represent rural as well as urban areas and because they are in close agreement with earlier surveys and more local reports.[3]

Burden of the handicapped. Of the 5 million persons in this country who are handicapped by physical defects, 623,500 are wholly incapacitated. This total includes 356,400 men and 267,100 women:[4]

MAJOR PHYSICAL HANDICAPS

Type of Impairment	*Males*	*Females*	*Total*
Orthopedic	208,500	132,500	341,000
Total deafness	77,100	70,900	148,000
Blindness in both eyes	70,800	63,700	134,500
Total	356,400	267,100	623,500

Although it is much more difficult to determine the minor handicaps by a census count or to distinguish between the degrees of such handicaps, the National Health Survey has estimated a total of 4,374,300 persons with such defects, divided between the types of handicaps and the sexes as follows:

MINOR PHYSICAL HANDICAPS

Type of Impairment	*Males*	*Females*	*Total*
Orthopedic, non-disabling	1,636,100	626,500	2,262,600
Partial deafness	886,200	762,900	1,649,100
Blindness in one eye	311,700	150,900	462,600
Total	2,834,000	1,540,300	4,374,300

When handicaps are enumerated from other than the medical point of view—for example, from the standpoint of employability of men in industry, the military capacity of youth or young adults, attendance records of school children, or the health and vitality of

[3] H. A. Rusk and E. J. Taylor, "Physical Disability: A National Problem," *Am. Jour. Pub. Health,* Vol. 38 (1948): 1381-1386. M. Gover and J. B. Yawkey, "Physical Impairments of Members of Low Income Families," *Pub. Health Rpts.,* Vol. 59 (1944), No. 36, pp. 1163-1184. The earlier reports are: E. Sydenstricker and R. H. Britten, "The Physical Impairments of Adult Life," *Am. Jour. Hyg.,* Vol. II (1930): 73-135. This study was based on male, white life insurance policy holders. ———, "Physical Impairments and Occupational Class," *Pub. Health Rpts.,* Vol. 45 (1930), Reprint No. 1404. R. H. Britten and J. C. Goddard, "Rates of Physical Impairments in 28 Occupations, Based on 17,294 Medical Examinations," *Pub. Health Rpts.,* Vol. 47 (1932), Bull. No. 1.

[4] B. D. Karpinos, "The Physically Handicapped," *Pub. Health Reports,* Vol. 58 (1943), No. 43, pp. 17-18.

housewives—the problem of physical defectiveness is much more extensive.

Since public attention has been largely devoted to the blind, the deaf, and the crippled, each will be given brief consideration here. As a matter of fact, their problems are well adapted to joint analysis because they have elements in common in addition to economic need and special education. The causes of their handicaps are largely the same, being disease, congenital or acquired defectiveness, and accidents, and consequently preventive measures will be similar. Victims of these conditions differ chiefly in their response to treatment, some being more adjustable than others.

Blindness. If a person has five per cent or less of normal vision, he is considered blind. According to the National Society for the Prevention of Blindness, there are 250,000 blind children and adults in the United States. However, the total number who suffer impaired vision is much larger. It includes 300,000 industrial workers who have eye injuries each year, about 800,000 persons who are losing their sight because of glaucoma, and 4,500,000 school children who need eye care.

Humanitarian sympathies are easily aroused by the blind because visual defects and their social handicaps are obvious. Although for these reasons more resources have been made available to the blind than to persons with other physical defects, blindness is least adjustable. However, since 1900 it has decreased in proportion to population and the rate is now about 1.75 persons per 1,000 population.

CAUSES OF BLINDNESS

Adults	*Children*
Specific diseases or defects	Congenital
Cataract	Specific diseases or defects
Choroid and retina	Cataract
Atrophy of optic nerve	Diseases of the optic nerve
Glaucoma	Diseases of conjunctiva
Cornea	Infectious diseases
Infectious diseases	Ophthalmia
Accidents	Syphilis
Noninfectious diseases	German measles
Vascular diseases	Accidents
Diabetes	Neoplasms
Congenital	Noninfectious diseases
Poisoning and malformations	Poisoning

Sources: Report of Interdepartmental Committee on Study of Problems of and Services for the Blind, California State Department of Education, Mental Hygiene, Public Health, and Social Welfare, Sacramento, 1946, pp. 62-66. Consult for supplementary surveys, *Social Work Yearbook,* Russell Sage Foundation, New York. Biannual reports.

The chief causes of blindness are specific diseases of the eye, general constitutional diseases, congenital defects, accidents, and aging. Among adults the leading causes are general diseases, such as the vascular diseases, diabetes, smallpox, and influenza; specific diseases or defects of the eye, such as cataract and diseases of the retina and conjunctiva; and accidents. Among children the leading causes are general diseases, congenital defects, and specific diseases of the eye.

In this country approximately seven tenths of all blindness is due to disease, two tenths to accidents, and one tenth to congenital conditions or old age. Important social facts that partially clarify the character of this problem are: (1) the sex ratio, which is 111 blind males for every 100 blind females, (2) employability: 11.0 per cent are reported employed, (3) economic status: 68.0 per cent of the blind population are located in families with incomes that must be supplemented under provisions of the Social Security Act, and (4) age distribution: nearly 70.0 per cent of blindness occurs in the age group over 50 years. Thirty-five per cent of this number were blind before they reached the age of twenty.

Blindness has many causes and generally there will be two or more causes in the case history of each blind person. For this reason it cannot be approached as a separate problem. Both treatment and prevention require widely different measures. The hopeful aspect is that it has been decreasing for many years and that most of its causes can be prevented. During the last fifty years four fifths of blindness has been due to trachoma, corneal ulcer, glaucoma, cataract, atrophy of the optic nerve, and ophthalmia neonatorum (an acute eye infection of the newborn). Of these, trachoma, which is a highly virulent infection associated with poverty, unsanitary living, and crowding, and ophthalmia neonatorum have responded to relatively simple treatments and no longer appear among the leading causes. Glaucoma is the disease of the eye most frequently causing blindness, and for it there is no effective treatment.

The others require surgery or the prevention of constitutional deficiencies. Many infectious and degenerative diseases also may result in blindness. For example, it is well known that venereal infections are related to blindness, and the compulsory treatment of the baby's eyes at birth has largely eliminated them as causal factors. Among causes that have responded least to current preventive agencies are industrial and other accidents. Although blindness is often associated with heredity, there is little evidence that a eugenic program, limited to restrictions on the marriage of the blind, would make any material reduction in its prevalence.

Deafness. An individual is classified as deaf or hard of hearing when his impairment is so serious that the sense of hearing is of little or no use. Like blindness, most cases of the hard of hearing could be prevented. Unlike blindness, deafness tends to increase proportionately to the growth of population. The National Health Survey reported that acquired deafness increases with age at a constant rate.

From these rates and other estimates, it is reckoned that there is a minimum of at least one and one-half to three million children and adults with hearing difficulties. School surveys report three to ten per cent of the school population. The Federal Office of Vocational Rehabilitation has noted that fifteen per cent of the adults applying for rehabilitation service have some degree of deafness. And when a different interpretation of hearing loss is used, the New York League for the Hard of Hearing estimates that there are twenty-six million with a handicapping loss of hearing.[5]

Deafness and blindness differ in many respects, particularly in the personal and social problems to which they give rise. There are three principal classes of the deaf: individuals who are unable to hear and speak; others who are able to speak but who became deaf in childhood; and the partially deaf whose defects may be corrected by auditory devices. Deafness is essentially a problem of childhood. About one fourth of the cases are the result of congenital defects, and nearly one half of the total become deaf before ten years of age. In a study of congenital and acquired deafness, conducted under the auspices of the American Medical Association, the following proportions were assigned: to the congenital, 45.5 per cent; to the probably congenital, 16.3 per cent; and to the acquired group, 38.2 per cent.

Deafness also differs from blindness in its causes. From one third to two fifths of the causes of deafness are ascribed to congenital conditions and heredity. Hereditary recurrence is more frequent than in blindness, or at least deafness has a tendency to recur in families more frequently than does blindness. Heredity as a cause of deafness, however, is not clear cut. Of the conditions predisposing to deafness, otosclerosis (hardness of hearing due to calcium deposits) is about the only factor that is considered by geneticists to be hereditary. The other causes are a variety of communicable diseases—colds,

[5] H. Davis (Ed.), *Hearing and Deafness,* Murray Hill Books, New York, 1947.

mumps, measles, scarlet fever, meningitis, influenza—which may result in infections of the middle ear. Only a small percentage of deafness is attributed to accidents.

Economic relief measures are as necessary in the case of deafness as in the other handicaps. This is because the incidence of impaired hearing is 25.0 per cent to 112.0 per cent higher among low than among other income groups. In addition, considerable attention has been given to the alleviation of the social isolation that so often is a primary hazard of the deaf. Other specific efforts include campaigns to control the infectious diseases, prompt treatment of inflammatory conditions of the ear, and further research into the nature and conditions of congenital deafness.

The crippled. As stated above in the review of the total distribution of handicaps in the population, there are about 341,000 persons with major and more than two million with minor orthopedic handicaps. The problems of rehabilitation and prevention are complicated not only by the variety of these defects and their numerous causes but also by the fact that they occur among children, the middle-aged, and the old. Treatment, accordingly, generally overtaxes the resources of the best-organized society.

Both the nature and the frequency of the problems of orthopedic handicaps were shown in a survey of New York City in 1919. At that time a rate of seven crippled persons per 1,000 population was found. Comparable and more recent surveys lead to the same general conclusions. Not only are the crippled much more numerous than the blind and the deaf, but a large number are disabled from birth or early childhood. In the New York study sixty-three per cent of the crippled were under sixteen years of age.[6]

Causes of these defects also vary by age groups. General conditions are tuberculosis, rickets, infantile or other forms of paralysis, congenital deformities, and accidents. Accidents, both industrial and nonindustrial, are more frequent causes in upper age groups, while among children infantile paralysis is the major factor.

In the distribution of causes, revealed by the National Health Survey, the dominant role of disease is obvious. Among males the

[6] "Why Cripples Are Young," *The Survey,* Vol. 44 (1920): 633. Equally high or higher rates may be noted in: Craig, M. L., "Absenteeism in the School Health Program," *Jour. Health, Phys. Educa., and Recreation,* Vol. 20 (1949): 638-39. E. W. Dolch, *Helping Handicapped Children in School,* Garrard Press, Champaign, Ill., 1948.

two leading causes are apoplexy and occupational accidents, among females, apoplexy and home accidents.

CAUSES OF INCAPACITATING ORTHOPEDIC IMPAIRMENTS

	Per Cent Distribution			
	Males		*Females*	
Accidents	43.0		30.9	
Home		4.1		13.3
Occupational		23.6		2.4
Automobile		8.6		6.6
Disease	53.7		69.0	
Apoplexy		34.7		42.9
Infantile paralysis		4.9		8.5
Congenital		4.0		5.8
Others	3.3		0.1	
War wounds		2.8		...
Total	100.0		100.0	

Source: B. D. Karpinos, *op. cit.,* p. 11.

The methods of treatment and prevention of these predisposing conditions do not differ markedly from the measures adopted for blindness and deafness. This is especially true in the case of crippled children, whose problems can be reduced by the elimination of infectious diseases; this does not apply to adults, however. Preventive measures in the case of adults are identical with the methods of a preventive program to maintain general health and to reduce the accident rate.

Frequency of minor physical defects. From a number of special studies of physical defectiveness in various age groups, a wholly different class of substandard persons has been identified, consisting of minor cases of defectiveness. These minor defects, which are widely distributed among persons who are ordinarily considered normal, cause an unknown amount of inefficiency and suffering, and indicate a field for remedial and preventive medicine hitherto neglected. The defects are called minor only in relation to their immediate effects and by contrast to the gross handicaps of the blind, the deaf, and the crippled.

This approach to physical defectiveness is largely a problem of child welfare. Although the connection between the defects of children and the ill health, defectiveness, and premature mortality of adult life is not definitely known, the fact that children should possess good health during the formative years is clearly established.

From this point of view, it is believed that in their ultimate consequences minor defects are no less significant than the physical diseases of childhood.

Distribution among adults. One of the most comprehensive inventories of the kinds of physical defects among the adult population resulted from the Selective Service examinations of men drafted for military service during the World Wars. Although the two examinations are not exactly comparable in numbers, age range, or rules regarding deferment, their findings as to distribution and types of defects are considered valid and representative.

In the following table, the first ten causes of rejection are listed. The per cents in the first column for World War I are based upon the "second million" examined; those in the second column for World War II are based upon 2,700,000 examinations. These reports will be supplemented by a comparable list, distributed for Negroes and whites, for the first three million examinations in World War II.

TEN LEADING TYPES OF DEFECT AMONG DRAFTED MEN

	Per Cent Distribution	
	World War I	*World War II*
Musculoskeletal	14.2	9.6
Syphilis	...	10.7
Cardiovascular	14.1	8.3
Eyes	11.6	6.8
Tuberculosis	8.4	3.4
Underweight	7.4	...
Feet	7.1	...
Hernia	5.6	7.6
Neurological	...	7.0
Ears	4.5	5.0
Mental deficiency	4.1	4.3
Mental and neurological disease	3.9	18.9
	80.9	80.6

Source: G. St. J. Perrott, "Findings of Selective Service Examinations," *Milbank Mem. Fund Quart.*, Vol. 22 (1944): 358-366. Adapted from Tables 1A and 1B, pp. 359 and 360.

In spite of changing medical standards in this comparison, the results are fairly similar. The ten leading classes of defects account for four fifths of all rejections. This rejection rate (30 per cent in War I and 52.8 per cent for the first three million in War II) is considered high. Both statisticians and health authorities agree that there has been no improvement in the health of young adults. Both reports also show that the leading disabling conditions have been just about the same. The two exceptions are the appearance of foot disorders and underweight on the War I list, and the appearance of syphilis and an increase in mental diseases on the War II list. The explanation of the latter is that so much difficulty arose during World War I because of psychoneurotics that they were more carefully screened during the World War II examinations. Also to be noted is the significant decline in tuberculosis since 1918.

Other similarities in the two reports show that many defects (skin, teeth, respiratory, and weight) are minor so far as general health is concerned and would not disqualify the individual for military service or hinder his performance in a civilian occupation. Two other comparisons show that there are a few more defects in the rural than the urban population and that farmers and unskilled workers have more defects than professional, supervisory, skilled, and clerical vocations.

Among the 52.8 per cent of the first three million registrants in World War II who were rejected for any type of military service, the following distribution of defects and disease were found:

Major Defect or Disease	*Per Cent Distribution*	
	White	*Negro*
Mental disease	18.6	10.1
Manifestly disqualifying defects	11.3	7.3
Mental deficiency	9.5	31.8
Musculoskeletal	8.3	4.4
Cardiovascular	6.8	5.6
Hernia	6.2	3.3
Neurological	5.6	2.7
Eyes	5.5	2.9
Ears	4.7	0.6
Syphilis	3.1	19.2
Tuberculosis	3.0	1.4
Lungs	1.9	1.1
Underweight or overweight	1.7	0.5
All others	13.8	9.1

Source: L. G. Rowntree, "Rheumatic Heart Disease and Physical Fitness of the Nation as Seen by Selective Service," *Jour. Pediat.*, Vol. 26 (1945): 220-229. For another list by the same writer, "Psychosomatic Disorders as Revealed by Thirteen Million Examinations of Selective Service Registrants," *Psychosomatic Med.*, Vol. 7 (1945): 27-30.

This comparison shows that rejection rates for Negroes for all causes was slightly higher than for whites (20 per 1,000 population for Negroes; 19 per 1,000 population for whites). Defects that were more often found among Negroes were cardiovascular, genitalia, syphilis, other venereal diseases, mental deficiency, and foot disorders. Defects that were more numerous among whites were eye, ear, teeth, tuberculosis, hernia, mental disease, neurological defects, musculoskeletal, endocrine, and weight.

Studies of defects, especially those of the United States Public Health Service, of these young adults when they were children show that such defects as underweight, poor nutrition, bad posture, and tooth and eye defects have good prognostic validity. Young men in the draft who had a record of poor nutrition and posture as children had a fifty per cent higher rejection rate than those not so handicapped; and those with underweight as a children's defect had a sixty per cent higher rejection rate.

Interesting and significant sectional differences were found in the geographical distribution of a few major defects and illnesses. The Northwest was distinguished by deformities caused by accidents, flatfoot, and goiter. In the Southwest, tuberculosis, drug addiction, hernia, and tonsilitis were most prevalent. The Southeast had an abnormally high proportion of venereal disease, hookworm, blindness, arthritis, underweight, mental deficiency, pellagra, and hernia; and the Northeast was characterized by congenital defects, underweight, tuberculosis, defective teeth, and syphilis.

Examinations among applicants for service in the United States Navy show essentially the same types and distribution of defects. Among the physical defects occurring most frequently as causes of rejection are, enumerated according to their incidence: defective vision, flatfoot, defective teeth, deformities, and heart disturbances.[7]

Within the industrial population, similar defects occur with greater frequency and severity, since the groups examined are more representative of normal age distributions. The table on page 60 gives the percentage of physical defects among two groups of workers. The first group includes over 100,000 adult males in the prime of life. These examinations were conducted by the Life Extension Institute. The defects affecting the largest proportion of men were abnormal tonsils, defective teeth, hypertrophic rhinitis (enlarged turbinates), digestive disturbances, defective vision, and albumin in

[7] National Industrial Conference Board, "Sickness Insurance or Sickness Prevention?" Research Rpt. No. 6, 1918, p. 6. C. B. Davenport, "Defects Found in Drafted Men," *Sci. Monthly*, Vol. 10 (1920): 7-8. "Summary of Data of 19,923 Reports," *Selective Service System*, Washington, 1941. E. E. Hadley and others, "Military Psychiatry," *Psychiatry*, Vol. 7 (1944): 379-407; this article gives regional distributions.

the urine. Of more immediate significance were the small percentages of serious disabilities. Serious heart impairments, for example, occurred in only two per cent of the group, and hardening of the arteries in three per cent.[8]

PHYSICAL DEFECTS AMONG INDUSTRIAL EMPLOYEES

Physical Defects	*Percentage with Defects* Among 100,000 Workers	Among 10,143 Workers
Nose and throat	45	69.7
Eye and ear	40	37.3
Teeth	39	91.3
Digestive	34	23.5
Hernia, varicose veins, etc.	19	41.3
Respiratory	16	8.5
Other circulatory	14	11.0
Skin	10	8.1
Heart	6	9.4
Miscellaneous	..	20.4

The same major and minor defects appeared among the second group—10,143 industrial workers—and were also shown in a study by the Metropolitan Life Insurance Company of 16,662 policyholders.[9] It is important to remember that these serious and potentially fatal defects occurred among selected white workers (professional men, business men, and skilled workers) who were actually engaged in their occupations at the time of the examination.

The high incidence of physical impairments among workers who are apparently physically efficient presents a major health problem. In the insurance group of 16,662 men, a special investigation was made to determine the probable causes of these impairments. The group was considered representative of the white adult population, because sixty per cent were more than thirty-four years of age. Two general facts relative to causation were discovered. Minor and moderate defects were very common among young men, but the greatest number of serious and advanced defects occurred among the upper age groups. In both the younger and the older groups many

[8] A. B. Mills, *Extent of Illness,* Committee on the Costs of Medical Care, Pub. No. 2 (1929): 13. R. H. Britten and L. H. Thompson, "A Health Study of Ten Thousand Male Industrial Workers," *Pub. Health Rpts.* (1926), No. 162, p. 84.

[9] L. I. Dublin and others, "Physical Defects as Revealed by Periodic Health Examinations," *Am. Jour. of Med. Sciences,* Vol. 170 (1925): 576. E. Sydenstricker and R. H. Britten, "The Physical Impairments of Adult Life." *Am. Jour. Hyg.,* Vol. II (1930): 73-135. (A study of 100,924 adults.)

errors in personal hygiene were noted as probable causes, such as a faulty diet, inadequate exercise, overwork, and overfatigue.

As a rule, the rural population is burdened by the same general types of defects, especially in the low-income groups.[10]

These findings led to another special study: of the relationship between overweight and physical defects. As overweight tends to increase with age, it furnished a clue to the increase in the number of defects in the upper age groups. The defects indicate the combined result of senescence, overweight, and increasing strain upon the circulatory and renal systems. Seventy-five per cent of the persons who were overweight had serious and advanced physical defects. There were, for example, an unusual number with enlarged hearts, functional murmur of the heart, high blood pressure, and arterial thickening. Overweight and high blood pressure are thus associated with diseases of the heart, blood vessels, and kidneys, and with Bright's disease and apoplexy. In addition, twenty per cent of those overweight had moderate defects requiring medical supervision. None of those with normal weight showed conditions as serious as these.

By these surveys of incidence and types of physical defectiveness among adults, the need for early treatment is clearly demonstrated. Early treatment is imperative because most of these defects can be eliminated in the early age groups by medical or surgical methods, and their irremediable complications thus prevented. This conclusion redirects the attention of public health to the incidence of physical impairments among children.

Distribution among children. The occurrence of defectiveness among children not only takes place at an early age but in an unusually large proportion of the population. According to various community surveys the total incidence of these defects is between two and four per thousand of the general population in urban areas and between two and seven per thousand in rural counties.

The most noteworthy difference between the defects of children and those of adults is the fact that there are comparatively few cases

[10] Mary Gover and J. B. Yaukey, "Physical Impairments of Low-Income Farm Families," *Pub. Health Reports,* Vol. 59 (1944), No. 36. United States Dept. of Agriculture, *Better Health for Rural Living,* Washington, D. C., 1946. Compare with: G. Brighouse, *The Physically Handicapped Worker in Industry,* California Institute of Technology, Pasadena, 1946, and editorial in *Jour. Am. Med. Assoc.,* Vol. 143 (1950): 974, which states that there are between seven and eight million handicapped persons in the working population.

of serious conditions among children. This is shown in the distribution of physical handicaps among children in the Pittsburgh Public Schools. Although this distribution is not a fair representation of the prevalence of major defects (for which special schools or classes are provided), it does show the extensive occurrence of minor physical handicaps. In this report the great majority of handicaps are defective teeth,[11] diseased tonsils, defects of nose and throat, and visual and orthopedic defects:

Physical Defects	*Number of Defects*	*Per Cent*
Diseased tonsils	10,685	31.9
Nose and throat	8,754	26.1
Visual	4,627	13.8
Orthopedic	2,154	6.4
Glandular	1,777	5.3
Oral (other than teeth)	1,620	4.8
Heart	1,423	4.2
Hearing	1,351	4.0
Ear	426	1.2
Chest	277	0.8
Abdomen	249	0.7
Pulmonary	224	0.7
Total number of defects	33,567	100.0–
Number of children examined	52,508	

Serious defects of children are poliomyelitis, cerebral palsy, trauma, clubfoot, and osteomyelitis. These five conditions account for more than one half of all crippled children. Since they develop mainly from prenatal or birth injuries, the hopeful outlook is that they can be prevented or corrected by surgery. Since 1900 one of the primary types of children's defects (those of bones and joints) has been reduced considerably by control of infectious diseases, improved nutrition (and the reduction of rickets), and from improved prenatal care. Credit for this success is given to the combined operations of the National Foundation for Infantile Paralysis, the National Society for Crippled Children and Adults, and the United States Children's Bureau.

[11] Based on a slightly larger number of children examined (53,894), 83.1 per cent had dental defects. "Report: School Board Examiners, 1949–50," Pittsburgh Public Schools, Pittsburgh, Pa., 1950. Compare with findings in the school population of Cincinnati: J. Hertzman, "High School Mental Hygiene Survey," *Am. Jour. Orthopsychiatry,* Vol. 18 (1948): 251. The incidence of speech defects among school children is about 10 per cent; consult: I. W. Karlin, "Stuttering—The Problem Today," *Jour. Am. Med. Assoc.,* Vol. 143 (1950): 731-36. K. C. Garrison, *The Psychology of Exceptional Children,* Ronald, New York, 1950, p. 334.

Because of such health gains and the current records of minor handicaps in children, two conclusions have been reached. The first is that minor defects are exceedingly common; the second, that when some of those minor conditions are uncorrected they become the major causes of impairments in later life. These conclusions are effectively presented in Mills' summary:

> Among school and preschool children examined in six different surveys, from 65 to 95 per cent have one or more defects. In four of the groups surveyed, defective teeth are found in over 50 per cent of the children. One third have enlarged or diseased tonsils. When vision is carefully checked by an examination made after the use of "drops," 95 per cent of the children are found to have some degree of hyperopia, myopia, or astigmatism—defects, congenital in many cases, which are serious enough to require glasses for 34 per cent of them. Other tests of vision, being much less thorough, reveal only 6 to 36 per cent with visual defects. In some of the groups surveyed, adenoids affected 10 to 35 per cent of these children, conjunctivitis 3 to 16 per cent, and defects of nutrition 4 to 18 per cent. A recent study has shown that children who have, or have had, diseased or enlarged tonsils suffer much more frequently from rheumatism, lumbago, neuralgia, neuritis, heart diseases, and ear diseases than those with normal tonsils.[12]

This quotation stresses a few of the consequences of physical defectiveness and indicates that one of the most successful agencies in health insurance is the correction of these defects among children and adolescents.

Relation of social problems to physical defects

From the total unadjustment of the blind and seriously crippled, the unfavorable consequences of physical impairments gradually diminish until their influences cannot be differentiated from other causes of personal inefficiency. Comparing physical disability with other causes tends to make it a secondary and not a primary factor in social problems. Of the general results that are traced to physical handicaps, the economic disability of the blind has already been mentioned; the equivalent problem of the deaf is their cultural and social isolation; and of the crippled their occupational unadjustment. But none of these consequences is inevitable. When they do occur with unemployability, poverty, and family or personal

[12] A. B. Mills, *op. cit.*, pp. 14-15. "Orthopedic Impairments Among Children," *Statis. Bull.*, Metropolitan Life Insurance Company, Vol. 29 (May 1948): 7-9.

demoralization, other conditions than physical defects are usually present.

In many studies of the adjustment of the seriously disabled, they are found to be among the most secure both socially and personally. Such individuals either begin with a mature, wholesome personality or, after their handicap, they have been able to achieve maturity. Since there are so many cases of this type among persons with major and minor disorders, it is safe to conclude that no handicap sets insuperable barriers to comparative social competence.

It is true that the serious handicaps result in lowered economic status and sometimes in complete economic dependence. When either of these situations occurs, it is also true that the family has additional burdens, such as loss of income or of contributions to household work, and the need to provide adequate housing, nutrition, and medical and other care. Hence the programs of workmen's compensation and of Social Security are provided.

When physical defects and a cluster of personal and behavior problems are discovered in the same person, there is a tendency to find more instances of frustration and maladjustment than among the nonhandicapped. However, these tendencies need not result in warped personalities. What actually develops in any case of physical defectiveness hinges largely on the cultural background and the personal-social relations of the individual. These characteristics have much more force in determining the psychological outcome than the disability itself.

A study of World War II amputation cases stresses this correlation. Six months after the amputation, fifty per cent of the individuals had emotional conditions especially injurious to their social adjustment. However, case study revealed that the same individuals manifested about the same type of behavior prior to the amputation. In other words, previous personality deficiencies proved to be important factors in determining the course of post-injury rehabilitation.[13]

Numerous studies of disabled and normal housewives, delinquents and nondelinquents, children with poliomyelitis, and handicapped college students point out that there may be a greater dependence of the handicapped person on his family and for this reason some tendency toward immaturity. Also, marriage and

[13] J. R. Rees, *Shaping of Psychiatry by War,* Norton, New York, 1945, pp. 100 ff.

employment may be conditioned by the handicap. Otherwise, there are no inevitable consequences of emotional dependence or of fears and worries. There is no way by which delinquent and non-delinquent children or adjusted and unadjusted college students can be distinguished solely on the grounds of physical defects. As a rule, personal, social, educational, and vocational adjustment are not exclusively the outcomes of physical normality or degree of handicap.[14]

Personal problems of the handicapped often discovered in all age groups are anxiety and tension, withdrawing behavior, shyness and selfconsciousness, refusal to admit disability, feelings of inferiority, emotional and sexual immaturity, isolation and friendlessness, attention-seeking, aggressiveness, and suspicion.

Frequently the studies of the adaptability of the handicapped conclude that it is a combination of maturity and intelligence that determines what the individual can become. Blindness, for example, as a single factor does not lead to abnormal behavior or social maladjustment. In fact the adjustment of the blind seems to be correlated directly with maturity and intelligence. From one report of newly blinded soldiers, six of every ten reacted in a mature manner without fear, anxiety, or depression, two deteriorated into a severe maladjustment, and two had borderline emotional disturbances.[15]

Personal problems of blindness, therefore, are found only in a minority. These problems are, or are conditioned by, alcoholism, mood changes, aggression, excessive dependency, apathy, unrealistic attitudes, and confusion. Psychiatrists account for this difference between the relatively normal and handicapped blind by pre-existing neurotic or psychotic traits, by guilt or remorse, by blindness that was developed from disease or noncombat causes, by partial vision (too slight to be useful), by false prognoses and incomplete understanding by the individual of his disability, and in a few cases by the sympathetic but misguided interferences of relatives. These observations are supported to some extent by the fact that partially

[14] R. G. Barker and others, *op. cit.*, Chap. 3. N. Doscher, "Adjustment of the Physically Handicapped College Students," *Mental Hygiene*, Vol. 31 (1947): 576-81.

[15] B. L. Diamond and A. Ross, "Emotional Adjustment of Newly Blinded Soldiers," *Am. Jour. Psychiatry*, Vol. 102 (1945): 367-71. D. H. Morgan, "Emotional Adjustment of Visually Handicapped Adolescents," *Jour. Ed. Psychol.*, Vol. 35 (1944): 65-81.

sighted children have more conduct problems than the blind or the children in sight-saving classes.

Although findings about the deaf are not so uniformly supported by research, comparisons of individuals with normal hearing and those who are deaf or who have degrees of deafness reach the same conclusions as those just noted for the blind. What impaired hearing can do to the individual varies with his intelligence and maturity. Problems normal to the deaf are their isolation, lack of emotional stimulus because of the absence of sound, and tension and fatigue because of efforts to maintain a relatively normal status.

Abnormalities of personality and social adjustment among the deaf or hard of hearing are precisely like those of the socially defective normal children and adults. Deaf or hard of hearing children are often found to be emotionally unstable, inattentive, suspicious, melancholy, immature, and fearful. Similar conditions among adults are despondency, a sense of inferiority, hopelessness, introversion, resentment, and supersensitiveness. They are also described as listless, egocentric, submissive, and neurotic.[16]

The employment of the deaf is not affected as seriously as their earnings, which decrease with increasing degrees of deafness. Employers express the opinion that deafness is a block to promotion in at least thirty per cent of the cases, and that the deaf are best suited for unskilled work. Here, then, as in the case of the blind, is demonstrated the need for vocational education and training, since their legal protection under compensation laws puts them in an unfavorable position to compete effectively with the nonhandicapped worker.

Problems of the crippled child and the speech defective are very similar to the above when they are aggravated by immaturity or intellectual deficiencies, and they therefore will not be discussed further.[17]

[16] R. G. Barker and others, *op. cit.*, Chap. 5. E. W. Coughlin, "Some Parental Attitudes toward Handicapped Children," *The Child*, Vol. 6 (1941): 41-45.

[17] L. F. Cain, "The Disabled Child in School," *Jour. Juvenile Research*, Vol. 4 (1948): 90-94. F. G. Koenig, "Social Consciousness in Relation to the Physically Handicapped," *Jour. Excep. Child.*, Vol. 15 (1949): 144-147. H. A. Greenberg, "The Management of the Emotional Problems of Crippled Children," *Am. Jour. Orthopsychiat.*, Vol. 19 (1949): 253-265. W. W. Roberts, "Interpretation of Some Disorders of Speech," *Jour. Ment. Sci.*, Vol. 95 (1949): 567-588. M. M. Ross, "Stuttering and the Pre-School Child," *Smith College Studies in Social Work*, Vol. 21 (1950): 23-53.

Occupational adjustment of the handicapped

As yet the problem of adjusting the handicapped person to an occupation has not been solved. This is not surprising, because solution enters the broad fields of vocational education and guidance, which for normal persons are largely unexplored. Authorities are reluctant to accept any definite list of vocations for disabled persons, because of individual differences within groups of handicapped persons and because of variations within similar types of employment. Until conditions of employment, as they are related to health, hours, wages, prospects for advancement and degrees of skill, are more thoroughly studied, little specific data can be furnished on this subject. A second serious lack is definite knowledge concerning the ability of different types of handicapped persons to perform suggested tasks. To date the experience with different kinds of persons in various jobs indicates that the personal factor is the chief determinant of occupational adaptability.

Since physically handicapped persons differ from one another as do normal persons, their occupational adaptability is determined more by their mental and temperamental characteristics than by their handicaps. An enumeration of jobs held by the handicapped is the least important factor in developing a program of rehabilitation. Of greater consequence is the person's intelligence, ambition, interest, and morale. The importance of the latter is sometimes overemphasized by popular accounts of what a few exceptional handicapped persons have been able to accomplish. The steeple jack who continued in his occupation in spite of the loss of an arm, chauffeurs with serious amputations, and the many successes of the blind in manual tasks are illustrations. On the other hand, there are instances where men with minor disabilities could not be adapted to the simplest manual or clerical jobs, even after prolonged training. Such contrasts are useful in demonstrating that intelligence and temperament are able to compensate for many physical barriers to occupational usefulness.

Disabled applicants for work are usually refused employment for the following disabilities: (1) anemia, underweight and overweight, (2) tuberculosis, (3) heart disease, (4) hernia, (5) defective vision, (6) defective hearing, (7) epilepsy, (8) marked orthopedic defects, such as the crippling of arm, leg, hands, feet, (9) rheumatism, (10) skin diseases and varicose veins, and (11) high blood pressure.

Since the work opportunities of the handicapped are limited for all these reasons, numerous efforts are made to show that handicapped workers also have many favorable qualities and that in many respects they are equal or superior to the nonhandicapped worker. One study shows that the average handicapped worker has a better work record in stability on the job, fewer absences, fewer accidents, slightly greater increases in earnings, and equal production records. There are also some less favorable differences; for, example, he makes more claims and receives more compensation, and the cost of his employment is greater in hiring, placement, and arranging special equipment.

These advantages and disadvantages of the handicapped in industry are largely responsible for many current efforts to expand work opportunities. The War Manpower Commission conducted an extensive campaign in this direction, and since the improvement of employment opportunities after 1943 the United States Employment Services have adopted similar tactics.

Since World War I there has been considerable expansion in the program of rehabilitation. Generally this development has been supported by federal legislation and funds under the control of the Federal Board of Vocational Education. It has had four definite aims: (1) to make the program more inclusive of specific disabilities, (2) to provide medical services, (3) to extend the training divisions, and (4) to obtain more funds for these activities. Favorable results have been immediate. There are now increasing numbers of disabled people in many more different occupations and industries. Their average earnings have increased. And in many cases through re-education, the disabled are returned to their employment with more skills.

Many companies have adopted special provisions for the readjustment of the handicapped, and several states operate bureaus not unlike the Federal Board.[18] The New Jersey Rehabilitation Commission, one of the first to be established, offers among other services a diagnostic clinic to determine the physical, vocational, and social adaptability of the worker. Connecticut has a similar organization.

[18] E. Ford, "Why We Employ Aged and Handicapped Workers," *Sat. Eve. Post,* Vol. 215 (1943): 16-17. E. O'Connor, "Fifteen Years' Experience with Handicapped Employees," *Executives Ser. Bull.,* Vol. 22 (1944): 5-6. F. W. Novis, "Clinical Rehabilitation," *Survey Mid-Monthly,* Vol. 80 (1944): 313-314. *Self-Help for the Handicapped,* National Goodwill Industries, Milwaukee, Wisconsin, 1945.

In addition, there are numerous agencies that offer opportunities for home or sheltered employment. There are, however, many objections to this form of rehabilitation.

Great Britain in 1944 adopted a comprehensive plan for the readjustment of the disabled under its Disabled Persons Employment Act. This law requires an official registration of all disabled persons. Each employer is given a quota of disabled persons to whom he must give work, thus assuring equal work opportunities and minimizing unequal competition. Since this plan puts all employers on an equal competitive basis, the general reaction to it has been favorable and its psychological stimulus to the disabled has been excellent.[19]

An early report of the Federal Board of Vocational Education on Civilian Vocational Rehabilitation anticipated most of these developments in stating:

1. That the possibilities of placement are much better than is ordinarily supposed. Physical handicaps do not limit the person to unskilled jobs, nor are training programs necessarily limited to a few skilled or clerical jobs.
2. That the range of occupational adaptability is much greater than was hitherto considered possible. Neither the physical handicap nor the mechanical requirements of the work are the chief obstacles in placing handicapped men, the intelligence and morale of the person being more important.
3. That a thorough study of the individual and of the job precedes successful placement and rehabilitation.[20]

The report covers the social and occupational history of 6,097 handicapped persons, distributed throughout 628 different vocations. Listed in the order of their frequency, the following were the vocations followed by these persons:

1. Occupations in which blind and partially sighted persons were most frequently employed: weaver, broom factory, laborer (factory), chain maker, piano tuner, janitor, auto repair mechanic, clerical, mattress maker, chiropractor, lawyer, molder, musician.
2. Occupations in which individuals with defects of hearing were most frequently employed: domestic servant, linotype operator, general office work, janitor, lathe operator, laborer in storehouse, typist.
3. Occupations in which individuals with disabilities of the hand were

[19] "Employment of Disabled Persons in Great Britain," *Int'l. Lab. Rev.*, Vol. 49 (1944): 373-376.

[20] "A Study of Occupations," *Civilian Vocational Rehabilitation Series*. Bulletin No. 96, Washington, 1925.

most frequently employed: watchman, laborer, clerical, bookkeeper, auto repair mechanic, retail store, elevator operator, farmer, poultryman, welder.

4. Occupations in which individuals with disabilities of the leg were most frequently employed: shoe repairing, bookkeeper, auto mechanic, barber, clerical, watchman, teacher, labor (factory and mine), retail store, janitor.
5. Occupations in which individuals with disabilities of the heart were most frequently employed: general office work, clerical, watchman, stenographer, auto repair mechanic, jewelry engraver.

Summary

The problems of physical illness and defect represent a drain upon social resources that justifies the recognition of health or physical efficiency as a basic requirement in social competency. If attention is confined wholly to the enormous distribution of ill health, physical defectiveness, and lowered vitality as indexes of these problems, the conclusion cannot be avoided that current remedial and preventive agencies have been only partially successful. Even with their recent emphasis upon the elimination and prevention of disease, actual prevention, or the achievement of positive health, depends upon other social readjustments, of which a population program is regarded as an indispensable part.

Little or no attention has ever been given to the coordinate problems of health and population quality, nor has there ever been a single instance of a national population program in which quality has figured prominently. To a considerable degree the problem of quality has been left to individuals, with only a few social restrictions. Some nations have adopted a population program on a limited scale in order to maintain increasing numbers, generally for military purposes, and quality has always been incidental to this objective. Marriage customs, also, are not concerned directly with quality, although they do exercise a mild form of restriction. For a long time the problem of population quality remained a matter of academic interest, confined to discussions of heredity and environment. However, with the rapid increase of population during the last century, public attention has been turned to the possibility of overpopulation, and fears arising from this source are largely responsible for the growing interest in a positive population program.

It is probably correct to assume that the major illnesses and physical defects cannot be controlled except by means of such a program. Even the coordinated efforts of public and private health groups are unable to make significant reductions in the total number of the unfit, because their measures are largely remedial. This fact is obvious in the current organization of dispensaries and clinics, out-patient departments of hospitals, health centers, free medical service, convalescent and custodial care, district nursing, special schools for the defective, and vocational training and placement, which at their best are only factors in the rehabilitation of those who are to a considerable extent unadjustable. Similarly, such preventive measures as better living conditions, sanitation, adequate medical service, control over disease or accidents, improved vital statistics, periodic health examinations, health legislation, and popular health education often fail to reach the basic causes of ill health and defectiveness.

Blindness, deafness, and other handicaps are approaching an irreducible minimum, unless drastic controls are introduced to remove the conditions that tolerate their persistence. Such controls are being proposed constantly by eugenists and population theorists, who reduce most questions of population to biological problems. But society, as a whole, is unwilling to accept a mechanistic attitude toward human breeding, and opposes the radical proposals of population reforms. However, these reforms are radical only because we have never had a population program and because most of us have great difficulty in separating biology from morals. As a matter of fact, every social reform has encountered both of these obstructions; namely, accusations of radicalism and immorality. Since disease and defectiveness are universally accepted as undesirable characteristics of a normal society, it should not be difficult to effect deliberate controls over breeding. To a considerable extent this point has already been sanctioned by most social groups, but there is no overwhelming unanimity as to the means to be employed in the exercise of these controls.

From the foregoing discussion of the relative incidence of various major and minor illnesses and physical defects, two conclusions are justified: (1) disease is a cause of defectiveness, and (2) defectiveness predisposes the individual to the most incurable diseases—the degenerative. Because of their relationship, disease and defectiveness cannot be treated as isolated problems. Furthermore, both result in the same social unadjustments of economic and social dependency. For this reason, an improvement in population quality is about the only reform that would effectually cover both these sources of incompetency. And a population program that could achieve these results would unquestionably have far-reaching effects, especially in eliminating a portion of the unsolved problems of poverty, unemployment, and associated disturbances.

Bibliography

Barker, R. G., and others, *Adjustment to Physical Handicap and Illness*, Social Science Research Council, New York, 1946. Bull. No. 55. Chaps. 2-5 and 7.

Chevigny, H., and S. Braverman, *The Adjustment of the Blind,* Yale University Press, New Haven, 1950.

Davis, H., *Hearing and Deafness,* Murray Hill Books, Inc., New York, 1947. Part 6, "Social and Economic Problems."

Ewing, I. R. and A. W. G., *Opportunity and the Deaf Child,* University of London Press, London, 1947. English experience with deaf children.

Hawk, S. S., *Speech Therapy for the Physically Handicapped,* Stanford University Press, Stanford, California, 1950.

Mackie, R. P., *Crippled Children in American Education,* Teachers College, Columbia University, New York, 1945. No. 913. Chap. 2, "Characteristics of Crippled Children."

Sommers, V. S., *Influence of Parental Attitudes and Social Environment on the Personality Development of the Adolescent Blind,* Am. Foundation for the Blind, New York, 1944. Chap. 4, "Survey of Personal and Social Problems."

Wilson, A. J., *The Emotional Life of the Ill and Injured,* Social Science Publishers, New York, 1950. Case histories.

Yost, Edna, *Normal Lives for the Disabled,* Macmillan, New York, 1945. Chap. XIV, "Some Jobs the Disabled Have Chosen."

Rehabilitation

Bridges, C. D., *Job Placement of the Physically Handicapped.* McGraw-Hill, New York, 1946.

Doherty, W. B., and D. D. Runes (Eds.), *Rehabilitation of the War Injured,* Philosophical Library, New York, 1943.

Dolch, E. W., *Helping Handicapped Children,* Garrard Press, Champaign, Ill., 1948.

Ray, M. B., *How to Conquer Your Handicaps,* Bobbs-Merrill, Indianapolis, 1948.

Rusk, H. A., and E. J. Taylor, *New Hope for the Handicapped,* Harper, New York, 1949.

Soden, W. H. (Ed.), *Rehabilitation of the Handicapped,* Ronald, New York, 1949. Part IV, "Vocational and Social Rehabilitation."

United States Civil Service Commission, *Operations Manual for Placement of the Physically Handicapped,* Washington, D.C., 1944.

United States Department of Labor, Bureau of Labor Statistics, *The Performance of Physically Impaired Workers in Manufacturing Industries,* Bull. No. 923, Washington, 1948.

Questions

1. How may a specific disability affect the life of a person? Compare the cases of Beverly and Marcia in Barker, *op. cit.,* pp. 93-110.
2. What are some of the personal problems of the blind? Consult Sommers. What attitudes of parents are most helpful in the adjustment of the blind?
3. Does your community or state provide special services for rehabilitation?
4. Do the industries of your community offer similar provisions?
5. What is the chief cause of orthopedic defects among children in the country as a whole? In your state?
6. Why is it difficult to provide adequately for the cerebral palsy child? Consult Mackie (see bibliography).
7. Is your reaction favorable to the suggestion that facial disfigurement may lead to problems of conduct?
8. State the chief trends in the incidence of blindness, deafness, and orthopedic impairments since 1900. What is the explanation of these changes?
9. Are racial differences in the distribution of physical impairments great enough to require special services and study?
10. What are some of the emotional problems of the crippled child?
11. Possibilities Unlimited is an organization for the handicapped comparable to Alcoholics Anonymous for drunkards. Are the possibilities of the handicapped unlimited?
12. Do the tables showing the incidence and types of defects confirm the statement that the basic health problem is to control them before they lead to major defects or illnesses? What are the possible, contradictory arguments?
13. Does deafness increase as population increases?
14. In what age group is the problem of defectiveness most acute?
15. Is the geographical distribution of defects a good guide in research?
16. Can you explain why, in most surveys, urban adults and rural children apparently have the greatest number of defects?
17. Why are minor defects considered sources of major defects?
18. How are bodily conditions related to behavior and educational achievement? When are the defects of children most likely to cause behavior problems?
19. What are the principal obstacles to the occupational adjustability of defectives other than their handicaps?
20. How might a positive population program be organized? From what sources would opposition to such a program be most intense?

CHAPTER 4

MENTAL HEALTH

MENTAL ILLNESSES NOW RANK AMONG THE GREAT UNSOLVED PROBLEMS of public health. The numerous disturbances of body and mind were granted this recognition about the turn of the century through the combined efforts of neurology and psychology. Psychotherapy, especially psychiatry, came upon the scene for the medical treatment of the mentally ill, who hitherto had only the worst forms of custodial care. Their needs became questions of scientific interest. Hence, since 1900 the identification, treatment, and prevention of mental suffering have reached the proportions of "grave national problems."

In an elementary approach to these illnesses, three broad and overlapping types of mental distress are named: the psychoses, neuroses, and psychoneuroses. These conditions and their symptoms are as widely distributed as are the chronic and other physical illnesses. As already noted of these more obviously physical diseases, few people can be found who are not handicapped to some degree or at some time during their lives by the mental diseases.

This situation is apparent when the minor and major mental illnesses are described through their symptoms. As minor illnesses they include anxieties, fears, prejudices and worries. As major disorders, the only change in these symptoms is their severity. They become guilt reactions, phobias, delusions, and repressions.[1]

[1] For further analysis and comparison, consult: J. E. Wallace Wallin, *Minor Mental Maladjustments in Normal People,* Duke University Press, Durham, N. C., 1939, p. 21; and N. Cameron, *The Psychology of Behavior Disorders,* Houghton Mifflin, Boston, 1947, p. 64. In both books there are cases illustrating these conduct disorders in their comparative degrees of mildness and gravity.

Mental diseases as social problems

Mental diseases and venereal diseases are often compared in their medical and social aspects. Both are grossly misunderstood by most people. In spite of mental and social hygiene movements, they continue to be regarded as secret and shameful misfortunes. Consequently, it is necessary to clarify at the outset what the mental diseases are and are not.

The mental impairments are not new. They are found in the earliest and most primitive societies. However, it is probably true that some of them are aggravated and intensified by the strains and conflicts of contemporary living, a fact that is also true of some of the physical diseases.

Moreover, they are physical diseases, being one subdivision of them, in addition to infectious, degenerative, dietary, and other classifications, which are convenient groupings for diagnosis, treatment, and research. Nowhere in physiology, psychology, or medicine is the separation between the terms physical and mental other than a useful distinction to indicate that a special approach is being adopted and new techniques of treatment are required.

The term, mental diseases, also implies that there are mental disorders other than those usually distinguished as the neuroses or psychoses. The others are principally the different types of mental deficiency, epilepsy, chorea, neurasthenia, and other milder disorders. Although mental disease and mental deficiency may be found in the same person, they are two totally different mental impairments psychologically.

The common problems of the mental diseases are those that are best known by laymen or general physicians. They are described in everyday language as emotional or nervous disorders. This popular approach is important because the approved diagnostic terms and symptoms are both too technical and confusing.

Ordinary cases are the problems of patients who go to the general physician for organic illnesses. The patient is worried about his physical condition and is apprehensive of mysterious complications. Symptoms disturb him. He is annoyed with the requirements of convalescence. He is often uncooperative with the recommended treatment.

Other problems may present definite combinations of emotional and physical disorders. Here both physician and patient must decide whether the more serious problem is the emotional attitude or the physical illness, since either may determine the course of the other. This is the field of psychosomatic medicine, which includes both (a) physical conditions that are complicated by emotional upsets, and (b) emotional disturbances that may lead to physical changes.

A third group of patients are those who suffer exclusively from emotional disorders. But they conceal them by a variety of physical complaints. These disorders are the tensions and fatigue conditions that medicine cannot explain or treat. Often, too, it is beyond the scope of the physician or the insight of the patient to appreciate the basis of his anxieties and fears or to recognize the psychological foundation of his depression or other changes of mood.[2]

History comes to the rescue of the student through the case analyses by psychiatrists of numerous well-known persons. An example is Elizabeth Barrett. After a minor injury when she was twenty years old, she was bedridden until she was forty, suffering from "consumption." When Robert Browning courted and married her, she recovered so fully and quickly that at forty-one she went on a walking tour with him. And at forty-three she gave birth to a child.[3]

Comparable problems are suicides and near suicides, proneness to accidents, many forms of convenient allergy, hypertension, asthma, headaches, pains of the lower back, ulcers, and "black-outs" among individuals who want to escape responsibility for some act, who fear failure, who are too ambitious, and who revel in imaginary symptoms and diseases.

Quest for the normal

No one has ever been able to devise a wholly acceptable definition of mental normality and abnormality. Both terms, however, are used frequently as measures of social adjustability in connection with such indexes as economic security, good health, social maturity, or educational achievement. It is necessary, therefore, to make an

[2] D. G. and K. A. Humm, "Measures of Mental Health from the Humm-Wadsworth Temperament Scale," *Am. Jour. Psychiatry,* Vol. 107 (1950): 443. Here characteristics are given that help to distinguish the psychotic from the normal.

[3] W. R. Brain, "Authors and Psychopaths," *Jour. Brit. Med. Assoc.,* Vol. 2 (1949): 1427-1432. In the same category, this writer lists Goethe, Poe, Rousseau, Swift, Boswell, and Dickens among many others.

initial distinction between mentally normal and abnormal persons. Although mental condition is largely an enigma, even to the psychologist, the mental diseases can be defined and classified in terms of exceptional behavior.

When an individual persistently adheres to extremes in behavior or in attitudes, and when these extremes are nonadjustive (meaning illogical or unsuited to the situation in which they appear), such persons may be considered subject to some mental disorder. This conception of abnormality covers both mental disease and feeblemindedness. In either instance, the same types of nonadjustive behavior may occur, and frequently they can be distinguished only by prolonged clinical examination. For purposes of general classification, the normal and the abnormal—either the mentally ill or the feebleminded—are identified by characteristic types of behavior (physical or verbal), and certain typical symptoms are employed to distinguish dementia (mental disease) and amentia (feeblemindedness) from mental normality.

From the statistician's point of view, a person is normal when he may be classified with the average or majority of his society. Accordingly, there are many degrees of normality in physical, in mental, and in social life. There are normal vision and height, normal intelligence, normal emotional behavior, and normal responses to social codes. The statistician employs the bell-shaped frequency distribution to count and measure each of these characteristics. This point of view helps in an understanding of mental or intellectual variations that are commonly described as the mental diseases and mental deficiency. It provides for average and borderline groups of people.

The fact that normal physical, mental, and social conditions are blended by almost imperceptible degrees with the abnormal is shown by the wide occurrence of symptoms and traits of abnormality among the so-called normal classes.[4] In contrast mentally abnormal people are distinguished in four groups: (1) the psychotic, (2) the neurotic, (3) the feebleminded, and (4) genius types.

The term "mental diseases" is thus a broad and inclusive classification of those major and minor mental changes that occur within

[4] A. J. Levine, "What It Means to be Normal," *Jour. Clin. Psychopath.*, Vol. 9 (1948): 324-333. G. K. Morlan, "Statistical Concept of Normal: A Criticism," *Jour. Genet. Psych.*, Vol. 38 (1948): 51-56.

individuals who were originally endowed with a normal brain and nervous system.

Mental changes that produce mental disease may result from diseases of the nervous tissue or of nonnervous parts of the body. Consequently, as a biological concept, mental disease is not of unitary character; that is, there is no single mental disease, but many different mental diseases. The first type of mental disorders includes those mental diseases that usually occur with definite organic changes of the body. The second type includes functional unadjustments for which no organic change sufficiently serious to account for the disease can be found. These are also called the psychoneuroses by some psychiatrists. Perhaps it is well to point out at this time that it is useless to attempt an absolute distinction between the psychoses and the neuroses. Sometimes the two terms are used interchangeably, indicating that no invariable line of demarcation separates them. Organic and functional mental diseases blend into one another, the uncertain separation between them being similar to that between abnormality and normality.

Distribution in the population [5]

Because of rapid advances in hospital care for the mentally ill, it is generally assumed that the mental diseases are actually increasing. This impression is due largely to the spectacular nature of mental diseases, and in part to a growing public interest in their sources and prevention.

Prevalence (the number of active cases at a given moment) of specific mental diseases and of mental disease as a whole is computed from the total hospital population and the number of first admissions. From these figures, the number of other cases in the community and expectancy rates are estimated.

In one summary the following statements of incidence are quoted:

> One out of twenty people . . . will in the course of a lifetime enter a psychiatric hospital on account of mental illness.
>
> . . . another one out of twenty will be too ill to work for a shorter or longer time, but will not go to a hospital.
>
> . . . one person out of ten in the course of his life will . . . be in need

[5] R. H. Felix and R. V. Bowers, "Mental Hygiene and Socio-Environmental Factors," *Milbank Mem. Fund Quart.*, Vol. 26 (1948): 125-145. E. Y. Williams and C. P. Carmichael, "Incidence of Mental Disease in the Negro," *Jour. Negro Educa.*, Vol. 18 (1949): 276-282.

of treatment on account of a mental illness or incapacitating psychoneuroses.

. . . three to five persons out of every thousand suffer from epilepsy. . . .[6]

Specific reports of incidence. Other estimates are found in general surveys,[7] and in studies that are limited geographically. In the Selective Service reports, both types and severity of the mental disorders are given in the percentage distribution of selectees who were rejected for (1) grave mental or personality disorders or major abnormalities of mood—10 per cent, (2) psychopathic personalities—29 per cent, (3) psychoneurotics—54 per cent, (4) chronic alcoholics or drug addicts—4 per cent, (5) unclassified—3 per cent.

In a study at Harvard University of several thousand people in business or the professions, it was discovered that 62 per cent of the failures could be explained in part by personality difficulties or undesirable attitudes.

Other indexes of incidence are the evidence of personal and social failure in divorce and separation and in the number of patients of general practitioners whose complaints are psychoneurotic in origin. It is estimated that 30 to 60 per cent of the people who go to the doctor have complaints primarily of a psychoneurotic nature, and that one person in five goes to a doctor each year for some mental or nervous disorder.[8]

Are the mental diseases increasing? [9] The hospital rate of incidence from 1880 is furnished by the United States Bureau of the Census. According to this enumeration, the rate per 100,000 population of mental patients in state hospitals has increased more than

[6] Reprinted by permission of the publisher and The Commonwealth Fund from Thomas A. C. Rennie and Luther E. Woodward's *Mental Health in Modern Society*. Cambridge, Mass.: Harvard University Press, 1948, pp. 137-138.

[7] Such as the statements of incidence in the two preceding chapters, pp. 16, 51.

[8] T. A. C. Rennie and L. E. Woodward, *op. cit.*, p. 138. On p. 154 the authors state: "There are in the United States 600,000 patients in hospitals for mental illness . . . at least 1,000,000 others are sick enough for hospital treatment . . . [and] an additional 8,000,000 people who should be receiving psychiatric guidance. . . ." See also: J. W. Affleck, "Psychiatric Disorders among the Chronic Sick in Hospitals," *Jour. Ment. Sci.*, Vol. 94 (1948): 33-45. L. G. Rowntree, "Psychosomatic Disorders as Revealed by Thirteen Million Examinations of Selective Service Registrants," *Psychosomatic Med.*, Vol. 7 (1945): 27-30. G. Ulett, "Geographic Distribution of Multiple Sclerosis," *Dis. Nerv. Sys.*, Vol. 9 (1948): 342-346.

[9] In 1880 the rate per 100,000 of patients in mental hospitals was 63.7. This rate has increased each year. Consult: *Patients in Hospitals for Mental Disease*, United States Bureau of the Census, or the annual report: *Statistical Abstract*.

sixfold since that year. Although these rates show a rapid growth in prevalence, this increase is due in part to better hospital facilities and treatment, to increasing willingness of relatives of mental patients to make use of the hospitals, and in part to the increased average length of life. When adjustments are made for these and other factors, such as the aging of the population, there is little evidence to verify the suspicion of increasing prevalence. Careful examinations of various populations show no general upward trend either in this country or in Europe and nothing to indicate that the spread of modern living is leading to increased mental breakdowns.

The evidence of increase is limited almost wholly to the rate of first admissions. Whatever the actual trend may be, it is of course considerably less than this rate. Dayton concluded from his analysis of trends in Massachusetts that an increasing rate of one fourth of one per cent may be fairly accurate. The modesty of this estimate may be observed by noting how much more the rates of increase are for some of the degenerative diseases. Furthermore, any estimate must be reconsidered in the light of such developments as the increasing age of the population, better medical and custodial care, immigration, urbanization, and economic status.[10]

Much more disconcerting than such considerations of an increasing rate are the seriousness of certain specific mental diseases, their low recovery rates, the large number of persons who are receiving no medical or social supervision, and the faulty community control of paroled patients.

Age and sex variations. Since 1900 there has been a marked increase in first admissions to mental hospitals. There is an abrupt increase at age twenty, another at age thirty, and then a constant increase. This trend is explained by the changing age composition of the population which in turn helps to account for the rapid increase at age seventy.

Apart from the psychoneuroses that may be traced back to the earliest years of life, mental disease is rare in childhood and early adolescence. It is not a significant problem, so far as numbers are concerned, under age fifteen.[11] From this age and prior to age

[10] N. A. Dayton, *New Facts on Mental Disorders,* C. C. Thomas, Baltimore, 1944, Chap. 10. J. D. Page and C. Landis, "Trends in Mental Disease," *Jour. Abn. and Soc. Psych.,* Vol. 38 (1943): 518-524.

[11] For statistics on first admissions and the distribution by age and sex groups, consult: *Statistical Abstract,* United States Bureau of the Census, Annual Reports.

thirty, dementia praecox, manic-depressive, and epileptic psychoses, psychoses with psychopathic personality, and psychoses with mental deficiency are responsible for this first increase. Between thirty and forty, the psychoses associated with syphilis and alcohol replace dementia praecox and manic-depressive psychoses among the numerically significant diseases. In the next decade (forty to fifty), involutional psychoses are most frequent, and for the remaining years, there are the senile psychoses and psychoses with arteriosclerosis.[12]

In brief summary, the early years of life are marked by the functional psychoses. Mental illnesses of middle life are associated with social causes. And the psychoses of aging are generally the result of the degenerative diseases.

Three types of mental disease are apparently recurrent in all adult ages. The first is paranoia; the second is any dementing disease, such as dementia praecox, but this type is also a characteristic of involution and senile psychoses; the third is a disease of depression, also accompanied by excited periods, as in manic-depressive psychoses.

In the distribution of mental disease between the sexes, there are few differences, and the variations that are known are not significant in the search for causes. Schizophrenia and cerebral arteriosclerosis have about equal frequency among men and women. Men have a slight liability to alcoholic psychoses and general paresis. Women have a slight liability to manic-depressive and senile psychoses.

The incidence of psychoses among children is so slight that Louttit omitted this section in the revision of his book.[13] Only a fraction of one per cent is given in statements of various hospitals and clinics. When psychoses are diagnosed in children, the initial symptoms are the same as those of adult cases, and the course of the disease is also identical, except that an early onset is an indication of poor prognosis. In general, the behavior problems of children

[12] B. Malzberg, "Statistical Analysis of the Ages of First Admissions to Hospitals for Mental Disease in New York State," *Psychiatric Quart.*, Vol. 23 (1949): 344-365.

[13] C. M. Louttit, *Clinical Psychology of Children's Behavior Problems,* Harper, New York, 1947, pp. 531-532. O. S. English and G. H. J. Pearson, *Common Neuroses of Children and Adults,* Norton, New York, 1937. K. Cameron, "In-Patient Treatment of Psychotic Adolescents," *Brit. Jour. Med. Psych.*, Vol. 23 (1950): 107-109. J. L. Despert, "Anxiety, Phobias, and Fears in Young Children," *Nerv. Child,* Vol. 5 (1946): 8-24. S. Keiser, "Severe Reactive States and Schizophrenia in Adolescent Girls," *Nerv. Child,* Vol. 4 (1944): 17-25.

resemble the milder neuroses. Their causal background (generally disorganized family relationships) is the same, and the suggested treatment is also the same.

Types of mental disease

Specialists, as well as laymen and general physicians, are often confused by the technical names of the specific mental diseases.[14]

[14] H. Cason, "Characteristics of the Psychopath," *Am. Jour. Psychiatry,* Vol. 105 (1948): 211-19. A. Gordon, "Transition of Obsessions into Delusions," *Am. Jour. Psychiatry,* Vol. 107 (1950): 456-457. B. Karpman, "The Myth of the Psychopathic Personality," *Am. Jour. Psychiatry,* Vol. 104 (1948): 521-534. A. W. Stearns, "History of the Development of the Concept of Functional Nervous Disease During the Past Twenty-Five Hundred Years," *Am. Jour. Psychiatry,* Vol. 103 (1946): 289-308. "Revised Psychiatric Nomenclature Adopted by the Army," *Mental Hyg.,* Vol. 30 (1946): 456-476. P. Wittman and W. Sheldon, "Proposed Classification of Psychotic Behavior Reactions," *Am. Jour. Psychiatry,* Vol. 105 (1948): 127-128. The following list of mental disorders has been prepared by the American Psychiatric Association. It is useful for two purposes, one of which is the statistical classification of mental disease as organic or functional. The other contribution of this classification is equally significant, namely, in suggesting causation. This outline is an adaptation of the more than eighty subtypes enumerated under the main captions.

1. Psychoses with syphilitic meningo-encephalitis (general paresis)
2. Psychoses with other forms of syphilis
3. Psychoses with epidemic encephalitis
4. Psychoses with other infectious diseases (tuberculosis, meningitis, chorea)
5. Psychoses due to alcohol
6. Psychoses due to a drug or other poison
7. Psychoses due to trauma (shocks)
8. Psychoses with cerebral arteriosclerosis
9. Psychoses with other circulatory disturbances
10. Psychoses due to epilepsy
11. Senile psychoses
12. Involutional psychoses
13. Psychoses due to other metabolic diseases (glandular disorders, pellagra, exhaustion)
14. Psychoses due to new growth
15. Psychoses due to unknown agencies but associated with organic changes (paralysis agitans, Huntington's chorea)
16. Manic-depressive psychoses
17. Dementia praecox (schizophrenia)
18. Paranoia
19. Psychoses with psychopathic personality
20. Psychoses with mental deficiency
21. Psychoneuroses
22. Undiagnosed psychoses
23. Without mental disorder (epilepsy, alcoholism, drug addiction, pathological emotionality or sexuality)
24. Primary behavior disorders (habit, conduct, or neurotic disturbances)

For this reason there is a considerable tendency to avoid specific labels in preference for a statement of the behavior traits of each patient. Nevertheless, for statistical purposes in classifying first admissions, course of the disease, and recovery, the older terms are retained.[15]

This change emphasizes the desirability of identifying clinical types of general and specific obsessions or repressions. To illustrate this trend, Cameron's book is called *Behavior Disorders* rather than *Mental Diseases.* He simplifies the longer list from which the psychoses (enumerated in footnote 15) are selected by reducing them to eight generic types: (1) hypochondriacal disorders, (2) fatigue syndromes, (3) anxiety disorders, (4) compulsive disorders, (5) hysterical inactivation, (6) paranoid disorders, (7) schizophrenic disorders, and (8) manic and depressive disorders.[16]

Case A illustrates practically all these categories, showing that the symptoms are more important than the single, identifying label.

A, a man 40 years old, married and with two children, developed homicidal tendencies. For several weeks, before he sought medical advice, he had an obsession that he should kill his wife. In order to prevent this act, he would leave home, or lock himself in his room. During this time he was unable to sleep or eat normally. Finally he became so exhausted and depressed that he was unable to go to work. Because of his anxiety and fear that he might succeed in his homicidal desires, he went to a doctor, admitting that he was probably insane because he had sinned. He continued in this condition for several months and then committed suicide. The diagnosis at this time was melancholia and obsessive neurosis.

Conditions in the life history of a person, such as A, that lead to disorders of conduct are classified by Mittleman[17] as five types of

[15] The frequency of the major psychoses in recent years appears in about the following order. Recent changes can be checked by reference to the *Statistical Abstract.*

1. Dementia praecox
2. With cerebral arteriosclerosis
3. Manic-depressive
4. Senile
5. General paresis
6. Alcoholic
7. Involution
8. Psychoneuroses
9. Undiagnosed
10. With mental deficiency
11. Paranoia
12. With convulsive disorders
13. With other somatic diseases
14. With cerebral syphilis
15. With brain tumor

[16] N. Cameron, *op. cit.,* p. 11.

[17] B. Mittleman and others, "Personality and Psychosomatic Disturbances in Patients in Medical and Surgical Wards," *Psychosomatic Med.,* Vol. 7 (1945):

personality disturbances. These conditions may also be considered as causes of the mental illnesses: (1) Pre-existing personality disturbances aggravated by infection or trauma, (2) personality disturbances precipitated by infection or trauma, (3) personality disturbances in patients with serious defects in structure or function, (4) personality disturbances in patients with gross structural defects, and (5) trauma resulting from personality disturbances.

Specific examples of social causes in the mental diseases are given in a study of "reactive depressions."[18] These causes are:

1. Concern about illness or disability
2. Poor family or marital relationships
3. Financial worries
4. Sexual maladjustment
5. Poor work or school adjustment
6. Death of relative or friend
7. Illness of relative or friend
8. Painful symptoms
9. Social maladjustment
10. Unrequited love
11. Guilt about venereal disease
12. Fear of pregnancy
13. Children leaving home
14. Homosexuality

Other causes, symptoms and trends will be observed in a brief analysis of a few of these depressions and recessions.

Schizophrenia (split personality), known also as dementia praecox (early loss of mind), is a severe, widespread and mysterious disorder.[19] It is responsible for most admissions to mental hospitals, possibly as many as one third. There are numerous varieties and subtypes. It is hard to diagnose and treat, and since it tends to be deteriorating, recovery is not particularly hopeful.

There is no accepted interpretation of its causes. In addition to certain illnesses, strains, fatigue states, and pregnancy, such social conditions as worry about sex and sexual behavior, financial difficulties, and marital conflicts are often associated with its onset. It

---

220-223. See also, N. S. Kline and A. M. Ashton, "Constitutional Factors in the Prognosis of Schizophrenia," *Am. Jour. Psychiatry,* Vol. 107 (1950): 435.

[18] H. S. Ripley, "Depressive Reactions in a General Hospital," *Jour. Nerv. and Ment. Dis.,* Vol. 105 (1947): 607-615.

[19] G. W. Albee, "Delusions in Schizophrenia as a Function of Chronological Age," *Jour. Consult. Psych.,* Vol. 14 (1950): 340-342. B. Betz, "Strategic Conditions in the Psychotherapy of Persons with Schizophrenia," *Am. Jour. Psychiatry,* Vol. 107 (1950): 203-215. M. Garrison, "The Genetics of Schizophrenia," *Jour. Abn. and Soc. Psych.,* Vol. 42 (1947): 122-124. F. J. Kallman, "The Genetic Theory of Schizophrenia," *Am. Jour. Psychiatry,* Vol. 103 (1946): 309-321. A. Myerson, "Family Mental Disease in Private Practice," *Am. Jour. Psychiatry,* Vol. 103 (1946): 323-337. W. H. Haines and R. A. Esser, "Case History of Ruth Steinhagen," *Am. Jour. Psychiatry,* Vol. 106 (1950): 736-743.

also has an unusually high incidence in certain families, which gives some support for a constitutional factor or explanation.

In a study by Garrison of 1,087 cases, schizophrenia was found in 10 per cent of the parents and in a third of the immediate ancestors. When one parent had the disorder, 16.4 per cent of the children developed it. When both parents had the illness, 68.1 per cent of the children developed it. Schizophrenia was found five times more frequently among grandchildren of schizophrenics than in the general population. It was also found more often in the spouse of a schizophrenic, at least twice the normal expectancy. Garrison also reported a birth rate among schizophrenics that is considerably lower than the average birth rate, which is good evidence that this illness, by causing susceptible families to die out, tends to be self-limiting to some extent.

Case B is an example of schizophrenia. The diagnosis is acute catatonic excitement. B, a male, first complained of insomnia when he was in his late twenties. Since the condition continued for about two weeks, he was admitted to a hospital for observation. During the first week in the hospital he became tense, irritable, and disoriented. His disorder grew worse; he became dirty, engaged in silly talk and behavior, and threatened suicide. About three weeks after admission he became violent and the struggle that followed led to a series of events including cardiac arrest, cyanosis (suffocation), and death from asphyxiation. A final diagnosis included traits of involution and manic-depressive psychoses.

In Case C, an example of the menopausal women to be discussed briefly later on, it is easy to see the similarities in the basic psychoses. C had a history of being tense, excitable, and depressed at various times during her late thirties. After an operation in her fortieth year, her depressed moods came more often. She had crying spells that alternated with periods of hyperactivity. She lost interest in almost everything except her own symptoms. After admission to the mental hospital, these periods of depression and restlessness continued. She would improve only temporarily. All through her stay in the hospital, she was fully aware of time, place, and the nature of her own condition. She had no hallucinations or delusions. But no treatment was effective. Here is a record that resembles the schizophrenia, recessions, and depressions of the two foregoing cases, with some of the indications of manic-depressive psychosis. Upon C's death, diagnosed as caused by hypertension and cardiac insufficiency, her mental condition was described as involutional psychosis.

Alcoholic psychoses.[20] One of the main reasons why the mental disorders are viewed as great, unsolved public health problems is to be found in the alcoholic psychoses. Heavy and moderate drinkers, numbered in the millions, furnish a steady supply for hospital, clinic, and Alcoholics Anonymous; alcoholics are estimated to be about three-fourths of a million.

Causes usually cited are social drinking, bodily changes, strains, grief, or a variety of pathological predispositions. Although alcoholic psychoses tend to cluster in certain families, the experts argue from this fact that it represents a psychological rather than a constitutional liability. Most alcoholics have a history of distorted family relationships—of being pampered to the extreme or seriously neglected—and of inferior, insecure, and inadequate personalities.

The alcoholic type is generally either single, separated, or divorced. If he is married, there are few or no children. The peak incidence of alcoholism is in the early forties. As a rule, he is of better than average intelligence, but he is handicapped by emotional instability, immaturity, and frustrations. Associated conditions are anxieties, oversensitiveness, psychosexual guilt reactions, and an evasion of responsibilities. Associated social problems are extensive family damage, reduced income, frequent arrests for drunkenness, juvenile delinquency and other problems of children, costly errors of judgment, many difficulties in getting along with other people, and industrial inefficiency and absenteeism. Male drinkers are more consistent in their drinking habits than female alcoholics, but the latter have less control and show greater emotional immaturity.

[20] C. T. Prout and others, "A Study of Results in Hospital Treatment of Alcoholism in Males," *Am. Jour. Psychiatry,* Vol. 107 (1950): 14-19. L. E. Wexberg, "Psychodynamics of Patients with Chronic Alcoholism," *Jour. Clin. Psychopath.,* Vol. 10 (1949): 147-157. R. V. Seliger, "Present-day Status of Medical Psychological Aspects of Alcoholism," *Mental Hyg.,* Vol. 33 (1949): 570-576. S. Paster, "Alcoholism—An Emergent Problem among Veterans," *Mental Hyg.,* Vol. 32 (1948): 58-71. L. C. Duryea and J. Hirsch, "Problem Drinking: A Challenge to Psychiatry," *Mental Hyg.,* Vol. 32 (1948): 246-52. J. J. Smith, "A Medical Approach to Problem Drinking," *Quart. Jour. Studies in Alcohol,* Vol. 10 (1949): 251-255. M. P. Manson, "A Psychosomatic Determination of Alcoholic Addiction," *Am. Jour. Psychiatry,* Vol. 106 (1949): 199-205. L. R. Sillman, "Chronic Alcoholism," *Jour. Nerv. and Ment. Dis.,* Vol. 107 (1948): 127-149. E. E. Mueller, "Personality and Social Implications in the Life of the Alcoholic Veteran," *Quart. Jour. Studies in Alcohol,* Vol. 10 (1949): 258-267. H. W. Haggard and E. M. Jellinck, *Alcohol Explored,* Doubleday, New York, 1946, pp. 35 ff. "The Society of Alcoholics Anonymous," *Am. Jour. Psychiatry,* Vol. 106 (1949): 370-375.

In Mueller's study of the personal history of alcoholic veterans, he discovered the following social conditions during their childhood:

Repeated grade in school
Emotional
Abnormal attachment to mother
Broken home
Abnormal fears
Abnormal sensitiveness
Obsessional traits
Failure to engage in sports
Fainting spells
Sulky under discipline
Thumb-sucking
Difficulty with teachers
Truancy
Juvenile delinquency
Shunned girls after puberty

Observe how D complies with these predictive factors. In his early childhood, D's parents separated. He remained with his father and was noted for being shy and withdrawn and for a record of truancy. He began his career of drinking early and formed the associations wherein drinking is accepted. He never held a job long. After marrying, he contracted gonorrhea while his wife was away, and this marriage ended in divorce. His second wife liked to drink as much as he did and both became chronic alcoholics. During a brief stay in a mental hospital, his chief complaint was that he had no friends, group contacts, hobbies, or interests. Psychiatric examination revealed a deep sense of inferiority, complicated by self-pity. He continuously dramatized himself and showed a progressive deterioration in insight and judgment. Because he never stopped drinking, D was hospitalized many times, his longest period of abstinence being for six months after joining Alcoholics Anonymous. The final diagnosis was the obvious alcoholic psychosis with paranoid trends.

Alcoholics are sick people. Their social problem is one of prevention rather than cure. Since studies reveal that twenty to thirty per cent of the children who are brought up in the homes of alcoholics turn out to be alcoholics themselves, this correlation is considered sufficient evidence that prevention must begin with the education of parents and especially with their responsibility to avoid conditions pointed out by Mueller.

Epilepsy. Little is known about epilepsy. Because of its obscurity it is often compared with diabetes, except that it is not usually considered a disease. It is classified among mental disorders because of its frequent occurrence with various psychoses and with feeblemindedness. Nothing is known about its causes or treatment. Hence recovery is not emphasized in its care. Instead, the patient is taught to adjust to his type of seizure. These seizures are called grand mal, psychomotor, petit mal, and focal. They refer to the behavior of the patient during his seizure and to degrees of its severity. There is a technical description of these types in Lennox.[21]

The adjustability of the epileptic is determined by a number of physical, social, and personal conditions. So far as the seizures are concerned, their type, frequency, severity, time of occurrence, and age of the patient at onset are important in affecting his personality and his emotional stability. According to the nature of these variables, the epileptic develops fairly acceptable control or by diminishing degrees little or no control. When seizures occur in the daytime and are especially violent or repulsive, the epileptic is subject to considerable discrimination socially and occupationally, and he may begin to feel like an outcast.

The sociability of the epileptic is a result in large measure of adjusted family relationships and understanding parents. Overprotection leads to the same types of withdrawn, dependent, and submissive characteristics that more normal children are apt to acquire under similar misguidance.

Epilepsy interferes drastically with the individual's friendships, schooling, and employment. If attacks occur in the daytime or irregularly, he is restricted to special schools and sheltered workshops. There are also numerous impediments to marriage and to adjustment in marriage, regardless of hereditary questions that are as yet not well understood.

The mental handicap of epilepsy is greatest when attacks begin before the age of nineteen, when they are frequent and of the psychomotor type. These three characteristics make the type of epilepsy that is most difficult to treat.

Adjustment at work is better for patients whose medical handicap is marked and who are able to accept their handicap and remain relatively independent. Other factors that favor good work adjust-

[21] M. A. Lennox and J. Mohr, "Social and Work Adjustment in Patients with Epilepsy," *Am. Jour. Psychiatry,* Vol. 107 (1950): 257-263. S. Levin, "Psychomotor Epilepsy," *Am. Jour. Psychiatry,* Vol. 107 (1951): 501. E. M. Davidson and J. C. Thomas, "A Social Study of Epileptic Patients," *Jour. Soc. Casework,* Vol. 30 (1949): 380-384. G. C. Randall and W. C. Rogers, "Group Therapy for Epileptics," *Am. Jour. Psychiatry,* Vol. 107 (1950): 424 (on this page there is a statement of the mental, social and personal traits of 100 epileptics). J. Pinanski, "Vocational Problem of the Epileptic Child," *Nerv. Child,* Vol. 6 (1947): 105-144.

ment are: (1) the patient responds well to treatment, (2) he makes a good social adjustment, (3) he tells his friends and employers of his disorder, (4) attacks are one month or less in frequency, (5) his intelligence is average or slightly below, which puts him in a less taxing occupation (note in this connection a higher requirement in intelligence for effective social adjustment), and (6) he is able to drive a car and to do some hazardous work.

Conditions associated with good social adjustment of the epileptic are: (1) average or slightly better than average intelligence, (2) schooling beyond the eighth grade, (3) attacks occur at night, (4) medical handicap is slight, and (5) he has a good occupational adjustment.

Senile psychoses. Senile dementia may result from organic disturbances associated with advancing age or from functional disturbances unconnected with arteriosclerosis. The latter only are included among the functional psychoses. In general, the factors of old age and dementia are the chief identifying traits, since the different aspects of senile psychosis represent a cross-section of practically every mental disease and its symptoms. The types of senile dementia indicate its inclusive nature: (1) senile deterioration, which is simply the loss of memory or mental capacity, (2) senile melancholia, which involves a depression such as that of manic-depressive psychoses and also deterioration, (3) senile dementia, which occurs with delusions, hallucinations, and conduct disorders, (4) senile paranoia, characterized largely by delusions of persecution.

Age is the chief cause of this psychosis, and it rarely occurs in a person prior to the sixtieth year. When fully developed it manifests almost every diagnostic symptom—impairment of attention, inaccurate perception, loss of memory, illusions and hallucinations, loss of judgment, morbid irritability, and ideas of persecution, melancholy, and grandeur. Death usually occurs within five years after onset. Not all psychoses of the aged, however, are senile. Manic-depressive, paranoia, and others may appear in the advanced age groups.[22]

This class of disorders is attracting increasing attention because of its disproportionate increases in recent years. At present they

[22] N. A. Johnson, "The Growing Problem of Old-Age Psychoses," *Mental Hyg.*, Vol. 30 (1946): 431-450. B. Malzberg, "Mental Diseases Among the Aged in New York State," *Mental Hyg.*, Vol. 33 (1949): 599-614. R. V. Seliger, "Alcoholism in the Older Age Groups," *Geriatrics*, Vol. 3 (1948): 166-170.

make up nearly one fourth of all first admissions to hospitals. If this trend continues, it is likely that they will eventually supplant schizophrenia as the ranking mental illness. Old age psychoses also add enormously to the costs of hospital care. A year of hospitalization of an aged psychotic is the equivalent in care of two years for all other mental disorders, except the acutely disturbed. Reasons assigned for this increase are the chronic diseases, changes in the family making it impossible to provide the necessary home care, separation of children from parents under the present-day working and housing conditions of urban life, and a shift of family responsibility to the state under the current Social Security program.

Other noticeable recent changes are the increasing urban rate of old-age psychoses, the lowest rate of all being that of the farm population; increasing rates for all age groups over sixty, the lowest being for the married; and high rates among the least educated, the lower-income classes, Negroes, and foreign whites.

Psychoses due to drugs. The story of drug addiction reveals several classes of addicts and a variety of predisposing circumstances. There are six types of addicts: (1) normal individuals who are addicted accidentally through medication, (2) people with an unstable personality who seek excitement of a new experience, (3) psychoneurotics, (4) psychopathic personalities, habitual criminals, and sexual perverts, (5) alcoholics who may resort to drugs after a spree, and (6) psychotics who become addicted as the result of a serious mental disorder. In most of these types addiction is to opium, Indian hemp, or cocaine or one of its derivatives. Morphine, which is derived from opium, is the most widely used drug.[23]

As persons, drug addicts represent a cross-section of nearly every form of social demoralization. Their family background has an exceptional record of psychoses, neuroses, epilepsy, alcoholism, asthma, and migraine. Family life is disorganized. And the addicts themselves have a sorry record of chronic and infectious diseases (especially the venereal), poor nutrition, poor dentition, anemia, and injuries.

The average addict begins to use drugs in his twenties, and has an

[23] M. Levin, "Frequency of Drug Psychoses," *Am. Jour. Psychiatry,* Vol. 107 (1950): 128-130. M. Malzberg, "A Statistical Study of Psychoses Due to Drugs," *Am. Jour. Psychiatry,* Vol. 106 (1949): 99. M. J. Pescor, *A Statistical Analysis of the Clinical Records of Hospitalized Drug Addicts,* United States Government Printing Office, Washington, 1943. There is a Narcotics Anonymous, similar to that for alcoholics; it was organized, and has its office, in New York City.

average period of addiction of 12.5 years. Reasons originally assigned for the addiction in clinic reports are psychopathic personality, the desire to escape from everyday worries, accidental acquisition of the habit during medical treatment, and relief from pain. Relapse after treatment is more frequent than continued abstinence, the average duration of abstinence being 1.8 years.

Studies of drug addicts rarely find them to be the vicious characters that are so often popularized in literary fiction. As a rule they do not engage in crimes of violence. But they fail miserably in social adjustments. They are poor marriage risks. Their employment record is bad. And their leisure-time activities are demoralizing.

Levin believes that the total number of drug addicts in the population and in hospitals is larger than the statistics indicate. He came to this conclusion on the assumptions that either the condition is not recognized or it is confused with some other pathology.

The neuroses and the psychoneuroses. Like the foregoing functional diseases, neuroses and psychoneuroses represent a vast number of symptoms or kinds of unusual conduct. There is further similarity in that both groups have a neural (physiological) and psychic (functional) basis. Nor is there any clearcut separation between the psychoneuroses and the psychoses.[24] They are connected by a series of symptoms from the mildest daydream to the violence of a maniacal attack. In the number of cases afflicted by these common disorders, they exceed by far all other mental disturbances.

Ordinarily the psychoneuroses are divided into five subgroups: (1) psychasthenia, (2) neurasthenia, (3) hysteria, (4) anxiety neuroses, and (5) the psychopathic personality. None of these subgroups can be precisely distinguished from the others except through the generalization that each represents a group of maladjustments.

Psychasthenia means that maladjustment which is typified most frequently by mental debility or weakness. The person is dominated by indecision, fears, obsessions, morbid compulsions, feelings of inadequacy, and exaggerated doubts and fears. This condition occurs rarely before adolescence, and seems to indicate a general inability to face the ordinary responsibilities of life.

The most common of the psychoneuroses is neurasthenia. It means nervous exhaustion. It may be a result of physical fatigue or of the imagination. The neurasthenic is one who is generally slow

[24] For further discussion, consult: B. Karpman, footnote 14, page 82.

in his responses or who actually does lack physical vigor. Furthermore, he may show extreme introversion, self-pity, feelings of inferiority, and the tendency to withdraw from ordinary personal and social situations.

Hysteria is one of the oldest mental disorders in the history of medicine. It is also the least responsive to treatment, primarily because of its many forms and causes. Hysteria may simulate almost any symptom that the human body may have. It is briefly defined to include those cases of persons who have imaginary diseases in order to compensate for mental conflicts.

The causes of hysteria are intangible as well as numerous. A cause may be any interference to the development of adequate personality. There is no evidence that hereditary or organic conditions are of paramount importance. Recently, emphasis has been given to social and educational status as one of the most helpful explanations. This explanation is based upon the observation that most cases of hysteria come from the extremely favored or disadvantaged social and economic classes, wherein there is less discipline, less adequate parent-child relationship, less emotional stability, and greater opportunity for failure.

The principal manifestations of hysteria are: somnambulism; fugues (sleep-walking involving flight from some problem); multiple personalities; convulsive attacks; motor disorders, such as tics, convulsive movements, tremors, and paralyses; anaesthesis (loss of memory or sensitivity); visual and auditory disorders (hysterical blindness); and a number of other physiological disorders.

Anxiety neuroses are traced in general to feelings of insecurity or the imagined hostility of one's associates. They are the mildest of all the neuroses and are personified by the constant worrier.

Psychopathic personality is a miscellaneous category in which are grouped those persons who are unable to make satisfactory social adjustments. It includes individuals whose philosophy of life is inadequate, who lack what is called good social judgment, and also mild forms of the "crank type." There is no discoverable symptom of mental disease, and for this reason primarily it is used only when other descriptive terms are considered inappropriate.

Recovery. When a disease is revealed as organic in character, recovery depends upon whether medical or surgical therapy is able to treat or eliminate the physical cause. If any considerable destruction of tissue has occurred in the central nervous system, the mental disease is incurable. When the disease is functional, the outcome cannot be predicted accurately. With functional diseases, prognosis is less favorable. Ordinarily there are two consequences. In one group of functional diseases the lapse from mental normality apparently runs its course to recovery. But often recovery is uncertain, on account of periodic relapses or the cyclical character of the disease, as in manic-depressive psychoses. In the second type of functional diseases, the disease runs its course with progressive deterioration.

Cerebral syphilis, as an example or organic mental disease, responds to treatment precisely as does syphilis in general. A hopeful prognosis depends upon early recognition and treatment of the disease, its pathological type, and the age of the patient. When syphilis attacks the vascular system, prognosis is unfavorable, and when it is untreated, the mental disease develops rapidly, usually terminating in death after a period of two to five years. Recoveries are reported in one fourth to one third of the cases. In the other organic mental diseases the proportion of recoveries is generally higher. Many unusual cures by means of surgery have been reported among the focal infections, and a recovery rate of over fifty per cent is given for alcoholic psychoses. For chronic alcoholism the prognosis is poor.

Of the functional psychoses, manic-depressive and involutional mental disorders have the highest proportion of recoveries. Paranoia and senile dementia, except in cases of faulty diagnosis, have few or no recoveries. In the case of dementia praecox (schizophrenia) there has been a reversal of opinion concerning the possibilities of recovery. Until recently this disease was classified with the incurable psychoses. Although it is still recognized as a serious condition, there are some recoveries. Prognosis is most favorable when the disease is traceable to some obvious exogenous factor. Cotton's focal-infection theory of dementia praecox has met with considerable favor and is much used in the course of treatment. Penicillin, insulin shock, electric shock and other experimental treatments have been used extensively since 1930. On the whole, however, the patients suffering from this disease gradually deteriorate mentally and the majority of cures are more readjustments to life in the community than recoveries. In the case of the shut-in, introverted type, dementia praecox is incurable.

Of all persons admitted to mental hospitals, only fifteen to twenty per cent recover fully. The ratio of recoveries is slightly higher for females than males because of the larger number of cases of paresis among the latter. Moreover, it is estimated that mental disease with its associated physical disorders shortens life expectancy by nearly fifty per cent.[25]

Personal and social correlations

In introducing a synopsis of the conditions that have been found to be highly associated with mental disease or with abnormal personality traits, it is necessary to preface a warning. Such studies are apt to be misleading, because they are usually made of selected groups. Either they do not permit comparison with outside or control groups (normal groups), or their standards of measurement of abnormality or the choice of other social unadjustments to be used in comparison may be arbitrary. The following conclusions are cited, therefore, not as proof of absolute correlations between mentality and other conditions, but solely as a survey of the studies in this field.

Population factors. In addition to the sex and age relationships already noted, and an occasional reference to geographical distribution, there are also important nativity and urban-rural variations.[26]

[25] In reports of *Patients in Mental Institutions,* United States Bureau of the Census, published annually, the rank order of recovery for specific psychoses is approximately as follows:

Most Recoverable	*Least Recoverable*
Due to drugs and other poisons	Senile
With psychopathic personality	Due to new growth
Alcoholic	With cerebral arteriosclerosis
With other infectious diseases	General paresis
Manic-depressive	With organic changes of nervous system
Due to other metabolic diseases	With convulsive disorders
Psychoneuroses	With other disturbances of circulation
Traumatic	Paranoia
Involution	

W. E. Barton and others, "Need for Uniform Discharge Statistics in Public Psychiatric Hospitals," *Am. Jour. Psychiatry,* Vol. 106 (1949): 438. E. Frankel, "Outcome of Mental Hospital Treatment in New Jersey," *Mental Hyg.,* Vol. 32 (1948): 459-464. Both of these state reports confirm the national figures. Frankel states that the chance of release is best in the first year and worsens progressively with every succeeding year of hospitalization. Both sources report low rates of recovery in schizophrenia. See also: C. K. Aldrich, "Problems of Social Adjustment Following Lobotomy," *Am. Jour. Psychiatry,* Vol. 107 (1950): 459-461.

[26] B. Malzberg, *Social and Biological Aspects of Mental Disease,* State Hospitals Press, Utica, New York, 1940, Chapters 3, 6-9, and 15.

Hospital records indicate a higher proportion of mental disease among the foreign born than among the general population. However, little biological significance is attached to this frequency. It was primarily a result of an unselective immigration policy and the economic and social handicaps of immigrants in American cities. Nevertheless, cities continue to furnish the majority of hospital cases.

Moreover, specific mental diseases tend to occur more frequently in some nativity groups. In the New York hospitals, Italy, Ireland, and Germany, in the order named, furnish the greatest proportion of the foreign born among first admissions. Different ethnic groups are also more susceptible to certain psychoses, dementia praecox occurring more frequently among Slavs, Negroes, and Jews; manic-depressive psychoses among Germans and Jews; alcoholic psychoses among Negroes and Irish; and general paresis among Negroes, Italians, and Slavs.

When the distribution of all mental defects among nativity groups is compared with the distribution of specific diseases, it is found that those groups with a high rate of feeblemindedness have low rates of mental disease. Relatively high rates of feeblemindedness among Negroes, American Indians, and Mexican immigrants are accompanied by lower rates of mental diseases than for the general population in this country. On the other hand, the French, Germans, Greeks, Italians, Jews, Scandinavians, and Scotch in this country have a slightly higher rate of mental disease than the average for the United States.

When the rates of urban and rural areas are compared, the rural are found to have the lower incidence. Furthermore, there is a marked relation between increasing rates of mental disease and size of city. There is no generally accepted reason for this correlation except the explanation of complexity—the strain and struggle of a complex urban existence are too demanding.

In the working classes. As a cause of unemployment, lost time, unemployability, and labor turnover, mental handicaps are cited more often than physical illness or defects. In one comparative study of work records, those men who were classed as mentally or emotionally unstable were found to have poor industrial records in fifty per cent of the cases, whereas no case classified as mentally normal had a poor work record. Thus, mental disorders are associated with reduced earning capacity and low standard of living, the employment of wives, the need for poor relief, and various subjective characterizations of inadequate personality, such as laziness, shiftlessness, and inefficiency. Since most of these studies were concerned with other than hospital cases, the less disabling neuroses were more numerous than psychoses as factors in occupational unadjustment. Economic instability presents another problem in the trend of the mental diseases. Dependency, unemployment, or business depressions are considered significant causes of increased first admissions.[27]

Schizophrenia, according to Rabin, is the outstanding psychosis in producing these occupational handicaps. Nearly one half of all schizophrenics are in the semiskilled and unskilled occupations. Manic-depressive psychoses are high in clerical and service occupations. The psychoneuroses are high in the professional and managerial groups. All three of these disorders have about the same incidence in rural occupations. In skilled work the percentage of psychoneurotics and manics is nearly twice that of schizophrenics.

Among criminals and delinquents. One difference between nineteenth and twentieth century criminologists is a decided change in the opinion of the latter as to the role of mental disorders in criminality and juvenile delinquency. Originally, mental abnormality and criminality were recognized as practically synonymous. In a review of recent literature, Reckless has concluded that the claim for a close relationship between psychopathic personality and crime is "still not certainly discounted or validated." Wilson and Pescor are more positive in affirming that neurotics commit the same kinds of crime as nonneurotics, with the exception of pyromania, kleptomania, and such types of trespass as that of "peeping Toms."[28] Both

[27] N. A. Dayton, *op. cit.,* p. 368. T. A. C. Rennie, "Vocational Rehabilitation of the Psychiatrically Disabled," *Mental Hyg.,* Vol. 33 (1949): 200-208. L. W. Rockower, "Development of a Vocational-Rehabilitation Program for the Neuropsychiatric," *Mental Hyg.,* Vol. 33 (1949): 386-400 (The New York State Plan). A. I. Rabin, "Trends of Vocational Achievement in Mental Disorder," *Sci. Monthly,* Vol. 65 (1947): 213-16.

[28] W. C. Reckless, *Etiology of Delinquent and Criminal Behavior,* Social Science Research Council, New York, 1943, p. 9. J. G. Wilson and M. J. Pescor, *Problems in Prison Psychiatry,* Caxton Printers, Caldwell, Idaho, 1939, pp. 130-136. S. B. Maughs, "Psychopathic Personality: A Review of the Literature, 1940-47," *Jour. Clin. Psychopath.,* Vol. 10 (1949): 247-271. A. J. Arieff and C. G. Bowie, "Some Psychiatric Aspects of Shoplifting," *Jour. Clin. Psychopath.,* Vol. 8 (1947): 565. D. Silverman, "The Psychotic Criminal," *Jour. Clin. Psychopath.,* Vol. 8 (1946): 302-327. L. H. Cohen and T. E. Coffin, "The Pattern of Murder in Insanity," *Jour. Crim. Law and Criminol.,* Vol. 37 (1946-1947): 262-287. A. J. Arieff and D. B. Rotman, "Psychopathic Personality," *Jour. Crim. Law and Criminol.,* Vol. 39 (1948): 158-166.

in clinic and prison reports, the range of incidence of all mental disorders varies from fifteen per cent to thirty-five per cent, but the incidence of psychoses is low. Moreover, all these cases are complicated by other predisposing criminal factors, such as poor work records, marital discord, alcoholism, and poor sex adjustments.

Another point of view, suggested by Maughs, lays greater stress on social than emotional factors. He reports no specific complex of mental conditions that would lead inevitably to crime. In comparisons between psychotic and mentally normal prisoners, Silverman found that poverty, broken homes, and parental abnormality were the chief handicaps in the background of the psychotic, whose mental diagnoses were schizophrenia with paranoid and depressive symptoms. Psychotic prisoners also had a childhood history of abnormal behavior traits and poor school records.

A most immediate association between behavior disorders and criminality is noted in murder and shoplifting. In both crimes the pattern of conduct is irrational and there is no sensible motive.

In murder cases, the victim is usually a close relation who is killed because the murderer wants to protect him from grief or pain. There is no plan, and no effort is made to escape the consequences of the crime. In cases of shoplifting, as observed by Arieff, seventy-seven per cent of the individuals apprehended, most of whom were women, had marked emotional or mental disorders, largely of the acute anxiety state.

Delinquents [29] likewise are described more as morbid or thwarted individuals than as psychotic. In their studies the Gluecks report an incidence of slightly more than fourteen per cent of "mental disease and distortion." However, delinquents as a group do differ from nondelinquents in intelligence, neurotic tendencies, emotional stability, feelings of inadequacy, nervous manifestations, withdrawing tendencies, and emotional adjustment. And the aggressive delinquent is further distinguished by such traits as irritability, temper, selfishness, defiance, early rejection by parents, low home and community standards, and a prominent sex drive.

Among families. Partly because of social causes other than the

[29] A. J. Rosanoff (Ed.), *The Etiology of Child Behavior Disorders, Juvenile Delinquency and Adult Criminality,* Department of Institutions, Sacramento, Calif., 1941. S. and E. Glueck, *Unraveling Juvenile Delinquency,* The Commonwealth Fund, New York, 1950, pp. 272-275. F. C. Zakolski, "Studies in Juvenile Delinquency," *Jour. Gen. Psych.,* Vol. 74-75 (1949): 109.

marital or domestic, various mental disorders tend to run in families. This statement has already been made for alcoholism and schizophrenia. It also holds for the anxiety and depressive states. The incidence of these illnesses is not only disproportionately high in some families, but they are also responsible for numerous other kinds of family problems. This condition is the cause in some instances of family extinction.[30]

Variations in family status, as causes or results of mental disorders, are indicated by a study of 138 university students who were diagnosed as psychoneurotic and compared with the university population as a control group. The family backgrounds of these students were found to have an unusually large number of mental and social handicaps, which were considered to be of valid diagnostic merit since the university group as a whole had no such record. The distinguishing characteristics in these students' families were: (1) mental illness of one or both parents, (2) separation of parents or lack of harmonious relations between them, (3) mental illness in siblings or disturbed relations between siblings, and (4) parental interferences with the student's plan for marriage. No relationship could be found between the student's mental condition and such domestic conditions as being an only child, age and number of siblings, sibling favoritism, foreign birth of parents, death or prolonged illness in the home, or having relatives or others in the home.

Unadjusting personality traits are also significant barriers to marriage, as already observed in the fact that mental disease is more frequent in the single than in the married. The more common personal characteristics in this domestic situation are psychopathic background, unhappy relations with parents, a poor school record, neurosis in childhood, and a history of invalidism, alcoholism, or venereal disease.

Family problems immediately associated with the occurrence of mental disease in one or more members are numerous and demoralizing. According to Treudley, one family in five in the United States

[30] H. V. Ingham, "A Statistical Study of Family Relationship in Psychoneuroses," *Am. Jour. Psychiatry,* Vol. 106 (1949): 91-98. R. W. and T. Lidz, "The Family Environment of Schizophrenic Patients," *Am. Jour. Psychiatry,* Vol. 106 (1949): 332-345. O. Odegard, "Marriage and Mental Disease," *Jour. Ment. Sci.,* Vol. 92 (1946): 35-59. M. B. Treudley, "Mental Illness and Family Routines," *Mental Hyg.,* Vol. 31 (1947): 237-249. K. A. Zimmerman, "Importance of the Family in the Prevention of Mental Illness," *Milbank Mem. Fund Quart.,* Vol. 27 (1949): 133-141.

is so afflicted. In turn, the socio-economic status of the family is lowered, especially if the father is the patient. The children's school work and recreation are modified by the inevitable stigma of mental illness in the family, with its accompanying sentiments of guilt, shame, and inferiority, the probability of domestic discord, and the additional burden of medical care. If the children are in the adolescent years, their chances of occupational training and job-getting are interfered with appreciably and sometimes completely obstructed. In addition, there are problems of housing and household management (if the mother is the patient) which includes nutritional problems and the various other requirements in child care and training.

Among adolescents.[31] In mental hygiene surveys of the school population, there are few children who are considered to be psychotic. No more than half the group is reported with symptoms of the neuroses, even when these symptoms are more nearly what are ordinarily looked upon as the behavior problems of children. Indications of neurotic symptoms are more often found among boys than girls and among Negroes (the anxiety symptoms) than whites. The most frequently reported disorders are the anxiety manifestations, stuttering, and allergies. The social background of this group is the same as that already described for the adult psychotic, namely, a complex of social, economic, and cultural handicaps.

Among veterans. These adolescent difficulties, both more numerous and intensive, were outstanding among the problems of Selective Service Boards and of discharged veterans. In one group of seven hundred veterans discharged as neuro-psychiatric casualties, eighty-nine per cent were diagnosed as psychotic.[32]

[31] J. Hertzman, "High School Mental Hygiene Survey," *Am. Jour. Orthopsychiatry*, Vol. 18 (1948): 238-256. H. J. Baker, "Mental Hygiene Problems of Adolescent Boys," *Nerv. Child,* Vol. 4 (1944-45): 151-158. M. F. Farnham, "Preventive Mental Hygiene Role of the Family," *Nerv. Child,* Vol. 3 (1943-44): 111-118. This writer traces a large number of the mental upsets of soldiers, and hence of children in general, to the dominant and domineering role of the mother in the home—the overprotective parent is cited as a cause of the increasing maladjustment and conflict of youth.

[32] T. W. McDaniel and M. A. Diamond, "A Study of 700 Discharged Neuro-Psychiatric Casualties and Follow-Up," *Dis. Nerv. Sys.,* Vol. 9 (1948): 148-153. J. J. Geller, "A Statistical Analysis of 480 Army Psychiatric Casualties," *Jour. Nerv. and Ment. Dis.,* Vol. 109 (1949): 509-518. J. M. Caldwell, "The Problem Soldier and the Army," *Am. Jour. Psychiatry,* Vol. 105 (1948): 46-51. This report gives the psychiatric diagnosis of 35,048 soldiers who were confined for conduct disorders.

Abnormalities in their background were overwhelmingly against them. These abnormalities included a high proportion of childhood disabilities; poor school records; an occupational history of no skill, trade, or desire to learn; a record of unsatisfactory social adjustment prior to enlistment; an unusual incidence of acute and major illnesses; and a background of delinquency, including such abnormal sex adjustments as homosexuality.

After their discharge, their behavior continued in the same pattern. It was marked by generally unsatisfactory social adjustment, as indicated by arrests, nomadism, alcoholism, imprisonment, and "nervous abnormality." For more than fifty per cent of these veterans, their prospect of satisfactory civilian rehabilitation was considered to be poor.

The story of discharged women veterans is a close parallel.[33] Nearly ninety per cent of the women discharged for neuro-psychiatric difficulties were diagnosed as clinically abnormal with anxiety and depressive states. Their family backgrounds were also identical, with a history of neuroses in childhood and of a high proportion of neurotic or psychotic parents and siblings.

As explanations for the neuroses among these women, the chief predisposing environmental factors were marital problems, regimentation in the service, separation from their family, and the unsuitability of service employment.

Among menopausal women the major mental disorders are the depressive reactions. These are traced causally to such gross environmental factors as poverty or other economic problems, or to accidental circumstances, such as prolonged illness in the home or the death of a child. Among husband-wife relations, the conditions that are regarded as of causal value, are cruelty, alcoholism, impotence, desertion, unsatisfactory sex relations, and gambling.[34]

Among the sexually promiscuous.[35] Promiscuity is often used as one index of neurosis or of social and emotional immaturity. In a clinical examination of 620 individuals in a venereal ward,

[33] L. Rees, "Neurosis in the Women's Auxiliary Services," *Jour. Ment. Sci.*, Vol. 95 (1949): 880-896.

[34] K. Stern, "Personality Studies of Menopausal Women," *Am. Jour. Psychiatry,* Vol. 103 (1946): 362. Compare with: J. MacKinnon, "The Homosexual Woman," *Am. Jour. Psychiatry,* Vol. 103 (1947): 661-664. This is an autobiographical case.

[35] B. Safier and others, *A Psychiatric Approach to the Treatment of Promiscuity,* American Social Hygiene Association, New York, 1949.

this conclusion was amply supported. Evidence of promiscuity was obtained in the cases of nearly sixty per cent of the women and more than forty per cent of the men. Contrary to the general impression that such individuals are oversexed, few were reported as either "sensual or sensuous."

Their mental disturbances were for the most part those of neurotic conflict accented by anxiety and impulsiveness. They were impulsive and unrealistic in their vocational goals, in quitting jobs, in marrying, and in many other instances of unpredictable behavior. In both sexes just about the same abnormalities were reported. These impairments, in the order of their frequency, were: neuroses of various types, psychopathic personality, homosexuality, mental deficiency, and a few diagnosed psychoses.

Among suicides,[36] domestic difficulties are the major, immediate causes. There are also a number of economic problems and a history of illness. Alcoholism is prominent among male suicides and in about one third of the female suicides. In Wallinga's study, nearly one fourth were found to be psychotic, and case studies revealed the usual trend of prior mental illness and suicide attempts. This writer concluded that attempted suicide is nearly always an indication of emotional disturbance rather than of a desire to die. Many of those who attempted suicide, for example, used wholly harmless materials and seemed to want attention more than death. In Arieff's report, the main cause (citing the would-be suicides' own statements) was alcoholism and next in order were sweetheart trouble, neurotic complaints, and exhibitionism.

Summary

Mental illnesses are recognized both as adverse social conditions and as causes of social problems. As such, they have called public attention increasingly in recent years to the problems of mental hygiene. The task of restoring the mentally ill to mental health are the problems of psychotherapy.

As a social movement, mental hygiene and psychotherapy have two responsibilities, namely, to prevent mental disorders and to conserve mental health. Both the increasing number of persons

36 J. V. Wallinga, "Attempted Suicide: A Ten Year Survey," *Dis. Nerv. Sys.*, Vol. 10 (1949): 15-20. A. J. Arieff and others, "Unsuccessful Suicidal Attempts," *Dis. Nerv. Sys.*, Vol. 9 (1948): 174-179. This article gives the psychiatric classifications and the individuals' own explanations.

seeking hospital care and the costs of this remedial work show the need for prevention. The program of mental hygiene is essentially preventive. Its services, long recognized as accepted resources of social case and group work, are rapidly being adopted by other social, professional, educational, and industrial institutions.

There are two fundamental problems of mental diseases that are as yet unsolved, both of which bear directly upon a treatment program. One is the separation of mental illnesses into the divisions of organic and functional psychoses; the other, supplementary to this, is the problem of transmission, that is, of discovering whether these diseases are inherited, acquired, or both. If they are inherited wholly or in the majority of cases, mental disease is a problem of eugenics, and mental hygiene is complementary to the eugenic movement. If they are acquired through social or psychological experiences or through physiological factors, such as disease, inadequate diet, or toxins, our contemporary culture must accept the major responsibility for these problems and introduce the necessary reforms to protect itself against them.

Important achievements during the twentieth century offer the prospect of better understanding and control of these problems. These achievements,[37] more or less in the chronological order of their development, are the beginning of psychiatric social work in Boston in 1905 and the publication of *A Mind that Found Itself* by Clifford Beers in 1908. Publication of this book stimulated treatment and research and was responsible for the founding of the National Committee for Mental Hygiene in 1909.

Next, in rapid order, under the stimulus of World War I, the child guidance and mental hygiene movements spread throughout the nation. Clinical psychology largely supplanted its philosophical and metaphysical forerunners. Internships were established for clergymen, probation and parole officers, and other professional advisers in schools, colleges, and in trade and industry (the personnel and counseling movements). Rural mental hygiene, the development of shock and other chemical or mechanical therapies, group therapy, the acceptance of psychiatry and psychiatric education in

[37] F. A. Freyhan, "Psychiatric Realities," *Jour. Nerv. and Ment. Dis.*, Vol. 109 (1947): 482-492 (this is a fifty-year review). W. Overholser, "Historical Sketch of Psychiatry," *Jour. Clin. Psychopath.*, Vol. 10 (1949): 129-146. See "Mental Hygiene," in *Social Work Yearbook,* Russell Sage Foundation, New York, published biannually. F. H. Sleeper, "Need for Research in Mental Disease," *Dis. Nerv. Sys.*, Vol. 8 (1947): 100-105.

the medical schools, and the foundation of the American Board of Psychiatry and Neurology were achievements of the 1930's.

Then, under the stimulus of Selective Service and the needs of the various military establishments during World War II, psychiatry became a recognized branch of all war services. Some important results were the establishment of the American Society for Research in Psychosomatic Medicine in 1943 and the People's Committee for Mental Hygiene in 1945; the reorganization of the Veterans' Administration; the National Mental Health Foundation; the National Mental Health Act; and to promote research, the National Mental Health Council and the Psychiatric Foundation.

During these postwar years many states introduced their own mental hygiene programs. These innovations made provisions for the more strategic location of hospitals, which included new building designs; extended the services of the hospitals; furnished training for personnel; made more opportunities for early treatment through the revision of commitment laws; and introduced research, preventive, and educational projects for the community-wide, mental health needs of the public.[38]

In 1946 the National Mental Health Act was passed, and a National Mental Health Council was appointed. This act provides for a National Mental Health Institute, under the United States Public Health Service, to institute a research and training center, and to supply grants-in-aid to public and private agencies for research and training throughout the country. This step is regarded as the most significant development of the century in the attack upon mental disease, since heretofore for every dollar spent on research one hundred dollars were devoted to the care of the mentally ill in institutions, and since it will unify the work of the different states, which had previously operated without any uniform plan.

This concerted national and state program of education, treatment, and research is expected to correct the present chaotic system of private psychiatric practice by introducing standards for certification or licensing.

Until this goal is reached and mental hygiene becomes an ac-

[38] F. F. Tallman, "A State Program of Mental Health," *Mental Hyg.*, Vol. 32 (1948): 271-278. Council of State Governments, *The Mental Health Programs of the Forty-Eight States,* Chicago, 1950.

cepted phase of everyday education, self diagnosis and therapy may be of some value. Good mental health is described by such evidences of emotional and social maturity as:

You do not complain of aches and pains when there is no discoverable cause for such indispositions, or conversely, you are almost always willing to admit a fair quota of social health.
You do not worry about death.
You are neither opinionated nor inclined to want to force your opinions on others.
You are not readily oppressed by vague fears.
You are not the worrying type.
You are not upset, as a rule, by minor interferences with routine.
You enjoy being with people.
You do not regularly complain of sleeplessness or over-fatigue.
You are even-tempered.
You are able to give enough attention to required tasks so as to complete them with a fair degree of efficiency and speed.
You do not make excuses on the grounds of never having had a chance.[39]

Bibliography

Deutsch, Albert, *The Shame of the States,* Harcourt, Brace, New York, 1948. Part I, "What Mental Illness Means."

———, *The Mentally Ill in America,* Columbia University Press, New York, 1949. Chap. 14.

Dicks, H. V., *Clinical Studies in Psychopathology,* Williams and Wilkins, Baltimore, 1947.

Dorcus, R. M., and G. W. Shaffer, *Textbook of Abnormal Psychology,* Williams and Wilkins, Baltimore, 1950. Chap. 10, "Classification and History of Mental Diseases."

Dunbar, Flanders, *Mind and Body: Psychosomatic Medicine,* Random House, New York, 1947.

Fry, C. C., *Mental Health in College,* The Commonwealth Fund, New York, 1942. Chaps. 7 and 9.

Garrison, K. C., *The Psychology of Exceptional Children,* Ronald, New York, 1950. Chap. 19.

Lemkau, P. V., *Mental Hygiene in Public Health,* McGraw-Hill, New York, 1949. Chaps. 1 and 12.

Mann, Marty, *Primer on Alcoholism,* Rinehart and Co., New York, 1951.

May, Rollo, *The Meaning of Anxiety,* Ronald, New York, 1950. Chap. 7, "Case Studies Demonstrating Anxiety."

[39] Similar and more specific guides can be found for particular age groups such as those listed as indicators of sound mental hygiene for adolescents on page 158, for the aged on page 240.

Mikesell, W. H. (Ed.), *Modern Abnormal Psychology,* Philosophical Library, New York, 1950. Chap. 2, "Psychotherapy." Chap. 15, "Manic-Depression of Famous Men." Chap. 25, "Mental Hygiene and the Future."

Overholser, W., and W. V. Richmond, *Handbook of Psychiatry,* J. B. Lippincott, Philadelphia, 1947. Chap. 2.

Shore, M. J., and others, *Twentieth Century Mental Hygiene,* Social Science Publishers, New York, 1950.

Steiner, L. R., *Where Do People Take Their Troubles,* Houghton Mifflin, Boston, 1945.

Wechsler, I. S., *A Textbook of Clinical Neurology,* Saunders, Philadelphia, 1944. Part V, "Neuroses."

Wolf, W., *The Threshold of the Abnormal,* Hermitage House, New York, 1950. Chap. 1, "Aspects of Normality." Chap. 18, "Normal and Abnormal Personality."

Wortis, Joseph, *Soviet Psychiatry,* Williams and Wilkins, Baltimore, 1950. Chap. 12.

Biographies and Autobiographies

Abrahamsen, David, *The Mind and Death of a Genius,* Columbia University Press, New York, 1946.

Brown, Henry C., *A Mind Mislaid,* Dutton, New York, 1937.

Graves, Alonzo, *The Eclipse of a Mind,* Medical Journal Press, New York, 1942.

Krauch, Elsa, *A Mind Restored,* Putnam, New York, 1937.

Lindner, R. M., *Rebel Without A Cause: the Hypnoanalysis of a Criminal Psychopath,* Grune and Stratton, New York, 1944.

Maine, Harold (pseud.), *If A Man Be Mad,* Doubleday, New York, 1947.

Meier-Graefe, Julius, *Vincent Van Gogh: A Biographical Study,* Literary Guild, New York, 1933.

Small, V. R., *I Knew 3,000 Lunatics,* Farrar and Rinehart, New York, 1935.

Wilson, M. I., *Borderland Minds: An Ex-Patient from Blackmoor,* Meader, Boston, 1940.

Woodson, M. M., *Behind the Door of Delusion: A Story of Inmate, Ward 8,* Macmillan, New York, 1932.

Questions

1. Is the contention that mental illness is increasing sufficiently supported by facts?
2. What does age have to do with some of the trends in specific psychoses?
3. Can you explain the nearly equal rates of mental illness in the sexes? The smaller incidence among children? In rural areas?
4. Which classification of the mental disorders is preferable for statistical study? How does the term, insanity, fit into your preferred list?
5. What psychoses are most and least recoverable?
6. Does the list of social causes, cited by Ripley (see footnote 18) impress you as sociologically sound?

7. State all the facts indicating the tendency of certain families to be more susceptible than others to the psychoses?
8. What problems tend to make alcoholism? What problems are caused by it?
9. What are the major social problems of the epileptic?
10. Point out all the occupational handicaps of the mentally ill.
11. Would you conclude that it is easier to overcome the habit of alcoholism than drug addiction?
12. What are the various meanings and disorders of hysteria?
13. What type of schizophrenia is least recoverable? Why?
14. Does the conclusion about mental disease and crime seem reasonable? If you disagree, construct the elements of a counterargument.
15. Does it seem reasonable to you that the single should be more liable to mental illness than the married?
16. Which is the more nearly correct? Divorce is a cause of mental breakdowns, or mental breakdowns are a cause of divorce.
17. Do the Selective Service findings convince you of the need for a eugenics program?
18. Are there any mental diseases that develop into conditions that resemble feeblemindedness?
19. Under what conditions is it feasible to parole mental disease patients or to allow them to remain in the community?
20. Why is it necessary to distinguish between the psychoses and the neuroses?

CHAPTER 5

MENTAL DEFICIENCY

FEEBLEMINDED PEOPLE NEVER KEEP DIARIES OR WRITE LIFE HISTORIES. There is no story of *A Mind Restored.* No examples of rehabilitation occur in which they can take pride. Their condition is more or less static, is more inclined to become worse than to improve, and there are no compensations such as the blind, the crippled, or the deaf may have by way of consolation. In brief, the problem of the feebleminded is their feeblemindedness. No other calamity, personal or social, could be more damaging.

There are numerous instances when a family's skeleton is not kept in a closet, when for example its handicapped member is a Helen Keller, a Steinmetz, a Harold Russell, or an E. R. Carlson (whose autobiography is mentioned in footnote 2 of Chapter 3, above). No comparable case appears among the feebleminded. Moreover, nature has stacked the deck against him and his type of disordered personality. The feebleminded individual has a body that is often deformed; he is more subject to illness and to degenerating impairments than the normal person; and if he does have enough intelligence, it too is affected by the same disorders of emotions, conduct, and psychoses as the individual of average intelligence.

As a rule when society spends money on its "natural" dependents, it assumes that the investment is sound and the return will more than make up for the costs. This is not so with the feebleminded. They are a constant burden, increasing in cost as they grow older and increasing with each generation if the birth rate follows the fears of the eugenists.

The feebleminded are handicapped in other ways, too. There is no national plan for their needs. There are, it is true, some excellent state projects, but they are usually limited to a type of educational, custodial, or medical care and are not complete programs. There is no Aments Anonymous. Research is slight compared with that for deafness or poliomyelitis. The only organization regularly concerned with them is the American Association on Mental Deficiency, organized in 1876. But its membership is less than 1,500 individuals, most of whom are people associated with institutions for their custody. And its main, official job is the publication of the *American Journal of Mental Deficiency*.

In short, the feebleminded are hazards to themselves and to the society that produces them. Each person who devotes his life to their care is one less person in productive undertakings. In the opinion of many eugenists, for every feebleminded child one normal child apparently fails to be conceived.

The nature of mental deficiency

Mental deficiency and its problems refer to a broad group of differences in intelligence. Other terms, as synonyms or as names of classes of the mentally deficient, are mental subnormality, feeblemindedness, intellectual retardation, and amentia. When medical, psychological, and social definitions are used, the classes of the mentally deficient are distinguished from the population as a whole as individuals whose intelligence is limited because it never developed.

This distinction is useful because it helps to separate the mentally defective from other defective classes. The latter may suffer mental deterioration or even retardation in the course of their illness or handicap. But they were not mentally deficient originally.

The introduction of intelligence tests in 1904-1905 suggested that deficiency is a matter of degree. Ordinarily, mental disease and deficiency are two separate conditions traceable to different causes. But there are individuals on the margin of low intelligence and subnormality who require careful clinic and social study before they can be called dements or aments.

There are two primary areas of overlapping impairments. In dementia there are forms of mental disease (the dementing illnesses), leading to a deterioration of the central nervous system, which are scarcely distinguishable from feeblemindedness. Likewise, among the feebleminded, there are forms of congenital and acquired mental deficiency, arising from congenital syphilis and prenatal injuries, that have all the principal traits of mental disease (in cause, development, and outcome).

Ordinarily, therefore, mental deficiency and feeblemindedness can be used interchangeably to mean degrees of low intelligence. These variations may be recognized as mental arrest, abnormality, or deterioration. Authorities continue to use these terms with slightly different meanings, and most of them no longer employ the term "amentia." This change is largely due to intelligence tests that distinguish classes of the feebleminded numerically as those at the lower end of a frequency distribution of intelligence (the bell-shaped curve). Because of intellectual shortcomings, the feebleminded will also vary in their emotion, volition, insight, originality, temperament, skill, motility, and in other physical and sensory traits [1]

Mental deficiency and its problems

This close similarity between the various classes of mental invalids should forestall hasty generalization about them as a group and about the problems that cause them or the problems that they create. There are four introductory considerations to be remembered in the study of the feebleminded. One, as already noted, is that they are not a homogeneous group. Instead, there are several kinds or degrees of feeblemindedness, and the problems of each type are equally different. A second reminder is that feeblemindedness is not a unit-character in heredity or in its other biological aspects. A third consideration is that the idea of the incompetence of the feebleminded is more important socially than it is intellectually; for example, a person may be feebleminded in one situation and normal in another. A fourth point of view is the observation that the intelligence level is only one of the helpful approaches. This conclusion is most vividly noticeable in the search for causes or in the study of clinical cases.

For all these reasons, Doll recommends that the concept of the social competence of the feebleminded should be added in the

[1] E. A. Doll, Chap. 17 in L. Carmichael (Ed.), *Manual of Child Psychology*, Wiley, New York, 1946. V. E. Fisher, *Introduction to Abnormal Psychology*, Macmillan, New York, 1937. S. I. Franz, "The Abnormal Individual," in C. Murchison (Ed.), *Foundations of Experimental Psychology*, Clark University Press, Worcester, 1929. G. D. Stoddard, *The Meaning of Intelligence*, Macmillan, New York, 1943.

interpretation of their individual handicaps or as an explanation of their social problems. This point of view suggests a multiple approach. It includes physical or biological conditions in arrested development. It is a measure of constitutional deficiency. It covers degrees of retardation in intelligence, and it is a criterion of educational and occupational ability or other types of social and personal maturity.

Mental deficiency or feeblemindedness, therefore, means both low intelligence and inability to acquire certain social habits.

Any one case study is apt to be misleading because it does not give equal illustration to the varied types of feeblemindedness and its causes. The following is an example of feeblemindedness and psychosis. The boy was sixteen years old before his parents were obliged to place him in an institution for the feebleminded, where he was classified upon admission as a moron. His family had no history of mental deficiency, but the boy had had influenza and convulsions in his second year. There were no other developmental difficulties except delayed speech. He always attended special schools where his record was good.

Clinical examinations during the first few months at the school for the feebleminded revealed organic brain lesions. His conduct was more and more subject to periods of excitement resembling the manic cycle. At times he would be quiet and submissive; on other occasions he would talk excitedly and become violent. At the end of six years, during which this condition continued, the patient died of bronchopneumonia.

In the institution, the first clinical diagnosis was mental deficiency with sex abnormalities. After five years of study, when signs of marked emotional disturbance and confused thinking were numerous, the diagnoses was changed to mental disease with psychosis.

This and similar cases may be confusing, because the feeblemindedness may be made identical with psychosis or identified with the social and economic environment in which it appears. In short, feeblemindedness may be made at one and the same time the cause and the result of conditions that are used to explain it.

Because of this misinterpretation of feeblemindedness as a descriptive term and of the curious tendency of certain persons to consider it a simple unit-character, the result of either heredity or environment, it will be desirable to summarize the literature that describes feeblemindedness as a defined mental and social status, and discusses its chief subtypes and their most frequent causes. This is a necessary step prior to an evaluation of the social significance of feeblemindedness.

This uncertain background of feeblemindedness is also confusing when an effort is made to state clearly the causal complex in which it is nourished and the problems that it complicates.

Historically, feeblemindedness has been identified with every major social problem. It is identified with poverty or low economic and social status, with disorganized families, and illiterate, immoral, and incompetent parents, with illness, and with every pathology in the kingdom of evils.

Although this historical confusion has now been fairly well eliminated, these theories reappear time and again to give *the* explanation for some notorious and fearful happening, such as a series of sex crimes, hasty marriages, illegitimacy, or family breakdowns.

One series of initial problems is to be found in remedial and preventive programs. These vary from efforts to educate and supervise the individual to mass programs of social control. Much of the earlier emphasis was placed upon eugenic measures, which were wholly ineffective because they were never applied. In addition, there has been a pronounced reluctance to recognize a most important source of feeblemindedness in natural social processes, such as urbanization, harsh and unstimulating environments, and the increasing complexity of social organization. When the latter sources are fully recognized, in conjunction with the graded concept of abnormality, a major cause of "new defectives" will be found in current social transitions to which certain individuals are unadjusted. On a small scale, examples of this type of defective may be found among those individuals who are normal in a rural community (and are able to meet the ordinary demands of life) but who become subnormal if they migrate to the city and are judged by the more exacting standards of an urban environment.

Another apparently incomprehensible social attitude which is widespread and an integral part of the problem of feeblemindedness is the reluctance of the public to adopt definite means of regulation. There are not enough institutions for custodial or educational purposes, and those now in existence are handicapped by overcrowding. Nor is there an adequate case-work program for parole and supervision in the community. In our public school system special classes for the retarded have been established, primarily to prevent interference with the progress of normal children. But there is a marked difference between the public attitude toward the support of these classes and the attitude toward special classes for the blind, crippled, or deaf.

This difference can be traced to several facts, primarily to the serious doubts as to the value of education for the mentally handicapped. In addition, the public is fearful that the consequences of such training will be increased delinquency, and that the training, by giving the feebleminded economic security, will facilitate an increasing birth rate among them. If, however, education is not a successful remedy, there is no alternative other than permanent segregation or some of the devices that are contrary to current moral codes. Corresponding with this hesitancy in the organization of remedial agencies is an equal distrust on the part of the public towards prevention. Public opinion has also refused to endorse drastic measures for the control of feeblemindedness. For this reason it distrusts suggested preventives. It seems to prefer the occasional act of violence or sexual crime which the higher grades of the mentally retarded commit as the lesser of the hazards.

Who are the feebleminded?

For purposes of general classification, a feebleminded individual is defined as one who is considerably below the mental average of his cultural group. Technically, the feebleminded are those individuals whose brains are undeveloped or whose cerebral and mental maturation is slow. This definition recognizes two variations: (1) degrees of abstract intelligence, (2) degrees of intelligence as determined by comparison with varying community standards.

In the light of the second variation, feeblemindedness may be defined or interpreted from several different points of view. This is primarily because of the fact that there are several gradations of intelligence within the general classification of mental deficiency. As a supplement to Doll's fourfold interpretation, Fisher suggests five criteria: the legal, medical, social-economic, pedagogical, and psychological.

Definitions from each of these points of view are useful in showing that mental deficiency is not a unit-character. Legal definitions of idiocy serve to distinguish those individuals who are legally less responsible than the average person. However, they are not of much value, because of their subjectivity. Tredgold's definition is cited by Fisher as an authoritative medical criterion:

> [Feeble-mindedness is] a state of restricted potentiality for, or arrest of, cerebral development, in consequence of which the person affected is incapable at maturity of so adapting himself to his environment or to the requirements of the community as to maintain existence independently of supervision or external support.[2]

As a social-economic definition, that of the Royal Commission of Great Britain, adopted in 1904, may be cited:

> A feeble-minded person is one who is capable of earning a living under favorable circumstances, but is incapable, from mental defect existing from birth, or from an early age, (a) of competing on equal terms with his normal fellows; or (b) of managing himself and his affairs with ordinary prudence.[3]

The chief objection raised by Fisher against these three definitions is that in each instance a sharp distinction between deficient and normal intelligence is implied, without adequate recognition that there is no such distinction in reality.

Pedagogical and psychological criteria remove this difficulty by considering gradations of intelligence from the lowest to the highest through comparison, and as deviations below and above an average. These criteria make an arbitrary distinction between the feebleminded and the normal. The first, the pedagogical, using classroom success as the basis for determining mental level, is largely subjective. The psychological, on the other hand, endeavors to obtain quantitative measurements of intelligence by objective tests, the test score to be the final definition of feeblemindedness. Through these methods intelligence is measured by achievement in comparison with chronological age, resulting in the intelligence quotient (I.Q.), or mental age. When series of standardized tests are constructed, the arbitrary character of this distinction is considerably reduced.

Psychological criteria of intelligence, consequently, recognize only differences of degree between different classes of persons. While in theory no two persons have the same intelligence and only approximate measurements of intelligence can be established, it is cus-

[2] V. E. Fisher, *op. cit.,* pp. 448-458.

[3] G. D. Stoddard, *op. cit.,* p. 277, gives the revisions of this definition from the Mental Deficiency Act of 1927. Tredgold's definition is dated 1922 and was revised slightly in 1937.

tomary to divide a population into arbitrary classes, as in the following table:

THE MAJOR CLASSES OF INTELLIGENCE

Classification	*Score in Terms of I.Q.*
Genius or near genius	Above 140
Very superior	120–140
Superior	110–120
Normal average	90–110
Dull or backward	80– 90
Borderline deficiency	70– 80
Definitely feebleminded	
(a) Moron	50– 70
(b) Imbecile	25– 50
(c) Idiot	Below 25

Thus, using the psychological criterion, a feebleminded person is defined as:

> . . . One who has originally an intelligence quotient of 70 per cent or less, and whose status falls in the lowest 2 per cent of human intellect.[4]

There is some difference of opinion as to the numerical score that should be accepted as the upper limit of deficiency. An I.Q. of 75 is recognized as this limit by the American Association on Mental Deficiency.

In his review of these several approaches, Kanner suggests the recognition of three classes: (1) absolute feeblemindedness, (2) relative feeblemindedness, and (3) apparent feeblemindedness (pseudo-feeblemindedness).[5]

Classes of feebleminded persons

By the use of these classes, the three usual divisions of idiots, imbeciles, and morons are regrouped and distinguished by more elastic traits.

Absolute feeblemindedness is limited to the categories of idiots and imbeciles. These types are easily recognized and are considered to be defectives in any society. They are in need of constant care, because no treatment (glutamic acid included) has succeeded in modifying their intellectual status.

Relative feeblemindedness includes those whose status is largely

[4] V. E. Fisher, *op. cit.*, p. 454.

[5] L. Kanner, "Feeblemindedness: Absolute, Relative, and Apparent," *Nerv. Child,* Vol. 7 (1948): 365-397.

determined by prevailing social standards—the moron, borderline, and dull-normal classes. They are not identified by distinctive personality traits. Their ability varies, and as a rule they can be detected only by scholastic or intelligence tests. Their variability is considerable: they may be "stable or unstable, secure or insecure, placid or moody, aggressive or submissive." Some, possibly all, of them may become adjusted in routine situations or in a society that is simpler than our own.

Apparent feeblemindedness (pseudo-feeblemindedness) includes those individuals who either fail in an intelligence test or are incorrectly diagnosed. Often this condition is confused with, or caused by, hearing or speech defects, severe illness, brain injury, and other physical handicaps.

Establishing the limits between these subclasses or between the feebleminded and borderline cases is a matter of considerable practical importance. While it is relatively easy to distinguish idiots and imbeciles, there is need for multiple tests prior to the classification of a person as a moron, borderline type, or dull normal. This distinction at best is only a matter of judgment, and consequently the diagnosis of intelligence tests should be checked by medical examination and social history. Legal restrictions placed upon the feebleminded, as well as the solution of social problems presented by them, make the distinction between the borderline and lower grades more than a technical problem.

The idiot is a person whose intellectual level is lower than that of an average three-year-old child. There are several definite physical and social characteristics by which this lowest grade of subnormality may be identified. The frontal brain does not develop to the same extent as in most children. Incidental to this lack is a corresponding retardation in mental growth. In the lowest forms of idiocy, the person is responsive only to the simplest stimuli, living at what is practically a reflex level. As a rule such persons are utterly incapable of self-help, being unable to learn to talk or walk. Most of them are unable to feed or clothe themselves. In some instances there is a slight mental and social capacity, but this is restricted to simple expressions of need for bodily attention.

The imbecile is a person whose mental level corresponds to that of children from three to seven years of age. His capacities also correspond roughly with the attainments of average children within these limits. By sufficient education the imbecile can be trained to many manual tasks. His reactions, however, are simple and direct. Few can learn to perform related operations. The imbecile can learn to read simple statements and to write his name, but he is practically worthless economically and cannot earn a living under ordinary conditions. Consequently, his occupations are limited to work under close supervision. Socially, he can be adapted to the elementary conventions, but he has few inhibitions and no ability to "reason why" about conduct.

An example of absolute feeblemindedness, cited by Kanner, is that of a boy whose father was described as of average intelligence and the mother slightly below average. This boy was slow to walk or talk. He acquired bowel control but never mastered bladder control. He could feed himself but could not dress or undress without help. He entered school at six but obviously was unable to learn. He was classified as a typical Mongolian idiot.[6]

Another special class is the *idiot savant*. He may have some special ability for which there is no explanation, such as making mental arithmetical computations rapidly and accurately or naming the day of the week of some particular date, e.g., of January 1, 1900. Apart from this capacity, however, the *idiot savant* has all the handicaps of his usual imbecile classification.

The third type of feebleminded, the morons, range in mental age from the imbecile class to the low normal types. In general, they correspond in initiative and intelligence to the average ten-year-old child, the upper limit not exceeding a twelve-year mental age. They merge into, and are confused with, the borderline group. These two mental classes present the most serious problems in community education and control, because great variations in ability and social adjustment occur. The morons are the only group that has some individuals who may become relatively adjusted to routine activities. Some may go as far as the fourth or fifth grade in school and may be trained in semiskilled occupations. At the same time they require a great deal of supervision and have the greatest incidence of failures in the attempt to become adjusted. Morons circulate practically without restriction, exercising in some instances a most demoralizing influence upon the community and upon those who are obliged to associate with them.

An example of relative feeblemindedness, cited by Kanner, is

[6] There are photographs of most of these clinical types in E. A. Doll, *op. cit.*, pp. 846 ff.

an only child of normal or superior parents. There is no history of previous feeblemindedness or of psychosis in the family. Both parents are rated above average economically and educationally. Although he was slow to talk, the boy did good work in the pre-school years at nursery school and kindergarten. But he could not do first-grade work and was recommended to a special school for retarded children. All through this period, the boy was healthy, pleasant, obedient, and in every respect a good boy. He is typical of the individual who can develop well up to a limit beyond which he cannot go, regardless of encouragement or special teaching.

A case of apparent feeblemindedness resembles this type of defectiveness closely. This boy also was slow to learn to talk. Specialists diagnosed him as slow, spoiled, feebleminded, or hard of hearing. After a series of tests he was found to be "word deaf," although he was not actually deaf. Upon admission to a school for the deaf, he learned to use words and to read and write up to the achievement of his chronological age group.[7]

As the several criteria of subnormality have demonstrated, no hard and fast division can be made among the three classes. They represent a merging in educability and in social responsibility. Although each type is compared with normal children of a certain age level, the retarded have problems wholly unlike those of normal children because of their differences in emotional and sexual, as well as in mental, makeup. When those individual differences are taken into consideration, a further subdivision of the retarded can be made. Thus, E. A. Whitney has prepared the following classification, based upon such differences as age, sex, degree of self-help, occupation or industrial skill, behavior adjustments, social conformity, and parental responsibility: [8]

1. Helpless low-grades; those who are economic burdens and sometimes an actual menace.
2. Unadjusted high-grades with behavior problems.
3. Physically handicapped high-grades.
4. Well-adjusted young high-grades.
5. Well-adjusted, old high-grades.
6. Aged high-grades.

[7] L. Jackson, "Non-Speaking Children," *Brit. Jour. Med. Psych.*, Vol. 23 (1950): 87-100.

[8] E. A. Whitney, "Presenting Mental Deficiency to Students," *Am. Jour. Ment. Def.*, Vol. 50 (1945-46): 55-58.

7. Clinical types, including such cases as orthopedic complications, endocrine types, remediable birth injury, congenital syphilis.
8. Psychiatric types, including the epileptic and psychopathic.

This classification is suggestive in showing critical complications in the physical and social adjustment of the subnormal.

Clinical types. An enumeration of rarer, clinical types of feeblemindedness is useful both for completeness and as an initial introduction to its causes. As will be noted later, they are much less numerous than the moron or borderline cases, but their dramatic nature more than compensates for their infrequency. These types include (1) Mongolism, (2) intracranial birth lesion, (3) microcephaly, (4) hydrocephaly, (5) cretinism, and (6) familial mental deficiency.

Mongolism or Mongolian idiocy is so named because this class of feebleminded have some of the physical traits of the Mongolian race. They occur about once in every 1,000 live births; their intelligence quotient is between fifteen and twenty-nine. The most significant social facts about them are that two Mongolian idiots are rarely born in the same family and that their life span is short, averaging fourteen years.

Intracranial birth lesions account for about the same number of the feebleminded as Mongolism. The mental capacity of this class extends from idiocy to the upper range of mental deficiency. Although this source of the mentally deficient was recognized long ago, only recently has any research been devoted to it.

Microcephaly is easily recognized by the small head of its victims. Their mental range extends from high-grade idiot to low-grade imbecile. Their number exceeds that of victims of Mongolism, being about one in every 250 mental defectives.

Hydrocephaly is also readily recognized by the large head of the individuals in this group. Their mental age varies from idiot to moron levels. Their number is about the same as that of microcephalics.

Cretinism is a type of feeblemindedness that develops with marked thyroid deficiency. It is so named because it was first identified on the island of Crete. It is a less frequent condition than either of the two foregoing types. Since one of its causes is known, there have been instances of distinct physical and mental improvement through thyroid treatment.

Familial mental deficiency is the most numerous of the clinical types. It is sometimes called aclinical (by Halperin, for example), because it involves only retarded development and is not marked by physical or psychiatric disturbances. This is the type that is most in need of study but which has not been studied to any great extent because too many of its victims are either not in institutions or otherwise identified.

In a classification of 338 clinical varieties of mental deficients, Halperin used the following types or sources: [9]

	Per Cent
Aclinical or familial	45.0
Intracranial	26.6
Mongolian	8.3
Cranial—microcephaly hydrocephaly	5.3
Psychiatric	5.0
Miscellaneous—toxemia, congenital	4.7
Endocrine dystrophy	2.7
Congenital syphilis	2.4
	100.0

Extent of feeblemindedness

With the adoption of standard psychological tests, estimates of the incidence of feeblemindedness in the population as a whole or in special groups have become much more uniform and complete. Nevertheless, most of them remain not much better than reasonable guesses because of the wide and unknown distribution of this condition.

According to the bell-shaped frequency curve, the number of superior and inferior individuals gradually diminishes from a median score. So far as the feebleminded group is concerned, this distribution shows that there are fewer idiots than imbeciles, fewer imbeciles than morons, and fewer morons than dull-normal or borderline cases. From the studies of the British Royal Commission, the distribution among 100 cases of mental defectiveness is reported to consist of 6 idiots, 18 imbeciles, and 76 morons. Among each 100 institutionalized cases in this country, according to Doll, 10 are idiots, 30 are imbeciles, and 60 are morons.

Conservative estimates of the actual number of the feebleminded place the total at 2 to 6 per cent of the American population. This range includes a minimum number of the lowest types and a maximum for those in the community who are not recognized or classified. Most observers accept these limits for the current population and as the proportions in its future growth to the year 2,000. A

[9] S. L. Halperin, "Human Heredity and Mental Deficiency," *Am. Jour. Ment. Def.*, Vol. 51 (1946-47): 156. Adapted from Table 5.

minimum of about one per cent, according to Whitney, requires institutional care or special supervision and training, and another one per cent is sufficiently retarded to need special education if a margin of economic and social efficiency is to be achieved.[10] There are few comparable figures for other countries. In Great Britain in 1920 it was estimated that 1.5 per cent of the population had I.Q.'s below 70 and that by the year 2,000 this proportion would be between 3.3 and 4.1 per cent.

Prevalence in rates per 1,000 population, reported since 1900, gives a more tangible understanding of this distribution and the incidence of specific types:

PREVALENCE OF FEEBLEMINDEDNESS

Area	*Year*	*Rates Per 1,000 Population*
United States	1900	5.0 (before I.Q. tests)
United States	1910	10.0
England and Wales	1908	8.0
United States—Selective Service	1918	12.0
England and Wales	1929	8.0
England and Wales	1929	6.7 urban
England and Wales	1929	10.5 rural
South Dakota	1929	12.9 (school population)
Baltimore	1936	6.8
Tennessee	1938	8.2
Baltimore	1938–43	8.1 males, 6.3 females
Illinois	1940	4.0 (school population)
United States—Selective Service	1942–43	10.7 whites
		19.0 Negroes

Sources: E. A. Doll, *op. cit.*, pp. 263-267. P. Lemkau and others, "A Survey of Statistical Studies on the Prevalence and Incidence of Mental Disorder," *Pub. Health Rpts.*, Vol. 58 (1943), No. 53, pp. 11-12. J. Downes, "Causes of Illness among Males and Females," *Milbank Mem. Fund Quart.*, Vol. 28 (1950): 417. G. Perrott, "Findings of Selective Service Examinations," *Milbank Mem. Fund Quart.*, Vol. 22 (1944): 362.

In the Baltimore study the distribution by types is as follows:

Intelligence Rating	*Rate Per 1,000 Population*
Idiot	0.28
Imbecile	1.89
Moron	2.43
Unclassified	2.09

This study reported a sex ratio of about 7 males to 6 females, and a frequency of types similar to that of the British Royal Commis-

[10] E. A. Whitney and R. E. Caron, "A Brief Analysis of Recent Statistics on Mental Deficiency," *Am. Jour. Ment. Def.*, Vol. 51 (1946-47): 713.

sion, namely, morons are four times more numerous than imbeciles and imbeciles are four times more numerous than idiots. The validity of these findings is confirmed by the records of first admissions to state institutions in this country.[11]

When estimates are made for both feeblemindedness and other forms of psychometric subnormality, about fifteen per cent of the population is grouped within a mental age less than twelve years, or an intelligence quotient below 85 on the Stanford-Binet scale.

These variations in estimates are due largely to the use of different criteria in the definition of feeblemindedness and to the fact that there is no complete registration of the feebleminded who are not in institutions. Estimates based upon the institutional population are not significant; nor does the fact of an increasing institutional population imply a general increase. On the latter point there is no available information. When the psychological definition, an I.Q. of 70, is taken as the dividing point, an incidence varying from 0.5 to 3.0 per cent is as accurate an estimate as current studies permit.

Causes of feeblemindedness

Mental defect in feeblemindedness is nothing more than a symptom, and like other symptoms, must be related to causes. Although structural anomalies rank among the most definite causes of defectiveness, many of the feebleminded have neither structural nor functional peculiarities. It is estimated that fully ninety per cent have no characteristic clinical traits. However, many idiots and some imbeciles do have both anatomical and physiological abnormalities, but the moron is usually as normal in these respects as persons of average intelligence and cannot be detected by facial or other physical characteristics.

As indicated by the problems associated with feeblemindedness and by its clinical types, the search for causes has been in heredity or other genetic factors and in environment, either prenatal or postnatal.

Heredity was originally the most frequently mentioned source. But its explanation, notwithstanding technical language, has always been uncertain in contrast with medical, pathological, serological, histological, biochemical, and endocrinological explanations. Esti-

[11] *Patients in Mental Institutions,* United States Bureau of the Census, Washington. In this annual publication, the distribution of types, as given in the Baltimore study, is further subdivided by sex.

mates of the amount of feeblemindedness resulting from heredity vary with different authorities and at different periods from twenty-nine per cent to ninety per cent. They are confusing because the same definition of feeblemindedness is not used. W. E. Castle makes about the most definite statement by including feeblemindedness under the caption, "Subject to heredity, but to what extent or how inherited uncertain."[12] A quotation from Morgan is added as perhaps the most authoritative opinion on this subject. Morgan says:

> Until more definite information is obtainable concerning mental traits and emotional reactions, some of us remain sceptical of the crude and often forced attempts that have been made so far to determine what is inherited and what is acquired after birth.
>
> A comparison of the facts of Mendelian heredity relating to plants and animals with what is known of human heredity leaves no doubt, as far as physical characters are involved, that the same rules apply to both. . . . But it is extremely hazardous to carry over this inference to the psychic character of man, where there is *no certainty as to what extent his behavior is determined by heredity and by environment.*[13]

The general range of causes as noted in the literature in the 1880's and as interpreted today is given by Whitney under eleven headings.[14]

CHANGING INTERPRETATIONS OF CAUSES

	Per Cent Distribution in the	
	1880's	*1940's*
Birth trauma	14–20	3–5
Heredity	64–75	55–65
Alcoholism	3–12	3–5
Syphilis	2	2
Tuberculosis	6	4
Epilepsy	3	2
Diphtheria	5	—
Consanguinity	5–7	—
Endocrine	—	5

This obvious shift to nonhereditary explanations is the most hopeful because it stresses primarily those conditions that are more sub-

[12] W. E. Castle, *Genetics and Eugenics,* Harvard University Press, Cambridge, 1921, p. 273.

[13] T. H. Morgan, in C. Murchison (Ed.), *Foundations of Experimental Psychology,* Clark University Press, Worcester, 1929, p. 36. Italics by the present authors.

[14] E. A. Whitney, "Mental Deficiency in the 1880's and 1940's," *Am. Jour. Ment. Def.,* Vol. 54 (1949-50): 151.

ject to study—such as biological processes of reproduction, gestation, and general bodily growth—or the conditions that modify them.

Among these conditions now being explored are maternal pelvic irradiation, German measles, the Rh factor, and numerous accidents or injuries during labor that may cause some injury to the brain. Halperin is convinced that idiocy is a result of "some severe injury to the central nervous system," and that the early appearance of convulsions, chorea, and muscular dystrophy is also associated causally with the more serious forms of mental defect. As a result of a study of two hundred autopsies, Benda cites vascular lesions, encephalitis, and abnormalities of the spinal cord among probable causes of idiocy or imbecility.[15]

The chief postnatal causative factors of feeblemindedness are traumata, toxins, infections, endocrine disturbances, convulsions, encephalitis, and malnutrition. Trauma refers to blows, falls, shocks, or injuries that affect the nervous system, and are used as explanations of defectiveness when no other cause can be assigned. Among the more prominent of these conditions are trauma at childbirth, caused by protracted labor or instrumental delivery, which may cause brain injury and injuries to the cranium, resulting in the fracture of the skull or lesions and hemorrhage of the brain. Toxins that may poison the brain, in addition to those resulting from syphilis, alcoholism, and drug addiction, result from measles, scarlet fever, diphtheria, influenza, meningitis, and other infectious diseases. Few clinical cases are known to be caused by these toxins alone. These acute infectious diseases during childhood are also associated with impaired sensory functions, with mental defects, and frequently with epilepsy. Endocrine dysfunction has already been mentioned in the case of cretinism. Investigations relative to malnutrition have made no startling discoveries as to its direct causative influence. Restricted diets apparently constitute a more serious handicap to feebleminded than to normal children; that is, children of normal parents have been found to resist extreme malnutrition with slight consequences upon mentality. On this subject, some positive cases of improved intelligence are reported among the younger children of mothers who have given birth to several defective children, and this improvement is accounted for by a combination of prenatal and postnatal medical care and supervised nutrition.

[15] C. E. Benda, "Ten Years Research in Mental Deficiency," *Am. Jour. Ment. Def.*, Vol. 51 (1946-47): 170-185.

With the exception of a few clinical types, most cases of feeblemindedness are the result of multiple causes. The inability to differentiate rigidly between heredity and environment in this problem is not unique. Students can protect themselves from the dogmatists on either side by separating what is known from what is unknown. Although the foregoing review of causation has not named the several leading causes in the order of their importance, it has supplied an outline of groups of probable causes, and at the same time has provided a basis for the elimination of hearsay evidence. Of two facts we are certain. Interbreeding, such as cousin marriages, may be listed among the factors that do not cause feeblemindedness. No study has ever substantiated this folk belief. Similarly, emotional shock to the mother during pregnancy (maternal impressions) is also classified among the superstitions.

Social significance of the feebleminded

In the past, many social problems have been explained wholly or in part by the presence of the feebleminded. Now most of these generalizations have been modified by studies that have produced the findings given in the preceding sections of this chapter. One of the chief reasons for this change in point of view is that the definition of feeblemindedness includes within it subnormality in dependence, responsibility, self-discipline, and self-support; in brief, subnormality in personality and in social relations. For good or evil, the feebleminded continue to be a considerable group in the population. It is important to know about their liabilities in order to provide adequately for their training or for preventive programs. But no achievement is made when they are charged with liabilities that are implicit in their defined handicaps.

Here are the personal characteristics of the feebleminded that must be used in interpreting any indictment of their danger to society. Their intellectual limits are indicated by intelligence-test scores and by restrictions on their maturing that these limits impose. These limits are *relatively constant.* As a class, the feebleminded are emotional rather than deliberate. They are unable to generalize, and for this reason they are unable to profit by experience or to adapt themselves to new situations. Even in trivial tasks they require constant oversight. They have no initiative. They are impulsive and emotionally unstable. They are highly suggestible but they cannot anticipate or foresee results. They have no critical ability.

Their attention is of short duration, easily distracted, and wholly superficial. They cannot be trusted to report the truth as witnesses. They have no comprehension of group responsibility or of cooperation in a group. They cannot think abstractly.

Among the more usual social problems with which their condition is identified—problems to be expected in a mentally subnormal group—are broken homes or deplorably disorganized domestic relationships, sexual immorality and other disorders of conduct in whatever group they may appear, economic uselessness as producers, delinquency and crime, demoralizing leisure-time activities, high rates of sickness, and physical defectiveness.

Is intelligence a constant? Not enough research on the social calamities of the feebleminded or their individual differences has been carried out to acceptable conclusions. But in the single item of intelligence there has been an enormous amount of testing and comparing. The results, however, are none too definite. Different researchers come to the conclusions that the intelligence quotient is a constant, that it decreases, or that it can be improved.[16]

In their study of the constancy of intelligence among mental defectives, Sloan and Harman found that as a rule test scores do not remain the same. On the contrary they tend to decrease as chronological age increases. In their group of defectives, twice as many lost as gained in the I.Q. test scores, an average loss of 2.6 points. The authors of this report reach the conclusion that their findings are in agreement with the majority of other comparable investigations. Or, in other words, a problem of the feebleminded is their gradual mental deterioration.

One study that conspicuously fails to agree with the majority is the report by Schmidt. In this study, 322 children, whose age range at the beginning was 12 to 14 years and whose mental age ranged from 27 to 69 I.Q., were provided with a special educational course and were observed in their later, postschool careers for five years.

During the school period these children made a gain of three years and eight months in composite educational achievement. This amounts to an academic achievement of about the fifth-grade level,

[16] V. M. Axline, "Mental Deficiency—Symptom or Disease?" *Jour. Consult. Psych.*, Vol. 13 (1949): 313-327. W. Sloan and H. H. Harman, "Constancy of I.Q. in Mental Defectives," *Jour. Genet. Psych.*, Vol. 7 (1947): 177-185. B. G. Schmidt, "Changes in Personal, Social, and Intellectual Behavior of Children Originally Classified as Feebleminded," *Psych. Mono.*, Vol. 60 (1946), No. 5.

whereas in terms of the group's average I.Q. (51.7), only a third-grade achievement was expected.

In addition to this school growth, the children improved in personal adjustment, as noted by range and increase of leisure-time interests, more pleasing personal appearance, and increased responsibility for personal activities. They were able to gain noticeable freedom from their previous dependence upon their families and to display both willingness and ability to obtain and carry on part-time employment. In group relationships they improved in conduct and they reached a competency in group activities almost equal to that of normal children. By objective tests they succeeded in reaching a capacity for social and personal adjustment that was comparable to the average achievements for their age group.

By the end of the postschool period, 27 per cent had completed a four-year high-school course; 5.1 per cent had continued high-school training; 20.1 per cent were still in school attendance. Of those who were working, 83.4 per cent were regularly employed, one third in skilled occupations, one third in clerical, and of the remainder some were in managerial, supervisory, or other types of work requiring both precision and responsibility.

By the end of the study, 59.7 per cent were classified as low or high normals, 26.7 per cent as dull, and only 7.2 per cent remained in the original feebleminded category. In their range of achievement in academic, vocational and social activities, this group was equal to the adjustment of the average adult.

Familial feeblemindedness. Before intelligence tests furnished the tools by which the feebleminded could be classified as the obviously defective clinical types and the not-so-obvious higher types of retarded or slow learners, many geneticists considered feeblemindedness to be a unit-character that is peculiar to certain families (as noted above in the review of hereditary factors). Now this position is radically modified. It is probably the most important new fact about the feebleminded that has come to light during the last half century.

A conclusion, now widely accepted, is that the lower grades of the feebleminded have few or no children. The highest birth rates of all the mentally retarded groups are those of the borderline and low-average groups. Moreover, idiots and imbeciles are produced for the most part by families of average or above-average intelligence with few or no other defective siblings. This fact was emphasized in the discussion of the familial type of mental retardation—a type that is derived from the low-average population, which has no apparent genetic basis for it. If a hereditary basis is to be found, it is probably limited to a few families.[17]

It is known, for example, that defective and inferior parents have a large proportion of children of moron level. The siblings of these morons are also inclined to be defective or inferior. This consequence is a combination of mental and socio-economic inferiority. The more defective the parents are, the more defective children are produced. When normal parents do have one defective child, they are seven to ten times more likely to have another than parents who have had no defective children. It also follows that under assortative mating, that is, the mating of one parent who is defective with one who is either inferior or normal, few defective children are born. Similarly, the higher the socio-economic level of the parents, the higher the average I.Q., and the fewer the number of children with an I.Q. of 70 or below.

These conclusions are illustrated in part by Halperin's investigation of the mental status of the parents of 631 defective children, mentioned in footnote 17. As indicated graphically, 43 per cent of the parents were average or above, 41 per cent were inferior, and only 16 per cent were defective.

Present day knowledge of general vital rates supplements these conclusions. Many of the inferior classes have excessively low birth rates; as, for example, epileptics or the mentally ill. In the lower grades of feeblemindedness, because of segregation, the birth rate is practically zero. Other factors also interfere with the increase of the feebleminded. There are more stillbirths and a higher infant mortality rate among the feebleminded than in normal stock. About one fifth of the mentally defective children die during their first year from asthenia or infectious diseases. Their general death rate is also higher for other age groups, especially up to the twentieth year. Mental defectives as a class are generally short-lived.

One report on the life-span of 768 institutional cases found the average life-expectancy of idiots to be 19 years and of imbeciles to be 26.6 years. However, because of the care that they receive in a

[17] A. Myerson, "Family Mental Disease in Private Practice," *Am. Jour. Psychiatry,* Vol. 103 (1946): 323-337. S. L. Halperin, "A Clinico-Genetical Study of Mental Defect," *Am. Jour. Ment. Def.,* Vol. 50 (1945-46): 8-26.

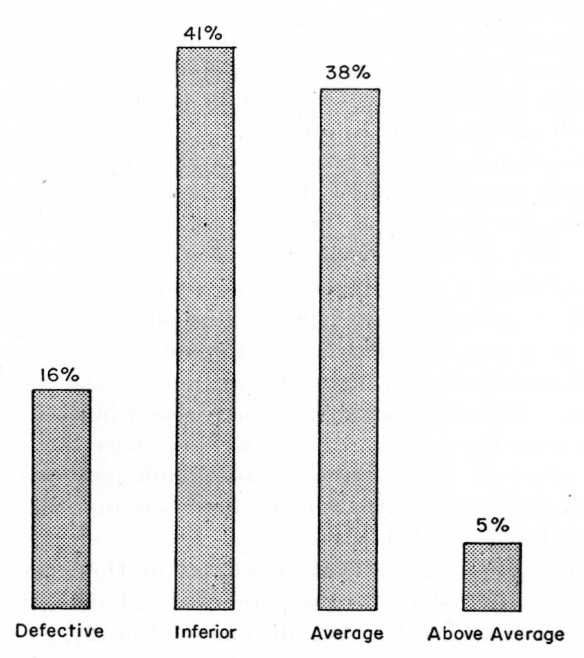

Mental Status of the Parents of 631 Defective Children

protected environment, some defectives survive for many years beyond these averages.[18]

References to the great fertility of the mentally inferior usually apply to high-grade defectives—morons and borderline types—whose birth rates are higher than the average for the general population or that for the middle or well-to-do classes. But before this fact can be interpreted to mean a natural increase, the death rate must also be reckoned with. Earlier marriages, failure to restrict the birth rate, and large families among the high-grade defectives are offset by the counter-selective factor of the death rate, and the contention of alarming increases and the calamitous doctrine of racial degeneration are only weakly supported by the facts.

An inventory by Town of the problems presented in familial feeblemindedness showed that in 141 families (1) there was an exceptionally high child-mortality rate, (2) 28 families were broken

[18] O. J. Kaplan, "Life Expectancy of Low-Grade Mental Defectives," *Psych. Record,* Vol. 3 (1940): 303.

by desertion, divorce, annulment, separation, or abandonment, (3) housekeeping conditions in more than a third were considered "flagrantly" bad, with many cases of malnutrition, (4) illegitimate maternity was discovered in 51 families, and incest or prostitution in 21, (5) a child was removed from 20 families for neglect, (6) instances of criminality were reported for 38 families, and in 20 others regular instances of physical violence toward members of the family.[19]

When a normal family has a defective child, the experience is apt to have dismal consequences. Generally the condition is not recognized at first, and when realization of the child's inferiority eventually comes to light the parents try to protect their ancestry by thinking of some accidental cause. The child had measles or convulsions or was hit on the head by a hammock. Often parents consider themselves at fault. They fear public opinion and for all these reasons are in no mood to make the child's life in the home as happy and agreeable as possible. One of the most difficult problems of the social worker in cases of this sort is to educate these parents to accept the child and rear it as normally as conditions permit.

An example of familial feeblemindedness, and also one of its rare clinical types, is a boy who was placed in an institution when he was eight years old because he could not get along in school. His parents were normal physically and mentally, though they had no education and were not well off economically. One other child had been placed in the institution with the diagnosis of spastic paralysis with mental deficiency.

In the case of the first boy, there was no history of illness, shock, or accident that might explain his misconduct and poor school record. At school he had been aggressive and noisy; he had numerous temper tantrums and was constantly irritable. He had no capacity to learn. When he was transferred to the institution, intellectual deterioration was progressive, with accompanying loss of motor control and marked aging until his eighteenth year, when he died of influenza. Cues to the familial character of this case are the defective sibling, the negative preschool history, and the average or better mental status of the parents. As a clinical variety, this case was diagnosed as neuronal lipidosis, which means a deteriorating neural

[19] C. H. Town, *Familial Feeblemindedness,* Foster and Stewart, Buffalo, 1939, Chap. 2.

condition combined with organic structural changes. It is rare, relatively obscure as to basic causes, and is regarded as a problem of metabolism, biochemistry, and psychosomatics.

Occupational adjustment. In its industrial and occupational connections, the distribution of intelligence has been used to explain three important facts about the working population. One is the concentration of the lower mental types in the unskilled and casual occupations. A second is that the majority of the intellectually superior are from the highest occupational groups. A third shows that intelligence is not wholly limited to the superior occupational groups and that there is constant mobility from the lower classes up the vocational ladder. Numerous recruits to professional and managerial positions are the sons of fathers in agricultural, skilled, and semiskilled work.

The relationship between the intelligence of children and the occupational status of parents is shown in the following distribution: [20]

OCCUPATIONS OF PARENTS ARRANGED ACCORDING TO THE INTELLIGENCE OF CHILDREN

Mean I.Q.	*Parents' Occupations*
Children—white	
111.3-113.9	Professional, accountants, auditors, bookkeepers
105.7-107.4	Managers, clerks, engineers, foremen, insurance personnel
100.9-104.0	Merchants, bus drivers, owners and partners, railroad workers, state police, salesmen
89.9- 99.8	Contractors, barbers, factory workers, technicians, housewife, trucking and truck drivers
Children—Negro	
92.0- 94.8	Bakers, butchers, professional
86.0- 88.5	Tailors, barbers, cleaners
82.5- 84.9	Carpenters, painters, railroad workers, mechanics
80.3- 82.3	Salesmen, truck drivers, laborers, factory workers, domestic service
79.6	Unemployed

Kennedy's comparative study of the occupational adjustment of morons and nonmorons is a good analysis of the abilities and limitations of the high-grade retarded individual.[21] This study was

[20] A. M. Jordan, "Efficiency of Group Tests of Intelligence in Discovering the Mentally Deficient," *High School Jour.*, Vol. 31 (1948): 75-94. Table 4, pp. 80 and 85. Adapted.

[21] R. J. R. Kennedy, *The Social Adjustment of Morons in a Connecticut City,* Social Service Department, State Office Building, Hartford, 1948.

controlled throughout so that the compared groups were similar in all respects except their mental level.

Most of the morons were employed in unskilled or semiskilled occupations. There were a few in clerical, sales, and in minor supervisory jobs. Both moron and nonmoron groups had about the same earning power, but the latter tended to change jobs somewhat more frequently.

In the employers' estimation of their abilities, there were uniform reactions to the effect that morons were inferior in learning, judgment, efficiency, absenteeism, tardiness, co-worker relations, speed, and accuracy. A few morons could equal the efficiency of nonmorons in accuracy and speed, just as a few of the nonmorons were below average in both of these characteristics. Some employers expressed the opinion that morons as a class were qualified to fit into more-skilled occupations.

On the basis of these discoveries, Kennedy concluded that most morons can be self-supporting and economically independent. Although they are less well adjusted to social conventions than to employment, they are not serious threats to society. Because of their occupational success, therefore, they should not be classed among the feebleminded.

A social background that has some predictive value for the successful occupational adjustment of the mentally retarded individual is favorable home environment and parental acceptance and guidance. Good personal traits on the job are caution, ability to adapt to routine jobs, and resistance to fatigue. General personal characteristics also favorable to employment are physical attractiveness, even temper, and being not too forgetful.[22]

Delinquency and criminality. It is now generally conceded that feeblemindedness as a single cause is not an important factor in delinquency and crime. Although a large number of delinquents and criminals may be defective, their behavior is due to the same factors that account for crime in general, namely, a coincidental cluster of events.

Moreover, in both delinquency and crime, the majority of the defectives are the dull-normal types, the lower grades being infrequently represented. And this dull, borderline group is further dis-

[22] H. Michael-Smith, "A Study of Personal Characteristics Desirable for Vocational Success of the Mentally Deficient," *Am. Jour. Ment. Def.*, Vol. 55 (1950): 139-143.

tinguished from lawbreakers as a whole by the fact that it engages mostly in sex crimes or crimes of violence. When the entire group of defectives is examined, their rate of arrests is surprisingly low. This fact has been noted in the studies made by Healy and the Gluecks who found from less than ten per cent to slightly more than thirteen per cent of defectives among their delinquent groups. The same conclusion is also reported in the studies of prison inmates. And in both, the great majority of the defective offenders were morons.[23]

Even though most delinquent children in the public schools are mentally retarded, it does not follow that all mentally retarded children are delinquent. And in the combination of delinquency and defectiveness there are several other causes that fully explain the delinquency. A school survey of delinquent defectives in Detroit showed that less than 20 per cent of all the mentally retarded were in special classes for the delinquent or were behavior problems. In other words, more than 80 per cent of the mentally retarded are not delinquents.[24] Among the conditions that are associated with defectiveness as favorable to delinquency are bad home conditions, personality difficulties, poor heredity, poor physical condition, mental retardation, mental defect, endocrine disturbance, early illness, and bad companions. These factors, in the order given, were enumerated by Blanchard and Paynter in a comparison of 250 children who were considered problems at home or in school (28.2 per cent of whom were mental defectives), with a control group of 337 nonproblem children (5 per cent of whom were defectives). In the above list, mental retardation refers to cases of children who were not defective but who were so intellectually retarded that they were unadjusted to the school curriculum.

In a special study of the social adjustability of the feebleminded it has been shown, in addition to the above findings, that normal children tend to be arraigned for certain offenses (crimes against property) much more frequently than the subnormal. Moreover, in both groups a great majority come from poverty-stricken homes. Of 432 delinquent subnormal children, Miss Powdermaker reported

[23] Mandel Sherman, *Intelligence and its Deviations,* Ronald, New York, 1945, pp. 104-107. A. E. Grigg, "Criminal Behavior of Mentally Retarded Adults," *Am. Jour. Ment. Def.,* Vol. 52 (1947-48): 370-374.

[24] C. S. Berry, "Care of the Mentally Retarded," *Proceedings,* National Conference on Social Work, 1925, p. 441. K. C. Garrison, *The Psychology of Exceptional Children,* Ronald, New York, 1950, pp. 190-196.

that 68 per cent came from homes "obviously inadequate because of gross neglect and cruelty, chronic alcoholism, psychotic or mentally defective parents, criminality, antisocial sex conduct, or marked poverty," as shown by the table of adjusted and unadjusted parents[25] in the following summary.

		Per Cent
Parents socially adjusted		27
Unadjusted parents		73
Mentally defective	13	
Other unadjustments	40	
Home broken by death	20	
Total		100

The total of 13 per cent for the mentally defective may be taken as the maximum contribution of feeblemindedness to delinquency and crime.

Proneness to psychoses. Feeblemindedness is not a condition that insulates its victims from other mental abnormalities, such as the psychoses. Many studies have been made of psychotic defectives, especially from the point of view of the relation between intelligence and mental stability. Symptoms of all major psychoses, with all their deteriorating effects, have been found in mental defectives. Such cases also are appearing or at least are being recognized with increasing frequency.

Observations have been made of the feebleminded with schizophrenia, epilepsy, emotional disorders, manic states, and paranoid trends. The chief difference between them and the usual psychotic is that they do not develop as a rule the exaggerated types of symptoms of self-esteem, nor are their depressions and elations as profound or persistent. In motor behavior, however, their conduct is often as exaggerated as that of the psychotic of normal intelligence. Although psychoses are frequently observed in the feebleminded, there is no evidence that their liability to them is any greater than that of the intellectually normal.

The most numerous cases are those of the feebleminded epileptic.

[25] P. M. Blanchard and R. H. Paynter, "The Problem Child," *Mental Hyg.*, Vol. 8 (1924): 26-54. F. Powdermaker, "Social Adjustment of the Feebleminded," *Annals, Am. Acad. Pol. and Soc. Sci.*, Vol. 149 (1930), Pt. 3, pp. 62-63. K. O. Milner, "Delinquent Types of Mentally Defective Persons," *Jour. Ment. Sci.*, Vol. 95 (1949): 842-859. A. M. Shotwell, "A Study of Psychopathic Delinquency," *Am. Jour. Ment. Def.*, Vol. 51 (1946-47): 57-62.

Manic-depressive psychoses are generally limited to the high grades, while schizophrenia appears in all grades except the lowest.

The chief effect of psychosis on the feebleminded is to hasten their deterioration. They become more untidy, erratic, destructive, excited, restless, and aggressive. They are mute more often and for longer periods, and other symptoms, too, are apt to be prolonged. These tendencies hold for all but the upper grades, whose behavior is more like the nondefective psychotic.

This combination of feeblemindedness and psychosis is illustrated in the disordered conduct of a boy seven years old. He is one of three children and he developed normally until his sixth year. There was no history of abnormality at birth or of the usual predisposing conditions and illness of the preschool years. He learned to walk and talk at an appropriate age, but he failed to make normal progress in talking after age four. At six, shortly after he began school, there is a record of a head injury about which little could be learned. Thereafter his conduct became so disorderly that he was transferred to a private school.

At this school he was diagnosed as a juvenile schizophrenic with mental deficiency, his I.Q. being 59. In school his work was often good with play materials, but it was regularly poor in academic subjects. His speech was slurred. Frequently he would not respond to questions at all. At times he would be noisy and then go to the other extreme of daydreaming. Other children irritated him and he never could learn to get along with them. His attention span was brief. The explanation for his low I.Q. was this inattentiveness and inability to respond to questions. Without the prolonged observation in this special school he would have been classified as being only mentally retarded. But with the additional cues noted in his play, compulsions, irritability, inattentiveness, and verbal blocking, the diagnosis of schizophrenia was indicated.

Study of the boy's family confirmed this diagnosis by discovering that the father and a brother had been in institutions for brief periods because of mental illness.

Custody, prevention, and control

Since feeblemindedness is the admitted result of a combination of hereditary and environmental conditions, the elements of a program to control them must pay attention to a variety of causes. Correlations between numerous other unsolved problems and feeblemindedness reinforce this need. However, society must never overlook the fact that the feebleminded continue to have a social significance for the same reasons that the poor are economically dependent and the sick are physically unfit. Competition puts too vigorous requirements upon each of these groups in demanding exactly what they do not have.

It is no longer considered profitable to show that the mentally deficient are economic, educational, and social misfits. Their classification is a blanket recognition of all these liabilities. For this reason society is encouraged to put aside its traditional belief that a certain minimum of the population must inevitably be of low calibre, and to substitute therefor a remedial and preventive program that is both efficient and acceptable to prevailing social standards.

Studies in causation have already been conducted with sufficient precision to show that the bulk of the feebleminded population is being produced by conditions that are wholly respectable. Not all, or even a majority, of defectiveness is a result of the universally deplored vices. When to this knowledge is added the fact that medical treatment (with a few notable exceptions) is ineffective, it becomes apparent that society is faced with the problem of prevention or complete control. From these circumstances one would assume that prevention would be welcomed, but such is not the case.

Under present conditions, education and special training are emphasized for the high-grade types; for the lower types, special training and institutionalization; and for the lowest grades simply permanent segregation. However, these suggested provisions are still largely objectives and are not systems already enforced. Because of the cost or because their families are reluctant to take advantage of this relief, only a small percentage of the feebleminded are institutionalized. It is estimated that about ninety-five per cent of the feebleminded remain in the community.

Hence, the community control of feeblemindedness is a major problem. This is the most serious consequence of a half-hearted program, and it appears rather ironic when the possibilities of this loose community supervision are contrasted with the current myths as to the hereditary menace of the defective. Apart from a preventive program to counteract those social processes that continue to add to the supply, there is no system other than institutionalization, even for some of the high-grade types. Yet this is precisely what the different states in this country have refused to adopt, and consequently the problem of supervision is largely the responsibility of the local community.

With the introduction of experimental programs, one of the first steps to be suggested was the placement of the feebleminded in the community, subject, however, to two provisions—adequate institutional training and continuous supervision. For economic reasons, trial placement has frequently been introduced, and this is the current policy of several states. Although placement is wholly tentative, three requirements are recognized as indispensable to the experiment: (1) ability to support oneself, (2) ability to regulate one's living without financial or supervisory assistance from family or agency, (3) ability to live without infringing upon the law to the extent of arrest and commitment to some correctional institution. Placement under supervision has proved to be a notorious failure. One survey of placement revealed success in fourteen per cent of the cases, but in these no common element could be found to account for the success. Success is not due to length of time spent in the institution, to the training received, mental age, emotional makeup, type of work, or supervision.[26]

A suggested alternative to permanent custodial care or failure in the community requires a combination of intensive training and supervision. What is needed is an industrial plant where the vocational training provided by institutions can be put into practice under supervision. Here the graduates of schools for the mentally handicapped could be employed, living either in their own homes or in colonies. Such a plan for the adjustment of the feebleminded has several favorable qualities, because it is not based upon the assumption that they must be adjusted to existing social conditions. A modified form of this idea has been conducted in London. It is patterned after industrial workshops, which have been in operation for the blind and crippled for some years. This substitute for institutionalization is more practical and humane and, from our present knowledge of the success of placement, is safer for the individuals who are employed in this manner.

[26] C. J. De Prospo and R. H. Hungerford, "A Complete Social Program for the Mentally Retarded," *Am. Jour. Ment. Def.,* Vol. 51 (1946-47): 115-122. L. S. Selling, "Use of Community Resources in a Small Community to Aid the Future Adjustment of Mentally Deficient Cases," *Am. Jour. Ment. Def.,* Vol. 54 (1949-50): 101-107. H. Neuer, "Prevention of Mental Deficiency," *Am. Jour. Ment. Def.,* Vol. 51 (1946-47): 721-730.

Among other remedial programs, the proper care of defective children is stressed as a first step towards prevention. In these programs there is provision for clinics where cases can be diagnosed early and where psychiatric and social studies can be conducted. The clinics are supplemented by hospitals, training and custodial institutions, and intensive supervision in the community. Medical care for the early diagnosis and correction of physical defects is, of course, imperative. Within recent years, particularly since the organization of behavior clinics, increasing attention is being given to habit training, and incidentally to the training and personal equipment of the social workers who are charged with the education and supervision of the defective child.

The undertakings of a community program, such as the Illinois or New York plans, include:

1. Improved facilities to identify the mentally deficient.
2. Centralization of supervision, care, and planning.
3. Specialization of institutional services to meet needs of the different classes.
4. Expansion of home and foster-home programs.
5. Increased emphasis upon the responsibilities of the public school system.
6. Education of the public for a better understanding of the entire problem.
7. Expansion of such rehabilitative services of the institution as vocational guidance, training, and placement.
8. Education of parents who have the custody of feebleminded children.
9. Teacher training.
10. Research.[27]

Preventive programs, which are recommended as supplements to custodial and community care, are concerned with health and education as well as with steps to reduce the number of the defective. One suggestion is improved maternal and child health through prenatal and postnatal care. Another is a direct campaign to control malnutrition, brain damage, endocrine disturbances, and meningitis, encephalitis, measles, and syphilis, all of which are accepted as direct causes. A third is improved medical and obstetrical service. A fourth is marriage counseling. A fifth includes the more radical suggestions of birth control, eugenics, and sterilization.

Advocates claim that eugenic sterilization is the only substitute

[27] E. L. Johnstone, "What Shall We Do with the Mentally Deficient?" *Mental Hyg.*, Vol. 30 (1947): 301-302.

for inadequate institutionalization and incomplete supervision, that it is the only preventive against the increase of defectiveness. Eugenic sterilization is the prevention of procreation, as distinguished from therapeutic sterilization, which is employed to improve the physical or mental condition of the person. The majority of state laws are eugenic; one half are eugenic and therapeutic; and some states apply their laws to a variety of conditions, such as mental disease, sexual perversion and drug addiction, and as a punishment for certain crimes. California still leads all states in eugenic sterilization, although it is estimated that the total number of mental defectives to whom this law is applied is considerably less than one per cent of the total.[28]

Summary

Mental deficiency is a general and permanent condition of social incompetency. It is an outgrowth of mental defects. These in turn may be a result of physical defects or arrested physical development, though this is not always demonstrable. As contrasted with other classes of social incompetents (the physically defective, such as the blind and the deaf, or those who are problems because of inadequate social environment), the feebleminded are a primary menace to sound social organization in so far as self-management and self-maintenance are demanded by society.

When the several problems of the feebleminded are clearly set forth, there is no apparent reason for placing them among the major social problems. From the standpoint of numbers involved, feeblemindedness cannot be so classified. Furthermore, its real seriousness rests upon the failure of the public to adopt sufficient preventive measures, the many biased and preconceived ideas concerning its sources and complications, and the absence of fundamental biological research as to its real nature.

Considering the advancement that has been made in the study of feeblemindedness during the last two decades, the changing attitude toward its social status as a community problem, and the rise of the

[28] F. O. Butler, "A Quarter of a Century's Experience in Sterilization of Mental Defectives in California," *Am. Jour. Ment. Def.*, Vol. 49 (1944-45): 508-513. I. B. Hill, "Sterilizations in Oregon," *Am. Jour. Ment. Def.*, Vol. 54 (1949-50): 399-403. M. Woodside, *Sterilization in North Carolina*, University of North Carolina Press, Chapel Hill, 1950. Other states reported with high rates of sterilization per 100,000 population are Georgia, Virginia, and Utah. Human Betterment Federation, *Newsletter*, Vol. 2, June 1951.

general opinion that some form of control is indispensable, the outlook for the eventual reduction of this problem is really hopeful. Even though at present there is no agreement upon any single preventive measure, it is nevertheless true that as general public health programs are expanded, control over the causes of feeblemindedness will be partially realized. On the whole, feeblemindedness is a problem of social policy. When humanitarianism permits the application of available knowledge, it will finally be classified among the rare and exceptional accidents.

During the current century the important steps toward this goal are: (1) invention and standardization of psychological tests (1904), (2) development of mental-hygiene and child-guidance clinics (1908), (3) speech correction in public schools (1911), (4) special classes for epileptics (1906), (5) first laws for selective sterilization (1909), (6) special educational provisions (1911), (7) expansion of state schools, (8) development of scales of social maturity (the Vineland Social Maturity Scale, 1935), (9) establishment of statewide programs for treatment and study, (10) the beginning of clinical research.

Bibliography

Buck, Pearl, *The Child Who Never Grew,* John Day, New York, 1950. The story of a mentally deficient child.

Kanner, L., *A Miniature Text-book of Feeblemindedness,* Child Care Publications, New York, 1949.

Overholser, W., and W. V. Richmond, *Handbook of Psychiatry,* Lippincott, Philadelphia, 1947. Chap. 4.

Penrose, L. S., *The Biology of Mental Defect,* Sidgwick and Jackson, London, 1949.

Sarason, S. B., *Psychological Problems in Mental Deficiency,* Harper, New York, 1949.

Spiegel, E. A. (Ed.), *Progress in Neurology and Psychiatry,* Grune and Stratton, New York, 1948. Chap. 28 is by C. E. Benda.

. . . . .

Doll, E. A., "What is a Moron?" *Jour. Ab. and Soc. Psych.,* Vol. 43 (1948): 495-501.

Farrell, M. J., "Need for Research in Mental Deficiency," *Dis. Nerv. Sys.,* Vol. 8 (1947): 118-122. The Rh factor.

Heilman, A. E., "Parental Adjustment to the Dull Handicapped Child," *Am. Jour. Ment. Def.,* Vol. 54 (1949-50): 556-562.

Jastak, J., "A Rigorous Criterion of Feeblemindedness," *Jour. Ab. and Soc. Psych.,* Vol. 44 (1949): 367-378.

Jensen, R. A., "Clinical Management of the Mentally Retarded Child and the Parents," *Am. Jour. Psychiatry,* Vol. 106 (1950): 830-833.

Lovell, C., and C. P. Ingram, "A High School Program for Mentally Retarded Adolescent Girls," *Jour. Ed. Res.,* Vol. 40 (1947): 574-582. The Rochester, N.Y., plan.

McKeon, R. M., "Mentally Retarded Boys in War Time," *Ment. Hyg.,* Vol. 30 (1946): 47-55.

Pense, A. W., "Developments in the New York State Program for the Institutionalized Care of the Mentally Defective," *Am. Jour. Ment. Def.,* Vol. 54 (1949-50): 26-30.

Tizard, M. A., and N. O'Connor, "Employability of High-Grade Mental Defectives," *Am. Jour. Ment. Def.,* Vol. 54 (1949-50): 563-576; Vol. 55 (1950): 144-157.

Whitney, E. A., "Historical Approach to the Subject of Mental Retardation," *Am. Jour. Ment. Def.,* Vol. 53 (1948-49): 419-424.

Wilder, J., "Malnutrition and Mental Deficiency," *Nerv. Child,* Vol. 3 (1943-44): 174-186.

Willoughby, R. R., "Rhode Island's Experiment in Registration," *Am. Jour. Ment. Def.,* Vol. 50 (1945-46): 121-125.

Wittman, J. V., "Intelligence Disorders of the Feebleminded," *Am. Jour. Ment. Def.,* Vol. 53 (1948-49): 610-616.

Questions

1. Why are the feebleminded not considered a homogeneous group?
2. Can you describe different situations in which a retarded person might be normal?
3. For what reasons does Fisher suggest five criteria of feeblemindedness? Give examples and problems that are peculiar to each criterion.
4. Which types of the defective are the most obvious because of their appearance?
5. What is pseudo-feeblemindedness and its probable causes?
6. State the essential abilities and limitations of the moron.
7. What does Halperin's list of causes suggest as to the social nature of feeblemindedness? Its biological nature? Its association with brain damage?
8. Do studies of prevalence show that feeblemindedness is increasing?
9. What is the sex distribution of feeblemindedness?
10. What are the chief differences in the interpretations of cause today and in the 1880's?
11. In the question of the constancy of the I.Q., whose point of view do you find most credible?
12. What is familial feeblemindedness?
13. In what type of families do most idiots and imbeciles appear?
14. Do idiots and imbeciles reproduce their kind?
15. What is the normal family's reaction to the birth of a mentally deficient child? Does it tend to discourage further reproduction?

16. Do you accept the findings relative to fathers' occupations and children's intelligence?
17. What are the liabilities of the typical moron on the job? Do morons have as good a work record as the physically handicapped?
18. Would it be reasonable to say that a certain crime was committed by an insane idiot?
19. Compare the Rochester plan with the prospects indicated by Miss Schmidt's study.
20. Can you construct a program that would be both socially acceptable and sociologically approved?

PART 2

PROBLEMS ACCENTED BY AGE

Introduction

THE AGING OF A PEOPLE CALLS ATTENTION TO TWO BROAD CLASSES OF problems. The first is personal and deals with the problems of the aging individual. The second includes those of aging populations.

No population or social class is exempt from the hazards of these changes. Hence the continuous search for adjustments or compensations. Insurance statisticians do not hesitate to suggest that these problems are the kind that either the individual or society can anticipate and, to some extent at least, control through timely precautions.

In this section, four illustrative problems are selected—the problems of average children, of delinquents, of college students, and of the aged.

Nearly every social observer has noted the inevitable correlates of aging. Shakespeare both named and defined the several ages of man and described most of their current liabilities. In his novel, *H. M. Pulham, Esq.*, Marquand went a step further and discussed some of the personal reactions to aging and some of the social changes that aging brings about in the family and in relations between parents and children.

Questions of both types of aging are numerous. They appear under such titles as the new criminality, the lost generation, new diseases, emancipated women or classes, the crisis of the child, the insecurity of the aged, forgotten people, the perils of the gifted individual, the submerged tenth—or possibly third—of a population, or the dangerous age. Analysis of such problems almost always proceeds through comparison: new challenges versus the routine of a simpler society—challenges to which both societies and individuals must adjust if they are to reach their full expectation of life.

CHAPTER 6

CHILDREN'S PROBLEMS

A LOT IS KNOWN ABOUT THE MAJOR PROBLEMS OF CHILDREN BECAUSE they receive the attention of the experts. These problems are the critical disorders that bring the child to clinic, hospital, or custodial institution where physical, mental, or social problems can be explored thoroughly. But the needs for adjustment or the minor problems of the child at home or in his other social contacts are comparatively unstudied. Yet some of the most perplexing questions of child care develop from these physical, mental, emotional, and social liabilities of the average child. They demand early detection and prompt treatment if they are to be prevented from becoming major obstacles to successful adjustment in the upper age groups.

Since the recognition and initial treatment of these problems are almost wholly in the control of parents, they are often neglected in the hope that they will be outgrown. Or, worst of all, parents and teachers sometimes interpret the symptoms of many difficult problems as evidences of sound discipline and wise management. For either reason, problems of the average child may run their course and reach a stage that defies the resources of the specialist in guidance.

Therefore the chief aim of current programs in child welfare is to show what the problems of normal children are, the age when they may be expected, their frequency, severity, and duration, and the guides that parents may employ in organizing an effective routine in child care. Each of these is basic to a preventive program, since two of the best precautions that parents can observe are to know

(1) the approximate range of problems to which the average child is exposed, and (2) when these problems usually occur as a normal part of his growth.

The normal child and his needs

Each year since 1900 the average or normal child has been one of two to four million children in the same age group. In 1900 the total number of children born was about 2,750,000. The number born each year varies because of such factors as the declining birth rate and the variations in marriage rates due to business depressions and wars. In the past five decades the largest number of births was nearly four million, in 1947. In the table below, the proportions of children in the different age groups are given for 1940 and 1950; estimates for the year 1955 show some of the effects of the changing birth rate. From the point of view of numbers alone, it is clear that child care is a major national enterprise.

AGE GROUPS OF CHILDREN AND YOUTH IN THE POPULATION OF THE UNITED STATES

Age Groups	*Per Cent Distribution of the Total Population*		
Years	*1940*	*1950*	*1955*
0–4	8.0	10.8	7.8
5–9	8.1	8.8	10.5
10–14	8.9	7.5	8.9
15–19	9.4	7.1	7.3
Total number (000 omitted) under 20 years of age	45,327	51,658	53,778

Source: United States Bureau of the Census, "Forecasts of Population and School Enrollment in the United States," *Current Population Reports,* Series, P-25, No. 18, Feb. 14, 1949, p. 12; United States Bureau of the Census, "General Characteristics of the Population of the United States," *Preliminary Reports,* Series PC-7, No. 1, Feb. 25, 1951, p. 6.

Another noteworthy observation that is important in a study of the problems these children may not avoid is that most of them are normal. This statement does not mean that the majority of children are alike or normal in the same respects. They are, however, normal within many degrees of difference.

A child is called "normal" in spite of the fact that he may be handicapped by numerous minor defects or temporary illnesses, or by life in a home where the personalities of the parents and the variations of economic and social position of his family may favor or deter his social growth. His status as an average or normal child is conceded when his defects (physical, mental, emotional, and social) do not fall below the minimum limits of four tests.[1] These tests of normal or average social adaptability are derived from (1) physical tests of bodily efficiency and absence of disease, (2) mental tests of intellectual normality, (3) relative freedom from neurotic and psychotic symptoms, and (4) emotional maturity. A direct test of a child's social maturity or adjustment is suggested by his behavior and his responses to the following questions: Does the child's difficulty persist too long? Does he fail to respond to common-sense methods of management? Is his conduct logical and appropriate to his social situation?

No census has ever ventured an exact estimate of the number of babies who are normal at birth. But by age five or six and for the school population as a whole, the consensus of the experts is that eighty per cent or possibly eighty-five per cent of all children are normal. This is the proportion of the children who are exempt from the designation subnormal, but who are candidates to be the victims of all the other social difficulties that are predicted in such sober actuarial terms as: (1) one million will have serious mental breakdowns, (2) four to five millions will be criminals; (3) two to

"He's three weeks ahead of Karen when she was his age, one week behind Ricky, six days ahead of George, four days behind Samuel, two days up on Henry, and eight days behind Alex That makes him just about normal."

Reproduced by permission of Better Homes & Gardens. *Copyrighted.*

[1] M. Levene, "Normality and Maturity," *The Family,* Vol. 21 (1940-41): 18-19.

fifteen per cent will be unemployed at various times in their lives.

As a rule, the child who is going to become one of the liabilities can de detected in advance. He is the child who is slow to achieve the basic habits of infant hygiene. As a preschool child, he is inclined to have difficulties in his play groups. As a school child, he continues to have the same difficulties in making favorable adjustments with other children. He is usually retarded in learning. He is inattentive and is apt to have numerous conduct disorders both at home and in school. The same varieties of social immaturity continue to appear during adolescence and in young adulthood. This type of individual, regardless of his age, is the one who is repeatedly confused by his own difficulties. When they are pointed out to him, he fails to understand them; he is apt to rebel against authority and usually does not respond well to suggested treatment.

These everyday difficulties of the child and of the adults who are responsible for him are to be located in each area of problems outlined in Chapter 1 as the common hazards of all people.[2] These are the ordinary obstacles in social adjustment that society often fails to recognize as problems either because the majority of children succeed in making satisfactory accommodation or because they acquire adequate compensations.

There are two other indications of problems in prospect for the average person. They usually involve common everyday social relations, and they are basically social rather than problems of illness, mental disturbance, or emotional tension.

The needs of the child, as they are determined by standards of adult responsibility, point out the likely sources of handicaps in the future and the challenges to education and guidance. According to the Educational Policies Commission of the National Education Association, the needs of all youth are:

1. Education for civic responsibility and competence.
2. Understanding of family relationships.
3. Understanding of the main elements of American culture.
4. Instruction in healthful living.
5. Occupational guidance and training and orientation to current economic conditions.
6. Development of rational thinking.
7. Insight into ethical values.[3]

[2] See Chap. 1, above, p. 8.

[3] *Education for All American Youth,* National Education Association, Washington, 1944, pp. 16-17.

Religious and moral values play an important part in human behavior. Nevertheless, the impact of such values on the development of the child has not received the same attention by the students of child development, as biological or emotional factors.

By age three or four the child begins to have some realization of the religious factors in the culture. No child can ignore these religious matters completely. Parents who are antagonistic to organized church groups must make decisions on what to teach their children concerning the nature of religion. Recognizing the need that children have to conform to the group, many such parents are caught on the horns of a dilemma. In many respects the problems associated with moral and religious values, as they are to be taught to children, are not children's problems but parents' problems.

Since World War II, there is evidence of an increasing awareness by the American people of the need for a reaffirmation of religious and moral concepts. In the opinion of large numbers, "science can not save us." The unleashing of the power of the atom has caused a questioning of the values by which men live. Such historical incidents make the question of religious training for the young an important one.

Children learn to react to religious and moral issues as adults teach them to react. When parents have differing religious and moral insights, the differences are reflected by conflicts in the children. It is probably true that unless adults can give to children religious and moral insights which have meaning to them, a significant area of adjustment is being neglected.

What are their prospects?

What the experts in child study establish as the needs of children are essentially the same as the hopes of parents. The child should have a sound body, good health, mental ability, emotional balance and control. He should have what may be called social intelligence or maturity proportionate to his age, together with the social relations essential to the acquiring of this maturity. These qualities, on the one hand, are the goals of child care, and, on the other, the measures by which a child's deficiencies can be detected or anticipated.

An inventory of the characteristics of normal social growth that are the specific standards or goals of child-rearing includes a reasonably adequate share of:

1. Strength and vitality
2. Skill in bodily coordination
3. Independence and originality
4. Alertness in play or work
5. Curiosity and imagination
6. Persistence in an assigned task
7. Ability to profit by experience
8. Ability to apply experience to new situations
9. Good self-expression without being self-conscious
10. Emotional poise
11. Ability to get along well with others
12. Popularity in peer groups
13. Reliability
14. Ability to adjust to changing conditions
15. Ability to defend his own rights and to adjust to authority
16. Neatness and cleanliness

An inventory of the negative qualities of the average child is supplied by the opposites of these characteristics. In various combinations they distinguish three special classes or sources of children's problems.

One type includes the conditions that have their origin in infancy or early childhood. They are the problems that do not disappear with growth as rapidly as the accepted rate of social maturing requires. Unadjustments of this kind appear in health and bodily vigor, emotional control, learning, and social habits. They can be separated from those of the next class as being less social in origin but equally social in their effects.

A second type includes those problems that are the direct outcomes of faulty social learning. The child is unable to develop an independence and social competence that his chronological age demands. Failures in this area and period of growth take on exaggerated significance the longer that they persist. In turn, they become the causes of many perplexing inferiorities and frustrations in adolescence and adulthood.

The third class of children's problems is less specific. They are the temporary problems and mistakes that most children will experience in passing from one age group to the next, as for example in leaving home for school, entering high school with its different academic and social requirements, going to college, or choosing and finding employment. Socially average or superior children are readily detected by their ability to meet these situations with considerable poise and maturity.

Since this class of problems includes the minor irritations, annoying mannerisms, and unpleasant habits that adults dislike to discover, the children in this category are also easily observed. They are the ones who enter school with numerous infantile habits and who reach adolescence or adulthood without sufficient maturity to eliminate these disagreeable characteristics or to make adequate compensations for them. As a rule, the social adjustability of this class of people is limited in the same sense as if they were impaired physically. For them social adjustment often means isolation in a few social groups that can tolerate their inadequate personalities and marginal social acceptability.

Areas of childhood insecurity

Parents, who have the best opportunity to observe and record the problems of children, rarely take time to make this contribution to child study. As a result, teachers, physicians, psychiatrists, and psychologists who meet children in groups are the primary observers and reporters. In recent years they have come to the conclusion that most of the social disorders of the child are outcomes of his social contacts. If a school child of average family background is failing to acquire the social habits necessary to normal maturing, in eight out of ten instances the reasons are to be found in his social relations; in the two other instances the explanation is either poor health or inferior intelligence.

Most of these problems, whether they are recognized at first as mild or serious disorders, are usually described as being the results of "poor training and discipline." This diagnosis is a useful guide. It indicates, or confirms the agreement of observers as to, the chief sources of problems. At the same time it suggests the methods of prevention or, if unable to prevent the problems, the course of treatment.

These problems are classified in Tables 1 and 2 on the following pages. In a few instances the same problem appears in both tables in order to show either its severity or time of onset. Table 1 gives the comparatively serious problems, and Table 2, the less serious but comparatively frequent problems of normal children. They are separated according to their primary sources as physical and health, mental and emotional, and social conditions.

The criterion of severity in Table 1 is the difficulty of treatment, prevention, or social adjustment. Occasionally a problem in this category immediately classifies the child as subnormal. Often, however, these problems are no more than symptoms of underlying and obscure defects.

Conditions listed in Table 2 are generally of the milder variety, which in many instances would not be called problems. They deserve and are given attention because of their complications. Sometimes they can be as critical as the most obstinate of the maladjusting disorders.

TABLE 1

COMPARATIVELY SERIOUS PROBLEMS OF CHILDREN

Age Groups	*Physical and Health*	*Mental and Emotional*	*Social*
1 to 5 years The preschool child	Rickets Undernutrition Vitamin and mineral deficiencies Blindness Deafness Speech defects Rheumatic fever Allergies Encephalitis	Mental deficiency Epilepsy Food fads and unusual food habits Temper tantrums Tics	Poverty Broken homes Rejected children Running away
6 to 11 years The school child	Appendicitis Meningitis Enuresis Poliomyelitis Accidents	Convulsions Vomiting Cruelty Fire setting	School problems Over-age pupils Retardation Truancy
12 to 17 years The adolescent	Deviations from normal growth Malnutrition Muscular and skeletal defects Heart disease	Sex problems Neurotic personality	Stealing Delinquency
18 to 24 years The young adult	Tuberculosis Pneumonia		

Reading the problems in their vertical arrangement gives some idea as to their onset or the severity of the complications at a later age. Rheumatic fever in the preschool period and heart disease during adolescence are one example of this sequence. Reading them horizontally indicates to some extent how problems of one class may lead to or aggravate problems in the other classes. The sequence between the deafness of children and their rejection has already been mentioned. Another sequence is undernutrition or malnutrition, food fads, and school problems.

TABLE 2

Relatively Frequent Problems

Age Groups	*Physical and Health*	*Mental and Emotional*	*Social*
The preschool child	Weaning Eating Sleeping Elimination Enuresis Teething Defects of ear, eye, and teeth Allergies Colds Bronchitis Chicken pox Diphtheria Measles Mumps Pneumonia Influenza Scarlet fever Whooping cough Digestive diseases Accidents Poor posture Poor nutrition	Thumb sucking Nail biting Fatigue Excitability Too active Negativism Teasing Screaming Whining Nagging Speech defects Nervousness Excessive crying Temper tantrums Masturbation Emotional dependency	Family problems Parental mismanagement Interferences of relatives Inadequate supervision Oversolicitude Domination Jealousy Aggressiveness Resistiveness Anger Disobedience Quarreling Fears Lying School problems
6 to 11 years The school child	Poor appetite Poor eating habits Defective vision Eyestrain Defective tonsils Tooth decay	Showing off Inattentiveness Problems of sex	Inability to get along with other children, to make friends, to play, to use money Lack of respect for property Failure to cooperate Bad companions Conflicting cultural standards
12 to 17 years The adolescent	Inadequate diet Accidents Poor posture Skin diseases Colds Bronchitis Liability to heart strain	Laziness Indifference Lack of ambition Overconfidence Fatigue Immaturity (childishness) Worries	Conflicts with parents Inadequate family life Academic problems Inadequate leisure-time activities

Age Groups	*Physical and Health*	*Mental and Emotional*	*Social*
			Choice and preparation for vocation Preparation for marriage No scholastic aptitude Inadequate social knowledge
18 to 24 years The young adult			Homesickness Ignorance of vocational opportunities Inability to see and understand own problems

Both tables are primarily useful for illustrative purposes. As analytical guides, they are obviously limited. In the first place, the indication of the time of onset is only approximate. However, if any problem is known to occur at some other time, as for example heart disease before age five, unusual fears during the middle grade-school period, or inattentiveness during adolescence, invariably this oddity in timing will be an important clue to the problem's severity and resistance to treatment. Other trends that the tables do not show too precisely are how problems can be intensified and become chronic, how a problem in one class, such as a health problem, can lead to an emotional problem and then to a problem of social retardation, or how combinations of problems can take place. These defects in the tables point to the need for further studies that are either adequate samples or controlled comparisons.

Personal and behavior problems

After infancy, each period and each year are subjected to increasingly exacting social tests. As the array of social liabilities in the tables shows, the possibilities for social maladjustment are more numerous than are the hazards of physical or mental health. During the preschool years, the individual must eliminate the dependence and other immaturities of the infant in order to be prepared for school. During the grade-school years, self-discipline in addition to the tools of learning must be acquired in preparation for adolescence and high school. During adolescence, the other foundations of the adult years are to be achieved. They include, in conjunction with the fundamentals for further education, the bases of vocational choice, adjustment to an occupation, courtship, and marriage.

In each of these age groups, an indication of serious unadjustment is the inability to get rid of the traits and habits of the previous period and the tendency to carry them over into years when they are wholly out of place. Radical examples are the school child who acts as if he were scarcely weaned or the adolescent who cannot read and who continues to depend on his parents for sixth-grade levels of guidance. The same social retardation is found in the college population and in adulthood. It explains the jealousies, temper tantrums, sensitivities, and other immaturities in these age groups.

The preschool child has to learn first of all how to get along with other children and with a few adults other than parents. In this training the values of the play group and kindergarten are demonstrated. According to the reports of observations of children in these groups, the ten most common problems of the preschool age are:

1. Temper displays
2. Feeding problems
3. Disobedience
4. Stubbornness
5. Enuresis
6. Sulking, crying, or whining
7. Finger sucking or nail biting
8. Being too dependent on adults
9. Sleep problems
10. Destructiveness [4]

Most of these difficulties are results of inadequate training and guidance prior to the preschool period. All of them are indexes of conditions that interfere with the child's sociability and with his social acceptance by adults.

Even in these early years there are distinctive sex differences. Boys are reported with a greater share of conduct disorders than girls. Of their particular shortcomings, questions of obedience and conflicts with authority are the most numerous. The preschool girl more often than the boy is the victim of fears and anxieties.

If the preschool child is usually friendly with other children and makes his contacts with some degree of ease and poise, and if he has a good personal appearance and the beginnings of a sense of

[4] Ethel Kawin, *Children of Preschool Age,* University of Chicago Press, Chicago, 1934. Adapted from pp. 265-266. See also: W. Wolff, *The Personality of the Pre-School Child,* Grune and Stratton, New York, 1946.

humor, he is generally given a passing grade for admission to the school group. But if he fails in these tests or if he has frequent changes of mood or makes contacts too aggressively or too timidly, these traits are regarded as the likely symptoms of later maladjustment.

The grade-school child. This period is important because of its continuous demands on the child for balanced growth. As a matter of fact, the middle years of childhood represent a period of significant physical growth and emotional maturing as well as of social growth and academic learning. But only recently have schools begun to give attention to the social needs and development of the grade-school child. Entering school is in Gesell's opinion a sociological event [5] by which he means a critical social test of the child's capacity for complete growth.

If the immaturities of the six-year-old are compared with the mature traits of the twelve-year-old, the reasons for Gesell's opinion are readily understood. There is no period of growth when the child is submitted to more exacting requirements, not the least of which are the social acquisitions of interests, self-control, and understanding of group relationships. In these requirements, the grade-school period has acquired some of the responsibilities hitherto assigned exclusively to adolescence.

The primary problems of the grade-school child are therefore defects and failures in social growth, the more frequent difficulties being:

1. Lying
2. Inability to get along with other children
3. Shyness
4. Enuresis
5. Daydreaming
6. School work below ability
7. Inattentiveness
8. Truancy
9. Stealing
10. Overactivity [6]

Explanations of these problems from the standpoint of their origins are derived from (1) the child's family, including an inventory of parents' problems to show how they are transferred directly to the child, (2) the child's own personality makeup, as judged by

[5] Arnold Gesell and F. L. Ilg, *The Child from Five to Ten,* Harper, New York, 1946. Chaps. 6-10 give the norms of achievement for each of the grade-school years.

[6] M. J. Fitz-Simons, *Some Parent-Child Relationships,* Teachers College, Columbia University, New York, 1935. Adapted from Table 21, pp. 92-93.

physical health, personality, mood, and intelligence, (3) the child's social relations, as noted in his conduct at school, in his companions and play participation, in his failures in school subjects, and in his delinquencies.

Traits of good adjustment during the grade-school years are: self-reliance, self-confidence, sense of personal security, social skills, and an absence of nervous symptoms and withdrawing tendencies. When the average child is examined for these characteristics and a minimum of the typical problems of this period, rural children on the whole are reported with a better score in social adjustment than urban children.[7]

Adolescence can be defined as a period of emotional growth and social maturing as well as of physical growth. The problems of adolescence, accordingly, may be of two broad kinds: one, the failure to achieve adolescent expectations in any of these respects, and second, the inability to acquire the standards that adults have established.

Either deficiency usually points to unresolved problems of prior age groups. Immediate tests of an adolescent's success are his demonstrated abilities and skills in meeting the obligations and in making the decisions of this age, such as continuing in formal education, beginning vocational training and preparing for an occupation, deciding whether to go to college and choosing the college, mastering the characteristic emotional puzzles of this period, developing friendships, and sometimes in marrying.

It is the experience of nearly all adolescents to have difficulty in meeting some of these problems through their own devices, in knowing when to accept advice and when to resent it, and, finally, in steering a course midway between enthusiasms and ignorance when questions of confused values and contradictory community standards are observed.

Whenever conditions of adolescent inferiority are enumerated, they generally include such common complaints as ineffective study habits, too much time spent in recreation or entertainment, lack of vocational interests, need for sex instruction, unfavorable home backgrounds, problems of physical health, and questions about

[7] A. R. Mangus, "Personality Adjustment of Rural and Urban Children," *Am. Sociol. Rev.*, Vol. 13 (1948): 566-575. L. A. Pechstein and D. M. Munn, "Measurement of Social Maturity," *El. School Jour.*, Vol. 40 (1939-40): 113-126.

friendships and dating—problems in many respects like those that demonstrate inferior ability and achievement in earlier years.

Traits of the adolescent that are cited as the best evidence of sound social development are:

1. Mental ability
2. Studiousness and ability to remember
3. Persistence
4. Accuracy
5. Ability to work independently
6. Desire to do good work
7. Social maturity
8. Ability to plan [8]

Characteristics of the mature adolescent are:

1. Ability to see things from the point of view of other people.
2. Objectivity toward one's self.
3. Ability to select suitable, long-term goals.
4. Ability to make adjustments to situations.
5. Ability to meet unexpected stresses and disappointments.
6. Ability to give as well as to receive affection.
7. Ability to form opinions based upon sound reasoning.[9]

Vocational interests and problems

Most children of high-school age have little or no knowledge about occupations or about the training or requirements for admission to different occupations or professions. As a rule, they are most familiar with the traditional occupations or professions of their community or with those which for the moment have unusual prestige. Their initial choices, consequently, are mainly concentrated on a few of the most overcrowded occupations, and the result is that there is almost always a lot of difference between the vocations that they enter and their original vocational choices.

Boys are most likely to choose professions or clerical and public-service occupations in excess of the opportunities in these fields. They are also inclined to follow their fathers' occupations when these occupations have prestige or when they are traditional in the community. Girls choose such occupations as teaching and clerical and secretarial work. In many inventories of occupational choices—which are primarily important because they indicate the need for

[8] H. G. Gough, "Factors Relating to the Academic Achievement of High School Students," *Jour. Educa. Psych.*, Vol. 40 (1949): 65-76.

[9] Ruth Strang, "Manifestations of Maturity in Adolescents," *Mental Hyg.*, Vol. 33 (1949): 566-569.

vocational guidance—one-third to one-half of the high-school boys and girls will choose professions first.[10]

In addition to the questionable wisdom of their initial choice, other vocational maladjustments are the selection of a vocation that is poorly suited to the individual's health or personality, that is beyond his skills either manual or academic, that is above or below his intelligence, that has requirements for further training that the individual cannot afford, or that is selected under the dominance of parental persuasion.

There are five trends in the vocational choices of adolescents that also serve to clarify some of their difficulties. One is the tendency already noted to select occupations which are supposed to have greater social prestige than those of their parents, without regard for the opportunities or demands of such vocations. A second observation is that as adolescents mature they become more realistic in their choices. The third is that individuals of lower intelligence regularly make the most errors in vocational choice, and, conversely, the fourth is that children of high intelligence have the highest vocational aims and the best choices. The fifth is that girls tend to be more realistic than boys in choosing vocations that have the most openings and that are in closest agreement with their intelligence and school work.

Summary

Although the increasing interests in child welfare have labeled the past several decades as the century of the child, little is known in an objective way about his problems. The reasons for this lack of information are not hard to find. Too often, current knowledge is based upon conditions of the child that can be examined because children assemble in certain places where they can be observed. Other habits and problems peculiar to the more inaccessible situations are neglected.

Another obstacle to objective social study of the child is in the point of departure. Sometimes the studies are based on inspiration

[10] R. E. Eckert and T. O. Marshall, *When Youth Leave School,* McGraw-Hill, New York, 1938, p. 229. W. A. Bradley, "Correlates of Vocational Preferences," *Genetic Psych. Mono.,* Vol. 28 (1943): 101-169. M. E. Young, "Some Sociological Aspects of Vocational Guidance of Negro Children," *Jour. Negro Educa.,* Vol. 15 (1946): 21-30.

or sentiment, controversial philosophical approaches, or prejudiced and one-sided observations.

Another zone of confusion is the original nature of the materials to be studied. The American family is not a unit in composition, social status, economic position, culture, or interests. In addition to this diversity in the most socializing of the child's contacts, it must be recalled that many children do not understand or live by the values of their parents or of adults as a class. Parents and other adults often establish rules for the child that they would rarely accept for themselves. Moreover, regardless of their origin, values and rules change in contemporary society, either through the impact of changing culture or through temporary upsets in the household when parents are worried, confused, or tired.

In Tables 1 and 2 the conditions and difficulties of child care are summarized to show the usual problems and questions that parents bring to the specialist.

As Table 1 indicates, the onset of some of the serious problems would remove the child immediately from the range of the normal. Such is true in the case of feeblemindedness, epilepsy, and possibly such an apparently inoffensive disorder as truancy. With only a difference of degree, the same observation can be made about some of the minor problems in Table 2. Unless they are detected and treated in time, they can create conditions of social maladjustment that are as subtle, complicated, and demoralizing as some of the more obvious disorders. As a rule, however, these developmental complications have to become so serious that their first recognized appearances are in cases of family disorganization, educational or occupational maladjustment in the young adult years, mental breakdowns, or criminal conduct.

Both tables tend to reinforce each other in stressing the critical nature of the child's early training, especially if it is inferior. In this respect the relationship between parent and child is no different than in earlier generations. The reason for current emphasis upon this relationship is that all the evidence of child study has shown that no other background of the child is of equal significance in his successful social adjustment. Because of this conclusion, the observation is made that "a child's level of adjustment depends little upon the extrinsic features of the day and little even upon his health. It depends much more upon the wholesomeness of his upbringing in the home, . . . the security and confidence and affection given him by his parents."[11] It is the child without this background who gives the impression of inadequacy and immaturity in his encounter with new experiences.

Resources now available for the study and treatment of the problems of children include a number of research agencies, child-guidance clinics, the visiting-teacher division of the public school system, private child-welfare agencies and protective services, character-building agencies, organized recreational opportunities, and vocational and employment offices.[12]

Bibliography

Ackerson, Luton, *Children's Behavior Problems,* University of Chicago Press, Chicago, 1942.

Bossard, J. H. S., *The Sociology of Child Development,* Harper, New York, 1948.

Child Study Association of America, *Parents' Questions,* Harper, New York, 1947.

Dennis, Wayne, "The Adolescent," Chap. 12 in L. Carmichael (Ed.), *Manual of Child Psychology,* Wiley, New York, 1946.

Langdon, G., and I. W. Stout, *These Well-Adjusted Children,* John Day, New York, 1951.

Lozier, R. V., *Pointers for Parents,* Lippincott, Philadelphia, 1947.

Midcentury White House Conference on Children and Youth, *Children and Youth at the Midcentury,* National Publishing Company, Washington, 1950.

Zeligs, Rose, *Glimpses into Child Life,* William Morrow, New York, 1942.

. . . . .

Gardner, G. E., "Mental Health of Normal Adolescents," *Mental Hyg.,* Vol. 31 (1947): 529-540.

[11] M. A. Shirley, "Children's Adjustments to a Strange Situation," *Jour. Abn. and Soc. Psych.,* Vol. 37 (1942): 217.

[12] In addition to governmental agencies, the following suggest the developments in this field: American Academy of Pediatrics; Child Welfare League; Child Study Association of America; National Congress of Parents and Teachers; National Council on Family Relations; Play Schools Association; Boy Scouts and Girl Scouts; Alliance for Guidance of Rural Youth; American Youth Hostels; Young Adult Council of the National Social Welfare Assembly; Save the Child Federation; Elizabeth McCormick Memorial Fund (an organization established in Chicago in 1908 to promote programs in all aspects of child care, research, and training of personnel).

Maddy, N. R., "Comparison of Children's Personality Traits, Attitudes, and Intelligence with Parental Occupations," *Genetic Psych. Mono.*, Vol. 27 (1943): 3-65.

Midcentury White House Conference, "Child and Youth at Midcentury," *Jour. Home Econ.*, Vol. 42 (1950): 710-713.

Minnesota Commission on Higher Education, *Higher Education in Minnesota,* University of Minnesota Press, Minneapolis, 1950. Chapter 5, "What Happens to Minnesota's High School Graduates—Nine Years Later."

Schwartzman, J., "Abnormalities of Adolescence," *Jour. Pediat.*, Vol. 21 (1942): 93-102.

Williams, M. J., "Personal and Familial Problems of High School Youths," *Social Forces,* Vol. 27 (1949): 279-285.

Questions

1. Why is it that parents are often slow to recognize problems in their own children?
2. How are the so-called serious problems of children identified and distinguished?
3. Do you recognize any similarity in the socially adjusting traits of preschool, grade-school, and high-school students?
4. Is it possible to predict success in college by a student's record in high-school or earlier years? Consult: Phearman, L. T., "Comparisons of High-School Graduates Who Go to College with Those Who Do Not," *Jour. Educa. Psychol.*, Vol. 40 (1949): 405-414.
5. How is the definition of normal children formulated?
6. What are some of the primary responsibilities of the family in child-training?
7. Is there any demonstrated relationship between the economic and social status of the family and the child's school record? His school problems? His occupational choice?
8. Is there any demonstrated relationship between a child's sociability and his success in school work?
9. What are some of the indications of a child's sociability?
10. Why do observers report more conduct disorders among boys and more emotional disorders among girls?
11. Do teachers, parents, and psychiatrists tend to differ or agree on the basic needs and problems of children?
12. As you review the history of child study and guidance, do you agree that both are subject to criticism under the caption "too little and too late"?
13. What trends in the nineteenth century tended to focus interest on the child and his problems?

14. What has happened to the notion that adolescence is a period of unusual stress and strain?
15. Can you suggest a course of child-training that would minimize or eliminate parent-youth conflict?

CHAPTER 7

JUVENILE DELINQUENCY

JUVENILE DELINQUENCY IS A SUBJECT OF CONTINUOUS POPULAR APPEAL. It is regarded as a major personal problem or as a dismal social failure. Analysis proceeds from several points of view.

There is the one-word interpretation: neglect.

Sometimes it is described as a direct result of learning from adult misconduct. The child is as little inclined to obey rules as his parents.

From a broader perspective, delinquency is identified with various behavior disorders of children. It is of the serious, aggressive variety.

Another definition has it that delinquency is a new problem. It arises with new values, new rights, new responsibilities, and the new social and moral risks of contemporary society.

Harry—seven years old, of normal intelligence, and with no medical or psychological disturbances—illustrates each of these interpretations. His parents referred him to an agency, because they were unable to manage him. There he showed the typical delinquent symptoms of confusion, tension, and conduct disorders.

Outstanding trends in his background were truancy, running away, stealing, and continuous mischief. At home he was disorderly, destructive, and aggressive.

After Harry entered a training school, his parents were divorced. The mother was described as an unhappy, unadjusted person who rejected Harry, although she admired his aggressiveness. The father, also a social misfit, was an alcoholic and abusive, but remorseful and submissive when sober.

Harry, therefore, is a perfect example of domestic discord, disorderly conduct, parental neglect, adult demoralization, complete rejection, and delinquency.[1]

Similarities between crime and delinquency [2]

Delinquency is separated from adult crime by an imaginary division that is based upon the assumption that age is related to increasing responsibility. The question of responsibility in either crime or delinquency has been debated for many generations. Its only importance is to show that delinquency is one aspect of the problems of crime. Like criminals, children are also held accountable for their misconduct.

In addition to early onset, crime and delinquency have many features in common. According to estimates of the statisticians, two per cent of all children have unusually severe behavior problems, eighty per cent of the behavior-problem children become delinquent, and eighty per cent of juvenile delinquents become criminals.

This record of social disorders during the early years of childhood becomes an important clue when attention is given to the enormous proportion of criminals who are in the age group from sixteen or eighteen to twenty-one. This fact alone is sufficient to convince almost everyone that there is something exceptionally wrong in a population or a society that can produce so many maladjusted youth.

Rates of recidivism (the repeaters) are also high in groups of both delinquents and criminals. Moreover, their distribution in certain economic and social classes is also fairly similar. Consequently, the administrative problems regarding repression and prevention are identical for each group. Other comparable traits are their evident and serious economic and social wastes, the complete failure of detention institutions in the treatment of their subjects, and the current inability to distinguish absolute types of potential criminals

[1] B. Bettelheim, "Harry—A Study in Rehabilitation," *Jour. Abn. and Soc. Psych.*, Vol. 44 (1949): 231-265. Although this case is cited at this point as a brief introduction to problems presented, it is actually an example of psychiatric analysis and treatment.

[2] L. J. Carr, *Delinquency Control,* Harper, New York, 1940. M. H. Neumeyer, *Juvenile Delinquency in Modern Society,* D. Van Nostrand, New York, 1949. T. Sellin (Ed.), *Juvenile Delinquency,* American Academy Political and Social Science, Philadelphia, 1949. C. R. Shaw and H. D. McKay, *Juvenile Delinquency and Urban Areas,* University of Chicago Press, Chicago, 1942. P. W. Tappan, *Juvenile Delinquency,* McGraw-Hill, New York, 1949.

among either juveniles or adults. Because of the last point of similarity, criminologists are prone to make crime essentially a product of social conditions, and hence preventable. The possibility of prevention is further indicated by the fact that there is a fairly definite sequence between juvenile delinquency and adult criminality. If a person is able to complete his apprenticeship to adulthood without developing criminal habits, he is almost certain not to begin thereafter.

A summary of comparable traits between crime and delinquency indicates their difference as one of degree only. It contributes also to our understanding of the crime wave. The basis of the crime wave is actually a matter of age. Its upward movement begins in youth; increases through the adolescent years, reaching its peak during the first two or three years of maturity; and declines gradually from this period until forty, after which its decline is rapid.

Juvenile delinquency is viewed solemnly, not because of any special difficulty inherent in its diagnosis or treatment, but because it reflects other forms of social disorganization that are its causes. Delinquency includes more than the direct violation of rules approved by society. Lying, stealing, truancy, running away from home, precocious sex habits, and a host of minor offensive behavior traits are forms of delinquency, or their immediate symptoms. But, underlying these conditions is the breakdown in familial, educational, economic, and other social processes that starts the delinquent on his career of lawbreaking. No interpretation of delinquency can separate it from these causes. Moreover, when it is noted that fully three fourths of the children in our schools do not complete their elementary or secondary education without manifesting some of these characteristics of delinquency, the problems that are usually called those of delinquents become really the problems of children in general.

Examples of the dissimilarity between the average and delinquent child are obvious in the crimes of some of the more notorious offenders. One youth of eighteen admitted the murder of five of his relatives. Two brothers confessed to more than forty burglaries, and when their mother learned of their record and tried to reprove them, one of the boys shot and seriously wounded her. A high-school girl, fifteen years old, who had large sums of money, was found to be operating a call-house.[3]

[3] For other examples, consult P. W. Tappan, *op. cit.*, pp. 18, 289, 532.

The nature of delinquency

Recent definitions, both legal and social, are united in making "delinquency" the equivalent of "problem children." This elastic interpretation covers those children who actually violate laws and are subject to arrest or court supervision and others whose behavior is not illegal but delinquent. From this point of view, delinquency is a definition of social rather than legal status. Indeed, if the same elastic definition were given to crime, few adults would escape being classified as criminals.

Most state laws accept this interpretation of delinquency, because it grants to the state the power to direct those children whose contacts or behavior may lead to serious offenses. Although the application of this law is limited by the economic or family status of problem children, it is a significant first step toward the prevention of delinquency. The result is obvious when the current law is compared with a law that must wait until a delinquent act is committed before a child is considered a ward of the state. Specific offenses are not significant in the legal or social description of the delinquent as a person. He may have violated some law in being a truant or a thief; he may have formed associations that are considered undesirable; or he may be "incorrigible." However, the modern concept of juvenile delinquency is synonymous with "behavior-problem children." Such children are differentiated from others of their age and cultural group by undesirable habits, personality traits, or behavior in the home, the school, or the community that may handicap their social usefulness and make a normal degree of adjustment impossible.

In this generic use of the term, "delinquency" is defined by an enumeration of the "rights of children" and by a statement of children's problems. Both show that the "good-bad" attitude that is usually associated with delinquency has been eliminated. In fact, an enumeration of the problems interfering with child welfare serves to prove the failure of society to secure for the child his rights. Children's rights represent standards in child welfare. Frequently, as in the case of the urban child, they are simply substitutes for those advantages that are natural to a small-population group. According to the *Children's Charter,* these rights include: (1) a normal home, meaning a safe, sanitary dwelling place, adequate standard of living, and wholesome parental relationships; (2) preventive and protective care of health; (3) an education that is graded according to individual abilities; (4) vocational guidance and training; (5) training of children and parents for successful parenthood, home making, and citizenship; (6) economic security; (7) intelligent treatment when problems occur; and (8) a community that recognizes and ensures these essential protections.[4]

Deviations from these standards are recognized as significant problems. They are intimately associated with delinquency in that they are important factors in the situations that produce delinquents. Accordingly, the broken home, the overpopulated home (too large a family in comparison with its income), infant mortality, parental neglect, the employment of mothers outside of the home, economic dependency, physical and mental defects, illegitimacy, detrimental leisure-time activities, and child labor are either causes of delinquency or in some way associated with it. Delinquency has been studied more than other problems of children primarily because of its connection with adult crime, but the repeated occurrence of these other conditions within the life of the delinquent has directed increasing attention to them. This clustering of problems indicates that child-welfare work in general is a preventive of delinquency, whether it be administered against it directly through behavior clinics and probation, or indirectly through the organization of community resources, such as child-guidance, family-welfare, child-health, or play-and-recreation movements.

The evolution of this contemporary attitude toward juvenile delinquency may be summarized under the following trends:

1. One of the most important among the increasing number of children's rights is the right to be treated differently from adults under criminal law. The recognition of limited responsibility has been extended to cover both the offenses for which a child may be held responsible and the treatment or penalty to be administered.

2. Special institutions and courts for the treatment of delinquents have arisen.

3. The distinction between delinquency and crime is due in part to the fact that delinquency is considered less dangerous to group welfare than crime, and in part to society's recognition of its own responsibility for many conditions leading to the delinquency of the child.

[4] White House Conference on Child Health and Protection, *The Children's Charter,* D. Appleton-Century, New York, 1930, pp. 46-48 (adapted).

4. In the early and informal application of state supervision, a wider variety of problems and children are reached than would be reached under the criminal law.

5. Legislation extending the definition of delinquency is an illustration of the gradual increase of state rights to protect the child, changing the legal status of the child and diminishing the former absolute control of parents.

Juvenile delinquency is defined specifically in two ways: one definition refers to types of behavior, the other includes a variable age group.

In the first phase of this definition, delinquency includes conduct and associations as well as violations against the law. By these additional provisions, the state exercises a control over many protective agencies, both remedial and preventive. A summary of various state codes shows that the following conditions are regarded as delinquency: violations of ordinances and laws; immoral conduct; habitual truancy; engaging in illegal occupations; associating with immoral people; exposure to crime; knowingly visiting or patronizing saloons, pool rooms, or houses of ill-repute; gambling; being on the streets late at night or in other places such as railroad yards; using vulgar, obscene language; staying away from home without parents' consent; behaving in such a way as to be a danger to himself or a nuisance to others; smoking in public; or begging.

Compared with crime, therefore, delinquency is not specific. Children who are ungovernable, who engage in acts of carelessness or mischief, who are neglected and in need of protection, or who associate with persons or conditions known to contribute to delinquency —all these may be defined as delinquents.

The second qualification, age, is equally elastic. Age limits usually range from eight to eighteen. Under the lower limit, a child is generally considered incapable of delinquency. At eighteen or above, the excuse of irresponsibility because of youth rarely holds. This range is supposed to be the developmental period during which the person is learning to adjust himself to society. Exceptions do occur, but only in the case of unusual crimes or because of extenuating personal characteristics of the offender.

Age and conduct, therefore, become even more specific descriptive factors when they are connected with mental, home, or economic conditions.

The Standard Juvenile Court Act was prepared by the National

Probation and Parole Association and endorsed in 1946 by the National Conference on Juvenile Delinquency to simplify the legal interpretation of delinquency. This act stresses the need to protect children from delinquency-producing situations. It reduces delinquent conduct to three types: violations of law or ordinance, staying away from home or being habitually disobedient, and truancy. By this innovation it seeks to accomplish two goals: to protect the child against the stigma of delinquency, and to ensure early and effective treatment.

An illustration is the following news report:

> PARENTS ARE HELD ON NEGLECT CHARGE
>
> The parents of three small children and another man who lived in squalor in a filthy room were held for court.
>
> Both parents were charged with neglecting minor children and the roomer was charged with beating one of them. The oldest, a child of five, said "Mother always buys wine when she gets her relief check and never buys us shoes."

Who is the delinquent?

The discovery and identification of the juvenile delinquent are usually the results of comparison. From the great number of behavior-problem children whose personal and social traits are closely similar to those of delinquents, comparisons are made between delinquents and nondelinquent, behavior-problem children, between delinquents and their nondelinquent siblings, between gang or group delinquents and solitary delinquents, and between delinquents who are repeaters and those who are single offenders.

As a composite type, the delinquent child suggests the following traits to be his personal and social characteristics:

1. He is superior in height, weight, general athletic build, and in health and vitality. He is not undernourished.
2. He is often retarded as judged by classroom standards, because he has no interests in ordinary school activities. But he is not

unintelligent or subnormal. By various tests he is shown to have creative skills and abilities.

3. He is generally defiant of authority, aggressive, self-reliant, and openly indifferent to rules.
4. He does not fear failure or defeat but considers himself able to look out for his own interests.
5. He is uncooperative and scorns the good opinion of others.
6. He is impulsive and has little or no self-control.
7. He is an extrovert, vivacious and lively; he explodes rather than broods.
8. He longs for adventure; this is one of his most distinctive traits.
9. He does not become delinquent through bad companionship. He seeks these associations and scorns the good boy.
10. His home life is often abnormal, either broken or overcrowded. The home is generally below the average of the neighborhood. One study found that only one third of the homes could be described as wholesome. On the other hand, one third were homes broken by death or the absence of one parent, and nearly all the others were described as abnormal or injurious from the standpoint of parental control. Parents as a rule had little or no formal education and in nearly one third of the families one or both parents were illiterate.
11. The home is one of conflicting and erratic discipline. Twice as many of the brothers and sisters of delinquents are apt to be delinquent as those of the nondelinquent.
12. He is more often the middle sibling than the first, last, or only child. Position of siblings in the family and its relation to delinquency are subjects that have received a lot of attention, but sibling position continues to be one of the most doubtful identifying traits.
13. Nearly one half of all problem boys have court records. Likewise, in many of the families of delinquents one or both parents had criminal records. Some studies put the total percentage of family delinquency as high as eighty-five per cent of all members.
14. The father's occupation is usually unskilled or semiskilled. In the 1945 re-survey by the Gluecks, sixty-eight per cent of the families were in the lowest self-supporting economic circumstances and nearly ten per cent were entirely dependent on poor-relief.
15. The mother is often employed outside of the home.

16. The family is mobile.
17. The problem boy is not inclined to work during his leisure time, even though the family is dependent.
18. He is unprepared for life vocationally, either by public or by disciplinary schools.
19. Early signs are temper tantrums, profanity, obscene language, early misconduct and early (before eight) delinquency.[5]

Of course, not all delinquent groups duplicate this list of traits. In general, behavior-problem children are in a predelinquent stage that is closely connected with truancy; and truancy is regarded by most psychiatrists as the kindergarten of crime. The Gluecks are of the opinion that significant predictive factors, as indicators of delinquency, during the predelinquent period are: (1) lax and erratic or overstrict discipline of the father, (2) absence of affection, or rejection by either parent, (3) the boy's nature: he is stubborn, extroverted, aggressive, defiant, suspicious, destructive, and emotionally assertive. Other personal traits also accorded high predictive value are restlessness, nervousness, quarrelsomeness, disobedience, and inattentiveness.

The nondelinquent or good child by contrast is less athletic, less healthy, has more neurological and psychoneurotic disturbances, is more dependent on others for encouragement and help, and is bound to his family by strong emotional and social ties.[6]

The social or gang delinquent differs both personally and socially from the solitary delinquent. His home life is easy-going, and not primarily characterized by emotional neglect. The home is generally situated in a low socio-economic neighborhood. It is this condition, in addition to the inadequate size of the home and insufficient income, that is considered the most important predictive factor in the case of the gang delinquent who is a repeater. Other problems associated with this type of delinquency, and presumably having some causal significance, are school problems, race discrimination,

[5] *Cf.* S. and E. Glueck, *Unraveling Juvenile Delinquency,* The Commonwealth Fund, New York, 1950, chapters 18 and 19. W. W. Wattenberg, "Delinquency and Only Children," *Jour. Abn. and Soc. Psych.,* Vol. 44 (1949): 356-366.

[6] W. W. Wattenberg and J. J. Balistrieri, "Gang Membership and Juvenile Misconduct," *Am. Sociol. Rev.,* Vol. 15 (1950): 744-752. F. C. Zakolski, "Studies in Delinquency," *Jour. Genet. Psych.,* Vol. 74 (1949): 109-17; 119-123. V. Birkeness and H. C. Johnson, "A Comparative Study of Delinquents and Non-Delinquent Adolescents," *Jour. Ed. Res.,* Vol. 42 (1949): 561-572. C. B. Spaulding, "Cliques, Gangs, and Networks," *Sociol. and Soc. Res.,* Vol. 32 (1948): 928-937.

weak religious controls, rejection by social and play groups, weak family relations (which include lack of supervision, immorality of parents, large families, and alcoholism), extreme emotional disturbances, feelings of personal inadequacy, poverty, inadequate recreation, and exposure to delinquent conduct.

The solitary or non-gang delinquent is a member of a tense and emotion-depriving home. This family situation is considered the most important predictive factor in the recidivism of these individuals. Other personal or social characteristics and problems in the background of the solitary delinquent are alcoholism in the family, the boy's slovenly appearance, indifference of the parents to the boy's activities, the boy's open show of dislike for both parents, inadequate recreation, and lack of a monetary allowance. The one respect in which this family is superior to that of the gang delinquent is its location in an average or better neighborhood.

Causes of delinquency

As these identifying characteristics indicate, the causes are not hard to find. Practically without exception the adolescent boy or girl who breaks the law and is taken into the custody of the courts has had the same childhood background—an early life in a broken home or in a family where social relationships have been inadequate, in neighborhoods of cultural conflict and poverty where delinquency is almost the tradition, where recreation is insufficient, and where this combination of factors leads to a training in unacceptable forms of behavior.

Various studies make these findings more intelligible when they reveal patterns of delinquency. There is no one absolute cause or one inevitable delinquency-producing situation. Often the particular traits and their combinations appear in the lives of nondelinquent children. Delinquency emerges from a combination of a number of these predisposing factors and susceptible children.

In spite of the fairly general acceptance of this conclusion, there are also many partial or one-sided explanations. Mental condition, economic determinism, heredity, glands, bad companions, and nativity are still being suggested as sufficient causes. There are also the more recent emphasis on defective education, religion, and recreation, and on the newer modes of communication, such as comic books, motion pictures, or television. In contrast with these "clear-cut" explanations, the emphasis of psychology and sociology upon a delinquency pattern is regarded as wholly theoretical. The following judicial explanation is an example of this contemporary logic:

> The presiding judge of the First Criminal Court, in sentencing a number of youths ranging in age from 16 to 20, asserted that in his experience gasoline and liquor were to blame for the excessive degree of crime among the city's youthful offenders. The remarks of the jurist from the bench are significant and worthy of note: "Most crime nowadays is committed by boys from 15 to 25 years old. Fifteen years ago criminals brought before the bar were from 35 to 65. The youths see [gangsters] and [racketeers] in big autos and fine clothes. Envious, they get guns and become hold-up men." [7]

One of the pioneering investigations into these multiple causes is the study of *The Young Delinquent* by Cyril Burt. He reported the discovery of 170 distinct factors in the delinquency process, of which 70 could be considered important. His major finding, however, was the right combination.

In comparing delinquents and nondelinquents, he isolated the causes of delinquency by their repetition in the lives of the former and their absence or milder occurrence among the latter. Delinquency, in other words, is not the consequence of exposure to predisposing conditions, which do not affect nondelinquents, but it is a surrender to a great number of these conditions.

Burt's Summary of the Major Causes of Delinquency [8]

	Per Cent Distribution	
	Delinquents	*Non-Delinquents*
Hereditary Conditions:		
Physical	53.1	31.8
Intellectual	35.6	8.2
Temperamental	42.2	19.7
Environmental Conditions:		
Poverty	85.5	53.9
Defective family relations	131.3	35.2
Physical conditions	145.1	84.5
Psychological conditions	380.4	111.3

[7] A. A. Bruce and T. S. Fitzgerald, "A Study of Crime in the City of Memphis," *Jour. Crim. Law and Criminol.*, Vol. 19 (1929), No. 2, p. 76. This quotation is modernized by the substitution of gangsters and racketeers for the original words "bootleggers and moonshiners."

[8] D. Appleton-Century, New York, 1925, pp. 578; 62-63. Per cents over 100 represent summations, indicating the number of times that groups of factors occur in the two classes. The table is only a partial reproduction of Burt's findings, showing differences between delinquents and nondelinquents.

This fact is shown clearly in the percentage distribution of Burt's major causes among both groups. The percentages also indicate the relative importance of these conditions between delinquent and nondelinquent boys.

Listed in the order of their importance, Burt enumerates the following specific causes of delinquency: (1) defective discipline, (2) general emotional instability, (3) family history of vice and crime, (4) intellectual dullness, (5) detrimental interests, (6) developmental conditions, (7) defective family relationships, (8) bad companions, (9) family history of insanity, (10) poverty and its concomitants, (11) physical infirmity of the child.

Similar results are reported in the comparison of delinquent and control groups in this country. In addition to gross environmental conditions, such factors as bad companions, sex, mental retardation, personality defects, adolescent instability, school unadjustments, and poor types of recreation are either causes or indicators of the causes in a delinquency pattern. These conditions appear among the 138 causes in the studies of the Judge Baker Foundation. In the table below, the percentage incidence of some of these causes in one group of 4,000 cases shows how they appear and combine in patterns of delinquency.

DIRECT AND PROBABLE CAUSES OF DELINQUENCY

Causes	*Per Cent Distribution*	
Directly Causative	*Boston Series*	
	I	II
Bad companions	64.0	67.0
Adolescent instability	18.4	15.5
Early sex experience	10.4	11.8
Extreme social suggestibility	7.6	3.8
Mental conflict	5.7	6.2
Other Probable Causes		
Poor types of recreation	21.4	20.4
Street life	11.6	11.5
School dissatisfaction	9.8	8.6

Source: W. Healy and A. F. Bronner, *Delinquents and Criminals,* Macmillan, New York, 1926, p. 281 (adapted). By permission of Judge Baker Guidance Center, Boston, Mass.

Recent analytical studies of causes are largely the contribution of behavior clinics, child-guidance bureaus, or institutions with case-work facilities. They are in substantial agreement with the point of view and the trends established by Burt and Healy. However, more attention is now being given to the frequency, intensity, and duration of delinquency-producing situations as objective factors and to emotional disorders as subjective causes or reactions.

Causal analyses of delinquency are valuable because they illustrate different approaches to the solution of the problem of delinquency. In recent years, several books on child guidance and children's problems have been published that indicate differences in point of view and in suggested treatment. In spite of these differences, there is practical agreement in their causal explanations as well as in their methods of investigation. Ordinarily, two methods are employed in clinical studies of the delinquency process. One, the life-story method, is a description of the individual offender from his own point of view. The other is the social case-history method.[9]

Types and prevalence of delinquency

The characteristic forms of juvenile delinquency are relatively few in number. There are, however, significant variations between sex and age groups. Stealing is the most frequent offense; it includes larceny, burglary, and automobile thefts. Other offenses against property are not numerous. Offenses against social regulations are also frequent, including unspecified delinquency and incorrigibility. Offenses against the person are few, even when sex offenses are added to this group.

Differences between the offenses of boys and those of girls consist primarily in the excessive incidence of sex offenses among girls. The

[9] Life histories: C. R. Shaw, *Delinquency Areas,* University of Chicago Press, Chicago, 1929. ———, *The Jack-Roller,* University of Chicago Press, Chicago, 1930. ———, *The Natural History of a Delinquent Career,* University of Chicago Press, Chicago, 1938, Chaps. 1-3. W. I. and D. S. Thomas, *The Child in America,* Knopf, New York, 1928. F. M. Thrasher, *The Gang,* University of Chicago Press, Chicago, 1936.

Case histories: J. G. Brill and E. G. Payne, *The Adolescent Court and Crime Prevention,* Pitman, New York, 1938. S. and E. Glueck, *Criminal Careers in Retrospect,* The Commonwealth Fund, New York, 1943, Chap. 2. S. H. Hartwell, *Fifty-Five "Bad" Boys,* Knopf, New York, 1931. W. Healy and A. F. Bronner, *Delinquents and Criminals,* Macmillan, New York, 1926. Joint Committee on Methods of Preventing Delinquency, *Three Problem Children,* New York, 1927. C. R. Shaw and others, *Brothers in Crime,* University of Chicago Press, Chicago, 1938, Chaps. 1 and 2. H. W. Thurston, *Concerning Juvenile Delinquency,* Columbia University Press, New York, 1942, Chap. 7. P. V. Young, *Social Treatment in Probation and Delinquency,* McGraw-Hill, New York, 1937, Chaps. 1 and 2.

chief offenses of boys are larceny, incorrigibility, and burglary; those of girls are incorrigibility, immorality, and running away.

TYPES OF JUVENILE DELINQUENCY, LISTED IN ORDER OF FREQUENCY

Type	*Percentage Frequency*
Delinquency, unspecified	74.5
Larceny	
Incorrigibility	
Burglary	
Auto theft	15.3
Immorality	
Truancy	
Running away	
Robbery	
Violation of parole or probation	
Assault	
Other sex offenses than rape	5.5
Disorderly conduct and vagrancy	
In danger of leading immoral life	
Rape	
Forgery	
Violation of liquor laws	
Homicide	
Drunkenness	
Carrying deadly weapon	
Violation of traffic laws	
All other offenses	4.7

Source: Classification in reports of the U. S. Children's Bureau.

Age is a significant factor in this sex distribution, indicating the operation of different causes of delinquency. Offenses committed by girls under twelve years of age correspond more with the offenses of boys than do those of older girls. Acts of carelessness or mischief (unspecified delinquency) decrease from the lower to the higher age groups, whereas sex offenses and violations of liquor or drug laws increase in both sex groups. Boys are classified in the incorrigible category at earlier ages than girls; few of the latter become delinquent under the age of ten. Truancy in both sexes occurs most often between the ages of fourteen and sixteen. Stealing continues to be the most frequent offense of boys in all age groups, but the forms of stealing vary with increasing age.

The age peak for delinquency among boys is seventeen. Girls have two high rates when they are classified by age. The first is at ages 18 and 19, the second and highest rate is at age twenty-two.

Another significant discovery is the fact that most arraignments for stealing include several boys. This suggests the factor of ganging in petty thefts. Among older boys not only does the form of stealing vary from that of younger ones, but the number who are jointly connected with an offense decreases with increasing age and experience.

In recent studies of juvenile delinquency, the following conclusions have been reached. There is a comparative rarity of delinquency as a serious problem, when its frequency is judged by arraignments in court. The minor character of the offenses with which children are charged is a noticeable feature of the cases. Approximately one third of the boys and one half of the girls are brought to court because of conflicts with parental authority.

Delinquency is one of the social problems for which no estimated number of cases can be given. Nor is it even fair to say *about* or *nearly* to modify a guess. The numbers of behavior-problem children from whom delinquents are recruited is unknown, in spite of many estimates. In order to begin an analysis of incidence, Carr suggests a classification such as (1) legal delinquents, (2) detected delinquents, (3) agency delinquents, (4) alleged delinquents, and (5) adjudged delinquents. This classification would permit a reckoning of incidence of delinquents who are truants, who are known to, or suspected by, the police, who are juvenile court cases, and who are either in detention institutions or on probation.

In recent years, between 250,000 and 300,000 delinquents have been handled by various courts. One to two million have either been known to, or suspected by, the police (this figure depends on the upper age of the delinquent class, that is, whether it is interpreted as eighteen or twenty by the courts). Two other evidences of extent are that one per cent of all children between the ages of ten and sixteen years pass through the courts, and that one in every hundred children is a police problem.

Accordingly, the actual number of children arraigned, or delinquency rates, do not give accurate estimates of delinquency and its problems. These figures must be corrected not only because of age and sex differences, which have already been noted, but also for urban and rural differences and for the racial or nativity distribution of the population. In addition, the rates of different states or regions vary because of differences in the age limits over which the courts have jurisdiction, the area (urban or rural) covered, the problems coming under the jurisdiction of the courts, and the development of other children's welfare agencies in the community. Marked increases in juvenile delinquency during the war appeared in communities having a large increase of population, though in most areas these increases were temporary. The failure of court statistics to reveal these increases is due in part to the improper compilation of reports and in part to the practice in some cities of clearing delinquency cases through other social agencies and in some instances through the public schools.[10]

Factors correlated with delinquency

Whether delinquency is interpreted generally to include all problems of children or specifically to mean a group of offenses committed by children, it is found to be intimately associated with several major social problems. The correlations between such conditions and delinquency have been used in the description of the delinquent as a person. They are also employed in the analysis of causes. However, it must be remembered that the association between delinquency and broken homes, race or nativity, rural-urban distribution of the population, mobility, ecological areas, business cycles, poverty and unemployment, war, adult criminality, recreation, schools, or other discoverable conditions may not be definitely causal.

For this reason, criminologists are interested in experimenting in the isolation of delinquency patterns—in discovering an environmental situation favorable to delinquency in which numerous factors are conducive to producing this condition. The situational approach, moreover, does not minimize efforts to discover specific personal causes, but regards the elimination of social causes as the most direct step that can be taken in a preventive program.

Studies of the delinquent as a person are unanimous in the conclusion that delinquency is the outcome of social stratification and selection. The almost uniform type of background of delinquents, in so far as their environmental contacts are concerned, confirms this assumption, and to some extent it explains the personal characteristics that brand the delinquent as a type.

Each of the following explored correlations is in reality a network of conditions in which the discussed factor is examined for its own outstanding contribution to delinquency.

Broken homes. As one of the major and most consistent correlates of delinquency, the broken home is a nucleus of many equally

[10] For a current statement of incidence, consult: *Social Work Yearbook,* Russell Sage Foundation, New York, published biannually. E. E. Swartz, "Statistics of Juvenile Delinquency in the United States," *Annals, Am. Acad. Pol. and Soc. Sci.,* Vol. 261 (Jan. 1949): 9-20 (on p. 11 there is a graph of court cases and arrests for the period 1938-47 that shows the increase during the war years and the decrease in the postwar period). W. A. Lunden, "War and Juvenile Delinquency in England and Wales, 1910-1943," *Am. Sociol. Rev.,* Vol. 10 (1945): 390-393.

demoralizing problems. These are crowding, housing, neighborhood, occupational status of parents, unemployment, educational deficiencies, and early employment of the child. In all studies previously mentioned, each writer shows that poverty, unskilled vocations of parents, and dependence on welfare agencies rank closely with the broken home as causes or correlates.

Since 1899 all inventories of delinquents' families are uniform in indicating a high relationship between broken homes (that is, broken by death, separation, or divorce) and delinquency. In that year a study discovered that 34 per cent of 1,300 delinquents were from such homes.

In 1923 the United States Census reported 56 per cent. In 1939 the United States Children's Bureau reported that 36 per cent of the boys and 50 per cent of the girls were from broken homes. In 1945 a study of 4,055 delinquents in Connecticut found one third to be in the same category. This trend, already noted in the studies of Burt and Healy, also holds for police records, court commitments, and institutional populations.[11]

These observers point out, however, that it is less the broken home as such that accounts for the delinquency than it is the broken home as a symbol of defective discipline, dissension, conflict, neglect, and emotional friction. This combination reveals one of the most insidious sequences to delinquency in the attitudes of parents and in the child's hostile reaction.

Business cycles. Why delinquency increases with periods of prosperity and decreases with depressions is none too clear. The most direct explanation is family disorganization which, as judged by divorce, also increases in periods of prosperity. Thus delinquency follows these trends in the family, possibly as a result of relaxed family discipline, working mothers, weakening family ties, more money for commercialized recreation, and alcohol. Other variables in this sequence, which occasionally add their share to the disorganization of the family, are abnormal conditions of employment, housing shortages, tensions of war, and higher incomes.

Since crime does not correlate with the business cycle in the same manner as delinquency, this is a significant difference yet to be explored.

Poverty. Together with its associated problem, unemployment,

[11] H. M. Shulman, "The Family and Juvenile Delinquency," *Annals, Am. Acad. Pol. and Soc. Sci.*, Vol. 261 (Jan. 1949): 25-27.

poverty is not considered so important as a cause, but it is stressed as an index of undesirable living conditions from which delinquency arises. Most delinquents are from homes of poverty or homes on the margin of poverty. However, associated conditions, such as blighted neighborhood, economic insecurity, family disorganization, emotional insecurity, and anti-social attitudes, are usually given greater weight than either poverty or unemployment in the pattern of delinquency.

Race and nativity. The role of race and nationality is similarly blurred by factors of economic status, discrimination, housing, cultural inferiority, mobility, crowding, and segregation. The foreign-born were ruled out long ago as major contributors to delinquency, and especially so now since they represent so small a proportion of the population. Until recently, children of foreign-born were conspicuous in delinquency statistics. However, as the number of foreign-born continues to decline, it is obvious that the number of children of foreign-born will likewise decline. The same clean bill of health has not been given the Negro, partly because of the high rates of delinquency among Negro youth in some localities. The conclusion to date is that Negroes become delinquents for the same reasons that whites do.

As soon as Negro mobility decreases and Negroes become the predominant group in a new area, their high rates decline and are stabilized on a basis comparable to that of the white group. This Negro experience has made a valuable contribution to causal study. It shows that any mobile, unstable, poverty-stricken people, regardless of race or nationality, will produce high rates of violation against law, especially when discrimination and ethnic tensions are at a high pitch.

Mobility calls attention to the rural-urban movement of the population since 1900 and to two results of the movement. One is that there are now more children in urban than in rural places. The second is the greater current significance of movements of population between cities and within cities.

As a single factor, transiency has rarely been considered a serious cause of delinquency. But it does point out groups that are necessarily liable to new and difficult adjustments and to demoralizing conditions that favor delinquency. Accordingly, studies show that in those places where population is increasing and is mobile, there is the greatest increase in delinquency. Also, as population becomes stationary or decreases, delinquency returns to its usual proportions. Both truancy and delinquency continue to be of interest from this point of view as indexes of a population that is directly exposed to crime-producing conditions.

This relation is partly confirmed by the lower delinquency rates of rural communities—only partly, however, because law-enforcing agencies are inadequate in most rural communities and also because of the greater control exercised by family, church, and school in rural areas. Delinquency is defined by the community and by law-enforcing agencies. Delinquency statistics are likely to reflect inadequacies in enforcing agencies as well as changes in the administration of the law.

Urban areas. Delinquency is not only an urban problem but it appears most frequently in the disorganized areas of the city. In the light of the ecological distribution of a population, it is highest in the deteriorated zone near the city center and diminishes gradually to the areas in outlying suburban sections. This trend is explained in the same way as such other urban problems as population distribution, tuberculosis rates, the distribution of the foreign-born and of Negroes, families on relief, and rentals and home ownership.

These correlates in urban delinquency are summarized in a study of housing and show that (1) delinquency rates tend to be higher where the economic value of housing (as judged by rentals) is low, (2) they are high in areas of high population density, (3) they are high in areas where the physical condition and equipment of the housing are poor, and (4) they are high wherever the rate of tenancy is high.[12]

War. According to court records, delinquency made spectacular increases during World War II. If the pre-war records are correct, these increases were as much as a hundred per cent in some localities, but a thirty per cent increase was about the highest average gain. However, this tendency toward increasing court rates had already begun before the war years, so that the obvious direct effect of war is to accent predisposing conditions. This intensification of certain social problems during war was noticeable abroad as well as in this country. Comparisons between localities that had large increases of population with those that had little or no increase lend credibility

[12] H. Harlan and J. Wherry, "Delinquency and Housing," *Social Forces,* Vol. 27 (1948): 58-61.

to the notion that some of the increasing delinquency was due directly to war conditions.[13]

Reasons assigned directly to war are the upsetting of ordinary living conditions brought about by war and its concomitant dislocations. In this respect, the effects of war are like those of a depression, namely, confusion in standards of behavior, the letdown of social controls, the recurrence of tensions and emotional distress, working mothers, family disorganization, family migration, and irregular school and recreational life.

Adult criminality. In the opinion of many criminologists, there is a direct and high correlation between the social indexes of adult crime and juvenile delinquency. Although it is impossible to prove that delinquency is learned from adult example or is influenced thereby, the correlation is close enough to merit attention. As Neumeyer explains it, delinquency follows tradition. If the community has a reputation for illegal conduct, delinquency follows the pattern and persists.

Those influences, most often cited, are the publicized examples of adult crime and corruption, and of flagrant violation of law by people in responsible positions. Newspaper reports of businessmen in black markets, open violations of price restrictions, income tax violations, white-collar criminality as illustrated by corporation frauds, and the scandalous misconduct of some of the military—all these are examples. In addition, there are the numerous instances of graft-ridden police, mayors jailed for "shakedowns," kickbacks in trade unions and the United States Congress, misuse of government property by city officials and prison wardens, the numbers racket, gambling, and "fixes" in the world of sports.

The moral in this implied correlation is that no program for the control of delinquency can be formulated without reference to adult example and its powerful influences.

Schools, recreation, and other correlates. All institutions, and the school especially, are supposed to give stability to the child and to engage in specific remedial and preventive activities. It is for this reason that truancy is regarded seriously both as a form of delinquency and as a step toward more aggravated misdeeds. In one study of delinquents, ninety per cent were so set in their dislike of school that it was considered a direct cause of their trouble. That

[13] A. L. Porterfield, "A Decade of Serious Crime in the United States," *Am. Sociol. Rev.*, Vol. 13 (1948): 44-45.

the school is failing the community is an obvious conclusion of such discoveries.

This conclusion is stressed even more when it is realized that the typical truant has all the traits outlined previously for the full-fledged delinquent. His home is usually as disorganized; his parents and brothers or sisters usually have criminal records; and there is also the customary record of retardation and conduct disorders.

Similarly, problems predisposing to delinquency—the serious behavior problems of children—are first apparent in the school. In the same way that delinquency is sometimes called a school for crime, schools are often considered the kindergarten. The reason for this accusation is that the child is frustrated by the requirements of the school and is trained in attitudes stressed particularly by psychologists as an outstanding predisposing condition in delinquency.

Similar but less conclusive statements are made about the church, public recreation or amusement, and various means of communication, but they are for the most part in need of further study and corroboration.[14]

Disposition or treatment of delinquency

There is little difference between the judicial treatment of delinquency and of crime. In both instances, courts adhere to a few legal methods of disposition. Consequently, these judicial dispositions are no more favorable to the prevention of delinquency than they are to the prevention of crime. One reason given for the failure to control either crime or delinquency is that too much reliance is placed upon the powers of the courts. The other is that courts persist in treating offenses and not offenders.

The limited resources of the courts are shown in the table below, which also shows that the general nature of judicial dispositions does not vary greatly from the penalties assigned to adults. In this summary of dispositions, the characteristic treatment of offenders is dismissal, probation, commitment to an institution, or assignment

[14] For the influences of other agencies involving moral risks, such as newspapers, comic books, salacious literature, radio, television, and the like, consult: M. B. Clinard, "Secondary Community Influences and Juvenile Delinquency," *Annals, Am. Acad. Pol. and Soc. Sci.*, Vol. 261 (1949): 42-54. C. J. Eckenrode, "The Achievement Is Delinquency," *Jour. Ed. Res.*, Vol. 43 (1950): 554-558. P. M. Smith, "Role of the Church in Delinquency Prevention," *Sociol. and Soc. Res.*, Vol. 35 (1951): 183-190. M. H. Neumeyer, *op. cit.*, pp. 168 ff. P. W. Tappan, *op. cit.*, pp. 150 ff.

to some children's agency. A few offenders are fined. Dismissed cases include cases closed without further action on the part of the juvenile court, cases over which the court has no jurisdiction, cases placed under the custody of parents, or cases committed to institutions with judicial commitment suspended. "Other dispositions" include miscellaneous methods, such as the assignment of the case to some other court or the placement of the child under the supervision of some individual other than a probation officer or parent.

DISPOSITION OF DELINQUENCY CASES BY THE COURTS LISTED IN ORDER OF FREQUENCY

Dismissed, adjusted, or held open without further action
Child supervised by probation officer
Child committed to an institution
Child referred to another agency
Restitution, fine, or costs
Other dispositions:
 Referred to another court
 Runaway returned
Disposition not reported

Source: Dispositions in the records of the United States Children's Bureau reports.

While, in theory, probation is the modern method of treatment and is the principal constructive effort of the court to prevent crime, its results vary considerably in practice. One comment upon probation states:

> The time spent in visits to the homes of probationers varies, but the average amount of time given by probation officers to the making of these visits is from ten to fifteen minutes.
>
> Probation officers may have all the elaborate definitions of what probation is that they may care to have, but fundamentally, probation is simply changing the habits of individuals and enlarging their group relationships. If the probation officer and probationer meet only occasionally, and home visits are infrequent and brief, can it logically be expected that the conduct of probationers will be revolutionized because they have learned the magic word "probation"? If probation supervision has been superficial and ineffectual—and superficial and ineffectual probation supervision is due generally to the failure of the proper fiscal authorities to provide for an adequate staff of probation officers—and the offender does not change his unsocial habits, have the court, the probation officer, and society given him a fair chance to make good? Probation technique must advance beyond the stage of ordering and forbidding, and this advance will be made only when communities provide adequate probation service.[15]

There is, as a matter of fact, little case-work treatment in probation or in detention institutions. To a limited extent, however, as

[15] Crime Commission of New York, *Crime and the Community,* Albany, 1930, pp. 90-91.

indicated by the proportion of other dispositions, child-welfare agencies with case-work facilities for diagnosis and supervision have been used for this purpose.

When the Juvenile Court was established at the beginning of the present century, it was regarded as a "sure cure" of crime. This presumption was necessary in order to secure public support, because not even the most fanatic advocate of the Juvenile Court believed that it could deal with more than one group of problem children, namely, the delinquent, and hence with more than one aspect of delinquency. Experience has shown the Juvenile Court to be as powerless as other courts to modify domestic, economic, or community factors in delinquency. Although there are few objective methods of measuring its effectiveness, the persistency of delinquency does not supply a hopeful index of its success. The court, however, cannot be branded as a failure; it operates under three distinct handicaps:

> First, it reaches only a small proportion of the child offenders in any given community; second, it reaches the majority of them at too late an age for the effective utilization of social therapy; third, it lacks the facilities to administer sound social therapy, save in rare cases.[16]

For these reasons, the Juvenile Court is a limited agency of control rather than a defective one. The most critical standard of its efficiency is its probation service.

There are two trends in the present treatment of delinquency. The first consists of efforts to reach the problem child in the predelinquent stage. The second advocates the study and treatment of the offender as a person, a method that is almost impossible to carry out under the present limited facilities of the court. While both involve the problem of determining the agency or agencies that are best equipped to assume these responsibilities, their actual working-out is largely a question of social policy or of local community resources. Some authorities urge that the public school, reinforced by visiting teachers and behavior clinics, should be the nucleus upon which these efforts are constructed. Other candidates for this work are private social agencies specializing in problem children, child-guidance clinics, and mental-hygiene societies.

Customary treatments suggested after clinical study generally recommend that the delinquent should be (1) kept in his own home

[16] *Ibid.*, p. 83.

under supervision of a social agency, (2) assigned to a parental school, (3) placed in a foster home, or (4) confined in a correctional institution or detention home. Other recommendations are health care, psychiatric supervision, vocational adjustment, educational correctives, or "other constructive direction."

There are various local and state experiments in the social, legal, or research approaches that may prove to be useful additions to current practice.

One of these innovations is the California law (1945) which holds parents or guardians equally responsible with the child. The social point of view on which this law is based is that delinquency is mainly a problem of gross neglect.

Another movement suggests an expansion of treatment resources. It is called the Youth Correction Authority and is sponsored by the American Law Institute. This Authority (established by Congress in 1950) recommends that a state agency should deal with all offenders under twenty-one years of age. It provides a board of specialists to decide each case, and it also promotes any service (educational, recreational or psychiatric) that would be indicated by these special studies.

Other suggestions include special adolescent courts, experimental court procedures as in the Brooklyn plan, self-government plans in the form of junior police or junior courts, and, in addition, the continuous drive toward improved and specially trained personnel in police, court, and detention institutions.[17]

This review of dispositions employed by the court and of other possibilities in treating the problems of delinquency calls attention to a fact that characterizes most social problems: society is slow to attack a problem early, to apply other than routine correctives, or to make its campaign nationwide.

Summary

In the suggestions that are made for the prevention of delinquency, several salient facts are revealed concerning its present status in social science and social work. Its connection with children's

[17] C. H. Z. Meyer, "The Brooklyn Plan of Deferred Prosecution for Juvenile Offenders," *Jour. Crim. Law and Criminol.*, Vol. 37 (1946-47): 478-480. J. O. Reineman, "Fifty Years of the Juvenile Court Movement in the United States," *Mental Hyg.*, Vol. 34 (1950): 391-399. P. W. Tappan, "The Adolescent Court," *Jour. Crim. Law and Criminol.*, Vol. 37 (1946-47): 216-229.

problems in general calls attention to its multiple causes and to the fact that it is more a consequence of other social problems than a distinct social problem in itself. These relationships with other problems stress external, environmental factors in the home, the neighborhood, and the school, which are considered its principal causes. But they do not supply any analysis of the processes out of which delinquency grows. Owing to this limited approach, delinquency may be regarded as a multiple problem, a pattern to be factored. Consequently, its treatment or prevention cannot be stated other than as a problem in social research.

As a problem in social research, and especially as a problem of changing social values, delinquency represents a cross-section of many typical classes of social problems. It can be used to illustrate the ill-effects of uncontrolled forms of social changes, or they in turn can be employed in the redefinition of delinquency. Thus, for example, delinquency can be interpreted as (1) one of the conduct problems of children, (2) a result of ineffective social organization, and (3) an outcome of numerous mental and emotional disorders of parents as well as of children.

Because of these basic problems that delinquency implies, constructive programs pay slight attention to law or to methods of its enforcement. Their emphasis, instead, is placed upon general social well-being and upon efforts to discover conditions that predispose to delinquency at an early period in the child's life. This approach suggests individual case study and treatment.

> We may best regard the field of delinquency and crime as one for human engineering, and the work to be done analogous to that required for any other engineering project.[18]

In accordance with this point of view, Healy and Bronner suggest the following procedure in the study and prevention of delinquency:

1. The education and training of personnel for research and treatment.
2. Collection of facts concerning the frequency and causes of delinquency.
3. Research as to the nature of these causes and as to methods by which human behavior may be controlled.
4. Development of a professional literature, in order to exchange the results of research.
5. Extensive case study of each delinquent.

[18] W. Healy and A. F. Bronner, *op. cit.*, p. 230.

6. Improvement of techniques of treatment.
7. Extension of resources in treatment, especially through trained personnel.
8. Coordination of administrative agencies.
9. Education of the public concerning the problems of the delinquent.

The preventive scheme, suggested by Cyril Burt, agrees with each of these proposals. Burt states in conclusion that:

Society must aim at prevention as well as at cure. Housing, medical treatment, continued education, the psychological study of children in the schools, improved industrial conditions, increased facilities for recreation, the cautious adoption of practicable eugenic measures, and, above all, sustained investigation into all the problems of childhood—these are but a few of the countless needs to be supplied, if delinquency in the young is to be not merely cured as it arises, but diverted, forestalled, and so far as possible wiped out.[19]

Or, as the Gluecks recommend in their most recent analysis, delinquency suggests above all else the need of the child for "loving care."

On the basis of their findings from clinic and court studies, they also recommend:

1. The need for a consistent and unified children's code.
2. The development of a scientific attitude on the part of the court as to the problems involved, clinical resources in treatment, and the social possibilities of effecting readjustment.
3. Improvement of hearings by having the probation officer present and verbatim records taken.
4. Systematic review of each case by the judge and probation officer.
5. Selection of court personnel on the basis of aptitude and professional training.
6. Complete records of treatment processes.[20]

Thus, delinquency is recognized as a social responsibility, and a well-coordinated scheme for the prevention of delinquency involves: (1) child guidance, (2) organization of preventive resources to attack the problem at its origins, (3) coordination of municipal, county, state, and national correctional and protective agencies, (4) detention, if it is considered necessary, of sufficient duration so that educational or reformatory measures may be effective, or, as may be required by some cases, provisions for permanent segregation.

[19] *Ibid.*, p. 587.

[20] *One Thousand Juvenile Delinquents*, Harvard University Press, Cambridge, 1934, pp. 244-252, 260-279.

Bibliography

Bell, Marjorie (Ed.), *Social Correctives for Delinquency,* National Probation Association, New York, 1946.

Deutsch, Albert, *Our Rejected Children,* Little, Brown, Boston, 1950.

Ellingston, J. R., *Protecting Our Children from Criminal Careers,* Prentice-Hall, New York, 1948.

Glueck, S. and E., *Unraveling Juvenile Delinquency,* Commonwealth Fund, New York, 1950.

Merrill, M. A., *Problems of Child Delinquency,* Houghton Mifflin, Boston, 1947.

Neumeyer, M. H., *Juvenile Delinquency in Modern Society,* D. Van Nostrand, New York, 1949.

Porterfield, A. L., *Youth in Trouble,* Leo Potishman Foundation, Fort Worth, 1946.

Shaw, C. R., and H. D. McKay, *Juvenile Delinquency in Urban Areas,* University of Chicago Press, Chicago, 1942.

Sheldon, W. H., and others, *Varieties of Delinquent Youth,* Harper, New York, 1949.

Sussman, F. B., *Law of Juvenile Delinquency: the Laws of the Forty-Eight States,* Oceana Publications, New York, 1950.

Tappan, P. W., *Juvenile Delinquency,* McGraw-Hill, New York, 1949.

Teeters, N. K., and J. O. Reineman, *The Challenge of Delinquency,* Prentice-Hall, New York, 1950.

. . . . .

Abraham, A. A., "Juvenile Delinquency in Buffalo and its Prevention," *Jour. Negro Educa.,* Vol. 17 (1948): 122-133.

Blue, J. T., "Relationship of Juvenile Delinquency, Race, and Economic Status," *Jour. Negro Educa.,* Vol. 17 (1948): 469-477.

Chute, C. L., "Fifty Years of the Juvenile Court," *1949 Yearbook,* National Probation and Parole Association, New York, 1950. Chap. 1.

Gardner, G. E., "The Community and the Aggressive Child," *Mental Hyg.,* Vol. 34 (1950): 44-63.

Jones, H. E., and others, "Radio and Movies," *1947 Yearbook,* National Probation and Parole Association, New York, 1948. Part 3.

Markey, O. B., "A Study of Aggressive Sex Misbehavior in Adolescents Brought to Juvenile Court," *Am. Jour. Orthopsychiatry,* Vol. 20 (1950): 719-731.

Monachesi, E. D., "Personality Characteristics and Socio-Economic Status of Delinquents and Non-Delinquents," *Jour. Crim. Law and Criminol.,* Vol. 40 (1949-50): 570-583.

Mullen, F. A., "Truancy and Classroom Disorder as Symptoms of Personality Problems," *Jour. Educa. Psych.,* Vol. 41 (1950): 97-109.

Pursuit, D. G., "A University and Law Enforcement Work Together in the

Control of Juvenile Delinquency," *Jour. Crim. Law and Criminol.,* Vol. 38 (1947-48): 416-422.

Williams, E. Y., "Truancy in Children Referred to a Clinic," *Mental Hyg.,* Vol. 31 (1947): 464-469.

Questions

1. What are the traits of the pre-delinquent child?
2. Are the factors in the life of the delinquent that are used for predicting the outcome of treatment supported by statistical evidence?
3. How does the gang delinquent develop as a social type?
4. Do you believe that you could distinguish the gang delinquent from the solitary delinquent by a personal interview?
5. What conditions almost always make a child susceptible to delinquency?
6. How does density of population affect delinquency rates?
7. Does the assertion by Neumeyer that delinquency follows tradition appeal to you as verifiable? If it is correct, how would it affect treatment?
8. In what respects do juvenile delinquency and adult criminality differ legally and socially?
9. How does the delinquency of boys differ from that of girls? Would a program organized to meet the needs of boys be equally preventive in the case of girls?
10. Show how the criminal is almost always the product of conditions that appear in juvenile delinquency.
11. Would the cost of adequate child guidance exceed the current costs of delinquency? By what methods may these costs be estimated and compared?
12. What preventive agencies are now in operation to treat the problems of delinquents?
13. What group contacts of children have high and low correlations with juvenile delinquency?
14. Why is an Adolescents Court recommended as a step in treatment?
15. What is the authority or jurisdiction of the juvenile court in your community?
16. What probation standards are observed in your community? Are probation officers trained for their specific tasks?
17. On the assumption that there is no single cause of juvenile delinquency, and hence no single remedy, construct a community program for its treatment.
18. How would you proceed to show that newspaper publicity (crime news) is or is not related to the prevalent types of juvenile delinquency?
19. What is the general sociological explanation of delinquency?
20. Do you accept the legal decision that the parents of a delinquent should be held accountable for the delinquency on the basis of neglect?

CHAPTER 8

PROBLEMS OF COLLEGE YOUTH

AN INCREASING NUMBER OF PARENTS IN THIS COUNTRY ARE ENTHUSIastic about advanced education for their children. This faith in a college degree and the willingness to make the sacrifice that it demands of most families are reassuring from many points of view. At the same time they reflect a current opinion and prejudice that may be no more permanent or socially practical than a catchy slogan.

This belief in education has been nourished for many generations in the hope that it can solve all social problems. In general, public opinion supports the notion that colleges do a good job and that most high-school pupils should be encouraged to take a college course. A college degree is a requirement for employment and advancement. Hence it is good. It means access to better jobs and higher income. From the public's point of view, vocational training is the basic purpose of the colleges. Other objectives are either not understood or they are ignored.

Problems that inevitably occur with these trends become obvious when it is realized that more young people go to college today than went to high school three decades ago. And this increase in numbers has taken place without equivalent increases in physical equipment or financial support and without corresponding adjustments in the educational program.

Goals of a higher education

The aims of the colleges are also confused in the minds of professional educators. They are by no means in agreement as to the content and objectives of an academic curriculum. Some cling loyally to the liberal arts for their contributions to human understanding, appreciation, and judgment. There are others who reject this tradition. They look upon the colleges as old-fashioned because they do not keep pace with changing social needs—specifically, to prepare the young for particular jobs.

This confusion in content, methods, and goals has been called the dilemma of the colleges. It is an outcome of a number of developments: the growing belief that a college education should be provided for more high-school graduates; the use of the colleges for the readjustment of veterans; the desire of the colleges to cooperate with the programs of military organizations; and the continuation of plans to train leadership for the needs of a peacetime society.[1]

What should American colleges do with their large, culturally different, and changing student body in order to satisfy the varying needs of students? Some educators maintain that the colleges should subtitute a more practical course for the liberal tradition. Others believe that a threatened loss of intellectual leadership can be offset by encouraging a sense of values essentially spiritual in nature. A third point of view holds that higher education merely reflects present-day society and that its responsibility is to follow society's dictates.

The report of the President's Commission is a broad interpretation of goals, methods, and facilities of higher education in America.[2] In this summary of the democratic perspective, education's function is to insure liberty and equal opportunity through the following services of a general curriculum:

1. Development of a democratic code of ethics.
2. Instruction for active participation in the solving of community problems (local and world-wide).
3. Knowledge of science, both physical and social, and the ability to think critically and constructively.
4. Appreciation of culture in general, of arts and literature in particular, and of effective self-expression.
5. Achievement of sound physical and mental health.

[1] L. J. Elias, "Democracy Hands the Colleges a Dilemma," *Bull. Assoc. Am. Colleges,* Vol. 34 (1948): 486-493.

[2] President's Commission on Higher Education, *Higher Education for American Democracy,* Government Printing Office, Washington, 1947.

6. Development of satisfying family, vocational, and other group adjustments.

Current needs of education as a social institution can be demonstrated most directly by a survey of contemporary handicaps and deficiencies.

Problems in higher education

During the 1930's the Carnegie Foundation conducted a ten-year study of the colleges in this country. One of the important findings of this study was the fact that there are more young people attending the high schools and colleges in the United States than in all the rest of the world. From the standpoint of numbers alone, therefore, any condition that is associated with an increase in school enrollments adds increasing importance to the responsibilities of higher education in America. It also accents the needs and problems of the youth who are participants in this change.

From the educational point of view, the Foundation's report included other startling findings. These conclusions will serve the double purpose of describing some of the needs of college students and of pointing out some of their handicaps.

Each finding is concerned with the preparation of young people for college work and their success in this undertaking. The report discovered: (1) that there is little relation between the time spent in college and the intelligence or achievement of students, (2) that many college seniors had lower grades on information tests than some high-school seniors, (3) that many college students had lower scores on these tests than twenty-five per cent of those high-school students who were not planning to go to college, and (4) that many college students, who indicated a desire to become teachers, had lower scores than thirty-six per cent of the high-school pupils.[3]

Before World War II and during the years covered by the Carnegie report, nearly a million pupils graduated from high school every year. Of this number, a third entered college, but less than one half of all entering students completed their college course. Over the years, only about thirty-five to fifty per cent of the students

[3] E. R. Embree, "Can College Graduates Read?," *Sat. R. Lit.*, Vol. 18 (1938), No. 12, pp. 3 ff. W. S. Learned and others, *The Student and His Knowledge*, Carnegie Foundation for the Advancement of Teaching, New York, 1938, Bull. No. 29, p. 37.

who enter all colleges at a given date are likely to take their bachelor's degree in regular course four years later.[4]

College Enrollment in the United States for Selected Years

Years	*Enrollment (000 omitted)*
1929–1930	1,101
1935–1936	1,208
1939–1940	1,494
1945–1946	1,677
1949–1950	2,750

Source: United States Dept. of Labor, Bureau of Labor Statistics, *Fact Book on Manpower,* Jan. 31, 1951, Table 21.

By this description of educational progress and of careers that are begun and not completed, the difficulties of college students are shown to be as important, from the numerical point of view at least, as those of any preceding age group. They will also be shown to be as varied and as hard to treat.

Those who do not go to college. One group of young people in whom the investigating commissions are interested is the lost generation, namely, those who do not have the opportunity to attend college. The belief that anyone can go to college who has the desire and the mental ability is not correct. One of the findings of the Commission on Higher Education (based on the Army General Classification Tests) is that at least thirty-two per cent of the population of the United States has the mental ability to complete an advanced liberal or specialized professional education.

From a different point of view, the factor of economic selection is stressed. In 1938, a report of the American Youth Commission showed that there is usually a close correlation between the father's occupation and the educational opportunities of children. In New York State more than half of the students in the top fourth of the high school graduating classes did not go to college. Findings in a Pennsylvania study show that while the most intelligent children have only a four-to-one advantage over the least intelligent in having an opportunity to go to college, the children of fathers in

[4] Between 1920 and 1940 the college population increased two and one-half times, or from 598,000 to 1,494,000. Since 1900 it has increased six and one-fourth times, and by midcentury 2,750,000 students were enrolled in colleges. R. Walter, "Statistics of Attendance in American Universities and Colleges," *School and Society,* Vol. 62 (1945): 412-419; Vol. 63 (1946): 177-181; Vol. 72 (1950): 401-413. Compare with: C. W. Reeder, "How Many College Graduates Will There Be Living in 1960?" *School and Society,* Vol. 72 (1950): 137-139.

the highest occupational category enjoy an advantage of more than ten to one over those in the lowest occupational level.[5]

This loss of talent is described in more detail by the studies of Warner and associates. In this survey, 56.8 per cent of the students of I.Q. 110 or above attending college are from homes above average in socio-economic status. This total is compared to 12.9 per cent of students of similar I.Q. who are from homes below average in socio-economic status.[6]

Whatever indexes of socio-economic status are used, such as jobs, housing, or neighborhoods, the conclusion is that the lower socio-economic groups do not contribute proportionally to the college population. Proportional representation is of course not significant in itself, but when it can be shown that intelligent youth who could benefit from a higher education are deprived because of insufficient financial means, then the need to offset economic discrimination is important. The President's Commission on Higher Education suggests that the real problem is one of devoting a larger percentage of national income to education and of enabling each family to earn a higher annual income. The Commission further suggests that the present system of scholarship and work programs be supplemented by a national plan of scholarships and fellowships.

Those who fail in college. Another group of students are those with whom college officials have immediate and continuous difficulties, namely, the failures. Of this group the most conspicuous are the youth who cannot make the step from school to college successfully and who discontinue their studies during the first year. In addition, there are special problems of another group who complete one or more years of work but who leave before graduation. Finally, there are the problems of the student who does complete his course and graduates, although he may be handicapped by numerous personal and social liabilities throughout his college years and thereafter as well.

[5] H. M. Bell, *Youth Tell Their Story*, American Council on Education, Washington, 1938. O. D. Henderson, "Equality of Opportunity," *Bull. Assoc. Am. Colleges*, Vol. 38 (1948): 239-249. L. Barber, "Why Some Able High School Graduates Do Not Go To College," *School Rev.*, Vol. 59 (1951): 93-96 (in Table 1, p. 95, the five leading reasons in a total of sixteen for not attending college are (1) finance, (2) lack of academic interest, (3) lack of serious purpose, (4) prefers to work, (5) college requirements). E. Sibley, "Some Demographic Clues to Stratification," *Am. Sociol. Rev.*, Vol. 7 (1942): 322-330.

[6] W. L. Warner and others, *Who Shall Be Educated?*, Harper, New York, 1944.

Why this large number of failures takes place or why others, in spite of handicaps, are able to perform acceptably is explained by ten requirements for success in higher education.[7] These requirements are: (1) health, (2) scholarly ability, (3) sufficient money, (4) stable family background, (5) religion, (6) morals and discipline, (7) personality, (8) social relations, (9) good living accommodations, and (10) a well-rounded social life as manifested by participation in recreation, reading, and school affairs. In the next section, these factors will be weighed as to their importance in making for success or failure.

A shortcoming in any one of these requirements often results in far-reaching and disastrous consequences. Initially, the record of the number of students who fail in college is a sign of economic and social waste. Furthermore, it points out three prominent defects in organized education. One is faulty preparation and selection at the high-school level, a second is a defective system of admissions by the colleges, to which high-school graduates, without the slightest understanding of, or desire for, higher education, are admitted. A third, also on the college level, is an inadequate system of advisory and counseling services, together with inadequacies of staff.

Causes of failure in college

Estimates of the number of college failures vary. However, over a period of years from fifty to sixty-five per cent of the students who enter college at a given time are likely to fail to complete their course.[8] Two major classes of causes are responsible for this loss. One includes educational difficulties and scholastic limitations leading to dismissal because of failure in class work. The second suggests major social difficulties, which embrace a variety of underlying economic, emotional, mental, and personal disorders.

The prevalence of such problems among youth of college age is much greater than is usually suspected. It has been estimated that fully one half to three fourths of all college students have emotional

[7] Hugh Hartshorne (Ed.), *From School to College,* Yale University Press, New Haven, 1939, pp. 46-47.

[8] United States Office of Education, *College Student Mortality,* Washington, D. C., 1938, Bulletin, 1937, No. 11. United States Federal Security Agency, Education Office, *Statistics of Higher Education in the United States,* 1945–1946, Biennial Survey of Education in the United States, Washington, D. C., 1949, p. 15. See recent surveys for current data.

difficulties that interfere with their efficiency in performing good college work. Ten per cent of college youth have mental maladjustments sufficiently serious to cripple their social usefulness and often to result in mental breakdowns. For a group that is presumably a highly selected one, these estimates do not suggest a favorable record of social competence.

One report is most enlightening from this point of view.[9] It is taken from a special study of fifty outstanding freshmen (outstanding because of their intellectual rating) who were followed to the end of their junior year in college. This study demonstrated that these brilliant students knew less at the end of their third year than when they entered as freshmen. They had less accurate information, and they gave other indications that their insights and understandings had been blunted. They possessed no adequate intellectual purpose or stimulus, and their entire stay in college was described as a period of chore-work and marking-time.

Other reasons for the general problems of college youth are the youthfulness of entering students, difficulties arising in connection with the first independence from home life, pressure of the family for college achievement, insufficient money, and uncertainty of vocational preference.

The relative importance of these circumstances that accompany success or failure is shown by the weights that are assigned to the ten requirements for academic achievement mentioned above. Their weighted order is:

Social relations	1.8	Health	0.63
Personality	1.1	Family and home	0.62
Living conditions	1.1	Religion	0.62
Recreation and leisure time	1.1	Finance	0.55
Scholarly ability	0.69	Morals and discipline	0.49

A similar study of problems among college students in clinics and out of clinics points to the same types of problems. The ranking of students' problems in clinical examinations was in order of the severity: emotional, motivational, and social; academic and sexual; schedule (inability to select or plan course work), discipline, and financial. Nonclinical students' problems were: social, emotional and motivational; academic and sexual; financial, health, and fam-

[9] E. R. Embree, *op. cit.*, p. 4.

ily.[10] Taylor reports a comparative study of students with all A's and another group with all F's. The factors reported as significant in this study were: (1) regular attendance, (2) attitude toward class work, (3) ability, and (4) study skills.

The emphasis given to social factors in college failure is to be expected. In order to gain some perspective as to major and comparatively insignificant conditions in social relations or personality that may account for the students' eventual failure, a list of these relatively frequent difficulties is given:

PERSONAL AND SOCIAL DIFFICULTIES OF COLLEGE STUDENTS

Absentmindedness	Feelings of insecurity	Peculiar or odd ideas
Abnormalities in attitude	Food fads	Procrastination
Bashfulness	Indecision	Sex problems
Daydreaming	Inferiority feelings	Speech inhibitions
Emotional conflicts	Morbid sensitivity	Superstitions
Fears	Nervousness	Timidity and worries

Source: J. E. Wallace Wallin, *Personality Maladjustments and Mental Hygiene,* McGraw-Hill, New York, 1935. Adapted from p. 120.

Other approaches to the direct causes of failures are made by an estimate of the most frequent causes for discontinuing college work, by inventories of types of personality that lead to maladjustment, and by a survey of those conditions that account for the success of college freshmen.

General conditions most often associated with college failures and with the discontinuance of college work are:

Vocation	School work	Daydreaming
Sex	Philosophy of life	Fears
Personality deviations	Parents	Speech
Finances	Self-consciousness	Too aggressive
Friends	Lack of concentration	Temper
Religion	Inferiority complex	Insubordination
Temperament	Health	Selfishness

Sources: George W. Hartmann, "The Classification of Adjustment Problems Among College Students," *Jour. Ab. Psych.,* Vol. 28 (1933-34): 64-69. K. L. Heaton, and Vivian Weedon, *The Failing Student,* University of Chicago Press, Chicago, 1939, pp. 162-195.

Common defects in personality most typical of the failing student are: (1) childishness and immaturity, (2) unusual worries and fears,

[10] Fred McKinney, "Four Years of a College Adjustment Clinic," *Jour. Consult. Psych.,* Vol. 9 (1945): 203-217. L. D. Taylor, "Why College Students Fail," *Jour. Higher Educa.,* Vol. 19 (1948): 425-427.

(3) social inadequacy as manifested by ignorance of the ordinary social courtesies, uncooperative actions, disobedience to college rules, being too aggressive or the opposite, or being unpleasant, disagreeable, and unattractive, (4) temporary emotional disturbances, and (5) inability to work alone or without constant guidance.

Most of these characteristics are conspicuous causes of failure. They achieve this explanatory value because they are for the most part *the unresolved problems of the high-school, grade-school and preschool years.*

The successful entering student is entirely different in personality and social background. He has just about the opposite of the failure's personal and social history. He is interested in intellectual and cultural subjects. His home background is favorable in two important respects. His parents have always been interested in his school work and achievements, but they have allowed him gradually increasing freedom from discipline. The home has maintained a better than average cultural status as measured by social, cultural, and religious contacts made available to the child. In addition, he enters college with a good high-school record in all subjects. He has also participated in extracurricular activities. On the negative side, he has not elected manual training or indicated an interest in mechanical subjects, both being interests that are generally correlated with the failing college student.[11]

Physical and mental health. Although the college years continue to rank with adolescence among the healthiest periods of life, minor illnesses are frequent. But, as shown above in the classification of the primary danger zones, ill health is ranked among the least frequent causes of failure in college. Specific illnesses that most often become handicaps are the same as those for adolescence in general, and of them the respiratory and digestive diseases are the most numerous.

Reports concerning the health problems of the college population include other equally important but less precise health hazards. For example, many college students are found to be at a low level of physical efficiency without their conditions being classifiable

[11] F. K. Shuttleworth, "Measurement of Character and Environmental Factors in Scholastic Success," *University of Iowa Studies in Character,* Vol. 1, No. 2, 1928, pp. 60-61. Leo T. Phearman, "Comparison of High School Graduates Who Go to College with Those Who Do Not," *Jour. Educa. Psych.,* Vol. 40 (1949): 405-414. K. K. Heidman, "Collegiate Success of High School Scholarship Winners," *Agricul. Ed. Mag.,* Vol. 21 (1949): 254-255.

under any one illness or defect. Others are reported with bad health habits, inadequate amounts of exercise and sleep, insufficient diets, and as being careless in obtaining necessary medical and dental services. In this connection, it should be noted that most colleges do not maintain sufficient health programs and facilities for the student population.

The situation of college students with respect to their share of physical defects is also similar to that of adolescent youth as a whole. They have a surprisingly large incidence of the common, indisposing minor defects that are found to be associated with poor health habits of youth in general. The four most frequent are defective hearing, overweight, flabby musculature, and anemia. These defects take on real significance when they are observed to occur most often among the failing group.

The college population is also a highly selected group from the standpoint of mental and emotional disorders. As already noted in the introduction to the broad classes of college students' problems, it has been estimated on the basis of clinical experience that fully fifty to seventy-five per cent of college youth are annoyed by minor emotional difficulties and that ten per cent have mental disorders that are sufficiently serious to cause mental breakdowns unless adequate treatment is provided.

Individual or personal problems, reported by the mental hygiene clinic as most likely causes of scholastic failure are: low intelligence, poor academic preparation, emotional maladjustment, sex difficulties, actual neuroses or psychoses, and disciplinary problems.

The reasons for the frequent mental or emotional upsets of college students are, in the records of the clinic, competition in scholastic life, other social changes brought about by the transfer from home to campus, bad home situations, physical changes of adolescence, constitutional emotional instability, and schizoid-reaction type of personality.

Problems of the students who seek service from a college mental hygiene clinic are substantially like those of the majority of the college population, except for the great emphasis on emotional problems. Personal, social, and academic problems are high in this order. Other problems that tend to be high are schedule, home, and vocational problems.

The college mental-hygiene clinic originally functioned in vocational and educational guidance. It was expanded to give psychological services to students in their adjustment to an academic program. Another trend has appeared—the clinic is becoming a recognized source of mental hygiene services and psychotherapy. There is a belief current among some educators that college experience prolongs infancy and that it provides a haven for individuals from an involved work or home situation. The college is used by some parents to escape their difficulties with a child, and the attempt is made to solve the problems of some individuals in need of personal guidance by using general college work as a therapy.[12]

Social and personal problems

In the records of student personnel service, the reports of various colleges show great similarity in the primary problems of college students. There are few or no important sex differences in the problems that are peculiar to men or to women. The only exceptions are certain cultural handicaps, such as the problems of the conspicuously foreign student and of the student who belongs to a group against which there are prejudices. Within this group, too, are the problems of the student who is from a home that is lower than the average college level, either economically or culturally, or which has been disorganized recently by some domestic crisis.

As a rule, neither the social nor the personal problems of college students can be stated as one major liability. Instead, scholastic, health, emotional, and social difficulties are usually found in the same types of students. Ordinarily, such problems appear as a sequence of events, resulting gradually in reduced efficiency or withdrawal from school. An example of this demoralizing combination of circumstances may be such a process as inadequate preparation for college, personal handicaps such as unimpressive appearance, difficulty in making the transition from high school to college standards, overwork, overfatigue, poor grades in the courses that are required for graduation or for advanced study.

The ordinary problems of entering freshmen are mainly social and educational. The latter are difficulties in adjusting to the different standards and policies of college routine, in adapting to dif-

[12] A. L. Rautman, "A New Role for the University Mental Hygiene Clinic," *School and Society,* Vol. 72 (1950): 209-212. H. M. Kallen, "College Prolongs Infancy," in W. Bower (Ed.), *New Directions,* New York, J. B. Lippincott, 1937. Karl Menninger, "Adaptation Difficulties in College Students," *Ment. Hyg.,* Vol. 11 (1927): 519-535.

ferent methods of teaching and teachers, in selecting a program of courses, in using the library, and in developing good habits of study. Social problems arise largely in connection with the new independence from family discipline and the novelty of college life. Associated conditions that may have distressing consequences are the inevitable homesickness, making new friends, achieving status, and seeking advice from proper sources.

The problems of upperclassmen cover a wide range of difficulties. Whatever the essential problem may be, it is usually intensified by academic or scholastic and financial handicaps. As outlined by advisers, administrators, and by students' own selection, their major problems are:

Vocational and Economic

1. Lack of qualifications for a chosen occupation.
2. Choosing an occupation that is overcrowded.
3. Lack of vocational interest.
4. Financial worries.

Intellectual

1. Low intelligence.
2. Defective background in tool subjects.
3. Deficient social knowledge.
4. Reading and memory difficulties.

Emotional

1. Inability to concentrate.
2. School work seems useless.
3. Inability to adjust to college regulations.
4. Discouragement and depression.

Physical Health

1. Digestive illnesses.
2. Defects of vision and hearing.
3. Fatigue.

Scholastic and Academic

1. Unable to budget time effectively.
2. Fear of examinations and inability to write examinations.
3. Inability to develop effective study habits, or to make a good impression in oral or written work.
4. Timidity in the classroom.
5. Lack of a clear-cut educational goal.
6. Inability to organize materials, to take notes, to adjust to lecture method, or to complete assignments.

Social

1. Inability to adjust well to associates or to make friends.
2. Too many extracurricular activities; not enough free time.
3. Too little recreation.
4. Commuting from home to college.
5. Disapproval of student activities and attitudes.

Personal problems. Elements in the personal problems of college students reveal many variations of these more general social unadjustments, particularly in emotional instabilities and frustrations. These specific personal handicaps are excitability, worry, poor adjustment to life in college, physical illness, oversensitivity and immaturity, scholastic deficiencies, fatigue, and sex maladjustments. The repetition of these conditions is shown in every list of personal problems. They also appear in the questions about which college students are usually curious as well as in their fears, most of which are as unreal and uncritical as those of the grade-school child.[13]

The most frequent personal problems of college students, as selected by themselves, are: (1) problems of personality, (2) choice of vocation, (3) choosing a program of study, (4) getting out of some difficulty, (5) methods of study, (6) sex knowledge, (7) changing courses, (8) religion and philosophy of life, and (9) self-support.[14]

These conditions become most demoralizing when they occur in certain combinations. One of these most disorganizing clusters of personal handicaps is identified by those traits that are found in college students who commit suicide. The unadjustments most often associated with suicide are worry, oversensitivity, shyness, marked fearfulness, overmaturity in attitudes, and fatigue.

Types of good personality adjustment illustrate the opposite of these characteristics. The adjusted college student is identified by a sense of responsibility, sincerity and directness of expression, constructive ideas in the face of difficulty, originality, and a genuine interest in people.

The prevalence of unadjusting personality factors in the college population may be judged in part by their occurrence among gradu-

[13] Ruth A. Hunter and David H. Morgan, "Problems of College Students," *Jour. Educa. Psych.,* Vol. 40 (1949): 79-92. W. A. Owens and W. C. Johnson, "Some Measured Personality Traits of Collegiate Underachievers," *Jour. Educa. Psych.,* Vol. 40 (1949): 41-46. A. H. Martin, "A Worry Inventory," *Jour. App. Psych.,* Vol. 29 (1945): 68-74.

[14] Daniel Katz and F. H. Allport, *Student's Attitudes,* Craftsman Press, Syracuse, 1926, p. 89.

ates. In one study of college graduates ten years after graduation, nearly forty per cent reported extreme sensitivity and twenty-five per cent stated that they were touchy, reticent, and constantly overtired.[15]

Unadjusting family situations. There are three types of problems in the college population that reflect direct influences of the family. All are connected with the skill of parents in training the child to good habits of self-help and self-control. Each in turn is a source of tension between parent and child unless it is handled promptly.

One class of problems arises from differences in attitudes and interests and from friction over social activities, college work, or manner of living away from home.

Another is traced to the type of home that continues to dominate the individual in affairs that long before should have become his own responsibility.

A third is caused by the home that protects youth too much from assuming a self-determining role.

Few students from these homes are able to make satisfactory adjustments to the impersonal nature of college life. It is for this reason that the difficulty of making the transfer from home or high school to college is mentioned constantly.

When college students express opinions as to how their parents might have contributed more fully to their college experience, they list these responsibilities and obligations of parents to children: parents should (1) encourage children to make decisions, choose their own friends, and assume responsibility for their own work, (2) train them in the management of money, (3) see to it that they have some familiarity with the college before they enter, and (4) give them the necessary preliminary experience in the customs and manners of life outside the family in order that they may be prepared to meet novel situations with some degree of elasticity.

Parents are urged, consequently, to try to keep themselves free from the narrow points of view that interfere with normal growth in relations with their children, to release them gradually from home influence throughout the adolescent period, and to study their children objectively.

Unfortunately most of the boys and girls who enter college have parents who are not college graduates. For this reason possibly

[15] C. Robert Pace. *They Went to College,* University of Minnesota Press, Minneapolis, 1941, pp. 68-69.

more than any other, there is need for college orientation by means of trained advisers for parents as well as entering freshmen.

Another problem of wider social significance is the waste involved when the two or three superior children of every fourteen who do not enter college fail to receive the training for which they are mentally capable. This is a problem partly because of financial selection, partly because some parents are opposed to a college education for their children, and partly because few colleges have facilities for the early detection and guidance of the potentially superior candidate.

The experience of one teacher in charge of a course for students who had difficulties in studying is significant. In one half of the cases of probation students, Pressey found that the family background played a significant part in bringing about failure.[16] Some of the most prevalent problems are: homesickness, the overprotective parents, the overly dominant parent, and failure to understand parental views.

The student who goes to college cannot divorce himself from his family merely by going to school. Early childhood is important in determining patterns of behavior. These patterns tend to persist in college situations and are important in the maladjustment of college youth. The solving of problems is then dependent on the student's realization of the importance of his family and his ability to see and understand a new situation and adjust to it.

Colleges are accepting responsibility to some degree for students with family problems. Counseling and courses are offered to aid in problem solving. A closer relationship between parents and institutions may be valuable in removing some problems whose source is in parent-student relationships.[17]

Interests and attitudes. Another way to study the social back-

[16] L. C. Pressey, "Some Serious Family Maladjustments Among College Students," *Social Forces,* Vol. 10 (1931): 236-242. S. H. Jameson, "Adjustment Problems of University Girls Because of Parental Patterns," *Sociol. and Soc. Res.,* Vol. 24 (1940): 262-271.

[17] Courses in marriage and family living have grown out of older courses on "The Family." In a study of 1,270 colleges and universities, 49.8 per cent had at least one course in the area of marriage education. H. A. Bowman, "Collegiate Education for Marriage and Family Living," *Annals, Am. Acad. Pol. and Soc. Sci.,* Vol. 272 (1950): 148-155. H. L. Pritchett, "The Adjustment of College Students' Family Problems," *Social Forces,* Vol. 10 (1931): 84-89. C. D. Williams, "College Students' Family Problems," *Jour. Home Econom.,* Vol. 42 (1950): 179-181.

grounds of college youth is through their interests and attitudes as these are manifested in their conversations and in a census of their likes and dislikes.

To college youth, social position or social status is the important thing, and this is the subject most talked about. Other topics more or less in the order of their interest are campus affairs, sex, recreation, morals, culture, money, employment, and home.

CONVERSATIONAL INTERESTS OF COLLEGE STUDENTS

Social position—honors, offices held, organizations.
Campus affairs—politics, gossip, studies.
Sex—social activities, clothes, sex problems.
Recreation—sports, travels, shows, stories.
Morals—religion, drinking, public affairs.
Culture—literature, art, debate.
Home—family, relations, home town.

An obvious conclusion from this inventory of interests is that the main business of going to college is infrequently a topic of conversation. When it is discussed, only trivial aspects of culture or education appear in the conversations.

There is continuous interest and generally a marked curiosity about matters of sex. Most of these interests are concerned with the facts of reproduction and with hereditary and congenital traits. Sex superstitions are numerous, and the student's actual knowledge of, or interest in, the normal aspects of personal sexual life or hygiene is meagre.[18]

Similarities of interest among college men and women are also noted in their attitudes concerning each other. Both sexes express a preference for attractive disposition and personality, equal moral standards, good health, and equal education. Neither sex values family connections or religion as much as might be expected. College men and women differ most in preference for economic ability and personal appearance, the former being chosen most often by women, the latter by men.[19]

Qualities of character noted in college leaders specify the traits

[18] F. I. Davenport, "Adolescent Interests," *Archives of Psychology,* No. 66 (1923). I. H. Anderson and W. F. Deerborn, "Reading Ability as Related to College Achievement," *Jour. Psych.,* Vol. 11 (1941): 387-396. S. M. Stoke and E. D. West, "Sex Differences in Conversational Interests," *Jour. Soc. Psych.,* Vol. 21 (1931): 120-126.

[19] W. C. Neely, "Family Attitudes of Denominational College and University Students," *Am. Sociol. Rev.,* Vol. 5 (1940): 517-519.

that are most popular. These qualities are originality, aggressiveness, common sense, cheerfulness, humor, emotional stability, trustworthiness, tact, and desire to excel. Traits negatively associated with leadership are readiness for anger, conceit, introversion, selfishness, pure-mindedness, uneven moods, occasional extreme depression, and excitability. Qualities most infrequently observed among leaders are radicalism, modesty, sensitiveness, or submission and extroversion (in their extreme manifestations).

Attitudes toward college work. In criticisms of college work by students, the curriculum is most often the object of adverse comment. Many courses in college are considered impractical, unimportant, and repetitive. Students believe that courses should be more adapted to their interests and that required course plans should be more flexible. They object to the stress that is put upon examinations. They believe that many instructors begin their courses above the student's intellectual ability and background. All these objections are connected with their frequent comments upon the indifference of many students to the academic aims of the college as a whole and specifically upon the occurrence of dishonesty in classroom work.

College students prefer those teachers who can present their subject clearly and interestingly. They like friendliness, patience, evenness of temper, a good manner of speaking, good personal appearance, and a sense of humor. They also expect the teacher to be tolerant of differences in opinion. Among the most disliked traits are cynicism, sarcasm, ridicule, any evidence of poor physical or mental health, and professional aloofness.

The real failures in college are the students who "pass" but fail to acquire either knowledge or maturity. This record of college mortality is often traced to poor instruction. Many persons teaching in colleges and universities would not be eligible to teach in grade or high school because of preprofessional requirements. In 1945 a survey of 305 colleges and universities revealed that in ten per cent of the institutions only ten per cent of the teachers had a Ph. D. degree. In ninety per cent of the institutions, forty-seven per cent or more of the faculty did not have a Ph. D. degree. These statements are given here as evidence that adequate education and training in research and teaching may be related directly to the requirements of efficient teaching. In order to remedy this situation, a preservice training program, a better recruitment selection and placement procedure, and a definite program of inservice training are suggested. Colleges are responsible to some degree for college failures. Not enough attention is placed on programs of selecting students; guidance programs are in need of review; and, as suggested above, a teacher selection and training program is indispensable.[20]

Dishonesty in college work has been reported so often that it assumes the proportion of a major problem. Cheating in examinations has been found to be associated with the fear of examinations, the competitive nature both of examinations and of the relationships between teacher and student, and the failure of the course to be clearly organized. Cheating also is most prevalent among poor students or those who work under the pressure of too many outside activities. It decreases with the amount and efficiency of supervision during the examination. However, there is a question of the value of supervision as the key to control. Removing the need rather than the opportunity, though a much more difficult task, would provide more-lasting results.

Conditions associated with low grades. Personal and academic characteristics that are found among students who do poor work in college are: (1) being a nonconformist, (2) starting an advanced education program for prestige rather than knowledge, (3) dislike of mathematics, science, and modern languages in high school, (4) insufficient study, (5) feeling that one is handicapped and (6) engaging in extracurricular activities as well as outside work.[21]

Conditions associated with scholarship. Aptitudes consistently found to be related to high grades or scholarship are intellectual curiosity, scientific approach, educational maturity, membership in political, social, or academic clubs, independent study and research, interest in contemporary affairs, certainty of vocational choice, sound judgment in the use of time, and emotional stability. The three outstanding negative characteristics are study difficulties, interest in informal physical activities, and participation in organized sports.[22]

[20] D. Chamberlin and others, *Did They Succeed in College?* Harper, New York, 1942. A. H. MacLean, "The Real College Failures," *N. E. A. Jour.*, Vol. 38 (1949): 444-445.

[21] K. K. Heidman, "Collegiate Success of High School Scholarship Winners," *Ag. Ed. Mag.*, Vol. 21 (1949): 254-255.

[22] Dean Chamberlin and others, *op. cit.*, pp. 191-92. D. C. Charles, "College Performance of Top Quarter High School Graduates," *Jour. Educa. Psych.*, Vol. 39 (1948): 82-91.

Vocational choices and fitness

College students as a class manifest no more understanding or ingenuity in their occupational aims than high school graduates. This handicap is apparent in their choice of programs of study as well as in their professed occupational goals. As in the case of high-school graduates, their first choice is for the overcrowded fields.

The typical vocational problems of college students are:

1. Planning to enter a vocation for which they do not possess the intelligence expected by graduate schools.
2. Planning to enter a profession involving subjects in which their grades are too poor to permit their admission to graduate work.
3. Indications of little or no interest in the type of work required by the occupation that they choose.
4. Indicating little or no interest in the technical literature of their chosen vocation.
5. Choosing occupations that they have practically no knowledge of and for which they possess few of the social requirements.

These problems show that there is a considerable gap between the students' ability or knowledge in their preferred fields and the requirements for admission to the vocation. Furthermore, there is practically no understanding of the average income to be expected in their vocation, and the poorer their qualifications, the more they are apt to overestimate prospective earnings.

This vocational ignorance points to the need for vocational guidance, counseling, and placement, all of which depend upon specific analysis of different vocations and a study of student's aptitudes.

Various studies have shown that college students ascribe little importance to counseling received in high school and that their vocational choice is not the result of a careful consideration of abilities or of guidance. Occupational indecision is a common malady among college students. Even after graduation it has been pointed out that approximately twenty per cent of college-trained personnel find their work drab and uninteresting. An additional twenty-five per cent are only mildly satisfied with their work.[23]

[23] L. P. Blum, "A Comparative Study of Students Preparing for Five Selected Professions Including Teaching," *Jour. Ex. Educa.*, Vol. 16 (1947): 31-65. N. B. Henry, "Job Prospects for High School and College Graduates," *School Rev.*, Vol. 56 (1948): 373-375. A. J. Walker, "Vocational Choices of Negro College Students," *Jour. Negro Educa.*, Vol. 15 (1946): 146-152. W. B. Webb, "Occupational Indecision Among College Students," *Occupa.*, Vol. 27 (1949): 331-332.

Highly intelligent college youth. Follow-up studies of children who were found to be superior in grade school and during adolescence have reported a continuation of this superiority in college and early adult years.[24] They differ most from average youth or adults in their interests and achievements as well as in their intellectual rating.

An outstanding characteristic of this group is acceleration in education, the superior group as a whole being two years younger than the average of their classmates. Gifted youth are most like the average in social traits. They are most readily identified as superior by their intellectual, volitional, and moral traits, and in the percentage who graduate. They continue to be selected as superior on the basis of health and good looks, social intelligence, personality appraisals (meaning an excess of favorable personality traits and a lower incidence of neurotic tendencies), realistic vocational interests, scientific aptitudes, social and leadership ratings, enjoyment of leadership, management of community activities, and receiving honors or appointments for research grants.

The most frequently reported problems of the superior college group are poor work habits, lack of interest, emotional maladjustments, and deliberate neglect of studies because of other interests.

Follow-up studies report conspicuous success for this superior group in adulthood, both vocationally and economically. It also has better than average records in family life and moral standards. As adults, too, they continue superior in duration of marriage, in the maintenance of satisfactory family relations, in emotional stability, and in accomplishments.

Many people are of the opinion that the good student as a type of individual is one who has adjusted to the ivory tower environment of the college but does not measure up to promise when faced with reality on the job. Many studies have pointed out a positive relationship between good scholarship and success, as success may be measured by vocational prestige. Any definition of success must of

---

M. I. Wightwick, *Vocational Interest Patterns,* Contributions to Education, No. 900, Teachers College, Columbia University, New York, 1945. J. L. Woodward and L. Harris, "Application of Opinion Research to Vocational Guidance," *Occupa.,* Vol. 28 (1950): 504-509. J. Stubbins, "The Relationship Between Level of Vocational Aspiration and Certain Personal Data," *Genetic Psych. Mono.,* Vol. 41 (May, 1950): 333-337.

[24] C. C. Miles, "Gifted Children," Chap. 18, in Carmichael, L. (Ed.), *Manual of Child Psychology,* John Wiley, New York, 1946.

course be an operational definition. A number of studies using income as this measure of success have shown that amount and quality of education are related to success.[25]

If college graduates are produced in increasing numbers, the problem of placing them becomes apparent. In 1940 the United States had three million living graduates; by 1968 the number is estimated to reach ten million. Can the United States also provide the kind of jobs college graduates have come to expect? Should college enrollments be restricted? Answers to these questions depend on many factors, including such things as the character of education to be given, the economic philosophy current, and supply and demand.

In 1940 the male college graduate earned about thirty-two per cent more than the average American income; by 1948 he was making only ten per cent more. By midcentury, bricklayers, railroad engineers, "rollers" in steel mills, and other skilled personnel were earning as much or more than many professional persons. Such factors may have repercussions on the system of higher education. When getting ahead plays such a large part in the motives for college attendance, it is to be expected that many students and parents may reconsider a college education in the light of possible future earnings of noncollege people.

Summary

Education ranks favorably among the social institutions in being able to rate its own effectiveness by the accomplishments of its personnel. Comparisons and rating can be applied to administrative programs, educational philosophies, the contributions of teachers or of research, and the success or failure of students.

This ranking and self-evaluation are important functions of the colleges because their interests have always been in scholarly achievements for human well-being. Educators are always concerned with the character and value of education as each of these qualities can be interpreted from the problems that beset college personnel before, during, and after their college years. The numerous studies of each of these periods are proof of the continuous efforts to improve college programs as well as to minimize ineffective requirements or to

[25] Donald Bridgeman, "Success in College and Business," *Personnel Jour.*, Vol. 9 (1931): 1-19.

modify outmoded traditional standards. Each study of the problems of college students also helps to clarify these objectives.

In the records from the negative point of view—those who are admitted to college without adequate preparation or interest and who discontinue, those who do not go to college because of lack of money or sufficient incentive, and those who complete their college program but graduate into a world of social, occupational, and emotional frustration—there is ample evidence of the need for improvement in the selection of personnel and for the reorganization of the curriculum.

The same standards and qualities are noticeable in the requirements for efficiency in high school, college, and the adult years. Their dependability as useful guides is assured because they are the qualities that also promise good adjustment in the individual's emotional, family, occupational, or wider social life.

In college work, successful adjustment correlates with good habits of study, coming to college with a well-chosen vocational goal, no excessive participation in social life, and an early decision as to programs of study that do not require any radical change in courses or objectives.

So far as home backgrounds are concerned, successful college students are found to come from families that have given them freedom and responsibility. Their parents, moreover, have employed understanding and guidance as discipline rather than domination or no discipline at all.

Judged by his intellectual maturity, the successful college student is described as one who can discover the facts in a difficult situation and who is able to think through a problem to its logical conclusion without the handicaps of emotional bias or interfering personal interest. Such students are further described as those who possess a wide range of information, facility in language, and the ability to appraise artistic and scholarly works in literature and science with some critical appreciation.

In the light of the goals formulated by the President's Commission (see page 193) and the needs essential to their fulfillment, a basic charge against higher education is that it exposes too many students to courses of study that they are unable to appreciate because they do not have the required knowledge, maturity, or academic skills. It neglects basic education for a curriculum that is largely materialistic. It produces graduates who want jobs and success but who are not willing to undergo the discipline that such goals demand. It fails to train the leadership that a society, confused by its own technological skills and social misunderstandings, needs most urgently.

From the point of view of one educator, the problem, at least in its broad social background, is clear: "Communities which spend millions for alcohol, cosmetics, and amusements, and what is left over for schools, are committing spiritual suicide." [26]

Bibliography

Babcock, F. L., *The U. S. College Graduate,* Macmillan, New York, 1941.

Barzun, Jacques, *Teacher in America,* Little, Brown, Boston, 1945.

Chamberlin, Dean, and others, *Did They Succeed in College?* Harper, New York, 1942.

Diehl, H. S., and C. E. Shepard, *The Health of College Students,* American Council on Education, Washington, 1939.

Foster, R. G., and P. P. Wilson, *Women After College,* Columbia University Press, New York, 1942.

Hamrick, R. B., *How to Make Good in College,* Association Press, New York, 1940.

Hartshorne, H. (Ed.), *From School to College,* Yale University Press, New Haven, 1939.

Harris, Seymour E., *The Market For College Graduates,* Harvard University Press, Cambridge, 1949.

Heaton, K. L., and V. Weedon, *The Failing Student,* University of Chicago Press, Chicago, 1939.

Held, D. C., *An Attempt to Predict the Success of University Freshmen in Their Adjustment to Scholastic Work,* Edwards Bros., Ann Arbor, Michigan, 1933.

Hollingworth, L. S., *Children Above 180 I. Q.,* World Book Co., New York, 1942. Chaps. 19-22.

Hollingshead, A. B., *Elmtown's Youth, The Impact of Social Classes on Adolescents,* John Wiley, New York 1949.

Leonard, E. A., *Problems of Freshmen College Girls,* Teachers College, Columbia University, New York, 1932.

McConn, Max., *Planning for College,* Stokes, New York, 1937.

MacIntosh, Archibald, *Behind the Academic Curtain,* Harper, New York, 1948.

McKinney, Fred., "Four Years of a College Adjustment Clinic," *Jour. Consult. Psych.,* Vol. 9 (1945): 203-217.

Minnesota Commission on Higher Education, *Higher Education in Minnesota,* University of Minnesota Press, Minneapolis, 1950. Chapter 8, "What Happens to Junior-College Students?" Chapter 10, "Students of

[26] *Time,* Nov. 1, 1948, p. 67.

Minnesota's Liberal Arts College": a follow-up study of former Minnesota Liberal Arts College students.
Moberly, Walter (Sir), *The Crisis In the University,* Macmillan, New York, 1949.
Pace, C. R., *They Went to College,* University of Minnesota Press, Minneapolis, 1941.
President's Commission on Higher Education, *Higher Education for American Democracy,* Government Printing Office, Washington, 1947. Vols. 1-6.
Rockwood, L. D., and M. E. N. Ford, *Youth, Marriage and Parenthood,* John Wiley, New York, 1945.
Sparling, E. J., *Do College Students Choose Vocations Wisely?* Teachers College, Columbia University, New York, 1933.
Strang, Ruth M., *Behavior and Background of Students in College and Secondary Schools,* Harper, New York, 1937.
Wallin, J. E. Wallace, *Personality Maladjustment and Mental Hygiene,* McGraw-Hill, New York, 1935.
Warner, W. L., R. J. Havighurst, and H. S. Loeb, *Who Shall Be Educated?,* Harper, New York, 1944.
Wrenn, C. G., and R. Ball, *Student Personnel Problems,* Farrar and Rinehart, New York, 1942.
Young, Kimball, *Personality and Problems of Adjustment,* Crofts, New York, 1940. Chap. 19.

Questions

1. What problems noted in other age groups are intensified in problems of college students?
2. What are some of the conflicts in value in current interpretations of the role of higher education?
3. Are any statements concerning problems of college students applicable to you? To your friends? Have you worked out any solutions to these problems? Where can you get information or aid in solving the problems?
4. Investigate the program of counseling and mental hygiene clinics at your college or university. What are the classes of problems with which they deal?
5. How are problems of higher education related to social class concepts and to analysis of professions in relation to social structure?
6. In what ways are the successful college students most like failing college students?
7. Analyze the demands for college graduates in specific professions over a period of twenty years. What types of vocations have the greatest demands for college graduates? Which have the fewer demands?
8. Do occupational interest and aptitude tests have any value in vocational guidance?
9. What current legislation can you find concerning the problem of discrimination in higher education?
10. What are the most significant predictive factors of college success?

CHAPTER 9

THE AGED

THE PROPORTION OF OLDER PERSONS IN THE POPULATION OF THE UNITED States has steadily increased and is likely to increase for some time to come. The average twenty-year-old can look forward to forty-five to fifty more years of life.

The fact of longer life is not an unmixed blessing. It borders on the paradoxical because a long life, which is considered good, also has its disadvantages. In this respect, aging and old age are typical social problems—in the numbers who reach the upper years, in their special needs, in the variable and contradictory social attitudes as to the values of being old, and in old age itself as a biological process.

In the latter connection, old age is a typical bio-social problem. It is a condition to which people must adjust since they cannot avoid it and there are no cures. The bodily symptoms of aging and the problems which accompany it are well known. But the causes of aging and old age are "insoluble problems."

Paradoxical, too, are the attitudes toward aging. Long life and the health and vigor that make it possible are always accepted as symbols of a progressive society. At the same time they create numerous campaigns to retard the aging process and frantic quests for elixirs of youth. But none of these efforts has ever been successful, and no centenarian has ever been able to furnish a recipe that would duplicate his good luck. Although aging is a normal process, defined as a progressive decrease of vitality, this normal process practically never occurs. Instead, senescence is a period of bodily damage and progressive inefficiency, the equal of which cannot be found in any younger age group.

Similarly paradoxical is the successful aging of increasing numbers of people. Rather than being proof that health, sanitation, nutrition, and public safety have produced a secure population, the result is a large number of people who are ill, defective, socially and emotionally disturbed, and economically dependent. The burden on the public treasury and upon private resources for their personal rehabilitation is one that has never been met fully or effectively.

Old age is supposed to compensate for these miseries by having its own special virtues, namely, few or no responsibilities, more leisure, fewer distractions, and a less tense existence. However, there is no evidence that anyone is eager to pay the price for these advantages. On the contrary, elderly people more often try hard to avoid them and to retain the appearances of youth.

Old age, consequently, is no certain sign of successful personal and social gains. To achieve it is a dubious advantage for a majority of the aged because they do not face their own problems graciously, nor are they able to eliminate the ill-effects through their own devices. In brief, the problems of the aged are questions of public welfare and control.

As the proportion of old persons in the population increases, they may become an asset to a nation or a social menace. What the outcome is to be in the future will depend upon public policy and the effectiveness and completeness of its planning.

Major problems of old age

Old age is a natural or normal condition. With one exception—the insecure cultural status of the aged—its pathologies are the same as those that occur at any other age period, but they are intensified by illness, family disorganization, unemployability, reduced income, and dependency. As a physical, mental, economic, or social problem, old age has been the subject of many books, but there has never been one that could supply the basis of an adequate plan for protection against its problems.

Under some forms of primitive social organization and in the Old World systems of patriarchal families, the aged had a definite and respectable cultural position. They were the elders, the carriers of folk wisdom, the sages. This position was lost to the aged by the same physical and social processes that multiplied their numbers. Accordingly, the chief social problem of modern society relative to the aged is to find some equivalent for that social position of usefulness. When physical impairments cause the retirement of the aged, these need by no means spell the end of their usefulness. Of this fact there are many illustrations.

Under any form of economic organization, only a proportion of the population is engaged in production. The power of consumption, however, is not so limited. Children and old folks are consumers: the former are potential producers; the latter have earned their keep by previous labor. Physically, mentally, and socially defective persons are consumers all the time and sometimes are never producers. But the care exercised for the latter is not at all comparable to society's responsibility for the young and the old. By contrast, one of the striking features of social welfare and reform is the relative neglect of the aged.

In one survey of the major problems of the aged, the following 4,007 conditions were found in a study of 1,935 aged persons:

PROBLEMS OF THE AGED

	Number	*Per Cent*
Inadequate homes	1,694	42.3
Physical illness	1,007	25.1
Economic need	623	15.5
Mental illness	352	8.8
Unsatisfactory family relations	260	6.5
Employment and other problems	71	1.8
Total	4,007	100.0

Source: H. H. Brunot, *Old Age in New York City,* Welfare Council, New York City, 1943, p. 41.

The social problems of this group are as varied as the several different classes of old people. And they are not problems that can be met by any one type of remedy. Economic competence, physical ability, mental capacity, and family adjustment must be taken into account. The economic is the major problem, because it is the most apparent. Moreover, prior to the factory system, economic superannuation or technological unemployment was practically unknown. But there are other equally important problems. Thus, no form of readjustment purely economic in character will solve all the problems of the aged. Physical and mental illness and lack of psychological adjustment and social adjustment present many serious difficulties. Compared with the latter, the solution of economic problems is simple. The others can be approached only through physiology, psychology, and sociology. But once economic security is gained, regardless of its costs, society will be well on the way to attack the problems of the aged from the other approaches.

Social and Personal Problems of the Aged

1. Impersonal relations in cities
2. Failure of industry to provide for elderly workers
3. Inability of children to support their parents
4. Urban housing: small dwellings and apartments
5. Emotional and social, as well as economic, insecurity
6. Chronic diseases and liability to accidents
7. Education of the public to appreciate the values of the aged
8. Recreational needs
9. Subjective reactions, such as feelings of inadequacy, depression, and self pity
   hypochondria
   anxiety and worry
   oversensitivity
   boredom and restlessness
   narrowing of interests
   social withdrawal
   loss of inhibitions, untidiness, and occasionally sex problems
   loneliness

Sex differences in the problems of the aged.[1] Distinctive social differences between aged men and women are discovered as primary indicators of their special problems and needs. Among men the chief disturbance is retirement, for which few are adequately prepared socially or emotionally. For women, because of their tendency to outlive their husbands, their most drastic readjustment is to widowhood. One result of this difference is that there are more elderly women than men without homes. They are obliged to live with their children or in institutions.

Other differences modifying the problems of the sexes are to be found in their preferences or personal traits. Women participate more in social activities than do men during their sixties, but in the seventies this condition is reversed and men have the more social

[1] R. S. Cavan and others, *Personal Adjustment in Old Age,* Science Research Associates, Inc., Chicago, 1949, pp. 60-61. In an essay in *Time,* Nov. 13, 1950, p. 31, on George Bernard Shaw, 1856–1950, there is an effective illustration of one problem of the aged, loneliness: "His great age was his last great turn, which could hardly conceal an appalling loneliness. All his contemporaries were dead. His wife had gone. He recognized how poor his contacts with human beings were, now he was without intermediaries. He was, in a sense, unhuman. He depended on servants whom he hardly knew. He came close at times to that terrible condition of the old in contemporary England, who discover that there is no one to depend on and for whom the mere mechanics of living have become tragically difficult." (Courtesy of *Time,* copyright Time, Inc., 1950.)

contacts. Men also have more companionships than women. A difference in economic attitudes is also noticed. Women tend to feel more secure economically than do men. Women report more physical handicaps, illnesses, nervous and neurotic symptoms, and accidents than men. They have more religious interests and more favorable attitudes toward religion. And oddly enough they consider themselves more unhappy and report less "zest for life." But men commit suicide much more often than women (a trend that starts in the early twenties with sharp increases in the fifties and sixties) and this condition is recognized as a fairly objective index of discontent, frustration, and a feeling of uselessness.

Old age defined

A person is no longer as old as he feels. This has been apparent in recent years since so-called "industrial old age," which is not identical with chronological old age, has become an important problem. Originally, the chronological limit was placed at 70; at this age people experience a decline in their physical or mental abilities, though they are still capable of self-help within the limits of their declining capacities. Most systems of private pensions or endowments recognize a lower limit for retirement and make age 65 the dividing point. Sixty-five is chosen because vital statistics show that at this age there are marked increases in rates of sickness and death, and the average individual 65 years old has given 45 years of productive labor. Industrial old age is a more elastic concept, sometimes going as low as the late thirties, and it will be mentioned among the newer insecurities of the aged.

In the New York City Survey, referred to above, the youngest person of the 1,935 was 47, the eldest 99.

Physiologically, aging is defined as interferences with normal metabolic processes in individual cells, the results being reduced, slower, or impaired functions of the circulatory system, of the kidneys, and of mental responses. This definition is in agreement with the popular impression of old age, and, in statements of old people as to how they first noticed aging, they most often mention difficulty in working, nervous ailments, sense-organ impairments, greater need for sleep, fatigue, impaired memory, fears, and loss of confidence.

Old age or its symptoms have been defined in other ways. They deserve some notice because they refer to the important social problems that are lost sight of in economic considerations. Among the various theories of old age, none has attracted more attention than those that have attempted to determine the period when actual senility sets in, as judged by lack of achievement. Perhaps no definition is better than the officially recognized age 65, however, since this is the age at which most pension plans take effect.

Another general interpretation is that old age begins when an individual is no longer able to maintain his share of those activities that are typical of the average adult. From this point of view, old age can be defined as a composite condition. One factor is physical disability. A second is declining mental ability. A third is the gradual giving up of social activities—usually work in the case of men and household management in the case of women—plus fewer community activities, changes in family status, and modified interests, plans, and goals. A fourth is also social, but largely because of a changing economic status. It may include economic dependence on others for support or management of funds, a position subordinate to younger people (to children or, in the case of old-age assistance, to social workers), living in an institution, and the dwindling of interests until they are largely identified with their children's activities.

Osler's idea of old age in terms of accomplishment and efficiency was neither new nor has it been abandoned.[2] Another and more recent term for age is "functional age." It is applied to such occupations as that of the airplane pilot. Here age is measured by vision, motor skill, and general mental ability. Thus, old age is more than physical infirmity, economic dependency, or social isolation. It is the period when the individual must adjust to a mode of living, when the lack of activity and interests may be demoralizing, and

[2] Prior to his retirement from Johns Hopkins University to accept an Oxford professorship, Osler said: "I have two fixed ideas. The first is the comparative uselessness of men above forty years of age. . . . My second fixed idea is the uselessness of men above sixty years of age, and the incalculable benefit it would be in commercial, political, and in professional life if, as a matter of course, men stopped work at this age." (Quoted by G. Stanley Hall, in *Senescence,* D. Appleton-Century, New York, 1922, pp. 3-4.)

A further social characterization of old age, describing different periods and beginning with 65, is quoted by Frances Bardwell in *Social Service Review,* Vol. 4 (1930): 203. "At that age we ceased to hurry; at seventy we discovered sunshine and lingered in it; at seventy-five we are fussy; at eighty, we demand; at eighty-five, we no longer demand, we have become a person who views the procession apart from it; at ninety, we wait apprehensively and expectantly; at one hundred we have a celebration and are congratulated; and from then on, the world seems to begrudge us our living."

when failure to achieve recognition gives rise to a philosophy of futility.

How numerous are the aged?

For an understanding of the numerical importance of the problem of the aged, three facts have to be considered. The first is that the aged constitute a relatively new problem. Only recently and in industrial countries have large numbers of the aged and dependent appeared. Their increase is traced to social and economic improvements and to medical advancement which, in combination, have brought about a remarkable decline in the mortality of younger age groups. In this country, the heavy immigration of adults during the last several decades has also been an important influence. The second fact has to do with the decreasing industrial opportunities for the aged, which make them natural dependents, resembling children in this respect. From this fact, a third becomes obvious: the aged are not pauperized in the same sense as other dependents. More than seventy per cent of the aged are in the 65 to 74 age group, and since there has been practically no improvement in life expectancy in the upper age groups, increasing mortality rates can be expected. Women experience greater longevity than men, hence their numerical superiority after age 65.

The aged are thus a new leisure class, and the aged dependent are those who can ill afford this leisure. These facts serve as the bases for a minimum program of economic and social rehabilitation.

In this country, the number of aged persons is increasing both absolutely and relatively. The total proportion of the aged 65 years and over is now approximately eight per cent of the population or 12.3 million people. The trends since 1900 and the prospects, as computed from census records and forecasts up to the year 2000 are:

THE AGED POPULATION
(65 years and above)

	1900	*1950*	*2000*
Number in millions	2.2	12.3	21.5
Per cent of total population	4.1	7.6	13.2

Sources: United States Bureau of the Census, and the special census publication, *Forecasts of the Population of the United States,* Washington, 1946, Series, P-46, No. 7.

These figures show that the aged are increasing faster than the general population, and the proportions of increase are indicated by the population pyramids for 1900 and 1980. In 1900, one person in twenty-five was 65 years and over; today about one in thirteen is in this group; and in 1980 there will be about one in ten.

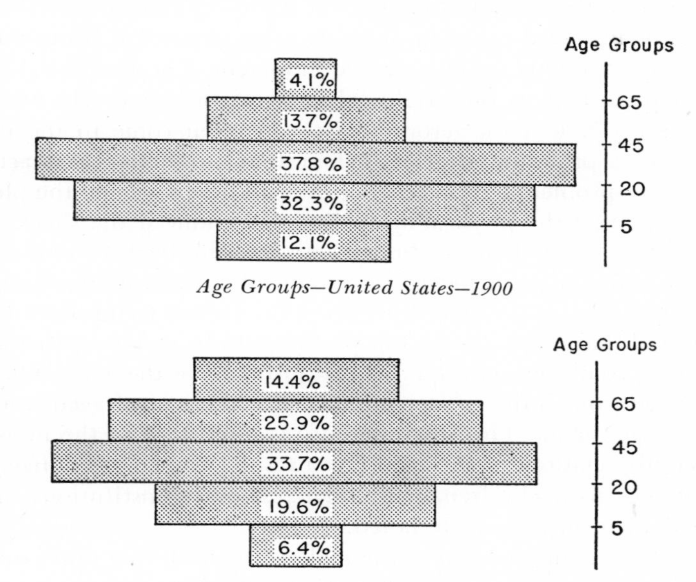

Age Groups—United States—1900

Age Groups—United States—1980

This tendency toward aging is not limited to upper age groups. It is characteristic of the entire population. As life expectancy increases, the median age is also increasing. In 1900 it was slightly less than 23 years. By 1950 it was slightly less than 30 years, and by 1975 it is expected to be about 34 years.[3]

Social hazards of the aged

The primary social hazards of old age are the changes that it brings about in economic and occupational status, in family and marital relations, in economic dependency, and in health. The first of these problems is largely a result of retirement, whether it is voluntary or forced. The second is generally the problem of widows and widowers and the breaking up of the home. The third is the ancient problem of poverty, since the average industrial worker is

[3] J. W. Mountin, "Public Health and Aging," *Pub. Health Rpts.*, Vol. 65 (1950), No. 25, pp. 795-802.

unable to save enough and is usually not, at least until recently, in a protected industry. The latter problem has been eased, if not solved, by the Social Security program of old age pensions and Old Age and Survivors Insurance. The fourth, the problem of health, is the major unsolved problem of the upper age groups. But it, too, has its hopeful note in the recent development of geriatrics.

As a hazard in its own right, old age, according to Dr. Martin Gumpert, a New York gerontologist, can often come to the individual as a profound shock.[4] When that psychological reaction occurs, this problem has precedence over all others. Then the physician must treat the physical symptoms that induced the shock and must restore the patient to as much activity as his health will permit.

In several studies of particular groups of people, dating back to the early works of Abraham Epstein,[5] a number of trends have been discovered that in turn point out problems to be reckoned with and the most promising plans for the readjustment of the aged. One of these conditions is the greater number of widows or of aged women than of aged men. This sex difference is important in the housing and family relations of the aged. As a result, women are obliged to find homes with children, with relatives, or in institutions more often than men, as already noted.

The equivalent problem of the male is the declining opportunity for gainful employment even though he may be willing and able to work. In the past, this old age employment put an excessive burden on children, poor relief, old age assistance, and pension plans. It continues to be a source of frustration, loss of interest in life, and concern about the individual's usefulness.

Both sexes are about equally handicapped in their inability to adjust socially. This unsatisfactory condition is explained in part by the low average of educational achievement of most old people, since the present generation of the elderly were in school (generally rural) when the average grade achievement was less than it is today. This educational liability modifies the aims of adult education programs to some extent and is a handicap to an individual's own resourcefulness. This unsatisfactory social adjustment is also indicated by few friendships, decreasing participation in social groups,

[4] "Nobody Gets Younger," *Time,* Jan. 24, 1949.

[5] Abraham Epstein, *Facing Old Age,* Knopf, New York, 1922. ———, *The Challenge of the Aged,* Macy-Masius, New York, 1922. ———, *Insecurity: A Challenge to America,* Smith and Haas, New York, 1936.

an inability to acquire interesting hobbies or constructive avocations, and by the almost universal absence of a wholesome social philosophy.

The problems of health are accented by increasing numbers of physical handicaps, more frequent and serious illnesses, more mental disturbances, and a general personal reaction among the aged that ill-health is their major burden.

In Cleveland, the Welfare Foundation introduced a program in 1944 to meet all these hazards of the elderly. This program is applied through a citywide organization of Golden Age Clubs. The members are in sole charge of the club activities, which include music, lectures, picnics, tours, and classes, and which are arranged so as to meet the needs of different cultural and educational groups. Hobby clubs have been formed under trained supervision, and they supply the same type of training as in occupational therapy. Hobby shops and a hobby show developed. Possibly of equal importance with these activities is the stimulus that they have given to other agencies to initiate avocational opportunities, such as the adult-education program of the public library, old age counseling services by the Church Federation, and the improved social program of the home for the homeless aged and chronically infirm.

Economic status of the aged

One of the most elusive problems is to determine the economic resources of the aged. The reasons for this difficulty are that the aged are widely scattered and that accurate reports as to their financial circumstances are given only for those who are on public relief or receiving other forms of assistance. In recent years, before and after World War II, about one in every four old people has received aid under the old age assistance provision of the Social Security Act. Another significant fact about the dependent aged is their regional distribution. Some states have a high rate of old age dependency —nearly 800 of every 1,000 old folks are on public assistance in Alabama, Colorado, and Oklahoma—while other states, such as New York, Connecticut, and Maryland, have had rates as low as 100 per 1,000.

In the study by Cavan,[6] which surveyed a group of old people in a more self-sufficient economic status than for the country as a whole,

[6] R. S. Cavan and others, *op. cit.*, pp. 47 and 52, Tables 12 and 13.

about one third of the total, 65 years and over, received public old age assistance, another third were employed and self-maintaining, and another third depended on their own resources or were supported by children and relatives. The sources of support for the whole group varied slightly, as the following separation by sex points out:

SOURCES OF SUPPORT OF THE AGED

Men	*Women*
Present earnings	Investments, annuities
Investments, annuities	Present earnings
Old age assistance	Old age assistance
Pensions	Children

By percentage distribution and by self-ranking, the economic status of this group is:

	Per Cent Distribution	
	487 Men	*732 Women*
Wealthy	1	1
Well-to-do	15	10
Comfortable	56	60
Enough to get along on	23	23
Dependent	5	6
	100	100

The insecure economic status of the total aged population, 65 years and over, for the entire country is shown more completely in reports of the Social Security Administration. According to its estimates, of the nearly twelve million individuals eligible for assistance, about five million, or forty-two per cent, are entirely without income; four million, or thirty-three per cent, are self-supporting; and three million, or twenty-five per cent, are dependent and are presumably supported by relatives. In the discussion below of old-age dependency, the chief sources of support for those not working will be given.

In both governmental reports and in the studies of selected groups, there is uniform agreement that the average standard of living of the aged is low. They also agree, and this agreement is supported by the personal reactions of the aged, that stability of income is more important to the aged than its actual amount. On the whole, the aged who have a small, regular income feel economically secure.

Occupational displacement. Most old people prefer to work if they are able. Only a small percentage retire voluntarily, and this reluctance to retire has been typical in the experience of old age benefit plans since the operation of the Social Security Act. It is this situation that leads most economists to conclude that industry should make special provisions for the able-bodied through part-time jobs.

Reasons for retiring according to Social Security records are: [7]

Lost job		53.2
Quit job		46.8
Health	34.9	
Wished to retire	5.5	
Other reasons, generally physical defects or mental condition	6.4	
Total	46.8	100.0

For a variety of reasons, the trend of modern industry has been in a direction opposite to the personal preference of the aged and has favored the gradual replacement of the upper age groups by younger workers. Important exceptions to the trend are in agriculture, forestry, animal husbandry, public service, professional service, domestic and personal service, and in special occupations, such as transportation, that have seniority provisions. Whereas, therefore, farmers, lawyers, justices, retail merchants, bankers, manufacturers, and a few other preferred groups continue to work after age 65 in greater proportions than would normally be expected, scarcely one fourth to one fifth of industrial and mechanical workers are employed at this age.

The reasons for this discrimination against the older industrial worker are numerous. Standardized and mass production eliminate the need for experience and skill, which are the two primary assets of the older worker. Moreover, the speed maintained by automatic machinery is too great for the older men. Technical changes in industry and, consequently, technological unemployment have materially reduced the number of employees over 45 years of age. This maladjustment of the older workers to new industrial processes has led many firms to adopt a hiring age limit, which is most disheartening to the worker because it makes chronological middle age the equivalent of industrial old age.

Another group of causes of occupational displacement is to be

[7] M. L. Stecker, "Beneficiaries Prefer to Work," *Soc. Security Bull.*, Vol. 14 (1951): 15-17.

found in the several humanitarian projects introduced by industry precisely for the purpose of eliminating the hazards of old age. Five of the six following causes of the economic insecurity of the aging worker fall within this classification: (1) introduction of pension and group insurance plans, (2) cost of workmen's compensation insurance, (3) the increasing demands of industry for physical fitness and mental adaptability, (4) the lower wage cost of younger workers, (5) the policy of promotion within the company, (6) the displacing of men by machines. Every one of these but the fourth represents an efficiency device adopted largely for the protection of the worker, but all of them in combination make the serious problem of occupational old age. Pension schemes, provided by industry for men 65 or over, qualify that the recipients of these pensions must have been employed by the concern for twenty to thirty years before retirement. In order to avoid responsibility for workers who could not fulfill this requirement, age limits are adopted that prevent the hiring of men who might become incapacitated prior to the time for retirement. Another factor, group insurance, which is being adopted by industry extensively, has a similar consequence—the lowering of age-limits—because of the higher insurance rates for older workers.

In a number of basic industries, definite age limits are observed in hiring. Usually the limit varies for degrees of skill, 50 being the upper age for skilled workers and 45 for unskilled. Although many industrial concerns deny the observance of any specific age limit, manufacturing and mechanical industries, transportation, and clerical employment show unusually small proportions of middle-aged or older workers, because they hire primarily from the 25- to 44-year-old group. Evidence of the latter tendency has been found repeatedly by social agencies concerned with the problem of industrial old age.

There is ample evidence that this employment trend runs counter to the facts concerning the occupational adaptability of the aged. During World War II many former employees who had been laid off were re-employed by industry, and their work record compared favorably with that of the younger group.

An almost impossible problem for the aged worker is to get a job after he has been released. As a rule, older workers keep their jobs more often than younger workers do when layoffs occur in slack times.

Numerous other conditions affect the employment of older workers, such as their assumed accident proneness and susceptibility to occupational diseases; their general physical condition; assumed reduction of skills with aging; ability to be retrained and the costs of this training in the light of their life expectancy; and friction with younger workers.

Extent of old age dependency. Old age has always been a major cause of dependency in industrial societies and in urban communities. It is a lesser cause in agrarian societies and in rural communities. This difference is a result in part of family solidarity and in part, as already noted, of the longer work life of agricultural peoples.

Mobility of population, which occurs under industrial and urban conditions, is also a factor in contemporary old age dependency. It breaks up families and makes the support of parents by children less possible, even if children were able and willing to assume this charge.

Other causes of old age dependency in the past have been the inability to save or acquire property, employment in industries without retirement or pension plans (or the inadequacy of such plans), and inability to maintain insurance or annuities with private companies.

According to a breakdown of the sources of support of the twelve million aged persons previously mentioned (of whom one in four is on public assistance and practically two thirds are without adequate income), the supplementary sources of support (supplementary to earnings, savings, annuities, pensions, and support by children or others) are federal civil service pensions, Army, Navy, Coast Guard, or other federal pensions, Veterans Aid benefits, pensions from state and local governments, and support by public welfare institutions.

Family status of the aged

At age 60 about two thirds of the men and two fifths of the women are living with their spouses in their own homes. The progressive loss of this family status with aging is their most tragic problem. Becoming a widow or widower means not only the breakup of the home but "a striking detachment and loneliness," and an inability to maintain equally satisfactory relationships in the homes of children, in institutions, or in other domestic accommodations. At ages 80 to 90, nearly one half of all men are widowers and three fourths of all women are widows (remarriage, separation, and divorce occur rarely in old age and are not factors that need to be considered either as modes of social readjustment or as conditions affecting domestic status).

A sample indication of marital status among the aged upon application for old-age assistance is furnished in the following distribution: [8]

MARITAL STATUS OF 591 APPLICANTS FOR OLD-AGE ASSISTANCE

	Per Cent Distribution
Married	11.4
Widows	48.2
Widowers	17.5
Separated	3.4
Divorced	1.1
Deserted	0.4
Spinsters	11.7
Bachelors	6.3
Total	100.0

Causes of old age dependency

In addition to the risky economic status of the aged, the chief causes of dependence are the chronic and degenerative diseases and the physical defects. These illnesses are equal in frequency to the highest rates of any preceding age group. They continue over a longer period of time. Convalescence is slower. And the rate of recovery is much less favorable than in younger groups. The illnesses of old age have other insidious characteristics that are peculiar to advancing years and that make their detection, care, and treatment most difficult. Among these liabilities and complications is the increase of mental diseases that accompany the physical breakdown of the body.

According to Vischer's observations, physical illnesses and the physical signs of senescence are twice as frequent as the mental. In order of decreasing frequency, they affect the following organs and functions of the body: motor coordination, nervous system (including defects of memory), sensory organs, skin, resistance to fatigue, sexual functions, circulatory system, metabolism, kidneys, and respiration. The insidious character of this deterioration of

[8] J. J. Griffin, "The Sheltering of the Aged," *Jour. Geront.*, Vol. 5 (1950): 30-43. A. L. Vischer, *Old Age*, Allen and Unwin, London, 1947, Chap. 1. J. H. Sheldon, "Old-Age Problems in the Family," *Milbank Mem. Fund Quart.*, Vol. 27 (1949): 119-132.

the body is noted by the facts that (1) most elderly people will have several of these illnesses or defects, (2) degeneration is slow but progressive, (3) often symptoms may be nonexistent or so few that they are not observed by physicians, and (4) there are few or none of the crises noted in the same illnesses in younger persons. Subjective symptoms, therefore, are considered to be more reliable in many instances than the objective signs. Among aged ill or defective people, these symptoms are loss of appetite, insomnia, tiring easily, crying spells, being melancholy, being nervous and forgetful, or worry about health.

Oddly enough, the special studies of selected groups do not find frequent complaints of ill health by the aged. Many individuals either regard themselves as in excellent condition or are satisfied with their health. Also, as would be expected, when complaints are made, the old can find a lot that is wrong with them.

The diseases reported among the leading causes of death for the entire population are also the major disabling illnesses of old age. These conditions are diseases of the heart, cancer, diabetes, cerebral hemorrhage, pneumonia, tuberculosis, nutritional diseases, and accidents.

Types of aged people and their adjustment

Classifying types of aged people is subject to all of the hazards of any form of classification.

A general classification suggested by Epstein recognized three major types: (1) the wealthy, whose only problem is social adjustment, (2) the great mass of the aged, who are theoretically independent because they do not seek aid but who are either near or below a minimum standard of living (for this group economic as well as social protection is required), (3) the institutional and pauper classes, recipients of public or private custodial or outdoor relief. Rubinow made a more extensive subdivision, indicating by the groups that are excluded the modern problem of old age protection. His five classes are:

1. Those whose earning capacity remains unimpaired. Although this occurs relatively infrequently, continued earnings avoid the problem of dependency.
2. Retired persons who have sufficient savings. Rubinow states that this group is more common in this country than in any other, but less common than is usually assumed.

3. Those who are supported by their children, requiring a group solidarity that is apparently breaking down.
4. Those depending upon public or private relief agencies.
5. Those depending upon superannuation schemes, industrial, civil, or military pensions.[9]

Those who are classifiable under any of these five classes, with the exception of the first, make up the group that is now eligible under Social Security provisions.

The various personal and objective circumstances in the lives of dependent old people furnish the basis for the classification of their main types. No single class can be identified by the personal factors of stupidity, ignorance, or folly. Rather, a chain of circumstances, in addition to incompetency and failure, is responsible for the final issue—chronic economic insufficiency, forced changes in occupations, the disappearance of trades, improvident helpmates, sudden illness or death of the wage earner, abnormal burden of dependents, industrial accidents, foolish investments, and character defects. It would be difficult, for example, to classify the numerous cases of dependent women who have spent their lives caring for parents or relatives. It would also be difficult to classify the case of a woman who invested all her money in the musical education of her daughter, because she felt that her own musical talents had been neglected, only to discover that the girl could never establish herself as a musician. Ordinarily, factors such as these are considered as a basis of subclassification in connection with the sources of support available to the aged.

Successful and planned retirement is the goal of most people and of all annuity programs. A good example and one worth a brief review is the experience of a retired physician.[10]

Dr. Peck practiced medicine for thirty years. Early in his working days he decided to retire at 60. He insured part of his financial security by an annuity of $150 per month to begin at age sixty. He insured the rest of his security by purchasing and operating a small farm which he selected after a careful search beginning fifteen years before retirement. On this farm he has a cow, chickens, and a vegetable garden. Without making this work all monotonous

[9] I. M. Rubinow, "The Modern Problem of the Care of the Aged," *Soc. Ser. Rev.*, Vol. 4 (1930): 169-182. See also R. S. Cavan, *op. cit.*, Chap. 6, for other illustrative types.

[10] J. Peck, "I Cured Myself of Working," *Saturday Evening Post*, Jan. 17, 1948, pp. 33 ff.

labor, he raises enough to break even on milk and egg production. The family's grocery bill for three persons is rarely more than $30 a month. He conscientiously limits his work day to three hours, the remaining hours being spent in resting, reading, recreation, or neighboring. He enjoys meetings of the Farm Bureau and confesses that he learns more from them than from any medical meeting he attended.

His philosophy for happiness is from the Bible: "For I have learned, in whatever state I am, therewith to be content."

When people retire, whether their financial status is assured or not, serious social disorders and personality defects may develop. In addition to being financially secure, a few in this group may be healthy, enjoy a favorable social environment, and hold an honored position in the community. Others upon retirement may develop demoralizing traits of frustration and become seclusive because they have nothing to do. Or they may be overprotected, which can be as damaging in some instances as loneliness. Or they may become the victims of anxiety states and other mental instabilities.

Notwithstanding the difficulty of meeting such needs, considerable headway toward the solution of these problems would be realized if it were possible to distinguish adequately the class of the economically dependent from those primarily in need of other social services. Then a thorough plan of treatment could be provided.

This plan, however, depends upon a knowledge of the conditions that identify the aged dependent. Such identifying characteristics might be used remedially to insure the economic and social adjustment of the individual; or preventively, perhaps in a system of adult education, to forestall preventable disabilities. Certainly, within such factors as age, sex, nativity, education, citizenship, residence, occupation, marital status, size of family, or some combination of personal traits, the basis of social adjustment could be established.

The circumstances that are most often found in the lives of the adjusted aged are: (1) good health and vitality and freedom from physical impairments, (2) agreeable social and emotional relations with family or friends, (3) having hobbies and outside recreational interests, (4) living in homes of their own, (5) having some useful activity (in addition to hobbies and recreation) that is like work.[11]

[11] C. M. Morgan, "Attitudes and Adjustments of Recipients of Old Age Assistance," *Archives of Psych.*, No. 214, 1937.

Conditions associated with unhappiness in old age are: (1) unsatisfactory marital status (divorce, separation, being unmarried or a widow), (2) poor health, (3) unemployment (in the case of men who want to work), (4) having too much spare time that is not taken up by hobbies or other recreation or by group associations, (5) living in rented homes, (6) being economically dependent, (7) unsatisfactory relationships with one's children.

Methods of insuring old age security

The chief methods of supporting the aged that have prevailed in English-speaking countries are the "natural" plans, such as savings, earning power during old age, and support from children or relatives; the almshouse and other public institutions; private homes (endowed, or with admission upon a fee basis); public and private outdoor relief; noncontributory pensions (military, civil, and industrial, including fraternal and trade-union plans); contributory pensions under the administration of the state; commercial life insurance; and noncontributory old age pensions.

Pensions. Industrial pensions are of three kinds: contributory, partially contributory, and noncontributory, or service. This movement for the protection of the industrial wage earner began in 1884, when the Baltimore and Ohio Railroad initiated its industrial pension policy. Although it has extended gradually to other industries, it is not a wholly satisfactory plan, either to the employer or to the employee. Even with recent adoptions, the number of pensioners is rather small. They include about ten per cent of the total labor force, or six million workers under more than 12,000 different private plans.

The plan of the Ford Motor Company is noncontributory, and provides the difference between a retired worker's Social Security benefits and one hundred dollars a month. This pension plan is significant in that it is likely to become the pattern that other company-union agreements will accept. Comparable plans on a large scale are maintained by General Electric, Standard Oil, and United States Steel, among the larger industries.

The motive stimulating the introduction of industrial pensions is conceded to be primarily economic—the maintenance of the stability and efficiency of working personnel. However, since this scheme contributes to the welfare of the employee, it is valuable. In so far as a pension plan interferes with advancement by transfer to another concern or with the mobility of labor, there are objections to its requirements for a certain number of years of service. Until a change is made in this respect, a large number of workers will be ineligible, and the plan's purpose of achieving the welfare of aged employees will be largely defeated.

Organizations of employees have also been instrumental in extending protection to the older worker through the establishment of homes, mortuary funds, insurance, and pensions. In 1927, the American Federation of Labor drafted an old age pension bill to be supported by organized labor. Pending the general acceptance of public responsibility for the aged, several trade unions have adopted methods to prevent their members from becoming public charges. Among the unions with old age pension plans are those of bridge and structural iron workers, bricklayers, electrical workers, granite cutters, printing pressmen and printers, street-railway employees, steel and automobile workers, and the railroad brotherhoods.

Pensions have also been used extensively for public service employees by the national, state, and local governments. Pensions for persons serving with the military or naval forces were officially recognized by the national government in the law of 1776. State and local pensions are adopted most frequently for public employees in the extrahazardous occupations. There was no system of pensioning under civil service until 1920. The gradual growth of this system is one of the chief arguments for a complete old age coverage, on the assumption that old age itself is a hazard. In reality, these pensions are a form of deferred payment, or a national but partial provision for old age. Serious objections are raised against the pensioning of special groups as a matter of social policy. The cost, moreover, is enormous by contrast to poor-relief, for which it is a substitute. An additional objection is that such pensions are distributed indiscriminately and violate elementary rules of ethical and actuarial practice. Other pension schemes, especially for teachers, have been provided whereby a fund is accumulated by the joint contribution of employer and employee, supplemented by endowment. The Teachers' Insurance and Annuity Association of America, founded under a grant from the Carnegie Foundation for the Advancement of Teaching, operates in connection with many colleges and universities of this country to supply annuities on a contributory basis.

Old age pensions and insurance

Because the systems of contributory or noncontributory pensions already in existence include only a small proportion of the population subject to the hazards of old age dependency, the movement for a national old age pension law or for some system of social insurance has been under way for many years and in nearly every industrial nation.

Old age pensions were first established in Germany as a part of the German National Insurance Plan, which was introduced by Bismarck as a prophylactic against the social democratic movement. Pensions were adopted under this plan in 1889 and were to be given without restrictions to those who reached the age of 70 and had paid premiums for 1,200 weeks. This is the contributory form of pension to which the employer, employee, and state contributed. Modified systems were introduced in succession by Denmark (1891), France (1905), England (1908)—following the example of her colonial possessions, New Zealand, Victoria, and New South Wales—Newfoundland (1911), Sweden (1913), and more recently by other nations.[12]

The plans vary in their contributory or noncontributory character, in the restriction or qualifications for the pension, and in the amounts paid. Denmark, for example, differentiated between the deserving and the undeserving poor, and required a residence of ten years and a record free from criminality and pauperism. In France, the system was never successful, because the contributions were too high to attract the majority of workers. In 1925, England made a radical modification of its pension system, making it compulsory, noncontributory, with no income qualifications, reducing the age limit to 65, and increasing the allowance. All these schemes are criticized because of the small amounts granted by the pension.

Movements to insure the economic independence of the aged were begun in the United States under the influence of the English system. By 1940, compulsory old age insurance systems were in force for some or all workers in thirty countries. For some time, Great

[12] For complete surveys of old age pension plans, consult report of the Twentieth Century Fund, *More Security for Old Age,* New York, 1937, Chap. 3 and Appendix A. H. W. Steinhaus, "Social Security Abroad," *Res. Coun. for Ec. Security,* Chicago, 1949. Bankers Trust Company, *A Study of Industrial Retirement Plans,* The Company, New York, 1950. "Preparation for Retirement: A Study of Post-Employment Adjustment," Standard Oil Co., New York, 1951, 12 pp. "Old Age Pensions," *Time,* May 22, 1950.

Britain had found it necessary to employ both old age poor-relief and noncontributory pensions. In this country, no effort to duplicate these protections was undertaken prior to the appointment of the Massachusetts Commission on Old Age Pensions in 1907. This example was soon followed by several other states. Finally, the movement approached a nationwide scale in the proposal that the federal government should grant aid to states with pension plans.

The first old age pension law, passed by Arizona in 1915, abolished almshouses and in their stead provided a pension of $25 and $45 per month, respectively, for men and women over 65 years of age. This act, however, was declared unconstitutional. Alaska adopted a similar plan during the same year. No further action was undertaken by the states toward this objective until 1923, when three states enacted pension laws (Nevada, Pennsylvania, and Montana).[13]

Concurrent with this legislative movement were a number of investigations during the 'twenties. As a rule, the proposals of this period advocated more extensive outdoor relief rather than institutional relief through almshouses. Two principles were finally accepted as essential to such legislation: (1) the adequacy of relief, and (2) the necessity of reduced administrative costs by efficient operation.

By 1934, twenty-eight states and two territories had old age legislation variously identified by such terms as pensions, relief, assistance, and security. By the time of the enactment of the Social Security Act in 1935, thirty-eight states and two territories had such provisions for a total of 408,502 aged persons.

Under this legislation ten benefits were provided—two insurance (old age and unemployment), three assistance (the aged, dependent children, and the blind), and four service (vocational rehabilitation, crippled children, maternal and child health, and public health). All of these services were administered by the states with federal aid except the Federal Old Age Insurance Plan. The latter is a contributory plan supported by both employers and workers. It is administered by the Bureau of Old Age and Survivors Insurance of

[13] For a complete digest of legislative experience, consult the report of the Twentieth Century Fund, *op. cit.*, pp. 174-175. For recent revisions, see publications of the Committee on Education and Social Security of the American Council on Education.

the Social Security Administration. As of 1950, three million persons were drawing benefits under its provisions.

At present and until Old Age and Survivors Insurance has a wider and more substantial coverage, individuals in the old age group depend upon a variety of supplementary sources of income. Now about two and one-half million are supported by old age assistance; three million by Old Age and Survivors Insurance; two million by children or others; one and one-half million by investments, annuities, and commercial insurance; and one million by private pension plans, or those that are maintained by federal, state, or local governments.

After the original amendments of the Social Security Act up to 1939, with the exception of the transfer of vocational rehabilitation to the Office of Vocational Rehabilitation in 1943, there were no major changes until 1950. At that time more occupations and workers were included, eligibility requirements were liberalized, and benefits and payments were increased. Old Age and Survivors Insurance operates in the same manner as the insurance and annuity programs of private companies. Since these operations involve many technical questions, no further description will be attempted at this point. Under these new provisions, forty-five million workers are covered.[14]

Summary

During the last several decades, emphasis has been directed mostly toward the economic problems of the aged. They were both the most obvious sources of distress and the most in need of solution. Current approaches to ensure a minimum of financial security and the prospects of more ample protection through annuities, pensions, insurance, and the Social Security provisions now bring to light other glaring omissions. Among these unsolved problems are questions of the employability of the aged and their potential usefulness as producers, of their health and mental hygiene, and of their social adjustment. On these matters little headway has been

[14] Consult: *Social Work Year Book,* "Social Insurance," for technical changes and extended coverage. See also: "Federal Social Security Act Amendments of 1950," *Mo. Lab. Rev.,* Vol. 71 (1950), No. 4, pp. 457-460. For a review and critical evaluation: L. Meriam and others, *The Cost and Financing of Social Security,* The Brookings Institution, Washington, D. C., 1950, Chaps. 9-11. J. Perlman, "Changing Trends under Old Age and Survivors Insurance, 1935-1950," *Indus. and Lab. Relations Rev.,* Vol. 4 (1951): 173-186.

made and most of them continue to be important problems in social research.

Growing old is obviously a greater risk to men than to women. Retirement is primarily a male problem, and it is a change for which men seem unequipped to make adequate plans or to approach from a sound mental-hygiene point of view. Though men are physically stronger and more aggressive in economic affairs than most women, they are not able to profit by these qualities in the upper age groups, as noted by their higher death rate, greater susceptibility to mental disease, and tendency toward suicide.

Most observers, therefore, are of the opinion that both men and women who have worked should not be forced into retirement by an arbitrary age such as 65 or by the provisions of some pension or annuity plan. Numerous plans such as the Forty-Plus Clubs, Opportunity Schools, the Not Less than 65 Clubs, and others are constantly being organized to spread the gospel and to find employment for people in these age brackets.

An assumption underlying these movements is that much of the world's achievement may still remain within the maturer capacities of the aged.

There are many studies that give examples of individual achievements by the aged that are far superior to the work of average men and that often excel their own earlier work.[15] And age continues to have its prestige in a number of vocations, such as judges, politicians, authors, physicians, generals, artists, and lawyers. However, it is still a matter of debate whether or not their work might not be done more efficiently by younger men. In Vischer's survey, the age of prime achievement varies from 41 for chemists to 58 for jurists and naturalists.[16]

Most unsolved problems of physical and mental health also complicate the employability of the old. The need in this connection

[15] A. L. Vischer, *op. cit.*, pp. 160-183. H. C. Lehman, "Some Examples of Creative Achievement During Later Maturity and Old Age," *Jour. Soc. Psych.*, Vol. 30 (1949): 49-79.

[16] A. L. Vischer, *op. cit.*, p. 161. The average age of peak achievement is: 41 for chemists and physicists; 44 for poets and dramatists; 46 for novelists; 47 for explorers and generals; 48 for actors and composers; 50 for painters and theologians; 51 for social reformers and essayists; 53 for physicians and statesmen; 54 for philosophers; 56 for astronomers, mathematicians, and humorists; 57 for historians; 58 for jurists and naturalists.

is research in the physiology of aging, in preventive medicine, and in sound nutrition.[17]

To acquire a more secure social life and a wholesome mental outlook, the mental hygiene rules are:

1. Keep up to the level of physical fiitness compatible with one's physical abilities.
2. Keep up your personal appearance.
3. Keep active.
4. Live within your physical means.
5. Stop bewailing loss of family, friends, and activities.
6. Read.
7. Take a full part in social life.
8. Seek new companions.
9. Acquire new habits and points of view.
10. Keep your independence.
11. Enjoy your possessions.[18]

Bibliography

Cavan, R. S., and others, *Personal Adjustment in Old Age,* Science Research Associates, Inc., Chicago, 1949. A study of middle-class aged; and a review of the basic literature.

Donahue, W., and Clark Tibbitts, *Planning the Older Years,* University of Michigan Press, Ann Arbor, 1950.

Dublin, L. I., and A. J. Lotka, *Length of Life,* Ronald, New York, 1949.

Gilbert, C. M., *We Over Forty,* Westbrook Publishing Co., Philadelphia, 1948. A discussion of hiring policies that discriminate against the older worker.

Kaplan, O. J. (Ed.), *Mental Disorders in Later Life,* Stanford University Press, Stanford University, Calif., 1945.

Lawton, George, *Aging Successfully,* Columbia University Press, New York, 1946.

Lieb, C. W., *Outwitting Your Years,* Prentice-Hall, New York, 1949.

Pollak, O., *Social Adjustment in Old Age,* Social Science Research Council, New York, 1948. A review of needed research; a selective bibliography.

Sheldon, J. H., *Social Medicine of Old Age,* University Press, London, 1948.

[17] A recommended diet sufficient for a person's minimum daily needs after 40 is:

Milk: 1 pint
Orange, grapefruit or tomato juice: 1 liberal serving
Green vegetable: 1 serving
Other vegetable: 1 serving
Eggs: one or more
Meat or fish: 1 serving
Butter or margarine: two or three pats

[18] R. T. Munroe and V. P. Williams, "Leading a Full Life After Middle Age," *Mass. Soc. for Mental Hyg.,* Boston, 1946 (a leaflet).

Stieglitz, E. J., *The Second Forty Years,* Lippincott, Philadelphia, 1946.
——— (Ed.), *Geriatric Medicine,* W. B. Saunders, Philadelphia, 1949.

Special Studies

Ford, N. D., *Where to Retire on a Small Income,* Harian Publications, Greenlawn, New York, 1950.
Gilbert, J. G., *Mental Efficiency in Senescence,* Archives of Psychology, New York, 1935. No. 188.
Gruchy, Clare de, *Creative Old Age,* Old Age Counselling Service, San Francisco, 1941.
Hutton, I. E., *Woman's Prime of Life,* Emerson Books, New York, 1937.
Maranon, G., *The Climacteric,* C. V. Mosby, St. Louis, 1929. Chap. 25, "The Critical Age of the Male."

. . . . .

Boyd, D. A., "Problems of Institutional Care of the Aged," *Am. Jour. Psychiatry,* Vol. 106 (1950): 616-620.
Cavan, R. S., "Family Life and Family Substitutes in Old Age," *Am. Sociol. Rev.,* Vol. 14 (1949): 71-83.
Chandler, A. R., "Attitudes of Superior Groups Toward Retirement and Old Age," *Jour. Geront.,* Vol. 5 (1950): 254-261.
Clague, E., *The Background of the Pension Problem,* United States Department of Labor, Bureau of Labor Statistics, Washington, 1950.
Dublin, L. I., and A. J. Lotka, "Trends in Longevity," *Annals, Am. Acad. Pol. and Soc. Sci.,* Vol. 237 (Jan. 1945): 123-133.
Granick, S., "Studies in the Psychology of Senility," *Jour. Geront.,* Vol. 5 (1950): 44-55.
Shanas, E., "Personal Adjustment of Recipients of Old Age Assistance," *Jour. Geront.,* Vol. 5 (1950): 249-253.
Simmons, L. W., "Attitudes toward Aging and the Aged: Primitive Societies," *Jour. Geront.,* Vol. 1 (1946): 72-95.
Stanford, W. R., "Aging: A Family Problem," *Soc. Forces,* Vol. 25 (1946): 61-65.
Tibbitts, Clark, "Aging and Living," *Adult Educa. Bull.,* Vol. 13 (1948-49): 204-212.

Questions

1. How is the aging of a population explained?
2. When is a population considered young, mature, old?
3. At what stage in their growth are France, Russia, China, the United States?
4. How is increasing life expectancy explained?
5. How is longevity explained?
6. How important as explanations of longevity are diet? Heredity? Occupation?
7. What research is being promoted by the National Committee on Aging? Consult in *Social Work Year Book* under "Aged."

8. Do women or men make the best adjustment to old age?
9. Why is old age called a period of many problems?
10. Does old age illustrate completely the elements in a definition of social problems?
11. If you were to choose one approach (of those mentioned in Chapter 1, above), which approach would you accept as most direct in the study of the aged?
12. Why are the chances of survival better for women than for men?
13. Does occupational displacement because of age ever occur before forty?
14. Do you consider the Social Security provisions adequate?
15. What are some of the family problems of the aged?
16. Why is isolation in old age called a problem?
17. What are some of the objective evidences of social adjustment in old age?
18. Do industries in your community maintain pensions? How do they compare with some of the national plans?
19. If a pension plan is not financially sound, what is the proof?
20. What major social changes hastened the growth of old age pensions on a national scale?

PART 3

PROBLEMS IN ECONOMIC ADJUSTMENT

Introduction

ALMOST ALWAYS THE FIRST EVIDENCE OF A GOOD SOCIETY IS AN EFFIcient economic system. When business prospers and there are no shortages in goods or services, the specific indexes of sound economic conditions are steady or increasing employment, income, and purchasing power.

The most frequently mentioned obstructions to this achievement are underproduction, black markets, cartels, runaway inflation, price subsidies, deficit spending, and high taxes. These inefficiencies assume numerous forms. Some are national and international in scope, such as depressions, currency problems, defaulting debtor nations, increasing costs of government, underdeveloped areas, wars and rearmament programs, unbalanced national populations, migrations, inadequate systems of distribution, and glutted markets. Others are usually the problems of smaller groups, such as interregional migration, housing inadequacies and congestion, family dependency, underemployment, minority group rivalries and conflicts, inequitable income distribution, occupational hazards, poverty, and poor-relief.

In this section, five of these groups of socio-economic problems are reviewed as illustrative of the frailty of present-day economic society.

No area of human enterprise has been explored more thoroughly for correctives than the sources of economic distress. Whatever solution may be introduced to prevent these problems or to forestall their ill effects, one rule is always of first importance in any plan of social reorganization. It is to be found in the observation that no social problem represents a simple series of causes and effects. Though every social problem has been exposed repeatedly to oversimplified analysis and elementary remedies, social problems of economic origin vigorously resist this type of treatment.

CHAPTER 10

POPULATION AND MIGRATION

DURING THE FIRST HALF OF THE TWENTIETH CENTURY THE POPULATION of the United States doubled in size. From a total of nearly 76 million in 1900 it increased to nearly 151 million by midcentury. This average annual gain of one and one-half million per year is a rate of increase that demographers consider to be a minor miracle in growth. The prospective goal of 200 million by the year 2000 should be achieved easily.

This total population was not a result of balanced growth. In the general death rate there was a small downward trend, but the birth rate varied from a low of seventeen per thousand to nearly twenty-six. These two characteristics are of primary significance, because the difference between them is the net or real rate of growth.

A third factor in population is migration. Its social significance rests largely on its continuity. Since frontier days the American people have been unusually mobile. This migration may be looked upon as evidence of social instability, of unsolved social problems, or of efforts to escape the congestion and discomforts of overcrowded regions.

A fourth factor is quality of the population. Emphasis upon quality is largely responsible for the setting up of minimum standards by which the biological, mental, economic, and social well-being of a people is maintained and the goals of a population program are established.

The population complex

Each of these four demographic factors determines major problems in the studies of population. From the earliest times, the connection between growth of population and national prestige has been regarded as of paramount significance. In brief, all problems of population affect every phase of national expansion. They are related to the use of land, economic production, income, standards of living, national security, and international war or peace.

Most census figures of increasing population are therefore simply the contemporary evidences of a long-time interest. Almost universally in human experience, people have taken pride in the sheer ability to reproduce. Many examples of this interest and of efforts to control growth and composition can be found in the earliest primitive societies.[1] No organized social group has been willing to leave population to the risks of chance or individual choice.

This one-sided conception of a society's need for numbers is the source of the most important problems in this field of biosocial relationships. Practically without exception all people have wanted an increasing birth rate and have introduced measures that they believed to be effective. Occasionally migration or colonization are encouraged, chiefly to bring about a more efficient distribution of population. With few exceptions in history, people are not concerned with death rates and their contribution to a pattern of population, or with differential birth rates, or with questions of population quality. In brief, no society has felt the need for a complete and consistent population policy, because growth is accepted at its face value as proof that no such policy is necessary.

As consequences of this historical point of view, there are two outstanding factors in a preliminary consideration of population: its growth and its mobility. Both are important, because of their bearing upon the balance between natural resources and numbers, and upon overpopulation and the need for colonization. Equally significant are the revolutionary effects of the growth and mobility of a population upon its biological constitution and composition.

Growth and size of population are regularly conceded to be important factors in the organization of human societies. In addition to their intimate relationship with the biological capacity of in-

[1] A. M. Carr-Saunders, *The Population Problem,* Clarendon Press, Oxford, 1922, pp. 139-161.

dividuals, they are connected as closely with the entire nature of group life and with the type of social activities that are fostered thereby. Scattered and sparse populations present social situations (activities, relationships, and problems) that are quite distinct from those of densely populated areas. In any society when population is too abundant or too heterogeneous, problems of economic and social misery are apt to occur in rapid succession, indicating precisely the type of life that corresponds with an inefficient or retrograde civilization.

Because of this close association between human population and culture, it is obvious that a well-balanced population and a sound population policy cannot be measured in terms of numbers alone. This conclusion is apparent in two basic laws of population, namely, (1) "Population varies directly with the means of life," and (2) "Population varies inversely with standard of living."[2] In order that both economic and other forms of culture should be reckoned with as well as numbers, recent emphasis is placed upon the qualitative aspects of population—upon the numbers of healthy, intelligent, economically useful, and socially adjusted people within given areas and cultures.

This shift in emphasis is the reason for the concepts of "standard population," "substandard population," and "optimum population" in recent literature.

A standard population is viewed in the light of facts in biology, genetics, geography, engineering, public health, medicine, sanitation, occupation, and cultural organization. Attention to population from this composite point of view reveals the following items as necessary to a modern policy: (1) the reproductive capacity of a people, which includes both fecundity, or physiological capacity to reproduce, and fertility, which governs the birth rate, (2) natural resources, especially as measured by prevailing standards of living, (3) vitality and health, (4) distribution of population by age and sex groups, (5) the distribution of population by economic, occupational, or other measurable social-class divisions, (6) the entire complex of cultural standards and values that may have some bearing upon reproduction, marriage, size of family, and associated factors.

A substandard population is described in negatives to indicate lower limits below which no healthy, self-maintaining group may

[2] E. B. Reuter, *Population Problems,* Lippincott, Philadelphia, 1937, p. 185.

fall. Broadly, and in the organization of minimum requirements of an optimum population, these limits are found in (1) the efficiency of economic productivity, (2) consumption and dietary habits, (3) housing, (4) family welfare, and (5) leisure time. Accordingly, an optimum population is a composite of growth or numerical changes and of social composition or quality.

This stress upon sound or unsound population programs and upon the desirability of determining an optimum population is reinforced in recent studies by two significant observations. One is to be found in the conclusion that population is no longer a matter that can be limited to one group of families, to social classes, or to one nation. Because of interracial and nativity competition and growing class rivalries, population has become an international problem.

A second observation is derived from the intimate connection between most social problems and population. Just as nearly every social problem can be measured in terms of units of population or rates, it is likewise possible to show many important connections between the incidence of social problems and increasing or decreasing numbers. Similarity, it is accepted as axiomatic that an adequately planned population—both in numbers and in quality—would go far toward the reduction of most social problems that hitherto have vigorously resisted all known treatments.

Growth of population

Even from a hasty survey of factors associated with population, it is apparent that growth of numbers is its most important historical problem. Generally, and throughout the major span of demographic history, emphasis is put upon its too slow growth. Occasionally in the past and most often in recent discussion, an assumed too rapid growth has been the principal subject of social study. As a matter of fact, any aspect of population may be regarded as a social problem.

One reason for this attitude is the close connection between the single fact of population and general cultural development. From this standpoint, population, in either its quantitative or its qualitative attributes, is associated with such important correlates of social problems as economic organization, political institutions, national rivalry in trade and politics, and geographical and social mobility.

Each of these aspects of population may be examined wholly apart from their supposed desirable or unfortunate social effects. When, however, they are reviewed in these connections, they become major social problems because they arise from the comparison of important and contradictory group judgments.

America's capacity to reproduce. During its comparatively brief span, the population cycle of the American people has moved in close accord with that of the world. There is the typical, initial stage of rapid expansion, a second period of increase at a decreasing rate, and finally a leveling in the rate of growth until it is practically that of a stationary population. In spite of those radical changes in the nature of population growth, there has been no equivalent alteration in the American policy toward the quantity or composition of its biological stock.

In American tradition primary emphasis is placed upon unrestricted growth. This point of view was in complete harmony with expanding industrial and national interests of a pioneering people. It was also favored by the abundance of natural resources and economic opportunity. With few exceptions throughout the history of American population theory, and at least for the period up to the Civil War, the accepted attitude endorsed natural increase and encouraged a policy of unlimited immigration.

The principal contradiction in this attitude was gradually recognized during the closing of the frontier. As free land grew scarce in quantity and quality, basic problems of an overpopulated country became noticeable for the first time. The strictures upon freedom of movement and economic opportunity, accompanied by diminishing returns (in spite of advancements in technical and scientific efficiency) and a falling standard of living, produced and accentuated all the problems that are typical of densely populated areas. In fact, most of the current problems of population can be traced to conditions that have been developing for at least a century and to the traditional lack of a consistent population program.

The population of the United States is recruited from an early period of high birth rates, the various streams of immigration, and the recent decades of reduced birth rates. Prior to the discovery of America, there were about one million people in this country. Since census records have been kept, the population has increased from about 4 million in 1790 to 151 million in 1950.

Population of Continental United States

(000 omitted)

1900	75.9	1940	132.0
1910	91.9	1950	151.7
1920	106.5	1960	164.5
1930	123.1		

Sources: United States Census, and forecast for 1960 in *General Outlook for the American Economy, 1949-1960,* Econometric Institute, New York, 1949, p. 5.

After the first few decades of experimental colonization, population increased during the colonial period about 30 per cent each decade. This rate of growth, which amounts to a doubling of the population each 25-year period, continued until the Civil War. That type of growth in American experience is an illustration of expansion when reproductive capacity reaches its highest rate—the only restriction being a high death rate.

The steady growth of the American population was interrupted during the decade 1860-1870. In the preceding ten-year period the rate of growth was 35.6 per cent. It decreased to 26.6 per cent for the decade ending in 1870. Between 1860 and 1890 the population doubled, and as already noted it doubled between 1900 and 1950. During the last five decades, rates of growth were nearly the same during the first three and the fifth decades, decreasing because of the depression to about half of this rate during the fourth decade.[3]

Rates of Population Growth—United States

Years	*Annual Per Cent of Growth*
1660–1860	3.5
1860–1890	2.5
1890–1910	2.0
1910–1930	1.5
1930–1940	0.7
1940–1950	1.4

Sources: I. B. Taeuber and H. T. Eldridge, "Some Demographic Aspects of the Changing Role of Women," *Annals, Am. Acad. Pol. and Soc. Sci.,* Vol. 251 (May, 1947): 24-34. The rate for the last decade is from the United States Census.

No single cause or set of causes is responsible for the retardation in population growth. Among the important immediate interferences are the slowing down of immigration, reduced marriage and

[3] W. S. Thompson, "The Demographic Revolution in the United States," *Annals, Am. Acad. Pol. and Soc. Sci.,* Vol. 262 (Mar. 1949): 62.

birth rates, a high military death rate, and the spreading of disease, all of which were direct effects of the Civil War. In subsequent decades, most of those conditions continued and were aggravated by the rising cost of living, cycles of unemployment, a gradually changing attitude toward family size resulting in smaller families, the urbanization of population, various particular circumstances of city life that interfere with the maintenance of large families, and, finally, the spread of birth control.

When the American population is viewed solely from the standpoint of its capacity for growth, it is noteworthy that a trend toward actual decrease began in some regions as early as the first decade of the nineteenth century. However, the rate of increase did not show a decline until a half century later, during the Civil War. When natural increase is separated from the contributions of migrations, it is apparent that population from that source began to decrease as early as 1830 and has declined steadily since that time. The importance of this change in reproductive capacity is frequently discounted because of the vast numbers of migrants whose rates of fertility for at least a generation or two in this country remained at nearly the same level as those of their home countries.

As a result of the interplay between natural increase and immigration, the history of the American population is one of increasing immigration and decreasing natural rate, which are its principal characteristics during most of the time after the colonial period. The American cycle is typical, consequently, of a rapidly increasing population at a steadily diminishing rate of increase. The precise combination of these agencies of natural increase and immigration is blurred and complicated by a high degree of internal mobility, and more recently by the advent of voluntary parenthood, or birth control.

The ability of America to reproduce itself can be estimated only after careful study of all the interacting forces. In this or any pattern of population, the most descriptive trends are those of birth rates, death rates, marriage rates, infant mortality, life expectancy rates, and other variables closely connected with them such as the age, sex, vital, and other biological or social factors in the composition of a people.

Capacity to produce population is an outcome of the combination, in a functional manner, of all the vital and bio-social determinants.

Precise factors in the complex pattern of population growth appear in the table below.

VITAL RATES OF POPULATION IN THE UNITED STATES

	1900	*1920–24*	*1936–1940*	*1946–1950* ‡
Births *	...	22.5	17.3	23.5
Deaths *	17.2	12.0	11.0	9.6
Infant mortality †	...	77.1	51.5	29.0
Maternal mortality †	...	6.9	4.7	0.7
Marriage *	9.3	10.6	11.0	11.2

* Per 1,000 population
† Per 1,000 live births
‡ All recent figures are provisional

Sources: Population Index, Vol. 15 (Jan. 1949): 98; Vol. 16 (July 1950): 266; Vol. 17 (July 1951): 235-241. United States Census, 1950.

Since 1940, the birth rate has increased and gained on the average 1.2 per cent per year from 1940 to its peak of 25.8 per 1,000 population in 1947. This gain is a combined result of the upswing of the business cycle and the increase in marriage occasioned by war. Statisticians are not too certain as to what the eventual results of this reversal of trend will be, but they are in general agreement that the complete effects on long-time population changes cannot be known for five or six decades.

From the point of view of natural increase, the real situation becomes clear-cut by contrasting the low birth rates of recent years with the rate of 35.0 per 1,000 population that prevailed during the first few decades of this country's existence as a nation. The death rate (general, maternal, and infant) is also decreasing. While this decrease accounts for an increasing population in spite of lower fertility rates, it is a source of much confusion concerning eventual trends in population. It is estimated, for example, that the death rate will finally be stabilized at about 15.4 per 1,000 population. The increase in deaths is based upon the aging of the population and the prospect that there will be no material reduction in the causes of death during middle life and old age.

Another accurate indication of population movements is the marriage rate. Even though marriage rates may vary as a result of depression or war, the fact of these temporary deviations from trend is less important than the general stability of family life as a whole and specific marriage rates of the different social classes. As a matter of fact, a principal characteristic of American marital status is a gradual trend toward uniformity. Sex differences and urban-rural differences are diminishing. However, judged by rural standards, urbanization is still a significant obstruction to large families, and this difference holds under urbanization for age, nativity, color, and sex differences in family patterns.

The foregoing account gives abundant evidence of the need for a population program. Such evidence is available from the standpoint of either numbers or quality. Ellsworth Huntington was of the opinion that the American population would be more sound both biologically and socially if there had been no immigration after the colonial period.[4] He believed that it would have achieved the same size through its own natural increase and that in addition it would have developed better economic conditions, higher standard of living, more home owners, less poverty and dependency, less crime,

EXPECTATION OF LIFE (IN YEARS) IN THE UNITED STATES

	White				*Non-White*			
	1901–1902	*1929–1931*	*1950*	*1970*	*1901–1902*	*1929–1931*	*1950*	*1970*
Males	48.2	59.1	65.9	71	32.5	47.5	58.6	69
Females ..	51.0	62.7	71.5	77	35.0	49.5	62.9	75

Source: "A Century of Progress in Longevity," *Statis. Bull.*, Metropolitan Life Insurance Company, Vol. 30 (1949), No. 10, p. 2. *Statis. Bull.*, Metropolitan Life Insurance Company, Vol. 32 (1951), No. 11, p. 6. Estimate for 1970 is from *Population Index*, Vol. 17 (July 1951): front cover.

grafting, and political demagoguery, and more intellectually capable stock. In other words, he concluded that America overlooked a great eugenic opportunity in becoming a melting pot. Without the constructive influence of a consistent population policy, it remains a land of demographic contradictions—of some groups enjoying the highest standards of living ever known, and at the same time "one third of the nation ill-housed, ill-clad, ill-nourished"; of overpopulated and underpopulated areas, of high birth rates from inferior stock and low birth rates or actual sterility in superior stock.

Composition of the population. All questions of population are in one way or another finally reducible to the two major problems of quantity and quality. While such movements as growth and migration are intimately connected with both composition and distribution, many other conditions in the makeup of a people are equally significant. Those conditions are apparent (1) in the life history of overpopulated and underpopulated regions or in degrees

[4] E. Huntington and M. Ragsdale, *After Three Centuries,* Williams and Wilkins, Baltimore, 1935, p. 75.

of density and sparsity of population, (2) in ethnic or racial composition, (3) in rural and urban groups, (4) in the interchange of blood stocks due to rural migration to cities or in the reverse of this movement, and (5) in age and sex changes. Specific connections between population and social problems may be reviewed through an analysis of the composition of the population, and especially of the most spectacular forms of composition in urbanization and depopulation.

If the man-land ratio, indicating density or scarcity of population, is considered an important factor in social stability, the maladjustments of a people that are revealed through this measurement become basic social problems. Similar diagnostic symptoms of combinations of social and population problems can be discovered in ethnic makeup and in sex and age distribution. All significant exceptional instances of mixed bloods and cultures or of unbalanced sex ratios become immediate areas of probable social maladjustments. They threaten social disorganization because no society has been able to maintain such an elastic culture that its institutions and customs can accommodate the extreme variations arising from these sources.

General accompaniments in this changing complex of the American population are:

1. An increase in the number of married persons.
2. An increase in the number of families.
3. Stabilization of the family on a three-child pattern.
4. A rapid development of economic plans to insure the economic security of the family.
5. Significant age changes; larger proportions of the population being over 65 and under 5 years of age, and
6. A sufficient proportion within the productive age groups, 20 to 64, to guarantee an adequate labor force.
7. A reversal in sex ratio, females now outnumbering males, but not sufficiently in the marriageable age groups to affect marriage rates.
8. Decline in the proportion of the foreign born from fifteen per cent in 1900 to seven per cent in 1950.
9. Health programs that promise to maintain current trends in reproduction.
10. Prospective changes in the differential birth rate (differences in the social classes), in equality of economic opportunity, in quality of population, and in attitudes of the upper classes toward small or childless families.

Migrations

Internal movements of population continue to follow the pattern established in the nineteenth century. After World War I they increased, and they reached a peak during World War II when the greatest movement in the history of American population took place—a record of more than seventy million changed residence during the 1940's. The causes of all these migrations are the same, namely, the quest for better economic opportunities. A forecast holds that this general pattern of migrations will probably continue for the next two decades.

There have been three primary migrations in this pattern. One is a continuation of the historic East to West movement. The second is the cityward migration from rural areas. The third is the movement from the South to the North. The area most affected has been the South both as a sending, and more recently as a receiving, region. Eight other migrations that are important although they are less continuous or involve fewer numbers are: (1) migrant agricultural labor, (2) migrant industrial labor, (3) recent movements from the South to the West, (4) movements away from the Dust Bowl area, (5) inter-regional movements, (6) urban to rural movements, (7) movements from farm to farm, and (8) the suburban movement—a recent major change in urban development.[5]

Causes of migration are revealed in part by its selectivity of individuals as migrants. Negroes are the chief migrants from the South to the North, and during World War II they were the chief migrants to the West Coast. They also participate in numerous regional (state to state) shifts. Males outnumber females as migrants, with the two possible exceptions of the rural movement to cities and movements from the South to war industries. Most migrants are young, the peak age being 25-29, and the same holds for families, that is, families with young children are more migratory than families with teen-age children.

Migrations also have some educational and occupational selec-

[5] H. S. Shryock and H. T. Eldridge, "Internal Migration in Peace and War," *Am. Sociol. Rev.*, Vol. 12 (1947): 27-39. In this monograph there are maps of these movements and indications of the tendency toward reverse movements. M. Hayes, "Regional Differences in Jobs, Income, and Migration, 1929-1949," *Mo. Labor Rev.*, Vol. 71 (1950), No. 4, pp. 433-437. Consult *Statist. Bull.*, Metropolitan Life Insurance Company, Vol. 32 (1951), No. 2, p. 5 for regional changes in population from 1850-1950.

tions. Individuals with the most education are the most migratory and they also migrate further. This rule holds for urban and rural, male and female migrants. The order of occupations in which migrants are found, listed in the order of most to least migratory, are professional, semiprofessional, domestic, clerical, salesmen, craftsmen, foremen, operatives, and nonfarm laborers. Occupational mobility, that is, shifting from one vocation to another, is twice as frequent among migrants as among nonmigrants.

Social correlates of a changing population

A long-time trend that is characteristic of the United States and of most Western European countries is the gradual decline in the birth rate. This trend is explained largely by economic changes and their social consequences, and in recent decades by changing attitudes toward family size and the burden of children.

In this socio-economic complex, more women marry but fewer children are born per family. This relationship occurs throughout the nation, for cities regardless of size, and for the rural population. This correlation is accounted for by the spread of the small-family system.

Another circumstance that supports this explanation of actual declines in the birth rate is the increase in marriage with little or no change since 1900 in the average age of women at marriage.

The negative or inverse relationship between income status and the birth rate is another long-time trend. Recent studies both here and abroad occasionally report birth rates among the highest class in income and education that exceed those of the next lower class. However, this variation is not interpreted as a reversal of the social class correlation or as sufficient to equalize the declining rates of the upper classes as a whole.

In a summary of all these correlations, it is concluded that "continued urbanization, increasing levels of living, expanded and more adequate educational opportunities, and the continued penetration of the values of the new ways of life into the still backward isolated regions and groups will probably operate to depress the national birth rate still further." [6]

The agricultural population. Conditions surrounding the life of rural peoples up to the last few decades have encouraged the tradi-

[6] I. B. Taeuber and H. T. Eldridge, *op. cit.*, pp. 32-33.

tional large-family pattern. As a result, the rural population has remained the most prolific group. The balance between increasing numbers and opportunity for employment has been maintained by migration to the city.

RURAL AND URBAN POPULATION—UNITED STATES

	Per Cent Distribution	
	Rural	*Urban*
1790	94.4	5.1
1850	84.7	15.3
1900	60.3	39.7
1940	43.5	56.5
1950	36.3	63.7

Source: United States Census.

The population problem involved in the rural situation is typical of the circular character of many social problems. Because the rural population has maintained a high birth rate in spite of economic changes, thus making a surplus population,[7] and because the urban population has a declining birth rate, the consequences of rural-urban migration bring about on the one hand (1) immediate, intensified competition for urban employment, (2) lowered fertility rates of rural migrants to the city, and, on the other hand, (3) a trend toward declining national population. Hence, the complex of bio-social and economic factors in population sets into operation a secondary series of ill effects, such as a reduced demand for farm products, lowered standard of living, more migration to the city, increased competition for employment, and a repetition of the cycle.[8]

NET RATE OF REPRODUCTION—UNITED STATES

	Rural			
	Farm	*Nonfarm*	*Urban*	*Total*
1905–1910	2.02	1.50	0.94	1.34
1935–1940	1.66	1.15	0.73	0.98
1942–1947	1.88	1.45	1.09	1.29
1944–1949				1.38

Sources: I. B. Taeuber and H. T. Eldridge, *op. cit.*, p. 27. United States Census, "Current Population Reports," Series P-20, No. 18, p. 5, June 30, 1948. *Population Index,* Vol. 16 (April 1950): 172.

[7] Such economic changes as mechanization of agriculture, technological improvements, depletion of soil, and the price structure of farm products. It is estimated that soil depletion is displacing 175,000 persons each year.

[8] O. E. Baker, "The Effect of Recent Public Policies on the Future Population Prospect," *Rural Sociology,* Vol. 2 (1937): 123-141.

The industrial population. The total working population (age groups 20 to 64 years) continues to grow. Two important sources of this increase are the addition of more women and a favorable work-life expectancy. The total work force of 63 million in 1950 is expected to increase by 1970 to 75 million. Hence, no inadequacies are anticipated from this source either for sufficient workers or for the military. However, one unresolved problem in this situation is the effect of the increasing employment of women upon the future birth rate.

Under 1900 conditions of mortality and labor force participation, an average man at age 20 could anticipate an additional life expectancy of 42.2 years and a work life expectancy of 39.4 years. By 1947 these age spans had increased to 48 and 42 years. With anticipated changes in work opportunities and in the age of retirement, these ages in life expectancy and in work years are reckoned at nearly 53 and 43 years respectively in 1975.[9]

The urban population. Immediate effects of all these changes in the composition and distribution of the population are to be noted in urbanization. By 1950, with more than 60 per cent of the population in urban places, the ratio of rural-urban distribution of 1900 had reversed itself. From projections derived from this shift, the prospects are that the American people will be urbanized eventually to the extent of 70 to 75 per cent of their total number.

The rapidity of this urban trend is accented by two findings of the 1950 census, namely, that four fifths of the total increase of population occurred in 168 metropolitan areas, and that the highest rates of increase were in unincorporated suburban areas and satellite cities.[10]

The school population. Recent changes in the birth rate are producing exceedingly unbalanced school-age groups. The results of these changes are most immediately observed in the uneven burdens that they put upon the school systems. In the decade 1950-1960, the child population, ages 5 to 17 years, will be increased by more than one third. This growth will mean a peak load for elementary

[9] H. Wool, "Trends in Pattern of Working Life, 1900–1975," *Mo. Labor Rev.*, Vol. 71 (1950), No. 4, pp. 438-442. E. Clague, "America's Future Manpower Needs," *Annals, Am. Acad. Pol. and Soc. Sci.*, Vol. 262 (Mar. 1949): 102-110. "Manpower for National Defense," *Statis. Bull.*, Metropolitan Life Insurance Company, Vol. 31 (1950), No. 8, pp. 1-3.

[10] P. M. Hauser and H. T. Eldridge, "Projection of Urban Growth and Migration in the United States," *Milbank Mem. Fund Quart.*, Vol. 25 (1947): 292-307.

schools by 1955. At that time the high schools will be overcrowded until 1960, and thereafter the colleges. The personnel and administrative problems of furnishing school accommodations and trained teachers will be the immediate tasks of education.[11]

FAMILY OR HOUSEHOLD POPULATION OF THE UNITED STATES

Year	*Number (in millions)*	*Year*	*Number (in millions)*
1900	15	1950	43
1920	24	1955	44
1940	34	1960	47

Sources: United States Census, "Current Population Reports," Series P-20, No. 35, Nov. 28, 1951. Paul C. Glick, "Estimates of the Future Number of Families," *Am. Jour. Sociol.*, Vol. 52 (1946): 236.

Institutional and dependent population. Another movement is the growing segment of population which is incapable of self-maintenance. It is true that in colonial days there were dependents: the aged, orphans, the poor, and the physically and mentally incompetent. With the growth of population and especially with the rise of cities, those classes not only have multiplied but have also brought into being a highly specialized and costly system of institutional care.

It may be a debatable question whether the dependent population is larger proportionately today than in the colonial period. But there is no controversy over the fact that new classes of dependents are constantly being recognized and that their numbers are excessively large. Here, in fact, is one of the most serious threats to the economic resources of government, not to mention the heavy burden of such costs to self-supporting people. Of the different types of persons requiring institutional care, the number of poor persons in almshouses and of dependent children under the care of public or private social agencies is probably decreasing. But the numbers of institutions for the aged, the sick (general hospitals), for specific illnesses (tuberculosis sanitariums), for the mentally ill, for mental defectives and epileptics, and for prisoners have been increasing in recent years.

According to a report of the Metropolitan Life Insurance Company, the ratio of natural dependents (of children under age 18 and

11 "School-Age Population to Rise for Another Decade," *Statis. Bull.*, Metropolitan Life Insurance Company, Vol. 31 (1950), No. 8, pp. 5-7. "Forecasts of Population and School Enrollment in the United States: 1948–1960," United States Bureau of the Census, Series P-25, No. 18, Feb. 14, 1949.

adults 65 and above) has increased each decade since 1910 and will continue to increase to 1960.[12]

Problems associated with changing population

Before a society can make readjustments in its institutional organization to recent movements in population, two types of information are needed. It is necessary not only to have an inventory of the component elements of population, but also to know certain basic bio-social facts and problems. Of the essential information that is preliminary to any complete knowledge of trends in population, the following have received most emphasis: (1) changing fertility rates, particularly as they affect the social-class composition and distribution of a society, (2) health and vitality, (3) the small-family system, and (4) sterility.

A review of these topics will serve a double purpose. They are, in the first place, introductory to a consideration of major current problems. They also present basic data that are indispensable to a summary of an optimum population or of the detailed requirements of a population program.

Changing fertility rates. Summaries of the various studies mentioned above indicate that:

1. Birth rates are highest in rural areas and lowest in urban areas, decreasing in proportion to the intensity of urbanization.
2. Birth rates are highest in the lowest social classes in all regions.
3. The white-collar class is not reproducing itself.
4. Unskilled laborers have a birth rate that is 15 per cent higher than necessary for replacement of numbers.
5. Professional classes, by contrast, have a birth rate that is 25 per cent lower than that necessary for replacement.
6. Childless and sterile marriages occur more frequently among the professional and business classes than among unskilled and agricultural people.
7. The heavy rural migration to the city acts as a sterilizing agency among the rural groups that might produce healthy and intelligent children.
8. The urban population as a whole is failing by 13 per cent to reproduce itself.

[12] "Trends in the Dependent Population," *Statis. Bull.,* Metropolitan Life Insurance Company, Vol. 31 (1950), No. 6, pp. 1-3.

9. Another important dysgenic consequence is obvious in the fact that those classes whose intelligence rating is on the average less than I.Q. 100 have an increasing birth rate while those classes over I.Q. 100 have a decreasing birth rate.
10. A compensating factor in this dysgenic trend is that infant mortality is higher in the lower classes but it is not sufficiently high to equalize the differential social-class fertility.

No adequate causal explanation for the declining fertility within the upper social classes can be given. It will be a temporary or permanent trend according to the nature of its causes. Among the causal factors usually enumerated are (1) competition for status in occupation and income, (2) education, (3) religion, (4) age at marriage and proportion of marriageable women who marry, (5) birth control, and (6) employment of women. Birth control is generally conceded major importance, first, because it is the only control that is definitely known to reduce fertility, and second, because it is the only factor that has increased during the period of diminishing birth rates. It is also argued that if birth control were uniformly distributed, the differential social-class fertility rates would gradually disappear.

Health and vitality. No policy in public health, social work, social reform, public education, or in population, can ignore the fact that major changes in the health and vitality of a people require compensatory adjustments in social life. That changes in health and vitality are often excluded from the provisions of public policy is usually due to the fact that they are not recognized or considered important. However, no one who is concerned with a population program can ignore the following demonstrated trends in American population:

1. The increasing expectation of life arising from the diminishing death rate of persons under middle age.
2. The unchanging character of the life span despite increasing life expectancy.
3. The likelihood that the general death rate has approached its lowest level and may increase because of the changing age distribution of the population and declining birth rates.
4. The recognition that environmental rather than genetic circumstances are the chief determinants of death rates.
5. The conservation of vitality rests upon the control of communicable diseases and the improvement of standards of living.
6. There is little or no hopeful prognosis in the task of reducing diseases among the upper age groups or the nervous and mental diseases.

7. The high prevalence of illness is a constant drain upon personal and social efficiency.
8. Progress in the conservation of vitality is largely dependent upon the control of diseases among children and young adults.[13]

The small-family system. The problem of the small-family system arises when fertility rates are so low that a population cannot replace itself. This is a comparatively new problem. Although there is evidence of the small-family system among primitive peoples, under such conditions it is an entirely different institution. The primitive small family occurs because couples are obliged to limit their families to accord with the requirements of a harsh physical environment. The modern small-family system is essentially a social consequence of economic insecurity.

When the large family became an economic deficit, economic motives stimulating a reduced birth rate were accentuated by developments in other social institutions. Such supplementary agencies are changing moral ideas, decline in religious controls, the trend toward the social equality of sexes, and the voluntary control of births. The difference, therefore, between the primitive and the contemporary small family systems is that the latter is chiefly a result of choice and planning.

Although the fall of the birth rate and the need for a program to recruit population can be traced almost exclusively to the small-family pattern, the system is by no means an ideal plan for the control of population. When parenthood is placed upon an intelligent basis, the so-called voluntary small-family system will become one of the most significant transitions in the history of the family. Up to the present, however, no adequate attention has been given to the basic problems of parenthood.

For this reason, primarily, the small family system is often regarded as mainly responsible for the various problems of differential class fertility rates, the maldistribution of population both in geographical regions and in age and social classes, and the implied threat of these consequences to population quality.

Since 1920 the number of large families (of seven or more children) has decreased by 60 per cent. Large families are now concentrated in the South, in agricultural regions, and among Negroes. Birth control, together with the well-known resistance of some family

[13] For an optimistic outlook: L. I. Dublin and A. J. Lotka, "Trends in Longevity," *Annals, Am. Acad. Pol. and Soc. Sci.*, Vol. 237 (1945): 123-133.

patterns to birth control, is the assigned reason for these general variations in fertility rates.

DISTRIBUTION OF THE CHILD POPULATION IN FAMILIES

Number of Children Per Family	*Per Cent Distribution* *Families*	*Children*
No child	45.4	0
One child	22.6	20.0
Two children	17.5	31.0
Three or more children	14.5	49.0
Total	100.0	100.0

Source: United States Census, 1950.

Sterility. Accurate information about sterility as a physiological problem or as a social fact is exceedingly scanty. In the Indianapolis studies, about ten per cent of all married couples were childless. During the last three decades from seven to fifteen per cent of all married women have been childless.[14] According to the researches of Farris, fifteen per cent of all males are either sterile or subfertile. He estimates that two thirds of all sterile marriages are due to this male deficiency.

There are numerous explanations of this infertility other than physiological deficiency; infertility may result from pituitary disorders, tension or nervousness, alcohol, venereal disease, or focal infections, but the explanation that seems to have the most unanimous endorsement among the scientists is an abnormally rich diet.

Miscellaneous associations. Although population and migrations in their extreme effects of overpopulation or underpopulation are associated with many specific social problems, this relationship may not be directly causal. Among the most frequently assumed accompaniments of major population problems are:

1. Economic problems, such as poverty; unemployment; business depressions; lowered standards of living; costs of rearing children; deficient natural resources; technological changes; and war.
2. Social problems, such as birth control; urbanization; stratification or segregation; overcrowding of regions, occupations, or social

[14] C. V. Kiser and P. K. Whelpton, "Social and Psychological Factors Affecting Fertility: A Study of Childlessness Planned and Unplanned," *Milbank Mem. Fund Quart.*, Vol. 26 (1948): 182-236. E. J. Farris, "Male Infertility," *Sci. Am.*, Vol. 182 (May, 1950): 16-19. E. J. Farris, *Human Fertility and Problems of the Male,* Author's Press, White Plains, New York, 1950.

classes; transportation; social security; waste; problems of leisure time and recreation; and changes in the social institutions, such as in religion, morals or in family bonds.

3. Health problems, such as sanitation; uncontrolled diseases, nutrition; eugenic standards; biological degeneracy; physical and mental defectiveness; and sexual problems.
4. Personal problems, such as individual values; competition; education; illiteracy; and confusion of moral standards.

Summary

Each topic of interest and each problem within the field of population are suggestive of the fact that no society ever had the foresight to establish a plan or program to protect and control population. But the idea of a planned population is not new. Throughout most of the literature on population, the majority of writers have been convinced of the importance of one major remedy and have rarely been concerned with a complete program. From Plato to Malthus, there are many one-sided explanations of what is now called an optimum population or a population policy. Many recent theories are similarly biased in favor of one exclusive system of control.

An optimum in population is a best population both in numbers and in quality. Wolfe's definition of an optimum population is that number of people who, with a known amount of natural resources and efficiency of the arts, would obtain the highest per capita return of consumers' goods or standards of living.[15] From this standpoint, the basic measure of an optimum population is economic efficiency, and population itself becomes a problem in economic engineering.

Even from this restricted point of view, population is not a result of economic conditions exclusively. Production, standards of living, the labor supply, markets, industrialization, and urbanization may be primarily economic criteria, but they are dependent upon, and are accompanied by, a wide variety of social circumstances.

The economic index is based upon a balance between numbers and the efficiency of a society's economic structure. Accordingly, it implies as important supplements to an economic measurement such factors as age and sex composition, housing standards, the distribution of wealth and income, efficiency of workers, amount and use of leisure, and the efficient operation of all social institu-

[15] A. B. Wolfe, "On the Criterion of Optimum Population," *Am. Jour. Sociol.*, Vol. 39 (1934): 585-599.

tions. A population optimum is, therefore, both quantitative and qualitative as well as economic and social.

In national planning, the merging of these different requirements is found most readily in suggested policies for the regulation of population.

The population policy of the United States is similar to that of most industrial countries, and for the most part has had but one objective: to increase numbers. It is possible to trace the growth of a more realistic policy in the gradual modification of this single aim. Such modifications are (1) the restrictive immigration policy growing out of efforts to prevent the immigration of criminals or persons with certain contagious diseases, (2) the Chinese exclusion act and the Alien Contract Labor law, (3) deportation and quota laws, and (4) the changing attitude toward birth control. Each step in the development of this policy is based upon a growing recognition of the need for qualitative regulations.

In the opinion of most demographers, there are three requirements of any population policy if it is to be an effective control over both quality and numbers: (1) a size of population that will permit a good standard of living, (2) a healthy population in which physical and mental deficiency is kept at a minimum, and (3) an efficient distribution of population in which a wholesome life is made possible to the full capacity of economic resources.[16]

Readjustments that are imperative for the realization of such objectives include:

1. Economic stability or the reduction of the various forms of social insecurity. A balanced national economy: which involves reorganization of rural life so that rural mobility may not be necessary on its present unselective scale.
2. Improvement of standards of living.
3. Improvement and extension of economic opportunity.
4. City planning in spheres other than physical equipment.
5. Eugenic education.
6. Encouragement of reproduction of desirable stock. Direct economic aid to families and children, such as medical care, adjustment of rent to size of families, food to meet nutritional needs, education as far as it can be undertaken, up to and including a college education.
7. Insuring the economic welfare of young married people.
8. Contraception and sterilization.

[16] Paul Meadows, "Toward a Socialized Population Policy," *Psychiatry*, Vol. 11 (1949): 193-202.

9. Adjustment of women's occupational activities to child bearing.
10. Further restriction of immigration.
11. Continuation of a eugenic inventory to determine individual or racial physical and mental differences, as a first step in an appreciation of social and personal differences.
12. Encouragement of attitudes favorable to the family and population replacement.[17]

Bibliography

Bontemps, A. W., *They Seek a City,* Doubleday, Doran, New York, 1945. Negro migrations.

Burch, G. I., and E. Pendell, *Human Breeding and Survival,* Penguin Books, New York, 1947.

Griffith, E. F., *The Childless Marriage: Its Cause and Cure,* Methuen, London, 1948.

Linder, F. F., and R. D. Grove, *Vital Statistics Rates in the United States, 1900-1941.* Government Printing Office, Washington, 1943.

Milbank Memorial Fund, *Postwar Problems of Migration,* The Fund, New York, 1947.

National Resources Committee, *The Problems of a Changing Population,* Government Printing Office, Washington, 1938. Effects of depression.

Notestein, F. W., and others, *Demographic Studies of Selected Areas of Rapid Growth,* Milbank Memorial Fund, New York, 1944.

Smith, T. L., *Population Analysis,* McGraw-Hill, New York, 1948. Chap. 18, "Internal Migration."

Thomas, D. S., *Research Memorandum on Depression Differentials,* Social Science Research Council, New York, 1938.

Thompson, W. S., and P. K. Whelpton, *Estimates of the Future Population of the United States,* United States National Resources Planning Board, Washington, 1943.

United States Bureau of the Census, *Population, Internal Migration, 1935-1945: Some Characteristics of Migrants,* Government Printing Office, Washington, 1946.

Vance, Rupert, *All These People: The Nation's Human Resources in the South,* University of North Carolina Press, Chapel Hill, 1945.

Questions

1. In what ways is population related to such problems as employment, standard of living, ill-health, or mental disease? Is migration also connected with them?
2. How do statisticians forecast future population?
3. Is a nation's population a matter of international interest?
4. Could internal migration affect a nation's growth?

[17] F. Lorimer and F. Osborn, *Dynamics of Population,* Macmillan, New York, 1934, Chap. 12.

5. What social or other changes accompany periods of rapid and slow population growth? Are these changes the causes of this growth?
6. What is a rate? What rate is the most sensitive index of population growth?
7. When did large families lose their popularity?
8. Is the suburban trend characteristic of your community?
9. Is the school system of your state able to meet the needs of its increasing child population? Does this uneven growth create a surplus of teachers?
10. Are dependent classes proportionately larger today than a century ago?
11. What social problems regularly occur in overpopulated areas? In underpopulated areas?
12. What are some measures (a) of optimum population (b) of quality of population?

CHAPTER 11

MINORITIES

A DEMOCRATIC SOCIETY IS THE SEED BED OF MINORITY-GROUP RIVALRIES. The seeds are human rights. "Among these are life, liberty, and the pursuit of happiness." Another is the right to organize and to strive for their realization. Whenever special privileges are claimed by one class or the rights of another are limited, minority groups and their problems develop.

Minority-group problems are world-wide. They spread like the plague. In their causes, onset, and development, they often resemble the life cycle of an unknown epidemic disease. Because there are no known preventives or remedies, they are "persistent, widespread, and serious" in all of their forms.[1]

Tensions in majority-minority group relations may be basically either racial or ethnic. Usually they are combinations of the two. In most instances their first and distinctive symptom is hostility. But this symptom is not clearcut. It ranges over numerous degrees of this emotion from suspicion and fear to hatred and bigotry. "Fear, ignorance, envy, suspicion, malice, jealousy, frustration, greed, aggression, economic rivalry, emotional insecurity, and inferiority complex are," according to Davis, "some of its traits." This emotional complex is the source of periodical waves of intolerance. They take place most frequently during periods of national unrest—of war, depression, or mass migration.

[1] R. M. Williams, *The Reduction of Intergroup Tensions,* Bull. No. 57, Social Science Research Council, New York, 1947, p. 105. Jerome Davis, *Character Assassination,* Philosophical Library, New York, 1950, p. 222. R. Bierstedt, "Sociology of Majorities," *Am. Sociol. Rev.,* Vol. 13 (1948): 700-710.

Initially, therefore, minority group contentions are typical social problems. In them the questioning of human values is obvious. They begin in a series of interests or causes and from these multiple sources they develop so slowly and innocently that the ultimate problem is rarely traced back to its precipitating origins. Their associated problems are also numerous and include practically every human need and social institution. It is not a matter of surprise that attempts at appeasement have been notoriously unsatisfactory.

In short, the problems in majority-minority relationships are typical examples of the social paradox. Their most contradictory element is perhaps the fact that they are as much the problems of the majority as they are of the minority. Either the majority or the minority may create a disputed issue with the assistance of the other. In the various combinations of majority-minority relations, there is a subtle line of cleavage in a psychological environment and a dominance of attitude. This demarcation may arise between groups that have lived together in peaceful adjustment for centuries.

In present-day societies there are dominant and large majorities, dominant and small majorities, suppressed majorities, minorities in majorities, and majorities in minorities. Add to this confusion of size and homogeneity such other variables as color, religion, or economics, and it is easy to see why the inconsistencies and contradictions of minority-group problems become even more paradoxical than ordinary social problems and continue to be more difficult to define, analyze, and solve.

Minority groups: types and origins

Since minority groups are different, numerous, and chameleon-like, there has been no great success in human societies at any period in precisely defining or limiting their identifying traits. No one word is broad enough to include their varieties or changing composition. Hence, minority groups are most exactly identified temporarily as special groups with particular problems. But this classification rarely calls forth the intelligent sympathy of dominant groups or stimulates the research necessary for the better understanding of their status and needs.

So long as such broad descriptive labels as racial, ethnic, cultural, or even minority continue to be vague, minority groups and their problems will be located in a number of popular but inexact terms. At present they appear under varying names that specify one of their prominent traits, such as geographic location, color, national origins, ancestry, religion, language, economic status, education, social or caste status, political affiliation, mobility, and also varying cultural designations signifying a manner of living or belief.

Size of group therefore is a relatively insignificant identification. Likewise, when the long view is adopted and the attitudes of different historical periods are compared, no other single label in the above list is an apt designation. According to authoritative observers, nationality differences are becoming of great importance today in the cross-currents of international relations. But they were of small significance in the Middle Ages or during the founding and early settlement of this country. Similarly, the orthodoxy that separated sects and religions in previous generations is seldom experienced today as the single or even major barrier between groups. In order to achieve a helpful conception of the makeup of present-day minorities, it is necessary to discover several identifying characteristics in what is called a pattern of intergroup relationships.

This inexactness or confusion of labels is the dilemma in the study of minority-majority group relations. Nearly every investigation is obliged to straddle this issue either by accepting a category that is not exact or by using one type of label, the religious for example, to include groups that are also recognized as minorities because of their economic, political, or educational situation.

This dilemma in the United States is no different from that of many other countries that have numerous groups in all the designations mentioned above. However, it is an open question whether the dilemma would disappear if all current differences vanished. Groups in all these categories have demonstrated extraordinary ingenuity in manufacturing differences under the least expected circumstances. Religious groups are divided by politics; fraternal societies are separated by local social customs; nationality and racial groups take opposing sides because of geographical location or economic preferences; sobersided scientific groups are breached by questions of ethics and vocabulary; and Phi Beta Kappa is split by the controversy over liberal education.

In recent summaries of the literature, this approach is simplified by fixing attention upon a few of the major minorities. Both Rose and Schermerhorn limit their study of the United States to no more than twelve groups or combinations of groups (the total of which makes up about one third of the population) as sufficient illustrations of the nature and problems of minorities.[2]

A base-line point of departure. There are numerous suggestions as to methods of locating and defining a nation's minority groups and of explaining their origins and solidarity. One of these newer perspectives is the historical-political outlook, which ascribes the present alignment of majority-minority groups to the growing importance of nationalism in world affairs. A second, which is increasing in emphasis if not in scientific accuracy, is the new psychology that traces its lines of demarcation to the same mental abilities or incapacities that are used to separate the mentally normal from the mentally ill.[3]

Two other approaches are suggestive because they indicate a composite background or base of operations in the detection and analysis of minority-group problems.[4]

The first is a combined statistical and sociological approach originally introduced by Woofter. It surveys minority groups and their prospects from a baseline as of the year 1910.

At that time five characteristics in majority-minority relations and in the changing population were paramount. There was a growing immigrant population with significant differences in its regional distribution (older settlers in the Midwest; newer immigrants in the industrial East). There was a relatively stable Negro group, increasing slowly and located mainly in the Southeast. There was a small and slowly increasing Indian population, most of whom lived on reservations. There was a small Oriental population largely confined to the Pacific Coast, and a small Mexican group in the areas along the border states.

In addition to these groups there were the economic, political, religious, educational, and other minorities that a population can

[2] A. and C. Rose, *America Divided,* Knopf, New York, 1948. R. A. Schermerhorn, *These Our People,* Heath, Boston, 1949. The groups are: Roman Catholics, Jews, Negroes, Mexicans, Southern Europeans, Indians, French Canadians, Puerto Ricans, whites from other areas of the Western Hemisphere, Japanese, Chinese, and minor Asiatic peoples.

[3] O. C. Cox, *Caste, Class and Race,* Doubleday and Co., New York, 1948. Examples of the psychological explanations are: G. Ichheiser, *Diagnosis of Antisemitism,* Beacon House, New York, 1946; and M. Samuel, *The Great Hatred,* Knopf, New York, 1940.

[4] T. J. Woofter, *Races and Ethnic Groups in American Life,* McGraw-Hill, New York, 1933, pp. 9-11. R. M. Williams, *op. cit.,* pp. 51 ff. Propositions 1, 4, 5, 6, 9, 11, 18, 22, 24, 27, 33. The eighth point is from pp. 7-8.

produce without the aid of immigration. Moreover, as early as 1910 symptoms of drastic changes were observable in or toward all these groups. The tradition of hospitality to immigration was waning. Majority groups were exploiting all minority groups both economically and socially. At the same time, small numbers of the minorities were climbing the economic, educational, and social ladder. Their growing prestige and demands for equality were already forcing changes in the attitudes of dominant groups as indicated by legal reforms, the number of community organizations designed to improve intergroup relations, and the growing authority of some minorities through their strategic political influence, ownership of property, business affiliations, or educational and professional status.

A second base line of interpretation is a combined social and psychological analysis, which may be dated at about the end of World War II. In this survey Williams reviewed the status of minority-majority group relations under a variety of descriptive generalizations, eight of which suggest the nature of the muddled situation at that time.

1. All individuals, possibly as many as four fifths of the American people, are either intolerant or entertain active notions of hostility toward certain social groups.
2. The greater the solidarity that exists within a group, the greater is the group member's hostility or prejudice against individuals not of this group or who belong to other groups.
3. Prejudice is learned. It is not necessarily a result of personal experience with members of minority groups.
4. Prejudice is a product of frustration, insecurity, visibility, contact, competition, and differences in values.
5. Tensions, associated with or rising from, rapid social changes, economic depressions, and social disorganization, lead to prejudice, discrimination, and hostility.
6. Rapid movements of population, especially when the migrants are visibly different and are numerous compared with the resident population, are likely to lead to conflict.
7. Militant opposition or conflict is most apt to arise in those classes that are one step higher in the economic scale than the invading minority and that are consequently most exposed to its competition.
8. The numerous local, regional, state, and national organizations

whose objective is to institute arrangements for the lessening of hostility and prejudice have not been conspicuously successful in spite of the millions of dollars expended in specific efforts to improve friendly relations.

These two points of departure are helpful in three respects. Without the handicap of naming specific groups, they suggest the criteria by which such groups can be observed in terms of their most likely difficulties. At the same time they name specific conditions that, either singly or in combination, are or make the problems of intergroup rivalry. Finally, each proposition points out to some extent that their solution will depend as much upon changes in subjective attitudes as upon improvements in basic injustices that are ordinarily labelled as the causes of these problems.

Minority group problems in the United States

As already noted, the problems of minorities do not differ basically from those of majority groups. If it is true that both types of groups are subject to changes in a cycle of relationships that are found in the life history of social groups as a whole, then the status of either the minority or the majority so far as its problems are concerned can be identified by its position in this cycle. At some time a minority group becomes a protest group and organizes to make its wants known. It is also identifiable by a number of objective needs and subjective characteristics, all of which are emphasized in a pattern or sequence of obvious group-making conditions.

In the broad view, minority group problems are, or are the result of, problems of population, mobility, urbanization, industrialization, economic competition, social adjustment, individual and group differences (and attitudes concerning these differences), segregation, discrimination, prejudice, and conflict.

These conditions make way for many different particular social problems, any one of which may be regarded as unusually severe because it appears in a group that is handicapped by inferior social status, or unequal political or other privileges in such a network as

Hostility
Ignorance
Indifference → Discrimination / Segregation → Tension —— Conflict.
Prejudice
Aggression

From this interplay of objective and subjective conditions there result inequalities and infringements in citizenship, employment, and occupations; discrimination in social opportunities, schooling, health services and housing; and other limitations imposed by a dominant culture when groups in power are fearful of their own security or suspicious of the ultimate consequences of rapidly changing social arrangements.

The sources of the problems are clearly those of inconsistent social values or double standards. Social problems resulting therefrom are typical of a disorganized society that is not sure of its own policies. On the one hand it resists assimilation; on the other it denies the desirability of cultural pluralism (which suggests that people of different cultures can live together amicably). This confused situation within the limits of a national society is similar to the unsolved problems of international politics and to the moral dualism that exist in a divided United Nations.

CHARACTERISTIC SOCIAL PROBLEMS OF MINORITY GROUPS

Institutional Problems	*Population Problems*
Economic and occupational opportunities	Migration
Income and standards of living	Birth, death, and other vital rates
Marriage and family relations	Intermarriage
Education	Exclusion
Political status	Segregation
Health	Refugees
Housing	Marginal peoples
Recreation	Assimilation
Transportation	Amalgamation

A pattern of majority-minority relations

Any list of social problems that pretends to identify the peculiar difficulties of a minority group is obviously subject to change as the group changes its social status. As the preceding outline indicates, specific problems cannot be diagnosed except for particular groups in known social situations. It is for this reason that an approach to the problems of a minority group through a pattern of relations is helpful.

Two examples of the societal patterns in which majority-minority problems have had their origin are those mentioned previously as the situations of 1910 and 1945. In the first period a pattern of relations is suggested by (a) the distribution of minorities, (b) their economic status, and (c) the hint of growing tolerance. In the second period, a noticeably different design is indicated in (a) the confession as to the continuity and ingrained character of intolerance, (b) the implication that a group's solidarity is a bulwark against assimilation or friendly relationships, and (c) the association between the problems of minorities and such complexes as frustration, insecurity, visibility, and contact.

Majority-minority problems in all countries are obviously enough the outcomes of some similar network of forces in a contemporary pattern. And the nature, persistence, and severity of the social problems of a particular minority can only be understood fully when its functional status in the pattern can be determined.

A Suggested Pattern of Majority-Minority Relations

1. Contact: the source of new and different social relations.
2. Conflict: resistance of a minority group to an assigned status.
3. Visible differences in appearance.
4. Differences in culture, customs, language, religion.
5. Competition involving personal and group interests; fears of loss of status, prestige, security, or of some encroachment upon material well-being.
6. Political status.
7. Size of minority group: for example, a small group does not acquire the status of opposition until it begins to compete.
8. Other population changes: migration, urbanization, intermarriage, or interbreeding.
9. Changing social and economic classes: a result of social mobility in and between majority and minority groups.
10. Other cultural changes: assimilation by minorities of the dominant culture, or their resistance to assimilation; changing standards in the culture of the minority.
11. Changing social values: as noted concretely in social legislation.
12. Social organization of the minority group: as in unions, fraternal societies, or cooperatives.
13. New technologies: such as the automobile, chain store, or public housing that permit minorities to enjoy a greater independence of majority dominance and that establish different personal-social relations and require new interpretations of segregation.
14. Admission of a few among the minority to a status nearly equal to that of the dominant group.

Consider by way of illustration the first two problems under the classification of population.

Migration that establishes new contacts and possible conflicts for the changing group is in itself a function of each of the other conditions. Consequently, whether being migratory is a social problem of the group or a means of social readjustment is an outcome that cannot be determined apart from a complete inventory of the changing societal pattern. For example, compare from the point of view of their respective readjustments and new problems the strikingly different migrations of European immigrants from the industrial East to the agricultural West, of the agricultural Negroes from the South to the industrial cities of the North, and the seasonal movements of agricultural or industrial workers.

Another source of constant friction between majorities and minorities is to be located in changing vital rates. A high birth rate in a minority is sometimes favored because it promises to provide a constant supply of cheap labor. At the same time and in some quarters it is feared as evidence of biological degeneration or as a source of excessive economic competition. Similarly, other vital indexes (depending on the social values that are favored at the moment) of health, sickness, infant death rates, or life expectancy may be used as proof of the basic vitality of a people or as evidence of its most undesirable traits.

Each of the other problems classified as those of population or of the social institutions can be restated in like manner in a pattern of competing social values and intergroup relationships.

Minorities within minorities

Rarely in the cycle of majority-minority group relations is it true that majorities are united in their opposition or that minorities present a concerted and organized front. Breaches in the ranks of either group occur, and the opportunity for concessions by the majority and gains by the minority is under way.

In order to stem this tide, the aggressive section of the dominant group employs isolation and segregation. These sources of majority-minority rivalry and unadjustment are constant causes of friction because they are never complete. The minority is not so isolated that it has not already discovered the advantages of a preferred status, and segregation is condemned as futile surrender.

There are many historical examples that demonstrate how a powerful majority can exclude a minority from privileges already guaranteed to it by law. But the same sequence can also appear in the reverse, and minorities can exclude majorities. The continuity of some minority-group problems is to some extent as much a function of internal minority-group dissension as it is of external group rivalries.

One extreme of this unstable balance between social groups is to be noted in those ethnic or cultural islands that are so named because there are few or no contacts between them and the external society. Rivalries and contentions that start with the already-noted pattern of increasingly numerous and closer contacts can be summarized under four generalizations:

(1) Any group, exposed to social changes, will react with varying degrees of conservation.

(2) Within both majority and minority groups, there are some involuntary and some self-imposed barriers to assimilation. Frequently, a minority clings to its own culture as its chief assurance of solidarity and survival.

(3) As a rule, segregation or exclusion is the device of the dominant group. Segregation, plus the historical tactic of divide and control, has been effective because it has led to

(4) Accepted orders of discrimination with their equally effective orders of prejudice.[5]

Contemporary illustrations of the special problems of minority groups from this point of view are to be found in the marginal person, the stereotype and scapegoat, and the refugee or displaced person.[6]

[5] A concrete example of a minority undergoing assimilation and at the same time acquiring traits that create the prejudices of a minority within a minority is given by Niles Carpenter, *A Study of Acculturalization in the Polish Group of Buffalo,* Monographs in Sociology No. 3, University of Buffalo, 1929. In this group, the prejudice was anti-Negro. In other groups, prejudice may be developed against another segment of its own group; note examples of group self-hatred in Rose, *op. cit.,* pp. 210 ff. Other types of minority group cleavage are orthodox versus the liberal; old against new immigrants; first against the second generation; organized labor against nonunion labor; or the clash between intelligentsia and conservatives.

[6] C. McWilliams, *Brothers Under the Skin,* Little, Brown, Boston, 1951 (on marginal peoples). *Impressions of the Writers' War Board,* The Board, New York, 1945 (stereotypes). Anonymous, "Note on Intergroup Conditioning and Conflict among an Interracial Faculty at a Negro College," *Social Forces,* Vol. 27 (1949): 430-433 (an account by a faculty wife of white-Negro faculty cleavage). C. S. Johnson, "Minority Groups in the United Nations," *Relig. Ed.,* Vol. 42 (1947): 306-310. S. M. Strong, "Negro-White Relations as Reflected in Social Types," *Am. Jour. Sociol.,* Vol. 52 (1946): 23-30. H. L. Sheppard, "The Negro Merchant: A Study of Negro Anti-Semitism," *Am. Jour. Sociol.,* Vol. 53 (1947): 96-99. F. L. Auerbach, "The Admission and Resettlement of Displaced Persons

The refugee or displaced person is a good example of all three types of minorities within a minority. Contemporary refugees are sometimes called stateless persons in order to call attention to their most peculiar status. Otherwise they resemble the religious, nationality, political, or racial minorities who have been prominent in every stream of immigration to this country.

Some of the problems of the refugee, which illustrate how minority-group problems arise in a sequence of contacts and of other related conditions in a pattern of cultural accommodation, are: (1) language, (2) acquiring the customs and values of the new society, (3) finding a suitable job, (4) adjusting to new social relations, friendly or hostile, and (5) adjusting to unfriendly attitudes, particularly those of earlier immigrants.

There are numerous other examples of minorities in the minority groups of this country: among French Canadians, illustrating the cultural adhesions of language and religion; among Jews who have subdivided on the basis of nationality origins, religious orthodoxy, and social class; among Negroes on the basis of length of residence, geographical region, and social class, as well as the more commonly observed differences in color; among Mexicans on the basis of occupation and length of residence; and the numerous divisions between first, second, and third generations of Orientals.

Adjustments of minorities

Minority groups have been granted a varying degree of social acceptance, the chief variables being those characteristics that determine their status in the cycle and pattern of intergroup relations. Concretely, the achievements of each minority are measured by their economic status, legal equality or educational opportunities, and by their capacity to blend culturally and biologically with majority groups.[7]

in the United States," Common Council for American Unity, New York, 1949. P. McCarran, "Displaced Persons: Facts Versus Fiction," Government Printing Office, Washington, 1950. M. Davie, *Refugees in America,* Harper, New York, 1947.

[7] The primary sources of the following analysis are: A. G. Hays, *Trial by Prejudice,* Covici-Friede, New York, 1933. M. R. Konvitz, *The Constitution and Civil Rights,* Columbia University Press, New York, 1947; and *The Alien and the Asiatic in American Law,* Cornell University Press, Ithaca, New York, 1946. President's Committee on Civil Rights, *To Secure These Rights,* Simon and Schuster, New York, 1948. Florence Murray (Ed.), *The Negro Handbook,* Current Reference Publications, New York, 1944, pp. 43 ff.

The right to work. Discrimination in employment is a constant complaint of minority groups in their struggle for existence. Heretofore, largely limited to casual jobs and to occupations with high rates of unemployment, minority peoples prosper whenever the labor market is booming and jobs are plentiful. At such times all minority groups have made some headway up the occupational ladder. A few individuals have entered the professions or have become proprietors of their own business. More have been able to obtain experience in the skilled crafts and some trade unions have modified membership rules in their favor.

Even after numerous favorable advances made by minority groups during the war years, the investigations of the Federal Employment Practices Committee reported continuous restrictions in employment. Discrimination in the hiring practices of individual employers or entire industries is the chief barrier to the equal right to work. One survey discovered admitted discrimination in (a) twenty-four per cent of the companies interviewed, though as a rule the discrimination would not be recognized as an established policy, (b) eighty-nine per cent of employment agencies operating in the largest cities, and (c) help-wanted newspaper advertising, even in states with laws that forbid this type of overt discrimination.

Discrimination is also put into effect by the placement practices of many industries and through company-union agreements for many different occupations. On this general relationship Hughes has concluded that while industry is always a continuous mixer of peoples, at the same time it is a chief agent of segregation and is almost universally a factor in racial and ethnic discrimination.[8]

On the job, discrimination is another serious restriction. It lowers the average income of the minority group considerably below the national average and limits promotion. While this practice is found most often in private industry, FEPC also discovered it in governmental work in spite of specific rules of the Civil Service Commission against such practices. Though many trade unions have liberalized their membership policies, numerous instances are found of a rigid upper limit beyond which minority-group individuals will not be advanced, general rules of promotion and seniority notwithstanding.

[8] E. C. Hughes, "Queries Concerning Industry and Society," *Am. Sociol. Rev.*, Vol. 14 (1949): 211-220. C. W. Summers, "Admission Policies of Labor Unions," *Quart. Jour. Econom.*, Vol. 61 (1946): 66-91.

Fair Employment Practices Laws are welcome as indications of changes toward a more democratic society. But as in the case of New York State, to give one example, these acts do not repeal numerous discriminatory laws that exclude minorities—in this instance noncitizens—from employment in such occupations as chauffeur, embalmer, watchman, realtor, billiard-room proprietor, and physician. The continuity of these minor laws shows the power of economic pressure groups and at the same time the legal paradox that admits an alien to residence but discriminates against his labor because of the law's assumed protection of public welfare. Illinois, New Jersey, and Florida, in addition to New York, are among the states with the greatest number of restricted occupations.

Discrimination against minority-group personnel, both in placement and promotion, is frequently reported in the military services. It was amply demonstrated in World War II despite declarations by all services to the contrary. After many public protests since that time against segregation, the War Department has issued the blanket statement that "it intends to continue its efforts to make the best possible use of available personnel resources in the post-war Army . . . without distinction as to race, religion, or color," a statement that has also been endorsed by the Navy Department (including the Marine Corps) and by the Coast Guard. In spite of these assurances, recruits from some minorities are still limited in the branches of the service and in the training schools to which they are admitted, and eligibility to advancement is at its best on a quota basis. Furthermore, segregation by regulation also continues to be the practice in the operations of the National Guard in most states.

Legal status of minorities. Whenever citizenship or the rights of citizenship are denied through eligibility tests of naturalization laws or through state laws that are contrary to the United States Constitution, the individuals thus limited suffer numerous other disabilities. Among the more important of these handicaps are the right to work in certain occupations, the right to own land, and the right to benefits under Social Security provisions or the various forms of state relief.

Foremost among the limitations of native-born residents in minority groups is the restriction on the right to vote. There were periods in the history of American politics when every male resident was permitted to vote whether or not he was a citizen. Gradually the franchise was barred to some because of race and to others by requirements that denied them access to the polls or by corrupt practices or irregularities in interpreting the qualifications for citizenship.

There are other discriminatory practices associated with this law evasion or nonenforcement of state laws, such as restriction from jury duty, personal insecurity through abuses of the police or by intimidation and threats of violence of lawless elements, and occasionally by more severe penalties in the courts.

These infringements on the lawful privileges of residents occur generally throughout entire regions in this country, regardless of state laws. There are three general patterns of state laws. Eighteen states have Civil Rights Acts that prohibit discrimination. Twenty states have laws that enforce segregation, and the remainder leave this issue to private discretion.

Cases of illegal discrimination are infrequently brought to court. When trial is sought (generally through the aid of some organized protest group), it is difficult for the prosecution to prove a violation of civil rights. Often the defendant will settle for the costs of damages as a more expedient procedure than a relaxation of the policy of exclusion. Some legal authorities regard this court situation as the most discriminatory of all, since the prosecution is required to prove discrimination when the acts of the defendant may be overcharging, discourtesy, house rules or some other wholly legal evasion of the law.

Historical and dramatic examples of legal discrimination and trial by prejudice represent every variety of legal evasion, fabricated evidence, and emotional bias. Outstanding among such cases during the present century, particularly because of the world-wide interest that they aroused, were the trials of Mooney and Billings, Leo Frank, Sacco and Vanzetti, and the Scottsboro defendants. In each the original charges were violence and murder, but secondary influences, such as labor conflict, anti-Semitism, communism, and Negro prejudice, so complicated these charges that each trial has been described as a network of falsified evidence, rumor, public demonstration, prejudiced juries, and special-group justice.

Education. Inequalities in educational opportunity are found at all levels of public and private instruction from elementary to the graduate professional schools. This discrimination is experienced by minority groups in two ways. One is inadequacy in the physical facilities and in courses of study. The other is the quota system of admissions. In some states this discrimination is maintained by a dual school system. In others it is maintained by limited segregation or by limited admissions.

The most unfortunate result of these practices is the varying quality of education that students of all ages receive. The same condition of inequality in educational services is known to occur under either system of discrimination and is demonstrated by differences in length of school term, transportation of students, extent of curriculum, per capita expenditures for education, teachers' salaries, or opportunities for advanced work and graduate study.

In states that do not have segregation, discrimination is carried on sufficiently to achieve a close approach to segregation through residential requirements, school districts, or separate classes. And in private schools and colleges, restricted admissions, which are based on geographical and socio-economic bases as well as on minority-group affiliations, also result in distinct hardship in individual cases and for entire groups.

These limitations tend to bring into being or to enforce restrictions in fraternities, athletics, dormitories, recreational and social activities, and occasionally in libraries, both in their use and in employment in them.

Graduate schools of law, medicine, and dentistry are accused of discrimination through the quota system more often than schools of engineering or business administration. One investigation of both undergraduate and graduate colleges states that "virtually all college and university officials are aware that discrimination is the rule rather than the exception."[9] In New York City the Mayor's Committee on Unity reported the same finding and expressed the belief that the situation is becoming worse each year.

Miscellaneous consequences of discrimination. Many minority groups are at a considerable disadvantage because of their low economic status in obtaining adequate health services or housing.

For years, high death rates, particularly infant and maternal, and high illness rates (especially from tuberculosis) have been serious handicaps of minority groups. Although much of this ill health is due to poor nutrition and overcrowding, it is traced in some measure to discrimination in medical facilities. Minority groups are

[9] D. Dodson, "College Quotas and American Democracy," *Am. Scholar* (Phi Beta Kappa publication), Summer, 1945.

not equally represented among trained medical personnel, and many hospitals and clinics refuse the use of their facilities to both practitioners and patients.

In most areas of this country there are similar complaints of discrimination in the use of recreational areas (parks, beaches, and playgrounds), in the availability of public services, such as restaurants, theaters, hotels, and stores, and occasionally in requirements for membership in churches, clubs, and fraternal societies.[10]

Opposition to minority groups is also regularly noted in restrictions on their residential areas. This restriction, in spite of rulings of the United States Supreme Court against the restrictive clause in deeds, is facilitated by controls over loans, the unwillingness of builders to construct homes, refusal of real estate companies to sell, as well as by open resentment against some minorities and even against public housing projects for them. In some large metropolitan areas it is estimated that fully eighty per cent of the residential property is covered by restrictive clauses. There is no surety under present legislation that either federal or state courts can control the discriminatory housing practices of private interests because of the numerous opportunities for law evasion.

Intermarriage

Opposition to intermarriage excites the purists among dominant groups more than any other type of social relationship. This attitude is, consequently, one of the chief supports of all forms of opposition, discrimination, prejudice, and segregation. As a result, there has never been very much intermarriage in the United States, even in those states that do not have laws forbidding it. Moreover, the tradition of inmarriage is firmly established in all social groups, the reason for this being group solidarity, which is the same condition that promotes the general aversion toward intermarriage.

Intermarriage is generally defined as marriage between individuals of different racial, religious, and nationality backgrounds. When it does take place with any degree of frequency, it usually indicates a mobile society, decreasing social solidarity, increasing personal emancipation, uneven sex ratios, and changing economic status. Although most statistics of intermarriage are unofficial and are derived from small-area studies, a general agreement of all these reports

[10] For examples, consult: *Segregation in Washington,* National Committee on Segregation in the Nation's Capitol, Chicago, 1948.

is that intermarriage has always been rare and in recent decades has been decreasing.[11]

These investigations also show that intermarriage follows definite sequences. When a group is large, its rate of intermarriage is low. The rate of intermarriage increases slightly as the group decreases in size, is urban, has an unbalanced sex ratio, or is exposed to rapidly changing conditions. There is no evidence that long-settled groups are tending to lose their identity for this reason.

When attention is given to other possible explanations, the following general trends are noted. From the point of view of sex differences in intermarriage, the tendency is for males to intermarry more often than females. This conclusion holds particularly for Negroes and Orientals. Urban rates of intermarriage are always greater than rural rates. Marriages between persons of different nationalities tend to be religious inmarriages and religious intermarriages occur most often when a particular religious group is small, the religion is liberal, and the sex ratio is unbalanced.

Racial intermarriage is most often an adjustment of the urban male—the smaller the racial group, the higher the rate of intermarriage. For both reasons of size and urban residence, Filipinos, Chinese, and Japanese tend to intermarry much more than Negroes. A striking sex difference in this connection is that the white male participates in miscegenation more often than does the white female. A final point that all studies consistently support is that there is no evidence of increasing interracial marriage.

The trend of marriage between nationalities is one of minimum occurrence among first generation immigrants, with increasing rates among the second and third generations. Among immigrants from Europe, their old-country geographical and cultural similarities and their geographical proximity in this country are favorable to intermarriage. Other social correlates are length of residence, similar economic status and education, and a waning of group compulsion. As already observed, most such marriages are between members of similar religious groups. This pattern of intermarriage has an incidence that is higher than either racial or religious intermarriage.

In religious intermarriage, the pattern is best described by its frequency in the different religions. Protestants have the highest

[11] M. L. Barron, *People Who Intermarry,* Syracuse University Press, Syracuse, N. Y., 1946. For a different conclusion, see *Time,* November 19, 1951, p. 95, which states that intermarriage between Protestants and Catholics is increasing.

rate, though most of these marriages are between the Protestant sects. Greek Orthodox and Greek Catholic are second; Roman Catholics, third, and Jews have the lowest rate. In these as in intermarriages as a whole, the favorable social conditions are emancipation of the individual, cultural similarity, uneven sex ratios, and the decline of religious conservatism.

As in all marriages, the chief factor is contact made possible by associations in school or employment; similarities in cultural background, language, and economic and social status; length of residence in the country; living in the same community or neighborhood; and similar recreational interests.

Passing

Passing is an adjustment of a minority group member that is effective when he can become identified with, and accepted by, the majority. Most passing takes the form of acculturalization, that is, the individual is assimilated by acquiring both the appearance and behavior traits of the dominant culture. It is a normal phase of social mobility and is usually encouraged, as for example in a program of Americanization. An exception is racial passing which in this country is the passing of Negroes who have only a small and obscure proportion of Negro traits.

Of these biracial hybrids, males are more likely to attempt to pass as whites than are the females. They are favored by better economic opportunities. And for this reason they are better able to change residence and to choose their friends. The near-white female may obtain employment as white, but she is less apt than the male to break completely with the Negro group and she usually marries within that group.

Most passing occurs during late adolescence or in early adulthood. It is easiest to pass in northern cities, and almost impossible in areas that are race-conscious. Passing is often for a special purpose, such as for employment or for service in restaurants and other public accommodations. It is also apt to be temporary, because the individual may choose to return to the Negro group rather than be constantly exposed to the tension of a new and strange role. Occasionally cases are reported when an individual will pass in a form that is called shuttling, during which he will be either white or Negro as business or social circumstances dictate.

According to Reuter's estimate, passing is infrequent but is not negligible.[12] More recent indications are that there is no widespread inducement for Negroes to attempt to pass or to become identified with the white group permanently. Often the number is grossly exaggerated. Conservative estimates hold that no more than ten per cent of those who could pass do so—a total of perhaps 2,000 per year.[13]

The sociological significance of passing is in its connections with marginal people and in the formation of marginal minority groups. All groups, dominant or minority, tend to produce their marginal types as a normal result of social differentiation. The net result is the production of another minority group, which then becomes subject to the same prejudices, problems, or advantages already described as typical of minorities.[14]

Programs and policies

The adjustment of intergroup relations is a basic sociological problem. But it has been rarely studied except in the pathologies of rioting and lynching. Hence it is poorly understood and is clarified by none of the generalizations that can be safely accepted in programs to relieve less complicated social problems. For all these reasons, and also because of their political implications, the problems of majority-minority groups are now being handled by numerous committees and councils. In this country their number is well over a thousand, but most observers are not enthusiastic about their achievements or prospects. Davis has classified thirty-seven of them that he believes should be of some constructive service, five in the field of education, five in employment, seven in labor, and twenty in the general field of religious, racial, and other minority-group relations.[15]

In brief, the situation of minority groups remains chaotic, because its problems continue to be viewed from discordant moral standards. There are the extreme positions of absolute separation and exclusion and the middle-of-the-road policies of good will and

[12] E. B. Reuter, *Race Mixture,* McGraw-Hill, New York, 1931, pp. 70-71.

[13] J. H. Burma, "The Measurement of Negro Passing," *Am. Jour. Sociol.,* Vol. 52 (1946): 118-122. E. W. Eckard, "How Many Negroes Pass?," *Am. Jour. Sociol.,* Vol. 54 (1946): 498-500. Note also the treatment of passing in *Lost Boundaries,* W. L. White, Harcourt, Brace, New York, 1948.

[14] D. E. Wray, "Marginal Men of Industry: The Foremen," *Am. Jour. Sociol.,* Vol. 56 (1949): 298-301.

[15] J. Davis, *op. cit.,* pp. 243-246.

understanding. The report of the President's Committee on Civil Rights is an excellent example of the latter, but it has not been accepted in Congress. Its simplified recommendations include (1) the protection of civil rights already guaranteed by the Constitution (rights to safety and security, citizenship, freedom of conscience, and equality of opportunity), and (2) education of the public to support the extension of these rights to all people.

According to Davis, the specific tasks of all such programs may be summarized in the following questions:

1. Is there discrimination because of race, creed, or color in employment and trade unions?
2. Are competent students being restricted in schooling because of quotas?
3. Are health and hospital facilities equally available to all citizens and licensed practitioners?
4. Are there segregated housing areas and discrimination in hotels and restaurants?
5. Does the law apply equally to all? Are all citizens equally eligible to jury service?
6. Is there intimidation or restriction in voting or in becoming a candidate for public office?
7. Is there segregation or discrimination in recreation?
8. Is the press free? Is there a newspaper monopoly?[16]

Under contemporary conditions, when national solidarity is reinforced by the dread of international communism and fear of a nationwide economic collapse because of the rearmament program, a new base line of minority-majority relations is apparent. One phase of this newer outlook is the endorsement of civil-rights legislation by increasing numbers in the majority groups and a stronger inclination to abide by the decisions of the Supreme Court. A second is the growing opposition to lawlessness by evasion and by violence. A third is an evidence of national maturity, which means the recognition of cultural pluralism wherein all social services will be provided for a population of recognized differences. A fourth is the increasing willingness to submit disputed questions to prompt and thorough investigation.[17]

Summary

Problems in majority-minority group relations have been clearly stated for many generations. Their general causes are known and

[16] *Ibid.*, pp. 239-40.
[17] *The Race Question*, Unesco Publication No. 791, New York, 1951.

are recognized as a medley of disturbances in the economic life of a people and in the emotional reactions of the individual. What is not understood with any degree of precision is how these causes may be removed so that people can live together in peace and dignity, despite differences in their appearance, belief, or contacts.

As sociologists have pointed out, at least since the time of Charles Cooley, people have learned how to live in primary, personal groups much more efficiently than they have been able to manage their secondary or impersonal relations. It is this capacity on the one hand and failure on the other that is credited with most of the problems of minority groups. Human beings do not make the same allowances for strangers that they are willing to make for intimates. At the same time, the convenient presence of strangers furnishes an excellent explanation for every form of social incompetence and for other irritating problems of the day.

The fact that the stranger needs no other visible identification is fairly sufficient proof that minority problems are not necessarily the result of unusual differences. No social groups ever treated each other more contemptuously or brutally than the colonial sects of the thirteen original colonies—yet in most respects these people were identical in culture, social and economic status, and religion.

Such historical examples, as well as the problems of the present, have stimulated numerous basic social studies of human prejudice. What is known so far is relatively elementary, and yet it furnishes a reasonably sound basis for further analysis.

Most people are prejudiced, and the source of this prejudice is found in early childhood. They learn to be prejudiced through the same contacts by which all other learning is acquired, through attitudes of parents, teaching in the schools, and influences of the neighborhood during the impressionable years from six to sixteen. Moreover, it is known that the usual precautions against the contagion of prejudice—such as religious instruction, occasional contacts with minority groups, or advertising devices showing individuals of different groups in friendly situations—are not particularly effective. Prejudice is too much a part of personality to be so readily dislodged. In fact, surveys agree in the observation that most people either do not realize their own quota of prejudices or generally underestimate them.[18]

[18] J. A. Bayton, "Personality and Prejudice," *Jour. Psychol.*, Vol. 22 (1946): 59-65.

For all these reasons it is desirable to recognize the appearance and spread of these problems from some tangible base line or to trace their connection with a pattern of potential causes or conditions that may eventually turn out to be the sources of their control. Such analysis, as a minimum contribution, serves to put any minority problem in an observable perspective, and removes to a considerable extent the fear and hostility that otherwise are apt to discredit both its study and solution because of the overload of emotional bias.

Whether minority-group problems are broadly social, or more narrowly those of economic conditions and psychological impressions, or combinations thereof is a question on which there is no certain knowledge. For this reason and because of the growing prevalence of open conflict between groups, these problems are recognized as deserving more attention as research projects. A good example of plan, scope, and objective of such an investigation is the program of the Race Relations Study of the University of Chicago.

This study, in cooperation with numerous national agencies and with other committees and research projects in the University, aims: (1) to test the theories of majority-minority group friction and to achieve a scientific foundation for the policies and programs of intergroup association, (2) to introduce this knowledge into the curricula of schools and colleges as a worthwhile area of teaching and learning, (3) to train leadership in the field of intergroup relations, (4) to encourage cooperative research and training in other universities, and (5) to institute experimental programs by which knowledge and techniques of intergroup relationships may be discovered and used in the testing of its policies.

Since no other social problem illustrates more effectively the damage of ignorance, the faith of the scholar is renewed by his confidence in the power of facts.

Bibliography

American Friends Service Committee, *Some Quaker Approaches to the Race Problem,* The Committee, Philadelphia, 1946.

Andrews, Bert, *Washington Witch Hunt,* Random House, New York, 1948.

Brown, F. J., *Discrimination in College Admissions,* American Council on Education, Washington, 1950.

Clark, Tom, and P. B. Perlman, *Prejudice and Property,* Public Affairs Press, Washington, 1948.

Crary, R. W., and J. T. Robinson, *America's Stake in Human Rights,* Bull. No. 24, National Council for the Social Studies, Washington, 1949.

Davis, Jerome, *Character Assassination,* Philosophical Library, New York, 1950.

Fisher, L. H., *The Problem of Violence,* American Council on Race Relations, San Francisco, 1947.

LaFarge, J. S., *No Postponement: United States Moral Leadership and the Problem of Racial Minorities,* Longmans, Green, New York, 1950.

Myers, Gustav, *History of Bigotry in the United States,* Random House, New York, 1943.

Myrdal, G., *An American Dilemma,* Harper, New York, 1944.

Ottley, Roi, *Black Odyssey,* Scribner's, New York, 1948.

President's Committee on Civil Rights, *To Secure These Rights,* Simon and Schuster, New York, 1948.

Scott, J. I. E., *Negro Students and Their Colleges,* Meador, Boston, 1949.

Weaver, Robert, *The Negro Ghetto,* Harcourt, Brace, New York, 1948. Residential segregation in the North.

Williams, R., *Reduction of Intergroup Tensions,* Bull. No. 57, Social Science Research Council, New York, 1947. Chaps. 1 and 2. This monograph has a well-selected bibliography, pp. 135-45.

Questions

1. Do you accept the general economic classification of minority group problems, or do you prefer some other?
2. How do the minorities and their problems in your community support either point of view?
3. Must a dominant group dominate education in order to preserve its power?
4. Is this statement a law of anti-Semitism: "the greater the national solidarity within any given state, the greater the likelihood of anti-Semitism?"
5. What is the meaning of group solidarity in the above context? Can you explain it sociologically?
6. Can you justify the quota system in education?
7. Why is the typical minority-group problem called a paradox?
8. By what channels do most minority-group individuals escape from their submerged status?
9. Analyze critically each of Williams' eight generalizations (see p. 272). Do you agree that they are substantially correct?
10. Will amalgamation solve racial problems?
11. Formulate a question about each of the problems of minority groups stated on page 274 and outline suggested solutions.

CHAPTER 12

INFLATIONS AND DEPRESSIONS

AT THEIR CRITICAL HIGH AND LOW POINTS, BUSINESS CYCLES CAN BE AS ruinous as major disasters. These two extremes indicate rapid economic change and unusual social instability. The business cycle as a whole corresponds closely in these respects to cycles in other conditions with which it may be related, for example, to variations in climate, disease, or group relations.

These personal, group, physical, and mental fluctuations have many similarities. For the most part they emerge from unknown combinations of causes. Their onset is unpredictable. Their development is not definitely periodic. Their consequences, invariably, are devastating.

In all these respects, the business cycle and its social consequences are typical social problems. Altogether they have brought into being a strange cycle of explanations, as inconsistent and sometimes as irrational as some utopian philosophies. They have also stimulated much of the most representative and objective social research.

Both inflation and depression are mass calamities, not unlike war, revolution, or famine. Each may appear at first as a harmless, relatively inconspicuous disorder. But before their climax is reached, they can aggravate almost every social problem and threaten the existence of a society. No person or institution can remain unaffected by their direct or indirect effects.

Inflation and depression, therefore, are specific social problems on a large scale. Opinions differ as to their ill-effects, because they frequently destroy the values that are the only barometer available for their measurement.

Inflation as a social problem

Inflation means high and rising prices. Its chief characteristic is too much money or purchasing power without sufficient increase in the volume of production. As results, the money cost of production increases and there are shortages in production.

Four major problems are associated with inflation. It is considered a cause of financial collapse and depression. It starts a spiral of wages trying to catch up with prices. It destroys the economic stability of workers on fixed incomes (especially those that have no bargaining power, such as unorganized workers), bondholders, and beneficiaries of life insurance, annuities, and pensions. It depreciates savings.

Little is known as to the combination of causes that result in inflation. In this country runaway inflation has occurred only during and after wars. Conditions that are most often associated with inflation are high costs of government and a large and increasing national indebtedness; high taxes (many of which are hidden in the costs of goods and services) and especially taxes that restrain private enterprise; public works projects; public payments to individuals for not working or to reduce production; regulations of exports and imports; controlled shortages; and hoarding. Because of the general nature of these conditions, inflation is generally worldwide when it does occur.[1]

Depression as a social problem

In comparison with periods of prosperity, depressions represent a number of disorganizing agencies. Some of these factors are called speculation, underconsumption, overproduction, hoarding, bank panics, mass production, a complex division of labor, excessive investments and overhead costs, competition, and low wages. Each one

[1] Because of these many complicating factors, most interpretive studies are historical. Consult: Anne Bezanson, "Inflation and Controls, Pennsylvania, 1774–1779," *Jour. Econ. Hist.*, Vol. 8 (1948): Supp. VIII, pp. 1-20 (in this report, the causes of inflation are given as shortages in production and cheap money). S. Rezneck, "Distress, Relief, and Discontent in the United States during the Depression of 1873-78," *Jour. Pol. Econ.*, Vol. 58 (1950): 494-512; and "The Depression of 1819-1822," *Am. Hist. Rev.*, Vol. 39 (1933): 28-47. K. D. Roose, "The Recession of 1937-38," *Jour. Pol. Econ.*, Vol. 56 (1948): 239-248. D. C. Seitz, *The Dreadful Decade*, Bobbs-Merrill, Indianapolis, 1926 (inflation in the 1870's). Department of Economic Affairs, "Inflationary and Deflationary Tendencies," United Nations, Lake Success, New York, 1949.

of these characteristics of depressions may be used to construct an explanatory theory of the business cycle, or they may be employed altogether to illustrate personal and impersonal consequences of a vast and planless social machine.

The rhythm of depressions and the regularity of their occurrence suggest one of the most usual characteristics of all social problems, namely, their apparent inevitability. During each decade of the last century and in each decade of the present century until 1940, there has been at least one major economic depression. Less serious depressions are even more numerous, occurring on the average every four or five years. These major and minor downward swings in economic efficiency are accompanied by, and largely described through, decreasing production, increasing poverty, decreasing standard of living, and increasing unemployment. Moreover, even during periods of inflation, production and standards of living have been regularly insufficient for human needs.

From superficial inspection of modern economic life, the demoralizing consequences of this insecurity are obvious. One, and perhaps the most outstanding, causal agency that is assumed to be chiefly responsible for depressions is defective industrial organization. The main defect occurs when industry fails to produce goods in harmony with changing markets and needs. Other defects and possible causes are the uneven distribution of income (the maldistribution of purchasing power), the instability of income, competition, defective organization of the labor market, risks in capital investments, rates of growth of total production, international exchange of goods, profits, indebtedness, credit, and the different sensitivity of producers' and consumers' goods industries to economic changes. At any rate, the opinion is widely held that certainty and security in any one of these economic spheres would go far in eliminating the ill effects of depressions.

The depression that began in 1929 focused attention of economists and laymen on the defects of industrial society. The general public is now more inclined to approve thorough and impartial study than ever before. In addition to such particular aspects of depressions as their intensity, duration, and worldwide extent, an interest in long-time economic and social consequences has put emphasis upon two major problems. One is the instability of our economic system in general. The second is concerned with specific economic and social consequences of depressions.

Attention to the disorganizing effects of depressions is fair proof of insecurity and change in modern life. It encourages, consequently, all efforts toward sounder social management, guidance, or stabilization.

In recent years many well-planned movements have endeavored to stabilize these cyclical changes. To date, however, they have scarcely accomplished more than an enumeration of leading obstructions to social security. Among the major problems that this approach to depression reveals, there are: (1) the changing demand for durable and consumers' goods, (2) lack of balance in the volume of both types of goods, (3) overproduction, (4) unemployment, (5) the correlation between insecurity of jobs and size of industry, (6) monopolies and controlled prices, (7) technological changes, (8) changes in the amount of labor supply, (9) competition between different classes of labor, (10) slackening in the growth of population.

These findings indicate major problems of depressions.

The nature of depressions

As a process, the business cycle is explained by basic economic changes. Though many probable causes both economic and non-economic have been cited, it is generally conceded that the principal cause is something within industry and commerce. One conclusion is obvious in the sequences of the business cycle: prosperity leads to crisis; crisis makes depression; depression encourages revival.

In this industrial setting any one cycle of prosperity, crisis, depression, and revival is simply an illustration of the range of forces that operate to make these sequences. In the depression of 1929, for example, the downward trend of business and the crisis are accounted for by the following coincidences: (1) the long-time effects of World War I, (2) its financial costs, (3) decrease of commodity prices, (4) the flow of gold in international exchange, (5) decline of agriculture, (6) industrial expansion, (7) expansion of trade and transportation, (8) decline in the demand for labor, (9) declining birth rate, (10) reduced immigration, (11) public debts, and (12) the extension of both public and private credit.

During the last hundred and thirty years there have been thirty-five cycles in the United States. A complete cycle is described by four dates: (1) the months during which expansion and prosperity occur, and (2) end; and (3) the months during which depression begins, and (4) ends. Although different indexes of the average duration of the business cycle reveal varying periods of length, in American experience the time period is between thirty-six and forty months, as indicated in the following table.

DURATION OF BUSINESS CYCLES IN THE UNITED STATES

Reference Dates		*Duration in Months*		
Peak	*Trough*	*Expansion*	*Contraction*	*Full Cycle*
June, 1899	Dec., 1900	24	18	42
Sept., 1902	Aug., 1904	21	23	44
May, 1907	June, 1908	33	13	46
Jan., 1910	Jan., 1912	19	24	43
Jan., 1913	Dec., 1914	12	23	35
Aug., 1918	Apr., 1919	44	8	52
Jan., 1920	Sept., 1921	9	20	29
May, 1923	July, 1924	20	14	34
Oct., 1926	Dec., 1927	27	14	41
June, 1929	Mar., 1933	18	45	63
May, 1937	May, 1938	50	12	62

Source: A. F. Burns and W. C. Mitchell, *Measuring Business Cycles,* National Bureau of Economic Research, New York, 1946, p. 78. During the first five decades of this century, there have been 219 months of contraction and 381 of expansion (the latter figure including all the fifth decade). Consult the graph of cycles prepared by the National Association of Purchasing Agents, Century Press, Toledo, Ohio, published annually.

Cycles are identified by classification according to their several phases as:

1. The 2-phase cycle—prosperity, depression.
2. The 3-phase cycle—prosperity, crisis, depression.
3. The 4-phase cycle—prosperity, crisis, depression, revival.
4. The 5-phase cycle—prosperity, financial strain, crisis, depression, revival.

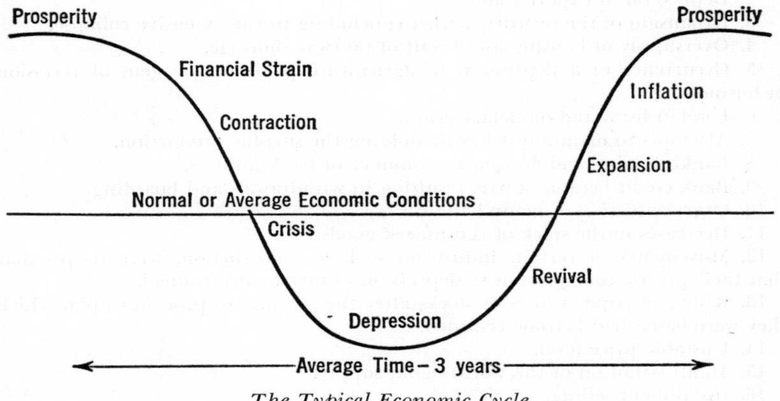

The Typical Economic Cycle

In such analyses it is customary to give each downswing of the cycle a particular descriptive label ordinarily noting some spectacular happening, such as the Jay Cooke panic of 1873, the railroad panic of 1881, the rich man's panic of 1903, and the prosperity panic of 1929. In addition, the recessions following a war have been called primary and secondary postwar depressions.

Likewise, periods of recovery are explained in part by distinctive names—the bank credit land boom of 1836-1837, the two periods of upswing because of California Gold inflation in 1851 and 1852-1854, railroad prosperity of 1888-1892, Coolidge prosperity, and war prosperity.

Causes of extreme fluctuations

When causes of economic instability are summarized, two general classes are isolated. In the first class are the economic, which include revolutionary changes in (1) the exploitation of new resources, (2) invention, (3) agricultural conditions, (4) credit, (5) war, (6) production, (7) banking operations, and (8) distribution. The second consist of noneconomic factors, such as (a) weather, (b) psychological factors in business, and (c) uncertainty.

Each of these general conditions and special features of depression is particularly noticeable in the depression of 1929.[2]

[2] J. M. Clark, *Strategic Factors in Business Cycles,* National Bureau of Economic Research, New York, 1934, pp. 111-123. As factors in the depression of 1929, Clark mentions:

1. Worldwide decline in prices before American depression.
2. Depression in export trade.
3. Expansion of the security market concluding in the extensive collapse.
4. Oversupply of housing as a result of postwar shortage.
5. Occurrence of a depression in agriculture prior to the general recession in business.
6. Foreign fiscal and monetary crises.
7. Attempts to maintain prices by holding the surplus production.
8. Banking crises and an unusual number of bank failures.
9. Bank credit became scarce, resulting in withdrawals and hoarding.
10. Overproduction of many basic stocks.
11. Decreases in the stock of consumers' goods.
12. Movements in certain industries, such as construction, were so peculiar that their precise contribution to depression cannot be determined.
13. Rising of paper values of stocks after the productive processes upon which they were based had become retarded.
14. Unstable price level.
15. Maldistribution of the world's gold supply.
16. Installment selling.

Cycles and especially the depression phase are also noticeable in other cultural and in several subcultural events. Comparable cultural upheavals are found in political agitation and revolution, in the income cycle, in occupational shifts and realignments, in social mobility, and in community organization. Many of these upward and downward movements have occurred so repetitively that they have been made the basis of long-range forecasts.

In several other different types of phenomena, similar cyclical movements have been observed. Some forms of animal life (fish, mice, and elephants) seem to thrive and then to diminish in numbers in definite periods. Weather in this country varies in a twenty-three year pattern. Cycles of epidemics include pneumonia and influenza (a three-year cycle), diphtheria (a cycle of six or seven years), and cholera, which is an annual event in India. Likewise, there are other cycles for vital rates (birth and death), changes in human weight, fashion, extremes of rainfall, climate, and for some forms of plant life.

The quest for an explanation of depressions is frequently directed to these noneconomic changes as well as to economic cycles, and also to the medley of influences out of which each different type of cyclical movement may develop. Similarly, this quest is often turned toward the recovery phase of cycles in order that the factors responsible for revivals and booms (or their equivalents in noneconomic conditions) may be determined.

The nature of recovery

Measurements of a return to improved business conditions are generally the same indexes that are found to be accurate in determining business recessions. Among the most sensitive of these symptoms of recovery are indexes of national income and real income, the cost of living, industrial production, employment, and unemployment. Occasionally, too, the revival of export trade, the investment in automobiles, and contracts for housing and other equipment are used. When all these indexes point to an upward trend in business, they are evidences of recovery.

Major characteristics of the upturn toward revival and a return of economic prosperity are:

1. The growth of old industries and the development of new ones.
2. Rising prices.
3. Increasing interest rates.

4. Increasing employment and wages.
5. Increasing public and private expenditures.
6. Increasing speculation.
7. Expansion of loans.[3]

In recent economic history, periods of prosperity are almost exactly counterbalanced by periods of depression. In one comparative study of cycles, covering the years 1890 to 1925 inclusive, the characteristic three-phase cycle is assigned the following distribution of prosperity, recession and revival, and depression: [4]

	Number	*Per Cent*
Months of prosperity	2,888	39.3
Months of recession and revival	1,756	23.9
Months of depression	2,700	36.8
Total	7,344	100.0

In contrast to the economic experience of most industrial nations, the United States has fared exceptionally well in its own record of depressions. On the average, this country has had a year and one half of prosperity for every year of depression. In the Swedish experience, for the years 1890-1913, 1.89 years of prosperity occurred for each year of depression.[5]

An exact barometer of economic recovery is difficult to formulate. Probably the chief reason for this difficulty is the uneven response of many economic conditions at the turning point of the depression and the unequal speed of their revival. Additional obstacles to precision in both measurement and prediction are the serious and costly social lags, as for example, the continuation of a heavy poor-relief load or of a large number of unemployed persons after prosperity is well on the way.

Because of variations in the movement of many economic and social indexes of recovery, it is customary to employ several other evidences of the normality or abnormality of business in addition to income, cost of living, production, and employment. Other suggested indexes include more specific measures of economic status and various social data, such as labor relations, inventions, popula-

[3] A. Achinstein, *Introduction to Business Cycles,* Crowell, New York, 1950, pp. 144 ff; pp. 236 ff.

[4] W. L. Thorpe and W. C. Mitchell, *Business Annals,* National Bureau of Economic Research, Inc., New York, 1926, p. 16.

[5] D. S. Thomas, *Social and Economic Aspects of Swedish Population Movements,* Macmillan, New York, 1941, pp. 153-154.

tion movements, social legislation, public health, dependency, crime, education, recreation, and travel.[6]

A suggestive theory on the nature of depressions and recovery is derived from the stage of industrialism or of economic stability that a country is able to achieve. According to this conception of economic changes, a country is exposed to relatively long cycles at the beginning of industrialization. Thereafter, cycles are progressively shortened as long as industrial and economic development is in its prime. As soon as the course of industry reaches a relatively stabilized period in its growth, cycles tend to have a longer duration. Industrial diversity and opportunity, consequently, are keys to recovery. And the duration of a cycle is a reflection of the elasticity of an industrial civilization.[7]

This theory is of further assistance in its interpretation of cycles of varying duration. In this respect it suggests their location within a cycle of much longer duration, as illustrated by the rise and fall of a population group, a government, or an industry.

CORRELATES WITH ECONOMIC CYCLES

PHENOMENA RISING OR FALLING WITH ECONOMIC CYCLES (LAGS DISREGARDED)		PHENOMENA ASSOCIATED BUT IN AN UNDETERMINED MANNER
Increasing with Prosperity	*Increasing with Depression*	
Alcohol consumption	Arrests	Attitudes and interests
Birth rates	Business failures	Crime, general
Crimes against the person	Church attendance	Death rates, general
Divorce and desertion	Crimes against property	Ill health or lowered vitality
Emigration	Housing deficiency	Infant mortality
Employment	Illegitimacy	Mental disease
Income	Lynching	Population, mobility and redistribution
Industrial accidents	Malnutrition	Social institutions (government, family, church, morals, etc.)
Labor liberalism	Pauperism	Tuberculosis
Marriages	Poor-relief, numbers and costs	War and revolution
Maternal mortality	Sickness	
Migration	Standards of living, restrictions in	
Strikes and labor disputes	Suicide	
Tuberculosis death rate	Transiency	
Wage rates	Unemployment	

Sources: This classification is derived from sources classified in the bibliography of this chapter under *Analytical Studies.*

[6] W. F. Ogburn and Abe J. Jaffe, "Recovery and Social Conditions," *Am. Jour. Sociol.,* Vol. 42 (1936-1937): 878-886. A review of 42 indexes of recovery.

[7] F. C. Mills, "An Hypothesis Concerning the Duration of Business Cycles," *Jour. Am. Statis. Assoc.,* Vol. 21 (1926): 457.

Correlates of business cycles

The social significance of inflation and depression is another equally important aspect in the study of business cycles. In addition to indexes that identify them as essentially economic phenomena, there are numerous studies of cycles of social welfare. Social cycles are derived from the discovery of upward and downward fluctuations in social phenomena, and have often been explained through social or psychological causes as well as through economic changes.

The chart on page 299 summarizes many of these social and sociopyschological phenomena. The trait that all these phenomena have in common is their tendency toward definite periodical changes of increase and decrease. Some of them, especially when lags are disregarded, seem to be sensitive indexes of economic changes. Accordingly, there are some social changes that vary directly with the movements of economic cycles, some increasing with prosperity, others increasing with depression. A third, more indeterminate classification includes social changes that seem to be associated with economic conditions but in which no precise positive or negative correlation can be found.

Various difficulties interfere with the establishment of correlations in the third classification. Some of these problems or conditions are too subjective. There is no adequate quantitative index by which they may be measured and compared. Others are too inextricably connected with a large social pattern or sequence. Occasionally, too, some social cycles fluctuate so inconsistently that their periodicity cannot be determined for comparative purposes.

A few social problems of business cycles are, consequently, readily identified by methods of exact correlation. Often, however, many of the most important of these problems can be only loosely associated with economic cycles and are scarcely more than the accompaniments of a period of social disorganization. This conclusion is especially true of the inflation period, when many of its worst traits are highly regarded as aspects of prosperity and of sound social organization.

Direct economic correlates. As summarized on page 299, the most accurate correlates between business cycles and social cycles are to be found in direct economic consequences. The most important cycles of social welfare include fluctuations in employment; in income and standards of living; in population movements, especially migration and transiency; in employer-employee relations, particularly with respect to labor conflicts and harmonious employer-employee cooperative enterprises; and in drastic changes within community organization and social-work practices.

In view of the fact that few observers dispute the connection between these social problems and depression, attention in remaining sections will be devoted to less obvious or tangible social correlates. These topics include the influences of depression upon family and child welfare, rural trends in the depression, health and illness during depressions, and a number of miscellaneous correlations.

Influences of depression upon family and child welfare

One of the most noticeable accompaniments of depression is the change in the marital status of the population. A specific effect is the reduction in the marriage rate, which in 1932 reached its lowest point in the marital records of this country. Other problems associated with this tendency and suggested as its explanation, in part, are the reduction of immigration, insufficient housing accommodations, and changing sex mores. The amount of reduction in marriage varies considerably between the social classes. It is greater in the older, economically established classes. Among other classes, in which the significant factor seems to be a low and indefinite economic status, there is no appreciable reduction in marriage during depression, and in some instances it even may increase.

Similar to this reduction in marriage is the cycle of divorce. Divorce coincides almost exactly with movements in the economic cycle, rising with prosperity, decreasing with depression. Apart from economic explanations of these changes, such as cost of litigation and alimony, the chief reason is presumably the firmer integration of the family that results from the necessity of facing common problems. In one study, eighty-seven per cent of the families were reported to be on a more solid foundation during the depression than prior to it. However, this assumed integration may be of a temporary character, concealing a host of latent, friction-making conditions.

Another sensitive vital rate is the proportion of births. In addition to the constant decline in the birth rate and in the average size of families, which has been going on for many decades, the birth rate has regularly declined below this usual trend as a result of adverse economic circumstances. This result is a composite product of social trends toward family limitation and of specific efforts to maintain a certain minimum plane of living. There is partial compensation for this decrease during depression in the increase of illegitimate births, with its associated problems of unmarried mothers and abortion.

General ill effects of depression upon the solidarity of family life may be summarized as follows:

1. Exhaustion of savings and credit.
2. Lowered planes of living from moving to cheaper houses.
3. Sharing homes with relatives and friends, resulting in excessive congestion.
4. Comparable reductions in other items of the budget: lower food standards, inadequate clothing, elimination of recreation, loss of insurance, loss of furniture, loss of homes partly paid for, and the sacrifice of special education.
5. Withdrawal of older children from school.
6. Development of serious health problems.
7. Problems arising with shifts from one vocation to another, and the search for supplementary work.
8. Ill effects from the reduced facilities of community agencies—hospitals and clinics, libraries, recreational opportunities.

Specific adverse effects upon children include: (1) malnutrition, (2) overcrowding, (3) insufficient health care, lowered vitality, and increased susceptibility to disease, (4) withdrawal from school, (5) unemployment of those eligible to work, (6) exploitation of child workers, (7) increasing predisposition to tensions and emotional instability, (8) lowering of moral standards and the loosening of parental control, (9) reduced recreational and other community resources.

A further handicap to the welfare of children is the employment of mothers in the families of unemployed men. In one report on this situation, a third of the mothers were found employed. Of this total, seventy-five per cent were employed outside of the home, with resulting inadequate parental care and insufficient supervision and protection. This consequence of the employment of women is only one of many that deserve consideration in any attempt to find the social costs of depression.

Other consequences of the depression upon family life and the well-being of children range over a vast number of subjective and intangible privations. These liabilities will probably not be understood or fully appreciated until they are revealed objectively in the costs of institutional care and in the occurrence of individual inefficiencies that will become realities during the next generation.

Rural trends in the depression

In general, the social organization of rural life in America, both in open-farm and in village communities, has been adjusted to the constant movement of large numbers of rural inhabitants to the city. This migration has occurred throughout recent history except in the year 1932, when the direction of this movement reversed and more people moved from cities to rural areas. Accordingly, while one reaction of rural people to depression is most noticeable in its influences upon mobility, it is well to note that other factors, before as well as during the depression, have also operated to change the nature of rural mobility. Jointly with economic recession are such rural changes as agricultural decline, reduction of land values, a slowing down in building and railway construction, exhaustion of natural resources, improved methods of transportation, and a competition increasing in range and intensity between urban centers and rural villages and towns.

When an attempt is made to estimate the particular influences of depression upon rural society, the most prominent result is the increasing population of rural villages. The population of rural villages is of mixed origin. It is recruited from cities and from surrounding agricultural areas. In the case of the city-to-village movement, urban residents make the change because of unemployment or because they desire to obtain cheaper living costs. In the case of the movement from open-farm regions to villages, the stimulus is the greater availability of work on governmental projects or more abundant poor-relief.

Additional specific inducements to this mobility are the occurrence of pestilence or drought, the mechanization of agriculture, and the trend toward subsistence farming.

Rural social problems of the depression are largely the accompaniments of these shifts of population. In addition to increasing problems of poor-relief, there are problems of schooling, house-overcrowding, social and economic conflict because of new social-class alignments, and lower standards of living. The last condition is largely a result of the engagement of many families in subsistence farming. Other rural problems are the decline of neighborhood activities, the decline of the rural church, the high rate of bank failures, the gradual trend toward an increase of partially employed people because of the establishment of small industries in the rural village, a growing number of employer-employee labor problems, and the emergence of the so-called youth problem. This relatively new situation in rural life includes a general lowering of morale and the lack of adequate economic opportunity. It also implies the inability of small population groups to organize and support necessary educational and recreational programs.

Health and illness during depressions

Although illness and poverty are often associated in a close cause-and-effect relationship, depressions tend to create a new class of poverty-stricken people, especially from the standpoint of their liability to disease. Comparisons between different social classes, or with the general population, show that the highest sickness rates occur among the depression poor. The toll of illness and physical deficiency within this class exceeds the illness rates of the chronic or predepression poor.

Three facts are commonly accepted concerning the sickness records of those who were forced into poverty by the depression: (1) families with unemployed or part-time workers have a higher rate of disabling illnesses than families with full-time workers, (2) families with a low income in 1932 had higher rates than the families in the more well-to-do income classes, (3) those families who were forced from fairly adequate incomes in 1929 to relative poverty in 1932 had the highest sickness rates. They also had a high incidence of such disabilities among children as malnutrition, deficient diets, and poor vision.

Among the less tangible evils of depression there are, of course, a variety of asserted benefits. With respect to illness or health, it is often stated that the enforced leisure of unemployment is a positive advantage to improved health and resistance. Much has been made of this professed asset. However, upon examination of the benefit of leisure in the case of specific illnesses, the advantage is found to consist primarily in a reduction of fatal accidents or of deaths from chronic diseases.

In opposition to this optimistic outlook is the point of view that the full costs of the national health bill, because of illnesses induced or complicated by depressions, cannot be known for many years. Though superficial evidence may show lower costs or even reduced mortality rates, such costs are actually in the nature of deferred payments. They are minimized by foregoing hospital treatment and necessary medical care, by postponing dental treatment, and by extensive self-medication.

Indisputable evidence concerning the depression as a cause of illness cannot be accumulated with any degree of precision. There is some indication in the slowing down of the rate of decrease of a few chronic diseases, especially tuberculosis, so that the real costs to health due to the depression may not be represented in impaired vitality or in increasing death rates until recovery is well on the way.

Miscellaneous correlations

A number of other social problems are also connected with depression in a causal sequence. But most of them, like illness, can be given no exact cause-and-effect description. In general, however, certain forms of delinquency or crime, a few types of mental disease or behavior problems, and suicide seem to have their roots in economic distress. But the degree of association in most of these noneconomic correlates is dependent to a large extent upon a particular economic index.

When unemployment is accepted as an index of depression, the most consistent correlation within the various classes of crime is that of theft, which includes burglary, robbery, and breaking and entering. Arrests, too, tend to rise and fall with an index of unemployment. Otherwise, there is no important connection between economic conditions and criminal conduct that cannot be explained more appropriately through other causal agencies. Crimes against the person show no tendency to increase during depressions, nor do such indexes of crime as court actions, admissions to jails, juvenile commitments, or admissions to prison.

As a single or important explanation, the depression does not figure prominently among the suggested causes of the major mental diseases. None of the increase in hospital cases can be traced to it. But depressions may be considered precipitating factors in cases requiring hospitalization and as factors in mild forms of mental and nervous disturbances, or in the more numerous maladjustments of behavior and personality.

When an unemployment index is used, some forms of mental disease apparently increase during years of depression. However, with an adequate system of poor-relief, admission rates decline, and the conclusion of the students of this correlation is that any circumstance causing widespread dependency will increase the rate of first admissions to mental hospitals.

Specific mental diseases reported in these first admissions during the depression are manic-depressive, traumatic, and alcoholic psychoses, psychoses due to drugs, and paranoia with cerebral arteriosclerosis, most of which have a low death rate and a fairly high recovery rate.

So far as there is a significant connection between the mental diseases and depression, it is to be found chiefly in the curtailment of treatment facilities. During the depression, the budgets of mental hospitals are reduced and building programs are discontinued. Consequences thereof are overcrowding, inferior standards, insufficient personnel, reduction of clinical, research, and training resources, and eventually a lower rate of recoveries. These results are the principal ill effects of depression upon the course of mental health.

Suicide is also a correlate of depression. It, however, is more closely associated with an index of business failures or other economic indexes of sudden crises than it is with unemployment or with more slowly maturing forms of social disorganization and pathology.

Summary

There is no agreement as yet among economists as to the real causes of business cycles or as to precautions by which their disastrous consequences may be avoided.[8]

According to the fiscal theory of the cycle, the ill-effects of a depression can be avoided or minimized by such undertakings as:

1. Old-age and survivors' insurance.
2. Free public employment services.
3. Unemployment insurance system.

[8] The most-discussed theory is the interpretation of Keynes, which associates business cycles with investment and other fiscal problems. It is the most controversial because of its support for deficit spending. Consult: J. M. Keynes, *General Theory of Employment, Interest and Money,* Harcourt, Brace, New York, 1936.

4. Insurance of bank deposits.
5. Minimum wage and hours legislation.
6. A high minimum wage.
7. Agricultural price support programs.
8. Resources developments, such as TVA.
9. Control over inventories by industry.

Inflation is subjected to cures of just about the opposite order. They are (1) reduction of government debt and a return to economy in government, (2) increased interest rates to create a balance in the high volume of purchases, (3) taxes should be reduced in order to encourage investment and production, (4) credit, (especially urban mortgages), public works, parity prices, government personnel, loans and subsidies should be reduced or eliminated, and (5) the free flow of goods on the market should be encouraged.

In many respects, both of these programs recognize that individual well-being and social adjustment are identical in their reactions to economic changes. In the case of both, the range of tolerance is markedly restricted. It is somewhat like the average person's limited tolerance to changes in temperature. Either above or below a rather narrow variation in temperature, the individual becomes uncomfortable unless precautions are taken. Likewise, the individual and society must adjust to variations in economic life whose upper limits of prosperity and lower limits of depression are inclined to be equally vigorous precipitants in the making of social problems unless the right correctives can be introduced.

Within the next twenty or thirty years the real social and economic costs of business cycles will probably be known with some precision. In the meantime, from current observations and prospects, a depression can be fairly adequately described as a gross pattern of insecurity that is essentially economic in nature. This preliminary and incomplete description is derived in part from the apparently fragile nature of the basic economic mechanisms. It is substantiated in detail by the many weaknesses in the foundations of contemporary economic society and in the radical extremes to which economic forces are liable. Each particular insecurity, whether it is called economic or social, points to the need for sound planning and efficient management in all phases of collective living.

Bibliography

Achinstein, Asher, *Introduction to Business Cycles,* Crowell, New York, 1950. Chaps. 14, 19, 20.

Estey, J. A., *Business Cycles: Their Nature, Cause, and Control,* Prentice-Hall, New York, 1950.

Larson, H. M., *Guide to Business History,* Harvard University Press, Cambridge, 1950. Section 66. An annotated bibliography of business conditions and depressions.

Mitchell, Broadus, *Depression Decade: From New Era through New Deal,* Rinehart, New York, 1947. Chap. 3, "Evolution of Relief"; pp. 25 ff. (Effects of Depression on Industry); Chap. 8, "Labor under the New Deal."

Moulton, Harold G., *Controlling Factors in Economic Development,* The Brookings Institution, Washington, 1949. Chap. 2, "Recurring Business Depressions"; Chap. 3, "The Great Depression of 1929"; Chap. 10, "Can Depressions be Prevented?"

National Assoc. of Manufacturers, "Paying—As—We—Go: A Program to Combat Inflation," Economic Policy Division, New York, Feb. 1951.

Waage, T. O., *Inflation: Causes and Cures,* H. W. Wilson Co., New York, 1949. Pp. 12-20, "What is Inflation?" by R. T. Bye; pp. 124-192, "Cures for Inflation."

Wecter, Dixon, *The Age of the Great Depression,* Macmillan, New York, 1947. A social history of the years, 1929-1941.

Wilson, Thomas, *Fluctuations in Income and Employment,* Pitman, New York, 1948.

Analytical Studies

Bernstein, E. M., "War and the Pattern of Business Cycles," *Am. Econ. Rev.,* Vol. 30 (1940): 524-535.

Brunner, E. deS., and Irving Lorge, *Rural Trends in Depression Years,* Columbia University Press, New York, 1937.

Clark, J. M., *Strategic Factors in Business Cycles,* Wolff, New York, 1934.

Habeler, G., "Prosperity and Depression," *League of Nations,* Geneva, 1941. Part I (Explanations); Part II (Comparative cycles of United States, United Kingdom, Germany, France, Sweden, Canada, and Australia from 1882 to 1935).

Hansen, A. H., *Fiscal Policy and Business Cycles,* W. W. Norton, New York, 1941.

Hexter, M. B., *Social Consequences of Business Cycles,* Houghton Mifflin, Boston, 1925.

Morgenstern, O., "On the International Spread of Business Cycles," *Jour. Pol. Econ.,* Vol. 51 (1943): 287-309. Susceptibility of the world economy to world business cycles.

Research monographs on crime, education, the family, migration, minority peoples, recreation, religion, rural life, social aspects of consumption, health, reading habits, relief policies, and social work. Social Science Research Council, New York, 1937. Bulletins 27-39.

Rundquist, E. A., and R. F. Sletto, *Personality and the Depression,* University of Minnesota Press, Minneapolis, 1936.

Smith, D. T., *Deficits and Depressions,* John Wiley, New York, 1936.

Smithies, A., "Behavior of Money National Income under Inflationary Conditions," *Quart. Jour. Econ.,* Vol. 37 (1942-43): 113-128.

Thomas, D. S., *Social Aspects of the Business Cycle,* Knopf, New York, 1927. Chaps. 1, 2, 3, 10.

Wilson, Edmund, *The American Jitters,* Scribner's, New York, 1932. Critical episodes in the functioning of capitalism.

Woytinsky, W. S., *Additional Workers and the Volume of Unemployment in the Depression,* Social Science Research Council, Washington, D.C., 1940. Pamphlet Series, No. 1.

Questions

1. How many of the characteristic traits of social problems as a class can you find in business cycles?
2. Which aspect of the business cycle has been studied more, inflation or depression?
3. What is the average duration of a business cycle? Why does the decade 1940-1950 vary from this average experience?
4. How does war affect the business cycle?
5. Do wars always cause inflation?
6. What influences do governmental controls have upon business cycles?
7. In what social phenomena are there cyclical trends?
8. What are some of the most sensitive indicators of impending depression? Of impending inflation?
9. Can you explain why tuberculosis is classified as unrelated to economic changes and its death rate is correlated with prosperity?
10. Why is transiency associated with depressions?
11. Is it reasonable that industrial accidents should increase in periods of prosperity?
12. What is the fiscal explanation of depression, recovery, inflation?
13. What typical social problems seem to be unaffected by economic changes?
14. What illustrations of the concept of cultural lag can you find in this chapter?
15. How do the social costs of business cycles differ from their economic costs?

CHAPTER 13

OCCUPATIONS

CONTEMPORARY SOCIETY IS ALWAYS MINDFUL OF ITS ECONOMIC FOUNdations. Children at play reflect this attitude when they count off: rich man, poor man, beggar man, thief. . . . People of all age groups recognize that few aspects of personal and social life remain uninfluenced by occupation and employment. Yet many leave these important choices to the same random chance as do children at play.

A man's occupation, in which approximately one-third of his daily life is spent, is more than just a way to earn a living. It influences habits of dress, mannerisms, vocabulary, marriage, recreation, and associations. Specific diseases have been shown to have a relation to occupations. Personality types as identified by stereotypes have been created around vocational peculiarities, such as teacher and clergyman.

In the treatment of this important personal and social problem, the following subjects will be considered: changing occupations, employment and unemployment, getting a job, income, labor-management relations, and vocational guidance.

Change in occupations

Any analysis of change or trends in occupations is made difficult by the numerous types of inconsistent classifications of occupations. Some categories are primarily vocational, others, primarily industrial, and still others, socio-economic.

Constant change is one of the most significant social aspects of the occupational life of the United States.[1] Change occurs in many different ways and is reflected in problems of full employment, labor-force growth, occupational trends, regional variation in jobs, income, and migration.

Occupational trends. Trends in occupations can be viewed from two points of view. One may be called a relatively long-term, the other a relatively short-term point of view. Long-term trends are changes in the proportion of the population engaged in major categories of employment, such as agriculture, service, and manufacturing. Short-term trends are illustrated by shortages in specific occupations due to such factors as mobilization and labor immobility. Each brings significant problems to individuals preparing for an occupation or changing occupations, and to national economic, political, and social policies.

One of the most outstanding trends has been the sharp decline in the proportion of the labor force engaged in farming. The relative change in farm and nonfarm population can be seen by comparing 1910 to 1950. In 1910, thirty-five per cent of the working population was farm population; by 1945 this figure had dropped to sixteen per cent and by 1950 to twelve per cent. The number of workers classified as farm workers in 1947 was approximately the same as in 1840.

The decreased proportion of agricultural workers can be understood in terms of changes in agriculture methods. Extensive mechanization and improvement in farm methods have resulted in

[1] L. Corey, "Changing Economic Group Positions and Socio-Political Relations in The United States of America," *Labor and Nation,* Vol. 5 (1949): 29-35. C. H. Grattan, "Factories Can't Employ Everybody," *Occupations,* Vol. 23 (Dec. 1944): 136-138. M. Hayes, "Regional Differences in Jobs, Income, and Migration, 1929-49," *Mo. Lab. Rev.,* Vol. 71 (1950): 433-437. F. H. Kirkpatrick, "Manpower: A 1951 Management Problem," *Occupations,* Vol. 29 (March 1951): 431-433. H. D. Kitson and others. "Distribution of Workers in Selected Occupations," *Occupations,* Vol. 25 (Dec. 1946): 154-156. *Mo. Lab. Rev.,* Vol. 71 (July 1950)—special section tracing fifty years' progress of American labor. United States Department of Labor, Bureau of Statistics, in Cooperation with Veterans Administration, *Occupational Outlook Handbook,* Bull. No. 940, United States Government Printing Office, Washington, D. C., 1948. Gladys L. Palmer, "New Light on Old Problems," *Occupations,* Vol. 28 (Feb. 1950): 281-283. L. M. Pearlman, "Occupational Trends," *Occupations,* Vol. 26 (Dec. 1947): 149-153. S. L. Wolfbein, "The Labor Supply of The United States," *Occupations,* Vol. 25 (March 1947): 321-324. Helen Wood, "Effect of Mobilization Program on Employment Opportunities," *Mo. Lab. Rev.,* Vol. 71 (1950): 680-681. ———, "Occupational Mobility of Scientific and Technical Personnel," *Occupations,* Vol. 28 (May 1950): 510-513.

increased productivity. The increase in productivity has released farmers for industrial employment. This fact, together with the high relative birth rate of rural communities, has made the agricultural population a major source of industrial labor supply.

Contrary to what might have been expected in view of an increase in manufacturing in the United States, there has been a sharp decline in the proportion of the labor force engaged in laboring occupations. This trend is likely to continue. The greater use of automatic machinery displaces manual workers. However, while the manual workers decline in proportion to population, the number of technical, managerial, and clerical employees rises. The number of mechanics, maintenance men and repair men to service the machines likewise has been rising. A major long-term trend has been a decline in manual workers with a corresponding increase in the proportion of workers engaged in semiskilled occupations. In 1910, proprietors and laborers represented the largest single occupational groups. By midcentury, operative and kindred workers had displaced them.

The first half of the twentieth century was marked by an increased proportion of workers engaged in the professional and clerical occupations. This upward trend was marked by an increase in employees in banking, insurance, real estate, clerical, sales, and administration. Strong upward trends in professional and semiprofessional workers are associated with the expansion of service industries. Professional employment has been growing and the trend is one of continued growth. However, professional and semiprofessional service continue to occupy a relatively low rank in terms of the number of opportunities available for large-scale employment.

Trends for clerical and sales workers are associated with the redistribution of employment by industry and the changes in occupations within industry. In fact, changes in occupations within industry are just as important as changes in employment between industries in their effect on occupational patterns. Salaried employees have multiplied because of the increased scientific nature of industry, the growing complexity of economic organization, and the increased growth in the function of government. Since 1929, employment in government has been steadily rising. When the classification of workers into agriculture, service, and manufacturing is used, the increase in service occupations is clearly noted.

Short-term trends are influenced by current national and international events. A good illustration of such a trend is in the shortages that exist in periods of mobilization. Mobilization for war and periods after a war point out existing trends and create dislocations in the labor market that are relatively short in duration. Mobilization during 1950 intensified pre-existing shortages of personnel. Such was the case in the health professions and elementary school teaching. The mobilization program called to employment persons who were unemployed, and together with a tight labor market, made demands for engineers, chemists, skilled metal workers, and railroad employees. Such conditions also caused a drain on occupations in which earnings were low and which occupied a low position in the prestige scale. Waiters, filling-station attendants, and sales personnel in stores deserted these fields.

Between Pearl Harbor and 1944 the occupational classification of one man out of five was changed. Immediately after World War II, employment in every occupational group rose. The smallest gains were in the groups that had experienced the greatest gains during the war—operatives, craftsmen, and foremen. The greatest gains were in those occupations that had lost their population during the war—retail trade and construction work for example.

Problems of women and children. World War II intensified two long-standing economic problems—the employment problems of women and children.

Midcentury represents approximately fifty years of an organized effort to control the social hazards of the employment of children. The minimum employable age has been pushed up, the workday and workweek have been shortened, the type of work and time of work have been controlled, and every effort has been made to provide high-school education for all. As of 1950, federal laws prohibited the employment of children under 16 in producing goods for interstate or foreign commerce. Child actors, newsboys, and children in agriculture outside of school hours were not included. Employment of children from ages 14 to 16 during out-of-school hours is controlled by regulations issued by the Secretary of Labor.

Children under 18 are prohibited employment in occupations declared by the Secretary of Labor to be particularly hazardous or detrimental to health. Federal laws are only a part of the picture. State laws must be considered for any adequate understanding.

Minimum standards proposed by the National Child Labor Committee include:

1. Compulsory school attendance to age 16 years for a consecutive term of at least 9 months.
2. A 16-year age minimum for employment during school hours.
3. A 14-year age minimum for employment outside of school hours.
4. A maximum 8-hour day and 40-hour week for minors under 18.
5. A maximum workweek of 18 hours for children under 16 years while attending school and of 24 hours for minors of 17, and regulation of night work.[2]

Many abuses of child labor during the war were due to the low standards and exemptions of many states and to the understaffing of enforcing agencies. The labor force of 66.2 millions in April 1945 was about eight million more than would have been expected from prewar trends. Women accounted for four million and teen-age boys for two million of the eight million extra. As late as October, 1949 there were nearly two million young persons, 14-17 years of age, employed in agricultural and non-agricultural occupations.[3]

Between 1910 and 1948 the total employment relative to population increased by three per cent but employment of women increased by almost one-half. Two-thirds of the women at work in 1910 were employed in manual occupations; less than half were so employed in 1948. While the proportion of children in the labor force has dropped, the proportion of women has increased. In 1900 women made up 14 per cent of the total labor force and by 1947 they made up 28 per cent. In 1900 children in the labor force, 14 to 15 years of age, accounted for 309 per 1,000 population; in 1950, 14 per 1,000 in the population.[4]

Problems associated with employment of women and children are not merely problems of numbers. The influences of an industrial society are at work as they affect the family. Social values are in conflict with reference to (a) the demands of industry, (b) demands of the school, (c) "the place of women," and (d) the working mother.

Mobility of the occupied population. Not only is change a

[2] "Youth Employment Standards in the Present Emergency," *American Child,* Vol. 33 (1951), No. 1.

[3] "Child Labor at The Mid-Century," *American Child,* Vol. 32 (1950), No. 7. "Employment of Minors: Minimum Wage Laws," *Mo. Lab. Rev.,* Vol. 71 (Dec. 1950): 701-704. G. L. Schermerhorn, "Child Labor Legislation Needs Help From N. V. G. A.," *Occupations,* Vol. 26 (Nov. 1947): 110-112.

[4] H. Ober, "The Worker and His Job," *Mo. Lab. Rev.,* Vol. 71 (1950): 17.

characteristic of occupations, but the people employed in occupations likewise manifest a considerable movement. It is estimated that two out of three of the eleven million young men who entered the labor market during 1940-1950 were replacing older men who dropped out because of death or retirement.[5]

Patterns of retirement and the conception of the work life of an individual will have effects on mobility within an occupation. Statistical data are lacking, but one needs only consider the work life of a professional athlete and that of a professional educator to be aware that the differential work life is a significant factor. In 1944 one out of six individuals occupying civilian jobs was employed in an industry group different from that in which he was employed in 1941. Seven million workers made changes in major occupational groups over this period. In 1947 an average of three-fourths of a million manufacturing workers left their jobs each month. Between Pearl Harbor and March 1944, more than a third of the labor group changed occupations, in comparison with less than one-tenth of the more stable professional group.

Professional persons do not change occupations as frequently as do other occupational groups. However, professional workers have a wide labor market and a high rate of mobility. Recruitment is done more through professional societies and college placement offices than by employment offices. Professional advancement also requires geographic movement in a number of professions.

It is important to the prospective job seeker to know that the greatest number of employment opportunities in most occupations are a result of vacancies caused by death, retirement, and transfer to another occupation.[6]

Employment and unemployment

Of recent industrial changes, probably the most important to the growing hazard of unemployment is the steady increase in the number of available employable workers in this country. In 1900 the total labor force represented 49 per cent of the population, and by 1950 it was 56 per cent.

[5] S. L. Wolfbein, "Measurement of Work-Life Expectancy," *Mo. Lab. Rev.*, Vol. 71 (1950): 193-195.

[6] S. Wolfbein, *op. cit.*, p. 194. H. Goldstein, "Estimate of Occupational Replacement Needs," *Occupations*, Vol. 26 (April 1948): 397-402. H. Wood, "Occupational Mobility of Scientific and Technical Personnel," *Occupations*, Vol. 28 (May 1950): 510-513.

In recent years unemployment has come to be recognized as one of the outstanding contemporary hazards in society as a whole, as well as in industry. It is generally conceded to rank among the leading causes of social distress, first, because of its frequent and widespread recurrence, and second, because of the increasing number of persons and occupations affected. It is one of the primary causes of poverty, and resembles the latter in that neither can be met successfully by charitable relief alone. In many respects, unemployment is comparable to war. This analogy holds in the numbers indiscriminately disabled by being thrown out of work, in the economic waste involved, and in the irreparable damage to personal and family security. The consequences of unemployment are thus seen to be leading factors in personal and social disorganization.

Prior to 1930, and especially during the prosperous 'twenties, unemployment was often regarded as a minor problem of short duration. As often, too, it was assigned to the personal inefficiency of the individual worker, and made a problem of poor-relief agencies. As a matter of fact, unemployment has been a constant feature of industrial organization for many decades. Probably a large share of its injurious consequences can be traced in this failure to recognize its permanent social causes and to the policy of inaction on the part of local, state, and national governments. The result has been the abandonment of local methods of poor-relief in favor of the Social Security Act.

General sources of unemployment that are discoverable in many surveys reveal the following classes of persons who are frequently exposed to this hazard:

1. Industrial workers.
2. White-collar workers.
3. Professional workers.
4. Special groups, such as Negro workers, women, the aged, and the young.

The major types of unemployment are summarized under the generalization, social disorganization. In preindustrial societies, especially prior to the organization of society upon a money economy, there was no comparable problem. This is the principal difference between unemployment and poverty as historical phenomena. Poverty has always been a menace to human society.

Unemployment, by contrast, is a relatively new cause of distress. When people worked directly with the commodities that they consumed, they may have been poor, but work was always plentiful, as regular as the individual's needs. Consequently, the folkways gave authority to the principle that a person should not be permitted to eat if he was unwilling to work. This ancient folk belief is only partly applicable today. At present thousands of men become workless in spite of their needs or willingness to work, because something is wrong with the machinery uniting the economic processes of production, distribution, and consumption.

Social disorganization refers to the inefficiencies arising from a minute division of labor and the specialization that it requires. These are not vague excuses for unemployment in the case of particular individuals. They involve basic social processes that are beyond the control of the individual. Few people can plan their lives so as to build an adequate protection against changes in the demand for labor. The first hazard is lack of skill. Skill or training is the best guarantee of steady work, but even specialized techniques become antiquated and useless during the lifetime of an individual. Age is the second hazard. Social disorganization, division of labor, and specialization are branded as fundamental causes of unemployment when trained, employable persons are unable to find work.

For steady work, the combination of youth and skill is the best unemployment insurance. Beware of the decades after forty. "If you are forty you need not apply. We want speed and production." Moreover, age and skill are often a bad combination, but age and no specialty are worse. In either case, presumably, there is something wrong with the person, not with the economic organization of society. He is ruled automatically beyond the age limit. This unsatisfactory situation is called "social disorganization," and its victims "social misfits."

The contemporary problem of unemployment is fundamentally caused by a lack of balance between supply and demand. Society has reached a stage in productive efficiency wherein the labor of large numbers of persons is not required. The labor surplus, rejected because of age, competition of younger workers, technical changes in industry, merging of corporations, business depressions, the moving of industry from one region to another (such as the shift of the textile industry to the South), or the gradual decline of an industry, constitutes the problems of enforced leisure, idleness, and unemployment.

Unemployment defined

Unemployment is involuntary idleness on the part of a workman who is able to work. Society requires a degree of economic competence of every adjusted person. At the same time, a corollary of this demand is the individual's right to work. This right is acknowledged by a definition of unemployment that differentiates between those who are unwilling to work—the idle—and those who are unemployable because of physical or mental incapacity.

When Louis D. Brandeis was Associate Justice of the United States Supreme Court, he made a liberal analysis of the reciprocal relationship between employer and employee in his description of the right to work:

> For every employe who is "steady in his work" there shall be steady work. The right to regularity in employment is co-equal with the right to regularity in the payment of rent, in the payment of interest on bonds, in the delivery to customers of the high quality of product contracted for. No business is successfully conducted which does not perform fully the obligations incident to each of these rights. Each of these obligations is equally a fixed charge. No dividend should be paid unless each of these fixed charges has been met. The reserve to ensure regularity of employment is as imperative as the reserve for depreciation; and it is equally a part of the fixed charges to make the annual contributions to that reserve. No business is socially solvent which cannot do so.[7]

From this point of view, the problem of unemployment is less extensive and is to be separated from the problem of the idle and from that of the unemployable. Idleness is a generic term. It develops from three sources—unwillingness to work by those who are capable of work, physical or mental incapacity of willing workers, and unemployment. This restriction limits unemployment to those who are capable and willing to work but who cannot find work because of general economic depression or because of industrial maladjustment within a particular plant or industry. It is unemployment in this sense and underemployment (part-time work), or irregular employment, that will be considered in the following sections.

Volume of employment and unemployment. Prior to 1930 and for the years 1897 to 1926, the rate of unemployment from all causes

[7] Quoted in the *Survey,* Vol. 42 (1919): 5.

and for all industries has been estimated to vary from a low of 5.3 per cent to a high of 23.1 per cent. The average for this period was about 10 per cent, and this average included all workers in manufacturing, transportation, mining and construction. During the depressions of these years, a total unemployment record as high as 20 to 25 per cent of all industrial workers was not exceptional.[8]

The normal amount of unemployment in this country during the past five decades has ranged from one million to two and one-half million workers in prosperous years, and from three and one-half to fifteen millions in years of depression.

The size of the labor force is a product of the pyramid of the population together with the values current concerning the employment of special categories of individuals, such as the old, the young, women, and the handicapped. The census defines the labor force as including those persons fourteen years of age and over who have a job or are looking for work at the time of the census. As of December 1950, the labor force was 64.7 millions; 62.5 in the civilian labor force, 54.1 million in nonagricultural pursuits, and 2.2 million unemployed.[9]

Trends in the labor force and number of unemployed is shown in the following table of estimates for selected years.

Trends of Employment and Unemployment in the United States For Selected Years

Year	*Number of Unemployed (in millions)*	*Total Labor Force (in millions)*
1920	1.4	41.0
1925	1.8	...
1930	6.9	48.0
1935	11.6	...
1940	10.7	52.8
1945	1.2	66.2
1950	2.2	64.7

Sources: J. H. G. Pierson, *Full Employment,* Yale University Press, New Haven, 1941, p. 17 (for the years 1920 to 1940). Recent numbers of the *Monthly Labor Review* are the sources for 1945-1950 estimates.

[8] P. H. Douglas and Aaron Director, *The Problem of Unemployment,* Macmillan, New York, 1931, p. 32. P. M. Hauser and R. B. Pearl, "Who Are The Unemployed?," *Jour. Am. Stat. Assoc.,* Vol. 45 (Dec. 1950), No. 252, pp. 479-500. W. E. Moore, "Current Items," *Population Index,* Vol. 17 (April 1951), No. 2, pp. 78-91.

[9] F. H. Kirkpatrick, "Manpower: A 1951 Management Problem," *Occupations,* Vol. 29 (March 1941): 431-433. *Mo. Lab. Rev.,* Vol. 72 (Feb. 1941), Table A-1, p. 211. United States Department of Labor, Bureau of Labor Statistics, *Fact Book on Manpower,* Government Printing Office, Washington, D. C., January 31, 1951.

Extreme variations in the volume of employment between different geographical areas, industries, and employed classes are shown most strikingly in various surveys. However, between 1929 and 1949, disparities in jobs and income between states were reduced to some degree. People in the North and West, on the average, were still better off than those in other sections, but new centers of manufacturing in Texas and California had expanded considerably.[10]

Types of unemployment

The foregoing variations in the number of employed persons can be traced to three sources of disturbance—seasonal, cyclical, and technological changes.

These are due in part to fluctuations in the character of modern industry; in part to the lack of coordination among its several divisions. Economic history has many illustrations of the comparatively rapid disappearance of some trades and the conflict and disorganization during the adjustment of the population to their substitutes. Sometimes, as in the change of a nation's principal economy from agriculture to commerce or to manufacturing, these changes go on slowly, and adjustments can be made without unusual hardship. Frequently, the change is revolutionary, a complete upheaval, as in the modification of the skilled hand trades by the machine. Most industrial change in contemporary civilization is due to this displacement, directly or indirectly.

During the last decade in this country, there have been noticeable decreases in the demand for labor in farming, mining, transportation, and manufacturing. In each of these classes of occupation, mechanization has increased productivity and reduced the labor force required. Distinct reductions in labor supply during this period have occurred in machine shops, iron and steel industries, rubber and glass works, tool works, sheet-metal works, sugar refineries, and occupations requiring musical ability. These decreases have been counterbalanced in part by the increasing demand for labor in the building trades, selling and servicing of automobiles, hotel work, public school teaching, life-insurance selling, and barbering and beauty parlor work.

Industrial stability depends upon the capacity of new industries to absorb the surplus labor of the old. When this process lags, or

[10] M. Hayes, "Regional Differences in Jobs, Income, and Migration, 1929–1949," *Mo. Lab. Rev.*, Vol. 71 (1950): 433-437.

the absorption is unequal to the labor displaced, unemployment is accelerated. A major portion of unemployment is due to unqualified industrial change.

Seasonal unemployment. Seasonal variations in the demand for labor make one of the most persistent causes of unemployment. They are also responsible for a large proportion of migratory labor and for the family distress that accompanies irregular work. Seasonal unemployment is usually thought of in connection with such specialized occupations as lumbering, farming, food industries, transportation, or the building trades. Practically speaking, no trade is without its period of inactivity alternating with a busy season. Work in mines, clothing factories, mills, canneries, docks, and automobile manufacturing plants is also among the leading seasonal occupations. This seasonality is traced to a variety of environmental factors, to variations in consumption and other social habits, changes in fashion, and climatic variations.

Seasonality is responsible for a large amount of normal unemployment—the variable minimum of 3.0 to 3.5 millions of persons. As a matter of fact, this type of unemployment is a problem of income more than of unemployment, since it can be anticipated and compensated for in part by savings. It occurs largely among the unskilled or semiskilled workers, reduces working hours, and is chiefly responsible for temporary or part-time work, casual labor, and dependency of families upon poor-relief. In this connection, seasonality, an overabundant labor supply, and an excessive labor turnover become one problem.

Unemployment due to trade or business cycles. As contributors to unemployment, trade cycles or business depressions are much more serious than seasonal factors. They account for an enormous reduction in employment, amounting to from one half to two thirds of the total on industry's payroll. Trade cycles are periodic, lasting from two to ten years. John R. Commons has described the rise and fall of the trade cycle as follows:

> Prices rise; wages rise; profits swell; everybody is confident and over-confident; speculation over-reaches itself; the future looks more assuring than it is; too many buildings and factories are constructed; then the inevitable collapse. Hundreds and thousands of workingmen are laid off. The credit system breaks down. Then the cycle repeats itself.[11]

[11] "Prevention of Unemployment," *Am. Labor Legis. Rev.*, Vol. 12 (1922): 19-20. "The Business Situation," *Survey of Current Business*, Vol. 21 (1941), No. 6, pp. 3-10. This source considers 1941 as the end of the depression.

During the last fifty-nine years unemployment has resulted from general industrial depressions on six occasions—in 1892-1893, 1904-1905, 1907-1908, 1913-1914, 1920-1922, and 1929-1941 (although there is a difference of opinion as to the terminal year of this depression).

Little is known about techniques of preventing either seasonal or cyclical unemployment. However, both are typical of the experience of all industrial countries. Apparently their elimination depends upon more basic changes in the organization of industry than have been proposed or introduced hitherto. Dovetailing industries that have slumps at different times of the year, spreading out labor, or accumulating reserve stocks are suggestions commonly made for relieving seasonal unemployment. Prior to 1935, nothing had been done on a national scale to offset the disaster of cyclical unemployment, other than poor-relief. When unemployment occurred with unusual severity in 1929-1934, no preparation had been made for this emergency. There was no unemployment reserve fund, no reserves for public work, and no public employment system. And, as already noted, there was no satisfactory method by which the rate of increasing unemployment could be determined.

Technological unemployment. Since the introduction of machinery in the textile industry, technological displacement has been a growing and unpredictable phase of the unemployment problem. The new technology is a product of the age of invention. While no precise estimate of its development can be made, it is measurable fairly accurately by the increasing number of patents.

A shortage of labor was the chief stimulus to invention, and the result is a growing surplus of labor. As a factor in unemployment, the new technology is largely an unknown quantity, owing to the short interval since its development and spread. Prior to the last decade, there were many instances of temporary unemployment caused by the introduction of machinery. Since 1920, the scale of industrial expansion and the number of men permanently displaced have been unparalleled.

During the last decade, inventions have saved more labor than capital. This consequence has influenced economists to become skeptical concerning the generalization, ordinarily made, that labor-saving machinery increases the demand for labor. For several years the supply of new jobs has been insufficient—from which it may be concluded that industry is in a period of increasing unemployment with increasing productivity. In other words, the employed classes are prosperous at the expense of an increasing volume of unemployment.

These changes are not limited to manual work. In clerical occupations there are calculating, check-signing, and bookkeeping machines, which are affecting the employment possibilities of the office worker. Robots are being substituted for salesmen, and the teletypesetter is threatening the printer.

Since the number of new inventions is constantly increasing, this type of unemployment will probably be more severe in the future than it has been in the past. Even movements of population, the tendency toward a decreasing rate of population increase, and changes in industry are apparently unable to offset its ill effects.

Lately, one of the consequences of technological unemployment has been the emigration of males forty-five years of age and over from the cities. This situation points to decreasing economic opportunity and to the shortening of the industrial worker's period of usefulness.

Technological unemployment is sometimes identified more broadly as an aspect of frictional unemployment. This term implies that there is a weakness and disorder in the organization of the economic system, the parts of which cannot be successfully coordinated. Shortages, bottlenecks, strikes, breakdowns of machinery, and accidents are the most obvious examples of these disorders.

Technological unemployment differs from seasonal and cyclical unemployment in that it is not recurrent. It is a permanent displacement that is constant and uncontrolled. This displacement of skill by machinery would be no cause for disturbance if the labor released were transferred to other jobs. But this transfer has not taken place. Not only are there insufficient jobs, but studies of the technologically unemployed have shown that a period of six months elapses before the majority are re-employed, and then they receive lower wages. Remedies suggested to overcome this factor in unemployment are higher wages, shorter hours, legislation to protect the unemployed through insurance, distribution of work, controls over seasonal fluctuations, and an increasing standard of living equal to the increasing productivity of industry.

Getting a job

The Division of Occupational Analysis, United States Employment Service, lists 22,028 defined jobs that are known by an additional 17,995 titles, or a total of 40,023 job titles.[12]

The number of defined jobs changes. New jobs are added and old ones discarded as the technology changes. Not only do the number of jobs change, but, as has been suggested, the character of occupations change. It is a complex vocational world that faces the youth concerned with finding a job. The individual himself is likely to be personally confused. A great deal of evidence suggests that young people do not choose jobs realistically.[13]

Realistic choice is hindered by, among other things, over- and underestimation of self, social status of jobs, and lack of knowledge about self and the vocational world. An approach to finding a job centers on knowing one's own capacities and knowing the job world. Relating these variables leads to specific techniques of seeking work. A considerable number of vocational guidance centers have been originated to aid in the process. Many aids are available in the analysis of self. The Cleeton Vocational Interest Inventory, for example, points out patterns of interest that are somewhat similar to the patterns for large numbers of persons engaged in that field of work. Other tests are available that provide insight into specific aptitudes and interests. Tests should be administered by trained personnel. Information derived from tests is a valuable aid in intelligently choosing a vocation. Other data in a personal inventory can be derived from (a) subject matter that is interesting and in which the person does well, (b) summer and part time jobs, and (c) critical comments from others.

There are many possible aids in the analysis of the vocational world. The *Dictionary of Occupational Titles* contains a large

[12] United States Employment Service, Federal Security Agency, *Dictionary of Occupational Titles,* United States Government Printing Office, Washington, 1949.

[13] J. Stubbins, "Lack of Realism in Vocational Choice," *Occupations,* Vol. 26 (April 1948): 410-418. R. Van Hamm Dale, "To Youth Who Choose Blindly," *Occupations,* Vol. 26 (April 1948): 419-420. W. E. Myers, "High School Graduates Choose Vocations Unrealistically," *Occupations,* Vol. 25 (March 1947): 332-333.

Several articles question the data on unrealistic choice. See K. W. Dresden, "Vocational Choices of Secondary Pupils," *Occupations,* Vol. 27 (Nov. 1948): 104-106. F. M. Carp, "High School Boys are Realistic About Occupations," *Occupations,* Vol. 28 (Nov. 1949): 94-99.

number of job descriptions. These descriptions were secured from direct observation, on-job analysis, and from occupational data obtained from employers, trade and labor associations, and public employment officers. A number of organizations specialize in occupational pamphlets. A partial list follows:

Science Research Associates, Chicago.
Commonwealth Book Co. Inc., Chicago.
Institute for Research, Chicago.
Occupational Index Inc., New York.
Bellman Publishing Co., Boston.
Morgan-Dillan and Co., Chicago.

More than 200 government publications are available.[14] Other sources are local, state, school, and private employment and counseling agencies.

A considerable literature is available on employers' preference and qualities sought by employers. In general, personal traits such as ability to get along well with others are stressed in this literature.

Certain facts should be kept in mind in considering the vocational world from the point of view of possible job opportunities:

1. Selection should be based on a variety of factors.
2. Fields of occupations should be considered.
3. Employers are interested in multiple skills.
4. Special training is more and more necessary.
5. Native aptitude and school subjects in which the individual does well should influence choice.
6. Many aids to job seekers are available in every community.

Social status of occupations. Social status of occupations may prevent a more rational measurement of qualifications in choosing a vocation. No analysis of social status can be complete without indicating the great importance, in the culture of the United States, of the occupations through which the economic function of the society is accomplished. There exists, in the literature of status, frequent reference to the importance of occupations in themselves and the importance of occupational derivatives in placing individuals in status positions.

Young people very readily learn that whatever is said about the social worth of any occupations, or the dignity of work, there does

[14] H. D. Kitson, "New Pamphlets on Occupations," *Occupations,* Vol. 24 (Oct. 1945): 14-16. W. J. Greenleaf, "Occupational Monographs Available Through the Federal Government," *Occupations,* Vol. 25 (April 1947): 388-392.

exist in fact a hierarchy of occupations based on social status. Numerous studies of occupational choice of high school students have emphasized an awareness of this hierarchy. It appears as a defiance of logic that a majority of high school students aspire to enter job categories that employ a minority of the employed. Nevertheless, on the other hand, a certain realism is expressed in their choices.

Scholars have recognized this occupational hierarchy and many attempts have been made to construct a ranking prestige scale of occupations. George S. Counts is generally credited with the first attempt at defining occupational levels based on prestige.[15] Counts used a judging technique. Forty-five occupations were chosen at random and six different groups of persons were asked to rank the occupations into nine groups of five, and then to rank the smaller groups on the basis of the occupations that were most looked up to. John A. Nietz,[16] in a study of occupational changes during the depression, used the same technique as Counts. The results of this study showed very few changes in social-status ranking of occupations. A number of studies of occupational status have been made since Counts' work. A review of these studies points out some interesting generalizations:

1. The most important fact is that, regardless of the specific method used, the age, sex, occupation, or geographic location of the raters, there has been a general uniformity of prestige that is striking.
2. While the specific techniques may vary, one cannot but be aware that the most-used method has been that of employing some form of judging.
3. In spite of the differing ranking expressed in different cultures, there has been an apparent uniformity of the prestige hierarchy in the United States during the last twenty to thirty years.
4. A comparison of studies is made difficult by the fact that different occupations were included in the rating scales.

Income

What families can and do live on is a topic of continuous interest to most people. The amount or distribution of a nation's income,

[15] George S. Counts, "The Social Status of Occupations: A Problem in Vocational Guidance," *Sch. Rev.*, Vol. 33 (1925): 16-27.

[16] John A. Nietz, "The Depression and the Social Status of Occupations," *El. Sch. Jour.*, Vol. 35 (Sept.-June 1934-1935): 454-461.

however, has little or no meaning unless it is associated with its sources in different occupations and its adequacy in affording minimum standards of decency.

Costs of living have been a subject of general complaint for many generations. In his satire *Phormio,* Terence (185-159 B.C.) made one of his characters look enviously upon the good old days when prices were low and goods abundant. Ever since the wants of man have depended upon money and its purchasing power, there has been continuous dissatisfaction with the scarcity of comforts on most planes of living.

The problem of maintaining a satisfactory standard of living is practically universal. It is basically an economic problem. But equally basic is the noneconomic culture of desires and satisfactions when incomes seem too small for comfortable living. In standards of living, there is a continuous interplay between economic and social culture, which cannot be neglected in the study of costs of living, planes of living, budgets, or standards. On the whole, it has been a problem of nearly every historical society and social class.

Often, however, standards of living are discussed as if they were wholly economic or social problems and not a combination of both. The economic approach is valuable and necessary. It fixes attention upon income, wealth, production, distribution, habits of consumption, and costs of living. Moreover these economic aspects of the problem are capable of objective study and measurement. Standards of living, on the contrary, are apt to be viewed as entirely a matter of personal whim—a question of how to spend income for necessities, comforts, and luxuries. But they also can be studied objectively when they are examined within the limits of a given social and economic society or class and are regarded as a study in comparative human values.

In general, economic culture sets the limits and social culture determines variations in planes and standards of living. This point of view may be illustrated by the question: How adequate is an annual income of $2,000 or $3,000 for an average family? Young people sometimes raise this question in planning to marry. Parents are regularly engrossed with the question of income in maintaining their family on a reasonably efficient plane. Older people consider it in making provision for protection against retirement or old age.

The monetary basis of standards

When such inquiries and the search for replies are made with reference only to the question of total income, the issues that standards of living involve are always obscured. Although income is the most definite and probably the most important factor in the evaluation of standards, there are, in addition, two other major considerations. One of these is the real money value of income, as measured by its purchasing power or by costs of living. This is the second element—the economic—in the problem of standards. The other is the social aspect, namely, individual or group concepts of the necessities required for efficient and wholesome living. In planning either budgets or standards, the limits put upon income by different habits of consumption cannot be neglected. Social workers, for example, often report families who will expend a disproportionate amount of income for one item, such as household furnishings, including television, or even insurance, to the utter neglect of routine necessities.

One measure of social well-being assumes that certain minimum standards of economic and social welfare are indispensable. These standards are complementary, one depending upon the other. Consequently, it is useless to exaggerate the prior importance of either through an overemphasis upon economic factors, such as income and costs of living, or upon social aspects of needs or habits of consumption. The fact has already been noted that poverty or low income sets up insurmountable obstacles to the achievement of standards for a great majority of wage-earning families.

Viewed as a composite product of income, costs, and group needs, standards are both objective and measurable. They become highly subjective and immeasurable, however, when they are treated solely as variable needs and as open to choice.

Wealth and income

Standards of living are practically synonymous with economic and social status, both of which are intimately connected with many social problems. The distribution of wealth and the distribution of income are consequently of significance, because they determine economic and social status to a large extent. Of these two economic factors, the distribution of income is the more discriminating index of social welfare. To know within limits how income is distributed is a necessary first step in the study of budgets and standards.

There is often confusion between wealth and income. Standards of living are considered low because they do not approximate the per capita amount of wealth indicated in statistical reports. It may be well to state that wealth in most of its forms is not distributable, at least in the same sense that income, its fluid product, is distributed. For this reason, standards are first compared with income, which is the individual's share in wealth and which is always much less than his hypothetical per capita ownership.

Both wealth and income, as economic concepts, are more easily described than defined. Most surveys or estimates of either make an introductory statement to the effect that one of the most troublesome problems is that of defining these commonly used terms. *Wealth* is recognized as an accumulation of goods or services, and includes wealth possessed by individuals, by groups or the public, and social wealth, which is described as the total stock of material goods possessed by society at any one time.

Related to wealth, and at the same time distinct from it, is *income*. Wealth is the source of income. Income is a more restricted concept, limited to those goods or services that are measurable in terms of money. Thus, income is described as consisting of wages, salaries, pensions, rent, interest, dividends, and profits. Although large incomes usually signify great wealth, the two may occur independently. Some wealth may yield no income, and some income receivers may possess practically no wealth. Since one of the most obvious social facts is the division of population into economic classes, we are interested more in the distribution of income than in the theoretical distinctions between wealth and income.

It is desirable, nevertheless, to continue this distinction between theoretical per capita wealth and the actual distribution of income in a preliminary discussion of standards of living. When these amounts are compared over a period of years, they reveal most strikingly the financial basis of present-day economic class divisions.

Real income is measured in goods and services that are consumed. Measurement, however, is difficult because there is no common denominator available. The best that can be done is an arbitrary weighting of selected items.

The unequal distribution of wealth and income is reflected in every analysis of income groups. It is difficult to compare in a meaningful way distributions from different sources and years. Different index numbers are used, and amounts have little meaning except as related to cost of living. Nevertheless, the observation can be made that inequalities of income have existed for a long time. Comparison for family income in 1929 and 1949 is shown in the table below.

DISTRIBUTION OF FAMILY INCOME 1929 AND 1949

	Per Cent of Families	
Income Class	*1929*	*1949*
Under $1,000	21.5	12.1
1,000-1,999	38.0	14.9
2,000-2,999	18.9	20.7
3,000-3,999	8.9	19.9
4,000-4,999	4.5	12.0
Over 5,000	8.2	20.3

Source: United States Census data.

The table on income distribution has more meaning when related to the table on Consumer's Price Index. The Consumer's Price Index measures average changes in retail prices of selected goods, rents, and services, weighted by quantities bought in 1934-1936 by families of wage earners and moderate-income workers in large cities, whose income averaged $1,524 in 1934-1936.

CONSUMER'S PRICE INDEX FOR SELECTED YEARS

Year and Month	*All Items*
1913 Average	70.7
1918 December	118.0
1920 June	149.4
1929 Average	122.5
1939 Average	99.4
1949 Average	169.1
1950 Average	171.2

Source: Mo. Lab. Rev., Vol. 72 (1951): 242 (see recent issues for current data).

Distribution of income and wealth are factors of social as well as economic significance. A review of social problems shows that the amount of income has a direct relation to social status, infant mortality rates, medical care, and amount of education received, and to other social conditions.

Labor management relations[17]

Between 1924 and 1927 a series of experiments were conducted at the Hawthorne Works of the Western Electric Company in Chicago. These dates are usually given as the beginning of a period that recognizes the fact that workers are not motivated only by the pay envelope. The worker has a desire to function in a work society where he realizes the purpose of his work and has a sense of personal importance in the accomplishment of the job.

Three approaches have been used: (1) Industrial Physiology, which is concerned with problems of health, (2) Industrial Psychology, which is concerned with problems of personal adjustment, and (3) Industrial Sociology, which is concerned with problems of interaction between segments of the industrial society.

The factory is regarded as a social system. Many of the social theories and methods of research that have been used in the study of other types of groups have been applied to the factory system. Attitudes developed in the work situation influence activities in other areas of social interaction and, contrariwise, attitudes developed in other areas of social interaction influence activities in the work situation. It must be acknowledged that informal groups will develop in any work situation and that these groups can be used for more harmonious personal relations. The experience of the Navy Employee Counseling Service has resulted in the announcement of certain principles of personal relations in industry.

1. The well-adjusted worker tends to be adjusted in other social relationships.
2. Productivity is an important factor in the status system of a modern factory.

[17] Sources for this section. F. J. Roethlisberger and W. J. Dickson, *Management and The Worker,* Harvard University Press, 1939. Elton Mayo, *The Human Problems of an Industrial Civilization,* Harvard University Press, 1933. ——, *The Social Problems of an Industrial Society,* Harvard University Press, 1945. E. B. Strong, "Individual Adjustment in Industrial Society; The Experience of the Navy Employee Counseling Service," *Am. Soc. Rev.,* Vol. 14 (1949): 335-346. J. C. Worthy, "Organizational Structure and Employee Morale," *Am. Soc. Rev.,* Vol. 15 (1950): 169-179. Herbert Blumer, "Sociological Theory in Industrial Relations," *Am. Soc. Rev.,* Vol. 12 (1947): 271-278. M. Dalton, "Unofficial Union-Management Relation," *Am. Soc. Rev.,* Vol. 15 (1950): 611-619. J. F. Scott and George C. Homans, "Reflections on the Wildcat Strikes," *Am. Soc. Rev.,* Vol. 12 (1947): 278-287. J. P. Goldberg and B. Yabroff, "Analysis of Strikes 1927-1949," *Mo. Lab. Rev.,* Vol. 72 (Jan. 1951): 1-7.

3. The productivity represents personal satisfaction and meaningful experience to the worker.
4. Previous subcultural values often explain an employee's inadequacy.
5. Fitness-of-duty examinations often highlighted an interesting fact. Transfer from one type of job to another was desirable, but difficult because of the loss of prestige or the learning of skills applicable in the past but inadequate for current duties.
6. Lack of proper training was more often responsible than lack of capacity for inadequate behavior on the job.
7. After a personally satisfactory relationship has been developed, it is often difficult for a worker to leave that relationship even when possibilities of advancement are presented.

The experience of Sears Roebuck Co. during 12 years of research on employee attitudes affirms many of the concepts discussed above. Sears Roebuck has found that certain types of difficulties follow certain types of changes in organization. Difficulties can often be predicted, and the sequence of events in which they are likely to appear are known. The conflict areas between management and labor can be resolved. Emphasis is placed on training leadership in an organized framework permissive of effective integration. A very complex organizational structure is one of the most important causes of poor management-employee relationships.

The problem of communication between management and workers is a significant area of possible conflict. The foreman and supervisor play an important part in translating management's views to labor and labor's to management. Because of this area of conflict, the character of such leadership is being studied.

Relationships between worker and management must also be viewed as a process between large organized groups. Big union organizations and management organizations influence the character of relationships in local industries. The alignment of those organizations is an important area of industrial relations. Nevertheless, it is likewise true that informal union-management relations on the plant level conflict with working agreements between the big unions and big management. Tacit evasion of contract by both sides has been shown to be related to lack of union consciousness and managerial incohesiveness. Wildcat strikes reflect the problem side of this lack of control. In 1944 there were 4,956 wildcat strikes, which set new patterns of labor conflict.

The character of strikes has been related to the struggle between organized labor and management. Before the establishment of collective bargaining, the strike was used as an effort by labor to obtain recognition. After the establishment of collective bargaining, the emphasis has been more related to the improvement of current working conditions. Warner and associates have shown that the strike is related to the cultural history of the community and industry as well as to the destruction of established patterns of everyday living.

Human resources in industry are considered more important as recognition grows of the importance of the needed satisfactions that work can bring. Skill in the art of communication in organized work situations is being investigated. It is now acknowledged that prestige, liking for work, and the companionship that work offers are as important as purely economic factors in job satisfaction.

Vocational guidance [18]

Young people must ordinarily make a choice of a vocation before they have adequate perspective or sufficient understanding of self. The vocational-guidance movement is designed to give aid in bringing order out of this confusion. The prospective employee needs aid in finding that portion of the varied occupational world in which he can function adequately. Furthermore, he needs aid in comparing his abilities to potential competitors in the field of his choice. Vocational guidance is rapidly becoming a technical process. Giving advice on the basis of personal experience alone is not adequate.

In response to this need, the universities now offer special training for potential guidance personnel. Vocational guidance is practiced in a variety of settings—high schools, colleges and universities, Veterans Administration, county and state guidance centers, and in private agencies. Many more adequately trained counselors are needed. In the school year 1945-1946, only 16.4 per cent of the

[18] Sources: D. S. Arbuckle, "Vocational Services in College," *Occupations,* Vol. 27 (Oct. 1948): 28-34. C. W. Failor and L. E. Isaacson, "The Veteran Evaluates Counseling," *Occupations,* Vol. 28 (Oct. 1949): 18-24. C. P. Froehlich, "Counselors and Guidance Officers in Public Secondary Schools," *Occupations,* Vol. 26 (May 1948): 522-527. M. C. McPherson and H. H. Randall, "A Community Counts its Workers: Occupational Inventory of Cuyahoga County, Ohio," *Occupations,* Vol. 26 (Dec. 1947): 162-164. N. Medvin, "New Techniques for Community Occupational Survey," *Occupations,* Vol. 26 (May 1948): 532-536. R. Strang, "Social Aspects of Vocational Guidance," *Sch. Rev.,* Vol. 58 (1950): 326-334. M. F. Baer, "Vocational Guidance in Group Activities; Distinguishing Values and Principles," *Occupations,* Vol. 25 (May 1947): 530-534.

secondary schools employed persons designated as counselors and guidance officers. Large high schools are adding counselors faster than the small ones, and the counselor pupil ratio is getting smaller. Vocational service in college also needs expansion. In one study of fifteen liberal arts colleges in Illinois, the following facts were revealed. Slightly less than one half of the freshmen and juniors responding had been informed about vocational opportunities and made aware of the qualifications needed. Specially appointed vocational counselors were serving in only one institution. Less than one fourth of freshmen had received vocational counseling from teachers, and this was considered of no value by 11.6 per cent of the students who had experienced it.

In another study of vocational guidance of veterans, a more favorable response was received. Fifty-seven and three-tenths per cent of the persons receiving occupational guidance in the V. A. Guidance Center in Colorado felt that the occupational information received had been valuable.

Vocational guidance, until recently, has stressed personal adjustment and success. The social aspects of vocational guidance are likewise important. The realization of a socially accepted self is an important function of skillful counseling. While aptitudes are significant, attention must also be given to emotional needs and social values.

A significant approach to vocational research and guidance has been community surveys of occupations. Between 1930 and 1940 public education agencies were responsible for the majority of surveys. In the decade of the 'forties, business groups, public and social agencies, and state employment services affiliated with the United States Employment Service conducted occupational surveys. An example of community research is that done by the Occupational Planning Committee of the Cleveland Welfare Federation. An inventory was taken of the number of persons employed in Cuyahoga County, Ohio on July 15, 1945. Estimates were made on the probable number that would be employed a year later. Occupational patterns of workers employed were developed. This information is of value to industry, to colleges and universities, to individuals planning to obtain work in the county, and to labor unions in apprenticeship training programs.

As in so many other aspects of guidance and therapy, understanding of the dynamics of group process is of value in vocational counseling. Vocational guidance through groups gives orientation to some people not reached by individual counseling. It can focus attention on individuals particularly in need of help, and it pools the experience of a number of people.

Many college students are reluctant to use the guidance facilities that are available. This reluctance stems in part from a skepticism of testing. As vocational counselors develop research and theory in new areas of guidance and as methods become standardized, it is likely that vocational guidance will be better understood. Individuals who understand their strength and weakness will approach occupations in which they can find personal and social security.

Summary

The occupation engaged in is one of the most significant aspects of an individual's life. Problems associated with the choice of an occupation—loss of work and personal unhappiness on the job—are likely to be considered as serious problems by individuals involved.

The number of workers available and their distribution are significant factors in the economic life of the nation.

As already shown, the number of persons engaged in specific occupations is subject to change. Our economy, founded on agriculture, changed to the factory system. Two major groups emerged—labor with its principal interests in wages and working conditions, and management interested in the return on investments. The resulting conflict has developed interest in labor-management relations. Shifting of influence between labor, management, and government reflect problems in this area.

From the point of view of the person, vocational training and guidance represent attempts at problem solving. Social security and unemployment insurance represent a corporate attempt at solving problems.

Bibliography

Bell, H. M., *Matching Youth and Jobs: A Study of Occuptional Adjustment,* American Council on Education, Washington, D. C., 1940.

Friedman, M., and S. Kuznets, *Income From Independent Professional Practice,* National Bureau of Economic Research, New York, 1945.

Ghiselli, Edwin Ernest, *The Validity of Commonly Employed Occupational Tests,* University of California Press, Berkeley, 1949.

Harris, Seymour E., *The Market For College Graduates and Related Aspects of Education and Income,* Harvard University Press, Cambridge, 1949.

Huff, Darrell, *Twenty Careers of Tomorrow,* McGraw-Hill, New York, 1945.

Kasper, Sidney H. (Ed.), *Job Guide, A Handbook of Official Opportunities in Leading Industries,* American Council on Public Affairs, Washington, D. C., 1945.

Kuznets, S. S., *Shares of Upper Income Groups in Income and Savings,* National Bureau of Economic Research, New York, 1950.

Mayo, Elton, *The Social Problems of An Industrial Society,* Harvard University Press, Cambridge, 1945.

Monthly Labor Review, Vol. 51 (July 1950).

Newman, S. C., *Employment Problems of College Students,* American Council on Public Affairs, Washington, D. C., 1942.

Research Council for Economic Security, *Social Security Abroad: Labor-Management Relations,* Publication No. 79, The Council, Chicago, 1951.

Reynolds, L. G., *Job Horizons, A Study of Job Satisfaction and Labor Mobility,* Harper, New York, 1949.

Ruggles, Richard, *An Introduction to National Income and Income Analysis,* McGraw-Hill, New York, 1949.

Watkin, Gordon S., "Labor in the American Economy," *Annals, Am. Acad. Pol. and Soc. Sci.,* Vol. 274 (March 1951).

Questions

1. What have been the recent trends in the occupation you are preparing to enter?
2. What are the laws of your state regarding employment of women and children?
3. What is meant by the statement that the number of unemployed is a function of source of information and methods of measurement used?
4. If you were to advise a young friend regarding occupational choice, how would you go about it?
5. What are the inadequacies of prestige scales of occupations?
6. How is income related to such social factors as amount of education, medical care, and so forth?
7. Consult current magazines and newspapers. From this reading can you draw any conclusions regarding labor-management relations?
8. Why must vocational guidance personnel take social factors into consideration?
9. Analyze the vocational guidance program of your school.
10. Consult census data for information on income distribution. How do recent data correspond to earlier figures on income distribution?

CHAPTER 14

ACCIDENTS

IN RECENT DECADES ACCIDENTS HAVE BECOME ONE OF THE LEADING causes of death. When fatal and nonfatal accidents are combined, this country is the undisputed record-holder. Because their costs reach an estimated total of seven billion dollars annually, accidents are recognized as a major economic problem.

But accidents also appear in two other types of problems. They create a significant challenge to public health and safety programs. In addition their combined ill-effects in industry, the home, and recreation make them a major social hazard.

Ordinarily accidents are defined as chance occurrences. That is, they are supposed to be events that are unexpected and cannot be foreseen. Even the briefest inspection fails to support this definition. Accidents do not just happen; they are caused. And among the more obvious of these causes, such personal conditions are found as carelessness, emotional stress, impaired vision or hearing, inattention, fatigue, ignorance, and underlying disease.

A newsworthy and pathetic example was the fatal injury of Margaret Mitchell, author of *Gone with the Wind*. The taxi driver who was responsible had committed twenty-one other traffic violations. Under any sensible program of law enforcement, he would have been recognized as a repeater and his permit to drive a car would have been suspended. Instead, the day after he was sentenced to jail for eighteen months on a charge of involuntary manslaughter, he drove the same taxicab into a truck.

Although the trend of accidents has been decreasing during the last fifty years, accidents as a whole or certain specific types still continue to be a triple hazard—in their tremendous economic costs, in their contributions to physical and health problems, and in their creation of numerous social and personal problems. Moreover, they make an important contribution to the theory of social problems. One contribution is their stress on the element of the accidental that is to be found in most social problems. Another is the element of repetition. Social problems as a whole seem to occur and repeat with unusually demoralizing effects within similar classes of persons who seem to be chronic victims of many different classes of problems.

Accidents remain within the field of social problems because they do not respond as a whole to current regulations or they do not decrease rapidly enough.

Accident facts [1]

The study of accidents is carried on by many different agencies. The National Safety Council, several insurance companies, the Federal Security Agency in its office of Vocational Rehabilitation, various state boards dealing with vocational education, and many different city agencies make regular reports on trends or rates, as well as on developments in the several specific forms of accident prevention.

Among the outstanding facts that have continued to identify accidents as a major problem are:

1. In spite of a decreasing trend, the numbers involved in accidents are enormous. Nearly 100,000 persons are killed each year; and more than ten times this number are seriously injured.
2. During the last four decades every major type of accident except automobile accidents and conflagrations has decreased.
3. Each year one in every fourteen persons sustains some reportable injury—or more specifically
4. Each day about 300 persons are killed in accidents, 1,000 are permanently disabled, and 25,000 are temporarily disabled.
5. In the analysis of all accidents by causes, the personal factor of carelessness ranks first.
6. Accidents from all causes rank among the first ten causes of death.
7. More children and young adults are killed by accidents than by any one disease.

[1] Unless otherwise noted, the sources of factual material are the references in the bibliography of this chapter.

8. The United States has always had a higher occupational-accident rate than any other comparable industrial nation.
9. Males contribute to accidents much more frequently than females; in fact, few records of sex differences in mortality are as great as the accident rate.
10. An unusually large proportion of all accidents is caused by repeaters.

Types of accidents

In the reports of the National Safety Council, four primary classes of accidents are recognized. According to their frequency, these classes are home, motor vehicle (with a subclassification, occupational and motor vehicle), public nonmotor vehicle, and occupational. In a standard total of 100,000 accidents, the approximate numerical and per cent distribution of these different types are: (1) home accidents, 35 thousand or per cent; (2) motor vehicle, 34 thousand or per cent; (3) public nonmotor vehicle, 17 thousand or per cent; and (4) occupational, 14 thousand or per cent.[2] The other kinds of accidents are concealed in this classification, such as catastrophes and accidents in sports, but they contribute little to total mortality records in spite of their dramatic appeal to public interest.

The numerical rank order of specific kinds of accidents is: (1) motor vehicle, (2) falls, (3) burns, (4) drowning, (5) railroad, (6) firearms, (7) poison gas, and (8) poisons other than gas.

The total annual accident bill is estimated to be seven billion dollars, the items including such direct and approximate costs as (1) loss of wages and future earnings, (2) medical expenses, (3) insurance costs, (4) property damages, and (5) indirect costs.

Occupational accidents

An adequate report of industrial accidents and of occupational accidents in general is impossible for two reasons. One is that accidents are interpreted differently by various state laws. The second is that in some states only compensable accidents are reported.

Although it is generally understood that an industrial accident is an injury that results in loss of time beyond the day or night shift in which it occurs, compensable accidents are injuries that entitle the injured person to compensation. Thus, variations in state laws

[2] National Safety Council, Chicago, *Accident Facts,* Annual Report, 1949, p. 19.

regarding eligibility or waiting period, or in the systems of record keeping and reporting, must be considered in estimating the total accident rate.

Both volume and variation of the accident rate have been traced to fundamental conditions of mechanization. Of these, three are cited. (1) The introduction of machinery to supplant hand labor and the reduction in the number of workers have increased the hazard per worker, and available figures indicate a much greater number and severity of accidents per person under mechanized than under nonmechanized conditions. (2) Automatic machinery requires a large amount of repair work, which is both dangerous and unstandardized. (3) Under mechanized conditions, industry tends constantly to speed up, which increases risks and exposure. Accident frequency is thus a correlate of mechanical production. Under current operating conditions, there may be a decrease in accidents per unit of production but an actual increase in numbers because production is increasing. Much has been made of speed as an impersonal factor accounting for the high accident rate since 1920. This explanation is substantiated by the tendency of rates to increase during periods of heightened industrial activity, when inexperienced men are employed, and by the falling of this rate when industry slackens and the inexperienced and inefficient are laid off.

Accident rates. As a substitute for the unavailable record of total accidents (including deaths, permanent disabilities, and minor incapacitating injuries), fatal accident rates are accepted as the best indication of trend in the total accident rate or in any specific type of accidents. The rates for total deaths from industrial accidents and from machinery accidents are reported by the Metropolitan Life Insurance Company in its *Statistical Bulletin.*

These rates cover the occupational experiences of all white males, fifteen years of age or over, insured by this company. During the period for which this information is available, 1912 to the present, the total accident rate shows a continuous downward trend at the rate of about one per cent per year. It has varied from a high of 36.6 per 100,000 population in 1912 to a low of 14.0 per 100,000 population by the midcentury. Machinery accidents have also declined throughout this period but by small annual decreases and with greater variations.

Refined rates of trend are obtained by the calculation of two special rates, supplemented by the qualitative evaluation of especially hazardous occupations. These special rates are the frequency and severity measurements of accidents. Frequency rates indicate the proportion injured (based upon hours of exposure) of the total engaged in industry. Severity rates differentiate between those accidents involving death, total incapacity, and minor losses, and are computed on the basis of time lost based upon hours of exposure. In this estimate, time lost in the case of death is given as the average life expectancy at the time of death, usually twenty years.

Although little is known about the total occupational accident rate, the experience of different occupations is fairly definite. Hazardous occupations, ranked in order of frequency from the highest to the lowest, are mining, construction, agriculture, transportation, public utilities, manufacturing, service, and trade. Both frequency and severity rates rank in these occupations in about the same order.

The most dangerous specific occupations both in severity and frequency are coal mining, other types of mining, lumbering, quarrying, construction, marine transportation, electrical utilities, air transport, foundry, and clay products (the rank order being from highest to lowest in severity). Occupations that rank high in severity but low in frequency are cement, air transport, and steel.

In farm work there are three primary sources of accidents. Machinery accidents lead all others by a considerable margin. In this respect farm work has become one of the most dangerous of occupations. Accidents involving livestock are second; and falls, third. These three hazards constitute seventy per cent of all the accidents in agriculture.

An index of the urban rate of accidents is provided by the National Health Survey. On one day of its survey in 81 cities, this investigation discovered that four per cent of the population was disabled by accidents, which would make an annual frequency of 16.3 per 1,000 persons.

In Rubinow's standard accident table, the average frequency of fatal accidents and of permanent and temporary disabilities is [3]

Fatal accidents	932
Permanent disability	4,875
Temporary disability	94,193
Total	100,000

[3] I. M. Rubinow, *The Quest for Security,* Holt, New York, 1934. Adapted from p. 47.

These numbers represent the standard accident experience of the industrial population and indicate that there are 106 nonfatal accidents for each fatality.

Causes. Accident-prevention campaigns isolate three general factors in causation: unsafe acts, personal, and mechanical. Unsafe acts include unnecessary exposure, improper use of equipment, and working on moving or dangerous equipment. Personal factors are primarily lack of skill or improper attitude. Mechanical conditions are defective equipment, improper guarding, and hazardous procedure.[4]

In the literature on industrial accidents, seven general factors are usually considered in describing causation:

1. Hours of labor and night work.
2. Speed of production.
3. Youth or inexperience of workers.
4. Psychic factors.
5. Temperature.
6. Ventilation and lighting.
7. Repetitive work, labor turnover, and defective machinery.

This list of causative factors summarizes the principal facts and hypotheses with reference to accident frequency. Many special investigations have shown a high positive correlation between the long working day, fatigue, and accidents. Of the other factors, speed and working conditions are simply aspects of mechanization, while youth, inexperience, and psychic factors refer to the highly intangible subjective causes. Although there is some evidence that illiteracy, carelessness, stupidity, and laziness are important factors in accidents, there are no experimental proofs of their contribution. Boyd Fisher's outline of the mental causes of accidents specifies the conditions usually mentioned as subjective causes:

1. *Ignorance*—of English; inexperience; mental limitations.
2. *Predispositions*—sense defects; mental sets (excitability, attitudes); subconscious errors; faulty habits (hurry).
3. *Inattention*—boredom; distraction.

[4] In a five-year summary of elevator accidents in Pennsylvania, unsafe acts and personal factors were found to account for 288, or 67.1 per cent, of the total 429 accidents. This contrasts with 88, or 20.5 per cent, mechanical causes, and 53, or 12.4 per cent, causes unknown. *Elevator Accident Summary,* Pennsylvania Dept. of Labor and Industry, Harrisburg, 1951. Unpublished report of the Elevator Division, Bureau of Inspection.

4. *Preoccupation*—worry; strife; mental disease.
5. *Depression*—disease; drugs; alcohol; faulty plant conditions; fatigue.[5]

The difficulty of establishing causation, under experimental conditions, is illustrated by the fact that all these mechanical and personal causes are usually interrelated in the explanation of any given type of accident. In other words, accidents rarely occur in a simple causal sequence, such as speed in production leading to fatigue and hence to accidents or disease. For this reason it is well to bear in mind both the mechanical and personal causes of industrial hazards. If these are considered separately, or if one factor, such as speed in production, is studied apart from the requirements of an occupation or from the personnel engaged in the work, isolated causes are apt to prove too much. As a matter of fact, recent investigations show that even the best of protective measures cannot reduce industrial hazard unless they are supplemented by constant attention to personal factors. Accident rates among inexperienced workers, among the foreign born, and among women furnish examples of this combination of objective and subjective causes.

For purposes of accident prevention, further investigation of causes is essential, especially to differentiate between mechanical and personal causes; but, for immediate safety plans, the following list indicates the direct causes of occupational accidents. This list gives the frequency of various accidents reported in the annual sum-

Specific Causes of Compensated Accidents

Handling objects and tools	Falling objects
Falls of workers	Dangerous and harmful substances
Mechanical apparatus	Stepping on and striking objects
Vehicles	Other or indefinite

maries published by the National Safety Council. In addition, compensation for types and degree of injury is given.

Automobile accidents

During the first five decades of its use, the automobile has been responsible for nearly one million deaths—by 1980 the second million will have been killed. It leads all specific causes in severity and frequency of accidents, in numbers killed or disabled, and in costs.

[5] Boyd Fisher, *Mental Causes of Accidents,* Houghton Mifflin, New York, 1922, p. 22.

This total bill of destruction puts it in a special class of hazards, comparable possibly only to a major disaster.

Most automobile accidents occur because of errors on the part of drivers. There are six primary causes: (1) excessive speed, (2) right of way, (3) alcohol, (4) disregard of traffic controls, (5) driving on the wrong side of the road, and (6) improper passing. This rank order is derived from the experience of accidents in cities. In rural areas, the three ranking causes of accidents are: (1) excessive speed, (2) driving on the wrong side of the road, and (3) alcohol.

The two ever-present factors in the majority of all automobile accidents are violations of law and alcohol. A summary of conditions that occur most often in all accidents shows that 57 per cent of the drivers who were involved in accidents were violating a law. And this proportion of drivers accounted for 71 per cent of all fatalities. Another survey showed that 17 per cent of the drivers and 23 per cent of adult pedestrians who were involved in fatal accidents had been drinking.

In the deaths of pedestrians the five most common situations are: (1) crossing between intersections, (2) crossing at intersections, (3) walking on a rural highway, (4) children playing on streets, and (5) coming from behind a parked vehicle.

For several years the same conditions have been reported as reasons for, or explanations of, this continuous high rate of fatalities and injuries. In addition to speed, the ten outstanding automobile accident facts are: (1) young drivers, 18 to 24 years of age, have a disproportionately high accident record, a condition that is responsible for higher insurance rates for families with drivers in this age group; (2) complacency and irresponsibility; (3) the higher proportion of male drivers; (4) three of every four accidents happen when the weather is clear; (5) drivers of passenger cars (that is noncommercial vehicles) are responsible for 75 per cent of all accidents; (6) higher accident rates for drivers in the rural areas, and higher rates for pedestrians in urban areas; (7) the recurrence of personal factors, since no more than five per cent of accidents can be traced to faulty mechanical condition of the cars involved; (8) higher rates at night than during the day; (9) the worst time for accidents is 5 to 8 P.M., and (10) the most dangerous days are Saturday and Sunday.

This combination of facts stresses the need for alert drivers and also calls attention to the accident-prone driver or pedestrian.

Home accidents

Primarily because home accidents as a class have ranked high both in costs and numbers, increasing attention has been devoted to them. Although they are much less spectacular than occupational or automobile accidents, they are equally fatal and more numerous. From insurance reports it is judged that nearly one-half of the ten million people who are injured each year sustain their injury in the home.

In spite of recent decreases in the rate of home accidents for all age groups and both sexes, they are still looked upon as a chief source of preventable deaths. This fact is accented emphatically by comparison. When they are compared to the number of deaths from appendicitis, poliomyelitis, the diseases incidental to childbirth, and the four leading communicable diseases of children, home accident fatalities are found to be two times more numerous than the combined total of this mortality.

The chief types of home accidents in the order of their frequency are: falls, burns, mechanical suffocation, poisonings (except gas), poisonous gas, and firearms.

Safety campaigns have apparently had some immediate effects in the reduction of these hazards. At any rate they have met with a generally better response than campaigns to reduce traffic accidents or accidents in some of the dangerous occupations.

Accidents in sports

As a rule, accidents that occur during play or recreation are concealed in some more-general statistical report. There are few or no reliable particular sources of information about them. However, public interest is easily aroused by publicity concerning accidents in a certain type of sport, especially if there is some unusually shocking example. On the whole, judged by the proportion of accidents to the number of individuals engaged in the sport, such accidents are far less serious than the foregoing types.

In the experiences of college sports, various studies have been able to reach general agreements as to their various risks. Sports are divided into three categories. The first of these classes, called very hazardous, include football, horse polo, wrestling, and lacrosse. The second is the highly hazardous, and includes soccer and crew. The third, or hazardous, category includes boxing, touch football, basketball, ice hockey, and heavy apparatus. Major sports that are typed as low, or minimum, hazard are handball, baseball, fencing, swimming, tennis, and volleyball.

The kinds of injury, enumerated in these reports, are always the immediate or obvious disorders. In order of their frequency, these injuries are sprains, strains, wounds, bone injuries, and internal injuries. There is no agreement as to the more concealed ill-effects, such as athlete's heart or brain injury, and no resource whereby these delayed consequences could be associated causally with a particular sport or a given minor injury.

Hunting accidents. In hunting accidents more information is available because of legal control exercised over those who are licensed to participate. From records of the Fish and Wildlife Service of the United States Department of the Interior, it is known that more than ten million people engage in the various forms of outdoor sport that require licenses. From these records, too, it is apparent that hunting is the chief cause of fatal injuries.

Hunting accidents amount to nearly one-third of the 3,000 annual deaths from firearms. In addition to this number, about 1,200 others are killed in the home during the preparation of the firearm for hunting. Of all hunting wounds, 45 per cent are self-inflicted.

A primary reason for this dreary annual record is that a license can be obtained for a small fee, since there is no other control except a minimum legal age. No concerted effort is made to insure that the licensed individual is familiar with firearms or that he has sufficient skill and knowledge of their use.

The latter cause of hunting accidents, namely, inadequate skill and knowledge, is cited as the primary cause of all accidents. Other causes are inadequate equipment, inadequate leadership, and finally those conditions that are unavoidable because of the nature of the sport.

Catastrophic accidents

As a rule, disasters are looked upon by the general public as accidents at their worst. In fact the opposite is nearer the truth. Catastrophes are classified with accidents only for statistical convenience because they are unexpected. Unlike the typical accident, they do not contribute appreciably to the annual mortality toll.

A catastrophe is defined as an accident in which five or more persons are killed. It is important to the study of social problems, because certain types of disasters, such as conflagrations, are recurrent and unusually destructive, and because there is no apparent method for their prevention or control.

Such, for example, was the world's greatest disaster, one of the outbreaks of the bubonic plague during the Medieval period. This particular epidemic was, however, but one of a long series of similar attacks of the plague that occurred periodically during the preceding four hundred years. But in this instance it swept over the entire continent of Europe. It is supposed to have claimed one-fourth of the population (estimated to be twenty-five million people) as its victims—the highest mortality record of any disaster in history—and, in the opinion of modern sanitary engineers, presumably could have been controlled by a good sewage system and soap and water.

Types and severity of disasters are indicated by a list of major disasters that in the recent history of the United States have caused more than 500 deaths.

Type	*Date*	*Area*	*Deaths*
Flood and tidal wave	Sept. 8, 1900	Galveston, Texas	6,000
Flood	May 31, 1889	Johnstown, Pa.	2,209
Shipwreck (Titanic)	April 15, 1912	Atlantic Ocean	1,517
Shipwreck (Sultana explosion)	April 27, 1865	Mississippi River	1,405
Hurricane	Sept. 12-17, 1928	Florida	1,180
Forest fire	Oct. 9, 1871	Pestigo, Wisconsin and area surrounding	1,152
Shipwreck—General Slocum burned	June 24, 1904	East River, New York	1,021
Shipwreck—Eastland capsized	July 24, 1915	Chicago River	812
Flood	March 28, 1913	Ohio and Indiana	732
Hurricane	Sept. 21, 1938	New England	682
Tornado	March 18, 1925	Illinois	606
Fire—Iroquois Theater	Dec. 30, 1903	Chicago	575
Ship explosion	April 16, 1947	Texas City, Texas	551

Accident proneness

All safety studies conclude that the personal factor ranks foremost among causes of accidents of all types. "Unsafe acts" of persons is the prominent condition in occupational, traffic, and home accidents as well as in sports. This combination of personal liabilities describes the meaning of proneness. It is derived from lack of knowledge, skill, or emotional balance, from improper attitudes, such as inattention, and from physical defects. Usually proneness is identified as lack of emotional balance. But other characteristics of accident-prone individuals are lack of knowledge and taking chances.

Studies in various parts of the country generally support the assertion that 80 per cent of all accidents are caused by accident-prone people. In one Detroit survey, for example, seven tenths of one per cent of all automobile drivers were responsible for 27 per cent of the traffic accidents. In a special study of taxi drivers, six per cent were found to be causing 72 per cent of the accidents. Similarly in industrial surveys, 29 per cent of the workers were responsible for 67 per cent of all occupational accidents. In one extreme instance, an individual was found to have had as many as 50 accidents in one year.

Specific characteristics of the accident-prone individual are indicated by a comparative summary of the case histories of automobile drivers with high and low accident records. Social and personal characteristics of the accident-prone driver are:

Family background: extremely disorganized; father was a poor provider, alcoholic, excessively strict.

Unadjustments in childhood: excessive juvenile delinquency; numerous fears.

School achievement: average.

Work record: frequent changes of employment; poor relations with employer.

Social adjustment: poor; few friends; principal hobbies—sports, drinking, gambling, dancing.

Sexual adjustment: inadequate, promiscuous, high venereal rate.

Health: average; nothing to explain a record of accidents.

Behavior: immature; given to eccentric dress; no personal concern for his own problems.

Driving habits: easily distracted; readily annoyed by other drivers; criticized own mistakes in others; raced other cars; frequent use of horn; discourteous; no concern for mechanical limitations of the car.

Philosophy: disliked discipline or routine; wanted to be his own boss; considered only the immediate future.[6]

[6] W. A. Tillman and G. E. Hobbs, "The Accident-Prone Automobile Driver," *Am. Jour. Psychiatry,* Vol. 106 (1949): 321-331. See also, A. T. Rawson, "Accident-Proneness," *Psychosomatic Med.,* Vol. 6 (1944): 88. E. M. Fuller, "Injury-Prone Children," *Am. Jour. Orthopsychiatry,* Vol. 18 (1948): 723. Consult for a comparison of the personal traits of injury-prone and noninjury-prone children.

Drivers with a low accident record (the control group) had none of these unadjusting traits. They were most like the accident-prone group in possessing average or good health and an average school record. In all other respects they differed from the accident-prone group in exhibiting those faculties that are considered to be evidences of maturity and self-control. They were well-adjusted in their family home, in their childhood associations, in their occupation, and in their marriage. Their hobbies and adult friendships were conservative. Their behavior traits and driving habits were the precise opposite of the accident-prone, and their philosophical outlook was distinctive in being primarily concerned with the welfare of others.

A review of the victim's own reasons for his accidents also stresses the facts of proneness and carelessness. Among various such confessions are the statements: "It was really my fault. . . ." "Perhaps I ought to have known better. . . ." "I can't remember ever having done anything wrong. . . ." "I only had a couple beers. . . ." "Some one is always running into my car. . . ." "I didn't see the other automobile; it was coming too fast. . . ." "I never had no accidents. . . ." [7]

Correlations of age, sex, and fatigue

Social correlates of the accident record help to demonstrate both its nature and ill-effects. In the report of the National Health Survey, the sex ratio of accidents was found to be 60.6 accidents for women to 100 for men. Accidents accounted for 7.6 per cent of the days of disability from all causes and were exceeded only by influenza and grippe as a cause of lost time. Families in the lower-income groups reported a higher accident rate than families in moderate circumstances. Of the total who suffered some injury, 12.4 persons per 1,000 had permanent physical impairments. Nearly one third of the orthopedic impairments were the result of occupational accidents.[8]

As already noted, the male accident rate is considerably greater than the female. Both in accident frequency and mortality, the accident rate among men has been consistently about twice that of

[7] Donald Armstrong and others, "Accident Prevention," *Pub. Health Rpts.*, Vol. 64 (1949), No. 12, pp. 355-389.

[8] R. H. Britten and others, "The National Health Survey: Some General Findings," *Pub. Health Rpts.*, Vol. 55 (1940), No. 11, pp. 21-22.

women. Two explanations are suggested: one is the greater exposure in occupations and sports; the second, the greater tendency to take chances.

This sex difference extends to all age groups from infancy up to age 75, when it is reversed. It increases steadily through all the years of childhood and reaches its peak at age 20 to 24, when the sex ratio is more than six to one. Particular accidents accounting for these differences are first, motor vehicle; second, occupational; and third, drowning, firearms, and air transportation. In only one type of accident, namely, falls, is the female rate greater than that of the male.

When age alone is considered, there are two distinctive differences. Young people and young adults have more accidents than the age group over 50. But they also recover in a higher percentage of the cases and they recover more rapidly than the older group. A second significant difference is that the accident death rate of the older group is twice that of age group 20-24, and, in addition, the rate of permanent impairments is also higher for the aged.

The particular accidents that continue to be the chief killers of children are: motor vehicle, children generally being in the street when the accident occurred; drowning; burns and explosions; and firearms.

Fatigue and accidents. There have been numerous studies of the relationship between fatigue and efficiency. In most of these reports a high degree of correlation has been shown to exist between the frequency of accidents and various measurements of fatigue—notably, length of the working period. A number of studies have concluded that accidents increase directly with the number of working hours, the former increasing in number and severity during the last hours of each working period.

This conclusion has been criticized on the score that the relationship is incidental and not causal. Attention to a third factor, speed of production, is the source of this criticism. In the original investigations of the relationship between length of working period and frequency of accidents, the factor of speed was neglected. Later, when this factor was included, a closer correspondence between curves of accidents and production was found than in the former studies of fatigue. But the primary importance of production has not eliminated fatigue as a causal factor. Cutting down the hours of labor from twelve to ten or eight has resulted in major reductions in accident frequency. Factors other than reduction of working hours have also been connected with corresponding decreases. In coal mining, both low production and fatigue were found to correlate positively with high temperatures. Through the introduction of ventilating systems, production was increased and accidents were cut down by one third. However interpreted or measured, fatigue remains an important contributory factor in the accident record.

Another supplementary explanation of accident frequency is called by Vernon the "psychic state of the worker." This category includes inattention, carelessness, and lack of responsibility of the individual worker. These factors were selected as important in the causation of accidents after a comparison of the accidents of day and night workers. During night work, accidents occurred more often in the early hours of the working period, a condition ascribed to carelessness and excitement. This apparent contradiction of the fatigue-accident sequence does nothing more than substantiate prior findings, such as those of Muscio:

1. Increasing rate of movement causes increasing inaccuracy.
2. Continuous work fails to show an inaccuracy curve similar to the accident curve.
3. A curve similar to the accident curve can be secured only by increasing the rate of work.[9]

Statistical studies in England and in this country stress both the factors of speed and the "psychic," or personal, element. In a summary of 73,000 industrial accidents in this country, 88 per cent were traced to personal causes, whereas the most liberal estimate assigned only 10 per cent to mechanical or material sources. Of this total, the remaining two per cent were classified as nonpreventable. Such a conclusion emphasizes the importance of skill, experience, and intelligence, as well as regulated speed of production, as necessary prerequisites to the minimizing of accidents. This conclusion is substantiated by the further discovery that the majority of accidents occur within a relatively small group of workers, who apparently are unable to avoid accidents.

Summary

During the past half century considerable advancement has been made in reducing the high toll of accidental deaths. In spite of a

[9] B. Muscio, *Lectures on Industrial Psychology,* G. Routledge and Sons, London, 1925, p. 36.

continuing and excessive number of deaths and disabilities, the outlook is much brighter than for most social problems. In fact, the study of accident prevention affords lessons and guides in social control that may prove to have valuable applications to social problems as a whole.

This improved record is a result of carefully organized plans that attack all forms and sources of accidents. Outstanding among recent social changes that are associated with decreasing accidents is the safety movement that was instituted first in industry about 1911 and that has been extended gradually to all the major causes of accidents. In addition, there have been changes in industrial methods, such as reduction in the hours of labor, better plant sanitation, and education of workers concerning hazards in their own jobs; the development of new and less hazardous industrial products; and a new medical specialty called industrial medicine. Other circumstances, also associated with the improved accident experience, are modernization of the homes, changes in the modes of public transportation, safety education in schools, and community-wide plans for safety, such as the Topeka campaign, the American Red Cross, the President's Highway Safety Conference, and the President's Conference on Industrial Safety.

From a personal standpoint, all these plans and campaigns can be stated in one suggestion, namely, each individual should become responsible for his own safety—a conclusion that is developed in the article "Don't Drive without a Mental License." [10]

The National Safety Council is a private, nonprofit association. Its members include manufacturing industries; transportation and insurance companies; government and civic agencies; traffic, home, and farm-safety organizations; schools; colleges; and individuals. Its purpose is a constant study of accident facts and their publicity, the organization of safety campaigns based upon this research, and advisory services that are designed to reduce or eliminate any type of accident. Its publications are numerous, and its directory of safety films is the most up to date and adequate.

The Topeka plan has been given wide publicity because of its immediately successful results. This campaign was instituted by the local chamber of commerce and other community associations in 1946 because of the high traffic death rate in 1945. In 1945

[10] Edith Roberts, in *Coronet,* Vol. 28 (Oct. 1950): 132-134.

Topeka ranked fifty-seventh in traffic safety among the 64 cities that are from 50,000 to 100,000 in population.

In addition to raising the necessary funds, the primary activities were the distribution of safety guides to all elementary schools, the preparation and distribution of a digest of traffic laws, and the widest use of all available means of communication (radio, movies, and public discussion) to educate the public.

As a result, traffic deaths were reduced by fifty-five per cent and Topeka achieved the fourth best record in traffic safety within its class of cities.

In the reduction of accidents, especially those of industry and the home, both the methods and possibilities of successful accident prevention are established. At present the particularly urgent areas in need of further study and research are the accidents of children, farm workers, and automobile drivers, and accidents in recreational activities. So far as current information is available, the reasons for these accidents are youth, inexperience, carelessness, and accident-proneness—factors that are easily detected. And as accident control programs have pointed out, each of them suggests its own necessary regulation.

Bibliography

Accident Facts, National Safety Council, 20 North Wacker St., Chicago, 6, Ill., Annual reports.

Blake, R. P. (Ed.), *Industrial Safety,* Prentice-Hall, New York, 1943.

Dunbar, F., *Mind and Body,* Random House, New York, 1947.

Huddleson, J. H., *Accidents, Neuroses and Compensation,* Williams and Wilkins, Baltimore, 1942.

Judson, H. H. and J. M. Brown, *Occupational Accident Prevention,* John Wiley, New York, 1944.

Kartman, B., and L. Brown (Eds.), *Disasters,* Pellagrini and Cudahy, New York, 1948.

Kessler, H. H., *Accidental Injuries: the Medico-Legal Aspects of Workmen's Compensation and Public Liability,* Lea and Febiger, Philadelphia, 1941.

Lippert, F. G., *Accident Prevention Administration,* McGraw-Hill, New York, 1947.

Neuschutz, L. M., *5,000,000 Accidents on the Home Front,* Beechhurst Press, New York, 1947.

Owen, S. J., *Safety for the Household,* United States National Bureau of Standards, Washington, D.C., 1948.

Seaton, D. C., *Safety in Sports,* Prentice-Hall, New York, 1948.

Stack, H. J., and others, *Education for Safe Living,* Prentice-Hall, New York, 1942.

United States Public Health Service, "Accidents in the Urban Home as Recorded in the National Health Survey," *Public Health Reports,* Vol. 55, No. 45, Washington, D. C., 1940.

Vernon, H. M., *Accidents and Their Prevention,* Macmillan, New York, 1937.

Williams, S. J., and W. W. Charters, *Safety,* Macmillan, New York, 1940.

Wolff, George, *Childhood Mortality from Accidents,* United States Dept. of Labor, Children's Bureau, Washington, 1945.

Yahraes, Herbert, *Make Your Town Safe!,* Public Affairs Committee, New York, 1947.

. . . . .

Armstrong, D. B., and W. G. Cole, "Can Child Accidents Be Prevented in Your Community?" *Am. Jour. Pub. Health,* Vol. 39 (May, 1949): 584-592. A community program of prevention.

Kent, F. S., "Engineering Aspects of Home Accident Prevention," *Am. Jour. Pub. Health,* Vol. 39 (Dec. 1949): 1531-1534. A proposed program.

Questions

1. Accident mortality and military fatalities are often compared. Do you consider this comparison valid or are they too different?
2. What education and training should an industrial hygienist have? A safety engineer?
3. Do occupational accidents occur more frequently when business conditions are slack or during business revivals?
4. Is there any connection between workmen's compensation laws, accident trends, and the safety movement?
5. What are the hazardous trades in your community or state?
6. Why is a standard accident table useful?
7. Do you agree that there is an element of the accidental in nearly all social problems? Cite illustrations from previous chapters, such as physical health, juvenile delinquency, or depressions and inflation.
8. Is it possible to compute rates of air transport fatalities that are comparable to those of other forms of transportation?
9. Is accident proneness essentially a mental, biological, or social condition?
10. Are the personal causes of occupational and home accidents the same?
11. Are the mechanical causes of automobile and railroad accidents the same?
12. Since occupational accidents have been reduced following various educational campaigns, is it reasonable to conclude that traffic accidents can be reduced by similar methods?
13. Point out what you consider to be deficiencies in the licensing of automobile drivers.

14. Is there any evidence that the hazardous sports may have ill-effects that do not appear until a decade or more after the sport is discontinued?
15. Can you account for or justify the practice that licenses an individual to use a firearm when he is ignorant of elementary precautions essential to his own safety and that of others?
16. Why are catastrophes classified as accidents?
17. Do you agree with the point of view suggested by Miss Roberts that a mental license or self-criticism is an effective support to safety in automobile driving?
18. Compare the decisions of your local courts with the compensations stated in *Accident Facts.* Are they larger? Is there a trend toward increasing amounts for fatal accidents and for serious injuries?
19. What organizations in your community are actively engaged in safety campaigns?
20. How do the safety activities of your community compare with the Topeka Plan? Consult pamphlet by Yahraes.

PART 4

PROBLEMS ACCENTED BY SOCIAL POLICY

Introduction

ANOTHER GROUP OF DISORDERED SOCIAL RELATIONSHIPS MAY BE OBserved in those problems wherein neither economic maladjustments nor bodily ailments are major or immediate causes or explanations. In general, this third class of problems may be identified by differences in culture and current social policy. They are called problems in social policy because they are located in that web of social relationships whose operations are dependent upon efficient economic culture but whose maladjustments arise most directly from other cultural activities and from an inconsistent system of moral or social values.

Important cultural problems may be discovered by a number of noneconomic standards. They include social problems in the major institutions of the family, government, education, religion, morals, and social work. They include the typical social problems in a dynamic society of cultural comparisons and conflicts. They include problems of the primary group in proportion as its services are replaced by secondary-group relations. In brief this category illustrates the broad generalization that all social problems eventually become forms of disorganized group contacts.

It is, of course, true that the simple expedient of instituting a fourth classification of social problems does not answer the many questions of ultimate causation. To the convinced economic determinist, the problems in this and the preceding section are simply by-products of economic status and organization. No one, however, denies the absolute necessity of a sound economic culture or the fact that important relationships of a noneconomic character do occur in everyday living. Consequently, the assumption that human difficulties may emerge independently of their economic setting urges a search for causes and cures within a pattern of many socializing agencies rather than within any one set of these conditions, regardless of their spectacular or fundamental character.

Additional areas from which particular problems might have been selected, if space permitted, are leadership, war, various national and international problems of a political nature, and numerous religious, educational, and local community problems. Many other problems can be identified, defined, and analyzed in harmony with the pattern suggested in Chapter 1.

CHAPTER 15

FAMILY PROBLEMS—PERSONAL

SOCIAL INSTITUTIONS ARE ALIKE IN THEIR TENDENCY TO ACCLAIM THEIR own superior achievements. Each one, government, business, religion, education, or the family, likes to assume that its own contributions are basic to a stable society. If there are serious social handicaps, the fault lies mainly in the backwardness or inefficiency of the other institutions. They are either too lenient or they may actually encourage the perversity of human nature.

A standard example of institutional self-esteem is to be found in the economic organization of society. Business leaders like to point out the efficiency of the system by such evidence as the increasing per capita production, the stabilization of employment at a figure much higher than was formerly considered possible, the doubling of take-home pay, and at the same time a substantial reduction in the work week.

Though most of the other social institutions would have difficulty in finding comparable statistics of their progress, the family is about equal to business in its positive signs of approved social change. There are such recent trends, for example, as the constantly increasing proportion of the population that is married, a decrease in the proportion of total marital breakdowns through divorce, separation, and widowhood, a high rate of remarriage of the divorced, and in recent years a significant rise in the birth rate.

One reaction to these achievements of the family states: "Altogether, the American people have a deep and abiding need for family life. Whatever the disruptive forces of contemporary society, they are outweighed by the strong desire for home and children." [1]

How families can be disrupted by current social disorders or by clashes in interpersonal relationships has been noted in numerous connections heretofore. If marriage and parenthood are normal goals in the social growth of the individual, they are also two of the most exacting tests of normal personality. All students of successful marriage, as well as the reports of marriage-counseling services, show that the personal and social requirements for adjusted marital and family relations are either complementary or just about identical.

Another test of family stability and of an individual's personal adjustment is to be found in the comparatively brief age span between the dependence of infancy and the maturity and self-control required in courtship and marriage. Both marriage and parenthood begin for some individuals in late adolescence. According to current trends, not only is the average age of marriage decreasing for the population as a whole (from 26 and 22 years of age for males and females respectively in 1890 to 22 and 20 in 1950), but many marriages take place within the age group from 15 to 19.

Successful marriages and stable family relations point out positively (as do unsuccessful marriages and broken homes negatively) that the necessary prerequisite is personal maturity. And to insure the continuity of the family on a basis of congenial relationships, the two most certain guides are understanding and companionship.

Personal and social differences in family life. Readily observed differences in families suggest the various sources of their stability or breakdown. These differences include:

1. Age of parents
2. Number, age, and sex of the children
3. Others in the home (relatives, boarders, and domestics)
4. Family income and standard of living
5. Housing
6. Neighborhood (rural or urban)
7. Occupation of father and of mother, if she is employed
8. Education of parents
9. Intelligence of parents
10. Health standards and habits
11. Dietary standards and home management
12. Adequacy of medical and dental care

[1] "American Family Ties Strengthened," *Statis. Bull.*, Metropolitan Life Insurance Company, Vol. 32 (1951), No. 3, p. 2.

13. Cultural status of the home, including the compatibility of husband-wife relations
14. Interests and attitudes of parents
15. Religion
16. Other social contacts

The significance of these objective and subjective indexes of family life and their importance in determining husband-wife and parent-child relationships are stressed continuously in research studies.[2] They point out consistently that members of the same family are apt to share four basic characteristics. These similarities are in health, intelligence, character, and social maturity. Although there is no clear-cut explanation as to why or by what means these effects take place, they are observed often enough to be considered accepted results of family influences.

The changing family

Differences in contemporary family life are associated with both the changing size and composition of the family unit. These differences modify the conditions that are recognized as problems of families and children and, in addition, alter the basic social services that parents must provide for children. They arise as a result of major social transitions, such as the urbanization or industrialization of a people.

One of the outstanding characteristics of the modern family is its decreasing size. The average family is composed of two parents and one or two children. These *normal* families include about four-fifths of all families reported in the United States Census of families or of households. Other family types are childless couples, parents with children and relatives or others in the home, the family with one parent (death, divorce, or separation), and one or two other relatively unimportant combinations of the above.

Changes accompanying this smaller family unit are of three kinds. There are major institutional changes, especially the economic and governmental, that modify the family as a social institution. These conditions alter the activities and responsibilities of particular fam-

[2] There are also numerous specific consequences of family relations. It has been noted, for example, that children develop a sense of security or insecurity, do good or poor school work, are aggressive or submissive, are accepted or rejected by groups, engage in delinquent or socially approved conduct, and acquire certain interests and values, such as vocational preferences, frustrations, or prejudices, because of family experiences.

ilies and in turn lead to changing personal relationships between husbands and wives and parents and children.

AVERAGE SIZE OF AMERICAN FAMILIES

Year	*Number of persons Per Family*	*Year*	*Number of persons Per Family*
1900	4.7	1930	4.1
1910	4.5	1940	3.8
1920	4.3	1950	3.4

Source: United States Bureau of the Census.

Changes affecting the family as a social institution include loss of functions of the rural and agricultural family, particularly in economic production, household management, and recreation; urbanization; increasing mobility of population; industrial changes; and an increasing number of competing interests.

Changes in the activities and responsibilities of the family that are generally the results of these institutional influences are radical modifications of the traditional family. They include increasing opportunities for the employment of women outside of the home. They make possible increasing leisure because of smaller dwellings and labor-saving devices. They bring about increased attention to child rearing because of the smaller number of children per family. They have multiplied the number of leisure-time activities outside of the home (parks, playgrounds, schools, clubs, and commercial amusements) in competition with those that were traditionally in the home or that may be restored to the home, viz., radio and television.

Changes in parent-child relations are illustrated by the following transitions: fewer associations with parents who work away from home; more intimate relations between mother and child if the father is away from home during working hours; waning of parental authority; increasing dependence of children on outside social contacts with the decreasing number of children in the home; child-dominated homes; fewer household duties for children; neglected children; types of helpers employed in the home or in the care of children.

Successful family life. When different types of family are compared in order to discover what makes for sociability or social adjustment in marital and parental relationships, certain characteristics stand out clearly as being most efficient in establishing the foundations both of successful family life and of normal personal growth. Some of these characteristics are the physical and economic resources of the family. Others are social and personal characteristics of parents and children that make possible the greatest number of stimulating social contacts.[3]

These essential factors in successful family life are:

1. *Physical and economic resources*
   (*a*) The family lives preferably in a single house.
   (*b*) The neighborhood is good and neighboring families are more or less on the same economic and cultural level.
   (*c*) Economic status is secure.
   (*d*) The family is not too large.
2. *Personal characteristics*
   (*a*) Both parents are healthy.
   (*b*) The intelligence of the children is high in relation to the average intelligence of school companions. They have good school records.
   (*c*) Parents are well educated and report a happy childhood.
3. *Social relations*
   (*a*) Parents have a variety of social interests outside of the home.
   (*b*) Children have a variety of interests, hobbies, and social contacts.
   (*c*) Family relations are congenial. There is no favoritism, and parents are the children's chief social influence.

When the specific traits of the successful home are examined in detail, the following rules of parent-child relationships are widely endorsed:

The home allows the children an increasing amount of freedom, as illustrated by a spending allowance, going away from home with other children, making choices and decisions.

[3] L. S. Cottrell, "Present Status and Future Orientation of Research on the Family," *Am. Sociol. Rev.*, Vol. 13 (1948): 123-136. P. C. Glick, "The Family Cycle," *Am. Sociol. Rev.*, Vol. 12 (1947): 164-174, and "First Marriages and Remarriages," *Am. Sociol. Rev.*, Vol. 14 (1949): 726-734. N. S. Hayner, "Regional Family Pattern," *Am. Jour. Sociol.*, Vol. 53 (1948): 432-434. A. B. Hollingshead, "Cultural Factors in the Selection of Marriage Mates," *Am. Sociol. Rev.*, Vol. 15 (1950): 619-627. J. T. Landis, "Marriages of Mixed and Non-Mixed Religious Faith," *Am. Sociol. Rev.*, Vol. 14 (1949): 401-407. P. H. Landis, "The Changing Family," *Current Hist.*, Vol. 19 (1950): 151-153. A. L. Porterfield and H. E. Salley, "Current Folkways of Sexual Behavior," *Am. Jour. Sociol.*, Vol. 52 (1946): 209-216.

Discipline is moderate, consistent, and uniform; and the standards of both parents are closely alike.

Counseling and supervision are graded to the needs of the child.

There is little or no friction between parents or between parents and children or between the children.

Parents as a rule are able to keep their own problems to themselves and do not hand them on to the children. At the same time, parents do not hesitate to talk over some problems with their children as a normal part of their introduction to reality.

The family is willing and able to modify some of its standards in order to comply with the pressure of outside affairs.

The home offers emotional security. It is not dominated exclusively by any one of its members.

The home is the customary center of social activities.

There is considerable evidence of respect and affection between the members.

Parents are especially careful in the supervision of the child's first social contacts in play, friendships, amusements, and in religious and club associations.[4]

Maladjusted families are described in general by the opposite of these characteristics. The combination of family characteristics that is usually found when parents and children are poorly adjusted includes ill-health of either parent; either parent is reported as being nervous or emotionally upset; children are punished frequently; either parent does things that the children dislike and criticize.

There is also some evidence that the absence of either parent from home or association with parents who have disagreeable personality traits may be conditions that are likely to lead to unsatisfactory school work and to difficulties in making friendships. These home conditions are found most often among school children who are handicapped by less than average intelligence, are over age for their grade, and who have a high record of failure in school subjects. Moreover, in a large proportion of cases, such children are also handicapped by other impairments, such as behavior problems, poor health, malnutrition, and physical defects.

[4] J. H. Collins and H. R. Douglas, "The Socio-Economic Status of the Home as a Factor in Success in Junior High School," *El. School Jour.*, Vol. 38 (1937-38): 107-113. E. R. and H. Mowrer, "The Social Psychology of Marriage," *Am. Sociol. Rev.*, Vol. 16 (1951): 27-36. M. L. Riser, "Lack of Parents and School Progress," *El. School Jour.*, Vol. 39 (1938-39): 528-531. M. B. Thurlow, "A Study of Selected Factors in Family Life," *Social Forces*, Vol. 12, (1934): 562-569.

Sources of family breakdowns

If none of the serious or pathological handicaps to successful husband-wife relations occurs,[5] the social demands of marriage often prove to be rigid tests of personal adaptability. They are, or introduce, changes in personal and social relations that may be neglected as trivial. But the records show them to be prominent among the reported causes of domestic discord.

In spite of the best premarital preparation or marriage-counseling service during the early years of marriage, questions arise for which there is no direct training except in terms of general principles. All normal married couples have to make readjustments; in the management of income, budgeting, choice of recreation and other leisure-time activities, accommodation between their own personal and family life and their new family relations and other social groups with which association was previously maintained, in the demands of the husband's occupation, and in the demands of the wife's occupation if she is employed outside of the home.

These are the most usual social sources of husband-wife disagreements and maladjustments when an approach is made from the standpoint of normal couples who are not plagued by biological, psychological, or emotional disorders.

A more critical survey of the problems of husbands and wives must take notice of all the immaturities and inadequacies that adults may bring to marriage. These liabilities can be traced sometimes to the earliest experiences of childhood. In the psychiatric literature, attention is often called to the supposition that problem children have problem parents. Hence, the first line of defense in the protection of the child is to assure the good adjustment of parents. In this connection, one of the first needs of the child is for normal association with both parents. A relationship that is limited to one parent is rarely sufficient.

[5] Physical, biological, and psychological factors in marriage are reviewed in the following sources: R. L. Dickinson and L. Beam, *A Thousand Marriages*, Williams and Wilkins, Baltimore, 1949; E. S. Gordon, "Physical Aspects of Marriage," Chap. 12 in H. Becker and R. Hill, *Marriage and the Family*, Heath, Boston, 1942; N. Himes, *Your Marriage: A Guide to Happiness*, Consumers Union, New York, 1940; E. D. Plass, "The Physical Aspects of Marriage," Chap. 11 in M. Jung, *Modern Marriage*, Crofts, New York, 1940; A. C. Kinsey and others, *Sexual Behavior in the Human Male*, Saunders, Philadelphia, 1948, Part III.

Specific marital tensions are discovered in a variety of sources. Their manifestations may be indications of either inadequacy or immaturity. Some tensions are related to sex, emotional upsets, or ill-health. Others may arise with, or from, insignificant conditions in the personal relations of the married couple—the "little things" so often mentioned in the polls or in the personal observations of judges, psychiatrists, and marriage advisers.[6] Frequent sources of disagreement occur in the social obligations that accompany marriage, home-making, and child care. In addition to any one of these factors which may become aggravated until it is a major friction, some authorities hold that a major social source of domestic unrest is due to uncertainty frequently discovered among married couples as to whether or not they should have married their partner. This situation, when it occurs, implies inability to make decisions and a general inclination toward personal and social instability.

Other criticisms of parents refer directly to their lack of information about the family. This informational handicap is used both to describe the bad parent and to indicate further sources of unrest. Of these criticisms, the ten that are cited most often are: parents have little or no training in child care, and for this reason they are not able to work out a mutually acceptable plan of child training; parents, furthermore, are accused of having little or no appreciation of the stages in child growth, of being poorly informed concerning human personality, and of having even less understanding of emotional training, mental hygiene, and sex education; consequently, it is asserted, parents neglect this necessary training of the child, avoid questions of vocational preparation, and make no intelligent endeavor to meet the issues that are involved in ensuring efficient social adjustment.

This bill of indictment is occasionally extended to include two other common defects of parents. It is asserted that they do not correlate the teachings of modern science with the teaching of religion, or if they attempt to do so, they succeed only in confusing the child or fostering in him an attitude of cynicism. It is also contended that they fail miserably in protecting the child from the

[6] These little things include nagging, extravagance, poor housekeeping, interferences of relatives and in-laws, drinking, night-clubbing, jealousy, neglect in child care, disagreements over religion, and such traits as being bossy, careless, and selfish.

distractions and speed of modern living and that they do not supply him with a workable social philosophy.

When types of parental behavior are examined to see what particular qualities are most associated with the social adjustment of children, three classes of parent-child relationships are distinguished.[7] These relationships are described as the rejected, the casual, and the acceptant, the latter representing the socially approved home.

The rejectant and casual types differ only in their degrees of unsociability, and are practically self-explanatory. Rejectant means the home in which parents are usually hostile, unaffectionate, disapproving, and emotionally distant. The casual relationship is illustrated by parents who vary in their reactions, sometimes being indulgent and at other times being autocratic or even rejectant. They are also the parents who cannot agree on methods of child care or discipline, but who indulge in babying, protectiveness, overanxiety, or devotion, with little or no appreciation of the child's developmental needs.

The acceptable family relationship is the democratic and not indulgent type. Its major characteristics are described by three contributions. It is above average in affection and confidence. It maintains an emotional objectivity, that is, it is not hostile, disapproving, or overanxious. Its social policy is one of freedom; the children are allowed as much independence as their maturity permits and they are subjected to a minimum of direct guidance.

Premarital indications of successful marriage

Although there is no one formula or prescription for the solution of the problems of husbands and wives or for the requirements of successful marriages, various studies are in agreement as to the conditions that are most hopeful indexes of marital happiness. These conditions suggest that in either sex the best matrimonial prospect is the socially adjusted, conventional, and conforming person.

A detailed outline of the background of such individuals includes

[7] A. L. Baldwin and others, "Patterns of Parent Behavior," *Psychol. Mono.*, Vol. 58 (1945), No. 3, pp. 1-75. Compare with A. D. Ullman and others, "Does Failure Run in Families?" *Am. Jour. Psychiatry*, Vol. 107 (1951): 667 ff. This article contends that an individual's problems are not especially conditioned by the family.

the following specific conditions. As a rule, a considerable portion of childhood is spent in a conservative community, preferably a rural or suburban area. The religious background is described as moderate, meaning that there is no tendency towards extremes of being too pious or too irreligious. There is a consistent membership in social groups, usually in two or more at the same time. Courtship is not a hurried affair; it usually extends over a period of two years. Both courtship and marriage are approved by the parents. Employment has been steady and has been sufficiently remunerative to permit savings. This prerequisite is necessary in order to give the new family a good economic start. Both before and after marriage, the occupation is a stable one. It does not require excessive mobility. In addition, it is a socially approved vocation, that is, it does not detract from the social position or prestige of the individual or family. The individual is the conforming type in that he is well adjusted to the social institutions and is so constituted temperamentally that he does not feel obliged to be seriously critical of their policies. His education in sex has come from conventional sources (usually from parents) and has been sufficient to prevent an attitude of shame or disgust or an accumulation of misinformation. And finally, the home life and the education of the good matrimonial prospect are rated good or superior.

Happiness of adults in marriage

The validity of these premarital indications of success in marriage is endorsed by several studies of family and marriage relationships. When adults come to marriage with a good share of the favorable premarital characteristics, another reassuring factor is to discover that the wish for a happy married life is foremost among their choices of the various satisfactions in life. Moreover, contrary to the inference that most married couples are doubtful as to their choice of partner, the majority of couples whose premarital prospects have been good are not in doubt on this score. Furthermore, they assign to themselves a high rating in marital happiness.

In the study of those satisfactions in life that married persons (who are college graduates) hope for most, both husbands and wives give the highest rating to the happiness of their married life. Other life satisfactions are similar for both sexes, as indicated in the table on p. 369. They value financial security, a good standard of living, and a comfortable home as necessary bases of well-adjusted marriage. The only sex difference is that men express a desire to be successful in their occupations and women select as their special choice success in child rearing. All these secondary preferences, it should be noted, are also regarded as important requirements for marital happiness.

CHOICES OF LIFE SATISFACTIONS BY COLLEGE GRADUATES

Goal	*Per Cent Distribution of Choices*	
	Men	*Women*
Happy married life	59	69
Comfortable standard of living	43	56
Financial security in old age	42	38
Making a good home for husband or wife	38	40
Financial success in work	54	—
Children one can be proud of	—	37

Source: C. Robert Pace, *They Went to College,* University of Minnesota Press, Minneapolis, 1941, p. 66.

A self-rating of 526 married couples in the study by Burgess and Cottrell shows a high proportion of couples who believe themselves to be well adjusted and happy in their marriage. This study of couples who have been married from one to six years deals with a young, middle class, native white, American, urban, predominantly nonneurotic, and in other respects homogeneous group. The results of their own happiness rating are: [8]

	Per Cent of Couples
Very happy	42.6
Happy	20.5
Average	14.4
Unhappy	13.5
Very unhappy	8.0
No reply	1.0
Total	100.0

Happiness in marriage is related to good health in childhood, enjoyment of, and success in, work, success in dealing with people,

[8] E. W. Burgess and L. S. Cottrell, *Predicting Success or Failure in Marriage,* Prentice Hall, New York, 1939, Table 13, p. 34. The validity of the use of the term happiness is discussed on pp. 30-32; comparisons with other studies are made on pp. 35-45. See also P. H. Landis, *Your Marriage and Family Living,* McGraw-Hill, New York, 1946. On pp. 172-173 there are reports of various studies indicating, as does the table from Burgess and Cottrell, that about 60 per cent of all marriages are rated happy.

popularity as judged by election to many offices, and love of nature.[9] It is also associated with certain characteristics of personality and with similarities between married couples in interests, social background, attitudes, and beliefs.

Characteristics of personality associated with happiness and unhappiness. Watson's account of marital happiness points out that the prospect of achieving a successful marriage is much more optimistic than is ordinarily assumed from the records of divorce and discord. The personal reasons for success or failure are given in the characteristics of husbands and wives who are rated as being happy or unhappy in marriage.[10]

Husbands and wives who are rated happy in their marriage share in common such traits as being emotionally stable, cooperative, conservative, methodical, and conventional in matters of sex, religion, and politics. Husbands are described in addition as being benevolent, equalitarian toward women, and willing and able to take the initiative and to assume responsibility. Other qualities of women are being kindly, sociable but not social climbers, willing to take a subordinate role, self-assured, and careful with money.

Unhappy husbands and wives are characterized as being emotionally tense; moody or variable in mood and sometimes neurotic; inclined toward radicalism in questions of morals, religion, and politics; oversensitive to social opinion; often confused by feelings of inferiority; and unmethodical. Other characteristics of husbands are domineering, lacking in confidence, irregular workers, do not take orders well from others, dislike to save, like to gamble, and tend to be antagonistic toward women. Women in this category are further described as egocentric; further, they tend to be joiners

[9] Goodwin Watson, "Happiness Among Adult Students in Education," *Jour. Educa. Sociol.*, Vol. 21 (1930): 79-109. Unhappiness was found to be associated with shyness, sensitiveness, and fears. Factors found to be unrelated to happiness are intelligence, school marks, hobbies, wealth, highly educated parents, number of children in the family, knowledge of academic subject-matter, participation in school athletics, and ability in dancing, cards, writing, music, or painting. Compare with R. B. Reed, "Social and Psychological Factors Affecting Fertility: Interrelations of Marital Adjustment, Fertility Control, and Size of Family," *Mil. Mem. Fund Quart.*, Vol. 25 (1947): 383-425.

[10] L. M. Terman, *Psychological Factors in Marital Happiness,* McGraw-Hill, New York, 1938, Chap. 7, pp. 369-374. This is a study of 792 married couples. It is a sample of the urban and suburban population in the middle and upper-middle cultural levels. L. M. Terman and Paul Wallin, "Validity of Marriage Prediction and Marital Adjustment Tests," *Am. Sociol. Rev.,* Vol. 14 (1949): 497-504.

of organizations but have small use for benevolent undertakings; they want to be considered important, and they are not antagonistic toward the opposite sex but are apt to be in search of romance.

Similarities between husbands and wives. Other personal and social characteristics favorable to happiness in marriage are given in the table below. In this table it is shown by coefficients of correlation that similarities in age, socio-economic status, education, intelligence, social interests, and certain beliefs seem to be important requirements for adjusted marriage. Although each of the other factors referred to in this table may also make a significant contribution to marital happiness, the table as a whole emphasizes the importance of a combination of characteristics (instead of one or a few factors). The reason for unhappiness, more often than for happiness, is found in an exceptional difference between couples in one of these characteristics or in the occurrence of a single major deviation or maladjustment.

DEGREES OF SIMILARITY BETWEEN HUSBANDS AND WIVES

Attitudes and Characteristics	*Correlation*	*Attitudes and Characteristics*	*Correlation*
Age	.905	Appearance	.413
Socio-economic status	.622	Visual acuity	.386
Communism	.602	Religious values	.380
Birth control	.585	Theoretical values	.370
Education	.574	Neurotic tendency	.299
Memory	.567	Weight	.274
Intelligence	.556	Economic values	.252
Associations	.468	Height	.241
Political values	.448	Aesthetic values	.234

Source: M. Schooley, "Personality Resemblance among Married Couples," *Jour. Abn. and Soc. Psychol.,* Vol. 31 (1936-37): 343.

Contrary to the more-or-less universal acknowledgment of the significance of certain personality traits in making happy or unhappy marriages, there is less agreement among the authorities as to the influences of these similarities in social status or attitudes.

Their importance, however, is confirmed in part by the ranking of the conditions that, in the opinion of husbands and wives, contribute most to happiness in marriage. These statements are the opinions of members of the American Association of University Women and their husbands.

Personal and social factors of marital happiness are found to be combined in the two primary qualities of understanding and companionship. What these words mean can be observed in two widely accepted indications of marital compatibility. One is the willingness of either husband or wife to admit the superiority of the other. The second is the tendency of both husband and wife to rate themselves above the average in most of the favorable personality traits.

IMPORTANT FACTORS IN MARITAL HAPPINESS

Factors	Rank Order as Preferred by Wives	Husbands
Social interests	1	1
Intellectual interests	2	4
Sharing of responsibility	3	2
Education	4	3
Attitude toward family	5	5
Religion	6	7
Ideals concerning material wealth and culture	7	8
Age of partners	8	6
In-laws	9	9
Childhood environment	10	10
Nationality of partners	11	11

Source: H. A. Houdlette, "The American Family Today," *Jour. Am. Assoc. Univ. Women,* Vol. 23 (1939): 140.

Of the chief circumstances in the personal and social history of married couples, Terman reported the following as the ten conditions most closely associated with happy marriages:[11]

1. Superior happiness of parents
2. A happy childhood
3. Absence of conflict with mother
4. Home discipline that was firm but not too harsh
5. Strong attachment to mother
6. Strong attachment to father
7. Absence of conflict with father
8. Parents were frank in matters of sex
9. Infrequency and mildness of punishment in childhood
10. Premarital attitude toward sex was wholesome and informed

Successful marriages

The characteristics of successful marriage resemble those that are also indicators of premarital social adjustment. How the pattern of childhood experiences and affectional relationships is connected with success in marriage is described by Burgess and Cottrell in their analysis of social types, cultural background, economic status, companionship, and sexual factors in successful marriages.[12]

[11] Lewis M. Terman, *op. cit.,* p. 372.
[12] E. W. Burgess and L. S. Cottrell, *op. cit.,* pp. 88 ff.

Social type. The person most adaptable in marriage is the socially mature and stable type. Indexes of this personal maturity are educational achievement, membership in group organizations, and participation in social affairs.

Cultural background. Similarities in cultural background are highly associated with success in marriage. Obvious differences in culture are as intimately associated with unhappiness as are the marked personality differences. Differences in education and religion, as independent factors, are not so significant among the sources of domestic discord as they are popularly suspected to be. They take on importance whenever they are aggravated by other disorganizing conditions. The cultural status of the husband is apparently more important than that of the wife as a determinant of success or failure in marriage.

Economic status. Regularity of income and stability of occupation (rather than the amount of income), a record of steady work, and economic security are favorable indications of successful marriage. In the case of the wife, a work record prior to marriage is more favorable than no work experience.

Companionship. In comparing the effects of age differences, courtship, and parental approval on marital success or failure, those marriages that are based on companionship were found to be more successful in harmonious social adjustment (in spite of differences that may occur in these other conditions) than marriages that are based on romantic ideals.

Sexual factors. The two outstanding correlations between sex and successful marriage are the absence of organic sexual defects and of interfering attitudes, and the type and sources of sexual knowledge that the couple has prior to marriage.

Miscellaneous factors. Other conditions associated closely with successful marriages are the desire for children, both husband and wife planning to work and working or, in the case of the wife, not planning to work and not working, living in a small city and in a single dwelling, buying or planning to buy a home, and not having many intimate contacts with parents-in-law. Of all these, the desire for children is the most highly related factor, whether or not the couple has children.

Evidence supporting these conclusions appears in the characteristics of families that seem most important to husbands and wives who consider their own marriage to be successful.

Characteristics of successful marriage mentioned by husbands are: (1) companionship with wife, (2) mutual understanding and accommodation, (3) love and sexual adjustment, (4) children, (5) specific traits of wife's character.

Characteristics of successful marriage mentioned by wives are: (1) companionship with husband, (2) interesting work and outside interests, (3) children, (4) specific traits of husband's character, (5) good management of money, (6) love and sexual adjustment.[13]

A detailed statement of the traits of personality and character in the rank order most preferred by husbands and wives is given in the study of the American Association of University Women mentioned previously.[14]

RANKING OF PERSONALITY TRAITS MAKING FOR SUCCESSFUL MARRIAGE

Personality Trait	*Rank Order as Preferred by Wives*	*Husbands*
Attitudes of cooperation	1	1
Good disposition	2	2
Sympathy toward problems of partner	3	4
Unselfishness	4	3
Attitude of frankness and cooperation in money matters	5	5
Ability to make and handle money	6	7
Habits of neatness and order	7	6

Most frequent problems in the successful marriage. Problems annoying to husbands whose family and marriage are considered successful are financial problems, which are mentioned much more often than any other, time and attention required by work, sexual adjustment, and problems of the wife's readjustment to the home after she has been employed outside the home.

Problems especially annoying to wives, are husband's temperament, financial problems, fatigue, housework and management of the home, jealousy, interferences of in-laws, and sexual adjustment.[15]

[13] Chase G. Woodhouse, "A Study of 250 Successful Families," *Social Forces,* Vol. 81 (1930): 511-532.

[14] H. A. Houdlette, "The American Family Today," *Jour. Am. Assoc. Univ. Women,* Vol. 23 (1939): 140.

[15] Chase G. Woodhouse, *op. cit.,* pp. 511-532. Compare with J. T. Landis, "Length of Time Required to Achieve Adjustment in Marriage," *Am. Sociol. Rev.,* Vol. 11 (1946): 666-677. In this report the rank order of difficulties of both husbands and wives are: (1) sex relations, (2) spending income, (3) social activities and recreation, (4) in-law relationships, (5) religion, (6) associating with mutual friends.

Unsuccessful marriages

Marriages that are regarded as distinctly unsatisfactory or unhappy have characteristics that are generally the opposite of those that are found in successful marriages. Lack of success is traced to a combination of two types of conditions—personality factors and material or circumstantial factors. Of these two sources, personality defects and conflicts in attitude are by far the most significant causes of marital discord. In brief summary, they are described by such terms as touchy, ill-tempered, hypercritical, or resentful of criticism, and they are compared with the common faults that identify the unadjusted adolescent.

Major personality differences. The most frequent complaints of husbands concerning wives and of wives concerning husbands suggest the chief personality defects in unsuccessful marriages.[16]

Husbands' complaints concerning wives. The wife nags, is not affectionate, is selfish and inconsiderate, complains too much, interferes with hobbies, is careless in her appearance, is quick tempered, interferes with discipline and is conceited and insincere.

Wives' complaints concerning husbands. The husband is selfish and inconsiderate, unsuccessful in business, untruthful, complains too much, does not show his affection or talk over matters, is harsh with the children, is touchy, and is not interested in children and home.

Other personality defects of the unhappily married person are being grouchy, demanding (always wanting one's own way), being critical of others or careless of the feelings of others, lacking in self-confidence, and easily excitable. In short, the personality and conduct of the unhappily married individual resemble the socially and emotionally immature types, characteristics that were found to be prominent among the unadjustments of behavior-problem children.

The primary sources of disagreement which may occur regardless of the happiness of the marriage are about (1) management of income, (2) recreation and use of leisure time, (3) family relations, (4) philosophy of life, (5) politics, (6) choice of friends, (7) religion, (8) ideals of conduct, (9) entertainment of relations and friends. These are the topics most frequently disagreed on by husbands and

[16] L. M. Terman, *op. cit.,* p. 99. See also H. M. McLean, "Emotional Background of Marital Difficulties," *Am. Sociol. Rev.,* Vol. 6 (1941): 384-388.

wives on the college level in a survey made ten years after graduation.[17]

More critical sources of marital discontent are indicated in the domestic situations that bring the family to the attention of a marriage-counseling agency. In general, these difficulties are fears, feelings of guilt concerning sex, personality difficulties, and conflicts with partner or relatives. Other problems in the order of their frequency are unwanted pregnancy, sexual problems (frigidity, contraception, venereal disease), inquiries about divorce, child guidance, sterility, adoption, and prenatal care.[18]

Summary: indications of good marital adjustment

From studies of success and failure in marriage, it is apparent that most unhappiness is to be traced to an ignorance of the conditions that most often make for discord and to an unwillingness or inability of couples after marriage to face their problems fully and frankly.

According to those studies that have tried to label, and to estimate the importance of, specific factors in happy marriages, these families have the highest rating of good social adjustment when the couples:

1. Have similar social and family backgrounds.
2. Have a good education and a similar educational background.
3. Frequently go to church, attend the same church, and may continue to go to Sunday school.
4. Have many friends, and each partner has a few but not too many friends of the opposite sex.
5. Have three or more memberships in social organizations.
6. Have six or more current interests.
7. Have several interests in common.
8. Have not been married previously.
9. Spent their childhood in the country rather than the city.
10. Had parents who were happy in their marriage.
11. Have a strong attachment for their parents.
12. Were approved in their marriage by parents on both sides.

[17] C. Robert Pace, *They Went to College,* University of Minnesota Press, Minneapolis, 1941, Table 6, p. 82. For a similar report, consult the unsigned article: "The Badly Educated Husband," *Family Life,* Vol. 8 (1948): 1-2.

[18] E. H. Mudd, "An Analysis of One Hundred Consecutive Cases in the Marriage Counsel of Philadelphia," *Ment. Hyg.,* Vol. 21 (1937): 202. See also G. P. Murdock, "A Comparative Anthropological Approach," in the series, "Problems of Sexual Behavior and Their Solution," *Jour. Soc. Hygiene,* Vol. 36 (1950): 133-138. A survey of premarital laxity as a social problem.

13. Had a long acquaintance before marriage.
14. Had a courtship of from two to four years.
15. Were engaged from two to three years.[19]

These requirements for the congenial relations of husband and wife are symbols of, not precise keys to, the essential conditions of social adjustment on the adult level. What they show most significantly is not the paramount or indispensable character of any one socially adjusting trait, but the need for the right combination on a mature basis.

Problems that interfere with the successful adjustment of parents are closely akin to the problems of children. Both are to be explained primarily by levels of maturity that are recognized as normal learning or achievement for different age and social groups. The only real difference is that in the family the good social adjustment of parents may be affected adversely by the presence of children, and likewise the good social adjustment of children may be affected adversely by incompatible husband-wife relations. This interaction between the generations is an illustration of how the immaturities of parents become the essential sources of the immaturities of children. Both are accounted for, and partly explained by, the absence of a well-planned system of child training.

All the social unadjustments in the family are traceable directly or indirectly to faulty child guidance. The example of the mother's employment outside of the home is but one of several conditions that may result in insufficient, or inefficient, child care. The studies of the employed mother are important in demonstrating that it is the quality, not the amount, of attention that is of most importance in the effective rearing of children. This difference is a matter of degree of parental oversight. It is further proof that the problems of parents and children are joint products of their maturity or immaturity.

Companionship, understanding, sound social discipline, and training, therefore, notwithstanding their subjectivity and variable interpretation, continue to be the important bases of effective family and parent-child relationships.

[19] R. E. Baber, *Marriage and the Family*, McGraw-Hill, New York, 1939, pp. 197-198. This is a summary of the studies by Burgess, Cottrell, and Terman. These conclusions are supported by recent studies as reported in the bibliography of this chapter.

Bibliography

Bossard, J. H. S., and E. S. Boll, *Family Situations,* University of Pennsylvania Press, Philadelphia, 1943.

Bowman, H. A., *Marriage for Moderns,* McGraw-Hill, New York, 1948.

Christensen, H. T., *Marriage Analysis: Foundations for Successful Family Life,* Ronald, New York, 1950.

Dickinson, R. L., and L. Beam, *One Thousand Marriages,* Williams and Wilkins, Baltimore, 1949.

Duvall, S. M., *Before You Marry,* Association Press, New York, 1949.

Fishbein, M., and E. W. Burgess, *Successful Marriage,* Doubleday, New York, 1947.

Kirkpatrick, C., *What Science Says about Happiness in Marriage,* Burgess, Minneapolis, 1947.

Koos, E. L., *The Middle-Class Family and Its Problems,* Columbia University Press, New York, 1948.

Popenoe, P. B., *Marriage is What You Make It,* Macmillan, New York, 1950.

Shryock, Harold, *Happiness for Husbands and Wives,* Review and Herald Publishing Association, Washington, D. C., 1949.

Skidmore, R. A., *Building Your Marriage,* Harper, New York, 1951.

Truxal, A. G., and F. E. Merrill, *The Family in American Culture,* Prentice-Hall, New York, 1947. Chaps. 6, 17, 20, 21, 24.

Questions

1. How may the family be affected by changing economic, legal, educational, or moral conditions?
2. Is there any proof in previous chapters that the family is sensitive to, or associated with, such problems as physical and mental health, mental deficiency, juvenile delinquency, occupations, business cycles, or minority group difficulties?
3. Why is the maturity of the person stressed as a primary requirement for stable family life?
4. What minimum combination of personal and social traits would you set up as a matrimonial barometer?
5. What primary societal conditions have led to the small family of contemporary society?
6. How many children must each family have to maintain a stationary population? A growing population?
7. Are there types of information that only parents can give children?
8. Do the findings of the premarital tests correlate with happiness in marriage and with successful marriage?
9. Which of the items in the premarital tests and in the criteria of happiness do you consider most valid and helpful as guides?
10. Which of these items are most accurately indicative of failing marriages?

CHAPTER 16

THE FAMILY—INSTITUTIONAL PROBLEMS

WHEN YOUNG PEOPLE MARRY, THEIR PRIMARY INTEREST IS IN EACH other. They have little appreciation or concern for the institution of the family or for marriage as a contract. Changes in the traditional family or in public morals suggest no immediate question for them, even though they are participants in these developments.

In their community relations most adults are like these youngsters. Such adults live in a limited world—limited in time and place and limited in their own personal maturity. Basic social problems rarely penetrate their consciousness because the irritations do not affect them directly.

Nevertheless, as suggested by personal strengths and weaknesses that individuals may bring to the family, both their success in marriage and the success of their own family are affected by domestic institutional trends in numerous ways.

The family is not just a collection of individuals reacting to the immediate demands of the day. In order to understand the family it is necessary to study its structure and its function as a social institution.[1]

Important problems of the institutional family include: the economic status of the family, health and intelligence in families, broken homes, housing, and leisure time. These problems may be identified in the changing cultural pattern of society, and most of them are discussed in the pages that follow.

[1] M. C. Elmer, *The Sociology of the Family,* Ginn, New York, 1945.

The institutional family

The family has been praised for every human virtue and damned for every human vice. However condemned or praised, it is always with us. The family is one of the most universal of human institutions. Every society has found it necessary to organize the relationships between the sexes and to provide for the responsibility of children. The family as a social institution represents a cultural uniformity. However, there has been a great deal of variability between societies and within societies.

There are differences in authority, system of kinship, forms of social control, marriage systems, and various conditions derived from relations with other social institutions. The family acts as an agency of cultural transmission. In this respect the individual family is selective. Segments of the culture are funneled to the individual through the family. This process is both deliberate and informal. The family must be able to adapt itself to change and at the same time to perpetuate its own traditions. For all these reasons, in modern urban society there is often a partial cultural break between generations.[2]

Not only does each generation not perpetuate itself in duplicate, but the family, acting as a mechanism for the transmission of culture, also changes in function. The family, once a unit of economic production and consumption, now, in the urban areas, is only a unit of consumption. Many educational, religious, and recreational activities formerly the responsibility of the family are now assumed by other social institutions. In addition, certain trends and problems of the American family are noted; among them are instability, specialization of function, secularization, urbanization, adaptability, and a trend away from the older authoritative family to the family based on companionship.[3] Such changes may involve problems over which the family has little or no control.

The family as a social institution continues to meet basic needs of society. These contributions are suggested in the previous chapter under the topic of "The Changing Family."

Is the family disappearing? Many people are disturbed about the

[2] R. E. L. Faris, "Interaction of Generations and Family Stability," *Am. Sociol. Rev.,* Vol. 12 (1947): 159-164.

[3] E. W. Burgess, "The Family in a Changing Society," *Am. Jour. Sociol.,* Vol. 53 (May 1948): 417-422.

instability of the family. Neglecting its favorable contributions, they ask the question, "Is the family disappearing?" This question is raised when people see the changing morality, the conflict between marriage as a sacrament and as a legal contract, and the many points of opposition between marriage as a personal agreement between two people and the family as a relationship between parents and children. When individuals feel that their personal happiness is threatened, there is little of societal compulsion or other values to maintain the marriage. The decreasing birth rate is regarded as a threat to the basic function of the family and as evidence of its possible disappearance.

Rates of delinquency, juvenile and adult, raise questions as to the personal functions of the family. Neither parents nor children, it is claimed, show enough respect for each other. All this criticism, intensified by the selfishness and brutality of the present, causes many backward glances to the family of the past.

The basic reason for concern is the fundamental belief that the family is still necessary for child education and personality development. This belief is reflected in the statement: "Best of all is the child's own home; failing that, a good foster home; and as a last resort, a good institution."

Proposals have been made to restore to the family all of its historical functions. Religious groups especially have urged the return of religion and moral instruction to the home. In fact, advocates may be found for the return of every function once carried on in the family circle. Another recommendation is the restoration of the family to the "prestige classes." The educated and economic elite are urged to assume family responsibility. A reflection of this point of view holds that: "Those who should have children don't; some of those who do, should not."

Experts admit the family is changing, but they do not agree on what it is becoming. One point of view holds that the family is likely to break up before the end of the twentieth century. This point of view sees a deterioration of the families of the "upper" socio-economic groups and threats of destruction of the families of the masses.[4] An opposite opinion is that, since the family is becoming smaller and its members are less economically dependent on

[4] C. C. Zimmerman, *Family and Civilization,* Harper, New York, 1947. J. K. Folsom, *The Family and Democratic Society,* John Wiley, New York, 1949.

each other, they become more emotionally dependent. This point of view concludes that the family is adaptable, and therefore admirably suited for survival. Aided and supported by the efficient services of other institutions and with limited and specialized obligations within the family, it now represents a cluster of social relations between husband and wife and children. Thus, the family emerges as a new and more stable unit. Families that survive the crises of transitional stages of civilization become new patterns of living together on a different basis of sound, healthy adaptability and resistance to moral collapse.

The family pattern. After World War II the marriage rate reached an all-time high—16.4 per 1,000 population. This rate was not only highest for any recorded year of this country's history, but the highest for the world, except for Hungary in 1919. The rate for Hungary in that year was 20.4 per 1,000 population. This figure emphasizes the long-time trend toward an increasing proportion of married persons in the population, and to a similar trend in the number of families. The trend is reflected in the table below.

MARRIAGE RATES, PER 1,000 POPULATION, IN THE UNITED STATES

Year	*Rate*	*Year*	*Rate*
1900	9.3	1930	9.2
1910	10.3	1940	12.1
1920	12.0	1950	11.2

Statistics on trends in number and size of families are dependent on definitions. A household refers to all the persons, regardless of their relationship to one another, who live in one dwelling unit. A family has been defined as a group of two or more persons related to each other and living together. Thus defined, there has been an increase of both families and households in the decade 1940-1950.

The typical household continues to be that with a married man as head. About seventy-nine per cent of the households in 1949 were husband-and-wife households, with or without other relatives or nonrelatives. About six per cent were headed by a man who was single, widowed, divorced, or married but not living with his wife. The remaining fifteen per cent were headed by a woman living alone or with relatives or nonrelatives. Ninety-four per cent of married couples maintained their own households in 1949. The remaining six per cent shared the living quarters of other persons or lived in hotels, rooming houses, and other quasihouseholds. About one-half of all families in the United States in 1949 had no children of their own under eighteen years of age living with them. Close to one-fourth of all families had only one child.[5]

Economic status of the family

The way a family earns its living and the way income is spent play a large part in its system of personal relations. Changing roles of husband and wife, the economic dependence and independence of women, the mother employed outside of the home, all can be interpreted among the changing economic reactions of the new family.

Who are the poor families? Personal income in 1948 in the United States reached a staggering figure of 414 billions of dollars. In such a period of prosperity it might be expected that everyone would enjoy a comfortable income. Yet in this period of plenty one out of every ten families received twenty dollars a week or less. Of the forty million families in the United States, ten million received less than forty dollars a week. There were 1,700,000 farm families with incomes under $1,000 a year, a quarter of them with five or more children. Despite fluctuations in total income, the trend of unequal distribution remains relatively constant.

When $2,000 or less is used as a criterion of low income, it is estimated that two-thirds of nonfarm low-income families fall into three groups. One group includes families in which the head of the family has been disabled by accident or disease. In the second group are the broken families, that is, families headed by women because of widowhood, desertion, or divorce. The third group is composed of families whose head is sixty-five years of age or more. Other families in the low-income group are families temporarily there for various reasons, and families of incompetents, misfits, and others who have trouble getting a job. Characteristically, then, low-income families are broken families, families of unskilled workers, and families lacking education.

All families have the same essential economic problems: to increase income; to secure the maximum in the form of food, shelter, clothing, and other goods and services; to insure that illness, acci-

[5] United States Department of Commerce, Bureau of the Census, *Current Population Reports: Population Characteristics,* Series P-20, No. 26, Washington, D. C., Jan. 27, 1950.

dent, unemployment, and old age do not remove the means of adequate livelihood.[6]

How families spend their income. The manner in which a family spends its income is just as significant as the income earned. Both in depression and inflation the puzzle of making ends meet continues to frustrate the home-maker.

In spite of the fact that families differ in consumption habits, in their budgets, and in educational standards, as well as in income, there are few or no comparisons to supply accepted rules as to what families ought to spend or where subsistence levels stop and standards begin. However a review of actual expenditures does supply guides upon both of these subjects.

AVERAGE MONEY EXPENDITURES OF FAMILIES AND SINGLE PERSONS IN CITIES, 1944

A. MONEY EXPENDED

INCOME GROUP	*Food*	(a) *Shelter*	*Clothing*	(b) *Household Operation*	(c) *Miscellaneous*
Under $1,000	$ 368	$231	$ 82	$ 74	$ 215
$1,000–1,500	506	285	157	97	324
1,500–2,000	646	328	231	124	443
2,000–2,500	747	379	268	141	503
2,500–3,000	908	424	353	193	633
3,000–4,000	1,034	484	456	232	737
4,000–5,000	1,147	546	621	297	1,028
5,000 and over	1,383	635	836	465	1,059

B. PER CENTS

INCOME GROUP	*Food*	(a) *Shelter*	*Clothing*	(b) *Household Operation*	(c) *Miscellaneous*
Under $1,000	39.9	23.8	8.5	7.6	22.2
$1,000–1,500	36.9	20.8	11.5	7.1	23.7
1,500–2,000	36.5	18.5	13.0	7.0	25.0
2,000–2,500	36.7	18.6	13.2	6.9	24.6
2,500–3,000	36.2	16.8	14.1	7.7	25.2
3,000–4,000	35.1	16.4	15.5	8.0	25.0
4,000–5,000	31.5	15.0	17.1	8.2	28.2
5,000 and over	31.6	14.5	19.1	10.6	24.2

(a) includes fuel and light
(b) includes furnishings and equipment
(c) excludes taxes, war bonds, and insurance

Source: Mo. Lab. Rev., Vol. 62 (1946), No. 1, p. 2. See Doris P. Rothwell, "Interim Adjustment of Consumer's Price Index," *Mo. Lab. Rev.*, Vol. 72 (1951), No. 4, pp. 421-429.

[6] R. L. Bonde, "Financial Plans in the Family Cycle," *Jour. Home Econ.*, Vol. 42 (1950): 25-27. H. Kyrk, "Economic Problems of the Family," *Jour. Home Econ.*, Vol. 40 (1948): 444-445. *Mo. Lab. Rev.*, "Low Income Families and Economic Stability," Vol. 70 (1950): 50-51. S. Slichter, "High Cost of Low Incomes," *Soc. Ser. Rev.*, Vol. 24 (1950): 257-259.

Between different income groups, food is only slightly variable in quality, though highly variable in quantity and cost. Shelter and clothing are slightly variable in quantity, but highly variable in quality and cost. Fuel and light are only slightly variable in quantity, quality, and cost. Among miscellaneous items, expenditures for education, religion, and recreation are slightly variable, while expenditures for health, vacations, insurance, and savings are highly variable. The study of variation in budgets and income leads further to the conclusion that, when income and occupational or social status are given, standards of living can be determined with a small margin of error.

Ten other factors besides income are considered in budget making or in the evaluation of standards:

1. Size of family.
2. Age and sex of children.
3. Occupation of the father.
4. Housekeeping skill of the mother.
5. Education of both parents and the standards of living in the homes from which they came.
6. Size of community, city, or town.
7. Marketing facilities and local costs of living.
8. Type of housing.
9. Social and religious customs affecting expenditures.
10. Personal choice.[7]

These are the relatively intangible sources of variation in budget making. All are important, especially those that, like the size of family, have a direct bearing upon income, or those that can be measured quantitatively.

From the spending habits of families, one can deduce generalizations that correspond in part with those established by Engel in 1857. After an examination of budgets of Belgian and Saxon working-class families, Engel formulated the following four laws in the variation of expenditures between different income groups:

1. The greater the income, the smaller the percentage outlay for food.
2. The percentage outlay for clothing is approximately the same, whatever the income.
3. The percentage for lodging or rent and for fuel and lighting is invariably the same, whatever the income.

[7] B. R. Andrews, *op. cit.*, p. 82. M. C. Elmer, *op. cit.*, Chap. 15.

4. As the income increases in amount, the percentage of outlay for sundries becomes greater.[8]

In 1911, Streightoff suggested a reversal in two of these laws, noting from American conditions that expenditures for clothing tend to increase with increasing income, while expenditures for housing and for fuel and light tend to decrease.[9] These revisions are confirmed by the data of the table on page 384.

By a comparative analysis of incomes and budgets, several much debated problems in standards of living are clarified. Income data show that few families in wage-earning groups are at all concerned with standards, if standards imply some degree of choice in expenditures or in quality of articles consumed. Most wage earners fall below the minimum standard of wholesome living, where standards first become apparent. They are chiefly concerned with budgets as planned expenditures.

A survey of economic competency through examination of prevailing income and standards of living leads to the conclusion that when both the latter are studied together, an accurate measurement of trends in social well-being may be computed. Standards lose their subjectivity, and variations in spending or in habits of consumption are found to be related to a series of known factors, of which the most important is family income.

One of the surprising facts is the apathy of the public toward the many problems of standards. Few families are at all concerned with systematized spending habits, budgets, or with the common facts of consumption, although organizations of home makers and some commercial associations (for intelligent advertising) have recently given some attention to wastes in retail buying. Perhaps the chief reason underlying public indifference is the attitude already mentioned, which on the one hand tends to overemphasize income as the only important variable in planning budgets, or on the other tends to regard estimated standards as too subjective to be standards.

Married women at work. Under primitive conditions, and practically without exception under every economic order prior to the industrialization of society, woman's social status was secure, both in industry and in the family. Woman has always been a worker whose services were as important as those of man. Although sex differences

[8] F. H. Streightoff, *The Standard of Living,* Houghton Mifflin, 1911, pp. 12-13.

[9] *Ibid.,* p. 20. C. C. Zimmerman, *Consumption and Standards of Living,* Van Nostrand, New York, 1936, Chaps. 5, 11, 15.

were recognized historically as a basis for specialization in industry or particular occupations as much as they are in the present, and although women were assigned "secondary positions" by societies in the past, there was never any question of their productive capacity or of their dependency.

Most people think of the dependence of the wife and children upon the earnings of the father as a time-honored custom. This belief is held to such an extent that the presence of women and children in industry is cited today as proof of the destruction of the modern family system. History's version of the economic copartnership between husband and wife gives an entirely different picture. The dependence of women and children upon the earnings of one male is a comparatively recent innovation. It is scarcely more than a century old, at least so far as the manual workers, who form the majority of the population, are concerned, and is more a product of industrial than of domestic changes.

Industrialism transferred the productive activities of the family to the factory. With this transition, women as a class lost their economic independence; they became dependent upon the wages of their husbands, and their labor was limited to domestic work. This economic change also accounts for the rise of the small-family system from the patriarchal or gross family (consisting of many relatives in one household), and for the insecure family status of single women, widows, and dependent children. "When woman ceased to be a producer, she became dependent."[10]

The social consequences of the industrial revolution entailed other changes in her social position. Marriage became a serious economic burden to the wage earner, rather than an advantageous cooperative enterprise. Women and children, who were largely self-supporting before, became "natural dependents." As a result, marriage itself came to be regarded as a source of livelihood from the woman's point of view. The employment of women and children, consequently, is no threat at all to the institutions of marriage and the family. In fact, any tendency toward employment is simply a return to the traditional industrial status of women. If, as Reuter and Runner contend, women become self-respecting as they become self-supporting, such employment is as much a matter of social necessity and personal choice as marriage or childbearing.

[10] E. B. Reuter and J. Runner, *The Family,* McGraw-Hill, New York, 1930, p. 435.

Married women work outside of the home not primarily because they want to but because economic circumstances demand it. The proportion of married women working for pay has been increasing for more than half a century. Women, especially those who are married, flocked to work in great numbers after World War II to combat the high cost of living. Slightly more than one-half of the 17,300,000 women working in nonfarm occupations in March, 1951 were married.

This increase has raised conflicts of value. Does the fact that married women work out of the home disrupt the function of the family? Does it affect the birth rate? The trend mentioned above is related to the long-term decline of the birth rate. Durard maintains that the future course of the birth rate will depend mainly on circumstances other than the number of employed women. In his opinion, public policy regarding employment of married women should consider the economic advantage to the nation of their employment.[11] Locke has shown no significant differences between the marital adjustment of wives who are engaged in full employment and those in full time housekeeping.

As indicated previously (Chapter 15), studies of the employed mother emphasize the quality, not the amount of attention as being most significant in effective rearing of children.

Marriage and economics. Jacob served seven years for Rachel and received Leah and yet another seven years before Rachel was his wife.[12] Here was a fusion of love and economics. In the history of marriage, economic problems are as significant as others.

While marriage has been linked to the "romantic fallacy" in the culture of the United States, there is no escape from the solid facts of economics. Full employment probably deserves a share of the credit for the marriage boom following World War II. Young girls have been urged in many varied ways to marry into a higher social class or at least not to marry "beneath themselves." But marriage within one's own or a related class is typical experience. Numerous studies reaffirm this statement of occupational endogamy.

There are few studies in the literature on the relation of education to divorce and separation. Burgess and Cottrell's study shows

[11] J. Durard, "Married Women in the Labor Force," *Am. Jour. Sociol.*, Vol. 52 (1946): 217-223. H. J. Locke and M. Mackeprang, "Marital Adjustment and the Employed Wife," *Am. Jour. Sociol.*, Vol. 54 (1949): 536-538.

[12] Genesis 29.

that higher education is correlated positively with better marital adjustment. However, Ogburn notes that the relation between education and family unity would be reduced if the factor of earnings could be eliminated.[13]

It should also be recalled that regularity of savings and steady employment are more significant than amount of income as indicators of probable family adjustment.

Economics and health. The amount of income a family earns is not merely an economic statistic. Length of life and good or poor health are closely related to these social and economic differences.

Certain diseases, particularly pneumonia, tuberculosis, and rheumatic fever, consistently appear more often among low-income families. The correlation between tuberculosis mortality by age and economic groups shows an inverse relation. This death rate is greater for adult males than for adult females. Each of these conditions suggests the presence of specific occupational factors, such as strain, postponement of medical attention, and greater extrafamilial exposure of males. Problems associated with tuberculosis are to be found in such familial problems as: separation from home, a sense of lowered status in the home, marital problems, and change of vocational plans, careers, and ways of living.[14]

Chronic illness has been shown to be related to socio-economic status both as cause and effect. Chronic illness creates an atmosphere in the family that may be detrimental to the individuals in the family. A child's reaction to the home situation created by psychoneurotic parents is unlikely to be conducive to either physical or mental good health.

Studies of public school children reaffirm the importance of family status in relation to health. One such study of Philadelphia public school children over a span of time, 1930-1942, indicates that dental decay, defective tonsils, defective vision, and nasal obstruction are correlated inversely with the ranking of parental occupation.[15]

[13] W. F. Ogburn, "Education, Income and Family Unity," *Am. Jour. Sociol.*, Vol. 53 (1948): 474-476.

[14] P. S. Lawrence, "Chronic Illness and Socio-Economic Status," *Pub. Health Rpts.*, Vol. 63 (Nov. 1948), No. 47, pp. 1507-1521. M. Terris, "Relation of Economic Status to Tuberculosis Mortality by Age and Sex," *Am. Jour. Pub. Health*, Vol. 39 (1948): 1061-1070. S. Bloom, "Some Economic and Emotional Problems of the Tuberculosis Patient and His Family," *Pub. Health Rpts.*, Vol. 63 (April 1948), No. 14, pp. 448-455.

[15] F. H. Lund and others, "Health Indices in Relation to Age, Sex, Race, and Socio-economic Status," *Jour. Soc. Psychol.*, Vol. 24 (1946): 111-117.

Economic status is an important index of environment. Such status determines to a considerable degree the amount and kind of food, housing, medical care, education, and recreation that the child receives. The adverse effects of economic status in all illness is most obvious in the very poorest families.

There exists some evidence in the sociological and psychological literature that companionship, affection, happiness, and common interests in the family serve to create those conditions that minimize the possibility of mental breakdown.

Broken families

In family living there are evidences of instability in many apparently normal, adjusted homes as well as in nearly broken or actually broken homes. The disorders of such families differ both in type and degree. What the eventual outcome may be—whether it is a demoralized family unit or person—depends upon the resourcefulness and adaptability of the persons concerned.

Most of the causes of broken homes and most family disorders are relatively minor in importance. As single events they would not lead to irreparable family damage. But any family does have unusual difficulty in weathering marital or family upsets when these isolated factors cumulate and combine. Then the most usual result is a rupture of marital and family ties. This rupture is also a matter of degree. It is graded from the discordant household in which parents and children live together under constant tension, to the friendly separation, and to the permanent separation of divorce, abandonment, or widowhood.

A changed social situation in the family is a matter of great importance to the student of family relations. Sociological study is interested in the nature of the change or disorder, what its sources are, and what attitudes accompany these changes.[16]

There are many forms of domestic crisis, conflict, and frustrations of personality in the family in addition to divorce, desertion, and widowhood. Such conditions are found in families broken by suicide, illegitimacy, excessive mobility, separation, annulment, confinement in an institution, in families of common-law marriage and of widowers, and in families that are broken by the placement of

[16] H. R. Mowrer, *Personality Adjustment and Domestic Discord,* American Book Co., New York, 1935, Chaps. 4, 11. E. R. Mowrer, *Family Disorganization,* University of Chicago Press, Chicago, 1927, Chap. 4.

children in foster homes. Since it is recognized that readjustments in all these domestic situations tend to be similar for the individuals who remain in the home, desertion and widowhood will be taken as typical causes of broken families. Both problems represent a drastic interruption of ordinary social relations in family life, and in their study or treatment the need for family conservation and counseling becomes obvious.[17]

Desertion as a social problem. Desertion has been described as the poor man's substitute for divorce or vacation. It has also been called an escape mechanism from an unsatisfactory domestic life. It may be either or neither. Desertion is class-limited, appearing with no great frequency outside of median and low wage-earning groups. In this respect, it differs from divorce and separation, and might be called an effort toward economic adjustment. It also may be temporary, chronic, or spurious (that is, pretended in order to secure poor-relief). Many different conditions have been cited as probable causes, and each of these must be examined thoroughly, because desertion is often viewed, like many other social problems, as a self-evident form of degeneracy.

In spite of the fact that desertion has a definite legal status and is usually regarded as a criminal offense, there are few complete studies either of the deserter or of the abandoned family. Most studies are taken from the records of family welfare agencies or domestic relations courts, wherein poverty or criminality is merged with the fact of desertion.

Some significant social factors can be derived from the records. Desertion is primarily a male characteristic. It is repetitive and many deserters have previous court records. Desertion is an urban phenomenon, occurring with housing congestion and overcrowded homes.

Since there are no national agencies and no one agency in the state or local community to deal exclusively with this problem, only indications of the incidence and trend of desertion can be given. In fact, the amount of desertion can be measured indirectly from its contribution to other problems more easily than it can be measured directly. The home broken by desertion is credited as being one of the primary causes of several problems. Prior to the estab-

[17] Lorraine Jennrich, *Case Work in Motherless Families,* National Conference on Social Work, 1936, pp. 158-166. E. N. White, "Experiments in Family Consultation Centers," *Social Forces,* Vol. 12 (Oct. 1933-May 1934): 557.

lishment of the Social Security program, when family welfare agencies were responsible for abandoned mothers and children, ten to thirteen per cent of the entire load of such agencies came from deserted families and nearly twenty per cent of their budget was expended for their relief. The deserted home has also an important connection with the dependency and delinquency of children in institutions and courts, and with the large proportion of mothers in industry.

The "perilous first five years" are even more hazardous in desertion than in divorce cases. The occurrence of desertion at an earlier period than divorce indicates the presence of serious conditions of maladjustment that require early diagnosis and treatment. The proportion of men and women under thirty years of age in deserted families (from thirty-nine to fifty-four per cent) corresponds closely to the proportion of desertions during the first five years of marriage.

Although opinion as to the influence of poverty and unemployment upon desertion is divided, and poverty is mentioned infrequently as a primary factor, occupational groupings are closely correlated with desertion. The skilled and semiskilled groups contribute a proportion of deserters that is considerably in excess of their distribution in the general population.

The problem of widowhood. Most historical summaries indicate a tendency on the part of the definers of social problems to designate certain conditions as the special problems of women or children. This has been the case with widowhood and with such other ancient difficulties as illegitimacy, unmarried motherhood, prostitution, and child dependency. Actually all these problems are aspects of a changing and unorganized or disorganized family. They continue to remain important because they point out basic defects in the social institutions.

Recent researches, moreover, show that there are few or no problems that can be called the special problems of men, women, or children. Usually they are the problems of social institutions in which sex or age factors are exaggerated either because of social status or individual differences.

The problem of widowhood illustrates this multiple origin of social maladjustments. Over the conditions that determine their social status, and especially over their vocational opportunities and the economic status of the family, women have had little control. In historical or contemporary aspects, the social problems of widowhood are practically coextensive with two social conditions: the insecure industrial and family status of women, and the problems of women in industry, both of which represent the institutional background of family dependency.

The two general reasons given for the larger number of widows is the higher death rate of adult males in the younger age groups, and the greater rate of remarriage among widowers. In recent census reports, there has been a slight increase in widowhood, due largely to the increasing proportion of the population in the upper age groups. This increase has little connection with the economic problem of widowhood, which is restricted primarily to younger women.

WIDOWS IN THE UNITED STATES (APRIL 1948)

Age	*Number*	*Per Cent*
Under 35	201,750	3
35-54	1,614,000	24
55 and over	4,909,250	73
Total	6,725,000	100

Source: "Widows and Widowhood," *Statis. Bull.*, Metropolitan Life Insurance Company, Vol. 30 (Sept. 1949), No. 9, p. 5.

WIDOWED, DIVORCED, OR SEPARATED PERSONS AS PER CENT OF EVER MARRIED, AGES 14 AND OVER BY SEX—UNITED STATES

	Men		*Women*	
Marital Status	*1940*	*1950*	*1940*	*1950*
Widowed	6.3	5.1	16.2	15.0
Divorced	1.9	2.2	2.3	2.7
Separated	4.8	2.8	4.2	3.3
Total	13.0	10.1	22.7	21.0

Source: Statis. Bull. Metropolitan Life Insurance Company, Vol. 32 (March 1951), No. 3, p. 3.

In April 1948 there were about 6.7 million widows in the United States. More than half of them had been widowed at least ten years. About one-fourth of the widows had not reached their fortieth birthday at the time of widowhood. Younger widows for the most part maintained their households. However, as the period of widowhood increases, more widows give up their own homes. Two factors are probably at work in this respect—it is increasingly difficult to earn a living as one gets older, and some widows move in with adult children. In 1948 one of every ten widows had the responsibility of caring for a dependent child. Almost half of widows with preschool children were in the labor force. There were about 2,000,000 widows in the labor force in 1948. Seventy-five per cent of them were employed as clerks, operatives, or service workers.

Recent Social Security legislation has improved the economic position of the widow but no security program can duplicate the money value of a husband earning an adequate wage. Systematic savings, life insurance, and other types of investments can safeguard to some extent the economic values of the home.

The possible family damage resulting from widowhood can be summarized under four problems. Widowhood is a problem of poverty due to the loss of husband's earnings. In the absence of normal parental relationships, widowhood presents a cross-section of the problems of the broken home. It is a severe strain upon family adjustments, both as the result of bereavement and as a problem of social readjustment. Finally, the problem of securing income, involving the employment of the mother and children, exposes the family to many physical, mental, and social hazards.

Housing

On the assumption that one third of families are ill-housed, then 15 million families need better housing. As of 1951 it would cost (at $1,000 per room) at least 90 billion dollars to provide for this immediate need.

The problem of housing is not new. It can be understood only in terms of the social and economic pattern of the country. Each generation's disregard of adequate housing, as well as improvements, become the housing problem of the next generation. Model tenements of 1880 became the monstrosities of 1900. There is every evidence that many modern apartments of 1950 will be the slums of the year 2,000.

The basic deficiencies of the substandard housing are usually defined in terms of crowding (more than 1.5 persons per room), inadequate water supply, toilet facilities, or heating, and other similar indices. It is recognized that overcrowding creates health hazards and a social setting favorable to the development of conflicts and tension. Contrary to popular impression, overcrowding is actually more prevalent in farm families. Farm houses are in poorer condition than nonfarm dwellings. In 1947, eighteen per cent of farm homes were in the need of major repairs and were without private bath and flush toilet, compared to six per cent of nonfarm homes. Indicative of the relative condition of farm homes is the fact that two-thirds of those homes lacked running water. Homes of Negro families are in worse condition than those of whites. Twenty-five per cent of homes occupied by Negroes were in need of major repair in 1947.

A record of improvement in the 1940's is indicated by the fact that homes considered in good condition or needing minor repairs increased from 82 per cent in 1940 to 90 per cent in 1947. The number of homes built increased after World War II. This increased number of homes brought an increase in home owners. In 1940, 40 per cent of the families owned their homes; in 1947, 55 per cent. This increase is partly due to the housing shortage of World War II. It is likewise true that the number of mortgages has risen, so that home ownership statistics may be misleading. Accompanying the improved conditions following World War II was a decline in the number of married couples sharing living quarters with others. However, in 1950 nearly six per cent of all married couples still lived with others.[18]

In spite of these indications of improvement, the concern of Congress and of public and private agencies points to glaring inadequacies in housing.

There are a number of popular fallacies about slum clearance and low-rent housing.[19] Some of these fallacies are:

1. The poor are a different race of people.
2. Poor people don't want good housing.
3. Poor people themselves, rather than the conditions under which they live, need reform.
4. Poor people like to be dirty. (The popular bathtub story.)
5. Good houses do not pay.
6. Clearing slums is a matter of rehabilitating worn-out structures.
7. Public housing alone is sufficient to clear slums.
8. To clear a slum, a public housing project must be built on a slum site.

[18] Housing and Home Finance Agency, *The Housing Situation: The Factual Background,* Washington, D. C., June 1949. M. A. Pond, "Housing and Health," *Am. Jour. Pub. Health,* Vol. 39 (1949): 454-458. Midcentury White House Conference on Children and Youth, *Children and Youth at the Midcentury, A Chart Book.*

[19] Housing and House Finance Agency, *The Relation Between Slum Clearance and Urban Redevelopment and Low Rent Public Housing,* Washington, D. C., Nov. 1950. L. Veiller, *Housing Reform,* Russell Sage Foundation, Charities Publishing Committee, New York, 1910.

Federal interest in housing. Until the 1930's the federal government's interest in housing was limited to routine reports, the supplying of information, and investigation of housing standards. During the depression part of the program to provide homes for low-income families was started under W. P. A. After 1933 the government halted foreclosures, encouraged home construction and loaned money for mortgage and repairs. The United States Housing Act of 1937 provided the first low-rent public-housing program in the nation. It was also the first nationwide effort to cope with slums. The policy of "equivalent elimination" was announced. This means that a slum dwelling must be destroyed for each new home erected.

The Housing Act of 1949 goes beyond the limited formula of 1937, which restricted slum clearance to public-housing operations. The attack was now to be private as well as public. The act of 1949 considers the improvement of housing conditions of all families as a basis of slum clearance. Slum clearance and housing are on a community basis rather than an isolated housing project. This act authorizes financial aid to local communities for the clearance of slums and for low-cost housing, and also introduces a program of assistance for farm housing. Contributions and loans were authorized enabling the construction of 810,000 additional units of low-rent public-housing over a six year period. This total is in addition to the 191,700 low-rent public-housing units existing in April 1949.

The Housing Act of 1950 expanded existing aids to housing and liberalized F. H. A. mortgage insurance for housing cooperatives and low-priced housing.[20]

Considerable conflict of values is expressed between the real estate interests and the advocates of public housing. Many critics of public housing call it socialistic, asserting that it destroys incentive. Advocates of public housing maintain that private construction failed to meet the need of low-income families. The 1949 Housing Act encouraged more private investors, and it has been

[20] "Federal Housing Policy Developments, 1932-1950," *Mo. Lab. Rev.*, Vol. 71 (1950): 682-83. R. J. Johnson, "The Housing Act of 1949 and Health Development Programs," *Pub. Health Rpts.*, Vol. 64 (Oct. 1949), No. 40, 1331-1336. 81st Congress, "Summary of Housing Act of 1950," *Senate Document No. 165*, United States Government Printing Office, Washington, D. C., 1950. Charles Abrams, *The Future of Housing*, Harper, New York, 1946.

recognized in statements from public-housing associations that the sphere of public housing is limited to the low-income groups.

Despite the number of housing census reports, a great deal of research is necessary in this field. The 1940 census of housing is frequently used as a bench mark for comparisons with other surveys. During World War II, more than 1,000 vacancy surveys were conducted. The Bureau of The Census conducted sample surveys in 1944, 1945, and again in 1947. In 1946 surveys were taken of veterans' housing.

Two of the most widely used systems of housing classification are the United States Housing Census and The Real Property Inventory Technique. Certain limitations have been noted in these systems. These limits led to the development of the appraisal method for measuring the quality of housing. This appraisal method is being used by increasing numbers of public health departments.

Research is necessary in housing and family patterns, housing and health, physiological aspects of housing, housing education and attitudes, economic and tenure aspects, and public and private housing. Numerous myths are current concerning the complex relation of slums to social disorder, the social effects of rehousing, and the financial liability of slums to the municipality.[21]

Home ownership. Even though home ownership reached a record peak at midcentury, numerous students have raised serious questions regarding its advisability. The hazardous nature of investing in property is noted. Mortgage abuses are called to attention such as exorbitant interest, the personal nature of the obligation, and the rigidity of the obligation. The other side of the ledger emphasizes that home owners are for the most part stable and secure. To the urban family it is a means of resisting the adverse effects of urbanization on family life. Home owners are more satisfied with their housing arrangements. People who have property interests are more likely to have community interests.[22]

[21] J. P. Dean, "The Myths of Housing Reform," *Am. Sociol. Rev.*, Vol. 14 (1949): 281-288. A. A. Twichell, "An Appraisal Method For Measuring the Quality of Housing," *Am. Sociol. Rev.*, Vol. 13 (1948): 278-287. L. F. Johnson, "Housing: a 1950 Tragedy," *Survey*, Vol. 86 (1950): 551-555. D. G. Carter, "Research Problems and Needs in Rural Housing," *Jour. Home Econ.*, Vol. 41 (1949): 447-448.

[22] T. Caplow, "Home Ownership and Location Preferences in a Minneapolis Sample," *Am. Sociol. Rev.*, Vol. 13 (1948): 725-730. L. Cohen, "Family Characteristics of Home Owners," *Am. Jour. Sociol.*, Vol. 55 (1950): 545-571.

Social correlates and housing. Housing is not merely a matter of economics, of politics, of plumbing and sanitation. It may "take a heap of living to make a house a home," but the fact remains that the house provides the area in which the social relations of a family are conducted.

Basic factors of housing adequacy are recognized as elements of physical health and social and emotional well-being. Blighted areas are focal points for crime, delinquency, and infant mortality. The coexistence of bad housing and bad health does not prove causal relationship. Nevertheless, every comparative study of poor housing and good housing adds to the bill of indictment of poor housing. A disproportionate share of public funds go to slum areas for extra police and fire protection, courts, sanitation, and social and health services. Children in slum areas are more likely than children of other areas to have serious health and social problems.

Housing needs are related to the life cycle of the family. Housing requirements begin to increase before the family has achieved its full economic capacity, and changes in requirements occur when economic capacity is on the wane.

One of the major criticisms of small houses is that they provide little privacy for members of the household. A family needs both areas for common meeting and areas of privacy. It can hardly be doubted that the form of the house will have a direct influence on the social relations of the members of the family.

It is a matter of concern that the voluminous data on housing have been accompanied by such a paucity of studies concerning social change accompanying change in housing.

Leisure time

A primary reason for the current emphasis that is being put upon the play life of the child and the recreational needs of adults is the association between play and social achievement. The industrialization and urbanization of society have increased the amount of time available for recreation. This increased time has not resulted in noticeable improvements in the use of leisure. The play life of adults and children is neither well conceived, restful, recreative, nor mature.

Lag between the theoretical importance of play and its actual realization in contemporary life is explained by an earlier philosophy that taught that the real business of life is work. This point of view produced the educational philosophy of vocational training and omitted what is now the equally needed training for leisure.

Play began to be considered seriously toward the end of the nineteenth century. At that time, its advocates felt obliged to prove its desirability and benefits. They explained play both philosophically and psychologically; children need to play because it is instinctive, because through it they are expending surplus energy, or because they are reliving the experience of the human race.

Play as a socializing agency. Fully two or more decades were spent in these apologies before play was recognized as a natural activity. The discovery was made that wholesome play is both a maturing process and an indication that development in later periods will be successful.

As an instrument of importance wholly because of its own wholesome socializing effects, play is now emphasized for various reasons. It is important to the health and normal bodily growth of the child. Through it the child acquires skills that are the basis of all learning, and play thus becomes an essential part of education. It is a means of instruction in a broad sense in training the child in those first social contacts necessary to all social adjustment, and hence is a means of instruction in the social, ethical, and aesthetic values. Implicit in all these contributions are its services as a means of relaxation. It is one of the ways of effecting a balance between work and fatigue in a complex and high-speed society. Play offers training in voluntary cooperation. It reproduces the activities, struggles and achievements of group life. It trains the individual to adapt his own interests and wishes to the requirements and interests of the group in which he is living and with which he will have future contacts.

When play life of the individual is examined critically, the most obvious conclusion is that society is far from realizing the goals that theory has so completely established. The actual number of play or recreational activities of the average individual is limited, and his membership in voluntary group associations is similarly restricted and lacking in stimulation. Perhaps the general characteristic of the status of recreation in this country is traceable to the average adult program, which is described as meagre, drab, nonrecreative, and of little or no value to the individual's personal and social development.

Because the home is the chief center of recreation for the young child, his play program and opportunities are limited by the average family's social philosophy as well as by insufficient resources for home play and by the cost of play materials. It becomes a growing source of complaint as children reach their teens or young adulthood and find no opportunity to center their recreational activities in the home. This is one of the reasons why the leisure-time activities of youth are described as consisting largely of shiftless idleness or sophisticated pleasure-seeking.

A second source of complaint is the predominance of passive activities in the commercialized amusements and in public recreation, in radio, movies, theatre, and the spectator sports, for example.

A third explanation for the narrow range of play opportunities is found in the deficiencies of social institutions other than the family. In spite of all that has been said about the educational, aesthetic, and moralizing values of play, the school and church still occupy a subordinate and secondary role as recreational centers.

Finally there is the general observation that society as a whole fails miserably in preparing the young for leisure.

Interests in the radio, movies, comics, and television. The radio enters millions of homes; the movies pull millions of families out of homes. Parents have been much concerned about the character of radio and movies because of their potential influence on children. How the radio or movies affect children depends mostly on listening habits in the case of the former, and the frequency of attendance in the case of the latter. Listening habits are conditioned more by the child's age and intelligence, the social status of his family, and the time that the program is offered than by the program itself. Movie attendance is similarly affected.

Precisely what effects either radio or movies may have upon the conduct of children is hard to determine because of the other variables in the life of the child. These variables may distort the findings or they may be the real sources of the observed disorders.

A generally accepted attitude toward both radio and movie programs is that their ill effects are most noticeable in children who are unstable for other social reasons or because of their own temperamental makeup.

The comic book has aroused the most anxiety among parents and educators because of its potential ill-effects upon either character or reading habits in general. Opposition to the reading of comics is considerably less now than it was a decade ago. At that time, the grammar was generally bad, the printing and paper were cheap, and the art work was crude. With improvements in all these aspects of makeup, opposition abated somewhat and was hastened by the discovery that a moderate interest in comic books is normal.

Parents and educators also learned by trial and error that trying to force a child to read worthwhile books is rarely successful. Finally, the conclusion was reached that about the only likelihood of abnormality in a preference for comic books is in reading them so much that other forms of reading or recreation are excluded.

The suspicion is abroad that television has deeply affected the habits of the families of the United States. Precisely what family habits have been affected are not yet known. Studies of the effects of television have been spotty, and all sorts of wild claims have been made. Tentative conclusions may be listed:

1. Families with television have had an increase in visitors but they have visited less.
2. Driving for pleasure has been slightly reduced after acquiring a set.
3. Sport events have been hit.
4. Movie going has suffered.
5. Families read less.
6. Viewing is a solitary activity. Families report less conversation.
7. Hardest hit of all has been radio. The chief reason given for listening at all to the radio is the superiority of radio news.

The solitary nature of much of recreation. Despite the theoretical claims of social values of recreation, much of contemporary leisure-time activity is of a solitary nature. The lists of recreation habits of adults lend credence to this point of view. Reading newspapers and magazines, listening to the radio, attending movies, visiting and entertaining others (playing bridge and the like), reading books, automobiling, swimming, writing letters, and conversation are listed many times as major activities. Thus, it is obvious that adults do not often choose social or organized group activities. They do list a preference for such recreations as games and sports, playing musical instruments, and the legitimate theatre, but most of these preferences are too costly for the average budget.

The role of leisure in social adjustment. What play is expected to contribute is suggested in part by the primary social changes of an industrial society. These changes are a complex of increasing population, increasing density of population, and the realignment of all institutions to this revolution. Altogether, they modify or aggravate most of the difficulties of children and adults who, among other social unadjustments, lack an adequate recreational program. Too often, people of all ages are defeated by the limitations of city life, space requirements, unplanned housing, and the financial cost of play.

What play is expected to contribute to a people is also shown in part by the individual needs and the reactions of the various age groups to existing play programs. A weighty proportion of the evidence for adequate play is discoverable in the social problems of children. It is of course shown more directly and obviously in their bodily, emotional, and mental needs. It is the absence of play, and the relaxation from tension that play supplies, that accounts for a young population with the problems of physical and social inadequacy that are revealed in the many health and social surveys of children.

A minimum recreational program is one that will meet the broad social changes of a society as well as the changing personal needs of the individual. Play at all ages must supply physical exercise, social contacts, artistic skills and appreciation, creative experience, mental stability, social hygiene, citizenship, character, and community well-being in general. While much of play life is not carried on in the home, the family as a major factor in the socializing and mental hygiene of the child has a responsibility to the child. The child must be taught to play. This teaching does not mean interference, but it does mean guidance and supervision. Play interests must be encouraged that have the possibility of developing into an adult leisure-time program. Such interests should be extensive and should allow for social, aesthetic, intellectual and physical growth.

Summary

The family, like education, has been blamed for every adverse social condition. Some groups believe that the family has outlived its usefulness and will disappear. Other groups are actively engaged in attempting to support and bolster the family. All agree that the family is changing.

Change in economic institutions complicates change in the family. The social consequences of the industrial revolution entail changes in the position of women. Problems of value are intensified in questions of the function of marriage, the size of the family, and poor health.

Desertion and widowhood represent historical aspects of the problem of broken families. There are neither federal laws nor uniform state laws in the area of desertion and nonsupport. However there are trends in social security and reciprocity between states toward this goal. It is difficult to estimate trends in desertion. Reports of social agencies cover only short periods. Changing definitions of desertion or changing legal concepts of abandonment add to the confusion.

The economic problem of widowhood is a function of three variables: (1) the changing economic status of the home and the consequent restriction of women to few occupations; (2) the total dependence of the modern family upon the wages of one worker; and (3) the inability of the widow with dependent children to find employment that will furnish sufficient income for family support.

Poor housing has been called *the* family problem of the century. Numerous popular misconceptions confuse the issue. Moreover, there can be no doubt that substandard housing continues as a correlate of many other social problems.

A major function of the family is the socialization of the child. Because of this fact, problems of recreation assume significance. The family is regarded as necessary for child education and personality development. Parents therefore are concerned about the leisure-time pursuits of children. Play is regarded as important to the health and bodily growth of the child.

Regardless of change and the variety of social problems, the family will, in all probability, continue to be a basic social institution.

Bibliography

Abrams, Charles, *The Future of Housing,* Harper, New York, 1946.

Angell, R. C., *The Family Encounters the Depression,* Scribner's, New York, 1936.

Elmer, M. C., *The Sociology of the Family,* Ginn, New York, 1945.

Folsom, J. R., *The Family and Democratic Society,* John Wiley, New York, 1949.

Koos, Earl L., *Families in Trouble,* King's Crown Press, New York, 1946.

Veiller, L., *Housing Reform,* Russell Sage Foundation, Charities Publishing Committee, New York, 1910.

Zimmerman, C. C., *Family and Civilization,* Harper, New York, 1947.

. . . . .

Kiser, C. V., and P. K. Whelpton, "Social and Psychological Factors Affecting Fertility. Part IX, Fertility Planning and Fertility Rates by Socio-Economic Status," *Milbank Mem. Fund. Quart.*, Vol. 27 (1949): 118-244.

Lawrence, P. S., "Chronic Illness and Socio-Economic Status," *Pub. Health Rpts.*, Vol. 63, (Nov. 1948), No. 47, pp. 1507-1521.

Ogburn, W. F., "Education, Income and Family Unity," *Am. Jour. Sociol.*, Vol. 53 (1948): 474-476.

Pond, M. A., "Housing and Health," *Am. Jour. Pub. Health.*, Vol. 39 (1949): 454-458.

"Widows and Widowhood," *Statis. Bull.*, Metropolitan Life Insurance Company, Vol. 30 (Sept. 1949), No. 9.

Worchester, D. A., Jr., and R. J. Lampman, "Income, Ability, and Size of Family in the United States," *Jour. Pol. Econ.*, Vol. 38 (Oct. 1950): 436-442.

Questions

1. What different forms of marriage and the family have occurred in history?
2. Compare widowhood with desertion and divorce as family problems.
3. Into what occupations usually considered those of men have women recently entered?
4. Is commercial insurance an adequate protection for the problem of widowhood?
5. Are employers justified in discriminating against married women?
6. Where are the areas of poor housing in your community? What are the social correlates of poor housing there? Are there any plans for improvement?
7. How does your family spend its leisure time? Do your findings agree with the problems discussed in this chapter?
8. What are the differing opinions current regarding federal participation in low-cost housing?
9. How has television affected the family life of your friends?
10. In your opinion, is the family disappearing?

CHAPTER 17

FAMILY PROBLEMS—DIVORCE

DIVORCE IS A MULTIPLE PROBLEM. WHENEVER ADULTS ARE ASKED TO choose among the various satisfactions of life, most of them state a preference for a happy marriage. However, for growing numbers this goal is not realized. The divorce rate has increased steadily since records have been kept. And it is this trend that leads many people to question whether divorce is a social problem or a solution of various problems in personal relationships.

From either point of view, divorce has a long and peculiar legal history. It is also representative of a strange mixture of personal frictions and social disorders. In the three primary types of broken families (death, separation, and divorce), divorce is the only type of dissolution that has gained proportionately in recent years. Observers of this trend are often forced to describe it both romantically and socially by the first part of the couplet: "Parting is such sweet sorrow. . . ."

Statistics fail miserably in demonstrating either the frequency or the severity of this domestic revolution. During the last fifty years in the United States and in other countries with similar demographic tendencies, there has been an accelerated trend in the proportion of the population that is married and decreases in the proportions of the single and widowed. But the small quota in the marital status "divorced" is by no means indicative of their actual numbers when it is noted that nearly four million marriages were legally dissolved in the United States during the decade 1940-1950, and that a majority of the divorced remarry.[1]

[1] P. C. Glick, "First Marriage and Remarriage," *Am. Sociol. Rev.*, Vol. 14 (1949): 733. This survey shows that nearly three fourths of those who obtained

MARITAL STATUS OF PERSONS IN THE UNITED STATES
(15 Years of Age and Over)

	Per Cent Distribution Males			*Per Cent Distribution Females*		
	1900	*1940*	*1950*	*1900*	*1940*	*1950*
Single	40.2	33.2	26.2	31.2	25.8	19.6
Married	54.5	61.2	68.2	57.0	61.0	66.1
Widowed ...	4.6	4.3	4.0	11.2	11.5	12.1
Divorced	0.3	1.3	1.6	0.5	1.7	2.2
Unknown ...	0.4	—	—	0.1	—	—
	100.0	100.0	100.0	100.0	100.0	100.0

Source: United States Census

Divorce continues to remain in the category of social problems largely because of this legal, moral, social, and statistical confusion. In summary, the observations and recommendations of the White House Conference on family life are pertinent:

1. Our present divorce laws are producing widespread evils.
2. Domestic-relations laws instead of protecting family and marriage are a threat to them.
3. A committee of experts should be appointed to study the whole problem in the light of law, religion, medicine, education, and sociology.
4. The services of family and juvenile courts should be extended to meet the social needs that this problem (divorce) causes.[2]

In the same spirit of inquiry and prevention, the society of Divorcees Anonymous has concluded that seventy per cent of divorces can be prevented: "Divorce is like cancer. Catch it early and cure it; neglect it and the end is inevitable."

Historical background of divorce[3]

Separation, divorce, and remarriage reflect rapid as well as basic changes in marriage and family customs. As a question of public morals, these changes have received many different interpretations.

---

a divorce in the five years prior to the survey date had remarried. See also footnote 25 below.

[2] J. T. Zukerman, "Some Legal Aspects of Marital Discord," *Jewish Soc. Serv. Quart.*, Vol. 26 (1949-50): 81-90.

[3] In the following survey of the connections between divorce and the social institutions, authorities most often referred to are: M. C. Elmer, *The Sociology of the Family*, Ginn, Boston, 1945; E. Westermarck, *The History of Human Marriage*, Macmillan, New York, 1921; and the references in footnote 4 of Chap. 16, above.

One group of people, believing that the ills of the broken home are related to unsolved social problems in all the institutions, such as crime, juvenile delinquency, or mental disease, has branded divorce as the national menace.

A different outlook now widely prevalent is that divorce is a symptom of serious maladjustments in the family and in the personality.

There is consistent agreement, however, among all observers that divorce is a crisis, that it follows the rejection of the monogamous concept of marriage, and that, as such, it is a revolt against the old-fashioned family with its presumed permanency. But these observers do not agree either as to the inevitability, or the desirability of divorce as a solution of conflicts within and between the social institutions.[4]

In current tradition. Divorce may be studied in three perspectives. In its most usual interpretation it involves a transition to a less stable form of family life, heralded by such a temporary union as the companionate or trial marriage. Secondly, as a mode of personal adjustment, it may be regarded (especially for persons whose lives are unduly disturbed by such changes) as the necessary supplement to modern culture that parallels recent transitions in other institutions, such as industry, leisure, education, and communication. And, incidental to the two interpretations mentioned above, divorce may be related to multiple social problems, which are apt to make it appear to be the lesser of a number of evils.

In a discussion of any of these approaches to divorce, dissension arises because of two opposing views on marriage. Marriage is either a permanent relationship that does not admit of any dissolution effected by human intervention, or it is one that may be dissolved for certain specific reasons. Neither of these views can be accepted entirely without qualification. The first is a contradiction of the fact that marriage never has been universally regarded as permanent. The second has the obvious weakness of not being able to include restrictions that will give flexibility to modern marriage without actually encouraging irresponsible unions.

A further source of confusion concerning both marriage and

[4] As illustrations of these different concepts, compare the works by W. Gwynne, *Divorce in America under State and Church,* Macmillan, New York, 1925; and S. E. Goldstein, *Marriage and Family Counseling,* McGraw-Hill, New York, 1945, Chaps. I and II.

divorce is the fact that personal liberties and social obligations in these relations have always been at swords' points. If we regard either as a personal privilege and isolate it from the current restrictions imposed upon it by the group, only half of the problem, at the most, is being considered. Much of the literature on these subjects is beside the point, just as poverty and crime, as their treatments often indicate, are only half understood when they are interpreted merely in their individual connections. In addition, although it is a serious matter, divorce is often treated frivolously, as some contemporary novels or movies bear witness. Largely because of this confusion and superficial examination, the problems of marriage and divorce have been divided into separate categories of many ills rather than one or two related problems. That is, there are in this country at least forty-nine generic varieties of both, with other differences in Alaska, the Canal Zone, and Hawaii. This "legal-social medley" with its related problems has in turn become a conflict of principles—a moral issue in the place of a definable problem of social policy.

For this reason it is well to begin an analysis of divorce with a statement of the principles upon which marriage is based. If such an array of principles could be provided and accepted, then divorce might be discussed as a deviation from these norms, and accordingly sanctioned or condemned. Unfortunately for the clarity of this discussion, divorce has become a problem simply because no one series of principles underlying marriage is wholly acceptable to everybody. However, to have some definite basis for our discussion of the question, let us assume that the following five conditions are essential to marriage and that they may serve as a tentative description of the moral standards from which divorce is a radical deviation.

Essential Conditions for Marriage

First, genuine marriage must be intended. . . . Since marriage is a natural institution, it must be taken for granted that those who marry intend the natural union with all its consequences, known or unknown, unless any of these be expressly excluded.

In the second place, the parties must be physically capable of the marriage union. . . . If . . . impotence be discovered after the verbal contract has been made, this must be treated as null and void, and there is no marriage.

In the third place, the consent of the parties must be free, deliberate, and informed; otherwise there is no true contract. . . .

Fourthly, the parties must be free of any other tie of wedlock. This follows from the unity and indissolubility of marriage. . . .

Lastly, persons nearly akin to each other are incapable of intermarrying.[5]

It is safe to assume that the groups opposing or upholding the permanency of marriage would accept all of these conditions in theory. Divorce enters as a problem in the third condition, because, in basing the validity of the marriage contract upon free, deliberate, and informed consent, one presupposes (according to the advocates of divorce) a condition contrary to fact.

When the status of divorce is considered in its institutional setting, the situation is at once complicated by the mores of several institutions, each referring to its own interests in the family. The law supplies a legal basis for marriage and divorce, but cannot serve as a general control because it is limited to contractual relationships. Moreover, the law, being relatively uninterested in ethics, is opposed by the church. For centuries religion has considered the family and marriage to be under its special jurisdiction, in opposition to state control. In addition, family, economic, and educational mores have important bearings also upon the legal and moral status of divorce. Although theoretically there is a moral institution that enacts codes for all institutions, and hence would avoid contradictory moral principles, actually the separate institutions create their own morals without as much reference to the others as might be desirable, as in the case of divorce. This institutional conflict is the chief reason for the classification of divorce as a social maladjustment.

In its personal setting divorce is considerably less complicated. A person contemplating divorce has changed his mind rather than his personal code of morality. The moral issue involved hinges upon the question: Are there any contracts or social situations so intimately connected with group welfare that personal rights must be subordinated? Divorce is not necessarily a danger to marriage as an institution; but under the present condition of increasing divorce there is coming into being a changing form of marriage, a more flexible family, and possibly the need for a new type of social control to insure the permanency of marriage.

[5] Quoted by W. Gwynne, *op. cit.*, pp. 26-29. For the different kinds of legal divorce, consult H. Ringrose, *Marriage and Divorce Laws of the World,* Musson-Draper, London, 1911.

Earlier historical points of view. Among primitive and ancient peoples, wide variations occurred in divorce procedure, ranging from lax trial marriages to nearly permanent unions. But these customs were accompanied by equally dissimilar sexual standards before and after marriage, and for this reason it is impossible to generalize about the moral issues at stake. Although these systems are confusing because of their variety, there is no doubt as to the elaborate nature of unwritten law on the subject of divorce.

Among primitive people there were five customary practices. (1) In some groups both marriage and divorce were exceedingly loose arrangements. Marriage was frequently preceded by trial unions and could be dissolved without cause or formal action. (2) On the opposite extreme was the practice of indissoluble marriage, a custom prevailing among some of the lowest forms of savagery, the Australian aborigines and the Veddahs of Ceylon. (3) Another practice was divorce by mutual agreement; no cause was recognized as valid unless this agreement was reached. Childless marriages were the usual grounds for divorce under this system. (4) The absolute right of divorce was sometimes vested solely in the male, and was granted at will or upon slight pretexts. (5) A final general form of divorce granted an equal right to the wife.

Under any of the loose systems, property rights, family ties, religion, and moral codes tended to restrain extreme laxity. Moreover, among many of these tribes, divorce could be granted only for definite reasons, such as adultery or sterility. Often, marriage became indissoluble after children were born.

Ordinarily under every form of family group prior to the small-family unit, emphasis was put upon family solidarity, particularly by restrictions on the disposition of children and by economic restraints such as the loss of the dowry; and divorce was used conservatively. Under this emphasis, marriage was subordinated to the family. In one of the earliest written codes, that of Hammurabi (King of Babylon, 2250 B.C.), divorce was allowed to both husbands and wives on the grounds of sterility, neglect, disease, or adultery, but with restraints as to the disposition of property and children.

According to early Christian teachings, divorce was not entirely condemned or forbidden. Divorce was sanctioned for one reason, adultery, but under no circumstances was remarriage permitted. On this theoretical doctrine, the views of the disciples were consistent, and Christianity has been one of the chief influences in favor of permanent marriage. However, marriage and divorce in the medieval church were also modified by Jewish and Roman practices. Under the patriarchal family of the Jews, divorce was the prerogative of the husband, and under the Romans of the Empire, divorce was allowed by mutual consent, in both cases with the permission of remarriage. The medieval church attempted to steer a middle course, resulting in the recognition of unfaithfulness as a valid reason for a husband's obtaining a divorce. The equal right of the wife to secure a divorce for this reason was not expressly stated. Various interpretations by the early church fathers and the development of canonical law obscured the legal and religious right to divorce. In the first place, the church attempted to control marriage as an offset against Roman laxity. By the time of St. Augustine, the theoretical doctrine of indissolubility was accepted, but practice deviated from this extreme standard. Under the Christian emperors, legislation permitted divorce by mutual consent; for two centuries secular divorce was practically unmodified by Christianity, with the exception that the former Roman laxity was restrained on certain specific legal grounds. This combination of Jewish, Roman, and Christian doctrine was supplemented by German folkways, advocating mutual consent; and, as a consequence, the general principle of permanent marriage was neglected.

With the gradual development of canonical law, the doctrine of the indissolubility of marriage was restored. By 1164, marriage was listed as one of the seven sacraments; and by 1563 (at the Council of Trent), the church claimed priority over the state in its right to solemnize marriage and control divorce. A distinction was made between real and invalid marriages; divorce or annulment and remarriage were allowed usually upon three grounds: adultery, desertion, and cruelty. The sacramental theory of marriage and of its indissolubility is the current Catholic doctrine.

During the Reformation, the religious and moral views of the Protestant leaders, especially Martin Luther, were instrumental in modifying the strict religious interpretation of marriage. Luther was particularly vehement in contending that marriage was a civil contract, and he was responsible for a liberalism in the civil codes that he would otherwise have been the first to reject. However, the theological concept of marriage continued, even among Protestants, well into the nineteenth century. English reformers were much more conservative than Luther, concerning both divorce and remarriage, with the exception of John Milton, who, anticipating many contemporary reformers, considered divorce an individual matter:

> The just ground of divorce is indisposition, unfitness, or contrariety of mind, arising from a cause in nature unchangeable, hindering, and ever likely to hinder the main benefits of conjugal society, which are solace and peace.[6]

According to this doctrine, a new issue has arisen, to the confusion of ecclesiastical and civil authorities alike, and it is responsible for the chief social problems of marriage and divorce. When marriage is based upon mutual love and divorce upon its absence, the inconsistency of the average legislation, which is restricted to a few objective reasons, becomes apparent.

These were the leading religious and secular views concerning marriage, divorce, and remarriage that were brought by the colonists to this country. Current regulations are not only tinged by these old-world backgrounds but are also the product of the different state legislatures, which have operated more or less without reference to each other.

Who is the divorced person?

There are few published facts about the participants in unsuccessful marriages, and those now available describe a situation rather than the persons involved. Ignorance, sometimes called romanticism; unadjusting personal habits (immorality, laziness, alcoholism, or jealousy); mental differences; bad housekeeping; nagging; extravagance; physical deficiencies; age, religious, or nativity differences; low income; and sex are sufficiently specific in describing types of problems, but they are too intangible to identify the repeaters in divorce. Even case studies of divorce fail to provide the golden key to successful courtship and safe marriages; nor have recent psychiatric studies found any justification for or solution to the mother-in-law complex.

The divorcé is becoming less a matrimonial freak and more a standard marital status. As the increasing number of divorced persons in the general population shows, their proportion has increased steadily since 1900. Although a greater number of women than men are classified in census reports as divorced, this fact is due wholly to

[6] G. E. A. Howard, *A History of Matrimonial Institutions,* University of Chicago Press, Chicago, 1904, Vol. II, pp. 87-88. The foregoing history of divorce was adapted chiefly from this source: Vol. I. Chap. 5; Vol. II, Chaps. 11 and 15.

the remarriage of divorced males. Since 1900, this difference has decreased, and the proportion of males has tripled while that of females has only doubled. The ratio of divorced women to divorced men is not so great, however, as the excess of widows over widowers, because divorce occurs very frequently in the younger age groups.

One of the first points brought out by these statistics is that age is the most prominent factor in the description of the typical divorcé, and it is a most important source of increasing divorce. The greatest increase in divorce has occurred among people in midlife, between the ages of 35 and 55; fewer divorces occur in the younger or older groups. For women, the maximum number of divorces is in the 35- to 44-year group, and for men in the 45- to 65-year group. Moreover, divorce occurs within a few years after marriage: about two fifths during the first five years, and two thirds before the first ten years. Although the number of divorced persons who do not remarry is large, in cases of remarriage the lapse of time is short, usually between three and four years.

Divorce is an urban phenomenon. With few exceptions, it is more frequent and is increasing more rapidly in cities than in rural communities. This regional difference is diminishing slowly and is being replaced by the migratory divorce, a form that is encouraged by lenient divorce legislation of some states and by the sex ratio of different sections of the country.

Divorce varies definitely among different nativities and religious groups. From the averages of selected states, it may be concluded that Negroes have the highest divorce rates; foreign-born whites have the lowest; and the native born of foreign parents have rates lower than the native born. These differences are explained also by religious and social customs. Divorce is considerably more frequent among Protestants. An exception to the urban characteristic of divorce occurs in manufacturing cities, whose lower divorce rates are due, presumably, to the unusually large percentage of the foreign born in the urban population and to the employment of foreign-born women; both of these factors correlate with low rates. These facts are sometimes used as evidence that easy divorce laws do not encourage laxity in marriage but that divorce is more the natural outcome of unadjustment due to early marriage and differences in cultural background. Except in the manufacturing city, divorce correlates with the increasing density and mobility of population. It also increases from east to west and from north to south.

Childless marriages are also characteristic of the divorced; the actual figures indicate that they are twice as frequent among divorced couples. The proportion of childlessness is much greater than that revealed by unselected families, which ordinarily show a proportion of less than 20 per cent without children. For this reason, children are considered to be a primary deterring factor. In one survey, nearly two thirds of the divorced were found to be childless: 57.1 per cent had no children, and 20.4 per cent had only one child. Low birth rates may, consequently, be taken as one symptom of various social and economic changes that are likely to stimulate divorce.

Divorce also correlates with other general conditions—with occupation, income, and education, with periods of economic prosperity, and with war and postwar periods. It is most common in the same social circles that are distinguished by occupational insecurity and mobility and by high rates of mental disease, suicide, crime and delinquency. At its worst, divorce is used as an index of several of the pathologies. According to Dayton, the divorced have the highest rate of mental disease of all marital groups. And he concludes that they are also biologically inferior, having higher sterility rates and a shorter life expectancy.[7]

In summary, the typical divorcé may be described as middleaged, a resident of an urban community, native born, childless, and a Protestant. The implication that he had been married only a short time and is also a prospective bridegroom is more a compliment to than a reflection upon this social status.

Divorce rates

Different measurements of this domestic turnover show that divorces are distributed widely in all social classes. They occur with increasing frequency in countries that are experimenting with various social and economic reforms. Differences in the legislation of

[7] N. A. Dayton, *New Facts on Mental Disorders,* Thomas, Baltimore, 1940, pp. 218-220. Jessie Bernard, *American Family Behavior,* Harper, New York, 1942, pp. 98-99. "Divorce and Size of Family," *Statis. Bull.,* Metropolitan Life Insurance Company, Vol. 31 (1950), No. 2, pp. 1-3. When families are broken by divorce during the child-bearing period, the average number of children is one-seventh less than in those families that remain intact. P. H. Jacobson, "Marital Dissolutions in New York State," *Milbank Mem. Fund Quart.,* Vol. 28 (1950): 25-42. H. J. Locke, "Predicting Marital Adjustment by Comparing a Divorced and Happily Married Group." *Am. Sociol. Rev.,* Vol. 12 (1947): 187-191.

various states and nations also produce varying divorce rates. There is no one factor, legal, religious, ethical, or social, that is a complete and infallible diagnosis of the causes of divorce.

If divorce is a serious attack upon the stability of the home, there is the added danger that it is also one of the most frequent of modern crises. In recent years the divorce rate has risen constantly. Immediately after World War II, in 1946, it reached a record high of 30.2 per 100 marriages. The total number of divorces granted, as reported by the United States Census, is given in the tables below. These figures show the increasing trend, the tendencies to decrease in business depressions, and the sharp increases in periods of economic prosperity and in war and post-war years. Since 1880, divorce has increased five times faster than marriage and seven times faster than population.

Three comparisons by rates are used to indicate this increasing trend. Although no two rates show the same proportionate increase, because they are based upon different population groups, each is important as a check upon the others. One rate is obtained from the comparison between current divorces and marriages, and is often employed to prove "the rising tide of divorce." Thus, in 1888, there was one divorce in every seventeen marriages, and in 1900, one in every twelve marriages; in 1930, there was one divorce in every six marriages; in 1941, one in every five marriages; and, according to the rates of recent years, one in every three marriages will result in divorce within the first fifteen years of married life. This rate is twice that which prevailed prior to World War II and three times the rate prevailing in the 1920's. Since 1867 the divorce rate per 1,000 population has increased tenfold and reached its peak in the late 1940's.

As the rates per 100 marriages indicate in the trend since 1900, there is no escape from the conclusion that marriages are broken abruptly and in vastly increasing proportions during an age of social unrest.

Year	*Divorces per 100 Marriages*
1900	9.4
1910	10.3
1920	16.5
1930	16.0
1940	21.3
1950	25.2 *

* Provisional.
Source: United States Census.

A second and more logical comparison is the ratio of divorces to married persons. Over the period for which figures are available, the divorce rate has increased more than fourfold in this comparison —from 0.81 per 1,000 married persons in 1887 to 5.66 in 1950. However, these rates fail to distinguish those age groups that are actually contributing most to the divorce rate from older groups whose marriages are less liable to result in divorce. In spite of this limitation, it is considered the most accurate of the three measurements.

NUMBER AND RATES OF DIVORCE

Years	*Number of Divorces*	*Per 1,000 Population*	*Per 1,000 Married Persons*
1887	27,919	0.47	0.81
1900	55,751	0.73	2.00
1910	83,045	0.90	2.32
1920	170,505	1.60	3.95
1930	191,591	1.56	3.65
1940	264,000	2.00	8.44
1946	610,000	4.30	11.00
1950 *	422,000	2.80	5.66

* Provisional.
Source: United States Census.

A third commonly used rate, based upon the entire population, is given above, as rates of divorce per 1,000 population. Here again a steady increase is shown until 1940, and then the sharp upward turn of the war years. In both columns the proportion of divorces is shown to be several times greater than the rates prevailing five decades ago.

The national tendency toward increasing divorce is also shown by international comparisons. Although an increasing rate is by no means limited to this country, few nations have equalled the rate of the United States. With one or two exceptions, the United States has for years exceeded all other countries in both volume and rate. International comparisons are, however, less valid than the preceding measures of increasing divorce, primarily because of differences in divorce legislation and other differences in the economic, religious, and political status of the several national populations. When any nation experiences a comparatively high divorce rate, as have Russia (1920-1925), Japan, Austria, Australia, New Zealand, and France (1920-21), the social background is usually one of rapid changes. Divorce is a reflection of urbanization, increased employment of women, reduction in the average size of the family, and economic and political upsets, as these conditions affect divorce legislation and family mores.

NATIONAL DIVORCE RATES

	Ratio per 1,000 divorces to average annual number of marriages in the preceding decade	
	1920	*1945*
United States	165.5	323.9
Denmark	57.1	166.3
New Zealand	67.8	136.2
Switzerland	88.2	113.3
Sweden	38.1	109.9
Australia	29.1	105.6
France	132.1	101.2
Norway	40.8	79.0
Netherlands	41.8	68.2
Belgium	43.0	57.2
Scotland	22.8	52.6
Canada	7.2	49.6
England and Wales	10.4	42.3

Source: "World-Wide Increase in Divorce," *Statis. Bull.*, Metropolitan Life Insurance Company, Vol. 30 (1949), No. 4, p. 2.

Grounds for divorce

From the foregoing conflict between church and civil authorities, between theoretical and practical expediency, and between personal and group rights, it becomes obvious that there is not necessarily any relationship at all between the legal reasons or grounds for divorce and its real causes. This separation would be ludicrous, if it were possible to discover the latter. But an even greater hindrance to consistent action or to a national policy of divorce is the differences between the regulations of the various states. In the different states and other areas under the jurisdiction of the United States there are fifty-two separate sets of laws concerning both marriage and divorce, particularly unlike in their legal recognition of marriage and in their restrictions upon marriage and divorce. The persistence of common law is another source of confusion. In half of the states, marriages that are unlicensed and unrecorded are considered legal, or their legality is left to court decisions. And in equity courts not only is the attitude toward common law marriages variable, but sometimes the same court renders contradictory decisions. Obviously, under this loose interpretation of marriage there can be no national divorce legislation. To a considerable extent these differences indicate the archaic nature of legislation derived from European backgrounds and adapted to the needs of a frontier people.

There are nearly fifty different grounds for divorce, but no one state recognizes all of them. The most frequently cited legal reasons are adultery, cruelty, desertion, drunkenness, neglect to provide, conviction of felony, impotency, insanity, imprisonment, incompatibility, mental incapacity, pregnancy before marriage, and voluntary separation. Their interpretation also varies considerably among the different states. No court expects to grant decrees of divorce for other than these legal fictions, of which the following is an illustration. The wife based her action on the fact that she and her husband did not have the same friends and that he would not join her dinner parties.

"How did this affect you?" asked the judge.
"It made me rather nervous."
"Did you require the services of a doctor?"
"Yes, I did."
"That's enough," said the judge, "decree granted."

Lawyers go even further in their interpretation of these grounds, and a stock phrase often used by the divorce lawyer giving both the legal and the real reason is: "This man and woman will not and cannot live together." This elastic attitude toward divorce is indicated from another point of view by the peculiar status given to divorce in the New York State Constitution. Article I, section 9, is headed: "Divorce, Lotteries, Pool Selling, and Gambling, Laws to Prevent."

DISTRIBUTION OF GROUNDS PREFERRED IN DIVORCE CASES [8]

Grounds	*Per Cent*
Cruelty	44.0
Desertion	28.0
Adultery	8.0
Nonsupport	4.0
Combined or Miscellaneous	16.0
Total	100.0

Whether increasing divorce rates are omens of good or of evil cannot be determined from an analysis of the common grounds mentioned above, except by assuming that divorce itself is an evil

[8] This distribution of grounds for divorce is an estimated average for recent years. A synopsis of various state divorce laws may be found in several of the annual books of facts.

or by the discovery of its real causes. In other words, there is no logic in the present use of those grounds by the various courts. As divorce becomes easier to obtain, less serious charges are preferred and accepted by the courts. Thus, taking the country as a whole, cruelty has displaced adultery, and desertion is more frequently given as a reason than drunkenness. However, different states vary in their use of these grounds according to the limits of their statutes.

Conflict in divorce legislation

The chief similarity in the divorce legislation of most states is their use of a few major grounds. In nearly every other respect there are dissimilarities leading to serious complications. In many states the laws are inconsistent because they have become antiquated.

Two of every five cases of divorce are granted because of cruelty, but some states insist on physical cruelty, extreme cruelty, or cruel and barbarous treatment. Virginia, for example, recognizes cruelty as a cause, but a legal separation of three years under court order must precede the divorce. Other states extend cruelty to include minor nervous reactions, as illustrated by the courtroom dialogue reported above, or criticism of a husband's conversation or a wife's aptitude in the use of the family car.

Georgia requires a verdict of two successive juries before absolute divorce is permitted, even in the case of adultery. Maryland does not recognize cruelty, either physical or mental, as sufficient grounds; whereas North Carolina fails to include neglect to provide, cruelty, or drunkenness, preferring instead such charges as adultery, impotency, premarital pregnancy, and perversion. South Carolina reversed its position of no divorce and now accepts adultery, desertion, cruelty, and drunkenness as causes. New York, which limits divorce to an incontestable violation of the Seventh Commandment, restricts the interpretation of adultery by such impossible demands for evidence that absolute freedom cannot be obtained except by collusion and fabricated testimony—two legal entanglements that presumably make the divorce invalid. However, New York eases its strict law by a broad annulment proviso whereby marriages may be voided because of force, duress, fraud, bigamy, incurable physical incapacity, nonage, want of understanding, and insanity.

Differences in statutory limitations, in "proof required," in length of residence, and in the period that must elapse before the interlocutory decree becomes absolute are chiefly responsible for the current conflict in divorce and for the westward movement of the matrimonially unsettled. In the residence requirement there are extremes from two years in some eastern states to one year in most of the western states, not including divorce-conscious Nevada with its present requirements of six weeks, and Florida, ninety days.

Nevada and one or two competing states, which commercialize divorce by short residence requirements, privacy, and minor legal grounds, necessarily depend upon other states for their business. While these experiments may be wholly beneficial in casting reflections upon the unnecessary restrictions of other states, they discourage the liberal movement in general and arouse hysterical opposition, which connects gambling, free love, and home wrecking with divorce. Furthermore, the centralization of divorce in a few states causes conflicts between their easy laws and the marriage requirements of other states. When a divorced person returns to his own state and remarries, that state may declare his second marriage void under two circumstances: fabricated evidence and matrimonial domicile.

As a matter of abstract law, divorces secured by fabricated evidence—for example, in the establishment of fictitious residence—may be declared void in every state. Recent divorce scandals, which have branded certain courts as "divorce mills," have originated from this practice. Such divorces are voidable in the home state; and the reason that more interstate divorces are not declared void for this reason is that the "full faith and credit" clause of the federal Constitution establishes a comity whereby the decrees and judgments of the courts of one state are recognized as legal by other state courts. But this ruling does not cover fabricated evidence, collusion, or other frauds. Moreover, since every state has the right to determine the civil status of its own citizens, many of these divorces could be set aside, if the local courts or the defendants brought charges on the above grounds. The legal status of interstate divorces and of divorced persons is highly precarious, and the legality of remarriage or the legitimacy of children by subsequent marriages is equally questionable.

This situation has an important connection with the right to inherit property. Heirs by the first marriage may have the divorce declared void, thus making the second marriage bigamous and the children illegitimate. When attempts have been made to nullify divorces on grounds of fraud, they have usually been successful in every state.

A second source of voidable divorces is the legal fiction of "matrimonial domicile" established by the United States Supreme Court in the case of Haddock *vs.* Haddock (1905). This ruling held that:

> . . . no State is bound to take as conclusive a decree of divorce as is granted to one of its citizens by a court of another state if the other party to the action was not present in court, or was not personally served with notice within the State where the action was tried.[9]

Although most states have not enforced this decision, it has been applied by the New York, Pennsylvania, Georgia, North Carolina, and South Carolina. Thus, the civil and criminal status of a divorced person and the legitimacy of the children by his subsequent remarriage are dependent upon the whim or bias of his local state courts.

Because of the two foregoing limitations, the easy divorces of some western states, and Paris or Mexican divorces are regarded with suspicion. These sources of conflict led Turano to conclude:

> Many divorced persons in the United States live in glass houses which will stand only so long as no one attempts to demolish them with legal pellets.[10]

Referring to the same indefiniteness of the "once-married-always-married" rule, Arthur Train has written:

> To this we owe our present predicament to which anyone who has secured a divorce can never be wholly at ease after marrying a second wife, lest he wake up some morning and find that he is married after all to the first.[11]

And for this reason Train repeated *Punch's* advice to bachelors, making it equally applicable to the divorced who are contemplating remarriage—"Don't."

9 A. M. Turano, "The Conflict of Divorce Laws," *American Mercury,* Vol. 17 (1929): 461. H. S. Daggett, "Reflections on the Law of the Family," *Annals, Am. Acad. Pol. and Soc. Sci.,* Vol. 251 (May 1947): 120-127. Consult for discussion of the case, Williams *vs.* North Carolina, 317 U.S. 287, a decision supporting the Haddock case. See also: S. T. Bigelow, "The Case of Colorado *vs.* Rawlings," *Jour. Am. Bar Assoc.,* Vol. 35 (1949): 728 ff.

10 *Ibid.,* p. 462.

11 A. Train, "On the Trail of the Bad Men," *Scribner's,* New York, 1925, pp. 317-318. P. W. Tappan, "Divorced in Reno, but not in New York," *Forum,* Vol. 104 (1945): 97-102.

A national marriage and divorce law

One of the attempts to correct the confusion resulting from diverse state laws is the movement for a national divorce law, to be supplemented by a national marriage law. These laws are proposed as substitutes for the numerous different laws now governing marriage and divorce. The movement was begun as early as 1884, when the national Congress considered proposals for a constitutional amendment permitting national legislation on both subjects. At this time, opposition was raised on the score that neither marriage nor divorce could be handled satisfactorily by national legislation, because local legislation was too experimental to indicate the needs of the country as a whole. In 1906, a National Congress on Uniform Divorce Laws was called by the Governor of Pennsylvania, but no suggestion was made for federal action. The California Legislature in 1911 proposed an amendment to the federal Constitution, putting both marriage and divorce under federal control. Nearly every year from 1915 to 1922, similar amendments were proposed. In the latter year, the General Federation of Women's Clubs drafted a proposed law. These movements resulted in the Capper Bill of 1923. This national movement has been unsuccessful in securing legislative recognition primarily because the conflict is now reduced to the opposition to, or the advocacy of, easier divorce legislation.

An example of this opposition is illustrated by a bill introduced in the New York Assembly "for the study of New York divorce laws." It was not even admitted to discussion on the floor.

The tendency of most proposals is to put greater emphasis upon divorce and to treat marriage as an incidental item. However, the objections ordinarily brought against divorce legislation apply also to marriage laws. The debate hinges upon the standards to be adopted. No progress has been made because no agreement can be reached as to whether the standard of a national law should be modeled after the states with the most or those with the fewest restrictions. Naturally, the advocates of divorce favor the laws now in operation in Nevada, Arizona, and other western states. And the opponents of a national marriage law fear that the high standards now maintained in the administration of a few state laws would be materially lowered by inefficient federal administration and by failure to enforce specific mental and physical requirements for marriage now provided in the statutes of high-standard states. It is probably correct to assume that no immediate enactment of federal legislation will take place, because the people of this country represent extreme cultural variations. However, this statement does not imply that state legislation ought not to be revised. Politics in either of these issues presents a tremendous obstacle, because it plays upon emotions and upon probable consequences that might and do come to pass without the intervention of law, such as family disorganization, godlessness, and companionate marriage. While a national law would be of inestimable value in eliminating the inconsistencies and conflicts of current laws, reformers are encouraged by the possibility of experimentation through state legislation, since this revised legislation will eventually furnish the basis of a national act. One conclusion is surely justified by the trend of the divorce rate: that additional restrictions would certainly run counter to obvious changes in our matrimonial institution.

Divorce by mutual consent

Although the basic requirement of a national or a state divorce law is still a matter of opinion, most proposals recognize mutual consent as the first step in the enactment of a sensible and applicable act. This conclusion is founded upon the experience of the courts in interpreting our present laws, which in many instances and in spite of legal technicalities grant divorce when in the judgment of the court divorce is needed. And yet, when free divorce is openly advocated or attempts have been made to establish it, there is profound public opposition. No proponent of mutual consent or free divorce has ever endorsed this basis of divorce without precautionary measures, however, such as restrictions to prevent unwise or hasty marriages, and a period of separation before the divorce becomes legally effective. Ordinarily, the person who is most concerned about wholesome marriage and family stability is also an advocate of free divorce.

But divorce by mutual consent is not a recent innovation. The Romans adopted it under social conditions closely resembling those of our own times. Napoleon made it a part of his Code Civil. It also appears in the present laws of Russia, Switzerland (non-Catholics only), Belgium, Rumania, Norway, Sweden, Denmark, Portugal, Japan, and in some provinces of Mexico. This type of legislation developed in countries where religious influence was not associated with temporal power, and also where social rather than ecclesiastical doctrine was accepted as the basis of marriage. Mutual consent, or free divorce, means, in addition to the elimination of current restrictions, the recognition of maritally unadjusted persons; the absence of court fees and legal quibbling; the elimination of fraudulent testimony, collusion, and slandering. In short, freedom of divorce is really nothing less than the extension of a privilege always enjoyed by some economic classes. As Lord Bryce said with reference to divorce under the church:

> It was easy, given a sufficient motive, whether political or pecuniary, to discover some ground for declaring almost any marriage invalid.[12]

For some years Denmark, Sweden, and Norway have had national marriage and divorce laws. Divorce may be obtained by court action for one of several legal reasons, or by mutual consent. While the latter requires no court action, it is safeguarded by the requirement that the couple confer with the parish minister or some government official. If reconciliation is not effected, an agreement is reached concerning the custody of children and the division of property, and a decree of legal separation is given. After the couple has lived separately for a period, generally one year, a decree of divorce is granted. Since their introduction, these laws have apparently been successful and have had no serious consequences. Divorce is not considered an important problem, because it is judged only by legal criteria and not by moral or religious concepts. The majority of divorces are granted under the mutual-consent decree, and in none of the Scandinavian countries is the divorce rate high.

The most usual suggestion for the readjustment of law and court procedures in this country develops from the quest for the real reasons underlying the application for the divorce, from a desire to avoid the punishment element in divorce, and from the need to provide adequately for children. For all these reasons, most students of the family are of the opinion that mutual consent as indicated by living apart is the most sensible manner by which mismated couples can be identified and a marriage can be regarded as terminated. As further precautions, they recommend that each application should be studied for several months and that ample opportunities should be provided for reconciliation; if this is not possible, then a dignified settlement should be made.

Under this system there could be no contest in court, no excessive

[12] E. Westermarck, *op. cit.*, Vol. 3, pp. 330-331.

fees, no need to determine fault, sin, or incapacity, no occasion for collusion, humiliation, or connivance, and no debate about alimony, since both the care of children and a property settlement would be logical parts of the mutual agreement.

Causes of divorce

As already noted in the two preceding chapters, there are numerous personal and social conditions in the process of unsuccessful marriage and divorce. Like the preliminary processes of courtship and marriage and the process of readjustment after divorce, there are many spurious and accidental factors that confuse investigation and often defy all available techniques of study.[13]

In prior analyses, there is a substantial basis for the interpretation of specific personal causes. Something other than recognized legal grounds is apparently responsible for increasing rates. For example, one study has shown from an analysis of 9,237 actions for divorce that (1) divorce tends to be granted to any couple, provided they devote sufficient time and money, and (2) divorce litigation is primarily concerned with property rights, money payments or alimony, and custody of children.[14]

Personal causes of divorce. The investigation of personal factors in divorce invades the broader field of unhappy marriages, including the conditions that are responsible for divorce, separation, or domestic discord. Reporting on the study of 1,000 American women who are what might be called "the cultural American type—they are urban, of good family background and education, married to professional men of moderate income, each with one or two children," [15] Dr. Robert L. Dickinson concluded that fifty per cent were unhappily married and that the cause of their unhappiness was primarily sex or ignorance concerning sexual matters. Other factors frequently mentioned, such as occupation, income, management of children,

[13] In Chap. 15 above, these personal conditions are examined under such headings as sources of family breakdowns, characteristics of personality associated with unhappiness, and unsuccessful marriages. In Chap. 16, there are reviewed such broad social causes or correlates of unstable families as unfavorable economic and occupational conditions, changing family organization, inadequate housing, and improper uses of leisure time.

[14] L. C. Marshall and G. May, *The Divorce Court,* Johns Hopkins Press, Baltimore, 1933. A. M. Turano, "The Alimony Racket," *Am. Mercury,* Vol. 19 (1933): 237.

[15] R. L. Dickinson, quoted in editorial "On Judging Marriage," *Outlook,* Vol. 158 (1931): 297.

or interference of relatives, were considered of secondary importance. How completely the two factors of sex and ignorance account for divorce requires more thorough examination.

Mowrer's investigation of the factors involved in domestic discord gives a more extensive array of probable personal causes. Judging by their frequency in 1,573 families, he concluded that there were fifteen significant variables leading to divorce: abuse, drink, irregular habits (such as gambling), mental deficiency, bad housekeeping, nagging, family interference, uncontrolled temper, jealousy, extravagance, stinginess, excessive sex demands, sex refusal, children by former marriage, and evil companions. Other factors that are less significant only because they occur less frequently are: immorality, affinity, laziness, physical deficiency, slovenliness, venereal disease, discipline of children, age differences, inadequate income, sex perversion, restlessness, religious differences, and nativity differences.[16] Particular domestic problems are identified by combinations of these twenty-eight factors.

In Mowrer's study the blanket legal terms used by the courts are analyzed into their natural causes. Thus, in cases of divorce granted for desertion, the following natural causes are enumerated according to their frequency: [17]

Natural Causes of Divorce	*Per Cent*
Financial tension	40.2
Desertion for another	13.2
Dissatisfaction with home	10.9
Infidelity	10.5
Drink and cruelty	9.9
Refusal to leave old home	7.8
Irregular habits	4.4
Irregular work and drink	2.4
Forced marriage	0.7
Total	100.0

These personal causes of divorce are further summarized as tensions in the process of family adjustment. The four major tensions are described as: (1) incompatibility in response, (2) economic individualization, (3) cultural differentiation, and (4) individuation of life patterns. The divorce process is thereby reducible to the follow-

[16] E. R. Mowrer, *Domestic Discord,* University of Chicago Press, Chicago, 1928, p. 40.

[17] E. R. Mowrer, *Family Disorganization,* University of Chicago Press, Chicago, 1927, p. 63 (rev. ed. 1939).

ing symbolic pattern: loss of respect .... pattern of life tension .... cultural tension .... economic tension .... loss of respect .... religious tension ....sex tension.[18]

A personal confession showing one combination of these factors and the resultant pattern is reproduced in the following document:

> Our first mistake was in marrying too young. If we had waited another year or two, my wife would have had time to learn that she was inseparably bound to the church—the church that so wisely warns her children against "mixed marriages." As it was, we married during a lapse of faith on my wife's part, which made it possible for her to assure me quite sincerely that the formal waiver of rights over the education of possible children, which I had to sign, would have no more force than I should choose to give it. I was too young—only twenty-three. . . .
>
> The first child was on the way before the first year of our union had passed. The economic problem became acute and continued so through all the years that we remained together. . . . The frictions and anxieties that accompanied this family increase (there were six children in all) were aggravated by my ever-intensifying disapproval of the religious training to which the children were being subjected. . . . On the economic side, there was nothing in prospect for us but growing debts and ultimate ruin. There was at least a chance that the worst features of the threatening future might be avoided if we broke up the partnership and worked out a new solution.[19]

In this broken home, there were several specific personal causes that illustrate each of Mowrer's four tensions, and a pattern or fusion of individual and cultural forces that gradually led to separation. Here, too, is an example of the manner in which personal and objective causes may be related. Neither alone could be considered of primary importance, but both became most unfortunately effective by their combination in this family.

Prevention

Any considerable reduction in the divorce rate can only be realized by accepting one of two alternatives. Either marriage must be regarded as indissoluble, in spite of its failures, or a thoroughgoing system must be introduced to eliminate the causes of divorce. The former measure would simply overlook family disorganization, considering the shell of conformity as more important. From this point of view, substitutes for divorce or current proposals for an experi-

[18] *Ibid.*, pp. 196-226.
[19] "Divorce and After" (unsigned document), *The Nation*, Vol. 130 (1930): 211.

mental marriage would be taboo. But under no system of family reorganization would they be more than temporary expedients, because the tradition of relative permanency in marriage is founded not so much upon belief as it is upon the idea that it is a necessary prerequisite to the fulfillment of family responsibilities. Both companionate and trial marriages contain elements that should be a part of ordinary contemporary family organization; for example, the recognition of economic and other conditions making child bearing unwise during the early years of marriage. However, these forms of marriage cannot be successfully introduced until divorce may be secured by mutual consent and the public learns to tolerate experimental marriage. The main source of danger and of public opposition lies in the bias toward sexual experimentation without the expectancy of permanent unions or child bearing. Until there are radical changes in family and ethical mores, reform must be directed toward other preventives.

The elimination of divorce depends upon the determination of rules that will serve as guides to successful family life both before and after marriage. This conclusion is based upon the third requirement for marriage stated by Gwynne: "The consent of the parties must be free, deliberate, and informed." To achieve this goal, attention must be fixed upon the social problems of marriage, "Cure marriage, cure divorce." If adequate information were available on the various aspects of marriage, it is highly probable that divorce, now often considered inevitable or even desirable, would be reduced to a small fraction of its present importance.

Howard mentioned four types of ill-advised marriages that are fodder for divorce mills. The first are "light-minded" marriages by immature persons; the second are "tainted" marriages of those who are physically or mentally unfit; the third are "pseudo-romantic" marriages, instituted on the basis of medieval chivalry and perpetuated in part by the Hollywood interpretation of love and the family; and the fourth consist of "risky" marriages, in which there may be several definite factors likely to handicap success.[20]

In addition to the accepted physical and mental qualifications for successful marriages, there are four major social problems involved in these ill-advised marriages. Early marriage or child marriage has

[20] G. E. Howard, "Bad Marriage and Quick Divorce," *Jour. Ap. Sociol.*, Vol. 6 (1921): 1-10.

figured as one of the important causes of the broken home. Undue haste, clandestine marriages, and law evasion are other causes.[21]

Child marriage, for the most part, is a problem of girls; few boys marry before the age of sixteen. In this country, Richmond and Hall found over 600,000 marriages that could be classified as child marriages, one of the persons in each case being under sixteen years of age. In some states, children are permitted to marry earlier than they may leave school or go to work, although under the common law such persons are unable to make a contract that is legally binding. Often the legality of child marriages is left to indefinite common-law rules, or the marriage-license clerk is obliged to interpret whether or not existing laws are applicable to marriage licenses. This is a result of the historical unwillingness of states to exert too much control over marriage.

The chief cause of this problem is laxity in the issuance of marriage licenses and law evasion. Among 505 marriage licenses issued in Cleveland to girls under eighteen years of age, over one third were procured simply because false ages were given. A suggested corrective is a minimum age limit for the issuance of marriage licenses: eighteen for boys, and sixteen for girls if the parents consent.

The problem in the social control of clandestine marriages is to strike a balance between the rights of the person and public welfare. A marriage is clandestine when the authorities legally entitled to the knowledge are informed after it is contracted; this practice indicates one of the valuable features of the custom, formerly enforced, of publishing the banns. As in the case of hasty marriages, a wide variety of motives is responsible for such marriages. Prematrimonial cohabitation or pregnancy are frequent causes. A law known as the Secret Marriage Act has been passed in some states to meet situations arising from these marriages, providing for their secret licensing and registration. It is unsatisfactory to the extent that legal sanction is given to common-law marriages or to other extra-legal unions. Clandestine marriages often occur from the best of motives: to avoid the costs of expensive weddings, the humorous activities of helpful friends, or interference with professional study. Frequently, social agencies find marriages of this type among children who would be least suspected of such acts by their families. This type of marriage

[21] M. E. Richmond and F. S. Hall, *Marriage and the State,* Russell Sage Foundation, New York, 1929.

indicates the need for flexible legislation in the social control of marriage.

Hasty marriages—"marriage on the spur of the moment after drinking, marriage on a dare, prematrimonial acquaintance by correspondence only, marriage in a fit of pique, and marriage in jest" [22] —are frequently in the background of divorce and annulment. The administrative requirement of a waiting period between the issuance of the license and the marriage ceremony is enforced to prevent haste and its frequent consequences of misrepresentation or concealment of facts relative to age or physical condition. The chief objection to hasty marriages is that the persons concerned are unable to fulfill the elementary prerequisite of being *informed.*

Law evasion in marriage generally occurs through marriage outside the state of residence in order to avoid certain provisions of marriage laws, medical certification, or the prescribed interval between divorce and remarriage. Greater uniformity in marriage legislation between states is urged as a preventive against such law evasion.

Medical certification. A frequently suggested supplementary control over marriage is medical certification, which is also considered an indirect attack upon divorce. Strong disapproval of this measure has been voiced in every country where it has been proposed, because of the theory that persons about to be married should be informed as to each other's condition, and the decision of marriage then left to their own individual judgment. By the addition of a compulsory examination, this movement has become, in reality, an extension of the laws regarding physical qualifications, which prohibit marriage to persons not physically fit.

In 1913, Wisconsin passed a eugenic marriage law providing that no man should receive a marriage license unless he was certified by a physician to be free from venereal disease. A few states with similar laws include other physical defects and sometimes mental deficiency. Such laws are generally considered to be valuable in their educational influences, but they are criticized because of administrative deficiencies. In the original Wisconsin law, for example, women were excluded, examinations were inadequate, and the law could be evaded by marriage outside the state.[23]

[22] *Ibid.,* p. 151. C. Woodbury, "Lonely Heart is Vulnerable: Lonely-Hearts Racket," *Woman's Home Comp.,* Vol. 76 (1949): 4 ff.

[23] F. S. Hall, *Medical Certification for Marriage,* Russell Sage Foundation, New York, 1925.

At present, more than thirty states have premarital laws that require either a serological or physical test of both persons. Many states, however, have rejected the serological test for syphilis. Fourteen states have no premarital law. In its place they may require each applicant for a marriage license to present a sworn statement of freedom from venereal disease, or they may restrict marriage "in the presence of any venereal disease during the infective or communicable stage." [24]

Summary

Family disorganization is a consequence of incomplete tests for successful marriage and of the absence of information by which permanent marriage can be insured. It is no proof that marriage is a failure. During the early stages of family development, primitive people regarded the family primarily as an economic group, and developed economic tests to insure its permanency. The man had to be the supporter and defender; the wife had to be capable of child bearing and of the hard work required by primitive living conditions. These requirements for family life became factors in sexual selection. If personal or emotional factors existed, they were not recognized as essential to successful matrimony.

Therefore, in its origins, marriage grew out of the family's need to extend common interests in food getting and child rearing. This materialistic basis gave a stability to the family that has now disappeared with the separation of the domestic and economic institutions. Although marriage does not furnish additional tests of family stability, it makes a negative contribution in demonstrating that there is no historical reason why the modern family should attempt to adapt itself to any one theory of marriage.

This variability is precisely the trend that many students of family relations consider to be a most wholesome sign in current marriage adjustments. People now look upon marriage "for better but not for worse." Those who seek divorce do so not because they are dissatisfied with marriage in general but because they are dissatis-

[24] V. Nisbet and C. P. Brown, "Premarital Laws," *Pennsylvania's Health*, Department of Health, Pennsylvania, Nov. 1945, pp. 2-30. Comparative summary of all state premarital laws. Recent data on extension of these laws are given in the *World Almanac*. For discussion of the effectiveness of these laws, consult editorial on "Premarital Physical Examinations," *Eug. Rev.*, Vol. 40 (1949): 181-183, with reply by M. Woodside, Vol. 41 (1949): 57-58.

fied with a particular marriage. Increasing marriage rates, despite increasing divorce, are cited as a proof of this tendency.[25]

In addition to the fact that there are no workable tests or available data by which the person may exercise absolute precaution against the hazards of matrimony, Keller points out that no partnership is exposed to more possible causes of misunderstanding and incompatibility than the average married couple. If for no other reason, divorce will always be a necessary remedy for mistakes on this score, especially because the possibilities of unadjustment increase with the increasing complexity of our culture.

> There will always be, and ought to be, some of it [divorce]. There will be the least of it where there is the minimum of frivolous lightness in contracting the matrimonial relation; and there will be less flightiness, here as elsewhere, if the young are taught about their duties and responsibilities, instead of about their rights to enjoy at the expense of others and of society at large. Our chief defect nowadays is failure to realize that self-limitation and self-discipline are at least as expedient as liberty.[26]

Bibliography

Barnett, J. H., *Divorce and the American Divorce Novel,* University of Pennsylvania Press, Philadelphia, 1939.

Bergler, E., *Divorce Won't Help,* Harper, New York, 1948. Chap. 2, "The Futility of Divorce."

Bossard, J. H. S., *Marriage and the Child,* University of Pennsylvania Press, Philadelphia, 1940.

——— (Ed.), "Toward Family Stability," *Annals, Am. Acad. Pol. and Soc. Sci.,* Vol. 272 (Nov. 1950). Sections by Elliott, M. A., pp. 134-47, and Davis, K., pp. 9-21, on statistical trends.

Cohen, A. E., *Divorce and Alimony,* Michie, Charlottesville, Va., 1949.

Elliott, M. A., and F. E. Merrill, *Social Disorganization,* Harper, New York, 1950. P. 422, Types of decree; p. 430, Alimony; p. 441, Crude divorce rates, 1867-1948. Chap. 21, "After Divorce."

Frazier, E. F., *The Negro Family in the United States,* Dryden Press, New York, 1948. Chap. 18.

---

[25] I. M. Rubinow, "Marriage Rates Increasing Despite Divorce," *Current Hist.,* Vol. 29 (1928): 289-294. For recent continuations of this tendency, consult "Current Rise in Marriages," *Statist. Bull.,* Metropolitan Life Insurance Co., Vol. 21 (1950), No. 10, p. 3, and in the same source: "Postwar Marriage Trends," Vol. 28 (1947), No. 6, p. 1.

[26] A. G. Keller, "Divorce," *Outlook,* Vol. 154 (1930): 157. Compare this point of view with the theme in the story by Conrad Aiken, "I Love You Dearly," in *The Short Stories of Conrad Aiken,* Duell, Sloan and Pearce, New York, 1950, pp. 307 ff.

Gray, A. W., *The Family Legal Adviser,* Greystone Press, New York, 1950. A review and simplification of family laws.

Healy, E. F., *Marriage Guidance,* Loyola University Press, Chicago, 1948. Attitude of the Roman Catholic Church on marriage, divorce, and birth control.

Hollis, Florence, *Women in Marital Conflict, a Casework Study,* Family Service Association of America, New York, 1949.

MacKay, R. V., *Law of Marriage and Divorce,* Grosset and Dunlap, New York, 1948.

Sbarbaro, J. A., and E. Saltonstall, *Marriage is a Trial,* Macmillan, New York, 1947. Opinions of a judge.

Vernier, C. G., *American Family Laws,* Stanford University Press, Stanford University, California, 1931-1938.

Questions

1. Are parents responsible for the guidance of their children toward more stable marriages?
2. What are some of the responsibilities of the church and the school in helping to build more successful marriages?
3. Should divorce be as free (as dissoluble by mutual consent) as marriage?
4. What different forms of marriage and the family have occurred in history?
5. Is it reasonable to anticipate a time when family disorganization will be subjected to investigation rather than to trial in a court?
6. Would a standardized federal divorce law be practicable?
7. With what social institutions does the legal control over divorce come into conflict?
8. Are eugenic regulations concerning marriage indispensable? What are the minimum regulations now enforced?
9. To what extent can society protect itself against divorce by organizing premarital and preparenthood training courses? Are such courses possible?
10. What constructive services may the church, the family clinic, or mental hygiene contribute to the problems of divorce?
11. To what extent do child marriages occur in this country? On what different grounds may objections be raised against "ill-advised" marriages?
12. What are the chief elements of weakness in the administration of laws relating to marriage?
13. Should all state marriage laws be made uniform?
14. Compare some of the local plans to prevent marital breakdowns, such as those of Detroit and San Francisco. Consult references in Sbarbaro in the bibliography of this chapter.
15. Is a divorced person a good matrimonial risk? What are some of the personal traits that are prerequisites for success in remarriage?

16. What is a "divorce mill"?
17. Does the postponement of marriage for educational or economic reasons interfere with satisfactory family adjustments?
18. What is the connection between age at marriage and adjustment relationships? Under what provisions may a proper age be designated as most likely to ensure success of the marriage?
19. What is the chief objection to common-law marriages?
20. Do you agree that the essential conditions to marriage are "essential"? How might they be revised?

CHAPTER 18

CRIME—EXTENT AND VARIETY

"IT'S A CRIME" IS A POPULAR EXCLAMATION THAT IS OFTEN USED TO describe any deviation from the mores as well as crime and criminal behavior. To the average citizen it means any evasion of the code of good citizenship. River pollution, wild-cat real estate projects, traffic violations, lynching, or sexual deviations are examples. Thus it includes acts that endanger public morality or welfare as well as those that are definitely illegal. The average citizen agrees more with the *new* than with *legalistic* criminology.

From this mixture of moral, legal, and personal confusions, many journalistic headlines can be found in the record of American criminality. A statement often quoted is that two million major crimes and an unestimated number of unreported and unrecorded offenses are committed each year. If this record is correct, it amounts to 166 serious crimes per minute–serious meaning killings, robberies, burglaries, assault, and rape. In addition to its being the highest crime rate in the world, its costs (four billion dollars annually) place crime among the most expensive of social problems.[1]

There are three questions that are uppermost in the minds of

[1] E. J. Lukas, *Crime Takes But a Moment to Commit,* New York Society for Ethical Culture, New York, 1947. M. B. Clinard, "Sociologists and American Criminology," *Jour. Crim. Law and Criminol.,* Vol. 41 (1951): 549-577. D. R. Cressey, "Criminologic Research and the Definition of Crimes," *Am. Jour. Sociol.,* Vol. 56 (1951): 546-551. Volumes consulted in the preparation of this chapter are: R. S. Cavan, *Criminology,* Crowell, New York, 1948. Nigel Morland, *An Outline of Scientific Criminology,* Philosophical Library, New York, 1950. W. C. Reckless, *The Crime Problem,* Appleton-Century-Crofts, New York, 1950. E. H. Sutherland, *Principles of Criminology,* Lippincott, New York, 1947. D. R. Taft, *Criminology: A Cultural Interpretation,* Macmillan, New York, 1950.

people who are interested in the problems of crime and in their solution. First, What is crime? Second, Who are criminals and what social conditions are producing them? Third, How may society introduce the proper methods to prevent these costly and demoralizing social acts?

The mixed nature of crime. All studies show that crime arises because of a perplexing combination of personal and material conflicts. Lukas calls it a symptom of personality instability (immaturity, temper, or frustration) and of various disordered social conditions. Others may look upon it more individually as a confusion of attitudes toward human experiences. Nearly everyone agrees that no one factor or motive is sufficient to explain it.

This more general analysis is supported by the many differences in criminal behavior. Crime may be planned and operate as a business. Sometimes crimes are accidents and resemble the problem of accidents. Some occur incidentally in connection with sexual psychopaths, alcoholics, and drug addicts, or as normal events in the conduct of neurotics and psychotics. There are many instances when crime and sharp business practices are hard to separate or when crime is similar to political beliefs or activities. Occasionally it is like exaggerated forms of play.

An illustration is the case of the college boys who decided to put one of their classmates in his place. They invaded his living quarters and gave the victim a thorough beating, five hours after which he died of cerebral hemorrhage. Were these college students criminals, guilty of homicide, murder, assault and battery, or manslaughter? One of the boys was indicted for manslaughter. The court allowed the plea "no contest." The defendant was found guilty, and received a sentence of one to two years in prison, sentence suspended, and $500 fine. Both the defendant, his father, the defending attorneys, and sympathetic college officials thought that the court was too severe.

In answer to the first question, What is crime? it soon becomes clear that criminal conduct is not a fixed and unchanging form of behavior. It varies with the number of laws and with their enforcement. It also varies with interpretations of the law and with the enactment of new laws that make illegal many acts that previously were regarded merely as unsocial or immoral. This interpretation and new legislation are the sources of the *new criminality.*

Who criminals are

Criminals, like crime, are hard to identify by type because of the lack of records. There is the white-collar criminal—perpetrator of the new criminality, which includes "official" and "big business" organized crime—and the professional criminal, who may also be organized but not necessarily of the white-collar variety. There is the habitual criminal who may be organized and/or professional; this type is found in gangs, syndicates, rackets, and corrupt political groups. There are casual, occasional, and episodic (accidental) offenders; and finally the disorganized person, the non-malicious type, who because of some other condition, mental, sexual, or resulting from addiction, may engage in criminal conduct as an incident to his pathological career.

A preliminary answer to the second question as to who the criminal is supplies a cross-section of many different classes of culpable behavior. Most of this behavior is technically criminal. Some of it, however, is sheer ignorance, carelessness, or an evidence of a crass and befuddled culture. In further answer to the question, society tries to distinguish between criminal and noncriminal, but equally dangerous, conduct. Practically without exception, the studies of criminology stress the importance of the social backgrounds of people who are in conflict with the law in order to separate what is moral or immoral from the strictly illegal act.

Laws establish the essential characteristics of criminal acts in their definitions of those who are criminal or who are equally dangerous but noncriminal. Criminals must be of competent age, and their acts must be voluntary and intentional. In the case of some offenders, knowledge as to the nature of the offense is required in the definition of particular crimes, as well as degrees of fraud, negligence, and malice. There are numerous refinements of motive to signify degrees of criminality, such as willfully, knowingly, maliciously, wantonly, and feloniously.

A discriminating illustration of this refinement in the identification of criminality is the strange case of Alger Hiss. From a social, educational, and professional background of the highest type, he was brought to trial by way of a Congressional investigation because of perjury. Although he was originally investigated for the offense of espionage, he could not be tried on this charge since the law of limitations prevented trial for a crime that had been committed more than seven years before indictment. His guilt, conviction, and imprisonment are called a tragedy, not to excuse his conduct but to demonstrate how degrees of guilt can be established against one of a number of equally guilty conspirators in a period of hysteria and political unrest.[2]

Prevention. In answer to the third question, society is challenged with the task of constructing a social program of prevention. The object of this program is twofold, to diminish the number of criminals and to protect law-abiding citizens. In both instances, crime, criminals, and crime-producing social conditions are considered to be the general indications of social and personal disorganization.

The tendency of both crime and criminals is to repeat. This fact alone is enough to show that prevention has played no significant role in historical or current programs of rehabilitation. For this reason, three points of view are regarded as indispensable to a well-organized attack upon the roots of crime problems: (1) to seek out and remove the conditions that induce people to rely on law-breaking as their mode of social adjustment, (2) to make as comprehensive an attack upon crime in high places as upon the petty criminals who now are the majority in courts and prisons, (3) to fix public attention on the precriminal and predelinquent population so that prevention may be ensured by being applied at the most favorable time for the re-education of the potential criminal.

Crime as a social problem

A different approach of criminology looks with the objectivity and completeness of the preventive point of view upon crime as any violation of trust, public or private. It includes sharp commercial practices, cut-throat business organization or methods, national and international combinations to control trade, violation of ordinary ethics by elected or appointed leaders who are supposed to be above bribery or using their position for personal gain, or engaging in activities that may not be against any particular law even though they may threaten public welfare.

Crime as a problem in social policy is identified when it represents a source of social insecurity, a break in social solidarity (referring to the so-called inner enemies of society who defy both its laws and

[2] S. K. Ratcliffe, "The Tragedy of Alger Hiss," *Fortnightly Rev.,* Vol. 167 N.S. (1950): 169-173. Alistair Cooke, *A Generation on Trial: U.S.A. v. Alger Hiss,* Knopf, New York, 1950.

standards), specific injuries, or general crises—each of which stimulates efforts to deter, protect, prevent, or to rehabilitate society, criminals, or victims as particular social policies dictate.

Like antisocial behavior as a whole, crime is a liability to any organized society. It originates from many causes, most of which are institutional, since crime is defined in terms of legal and moral standards. Therefore, the general saying holds that crime increases with the number of laws enacted. But it is also connected with other institutions—with industry, the family, church, and school, and with many other personal and impersonal causes. When crime is viewed as a personal problem, basic elements in biological and mental characteristics are listed as causes. When crime is viewed as a social problem, it is considered to be a natural deviation from standards accepted as normal by the majority. This combined origin brands crime as a typical social problem like poverty or disease, a persistent, self-generating condition. For this reason it has flourished in spite of severe punishments.

Crime is now recognized as primarily a social product. But criminal law, stressing freedom of will, intent, responsibility, guilt, and innocence, has not supported this interpretation. Comparisons show that there were relatively few crimes in primitive society, and that crime increases with every additional prohibition in social evolution. Now, one of the most important questions is: when is an act illegal, or when is an individual guilty of a crime? Originally, crimes were regarded as definite acts. Blackmail, burglary, assault, and murder were crimes to be punished by fixed penalties. This point of view is changing. There is a growing tendency to draw no absolute line between criminal and antisocial behavior. The most definite fact about all crimes is that society considers them illegal under certain circumstances. These modifications are the chief sources of confusion, both in the application of criminal law and in the definition of specific crimes.

Recent emphasis upon the criminal as a person and upon crime-producing situations (the subjective and objective approaches) and less emphasis upon abstract criminal law have clarified these problems. They are now being recognized as clinical problems, to be diagnosed, as in the case of illness, with regard for personal differences, and to be treated accordingly. In the past, society has approached the treatment of crime from two directions, employing violent, inflexible punishment, or overflowing sentimentality. Neither of these systems has been effective. Consequently, an understanding of crime as a modern social problem rests upon the differentiation between legal and illegal behavior, a knowledge of criminals, and to some extent of their victims, and the ability to control those social processes responsible for lawbreaking.

The lawless community describes most of the social problems appearing in court records and in the local, state, and national investigations of crime commissions and Congressional committees.

In 1904 [3] the average American city was called a hotbed of graft, mismanagement, and public and private indifference to the evils in municipal operations. In a review of the same cities forty-three years later, Allen and his latter-day muckrakers described Boston as having one of the most venal and noisome city governments in the world, Chicago as a grimy and dreary dump and a frolicsome flesh-pot, San Francisco as graft-ridden with an incompetent police force, a municipal government that is overrun with clowning politicians and bungling phonies, and a transportation system wholly inadequate to its needs.

Other cities fared no better in this survey. One mayor, while under indictment for graft, was elected governor and then sent to Congress. Before his term in Congress had expired, he was re-elected mayor. He held both jobs until he was imprisoned on a charge of mail fraud.

Another mayor, who boasted: "I am the law," was elected for eight successive terms. His regime was so corrupt that the city gained the title of America's worst. Payrolls were loaded with political appointees until the cost of government became the highest of any city in its population class. The tax rate tripled in three decades; property values were raised one hundred per cent, and the highest per capita bonded debt was accumulated, with the result that the city had to pay premium interest rates to induce purchasers of its bonds. Gambling flourished; the police force was both large and incompetent; garbage disposal was inadequate; streets were littered; the school system was antiquated. Although rated a multi-

[3] Lincoln Steffens, *The Shame of the Cities,* McClure, Phillips, New York, 1904. Robert S. Allen (Ed.), *Our Fair City,* Vanguard Press, New York, 1947. Hans von Hentig, *The Criminal and His Victim,* Yale University Press, New Haven, 1948, Pt. 4. Compare these interpretations with: P. W. Tappan, "Who Is the Criminal?" *Am. Sociol. Rev.,* Vol. 12 (1947): 96-102.

millionaire, this mayor's salary never exceeded $8,000 and he paid no tax to the city.

Victims of crime under these and other unsavory conditions seem to aid and abet the criminal deliberately, as well as being indirectly prone to disaster. In his study von Hentig states that the largest class of victims are those people who are greedy, acquisitive, or sufficiently dishonest to be ready cooperators with criminal acts and schemes. They, too, want to turn a dishonest dollar, generally from the arguments that you cannot control human nature, the appetites, or the individual's biological urge to indulge in some of the forbidden acts. In addition, other classes of victims are youth, because of their inexperience; women, because of their sex; the aged, because of their savings and gullibility; immigrants, minorities, and dull normals, because of their suggestibility; the feebleminded, mentally ill, drug and alcohol addicts, because of their irresponsibility; and, finally, the wanton, the lonesome and heart-broken, and the pleasure or thrill seeker.

General classes of crime

Crime is most readily defined by an enumeration of the specific offenses that are considered by society as contrary to public welfare. Crime is any violation against public policy, and especially against the criminal law. According to Bonger:

> A crime is an act committed within a group of persons that form a social unit, and whose author is punished by the group (or part of it) as such, or by organs designated for this purpose, and this by a penalty whose nature is considered to be more severe than that of moral disapprobation.[4]

Since law is specialized both by definition and by application, the general nature of crime is best described by distinctions between civil and criminal law, criminal law and equity, felonies and misdemeanors, and delinquents and criminals. These distinctions show, furthermore, that the chief legal problem of courts and lawyers is to determine the real intent of the law.

Civil and criminal law. Based upon common, or unwritten, law, two systems of written law have evolved, and offenses are codified according as they are considered to be primarily against the person or the group. Civil law deals with offenses against the individual,

[4] W. A. Bonger, *Criminality and Economic Conditions,* Little, Brown, Boston, 1916, p. 378.

while criminal law deals with offenses against the public. This distinction is, of course, neither wholly valid nor clear-cut. It fails to differentiate between the relative seriousness of specific offenses, or to recognize that an offense may fall within both categories. Injuries against individuals are prosecuted by the civil courts as torts. Crimes, as injuries against the public, are prosecuted in criminal courts.

Criminal law and equity. Criminal law consists of prohibitions against specific acts. This is its major variation from the civil law. It prohibits such acts as murder, burglary, specific nuisances, or other acts, all of which are strictly defined. It also provides definite penalties. Unlike the civil law, the criminal law contains no inclusive prohibition against acts that might be injurious to social welfare. Accordingly, some acts may be legal and yet more serious than those that occur within the criminal law. The criminal law was originally intended to have universal and equal application to all offenders. It was soon recognized, however, that this was both unjust and impracticable, and there arose equity courts to allow deviations from codes in exceptional cases. Equity, consequently, is an attempt to adjust the law to special classes of persons or situations. The juvenile court is one of the best illustrations of the operation of equity in the administration of criminal law. To a limited extent, equity is also admitted in the adjudication of offenses by adults through the use of a parole and probation systems and indeterminate and suspended sentences.

Felonies and misdemeanors. Crimes are further classified by the criminal law into two categories: felonies and misdemeanors. The more serious crimes are called felonies; the less serious, misdemeanors. In general, variations in penalty are implied. The distinction between felonies and misdemeanors has, however, practically disappeared in criminal theory, largely because it has served no useful purpose either in distinguishing the actual seriousness of particular crimes or in furnishing a satisfactory basis for the treatment of individual offenders. However, as will be shown in the next chapter, one disposition frequently used by the courts in meting out punishments is to reduce a felony to a misdemeanor. As long as this practice is recognized by the law, felonies and misdemeanors are valid categories.

Criminals and delinquents. These variations in the application of criminal law to different kinds of conduct indicate efforts to adjust law both to individual differences and to persons in different social groups. Theoretically, such revisions endeavor to clarify the definition of what is meant by legal "intent" or responsibility, or what, broadly interpreted, is right or wrong. At present the distinction between criminals and delinquents is the basis of the separation between adult criminality and juvenile delinquency. Although delinquency usually refers to the offenses of children, it is also expanded to include offenses of other groups who could not be considered intentional or voluntary criminals, such as the feebleminded and psychopathic. Both concepts remain under the criminal law because of the recognition that they cover acts that the state must control.

In summarizing the characteristic elements of crime as a form of social and personal maladjustment, Sutherland points out four descriptive traits to be included in any definition: (1) Crime is constantly changing in content. (2) Specific crimes are acts prohibited by a group with the power to enforce observance. (3) Crime may be either an act of omission or an act of commission. (4) It consists of an overt act and a culpable intent.[5]

When specific crimes lose their significance in comparison with the wholesale operations of racketeering and the crime syndicate, attention is redirected to the nationwide incidence of criminality. From this point of view there are four general types of crime: professional, organized, white-collar, and political graft and corruption. These crimes are similar in several ways. Each represents an occupation or career and is often conducted on a large scale. They are almost exclusively predatory. Often they impress some observers as being crime of the Robin Hood variety, that is, the performing of sordid tasks as a necessary public service. For this reason they are sometimes called an inevitable part of social life. Finally, because of confusion and technicalities in the judiciary, they are often beyond the law. In short they are precise examples of subtle crimes of omission or commission.

Professional crime. A professional criminal is usually a thief. There are opportunities for his special services in many different occupations. Theft may take such forms as the activities of a pickpocket or a sneak thief in department stores or other establishments, shoplifting, extortion, passing illegal checks, or confidence

[5] E. H. Sutherland, *Principles of Criminology,* Lippincott, Philadelphia, 1947, Chap. 1.

games. It may also include illegal practices in law, medicine, or any profession. The chief similarity in all these activities is the use of nonviolent methods. The professional achieves this status, particularly in the eyes of his associates, when he gains sufficient skill to be successful and to evade arrest.

The case of "Dr." Faiman shows how the crime of the professional criminal differs, essentially in respectability, from the closely related form of white-collar criminality. In his career of malpractice, "Dr." Faiman sold an abortion paste that was dangerous because it contained a poisonous metallic salt. So long as operations were limited to a state, the doctor could not be indicted for this specific offense. But when he sold his preparations in interstate commerce, he was indicted for violating the pure food and drug law.

Organized crime. Although the professional criminal is often organized in the sense that he works with a small group of confederates, organized crime is different because it controls a large-scale illegal business and generally tries to monopolize a definite geographical area. Business operations include such activities as the drug traffic, prostitution, gambling, the numbers racket, control of the illegal manufacture of liquor, disposal of loot, numerous commercial rackets, and political graft. Murder, though much publicized as in Murder, Inc., rarely occurs in this category.

A representative example of organized crime is the criminal syndicate. On the surface it is a reputable business but its main line of goods and services are illegal. Its success depends upon public tolerance or indifference or upon bribery of public officials. Organized crime also includes the rackets that are forms of extortion, generally enforced by violence, against business or labor.[6]

Johnson's version of organized crime in the labor movement is an indictment of those leaders who misuse their positions for personal gain:

[6] Malcolm Johnson, *Crime on the Labor Front,* McGraw-Hill, New York, 1950. Case materials describe rackets in Hollywood and in the Longshoremen's Union, the Capone gang, and the Pittsburgh Beer War. Primary methods are described on pp. 2 and 3, including violence, bribery, control of both union and employers' association, misuse of funds, restraint on trade, and selling union contracts or strike insurance. Another source is: R. L. Neuberger, "What Labor Leaders Forget," *Reader's Digest,* Vol. 58 (April, 1951): 67-68. Other examples of organized crime are reviewed in: C. Thompson and A. Raymond, *Gang Rule in New York,* Dial Press, New York, 1940; P. S. Van Cise, *Fighting the Underworld,* Houghton Mifflin, Boston, 1936.

"who have been indicted for murder, kidnapping, rape, robbery, pandering, and every other crime in the books . . . they practice extortion, participate in gambling syndicates, demand wage kickbacks and bribes, engage in blackmail and murder. . . ."

They have no interest in the ordinary aims of the labor movement and they are equally indifferent to the broader interests of the consumer.

White-collar crime differs most from the two preceding types in its respectability and the comparatively high social status of the suspects. It operates above the law in the sense that it can be carried on without legal interference except in a period of hysterical crime probes. Influence is its chief stock in trade. It is ably supported by sharpshooting lawyers and by bribery or public indifference, and here, primarily, it is similar to professional and organized crime. It differs most from the latter in that it operates (more or less as a sideline) in conjunction with a reputable business.

White-collar criminals are the twentieth century's prototypes of the robber barons who flourished in the gilded age of American business expansion and exploitation. They operate on the indefinable border between legality and illegality. Their motto seems to be "never turn an honest dollar if the same profit can be as easily acquired by dishonest methods." Ponzi, Fall, Sinclair, Whitney, Insull, Musica-Coster, and Kreuger are prize examples.

This variety of crime has been called the legitimate rackets. It represents crime in general, however, through its use of dishonesty, misrepresentation, duplicity, direct or indirect bribery, embezzlement, tax frauds, bankruptcies, and illegal uses of money in general. It becomes effective and is coordinated by an individual in a position of public or private trust who violates that trust to his own advantage.

Evidence of the volume of such crime does not appear in the records of the police or courts. It is usually revealed in the studies of crime commissions and in the testimony of Congressional hearings or of trade boards. Professions, trade boards, athletic commissions, and even educational and religious organizations are often mentioned in these records. In Sutherland's opinion, the financial losses to society from this source are much greater than from ordinary criminality, and probably exceed the costs of corrupt government.[7]

[7] E. H. Sutherland, *White Collar Crime,* Dryden Press, New York, 1949. F. E. Hartnung, "White-Collar Offenses in the Wholesale Meat Industry in Detroit,"

Political graft and corruption. When public officials from mayors to congressmen are suspected of crime, investigating commissions, both national and local, are whipped into action. The charges that spur these probes are misappropriation of public funds, accepting bribes, padding payrolls, salary kickbacks from public employees for campaign funds or for the politician's own use, and accepting a percentage from the organized rackets or syndicates for protection.

Illustrations of political graft and corruption are numerous. Contemporary revelations rarely differ from the findings of the crime commissions since the 1920's. The story displays the same machine politics, corrupt elected officials, and mastermind political bosses who dominate the machines. Minor evidences of misconduct in office are frequently ignored as being a normal privilege of those who are lucky or shrewd enough to get elected. Major evidences, such as the governor who invited the Costello syndicate to manage gambling in his state in return for a liberal concession, fail to lead to indictments for crime either because no state or federal law is violated or no group has the courage to begin prosecution. Or when an investigation does take place, suspects are exonerated with excuses that their misconduct in office was slight or that they were only a little dishonest.[8]

Each crime commission regularly acknowledges that there is a nationwide and "sinister pattern of organized crime." It thrives on connivance through official corruption and on mobsters who are immune from prosecution. As the Kefauver committee observes, there are criminal gangs in practically every city, of which the two best known are the Capone syndicate in Chicago and the Costello syndicate in New York.

Their specialty is the control of gambling, which was chosen after experiments in many other rackets because it is most profitable, least illegal, and most readily organized through the pressure of

---

Am. Jour. Sociol., Vol. 56 (July, 1950): 25-34. The story of the Lustron Corporation, as told by *Time,* Feb. 12, 1951, p. 22 ff., is an example of white-collar crime in both a political and a business setting.

[8] E. L. Irey, *The Tax Dodgers,* Greenberg, New York, 1948. "I Never Sold Any Bibles," *Time,* Nov. 28, 1949, is the story of the Costello syndicate. "It Pays to Organize," *Time,* March 12, 1951, and "Crime Hunt on Foley Square," *Time,* March 26, 1951, are accounts of the Kefauver Committee report. In Dr. Cavan's account of organized crime, *op. cit.,* Chap. 6, no essential finding of the Kefauver report is omitted, though the book was published three years before the committee's hearings.

political machines, bribed police, and the willing cooperation of the betting public. As examples of this mode of operations, one sheriff in a Florida county was found whose bank account grew in a period of six years from $2,500 to $75,000, and a city police captain was discovered with a monthly take of $152,000. A former mayor of New York City admitted that large-scale gambling could not exist without police protection, and he confessed to having appointed proteges of the Costello syndicate to office.

Concrete results of the commissions are few and ineffective. Part of this inefficient record can be assigned to the incompatible federal and state laws. But a part of the responsibility must be assumed by the commissions who conduct their hearings loosely and in a setting of pageantry, exhibitionism, and hysteria. In the report by *Time* of the Kefauver investigation, dignity, outrage, denunciation, eloquence, tears, and applause appear with much greater frequency than due process of the law. There is loose use of evidence, a mixture of law and morals to the detriment of both, and a pseudo-trial of witnesses who have not been charged with any crime.

As results, the commissions accomplish little of importance. They furnish no new knowledge as to the nature or spread of organized crime. Reputations are damaged. A few minor political appointees are forced to resign, are demoted, or are indicted for perjury or income-tax evasion. And the only administrative unit that could handle crime of this magnitude, the federal government, continues to avoid consideration of laws involving satisfaction of human appetites, an avoidance founded on the Prohibition fiasco. From the federal point of view, gambling is a biological necessity and its control is left to the discretion of the states.

Specific crimes

Crime in its technical, limited, and legal interpretation is that which is designated in *Uniform Crime Reports.* This official classification will be given and discussed below. As an introduction to the next three topics, the following specific classes of crime are reviewed for their value in contributing to an understanding of the frequency, causes, and social aspects of criminality.

Homicide or murder makes more headlines in the public press because of its personal and exciting character than its frequency merits. In various studies murder is found to be an incidental crime, and the murderer is rarely a careerist or repeater. Most often murder is a result of trifling causes, such as momentary personal animosities, and is usually associated with brawls in which alcohol, jealousy, fits of temper, or domestic disagreements are a part, or it is an accident that occurs in connection with some other crime.[9]

These conditions are indicated in the records of the police, which show the following motives for murder:

	Per Cent Distribution		*Per Cent Distribution*
Altercation	34.3	Dispute—debt	2.6
Marital or passion	26.0	Dispute—gambling	2.2
Unknown	21.3	Dispute—drunken	2.0
Commission of felony	5.7	Indecent assault	0.5
Dispute or revenge	4.9	Mercy killing	0.5
		Total	100.0

Source: Annual Reports, New York City Police Dept., 1937-1940, pp. 6 ff.

An exceptional case is William Heirens, who gained nationwide publicity for the brutal murder of a little girl. Upon arraignment he pleaded guilty to thirty charges. He was sentenced for twenty-four burglaries (one year to life), for three murders (natural life), one robbery (one to twenty years), one burglary (one year to life), and one assault to commit murder (one to fourteen years).

After careful investigation he was adjudged legally sane, of average intelligence, emotionally insensitive and unstable, and with a gross sexual perversion. In the psychiatric report, special emphasis was given to his serious personal demoralization and an appalling immaturity.

Other crimes of violence or passion duplicate some of the exceptional traits of a Heirens and of murderers as a class. A closely similar group are rioters. Their primary characteristics are inferiority in intelligence, education, vocational status and stability, and domestic relations. Unlike murderers, many of them were repeaters with a number of prior arrests and convictions in their records.

Why people steal. Embezzlement as one form of theft is estimated to cost the nation about $400 million each year. As a rule, embezzlers have a good work record and are regarded as trusted employees. They become victims of a chain of circumstances involv-

[9] E. Frankel, "One Thousand Murderers," *Jour. Crim. Law and Criminol.,* Vol. 29 (1938-39): 672-688. H. Harlan, "Five Hundred Homicides," *Jour. Crim. Law and Criminol.,* Vol. 40 (1949-50): 737-752. F. Kennedy and others, "Psychiatric Study of William Heirens," *Jour. Crim. Law and Criminol.,* Vol. 38 (1947-48): 311-341; and Vol. 39 (1948-49): 49-51.

ing one or more of the following conditions: (1) gambling and/or drink, (2) extravagant living standards and careless spending habits, (3) unusual family expenses, generally for sickness, (4) undesirable associates, especially "fast" women, (5) inadequate income, and (6) lax accounting methods or company supervision.

Bank robberies, shoplifting, and relief chiseling follow similar patterns, although there are many variations in the precipitating condition.

Chiseling is a contemporary method of stealing, which is cited both as evidence of personal deficiencies and as a crime of the no-collar classes. In one case, several former farm workers in Wisconsin claimed and received unemployment insurance as shipbuilders, which they had been during the war. When they were dropped from the rolls of the unemployed, a federal representative of the Social Security Administration ruled that "They are entitled to stay on insurance until you can offer them jobs within their latest experience." [10]

Traffic violators are a special class of offenders, and they are also examples of personal immaturity. They are more accurately described as being accident-prone than as criminal. Yet from either point of view they are a costly and serious liability to public welfare. Their contributions to and understanding of crime includes their disregard of law, aggressiveness, egocentricity, inferior intelligence, ignorance of the law, faulty driving habits, ill-health and poor physical condition, and their liability to alcoholism and to some other evidences of psychopathic personality or mental disease.[11]

Military offenders. [12] There are several complementary studies of

[10] C. Stevenson, "Chiselers Endanger our Unemployment Insurance Program," *Reader's Digest,* Vol. 57 (Dec. 1949): 1-7. V. W. Peterson, "Why Honest People Steal," *Jour. Crim. Law and Criminol.,* Vol. 38 (1947-48): 95-103. A. Manes, "Insurance Crimes," *Jour. Crim. Law and Criminol.,* Vol. 35 (1944-45): 34-42. D. G. Morrison, "Dishonesty among Store Clerks," *Sociol. and Soc. Res.,* Vol. 33 (1948): 24-32. L. A. Pratt, *Bank Frauds—Their Detection and Prevention,* Ronald Press, New York, 1947.

[11] L. S. Selling, "Treatment of Traffic Offenders," pp. 510-516 in R. M. Lindner and R. V. Seliger (Eds.), *Handbook of Correctional Psychology,* Philosophical Library, New York, 1947. W. A. Tillman and G. E. Hobbs, "The Accident-Prone Automobile Driver," *Am. Jour. Psychiatry,* Vol. 106 (1949): 321-331.

[12] A. H. MacCormick and V. H. Evjen, "Statistical Study of 24,000 Military Prisoners," *Fed. Prob.,* Vol. 10 (1946): 6-11. M. J. Pescor, "A Study of Selective Service Law Violators," *Am. Jour. Psychiatry,* Vol. 105 (1948-49): 641-652. G. H. Weltner, "Millions of Guilty Men," *Harper's,* Vol. 194 (1947): 81-84.

military crime in the reports of military prisons, selective service violators, and black-market operations. On the whole, military crime is a cross-section of civilian crime.

Black-market operations were carried on far and wide in monetary exchange, clothing, jewelry, food, and cigarettes. The reasons given for this wholesale disregard for the rules were opportunity to make easy money, hatred of authority, occupational blues (disillusionment over asserted war aims), and resentment against the high wages of the home-front industrial soldiers, who also were suspected of making easy money.

The story of Major General Bennett E. Meyers added to postwar demoralization. Meyers had used his office of purchasing agent in the Army to become associated with a private aviation company. As a result of a Senate investigation, he was indicted for lying, evading income tax, and falsifying returns of the company that he represented indirectly through a dummy president.

Violators of selective service laws include three groups: technical violators, Jehovah's Witnesses, and conscientious objectors. Aside from those with obvious religious or conscientious scruples against military service, the group as a whole included men who had failed to comply with technical requirements of the law, who were either mentally ill or of inferior intelligence, who were careless or indifferent, who feared discovery because they were wanted criminals, or who were actual cowards.

Technical violators were the most numerous and were most like the average military prisoner. Few would have qualified for military service because of inability to meet physical requirements. In other respects, too, they had poor backgrounds, particularly from the standpoint of occupational and domestic adjustment. Many had offensive personality traits; some were chronic migrants, and a total of thirty-six per cent had served time for some misdemeanor or crime.

Both the conscientious objectors and the Jehovah's Witnesses shared in common a better than average intelligence rating and a considerably lower record of criminal offenses. The chief difference between these two groups was the higher incidence among the former of chronic medical or psychiatric handicaps and of sexual deviations.

Sex crimes.[13] Sex offenders usually have a record of various crimes in addition to those of sex. All the individuals in Abrahamsen's study had symptoms of mental or character disorders, complicated by traits of extreme brutality and sadism, and all resented authority. The majority, as in the case of William Heirens, could not understand, or would not admit a realization of, the motives for their behavior, and they showed no remorse.

Outstanding among the symptoms of their sexual offenses were a deprived and unhappy childhood—though many were reported as model children—a record of alcoholism in more than half the cases, and recidivism in one-third.

Women offenders.[14] Most students of criminology agree that, although the criminality of women may differ in nature and extent from that of males, much of it is hidden. It is concealed by the tendency of women to operate in association with male criminals, or observers are reluctant to report and police to arrest when women are individual offenders.

Typical female crimes are shoplifting and other thefts, prostitution, abortion, perjury, disturbance of the peace, sex offenses against children, homosexuality, accessory to rape, and infanticide. Little is known about the incidence of these crimes and the ratio of male to female arrests is considered unreliable, because much female criminality is either undetected or women offenders are not reported, arrested, or prosecuted.

Chief among the social characteristics of female criminality is the tendency to begin criminal careers later than men and to continue in them longer. More female offenders are married than male offenders, and there is some tendency for their social emancipation to correlate with increasing criminality. In other possible causes, such as broken homes, poverty, sex repression, occupation, and

[13] D. Abrahamsen, "A Study of 102 Sex Offenders at Sing Sing," *Fed. Prob.*, Vol. 14 (1950): 26-32. J. M. Reinhardt and E. C. Fisher, "The Sexual Psychopath and the Law," *Jour. Crim. Law and Criminol.*, Vol. 39 (1948-49): 734-742. E. H. Sutherland, "The Sexual Psychopath Laws," *Jour. Crim. Law and Criminol.*, Vol. 40 (1949-50): 543-554.

[14] Walter Bromberg, *Crime and the Mind*, Lippincott, Philadelphia, 1948, Chaps. 1 and 2, and pp. 167-173. C. Chesterton, *Women of the Underworld*, Stanley Paul, London, 1928. Otto Pollak, *The Criminality of Women*, University of Pennsylvania Press, Philadelphia, 1950. G. Zilboorg, "Masculine and Feminine," *Psychiatry, Vol. 7* (1944): 257-296. A. N. Foxe, *Studies in Criminology*, Nerv. and Ment. Dis. Mono., No. 76, New York, 1948. Chap. 2 describes the Gray-Snyder Murder Case.

intelligence, there is no condition which particularly identifies the female criminal.

Frequency of criminal behavior

The volume of crime is a subject upon which there ought to be reliable data. It is necessary, for example, to know whether crime is increasing or decreasing, and whether one community is producing more or less criminality than other communities of comparable size and makeup. Although several measurements of crime may be used to determine trends, such as arrests by the police, convictions by courts, or the number of persons imprisoned, none of these is an absolute index of its total extent.

One difficulty in the census of crime can be traced to the fact, already mentioned, that our conception of what constitutes a criminal act is a changing one. Furthermore, local variations in the enforcement of the law or in the efficiency of police, court, and prison systems prevent the discovery of state and national crime rates. There are two other obstructions to an exact quantitative census of crime. Many crimes are concealed or undetected, and consequently are not enumerated. The second is the overemphasis placed upon spectacular crimes. The intense emotional interest aroused by murder or the activities of gangsters leads to the more careful enumeration of the spectacular than of routine cases. Yet the latter are by far the more numerous, and, in their eventual effects, unquestionably the more serious. Moreover, the disappearance of some crimes (from the records) or the rise of new crimes for relatively short periods handicaps the numerical analysis of trends.

Since 1930 the Federal Bureau of Investigation has published statistics of crimes known to or investigated by local police. Although these reports observe a uniform classification, not all communities are represented, and there is a tendency for the crime of rural communities to be neglected. *Uniform Crime Reports,* however, do provide one index and a fairly acceptable classification of crimes.[15]

[15] United States Department of Justice, *Uniform Crime Reports,* Government Printing Office, Washington, D.C. Other sources are: United States Bureau of the Census, *Judicial Criminal Statistics,* which reports the disposition of cases by county courts (the last material, for the year 1945, was published in 1947); United States Bureau of the Census, *Prisoners in State and Federal Prisons and Reformatories,* which is a census of the prison population; and United States Department of Justice, *Federal Prisoners,* a census of individuals who are convicted of violations of federal laws.

CLASSIFICATION AND FREQUENCY OF CRIME

(Number of Arrests [000 omitted])

Offense	Arrests	Offense	Arrests
Drunkenness	181	Gambling	17
Larceny—theft	68	Offenses against family	14
Assault	58	Weapons, carrying	11
Vagrancy	49	Rape	9
Disorderly conduct	47	Forgery and Counterfeiting	9
Suspicion	45	Liquor laws	8
Burglary—breaking and entering	41	Prostitution	8
Driving while intoxicated	39	Other traffic laws	8
Robbery	20	Road and driving laws	7
Embezzlement	20	Criminal homicide	6
Auto theft	17	Narcotic drug laws	4
Other sex offenses	17	Stolen property	3
		Arson	less than 1

Source: United States Dept. of Commerce, 1950, Statistical Abstract, p. 139, Table No. 65.

Is crime increasing? In spite of the evidence of the widespread and hidden character of crime, there are no sources of information that lend support to the conclusion that crime is increasing.[16] There are numerous instances of cyclical variations, when total crime increases or decreases because of some unusual condition such as war, depression, or mass migrations. There are also marked fluctuations in the occurrence of specific crimes, sometimes because of a crime drive or because conditions in general favor a diminishing trend. Most observers agree that the problem of crime is not marked by a trend toward either increase or decrease or by changes in regional contrasts.

Regional or sample studies, of which there are many since 1900, generally endorse this absence of trend. In a Rhode Island study extending over the period 1897-1927, the trend of all crime did fluctuate cyclically, but there was no general increase or decrease. At the beginning of the study the rate was 149 crimes per 100,000 population, and in 1927 it was 148. Thompson reports a similar trendless characteristic of national crime rates in his summary of *Uniform Crime Reports* since 1929.[17]

[16] C. L. Thompson, "Is the Crime Rate Increasing?" *Forum,* Vol. CXI (June, 1949): 352-358. A. L. Porterfield, "A Decade of Serious Crimes in the United States," *Am. Sociol. Rev.,* Vol. 13 (1948): 44-54. ———, "An Index of Crime by States," *Jour. Crim. Law and Criminol.,* Vol. 37 (1946-47): 528-529; Vol. 38 (1947-48): 152-153.

[17] R. S. Cavan, *op. cit.,* pp. 264-265, presents a review of these trends. The use of costs as an index of crime was once customary. It is abandoned because of the distortion in the comparison of costs due to inflation and deflation.

As Porterfield shows, crime rates vary for many different personal reasons and because of numerous social changes in the makeup of a people.

Causes of crime

No topic in the historical literature of crime has received more attention than its personal and social causes. Another topic, classifications of crime, ranked a close second, mainly for its possible contribution to causal study. Combined explorations of psychology, psychiatry, and sociology are responsible for a changing interpretation. Now attention is devoted almost exclusively to the multiple-factor approach.

In this historical background, theoretical or probable explanations have neglected few conditions in the individual or environmental life history of the criminal—he is a born type, biologically determined, instinctive, the product of physiographic factors such as climate, or of social processes such as imitation-suggestion. Thus, human depravity, physical differences, inheritance, and mental and social differences appear prominently in causal analyses. In his summary of various single explanations, including those of heredity and mental and economic conditions, Sutherland points out that sex and the broken home are about as significant as any single cause, and that their contribution is less fundamentally causal than that of the factors that accompany them in a complicated social situation.[18]

In the search for the causes of crime, criminologists and social philosophers in general may be divided into two schools of thought. The first and the earlier, from an historical point of view, is the classical school. The second is called the "positive school."

Classical writers based their theory of crime upon the hypothesis that it is a matter of individual volition, the criminal weighing the advantages of crime against the possibilities of punishment. Under this social philosophy, punishment was severe and arbitrary. Since crime was a matter of innate depravity, reformation could be secured only by deterrence. This theory prevailed during the rise of current legal philosophy and has continued to be the basis of criminal law.

Positivism does not represent a uniform explanation of crime so much as a break from the classical emphasis upon its voluntary

[18] E. H. Sutherland, *op. cit.,* Chaps. 4-8.

character. The positive school includes a number of different theories, all of which are integrated by their stress upon non-volitional causes. This change in emphasis occurred gradually during the nineteenth century and consisted chiefly in directing the attention of students from the study of crime to the study of criminals. For this reason, all recent criminologists may be classified as positivists, regardless of their different points of view.

Mercier's emphasis upon temptation and opportunity as causes illustrates a point of view midway between the classical and the positive explanations:

> What we are now concerned to recognize is that criminal action, like all other action, is compounded of two factors—instinctive impulsion . . . and reasoned action.
>
> My opinion . . . is that crime is a function of two variables, viz., a certain temptable disposition on the part of the person who commits crime, and the temptation to which he is subjected; and that the more of one of these factors that is present, the less of the other is needed to bring about the result. In short, crime is due to temptation offered to temperament. This being so, crime is to be diminished, if at all, by diminishing temptation, including opportunity, and by modifying temperament. If my doctrine of the causation of crime is correct, there is no other way. Legislation can do little to diminish temptation to crime, but it can do much to diminish opportunity.[19]

There are three subdivisions under which the principal theories of the positive school regarding causation may be outlined:

1. Physical and biological causes.
2. Psychological theories.
3. Environmental explanations.

Physical and biological explanations. Lombroso introduced the positive approach to the causes of crime by the isolation of criminal types. According to this theory, crime is the result of atavism or reversion to primitive man. Lombroso's contribution, therefore, was his study of criminals rather than crimes. He did not trace causes to heredity, nor did he stress environmental influences. His notion of the physical basis of criminality occurred to him during the examination of the skull of a famous brigand:

> At the sight of that skull I seemed to see, all of a sudden, lighted up as a vast plain under the flaming sky, the problem of the nature of the crimi-

[19] Charles Mercier, *Crime and Criminals,* Holt, New York, 1919, pp. 25, 253-254.

nal—an atavistic being who reproduces in his person the ferocious instincts of primitive humanity and the inferior animals.

Briefly summarized, this theory holds that criminals are a distinct type. They may be identified by such physical stigmata as asymmetrical cranium, long lower jaw, flattened nose, scanty beard, and low sensitivity to pain. Lombroso was thus concerned with the physical, organic, and mental description of the "true criminal," as distinguished from normal persons, pseudocriminals, or unintentional criminals. He did not regard these stigmata as causes of crime but only as symptoms of physical or mental disorders underlying criminal behavior. Although under the pressure of criticism several modifications of this theory were made during his lifetime and later by his followers, Lombrosianism is still representative of the single-cause explanations.

In spite of its exaggeration, Lombroso's theory made a distinct contribution in stating four facts which are recognized as valid by later criminological investigations: (1) that many criminals are abnormal, (2) that it is necessary to make a multiple approach to the problems of crime, through several sciences, (3) that treatment or reform must be as varied as are criminal types, (4) that the inductive method is indispensable.

An attempt by Goring, an English prison physician, to check Lombroso's physical explanation, disproved the theory of anatomical differences, merging it with the broader theory of biological and hereditary causation. Goring examined 3,000 English convicts, measuring the various physical traits mentioned by Lombroso as indicative of criminality. No significant differences were found between this group and the noncriminal population, except that the convicts were slightly shorter in stature, weighed less, and were possibly of inferior intelligence. Goring concluded that "there is no such thing as a physical criminal type."[20]

His results led to the substitution of heredity for physical explanations. Goring's correlations between criminality and inherited traits became the basis for later attempts to prove that crime appears in families according to Mendelian ratios. As a result there was an overemphasis upon heredity and defective intelligence. Investigation failed to reveal specific inherited traits of criminality or any relationship between the criminal behavior of successive genera-

[20] C. Goring, *The English Convict,* Wyman, London, 1913.

tions in the same family, but it was a valuable stimulus in the search for causes by directing research into several new channels. Hereditary studies necessarily led to the examination of environmental factors and eventually were so combined through the extension of statistical and case studies as to form the present multiple explanation of crime.

Psychological causes. Closely resembling the physical and hereditary explanations are those that reduce crime to a mental condition. Many representatives of this group have concluded with Mr. Dooley that crime is the special prerogative of the simple-minded. Although extravagant claims have been made for the priority of psychopathic conditions as causes, nothing definite can be stated concerning them until the nature and origin of the psychopathies are better understood. For the present a consensus of observations holds that no specific complex of mental conditions leads inevitably to crime, with the possible exceptions of murder and shoplifting.[21]

Moreover, the facts concerning these "psychopathic" criminals have been gathered from criminals in institutions rather than from criminals as a class or by comparison with the noncriminal population. Until the latter contrast is made and the general population is found to be relatively free from mental abnormalities, mentality cannot be considered as the only cause. Sutherland states that both mental disease and crime may be methods of adjusting to social situations, or results of social interaction. Consequently they cannot be known fully until they are studied in connection with the social relationships from which they have developed.

Environmental causes. Factors omitted by the foregoing explanations of crime, or used to supplement them, have been included under the broad term "environmental." Among primary environmental factors often connected with crime are conflicting moral codes, variable cultural standards, ineffectiveness of law or public opinion as controls (by contrast with the force of the mores in primary groups), substitution of secondary for primary group relationships, isolation, mobility, segregation, lags and inefficiencies in such social institutions as the family, the church, and the school. Such specific items as the home broken by desertion, divorce, death, or loss of parental control, neighborhood and community disorganization, absence of wholesome recreation, poverty and its consequences,

21 See above Chap. 4, pp. 96-101, and Chap. 5, p. 131.

occupation, illiteracy, alcoholism, drug addiction, physical defects, and illness are to be included. These are sufficient to show that "environment" omits few of the conditions that have at one time or another been cited as prominent causes of crime. Their specific nature also indicates why the confirmed advocate of primary physical, biological, psychological causes does not take them seriously.

Yet environmentalists, like the others, have supported single factors and one-sided theories. This point of view is well illustrated by the economic explanation, a notion supported by Bonger and many earlier social philosophers. Bonger contends that economic conditions, namely, methods of production and distribution, are sufficient as ultimate causes of crime. Criminality, in other words, is an economic phenomenon. While other causes may be the predisposing or immediate factors, they can be traced eventually to defects in social organization resulting from economic inefficiencies. Bonger states:

> If it were principally the consequence of innate human qualities (atavism, for example) the pessimistic conclusion that crime is a phenomenon inseparably bound up with social life would be well founded. But the facts show that it is rather the optimistic conclusion that we must draw, that where crime is the consequence of economic and social conditions, we can combat it by changing those conditions.[22]

Thus, Bonger makes our economic system the explanation not only of economic crimes such as theft and fraud, but also indirectly of crimes of violence, of sexual, political, and pathological crimes.

Recent trends in the social sciences do not support this or any other effort to interpret social phenomena as the effects of one cause. Criminality is now generally considered, like other social facts and problems—poverty, mental disease, divorce, and the like—to be the result of many causes. For this reason there is no fundamental difference among the scientific explanations of causes, whether the approach is made through an examination of physical, biological, psychological, or social data.[23]

[22] W. A. Bonger, *op. cit.*, p. 669.

[23] H. Ellis, *The Criminal*, Scribner's, London, 1890, pp. 296-297. Ellis summarizes the environmental point of view as follows:

"Criminality, like insanity, waits upon civilization. Among primitive races insanity is rare; criminality, in the true sense, is also rare. Conservatism and the rigid cult of custom form as distinct a barrier against crime as they do against progressive civilization. . . . Like insanity, criminality flourishes among

Summary. No review of the causes of crime leaves the student in a very contented frame of mind. It is useful, however, to show that many definite and foolish notions have been accepted. These include the instigation of the devil, atavism, heredity, environment, and particular biological, economic, and social explanations, degeneracy, epilepsy, psychological obsessions, emotional instability, influence of the foreign born, imitation, and the like. Their variety is proof that little can be known about crime except from the analysis of specific cases. No social problem is more deeply imbedded in cultural differences than is crime. Hence its study offers a challenge to the student in his critical choice of evidence or in his support of untested hypotheses.

Crime remains largely within the unknown, both as to its nature and as to its remedy, because of our human bias toward fixed ideas. For this reason we will continue to suffer from statements such as that by Judge Kavanaugh, who holds that it is:

> . . . a demonstrable, scientific truth, that it is not the weakness of the human mind that makes a criminal, but the wickedness of the human heart.

Equally unsound is the wholehearted disavowal of this belief by Harry Elmer Barnes:

> There is not the slightest iota of freedom of choice allowed to either the criminal or the normal citizen in his daily conduct.[24]

Most devastating of all evaluations of causes is the conclusion, obtained from an examination of one hundred thirteen studies of

---

migrants, and our civilization is bringing us all more or less into the position of migrants.

"But the problem of criminality is not thereby rendered hopeless. Rather it is shown to be largely a social fact, and social facts are precisely the order of facts most under our control. The problem of criminality is not an isolated one that can be dealt with by fixing our attention on that and that alone. It is a problem that on closer view is found to merge itself very largely into all those problems of our social life that are now pressing for solution, and in settling them we shall to a great extent settle it. The rising flood of criminality is not an argument for pessimism or despair. It is merely an additional spur to that great task of social organization to which during the coming century we are called."

[24] M. A. Kavanaugh, *Criminal and His Allies,* Bobbs-Merrill, New York, 1928, p. 62; H. E. Barnes, *The Repression of Crime,* Doubleday, Doran, New York, 1926, p. 24.

criminal behavior, that criminals and noncriminals cannot be shown by test to differ in any personality trait.[25]

Social aspects of crime

Although no one factor except illegal conduct distinguishes criminals as a class, a summary of those conditions generally indicative of crime is a useful supplement to a review of causes. Numerous classifications of criminals have been made as a step in this direction. None of these is wholly satisfactory, but they do show the variety to be expected in this problem. The criminal types usually listed in these classifications are single offenders, habitual criminals, recidivists, criminals by chance and by opportunity, professional, political, and psychopathic criminals. Root suggested a psychological classification of crimes involving: (1) sustained and prolonged premeditation, (2) temporary premeditation, (3) impulse acts, (4) coincidental cluster of events, and (5) habitual dereliction.[26]

From statistical and case studies, typical characteristics of vast groups of the criminal classes have been found in connection with age, sex, residence, nativity (race), intelligence, education, economic and social status, and war or other crises.

Age. Adolescence and the early years of adulthood are the periods of greatest criminality. Crime reaches its maximum in the age group of 21 to 24, gradually increasing from the age of 10 and decreasing to the age of 44, after which the decrease is rapid. In recent reports of state and federal prisons, from 40 to 60 per cent of the prisoners are under 25 years of age. Statistics of arrest and convictions show the same general tendency. Among prisoners, the

[25] K. F. Schluessler and D. R. Cressey, "Personality Characteristics of Criminals," *Am. Jour. Sociol.,* Vol. 55 (Mar. 1950): 476-484.

[26] W. T. Root, *A Psychological and Educational Survey of 1916 Prisoners in the Western Penitentiary of Pennsylvania,* Pittsburgh, 1927, p. 34. D. Abrahamsen, "Family Tension, Basic Cause of Criminal Behavior," *Jour. Crim. Law and Criminol.,* Vol. 40 (1949-50): 330-343. H. A. Bloch, "Economic Depression as a Factor in Rural Crime," *Jour. Crim. Law and Criminol.,* Vol. 40 (1949-50): 458-470. V. Fox, "Intelligence, Race, and Age as Selective Factors in Crime," *Jour. Crim. Law and Criminol.,* Vol. 37 (1946-47): 141-152. A. H. Kratz, *Prosecutions and Treatment of Women Offenders and the Economic Crisis,* University of Pennsylvania Press, Philadelphia, 1940, Chap. 3. E. R. Moses, "Differentials in Crime Rates between Negroes and Whites," *Am. Sociol. Rev.,* Vol. 12 (1947): 411-420. R. E. Watts, "The Influence of Population Density on Crime," *Jour. Am. Statis. Assoc.,* Vol. 26 (1931): 12-13. A. L. Wood, "Minority-Group Criminality and Cultural Integration," *Jour. Crim. Law and Criminol.,* Vol. 37 (1946-47): 498-510.

rate per 100,000 population is highest for males 20 years of age and for females 19 years of age.

It is in the younger age groups, moreover, that serious offenses occur most frequently. Prison commitment records indicate that burglary, larceny, forgery, fraud, rape, and trespassing are often the crimes of persons under 20 years of age. The age group 21 to 24 has the highest rate for homicide, robbery, disorderly conduct, assault, carrying concealed weapons, gambling, adultery, prostitution, and malicious mischief. Fraud and forgery are highest in the group from 25 to 34 years.

For many years attention has been directed toward this early origin of crime as proof of the need for prevention, especially during the unsettled period between school and marriage or occupational adjustment. One point repeatedly brought out in studies of criminal careers is that most criminals begin as juvenile delinquents. This fact is substantiated in the several investigations by Healy and the Gluecks, and is the conclusion of Goring's study of the habitual criminal.

Sex. The social nature of crime is revealed again in its distribution among the sexes. Judged by arrest or prison records, crime is considerably less frequent among females. Approximately 9 times as many males as females are committed to prisons. Statistics of arrests in Massachusetts show a greater disparity, males figuring more often than females by a ratio of 15 to 1. In an analysis of crime in Canada during the years 1891 to 1930, it was found that 95 per cent of the crimes were committed by males.

There is also a difference in the types of crimes committed by males and females. Women are usually involved in offenses against sex morality, vagrancy, or violation of the drug laws. These sexual offenses explain the high incidence of female crime among persons under 20 years of age.

Crime as an urban phenomenon. Most studies of urbanization show a positive correlation between crime and the density of population. This trend, however, does not mean an absolute difference in the ratio of criminality between city and country, because the urban increase is largely due to the number of minor offenses possible. The city represents a combination of many factors favorable to this urban-rural difference. In addition to rural migration to the city, the breakdown of primary group contacts in large populations, more laws and stricter enforcement than in rural communities, there are such matters to be considered as urban mobility, the sharp contrasts between culture groups and between economic standards, lack of recreational facilities, and the presence of commercialized vice and amusements.

In his study of the relation between population density and crime, Watts concluded from Canadian rates during the period 1891 to 1930 that crime increases at a greater rate than population. During these years, population increased 115.9 per cent, in contrast to a 639.7 per cent rise in crime. In the judicial districts with the largest cities, the crime rate averaged 500 per 100,000 population; in the least populated areas it did not exceed 90. Prison commitment records for the United States show a high proportion of commitments from cities, over 75 per cent, especially from migratory classes. There is also considerable evidence that a large number of convictions occur among interstate migrants.[27]

Crimes increasing directly with the density of population are violation of drug laws, habitual offense, burglary, robbery, larceny, embezzlement, possession of stolen property, and general sex offenses.

Nativity. Although statistics of arrests and commitments show a high rate of criminality among the foreign born, Sutherland is of the opinion that foreign birth is not a major factor in crime. Two reasons are generally given for this opinion. Immigrants are usually adult males. Consequently, crime rates should be computed according to the proportion of adults in the population when comparisons are made with the native born. Moreover, immigrants usually settle in cities where either their economic status or the absence of normal home life might be decisive factors. When allowance is made for their distribution in the adult population, local studies of crime show in general that the foreign born have a lower rate of criminality than the native born for arrests, convictions, and commitments.

This conclusion holds for serious crimes as well as misdemeanors. Some foreign groups do have disproportionately high rates for certain crimes; for example, Italians and Mexicans for crimes of violence. A more important nativity trend, however, is the high rate of criminality among the children of foreign-born parents. Of the three groups, native born, foreign born, and native born of foreign or mixed parentage, the last has the highest crime rates. In other

[27] M. B. Clinard, "Rural Criminal Offenders," *Am. Jour. Sociol.,* Vol. 50 (1944): 38-45.

words, in criminal records this group is closer to the native born of native parents than to the foreign born.

Practically all observers have found an excessively high rate of crime among Negroes. The study of the Western Penitentiary of Pennsylvania found 575 Negro prisoners instead of the 42 which would have been the normal quota according to Negro distribution in the population. This is a frequency thirteen times greater than that of the white population. It is also admitted by these observers that statistics of Negro criminality are more unreliable than those of other groups. Negroes are arrested more frequently, at least for certain offenses, and are more easily convicted than are the whites, largely because of racial discrimination. Poverty, lack of education, residence in the worst sections of the city, low housing and living standards, and the inadequate care of Negro defectives are further reasons assigned for this criminality. Consequently, instead of racial comparisons and explanations, economic status, limited recreation, restricted employment opportunities, unadjustments to urban life, rebellion against discrimination, and frustration account for this difference in the races.

Intelligence. Variations in intelligence and mental defects no longer hold the prominent position formerly given to them as traits descriptive of the criminal. Although estimates of mental abnormality among prison populations are high, their range is too extensive to be convincing. Another source of faulty comparison is the more frequent detection and arrest of the defective criminal.[28]

Most studies fail to distinguish significant mental differences between the criminal and the general population. Earlier opinions to the contrary are explained through the absence or inadequacy of tests or by the fact that they were applied to selected groups. Criminals are found in all levels of intelligence. The distribution of intelligence test scores among criminals is the same as that of Selective Service, and the results of intelligence tests for prison populations are similar to those of noncriminals.

Three important contributions as to the relationship between

[28] J. G. Wilson and M. J. Pescor, *Problems in Prison Psychiatry,* Caxton Printers, Caldwell, Idaho, 1939. One half of the prisoners included in Wilson and Pescor's survey were considered normal mentally; four to fifteen per cent of the prison population were judged to be psychoneurotic. Here, too, the chief difference between mentally normal and abnormal prisoners was in the nature of their crimes, the former engaging more than the latter in crimes of dishonesty.

crime and mental condition are to be found in the connection between mental status and certain types of crime. Sex crimes are found mostly among those of low intelligence; fraud and murder, among the high-intelligence group; and burglary, larceny, and robbery are between these extremes.

Educational, economic, and family status. Crime is associated positively with illiteracy and inadequate education, poverty, and the broken home.

Illiteracy is twice as great among prisoners as among the general population. But illiteracy is no more important than is inadequate education. Haynes states that less than four per cent of the men at the Anamosa Reformatory in Iowa had a complete high school education and that less than one in 500 had a complete college education. The average educational attainment of these men was less than that of the sixth grade. Offenses also vary with degrees of education. Assault, homicide, and violation of liquor laws are numerous among illiterate prisoners, while those who have attended college are committed for embezzlement, fraud, and forgery in a large proportion of cases.

While economic or occupational status, like age or sex, may be wholly incidental in their association with crime, such conditions as low wages, irregular employment, family instability, and moral hazards do make high contributions. In a Texas penitentiary study, 76.8 per cent were urban workers, and there was a much larger proportion of unskilled workers than of the upper urban classes whose work is steady. Prison records for the entire country support this economic basis of crime, showing a close correlation between low income and unemployment and convictions. In the report of the Chicago City Council on Crime, the statement is made that the penal institutions of that city are filled with:

> . . . poor and petty criminals . . . who were sentenced . . . in the great majority of cases . . . because of their poverty and were committed because they were too poor to pay the small fines imposed upon them.[29]

High rates of crime are found for both adults and juveniles among persons unadjusted because of abnormal family relationships. Case studies of juvenile delinquents show that from one third to two thirds come from homes where these exist. Among adult criminals, few of whom had a normal family life prior to their commitment,

[29] F. E. Haynes, *Criminology,* McGraw-Hill, New York, 1935, p. 3.

there is a high percentage of divorce and desertion. Thus, the early separation from parents, poor and overcrowded homes, divorce, desertion, and inadequate parental control are considered important supplements to inferior economic status.

These factors describe the salient characteristics of the individual criminal. In general, he is a young man, native born, an urban resident of average intelligence, who is handicapped by inadequate education, irregular working conditions and poverty, and by broken family ties. Although each of these traits identifies sources of criminality, none may be regarded as an absolute cause. They show rather pointedly the small use of current punitive systems, and direct attention to other methods of treatment that might well be exploited as resources against crime.

Crime during crises. Crime not only appears as a crisis in the life of the individual but it tends to respond critically to all mass disorders. In his study of a decade of criminality, Porterfield shows that crime tends to increase and to behave erratically both during war years and in the turmoil of postwar adjustments. The same conclusion holds for other disorganizing social influences such as depressions, labor unrest, or mass migrations.

Specific illegal acts also vary widely under conditions of boom towns, overcrowded industrial areas, proximity to military camps, and other correlates of wartime activity, such as rationing, price controls, and inflation.

Many times the particular types of misbehavior under these conditions of distress are not called criminal. Often, too, the facts about both the conduct and the causes are suppressed. Under the strained social relations of war, the primary characteristic of crime is to become different as indicated by such occurrences as profiteering, selling inferior goods to the armed services and to the public, artificial shortages, combines to regulate production, black marketing, and cartels.

Most of the specific crime that does develop is an indication of social unrest that follows interruptions of family life, the mobility of population, and overcrowding. On the whole, it falls within the interests of the new criminology.

Summary

Crime is one of the most typical social problems. It satisfies all the theoretical requirements of multiple causation, widespread incidence, correlation with other problems, relativity (to time, place, and public opinion), persistence, subtlety, secrecy and hidden or masked nature, disastrous consequences, moral character, and challenge to experimental correctives.

In all these respects, too, it can be compared with divorce. Both, in addition, are causes and results of personal and social distress. Both are defined as legal as well as social facts. Both illustrate the provoking confusions that can arise to threaten the security or peace of mind of the divorcé or the suspected criminal when laws are unclear, contradictory, or changeable. Furthermore, the entire sequence in both that may result in a harmonious agreement between the legal and social definitions can be reversed—divorce by remarriage and crime by pardon.

There is another more personal and possibly more revealing similarity in both divorce and crime. It is sometimes called a proneness either to the disordered behavior of crime or to marital instability. Each is like accident proneness or the susceptibility to physical disease. For no particular or discoverable reason, some people have a greater liability than others—a liability that far exceeds chance occurrence. Wood calls this characteristic a result of cultural disorganization or personal frustration; Fox is of the opinion that a primary feature of all criminality is the social immaturity of all classes of offenders; Cavan reaches the same conclusion in stating that because some criminals never seem to mature they continue in crime until age leads to deterioration and a more ready compliance with the law. In all these interpretations of lack of maturity, these observers agree in meaning absence of judgment, self-control, or ability to suppress antisocial drives.

This delay in maturing or absence of integrated personality is illustrated by the reflections of an exprisoner.[30] This man was convicted of assault with intent to rob. He had the typical precriminal career, leaving school after the eighth grade, drinking excessively, an unsuccessful marriage, first arrest at nineteen, an unstable and mobile occupational experience. As he reflected on this background when he was about to be paroled, he wrote:

"It took me a long time to answer the question: What happened to me? and the answer didn't come all at once. When it did come, it was a shock. I was 42 years old and I was just beginning to grow up."

[30] "Home from Prison," *Coronet,* Vol. 30 (June, 1951): 109-111.

In the quest for important factors in criminality, possibly no more accurate indication will be discovered than this immaturity or the social and personal deficiencies that it involves. It shows itself in the tendency of criminals to be repeaters, in the tendency of crime to be concentrated within definite geographical areas, and in the tendency for criminality to respond immediately to changing social conditions.

Recidivists, repeaters in crime, constitute a large portion of criminals arrested, convicted, and imprisoned. Because of imperfect methods of identification and the lack of coordination among penal agencies between states or within the same political area, the precise amount of recidivism is unknown. From records of arrests and commitments, the average is stated to be more than fifty per cent. In other words, half of our criminals are plural offenders. Recidivism not only explains crime waves and the persistency of serious crimes, but is also helpful in identifying that portion of the criminal population which indulges in crime as a business, and in distinguishing those criminal types who, because of abnormal mental and social traits, require other than current methods of restraint.

In the twenty-year period covered by the Missouri Crime Survey, recidivism increased 100 per cent, and 31.9 per cent of the prisoners in the Missouri Penitentiary were serving second terms. An illustration of this failure of courts and prisons to detect the habitual criminal is shown in the following record:

Charge: Burglary and larceny.
Age: 30.
Convicted: 9–8–25, 25 years.
Previous record:
4–29–24 Convicted of larceny from person. Sentence, 2 years; released 6–28–25.
12–6–19 Convicted, charge not stated; sentence, 5 years; released 11–5–22.
3–7–16 Convicted of robbery, first degree. Sentence, 5 years; released 9–12–19.
9–5–12 Convicted of robbery, third degree. Sentence, 2 years; released 3–14–14.[31]

Recidivism occurs most frequently among the young, among those with relatively little education, among the single, and among those who are engaged in certain types of crime (professional and psychopathic criminals). Case X, quoted by R. F. Yeomans as an illustra-

[31] *Missouri Crime Survey,* Macmillan, New York, 1926, p. 527.

tion of the failure of our judicial and penal systems, is typical of the psychopathic criminal:

Case X—This woman, sixty years old, was sent to the Boston State Hospital from the Suffolk County Jail, where she had been held on a complaint of drunkenness. She had been examined by the court psychiatrist at the request of the sheriff.

In two months she was returned to court as recovered from an alcoholic psychosis, and was sentenced to three months at the state farm. This was the twenty-second sentence that she had served. In less than ten years she had had nine commitments to state hospitals. Her court record from 1905-1927 shows a total of 91 arrests, 88 for drunkenness, one for night walking, one for "bootlegging," and one for escaping from a penal institution. At the present time she is at the state farm serving her twenty-sixth sentence. The length of time that she spends at the state farm has varied from three days to seven months. The intervals between terms have varied from five days to ten months, in ten cases being under one month in length. She is known to have twenty-three aliases, so that some of her record may not be included in this review.[32]

Zones of criminality. Crime, like physical disease, becomes infectious and spreads under the stimulus of favorable conditions. Hence, the discovery of delinquency areas is an important step in establishing social and judicial prophylaxis or quarantine stations. According to studies in Chicago and other cities, this zone of criminality is identical with the zone in transition, an area just beyond the central business district which is in the process of being absorbed for business or industrial purposes. This region is distinguished by deteriorated housing, overcrowding, low living standards, disorganized family and community life, and the absence of constructive social forces.

This zone is the nucleus both of adult crime and juvenile delinquency. No other district has an equal crime rate of serious or minor offenses. Recidivism is also a product of the conditions associated with this area.

When the several social and personal predisposing factors are combined, they will probably produce a causal pattern consisting of: (1) the general effects of cultural change and social organization, (2) competing systems of behavior, and not individual traits or conditions, (3) cultural conflict, (4) differences in a person's associations, (5) his exposure to social disorganization, (6) the occurrence of social

[32] "Who are the 'Criminal Insane'?" *Mental Hygiene,* Vol. 14 (1930): 687.

crises, (7) mobility and heterogeneity of population, and (8) the occurrence of displaced or minority groups.

Bibliography

Unlike the publications listed in the bibliographies of other chapters, these volumes are listed because of their reference to special topics and problems that are not treated specifically in the foregoing discussion.

Bornstein, Joseph, *The Politics of Murder,* William Sloane Associates, New York, 1950.

Canavan, M. M., and L. Eisenhardt, *The Brains of Fifty Insane Criminals,* Department of Mental Health, Boston, 1942.

De River, Joseph P., *Sexual Criminal,* Thomas, Springfield, Ill., 1949.

Hamar, A. C. (Ed.), *Detroit Murders,* Duell, Sloan and Pearce, New York, 1948.

King, W. J., *Moral Aspects of Dishonesty in Public Office,* Catholic University Press, Washington, 1949.

Loth, D. G., *Public Plunder: A History of Graft in America,* Carrick and Evans, New York, 1938.

MacDonald, J. C. R., *Crime is a Business,* Stanford University Press, Stanford University, Calif., 1939.

Milligan, M. M., *Missouri Waltz: Inside Story of the Pendergast Machine,* Scribner's, New York, 1948.

Porterfield, A. L., *Crime, Suicide and Social Well-Being in Your State and City,* Leo Potishman Foundation, Fort Worth, Texas, 1948.

Vollmer, August, *The Criminal,* Foundation Press, Brooklyn, New York, 1949.

Questions

1. What items would you include in the total crime bill of your community?
2. Can you describe a crime that resembles some other problem more than it does a typical crime?
3. Do you agree that considerable crime is a result of public tolerance?
4. What are the legal requirements of a criminal act?
5. Is the Alger Hiss case an example of the new criminality?
6. In what crimes does success depend upon the willing cooperation of the victims?
7. Can you add to the identifying traits of the individual criminal?
8. (a) How do professional crime, white-collar crime, and organized crime differ?
   (b) How do urban and rural crime differ?
9. Why are many investigating commissions ineffective?
10. In what class of criminality would you place William Heirens?
11. Is relief chiseling a crime?

12. What are the primary personality traits of traffic offenders?
13. Is crime by a person in a position of public trust more serious than the same act by a private citizen?
14. Are conscientious objectors criminals?
15. What is typical female crime?
16. Why is it difficult to discover the total volume of crime?
17. Read the article mentioned in footnote 25. Do you agree that subjective traits of criminality are not clearly revealed?
18. Why did the classical criminologists search for and report so many unlikely causes of crime?
19. Do you agree that immaturity may be a basic factor in crime?
20. Can you reconcile this theory with the analysis of a crime pattern that concludes this chapter?

CHAPTER 19

CRIME—ADMINISTRATIVE CONTROL

STUDIES OF THE CYCLICAL OR CHANGING TRENDS OF CRIME SHOW THAT the public rarely supports a consistent policy of repression or prevention. Periods of violent protest because of some real or fictitious orgy of crime are followed by periods of comparative indifference. As results, there is little serious interest in the actual efficiency of administrative agencies that are supposed to maintain law and order, and problems in the adequate treatment of offenders are generally neglected.

A more precise indication of the several challenges that crime presents to a society is to be found in the conclusions of specialized criminologists. These observers agree that among the major administrative problems in the control and prevention of crime are such conditions as: (1) too few criminals are arrested and convicted, (2) crime costs are excessive, not the least of which is the maintenance of an expensive prison system, (3) methods of apprehension, court procedure, and treatment of prisoners are antiquated, and (4) too little attention is given to the study of the offender's real problems and too few trained people are available in each stage of crime-producing situations, from predelinquent or precriminal careers to detection, arrest, conviction, incarceration, and release.[1]

[1] Primary sources of the materials in this chapter are the references in footnote 1 of Chap. 18, above, and: S. Bates, *Prisons and Beyond,* Macmillan, New York, 1936. E. L. Brown, *Lawyers and the Promotion of Justice,* Russell Sage Foundation, New York, 1938. D. Clemmer, *The Prison Community,* Christopher, Boston, 1940. R. Fosdick, *American Police Systems,* Century, New York, 1920. Max Grünhut, *Penal Reform,* Clarendon Press, Oxford, 1948. F. E. Haynes, *The American Prison System,* McGraw-Hill, New York, 1939. B. McKelvey,

Most of these legal and social needs are illustrated by the career of Jack Callahan:

> . . . look at my own case: arrested eleven times in seventeen years and served but two terms—a two-year "stretch" and six months of a sixteen-year term. "Dutch" Anderson was arrested seven times in twelve years and served but two terms. . . . Jack ("Legs") Diamond was arrested twenty-three times in sixteen years with but one conviction, a term in the reformatory. How did we do it? Sharpshooting lawyers, crooked politicians and soft-hearted men and women who viewed us as poor boys who never had a chance when we were juveniles.[2]

Changing concepts of punishment

Punishment originated in the desire for revenge against personal injuries, but was gradually assumed as an obligation of the state. Thus, it consists of two concepts: a restraint, to be exercised by the majority over the individual; and pain or suffering, which is calculated to deter a repetition of the offense. The specific objectives of punishment are to put the criminal, either permanently or for a fixed period, where he can do no further harm; to instill in the criminal, and other persons as well, a fear of committing crime; and to reform the criminal in so far as that is possible.

In general, three types of penalty have been enforced: (1) physical torture, (2) social degradation, banishment, transportation, and imprisonment, and (3) financial losses. The history of these penalties shows considerable ingenuity in their application but little or no effort to make them adaptable to the offense or the person. Fines, for example, were originally assessed to compensate the injured person. They were gradually taken over by the state under its right to tax, and are used today in some offenses as a substitute for imprisonment.

In their historical applications, punishment and especially cruelty were employed indiscriminately.[3] Inanimate objects, animals, and

American Prisons, University of Chicago Press, Chicago, 1936. R. Pound, *Organization of the Courts,* Little, Brown, Boston, 1940. V. A. Rapport, "State-Wide Police," *Jour. of Crim. Law and Criminol., Vol.* 30 (1940): 706-711. Bruce Smith, *Police Systems in the United States,* Harper, New York, 1949. A. Vollmer and A. E. Parker, *Crime and State Police,* University of California Press, Berkeley, 1935.

[2] Jack Callahan (pseud.), "Colleges for Crooks," *Outlook,* Vol. 158 (1932): 140.

[3] E. P. Evans, *The Criminal Prosecution and Capital Punishment of Animals,* pp. 206-207. Dutton, New York, 1906. "Medieval penal justice sought to inflict the greatest possible amount of suffering on the offender and showed a

the dead were subjected to the same penalties that were presumed to regulate the behavior of man. This extensive use of cruelty was due to the theory that crime was either a matter of personal choice or the result of evil spirits. The punishment of witchcraft is an illustration of the latter theory. A section in the laws of Cnut indicates the same spiritual interpretation of crime. For a repeated offense, this code states:

> Let there be no other bot (fine) if he be foul (at the ordeal) than that his hands be cut off or his feet, or both, according as the deed may be, and if then he have wrought yet greater wrong, then let his eyes be put off, or his nose and his ears and the upper lip be cut off; or let him be scalped . . . so that punishment be inflicted and also the soul preserved.[4]

Thus, the history of crime resembles the history of medicine, with its bleedings, cuppings, purgings, and blisterings. Both were in search of a panacea for little-understood ills.

The chief difference between contemporary and medieval penology is the current effort to make the penalty fit the person as well as the crime. But no panacea has been discovered, and the new criminology covers a multitude of half-accepted doctrines. The chief modifying factors in modern penology are the emphasis upon the social causes of crime and, incidentally, the changing attitude toward individual responsibility. Both combine in their efforts to prevent crime through controls other than those embodied in the criminal law.

Criminal law is considered too inflexible, and its penalties too

---

diabolical fertility of invention in devising new methods of torture even for the pettiest trespasses. The monuments of this barbarity may now be seen in European museums in the form of racks, thumbkins, interlarded hares, Pomeranian bonnets, Spanish boots, scavenger's daughters, iron virgins and similar engines of cruelty. Until quite recently an iron virgin, with its interior full of long sharp spikes, was exhibited in a subterranean passage at Nuremberg, on the very spot where it is supposed to have once performed its horrible functions; and in Munich this inhuman instrument of punishment was in actual use as late as the beginning of the nineteenth century. The criminal code of Maria Theresa, published in 1769, contained forty-five large copperplate engravings, illustrating the various modes of torture prescribed in the text for the purpose of extorting confession and evidently designed to serve as object lessons for the instruction of the tormentor and the intimidation of the accused." R. G. Caldwell, *Red Hannah,* University of Pennsylvania Press, Philadelphia, 1947. An account of physical punishment in Delaware.

[4] George Ives, *A History of Penal Methods,* S. Paul, London, 1914, pp. 8, 70. A. W. Stearns, "Evolution of Punishment," *Jour. Crim. Law and Criminol.,* Vol. 27 (1936): 219-230.

rigid, to cover the various problems of modern crime. At the same time, its administration through several uncoordinated agencies is cited as an important source of inefficiency and abuse. These deficiencies are traced in part to the dependence of law upon the theory of individual responsibility, but no one has ever been able to set up the limits of responsibility for different classes of persons or to prove that there is no individual responsibility. However, major reforms in the actual operation of penal agencies are traceable to the gradual acceptance of limited responsibility. Perhaps the most drastic of these suggestions is that criminal law should be restricted wholly to the settlement of legal questions and should be separated from the punishment or treatment of crime. Under this plan, punishment would be a case problem for a board of experts.[5]

Administrative agencies

While in theory modern penology stresses treatment rather than punishment, it really differs from medieval systems less in this respect than in its multiplication of administrative agencies. In general, definite reforms have been realized in the abandonment of cruel and unusual punishments. But opposed to this humanitarian trend is the possibility that the criminal may avoid punishment entirely, even after arrest and conviction. This is an administrative problem, because of the lack of coordination between the several agencies to which the various steps in the process of punishment are assigned.

Administrative agencies consist of three principal divisions: the police, the judiciary system, and the prison. Each of these divisions contributes to or controls punishment. The police are organized in local, state, and federal units. Detective and identification divisions and detention institutions are connected with one or more of these units. Courts are concerned with the prosecution, and under their jurisdiction there are several specialized courts: police or lower courts; and superior, family, and juvenile courts. They also control the prosecution and the jury. Punishment is usually connected with one of the penal institutions (prisons, reformatories, or juvenile homes) or with probation and parole systems.

[5] For arguments for and against individual responsibility, consult: C. B. Farrar, "Criteria of Responsibility," *Jour. Crim. Law and Criminol.*, Vol. 21 (1930): 438-445. C. S. Kenny, *Outlines of Criminal Law*, Cambridge University Press, London, 1925, pp. 501-502. Other references in the *Jour. Crim. Law and Criminol.* are Vol. 19 (1928): 181-295; Vol. 20 (1929): 88-101; Vol. 21 (1930): 267-296; Vol. 28 (1937): 845 ff; Vol. 30 (1939): 634 ff.

The disposition of a case by any one of these agencies does not vary materially from earlier forms of punishment. Penalties most frequently employed are: a fine, a fine plus a short imprisonment, an imprisonment for various terms, an indeterminate sentence, a life sentence, a death penalty, a deferred sentence, or probation and parole. Possibly an incompleted trial should also be mentioned as a form of punishment. This disposition and others will be listed among customary methods by which the docket is cleared, although they may not fall logically within a classification of penalties.

The police

Being on the first line of defense between society and the criminal classes, the police fulfill several important functions in the detection and prevention of crime and in the enforcement of the law. This is a comparatively new subdivision among administrative agencies; the first organized force was that of New York City, which was established in 1844. Police functions are classified into two principal divisions, the administrative and the criminal. Administrative functions consist broadly of noncriminal activities, such as traffic control, licensing, special squads, and other supervisory work. All activities directly connected with the prevention, the suppression, and the detection of crime are listed under the criminal division.

In the performance of either of these functions, the police occupy an unenviable position. They are obliged to determine what laws are to be enforced, when a law is broken, when an arrest must be made, and what conditions must occur to prove a case in court. Because of this wide range of power and discretion, the police settle many cases out of court. This practice and their inability to obtain legal evidence of guilt are two serious loopholes in an effective system of crime suppression. The chief problems of police administration are to define the limits of police powers and to recruit a police personnel which is capable of exercising the discretion allowed by these powers. As a matter of fact, the police are called upon to perform many tasks that they are neither trained nor specifically authorized to do, simply because the strict enforcement of the law would overload the courts.

Moreover, the police are frequently held responsible for the entire prevalence of crime. They are chiefly criticized because they are the most obvious agents in law enforcement or because of their wide range of power. Incidentally, criticism constantly arises over particular methods used by the police that the public does not understand. This statement is especially true regarding direct public contacts, as for example, in the police application of the lecture system, although the criticism applies to traffic enforcement, which is an administrative rather than a criminal function of the police.

Four major police problems are: (1) the few arrests made in comparison with crimes reported as known to the police, (2) the disposition of cases by the police, (3) the caliber of police personnel, and (4) association of police with local politics and their alleged cooperation with graft and other criminal rackets. Each of these problems is connected directly with inefficiencies in other administrative agencies, especially with problems of prosecution.

One of the chief defects in the current organization of the police is the relatively small proportion of criminals who are apprehended. Published reports of studies of the ratio of arrests to certain crimes known to the police are not numerous, but these indicate that arrests infrequently take place in more than one of every two reported crimes. In one of the most intensive, nationwide surveys of criminality, which included 744,863 major offenses, it was shown that nearly three fourths of the offenders were never apprehended or arrested.[6]

The best method of measuring the effectiveness of the police is to compare the number of offenses cleared by arrest with the total number of offenses known to the police. It is important that the offense rather than the offender should be used as the unit, because the number of arrests is likely to be greater than the number of offenses. In Detroit, for example, there were 8,654 arrests in 1928 for 5,541 offenses, but 3,815 persons arrested were dismissed without prosecution.

The following ratios are shown for four cities, indicating the relative effectiveness of the police against different types of crime. Note

[6] National Crime Commission, *Relation of the Police and Courts to the Crime Problem,* New York, 1928, pp. 17-18. D. L. Kooken, "Ethics of Police Service," *Jour. Crim. Law and Criminol.,* Vol. 38 (1947-48): 61-74. E. W. Lester, "Some Aspects of American Police Problems," *Jour. Crim. Law and Criminol.,* Vol. 40 (1949-50): 796-809. J. P. Shalloo, "Modern Police vs. Modern Society," *Prison Jour.,* Vol. 25 (1945): 70-77. G. H. Sheehe, "Police Training for Recruits and In-Service Personnel," *Jour. Crim. Law and Criminol.,* Vol. 35 (1944-45): 281-296.

the striking variations, whether cities or crimes are compared: Buffalo with a ratio of 64.1 and Detroit with a ratio of 29.7 have the highest and lowest percentages of efficiency. Different ratios show either the efficiency of the police or the difficulty in apprehending certain types of offenders. In addition to low rates for each of the four offenses cited, automobile thefts also had exceptionally low clearance rates.

CRIME CLEARANCE RATES IN FOUR CITIES

(Ratio of offenses cleared by arrest to the total number of offenses in each group.)

	PER CENTS				
CITY	*Homicide*	*Robbery*	*Burglary*	*Larceny*	*Total*
Detroit	76.8	49.8	54.9	23.9	29.7
Cleveland	91.7	29.5	23.7	33.5	45.3
Baltimore	94.2	56.4	31.6	33.6	39.6
Buffalo	23.3	45.0	56.0	67.6	64.1

Source: B. Mead, "Police Statistics," *Annals, Am. Acad. Pol. and Soc. Sci.,* Vol. 146 (1929): 81.

Even lower rates occur in England and Wales, as the following comparison with St. Louis shows:

RATIO OF ARRESTS TO CRIMES KNOWN TO THE POLICE

	PER CENT	
CRIME	*England and Wales*	*St. Louis*
Burglary	25	8
Embezzlement	47	17
Forgery	37	8
Larceny	59	6
Manslaughter	100	32 (Manslaughter and Murder combined)
Murder	64	
Robbery	80	11

Source: Relation of the Police and the Courts to the Crime Problem, p. 6.

A second criterion of police effectiveness is the disposition of offenders in the lower or municipal court. One example of these dispositions is given by the Memphis Crime Survey, which included a total of 21,999 arrests for the year 1925. This record shows that more than 46 per cent were dismissed and another 46 per cent were fined; less than 8 per cent were left for other dispositions usually considered to be punishment. This distribution is the first indication of the actual content and distribution of punishment. It is typical of the experience of many cities and holds for felonies and misdemeanors, as will be noted later in the more recent crime-clearance rates given in *Uniform Crime Reports.*[7]

DISPOSITION OF 21,999 ARRESTS—MEMPHIS, TENN.

DISPOSITION	OFFENDERS *Number*	*Per Cent*
Dismissed	10,134	46.1
Fine	10,231	46.5
Held over to grand jury	1,246	5.6
Referred to other authorities	153	.7
Referred to federal authorities	46	.2
Referred to local police magistrates	189	.9
Total	21,999	100.0

Source: A. A. Bruce and T. S. Fitzgerald, "A Study of Crime in the City of Memphis, Tennessee," *Jour. Crim. Law and Criminol.,* Vol. 19 (1928), No. 2, Part 2, Chap. 5.

These inefficiencies of the police have been explained by their persistent use of antiquated methods. In his comparative study of European and American police systems, Fosdick calls attention to this fact. In addition, he and many others have expressed the opinion that a more efficient organization of the police depends upon higher standards in the selection and training of police recruits.

The Survey of Criminal Justice in Cleveland came to the conclusion that the quality of police personnel is largely responsible for ineffective police work. During this survey, the entire police force was examined by the Army Alpha Intelligence Tests. The results of the examination showed a strikingly low proportion of men in the upper intelligence levels, among both officers and patrolmen. Of the entire force, only 3 per cent were in grade *A,* and 13 per cent in grade *B.* These proportions were exceeded by Army privates. Furthermore, one fourth of the patrolmen were classified in grades *C*−, *D,* and *E;* this fact meant that they were incapable of completing the third school grade. Detectives fared worse than any other group in these tests. There were none in grade *A;* 27 per cent were in grades *B* and *C* +; and nearly 25 per cent were of markedly

[7] H. Heinzen and R. K. Rypins, "Crime in San Francisco," *Jour. Crim. Law and Criminol.,* Vol. 18 (1927): 75-91.

inferior intelligence. This situation emphasizes the need for police training schools and better methods of selecting and promoting recruits.

Other police problems are: the absence of effectual rural police; the lack of coordination between urban and state systems, especially in the case of mobile criminals; political control and appointments; personnel problems, including insecure tenure and low pay and few or no standards of professionalization; inadequate records; failure to maintain a good patrol system; and the absence of preventive police work.

The problems of the police in the words of one policeman, are stated bluntly in the following:

> The whole trouble is that the policeman is ordered by law to stop too many things. We have to watch people's morals. We have to protect them like babies instead of like grown-ups.
>
> In the newspapers now the policemen are being blamed for everything. I think all this dishonesty and racketeering is not so much because the police are incompetent, but because the people are worse today than they ever were. If anything goes wrong, a law is passed; then the citizen thinks his responsibility has ended; the police have the job from then on of enforcing the law. In my own city there are over 1,500 laws which I can arrest people for breaking. If we tried to enforce even half the laws that the people break we would lose our jobs in a day.
>
> I found out it was the easier way just to take the five dollars and tear up the tag at once. I don't feel wrong about taking a few dollars. In a way, it's like a fine. All the wealthy men in their big cars know someone with pull and get out of being fined by the judge anyway, so why shouldn't I make them pay on the spot? . . . I don't call that graft. The man in the automobile is doing the grafting. If I didn't take his money he would give it to someone else for helping him get out of a twenty- or fifty-dollar fine. If you want to know the truth, I don't see how you can blame a policeman for picking up a little easy money now and then. A policeman isn't any better than anyone else—nor worse.[8]

The courts: the judicial treatment of crime

As the foregoing discussion shows, the police is essentially an apprehending agency. Although it exercises control over some punitive powers, the effectiveness of the police is reduced considerably as shown by the comparison of offenses known to the police and the number of arrests and indictments.

[8] Anonymous, "All Cops Are Grafters," *Outlook*, Vol. 157 (1931): 590-591.

OFFENSES, ARRESTS, AND INDICTMENTS

(Based upon Reports of 1,652 cities with a population of 49,618,922)

Offenses	*Per Cent Distribution of 837,231 Crimes* Cleared by Arrest	Indicted
Murder	93.7	91.7
Manslaughter	85.1	81.5
Rape	80.2	75.3
Robbery	39.5	39.2
Assault	77.2	66.3
Burglary	29.0	21.9
Larceny	21.6	17.4
Auto Theft	27.3	22.6

Source: United States Department of Justice, *Uniform Crime Reports,* Vol. 21 (1950), No. 1, Tables 14 and 15, pp. 47 and 49.

Courts are the first significant agencies in the distribution of penalties. In the following section, all the dispositions assigned to 15,833 defendants, including penalties, are recorded. This study of crime in Rhode Island for a period of 30 years (1897-1927) shows the travel of each case from arrest to imprisonment or release. The disposition assigned by the court in each of these cases is given in the following table. While this material shows the actual content of punishment, it may also be used to test the efficiency of the courts: (1) in the repeated application of similar penalties to different crimes, and (2) in the proportion of incompleted cases, which is called the mortality record of the courts.

DISPOSITION OF CRIMINAL OFFENSES—RHODE ISLAND, 1897-1927

NUMBER OF PERSONS PUNISHED

	Offenses Against				
DISPOSITION	*The Person*	*Property*	*Sex Morality, Public Order*	*Miscellaneous Crimes*	*Total*
Not guilty	110	60	32	30	232
Incompleted	536	474	305	195	1,510
Bail	—	512	578	206	1,296
Deferred sentence	529	1,951	1,559	694	4,733
Fine	227	175	288	123	813
Probation or reform school *	190	1,946	304	150	2,590
Prison terms:					
Under one year	—	1,750	271	198	2,219
One year or more	823	1,213	242	141	2,419
Life	21	—	—	—	21
Total	2,436	8,081	3,579	1,737	15,833

* Of the total number of defendants under this classification, 2.4 per cent (378 defendants) were sentenced to the Reform School.

Source: Indictment and Docket Records, Superior Court of Providence and Bristol Counties, Rhode Island, 1897-1927.

Each type of disposition shown by this table requires a brief explanation. The general forms of punishment, now assigned by the courts, have already been stated. They usually consist of three dispositions: fines, imprisonment, or release (probation and deferred sentence). Other dispositions include the categories: "Not guilty" and "Incompleted."

If the defendant is found "Not guilty," theoretically, at least, the case is no longer of interest to the student of crime. In practice, however, there are many instances when cases that receive this disposition are of primary interest, because they present the most colorful aspects of crime: conditions that make it impossible to establish legal guilt. In the following classification, those defendants who were found "not guilty because of insanity" are also included in this group, but such cases are fairly infrequent, being twenty-two in number. One half of these dispositions were made in murder cases.

The "Incompleted" group includes those cases in which trial was never begun or never completed. In the docket records, such cases would appear under the following captions: "Capias ordered and issued," "Nol pros," "Jury disagrees," "Indictment quashed," or there would be no entry describing the development of the case. "Bail" is reserved to designate those cases, regardless of the time when they occurred, in which no disposition was made other than "Released under bail." They may be combined logically with the incompleted group. "Deferred sentence" includes those defendants who were assigned this penalty without regard to an earlier report in the record that indicated another offense for which they were committed or given another deferred sentence. "Fine" includes two other types of disposition: "Fine and short sentence" and "Fine and costs." For the purpose of brevity, those released on probation and the few who were committed to the reform school for juvenile delinquency are combined; the latter constitute only 2.4 per cent of this group.

Defendants who were given prison terms are classified under three captions according to their sentences: "Under one year," "One year or more," and "Life." The last group consists entirely of murder cases, since there is no death penalty in Rhode Island.

It is necessary to add that only the first disposition made by the court in completed cases is recorded. This record does not include treatment of recidivists but does furnish a picture of the frequency with which defendants are found not guilty and cases are incompleted, and in the completed cases, of the frequency with which different sentences are employed.

Summarizing the total number of dispositions found by the court during this period of thirty years, 232, or 1.5 per cent, of the defendants were found not guilty. This per cent is an enlightening commentary on a great majority of the cases that come before the Superior Court, of which the chief function is not to determine guilt or innocence but to discover some means of disposing of or punishing the defendant. Interpreted in this light, the actual disposition, treatment, or punishment takes on a new meaning and renders itself open to evaluation on a very vulnerable point, if the disposition is supposed to do what in theory punishment professes to do; that is, to deter criminal behavior or to exercise a moral influence upon potential criminals. The questionable character of each type of disposition is apparent in the uniform treatment of a variety of problems and people.[9]

Of the remaining cases, 2,806, or 17.7 per cent, of the total were incompleted, or the defendants were released on bail. This type of disposition is the mortality record or the proportion of losses. Those individuals who received a slight punishment (a fine) or who were given another chance (deferred sentence and probation) include 7,758, or 49 per cent of the total defendants. Prison terms of variable lengths were assigned to 5,037 individuals, or in 31.8 per cent of the cases. The general frequency of the different types of judicial dispositions is as follows:

	Number	*Per Cent*
Defendants found not guilty	232	1.5
Incompleted	2,806	17.7
Released	7,758	49.0
Imprisoned	5,037	31.8
Total	15,833	100.0

The frequency of these dispositions in the various categories of offenses is expressed on the next page. Attention to these frequencies, with particular reference to the incidence of the crimes to

[9] R. Hartshorne, "Jury Verdicts: A Study of Their Characteristics and Trends," *Am. Bar Assoc. Jour.*, Vol. 35 (1949): 113-117; F. J. Gaudet, "Sentencing Behavior of the Judge," pp. 449-461 in V. C. Branham and S. B. Kutash, *Encyclopedia of Criminology,* Philosophical Library, New York, 1949. "Convicting the Innocent," *Jour. Crim. Law and Criminol.,* Vol. 37 (1946-47): 408-412.

which they apply, will be helpful in evaluating the effectiveness of the various judicial methods. In the first column, crimes against the person, most of the defendants were charged with "assault with a dangerous weapon." Of these cases, 4.5 per cent were found not guilty; 22 per cent were incompleted; 38.8 per cent were released; and 34.7 per cent were imprisoned. In the second column, crimes against property, which are primarily cases of "breaking and entering" and "larceny," 0.7 per cent were found not guilty; 12.2 per cent

DISTRIBUTION OF CRIMINAL OFFENSES—RHODE ISLAND, 1897-1927
PER CENT DISTRIBUTION

DISPOSITION	*Offenses Against*				
	The Person	*Property*	*Sex Morality, Public Order*	*Miscellaneous Crimes*	*Total*
Not guilty	4.5	0.7	0.9	1.7	1.5
Incompleted	22.0	5.9	8.5	11.2	9.5
Bail	—	6.3	16.2	11.9	8.2
Deferred sentence	21.7	24.1	43.6	40.0	29.9
Fine	9.3	2.2	8.0	7.1	5.1
Probation or reform school	7.8	24.1	8.5	8.6	16.4
Prison terms					
Under one year	—	21.7	7.6	11.4	14.0
One year or more	33.8	15.0	6.7	8.1	15.3
Life	0.9	—	—	—	0.1
Total	100.0	100.0	100.0	100.0	100.0

were incompleted; 50.4 per cent were released; and 36.7 per cent were imprisoned. Of the crimes against sex (column three), 0.9 per cent were found not guilty; 24.7 per cent were incompleted; 60.1 per cent were released; and a prison term was given to 14.3 per cent. Of the miscellaneous group (column four), which is concerned primarily with minor thefts, 1.7 per cent were found not guilty; 23.1 per cent were incompleted; 55.7 per cent were released; and 19.5 per cent were imprisoned.

When each group of crimes is analyzed with particular reference to the type of crime that is most frequent, several general conclusions are obvious. (1) The proportion of defendants who are considered not guilty is very small in each group and diminishes accordingly as crimes are popularly considered of minor consequence. (2) The number of defendants whose cases are incompleted is large enough and varies enough between the groups to raise the suspicion that mortality of a case is due to other reasons than lack of sufficient legal evidence to convict. (3) In the proportion of defendants who are released through a system of fines, deferred sentence, or probation, which is by far the most usual form of disposition in each group, the question immediately is raised: To what extent are these vehicles of control adequate treatment of the many problems to

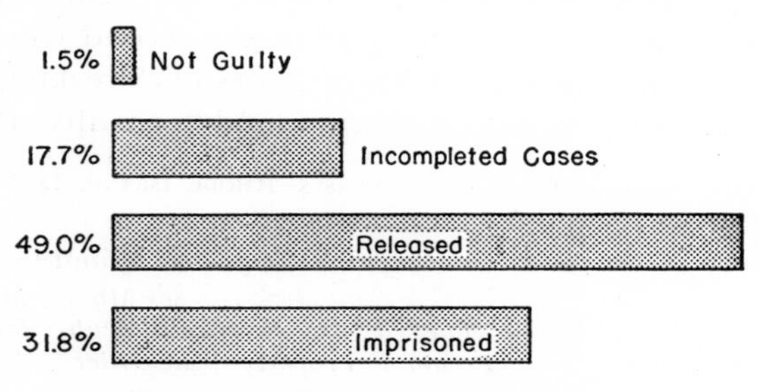

Relative Frequency of Various Dispositions

which they are applied? In the case of an offense against sex or public order, is there any reasonable connection between the usual treatment (deferred sentence) and the repetition of the offense? (4) A final conclusion, and one that is from many points of view the most interesting, reveals the comparative infrequency with which prison sentences are assigned. Ordinarily, imprisonment is considered a certain protection for society against the people who indulge in crime. Yet in a great majority of the cases it requires more than one offense to incur the risk of a prison sentence.

This disposition of criminals by the courts raises many questions about the content and purpose of punishment that cannot be answered at present. Every defendant whose crime merits attention from the superior court is a problem. Is the court, with its legal concepts and rigid punishments, equipped to deal adequately in any respect with such defendants? Is it a wise public policy that metes out deferred sentences or any other legal treatment without special study of the individual case? Law was one of the first bodies of knowledge to make "cases" the basis of its policies and is apparently going to be the last to make case analysis of individuals the basis of its treatment. Many authorities describe what law and the courts are supposed to do: to punish, to correct, to prevent, and to control. Under their present organization, there is no doubt that improvement has ample opportunity to show itself.

Among the most persisting of unsolved problems is the question as to effective methods of treating or preventing criminality. Whether current repressive and punitive agencies work as they are supposed to has never been adequately tested. Even in the more basic question of crime prevention, there is no assurance that the administration of criminal justice is in any way instrumental to its achievement.

Robinson maintains that the very concept of punishment is a handicap to the judicial treatment of crime for he says:

> Any one who has had an opportunity to examine the individuals who pass through our criminal courts knows that no two are alike. . . . Yet we subject them to pretty much the same dull routine.[10]

In this summary of the frequency of crimes and the disposition of the various grades of defendants, the fact that stands out glaringly is the indiscriminate use of certain methods of punishment. There is no evidence that any method is more desirable than another, and yet certain ones are constantly being employed simply because they always have been used or because there is a lack of sufficient ingenuity to devise other procedures.

One incident that occurs in the above records deserves special comment in this connection. A defendant was charged under the indictment "Habitual criminal" and was given a deferred sentence.

A review of 15,219 cases of women defendants, approximately the same number as appeared before the Rhode Island courts, records a comparable laxity in the operation of the courts. Of this total, 51 per cent of the cases indicted by the Grand Jury for serious crimes were eliminated by the courts and 49 per cent of the cases were given the following dispositions:

	Number	*Per Cent*
Probation	4,650	62.0
Jail sentence	2,285	30.5
Fine only	514	6.8
Other	53	0.7
Total	7,502	100.0

Official treatment of specific offenses also resembles the record of the Rhode Island courts. Offenders most often dismissed include those indicted for assault, embezzlement and fraud, sex crimes, and burglary. Offenders most infrequently brought to trial include those

[10] L. N. Robinson, "The Content of Punishment," *Annals, Am. Acad. Pol. and Soc. Sci.,* Vol. 125 (1926): 229-232. C. A. Rymer, "The Insanity Plea in Crime," *Am. Jour. Psychiatry,* Vol. 105 (1948): 420-425.

indicted for forgery, gambling, prostitution, robbery, carrying deadly weapons, murder, and drug violations.[11]

In summary, there are two conclusions from this study of the frequency of crime and punishment that merit attention. First of all, in each group of offenses there is one type of crime that makes the greatest proportion of indictments in each class. These numerous crimes in combination are responsible for increasing or decreasing crime rates. They supply significant cues both as to causes as well as to the effectiveness of present-day controls. Secondly, there is every indication in the rigid adherence to customary legal practices that punishments are assigned indiscriminately and that crime, and not the criminal, is the primary object of interest. If these conclusions are correct, it is proper to raise two questions: (1) how effective is the present system of judicial dispositions in repressing the most frequent of modern crimes, and (2) how completely does this system attack the causes of crime? Reference to one group of crimes, offenses against the person, will be helpful in an approach to these problems.

Disposition of violent crimes

Society is naturally very much concerned with the causes of violent crime. Although several major causes are suggested in criminological literature, "crimes of passion," as they are called, have not lent themselves to clinical study. For the most part, obvious causes, such as economic conditions, sale of firearms, psychopathic mentality, and the like, are cited, with no reference to specific causes or to the combination of associated factors in individual cases. If attention is limited to crime against the person, it is apparent that the spectacular crimes of murder and manslaughter have received much consideration, although such crimes are relatively infrequent in the total incidence of violent crimes. Principally for this reason, many of the books on criminal problems suggested in the supplementary readings of Chapter 18, above, are very inadequate pictures of crime. Dealing solely with spectacular crimes and even disregarding frequency within this sort of crime, their contribution is literary rather than scientific, because they stress the unusual and in

[11] A. H. Kratz, *Prosecutions and Treatment of Women Offenders and the Economic Crisis, Philadelphia, 1925-1934,* University of Pennsylvania Press, Philadelphia, 1940, p. 75. Compare with: B. Johnson, "Women Sex Offenders in New York Courts," *Jour. Soc. Hyg.,* Vol. 35 (1949): 374-380.

most instances the unsolvable aspects of crime. They add little or nothing to a knowledge of causes or to a system of punishment that would have repressed such crimes. It is necessary to turn from the spectacular to the usual types of violent crimes against the person, if the real causes of violence are to be discovered or if society wants to establish a sound program of treatment.

The next table indicates the relative frequency of crimes against the person that succeeded or failed to effect a homicide. Legally, there is a considerable difference between them. Actually, there is little. From the standpoint of the treatment of the person as a delinquent, there is none.

PUNISHMENT OF CRIMES AGAINST THE PERSON—RHODE ISLAND, 1897-1927

DISPOSITION	MURDER		MANSLAUGHTER		ASSAULT WITH DANGEROUS WEAPON		ASSAULT AND BATTERY	
	Number	*Per Cent*	*Number*	*Per Cent*	*Number*	*Per Cent*	*Number*	*Per Cent*
Not guilty	29	16.3	26	24.1	49	2.6	6	2.4
Incompleted	33	18.5	43	39.8	404	21.3	56	22.3
Fine	2	1.1	—	—	182	9.6	43	17.1
Deferred sentence	3	1.7	9	8.3	488	25.7	29	11.6
Probation and reform school	—	—	—	—	137	7.2	53	21.1
Prison terms:								
Life	21	11.8	—	—	—	—	—	—
Other terms	90	50.6	30	27.8	639	33.6	64	25.5
Total	178	100.0	108	100.0	1,899	100.0	251	100.0

In the disposition of these defendants, there is every indication of the same inelastic legal treatment previously mentioned. For example, in the number of defendants who were indicted for murder or manslaughter and who were found not guilty, there is some evidence that legal and not actual guilt is in question. These proportions are emphasized when they are compared with the relatively small number of defendants who were found not guilty on indictments for the use of violence in cases which did not result in homicide; namely, in cases of assault. Again, there is a large number of incompleted cases and of defendants who are given another chance. Because crimes against the person are considered more serious than some of the other crimes, a larger proportion of the offenders are given prison terms. But even with the threat of imprisonment or other sentences, the question that remains to be settled is: In what respect does such treatment of violence cure the lawless or prevent others from engaging in the same activities?

The menace to society in crimes of violence against the person is not so much that resulting from the occasional murder or manslaughter as that brought into play by the frequent use of violence, which is resorted to apparently for a number of unknown reasons. Because cases of assault are the most frequent types of crime against the person, and because the problems of restraining homicide (murder and manslaughter) are intimately connected with the general problems of violence, one case which typifies the origin of many cases of assault and of quasi-murder is presented from a recent newspaper report as a good instance of the difficulties involved in securing legal or any other disposition:

WOMAN ASKS NEW CHANCE FOR HUSBAND

After being slashed with a razor, Mrs. ________ wants her husband given another chance. . . .

After the assault on his wife, [the man] cut his own throat and was in a critical condition. According to the wife, her husband received a gash in the head during the World War and since that time "moonshine drives him crazy" but he is "a good and kind husband when sober, which he is most of the time."

Although she is always in fear of him when he is drunk, she wants him to have another chance. The argument between the couple which resulted in the indictment was the result of the wife's refusal to give him money and, as she started to run away, he drew a razor and assaulted her. . . .

It is for this class of people that society must provide more than legal treatment, if in the long run it is ever going to develop adequate control over the criminal. Whether or not the courts will give another chance, is the immediate problem. The whole matter requires a careful study of criminals as delinquent persons and not as legal persons. A number of factors condition and complicate any final disposition.[12]

"Mortality" and its causes

The belief is widely accepted that the efficiency of the courts cannot be evaluated by the single criterion of convictions. Other agencies or administrative devices are held to be equally responsible for

[12] C. C. Van Vechten, "Differential Criminal Case Mortality in Selected Jurisdictions," *Am. Sociol. Rev.,* Vol. 7 (1942): 833-839. In this comparison of Washington, D. C., and Minnesota, prosecutions for murders known to have been committed were one in three in Washington and one in five in Minnesota.

losses or mortality at this point. Moley states that the court records of mortality reflect the lack of coordination between police, magistrates, prosecutors, judges, and jurors.[13]

The fact remains, moreover, as a tremendous handicap to law enforcement, that many processes leading to and including trial favor the defendant more than the prosecution. In Chicago during the year 1926, the courts made the following disposition of 12,543 arrests for felony:

Released without punishment	85 per cent
—in the preliminary hearing	49 per cent
—in the grand jury	11 per cent
—in the trial court	20 per cent
—after guilt was established	5 per cent
Total receiving some punishment	15 per cent

In Van Vechten's comparisons, mentioned above, the same mortality or loss is indicated:

	PER CENTS		
	United States	*District of Columbia*	*Minnesota*
Crimes known to the police	100.0	100.0	100.0
Offenses cleared by arrest	25.0	35.7	34.8
Persons charged by police	20.0	19.0	—
Judicial prosecutions	7.0	7.5	7.1
Convictions	5.5	5.9	6.4
Sentenced to prisons	3.5	3.7	3.1
Prisoners received from courts	3.8*	3.6	3.4*

* Prisoners received exceeds those sentenced to prisons because it includes violators of probation or parole.

The failure to secure convictions when there is practically no question of guilt may often be traced to the varied functions of the prosecutor. When the travel of a case from arrest to final disposition is reviewed, the prosecutor assumes a position of vital importance. He is sometimes described as the real police surgeon, being connected with the mortality of cases in every administrative division of the law.

[13] For an evaluation of mortality studies, consult: W. C. Reckless, *op. cit.*, pp. 10-18. Other sources used in this section are: N. F. Baker, "The Prosecuting Attorney," *Jour. Crim. Law and Criminol.*, Vol. 26 (1935): 647-678; C. E. Gehlke, "Statistical Studies in Crime," p. 84 in S. A. Rice, (Ed.), *Statistics in Social Studies*, University of Pennsylvania Press, Philadelphia, 1930; R. Moley, *Politics and Criminal Prosecution*, Putnam's, New York, 1929, p. 31; "National Crime Commission, *op. cit.*, pp. 25-29; C. C. Van Vechten, *loc. cit.*

The prosecution of criminal cases is almost wholly within the control of the prosecuting attorney. At the beginning of a case, by refusing to issue a warrant, he may determine whether it will be continued or stopped. By this power, he exercises considerable control over the activities of the police. Furthermore, in most states, he takes an active part in preliminary hearings and in coroners' inquests. He may take a case from the magistrate's court directly to the grand jury. Or, by his refusal to participate, the case is likely to be lost in the magistrate's court. Discontinuance or mortality of cases listed under the caption "Dismissed for want of prosecution" is due directly to the activity or negligence of this officer.

In some states, he is totally responsible for the indictment of felony cases; in others, where indictment is secured by a grand jury, the prosecuting attorney not only dominates the grand jury but draws the indictment for their uncritical approval. He interviews witnesses, examines evidence, and bargains with the defense over the plea to be offered, and in the actual conduct of the case largely supersedes the judge, even to determining the charge that is to be given to the jury. In addition, he is frequently consulted by the judge in the determination of sentences and by parole authorities in granting pardons or paroles. He may also begin one stage earlier and engage in police work, such as investigating crimes, gathering evidence, and making arrests.

According to the Missouri Crime Survey, the relative importance of the prosecutor's office and other administrative agencies is shown by the final outcome of cases. In this study, 50 per cent were eliminated by the prosecutor, 12 per cent by the judge, and 38 per cent by all other agencies.

Subsidiary factors in the mortality record of the courts are the use of nolle prosequi, reduced charges, abuse of bail, and the antiquated indictment.

"Nolle prosequi" originated as a method of clearing the docket, when mistakes had been made, in order to reduce the number of cases pending. This method of disposition is a formal entry in the docket record whereby the prosecuting officer declares that he "will no further prosecute" the case. Although this procedure was originally limited to unusual cases as a check against injustice, it has been employed freely in large numbers of cases. In fact, the Cleveland Survey reported that a "blanket nolle" is sometimes authorized, by which hundreds of cases are dismissed at once.

Opposition to this practice has caused several restrictions upon its use and has resulted in the bargaining for pleas of guilt by a reduction of charges or by promises of leniency. Under this procedure, a felony may be reduced to a lesser felony or to a misdemeanor. At times, bargaining is carried on through a promise of early parole. In New York state during 1926, 37.5 per cent of the cases were changed to lesser offenses by this method. Reducing the original charge has gone on extensively in this state to avoid the strict interpretation of the Baumes Law, which provides that the fourth conviction on a felony charge shall be given a life sentence. The reduction of charges as a method of avoiding punishment is also illustrated in the 12,543 felony prosecutions in Chicago. Although only 2,449 indicted persons were convicted, 1,855 were convicted on reduced charges and only 594 on the original charges. Of this entire group of 12,543 persons, 3.1 per cent were punished for the offense originally charged in the indictment.

Abuse of bail is another source of incompleted cases, and especially of delays in trial. There are two reasons for the abuse of the bail system. One is that bail is not immediately collectible. This makes delays possible at a small cost, usually less than ten dollars. In the second place, after judgment has been declared in cases of forfeited bail, the amount collected is negligible. The Missouri Survey found that nine per cent of the forfeited bonds were reduced to judgment and that only six per cent of the amount reduced to judgment was collected. In Cleveland, three-fifths of one per cent of forfeited bail was collected.

The reasons given for this small collection are that many of the bonds are intrinsically worthless and that the machinery to enforce collection is inadequate. One professional bondsman is described by the Missouri Survey in the following terms:

1. His property was mortgaged for more than its assessed value.
2. He was delinquent in local and federal taxes.
3. He had a police record of twelve minor charges.
4. With property valued at less than $60,000, he was permitted to become surety for $670,295 in one year.

Another instance of antiquated and abused machinery is the wordy indictment, which, as Arthur Train explains, is due to the early system of paying by the word for the drafting of legal documents. An indictment serves the purpose of informing the defendant of his crime and of recording the point at issue. Indictments may be very long, and cases may be reversed if there is any deviation from its legal form. The involved nature of the indictment furnishes an excellent opportunity for contention in court and for appeals and delays because of technical errors. During a ten-year period in Missouri, twenty-eight cases were reversed because of technical errors in the indictment.

> It can be fairly stated that not a single one of the errors complained of, for which any of these twenty-eight cases were reversed, substantially affected the merits of the cases or deprived the defendants of any rights which they should have enjoyed under a fair system of criminal procedure.

Such minor errors as the omission of the word "the" or the improper spelling of a man's name are grounds for delay and reversal.

> To obviate this source of injustice, it is necessary to simplify the wording of the indictment making it consist simply of the charge and to refuse formal motions for appeal for reasons unconnected with the guilt or innocence of the accused. Some states have already adopted a simple form of indictment, as did England years ago.

Arthur Train gives the following example of a case in which delay was secured by a faulty indictment, although the error involved no question of innocence. He was called upon to prosecute a case of bigamy in which the man had married a woman, *A,* in New York. The defendant already had a lawful wife, *B,* in Chicago. The defense argued that *B* was not his lawful wife since he was married previously to a woman in Iowa. Through this triangular defense, an acquittal was secured upon the precise charge of the original indictment. This decision is additional evidence for the belief that the more criminal a person is, the less likely it is that he can be convicted and punished under current legal machinery.[14]

In his volume *Forgotten Crimes,*[15] J. W. Poynter furnishes a similar illustration. William Sheen was charged with the murder of a baby alleged to be "his infant son, William Sheen, alias Beadle." According to testimony and the registry of births, his child was Charles William Beadle. Therefore, the attorney for the defense contended that there was no proof that the child mentioned in the indictment was the child who had been murdered. The jury was

[14] A. Train, *On the Trail of the Bad Men,* Scribner's Sons, New York, 1925, pp. 314-315.

[15] Macaulay, New York, 1930, pp. 77-81.

instructed to return a verdict of "not guilty of killing as laid in the indictment." He was charged again for the same offense, and the crime was described in thirteen different ways and named differently in each, in order to avoid this flaw in the original indictment. On this charge the prisoner contended that "he had already been tried and acquitted for the murder of the same child as the one described in the present indictment." The jury returned a verdict that the child was known by "Charles William Beadle" as well as by other names, and the prisoner was discharged.

Massachusetts has made a significant innovation, which avoids some of these breakdowns in the machinery of justice, through the provisions of the Briggs Law. This law requires a competent mental examination, prior to the trial, of individuals who are indicted for capital offenses and of others who have been convicted previously of a felony. This procedure has many advantages. It furnishes the court with important information, thus reducing delays and costs. The "battle of experts" is eliminated. It also points to socially desirable dispositions. In addition, lawyers, prosecutors, and judges are trained to appreciate the need for individualization in the operation of justice. In actual operation, however, the effectiveness of this law is considerably reduced by the tendency of courts to disregard the findings of the mental examination and to commit some offenders who are mentally defective to penal institutions.[16]

Prisons[17]

There is no clearer proof, says Healy, of the non-existence of an applied science in the study of criminality than in the figures of

[16] P. B. Hagopian, "Examination of the Accused in Massachusetts, 1921-1949," *Am. Jour. Psychiatry,* Vol. 107 (1950): 336-339. W. Overholser, "The Briggs Law of Massachusetts," *Jour. Crim. Law and Criminol.,* Vol. 25 (1934): 859-883.

[17] N. Carlisle, "The Black Scandal of Our County Jails," *Coronet,* Vol. 22 (1947): 3-8. V. Fox, "Michigan's Experiment in Minimum Security Penology," *Jour. Crim. Law and Criminol.,* Vol. 41 (1950): 150-166. E. M. Gerlach, *Treatment of Adults Prior to Trial,* National Conference of Social Work, 1946, pp. 441-451. Howard Gill, "One Hundred Years of Penal Progress," *Prison Jour.,* Vol. 25 (1945): 12-21. S. and E. T. Glueck, *Juvenile Delinquents Grown Up,* Commonwealth Fund, New York, 1940, pp. 153 and 161. ———, *Criminal Careers in Retrospect,* Commonwealth Fund, New York, 1943, p. 151. F. E. Haynes, "Sociological Study of the Prison Community," *Jour. Crim. Law and Criminol.,* Vol. 39 (1948-49): 432-440. A. MacCormick, "The Prison's Role in Crime Prevention," *Jour. Crim. Law and Criminol.,* Vol. 41 (1950): 36-48. B. McKelvey, "The Prison Labor Problem," *Jour. Crim. Law and Criminol.,* Vol. 25 (1934): 254-270. L. N. Robinson, *Should Prisoners Work?,* Winston, Phil-

recidivism or in the failure of our penal agencies. This statement is especially applicable when the specific functions of prisons are analyzed. The prison serves three purposes—to confine, to reform, and to deter—which are not only contradictory but which actually prevent the permanent segregation of the habitual criminal.

Although no studies have succeeded in furnishing reliable estimates of the value of imprisonment, neither the testimony of prison officials nor that of inmates puts a high premium upon its achievements. Considering the prison as a last-resort method for the protection of society, Sutherland recommends that this form of punishment be used sparingly according to the nature of the individual criminal, and that sentence should be for life, except in special cases. His opinion is based upon the only information now available concerning the efficiency of prisons, such as rates of recidivism, or upon such conclusions as those of Glueck, who found that eighty per cent of the inmates confined in the Massachusetts Reformatory were not reformed five to fifteen years after their release.

Failure of the prison is traced to several outstanding defects, other than that of its multiple and nonspecific functions. Inefficiencies in prison administration and untrained personnel constitute a primary source of ineffectiveness. Mass treatment by inflexible routine, which is necessary for purposes of economical management, succeeds only in adapting the inmates to the prison, intensifying their loss of social status and their isolation, and preventing an exercise of personal choice fundamental in the gradual training of the person to live in society. Other specific defects are unemployment or idleness of prisoners and unsatisfactory living conditions, both of which interfere with the reformatory objectives of the prison, misuse of disciplinary measures, ineffective educational classes, inadequate medical supervision, and a general failure to adapt available resources of the prison to rehabilitation.

Although the trend in modern penology is toward individualization in treatment, any one of these general or specific defects in

---

adelphia, 1931. ———, "The Perennial Jail Problem," *Jour. Crim. Law and Criminol.,* Vol. 35 (1944-45): 369-374. G. Rudstedt, "The Swedish Prison System of Today," *Yearbook,* National Prison Association, 1947: 161-68. R. M. Simpson, "Prison Stagnation Since 1900," *Jour. Crim. Law and Criminol.,* Vol. 26 (1935): 870-882. Case Note, "Time Served in Prison Compared with Legal Sentences," *Jour. Crim. Law and Criminol.,* Vol. 27 (1936): 661-667. J. G. Wilson and M. J. Pescor, *Problems in Prison Psychiatry,* Caxton Printers, Caldwell, Idaho, 1939, Chap. 12.

prison management defeats the realization of this goal. For some years, prison officials have declared in favor of small prisons housing no more than 500 inmates. Nevertheless, overcrowding of much larger prisons is generally prevalent. In fact, this condition is typical of most penal institutions, prisons, reformatories, and county jails. In some instances, overcrowding has exceeded normal capacity by 200 per cent and is cited to be largely responsible for prison riots and for the description of prisons as places where inmates:

1. Live in idleness at the expense of the taxpayer.
2. Learn vice, immorality, and crime.
3. Degenerate both physically and mentally.

CAPACITY AND OVERCROWDING OF PRISONS

Federal Penitentiary	*Capacity*	*Prison Population 1928*	*Amount over Capacity*	*Per Cent of Excess*
Leavenworth, Kan.	1,700	3,416	1,716	200.9
Atlanta, Ga.	1,843	3,176	1,333	172.3
McNeil Island, Wash. ...	669	873	204	130.5

Source: A. W. Butler, "Prisoners and Prisons," *Ind. Bul. Charities and Corrections,* No. 175, Oct., 1929.

Perhaps for these reasons, the fact that few persons who are arrested and convicted actually receive prison terms is ultimately favorable to the control of crime. In one state survey, conditions of unusual laxity were uncovered. A warden was found to be supplying prison labor to private enterprises outside the prison and was eventually suspended for this offense. A manager of a prison shop was convicted for the sale of prison supplies to the public. One prison was described as the Ritz-Carlton among penitentiaries, and the following specific charges were made: (1) the real authority of the prison was maintained by a group of important convicts; (2) these individuals were assigned special cells from which they bought and sold the preferred prison jobs, controlled betting on ball games, prize-fights, and horse races and participated in the profits from manufactures and concessions of the prison; (3) they were entertained by prison authorities outside of the prison, going to theaters and sporting events in official cars; (4) they were permitted to visit houses of prostitution on the outside and to have women visitors in the prison; (5) furloughs and escapes could be purchased.

Public skepticism concerning the value of current penal methods may be due in part to such revelations and in part to the belief that imprisonment confirms the inmate in his criminal career or that early release defeats the purpose of imprisonment. There is no greater inconsistency in these points of view than in the tendency of the courts to assign the penalty of imprisonment in a minority of criminal cases, even for felonies. At any rate, the practice of assigning short prison terms, in addition to early release, makes it impossible to determine the influence of the prison as a reforming or deterring agency.

Few prisoners serve their full terms; most of them are released before they have served half of their sentences. There are various methods by which release may be effected. Generally, these consist of parole, commutation of sentence, and pardon.

In theory, pardon is used only when the prisoner is found to be innocent of the crime for which he was committed. Actually, it is employed for many other reasons, such as sickness, age of the offender, and family's need of prisoner's assistance; and it is used sometimes as a reward for becoming a witness of the state, to relieve overcrowding, and for other reasons wholly unrelated to the reform of the individual or his capacity to re-enter society.

This abuse of the systems of pardon and parole holds for major as well as minor offenses. From 1838, when the Rhode Island State Prison was opened, to the year 1927, 236 persons were sentenced for the crimes of murder, manslaughter, or assault with intent to kill. Of this total, 76 were committed for life (murder in the first degree); 39 for long terms (murder in the second degree); 120 for manslaughter; and one for assault with intent to kill. However, the use of pardon or parole has made considerable alteration in the actual sentences of these persons. Thus, of the persons sentenced for life, 48.7 per cent were pardoned after serving an average of 13 years. In the case of second-degree murder and manslaughter, average sentences of 18.9 years and 8.3 years, respectively, were reduced by pardon and parole to an average of 4 years.

PARDON AND PAROLE IN HOMICIDE CASES—RHODE ISLAND, 1838-1927

Homicide	*Pardoned*	*Paroled*	*Total*
Murder, first degree	48.7%	—	48.7%
Murder, second degree	20.5	15.4%	35.9
Manslaughter	25.8	15.0	40.8

These records show that the maximum penalty for violent crime is another legal fiction. In their provisions for early release, prisons are failing in their basic function of detaining the person and are actually undoing the work of the courts. This situation is due largely to the incompatibility of the three functions of the prisons, which collectively interfere with the efficient fulfillment of any one of them.

"Parole" is a conditional release from prison after a portion of the sentence has been served. Although the general principle upon which parole is based is the assumption that the person is capable of adjusting himself to society under supervision, few states observe this limitation. New York state, for example, grants parole to all prisoners; with the exception of unusual cases, eligibility for parole has no requirement other than the time element. Frequently, parole is introduced because it is cheaper than imprisonment.

Parole and recidivism

Considerable attention has been given in recent literature to an analysis of the success and the failure of persons on parole. Although it is impossible to name any combination of factors which guarantees that an individual will be ready for parole, case studies have shown that several conditions have some predictive value in determining success or failure. From a study of 3,000 men paroled from three Illinois institutions, Burgess concluded that first or occasional offenders are good parole risks and that the habitual or professional criminal is rarely successful under parole. In this study of 263 consecutive paroles, Borden found twenty-eight factors that were useful correlates of parole success. Factors correlating with failure on parole, in addition to prior criminal record, are abnormal mental conditions, irregular work records, unsatisfactory prison records, and parole under family or neighborhood conditions similar to those under which the original criminal activity occurred.[18]

[18] R. M. Allen, "Problems of Parole," *Jour. Crim. Law and Criminol.,* Vol. 38 (1947-48): 7-13. H. G. Borden, "Factors for Predicting Parole Success," *Jour. Crim. Law and Criminol.,* Vol. 19 (1928): 328-336. E. W. Burgess, "Factors Determining Success or Failure on Parole," *Jour. Crim. Law and Criminol.,* Vol. 19 (1928); No. 1, Part 2, Chaps. 26-29. Jerome Davis, "Towards a Rehabilitation Quotient for Penal Offenders," *Social Forces,* Vol. 14 (1936): 530-537. S. and E. T. Glueck, both volumes cited in previous footnote, and *After Conduct of Discharged Offenders,* Macmillan, London, 1945, Chap. 6. F. F. Laune, "The Application of Attitude Tests in Parole Prediction," *Am. Sociol. Rev.,* Vol. 1 (1936): 781-796. L. W. Sampson, "After-Careers of 424 Wisconsin Criminals," *Jour. Crim. Law and Criminol.,* Vol. 25 (1934): 607-620. A. C. Schnur, "Validity of Parole Selection," *Social Forces,* Vol. 29 (1951): 322-328. H. L. Witmer, "The

In the first comparative study of the Gluecks (1940), 20.3 per cent of the 1,000 delinquents succeeded on parole, 21.8 per cent succeeded on occasions, and 57.9 per cent always failed. In a second study (1943), 92.4 per cent of 500 male criminals failed to comply with the requirements of parole. In a third study (1945), in which the behavior of offenders was examined during three periods—prereformatory, parole, and postparole—total failure in each period respectively were 87.7, 56.1, and 62.1 per cent.

Conditions that are favorable to good social adjustment in the community also supply the guides to a rehabilitation program for prison. According to the studies mentioned in footnote 18 and the several studies of the Gluecks, the more important among these socializing factors are: (1) the educational status of the individual's parents, (2) intelligence of the offender, (3) the stability of the family (absence of conflict or broken family relations), (4) industrial skill and occupational record of the offender, (5) grade achieved in school, (6) economic status of the offender's family (parental), (7) absence of a record of childhood delinquency or school misconduct, (8) little or no mobility, (9) recreational habits, and (10) length of time the individual has been under legal supervision.

In the management of recidivists, most states depend upon an habitual-criminal act. This recourse became general policy during the 1920's. Through its enforcement a criminal can be detained indefinitely after two or three convictions, and if he is paroled, the parole may be revoked at any time. Since this law is mandatory in most states, it is criticised on two counts. Judges are inclined to reduce felony charges in order to avoid conviction, and district attorneys and lawyers for the defense are prone to bargain for indictments for lesser offenses.[19]

Summary

In an as yet unknown number of cases, current methods of punishment or control may result in rehabilitation. This result may be achieved because of the prisoner's improved health, education, vocational skill, or mental outlook. For the great majority of prisoners, less hopeful results are all too evident.

History, Theory, and Results of Parole," *Jour. Crim. Law and Criminol.*, Vol. 18 (1928): 24-64.

[19] G. K. Brown, *Recidivism: A Socio-Legal Survey of Its Definition, Incidence and Treatment in the United States*, University of Pennsylvania Press, Philadelphia, 1947, Chap. 3.

Crime prevention, therefore, rather than repression or punishment should be the objective of penal agencies that are being guided by the new penology. Likewise, numerous social institutions other than those directly concerned with law enforcement become important supplements in a preventive program. As most criminologists point out, crime cannot be abolished entirely because new forms of illegal acts will develop from changing economic and social conditions.

Although it is impossible to state precisely what new conditions will supplant the causes of contemporary lawbreaking, they will probably arise from increasing population, urbanization, and the changing social standards that accompany a new and different culture. Emphasis upon research and sound social planning can anticipate many of the newer crimes and to a considerable extent modify their causes. From this approach problems of crime, both in their origin and treatment, do not differ from any other problems in social control.

For the time being, the first steps in crime prevention should be directed toward a revision of criminal law and its administrative agencies.

One of the most noticeable obstructions to legal reform is the excessive fecundity of our lawmaking organizations. Laws are passed with little or no attention to their effectiveness, many being unenforceable. As a result, the average person is unable to know all the laws or even those that the police choose to enforce.

> During a recent five-year period there were passed over 62,000 laws, State and Federal, to interpret which required 65,000 decisions of courts of last resort, filling 630 volumes; our legislative harvest is upward of 15,000 statutes per annum.[20]

A second deficiency in the administration of the criminal law is the ineffectiveness of punishment because of its infrequent application. In addition to the probability of escaping detection and arrest, the criminal, when arrested, has five possible ways of avoiding conviction and, when under trial, has access to nine ways of avoiding the full legal penalty for his crime. After arrest, he may not be held by the police. If held for preliminary hearing, his case

[20] Arthur Train, *op. cit.,* pp. 153, 160-169. See also A. E. Stevenson, "The Problem of Law Enforcement: The Alliance of Crime and Politics," *Am. Bar Assoc. Jour.,* Vol. 36 (1950): 994-998.

may be discharged, dismissed for want of prosecution, or not billed, or he may be permitted to plead guilty to a misdemeanor. If he is placed on trial, the trial may result in failure to convict. If he is convicted, his sentence may be suspended; he may be released on bail which can be forfeited; an appeal may set aside the verdict; he may be released by a second trial; a sentence less than the maximum established by law may be secured, or he may be placed on probation. If he is sentenced to prison, he may be pardoned or paroled. This lack of coordination led to the following characterization of administrative needs:

> Instead of this loosely built rail fence through which criminals can break seemingly at will, what is needed, to use the language of the farmer, is "a fence, horse high, bull strong, and hog tight." [21]

The following are significant trends in the recent modification of criminal law:

1. Paring down the indictment so that it describes only the offense, with no elaboration of details.
2. Substitution of information for the indictment. This procedure eliminates the grand jury.
3. Gradual abandonment of trial by jury, especially in cases of misdemeanors. This change is being introduced more through the pressure of business than a changing belief in the justice of trial by experts.
4. Trial by jury is being speeded by entrusting the selection of jurors to trial justices. Provision is also made for alternate jurors to prevent mistrials by illness or death of the regular jurors.
5. Admission of expert testimony.
6. Rise of the public defender.

Significant developments in the changing attitude toward punishment include:

1. Increasing recognition that crime prevention depends upon individualization of treatment.
2. Introduction of preventive agencies in the community, such as behavior clinics, visiting teachers, juvenile courts, and various facilities under schools, recreational, and social work organizations.

[21] National Crime Commission, *op. cit.,* p. 10.

3. Efforts to forestall crime by eliminating the deteriorating influences of disorganized communities. Discovery of predelinquents. More adequate facilities for the treatment of problem children.
4. Combining the prison policy of restraint with educational and training programs whereby the prisoner may be rehabilitated during his prison term.
5. The movement to put legislation upon a scientific basis whereby the findings of the social sciences, medicine, and psychiatry may be incorporated in the law.
6. Introduction of case work in each stage of the offender's custody.
7. Extension of supervised parole and probation.
8. More adequate criminological researches and resources of research, such as the Chicago Area Project.

Among outstanding achievements in the administrative control of crime that have been introduced or made more efficient during the current century, the following are often cited: (1) The National Probation and Parole Association (1907); (2) State Police Systems (Pennsylvania, 1905); (3) Institution of the Federal Bureau of Investigation (1908); (4) Public and voluntary defenders (1913); (5) Police training systems (1917); F.B.I. school for local police (1935); (6) Institution of state and local crime commissions (1920); (7) Psychiatric and social work introduced (1921); (8) Use of scientific methods: radio (1921), identification and detection (F.B.I. Laboratory, 1932); (9) The Legal Aid Society (1923); (10) Uniform Crime Reports (1930); (11) Classification of prisoners and retraining programs (1930); (12) Interstate coordination of teletype systems (1934); (13) Behavior Clinics (1937); (15) Merit system and civil service status for police (Chicago, 1895); (16) Prediction studies in criminology (1920's); (17) Federal Youth Corrections Act (1950).

Bibliography

Frank, Jerome, *Courts on Trial: Myth and Reality in American Justice,* Princeton University Press, Princeton, 1949.

Kinder, R. M., and R. V. Selinger, *Handbook of Correctional Psychology,* Philosophical Library, New York, 1947.

Mannheim, Hermann, *Criminal Justice and Social Reconstruction,* Kegan Paul, London, 1946.

O'Donnell, B., *The Old Bailey and Its Trials,* Clerke and Cockeran, London, 1950.

Orfield, L. B., *Criminal Procedure from Arrest to Appeal,* New York University Press, New York, 1947.

Radzinowicz, Leon (Ed.), *Penal Reform in England,* Macmillan, London, 1946.

Sellin, Thorsten, *Pioneering in Penology,* University of Pennsylvania Press, Philadelphia, 1944.

Tappan, P. W. (Ed.), *Contemporary Correction,* McGraw-Hill, New York, 1951.

Timasheff, N. S., *Probation in the Light of Criminal Statistics,* McMullen, New York, 1949.

Ulman, Joseph N., *A Judge Takes the Stand,* Knopf, New York, 1936.

Wilson, D. P., *My Six Convicts,* Rinehart and Co., New York, 1951.

Wilson, O. W., *Police Administration,* McGraw-Hill, New York, 1950.

Special Studies

Collins, F. L., *Homicide Squad,* Putnam's, New York, 1944.

Duffy, C. T., *The San Quentin Story, Doubleday,* New York, 1950.

Kohn-Bramstedt, Ernst, *Dictatorship and Political Police,* Kegan Paul, London, 1945.

Lowenthal, Max, *The Federal Bureau of Investigation,* William Sloane Associates, New York, 1950.

Moran, Frederick A., *The Sex Criminal on Parole,* Division of Parole, Albany, New York, 1940.

O'Hara, C. E., and J. W. Osterburg, *An Introduction to Criminalistics,* Macmillan, New York, 1949.

Reynolds, Quentin, *Courtroom,* Gollancz, London, 1951.

Robinson, L. N., *Jails: Care and Treatment of Misdemeanant Prisoners in the United States,* Winston, Philadelphia, 1944.

Snyder, C. C., *Homicide Investigation,* C. C. Thomas, Springfield, Ill., 1949.

Teeters, N. K., *World Penal Systems,* Pennsylvania Prison Society, Philadelphia, 1944.

Waite, J. B., *Criminal Law and its Enforcement,* Foundation Press, Brooklyn, N. Y., 1947.

Questions

1. Can you suggest reasons why "crimes known to the police" exceed the number of arrests?
2. Is the question of legal evidence important in explaining this poor record?
3. How are police recruited or appointed? Are most police under civil service?
4. What is the "travel" of a case after arrest to final disposition?
5. Do the punitive or treatment resources of the courts seem to you satisfactory as methods of regulating crime?
6. Is the system of elected judges accepted as the best way to obtain competent personnel?

7. What are the various duties of the district attorney?
8. What does the disposition "not guilty" mean?
9. Under what conditions is a deferred sentence justifiable?
10. Would the sentence "suspended judgment" seem to be advisable in some cases?
11. Is the concept "cultural lag" useful in the analysis of antiquated legal procedures?
12. Under what conditions is probation used rather than a prison sentence?
13. What is the opinion of criminologists concerning systems of self-government in prisons?
14. When sterilization is employed in the repression of crime, do its advocates assume that criminal tendencies are hereditary? In what states is sterilization practiced?
15. In what administrative agencies connected with the police courts and the prisons can the methods of social case work be employed?
16. What individual and social characteristics are highly associated with good parole risks?
17. How successful are current systems of prison labor?
18. Does the indeterminate sentence decrease penalties?
19. What provisions does society now lack for the social adjustment of exprisoners?
20. In the light of scientific criminology, how would you formulate a preventive program?

CONCLUSION

Introduction

Both man and nature are responsible for conditions that are called social problems.

This point of view has been accepted for a long time. Some of the parables in the *Bible* are like current case histories; many ancient myths recall the moral indignation that is basic in every reform movement. More than 2,000 years ago, Aesop commented upon typical social problems in his *Fables*—problems that are questions of moral conduct and also basic social riddles.

Contemporary social problems resemble these fables both as stories and as moral insights. Often, however, the average citizen remembers the story but forgets or is confused by its moral. Most social problems are similar mixtures of opinion and moral conflict, as illustrated by Aesop in the story of the frogs and the bulls.

Two frogs saw two bulls fighting, and one said: "That fight is going to be dangerous for us frogs."

"Nonsense," scoffed the second frog, "we are frogs, they are bulls; their fight is no concern of ours."

"But when one of the bulls wins," replied the first frog, "he will chase the other into the marsh and trample us; then many of us will be killed even if the fight is not our affair."

Aesop made the point that little people almost always suffer when big people are in conflict. Or, he might have concluded that social problems are everybody's business. Some people are the victims; a few are responsible for social policy and control; but everyone is obliged to share the burdens of human misery and its numerous and fantastic social costs.

CHAPTER 20

KEYS TO SOLUTIONS

SOLVING PROBLEMS IS A FINAL STEP IN SOCIAL STUDY. SOLUTION HOWever is a rare event. It is limited by various imperfections in social analysis. Nevertheless, the public wants solutions and compares the sciences and arts on their merits from this point of view. The history of solutions that do not solve problems is for the most part an unwritten sector of all the sciences. Consequently, any attempt to suggest the keys to solution is necessarily provisional.

In spite of this dubious background, many people of good will are sincere in supporting their own particular understanding of problems. Their answers supply keys both in social research and in solutions.

Plato (427-347 B.C.) is often cited as a precedent. In his early publication, the *Republic,* he provided both a statement of human problems and a method for their control. Later on and after further observation, he prepared a revised interpretation in the *Laws,* thus changing his original concept of problems and their solutions. Almost all recent studies repeat Plato's experience.

The most concrete result of historical study is to show that human problems are also problems of science.

Prospects

In the light of such observations, students of society could not fail to detect that their own explanations, plans, or solutions often complicated, or became the problems of, a later period. For this reason primarily they were persuaded to adopt the methods and limits of scientific logic.

One of the most important results of this newer perspective was the transition from the stress on *the* social problem to *social problems.* At the turn of the current century, such titles as *The Social Problem* introduced numerous volumes on slums, poverty, the single tax, or votes for women. As in the Utopian philosophies, this limited approach to the problem often failed because it suggested its own solution without sufficient analysis.

The shift in recent studies from the single to the plural approach continues to be in a stage of only partial acceptance. Most people still prefer a simple interpretation and a single remedy. This change succeeded, however, in accenting the primary challenges of social problems as a class, namely, their numerous, obscure, and often unknown causes, their variable onset and development, and their complicated results, which more often than not have been recognized as the whole problem.

For all these reasons, students are agreed that every human society will always have its share of problems. This continuity is a primary basis for the conclusion that they can be studied and controlled.

Among various controls or solutions, the keys or answers are comparatively obvious. They include analysis or the factoring of each problem, prevention whenever a condition can be forestalled, adjustment when there is no other alternative, or planning. Frequently the most efficient recourse is nothing more ingenious than the use of undeveloped resources either in the social institutions or in maturing human personality.

No aspect of personality or human social organization has been neglected in the search for the elusive master key. A latter-day example is *The Prospect Before Us,* by John Dos Passos.[1] To Dos Passos, as well as in the opinion of Aesop's frog, the great danger to society is its Bigness. And the answer also is the same: everyone must participate in all aspects of community life; otherwise the individual and his liberties will be destroyed.

Analysis

As aspects of unknown or obscure causes, multiple origins, inadequate study, and imperfect controls, each problem in the questions introductory to Chapter 1 illustrates necessary steps in the analysis of social problems as a whole.

[1] Houghton Mifflin, Boston, 1951.

In comparing the public's expenditures for alcohol and medical care, attention is directed to the standards or moral values that a society tolerates regardless of their final costs in misery, demoralization, and physical degeneration.

In the struggle with the socio-medical problem of cancer, two guides are apparent: one, the obscurity of a problem in its sources; another, in its resistance to detection or prevention.

Deafness emphasizes the enormous frequency of most problems, as well as their relativity and increasing incidence with age.

The numbers of self-appointed practitioners in the field of mental health indicates the willingness of many people to exploit the weaknesses or needs of their fellow man, as well as the inability of the average person to distinguish between the charlatan and the honest practitioner.

Sterilization as a therapy points out how costly a problem can become when it is neglected and how ineffective a treatment can be when it is not applied promptly or completely.

Nonattendance of children at school is a typical example of how an institution that is often considered one of the most efficient of all social institutions can fail to maintain a minimum standard of efficiency.

Similar conflicts in institutional mores and efficiency are shown by the proportion of children in broken homes and by the failures in higher education.

Problems that increase with age or that seem to be peculiar to a particular age group point out both the broad range of social liabilities in man's physical nature and types of problems that appear at first as inevitable and unadjustable.

Likewise, the broad background of social problems in man-land ratios is equally representative of their widespread distribution in either historical or present-day societies.

That problems cannot always be solved even when the facts are known or adequate funds are available is shown respectively by the continuity of prejudice and the steady improvement in the American family's financial position. Another illustration is to be found in excessive amounts of economic competition, as indicated by such a statistical fact as inflation of currency which, because of its erratic character, is like:

The problem of accidents, hitherto discussed as a characteristic of all social problems in each stage of its development from causes to effects or from onset to its disastrous results.

In those problems that are notorious because they are more questions of choice than of physical, mental, or emotional normality, the social, economic, legal, and marital instabilities of a people are given prominent attention. They point out how financially costly and how personally and socially widespread such conditions can become when an element of indifference, ignorance, or confused moral opinion is permitted to persist and to intensify the everyday troubles of the average citizen.

Altogether, these introductory inquiries make a good case for an essential prerequisite, namely, objective study.

Problems beyond the range of science

Notwithstanding the fact that a problem may be both interesting and important, many major problems remain outside the possibility of immediate scientific analysis. If science is defined as a method of investigation, then the limits of the method must be acknowledged.

Problems such as gambling and choices in leadership are examples that thus far have not been adequately studied by methods of science.

Some form of gambling are approved, and those successful in this activity are acclaimed and given the highest honors that society can bestow. Other forms of gambling are defined by law as a business or as criminal. Some aspects of gambling are considered sinful or as outside the realm of vice by different people. This confusion is evident in religious, political, and economic groups as well as in sports.

A similar variance of opinion and confusion is noticeable in the studies of leaders, in methods of selecting them, and in their merits or contributions.

Comparable problems are suicide, war, political systems, and waste. Such problems are difficult to delimit, lack a systematic approach, are not adequately sampled, lack methods and techniques that are appropriate to the problem and the evidence, and are lacking in verification and prediction.

Methods of study

All these examples show one major handicap to observation and research in the social sciences. Each problem suggests its own approach or method of research in the collection and analysis of social facts. As a result, no definite mode of attack has been developed.

Today, as in the past, researchers find the answers to their questions by way of three analytical procedures—insight or intuition, authority or prestige, or the methods of science.

Each of these points of departure may be used separately or they may be united in one complete approach to the subjective facts of human experience and the objective facts of man's physical world.

Sources of inaccuracy are both confusing and demoralizing because experts at the outset tend to interpret problems from their own particular set of interests. As a result, typical social problems remain ill-defined. There is no uniformity in the treatment of subjective and objective facts. As a consequence, the difficulties of obtaining sufficient and adequate evidence abound, and the moral values by which each problem is initially brought to light are not reduced to a workable design.

This characteristic indecision is amply illustrated in research undertaken by government, especially in time of crisis such as depressions, inflation, war, or postwar adjustment. In the medley of opinions as to what science is and can do in human relations, experts frequently suggest the solution of inflation by depression, and vice versa. In the case of social problems associated with conflict, a panel of experts concluded that applicable scientific resources for conditions that first originate in the hearts of men should be limited to procedures in physics, chemistry, physiology, and medicine.[2]

At present, therefore, the procedure of social study is organized to avoid these obstructions and to establish a field of inquiry within the limits of its own subject matter and of valid techniques in research.

This routine includes:

1. The examination of sources of information.
2. The development of a systematic approach.
3. The definition of a problem and the limiting of conclusions of the study to a framework of observation—established by sources, approaches, and methods—in such a way that both the problem and the conclusions may be tested by repeated observations.

Thus, as many scientists recognize when they survey the unsolved

[2] National Science Foundation, *Report on Science Legislation to the Senate Committee on Military Affairs,* Report No. 8, Washington, D. C., 1946.

problems in their own work, the elements of all systematic investigation are honesty, objectivity, and critical judgment, plus observation, repetition, and proof. In his autobiography, *The Way of an Investigator,*[3] Dr. W. B. Cannon concluded that the indispensable conditions for methodical work are: curiosity, imaginative insight, critical judgment, thorough honesty, a retentive memory, patience, good health, and generosity.

Concrete results of this logic of social problems can be located in each class of problems and in each of the four sections that are adopted in the outline of this book. Infectious diseases, in contrast with degenerative diseases, are partly solved problems, especially when their specific causes are understood and they are not complicated by uncontrolled social conditions, by the inevitable ills of aging, or by dual systems of social values. In further illustration, population problems, fatigue, or tuberculosis may be considered midway between a condition of partly solved and unsolved problems, because each in its peculiar way is an example of partly understood causes and partly accepted controls. At the further extreme are such unsolved and possibly insoluble problems as mental disease, homosexuality, prejudice, or inflation.

In each of the latter examples, society is about as willing to accept another problem as the solution as it is to support a reasonable program for their adequate investigation. At this point it is worthwhile noting that problems may invite public attention for a number of irreconcilable reasons: because they lead to other problems or result from other problems; because nothing is known about them and they are described as mysterious; because they are looked upon as serious; because there are many victims; because there is no known or socially acceptable treatment; because they are unpredictable; and, among various other vague interpretations, because they lead to disputes in social values.

Mass plans

Searches for remedy or reform have one aim in common—the desire to solve problems. A plan for social guidance generally takes one of two forms; it may propose a broad program of social reconstruction or it may be less pretentious and consist of efforts to eliminate the causes or disastrous results of specific problems.

[3] Norton, New York, 1945, p. 43.

Current examples of social planning seem to be novel and distinctive largely because of their comprehensive applications. Contemporary social reform movements are actually unique in contrast to many historical reforms because of: (1) the size and complexity of the problem for which they propose a program, (2) the large number of people involved, (3) the magnitude of financial costs, and (4) the introduction of foresight and method.

All programs of constructive social change are based upon the assumption that society is organized, or is capable of being organized, to treat or to prevent its problems. The main sources of confusion are found in the choices of particular plans and goals.

Illustrations of mass plans are apparent in each major class of problems; for example, in such movements as public health, mental hygiene, eugenics, education, regional economic rehabilitation, social security, or universal military training. Each of these innovations varies in scope, in problems to be treated, in the handicaps that are to be avoided by its introduction, and in its social acceptability. For one or another of these reasons, the usual obstacles to planning are conflicts arising from (1) dissimilar economic interests, (2) variant cultural patterns, (3) the meaning of the facts which are basic to the organization of the policy, or (4) the interpretation of the eventual outcome of the policy.

The adaptability of a program (or the interpretation of its significance as a valid instrument of social change) may be determined by raising three questions. These questions enter into the preliminary analysis of every social plan:

1. How much of a problem can be analyzed and solved?
2. What other related problems will be solved?
3. What other problems will be created by the plan?

Of these questions, the first is by all means the most important.

The objective and significance of social planning may not be measurable to any important extent by its solution of problems. But it does set a minimum requirement for adequate social action, namely, that it should be able to present what the problem is a little more clearly.

Solubility of social problems. The answer of the social scientist to this challenge has never been wholly satisfactory. Generally, he has depended upon the rather doubtful claim that social phenomena are more complex than physical phenomena. Perhaps he should assume another attitude toward the comparative effectiveness of physical and social science and contrast the problems in these two fields. In this comparison, he can defend his own lack of achievement through the relative insolubility of his problems.

Social problems have been described as insoluble for three reasons. First, social scientists now realize that their techniques of observation and analysis—their science—are limited to repeated events. But no scientist laboring under these limits is able to state whether the result of a proposed action will be good or bad. Second, there is no basic system of social ethics or social welfare that supplies a sure index of "what ought to be done." Third, any proposed social change has a number of effects other than those that were intended. It is impossible to state scientifically whether some of these effects may not be worse than the problem that originally stimulated the change. For these reasons, the methods of abstract, or pure, science break down in the survey of social problems.

Or to repeat the point of view of Dos Passos, human societies and problems are too big, and people and social institutions are too inefficient, indifferent, careless, corrupt, selfish, or contradictory.

A few examples of relatively unsolved problems are:

1. Justice in the distribution of income.
2. Selection of people for positions of importance because of their competence.
3. Business depressions.
4. Social consequences of inventions.
5. Qualities of population that should be preserved by a planned policy.
6. Why pathological types of personality continue to thrive.
7. Why society cannot train citizens who will live in harmony with its conventions.
8. Why people are so susceptible to manias without any factual basis for their beliefs.
9. Racial antipathies.
10. Exploitation.

Summary

From the foregoing suggestions, it may be noted that social problems and reforms or plans have three traits in common:

1. Both are formulated or defined in terms of prevailing standards of social welfare or ill-being.
2. Both refer to the causes and effects of deteriorating living conditions that do violence to the mores.
3. Both represent important fields of social research and may be considered problems of social investigation.

Most people go through life undisturbed by such considerations. They do not question the customs or beliefs of their time, nor are they at all distressed by its problems.

There are many men and women, however, who are sincere in their desire to assist in the removal of gross human inequalities. But they are bewildered by the complexity of the social organization to be changed and are discouraged by their apparent inability to substitute good for evil. At least these sincere minorities think in such terms. And because they have not traveled the narrow road of science, they find themselves marooned in their thinking or random activities, rejecting the dogma of the radical and the dreams of the utopian. In addition, they are wholly confused by the aloofness of the scientist. Lest science be as sterile as its competitors, it too, perhaps, requires some reformation.

Broadly stated, the objective of the study of social problems is to discover how to eliminate undesirable social conditions and how to extend desirable social conditions. While it is true that no social problem can be analyzed or partly solved without the aid of highly specialized experts, it is equally true that no solution can be effectively introduced without the cooperation of a large number of sympathetic, though untrained, persons. Until science and art reach this point of cooperation, at least two encouraging suggestions can be made to this portion of the public. No social problem is as bad as its archenemy, the reformer, contends, and no social plan accomplishes the good that its advocates claim or the harm which its opponents fear.

NAME INDEX

(Names in footnotes and chapter bibliographies are omitted except when they serve as cross-references.)

SUBJECT INDEX

E

J

K

L

M